THE ENGLISH LEGAL SYSTEM

Sixth edition

Cavendish
Publishing
Limited

London • Sydney • Portland, Oregon

This book is supported by a Companion Website, created to keep *The English Legal System* up to date and to provide enhanced resources for both students and lecturers.

Key features include:

◆ termly updates
◆ links to useful websites
◆ links to 'ebooks' for introductory and further reading
◆ revision guidance
◆ 'ask the author' – your questions answered

www.cavendishpublishing.com/els

THE ENGLISH LEGAL SYSTEM

Sixth edition

Gary Slapper, LLB, LLM, PhD, PGCE (Law)
Professor of Law, and Director of the Law Programme,
The Open University

David Kelly, BA, BA (Law), PhD
Principal Lecturer in Law, Staffordshire University

Cavendish
Publishing
Limited

London • Sydney • Portland, Oregon

Sixth edition first published in Great Britain 2003 by
Cavendish Publishing Limited, The Glass House,
Wharton Street, London WC1X 9PX, United Kingdom
Telephone: + 44 (0)20 7278 8000   Facsimile: + 44 (0)20 7278 8080
Email: info@cavendishpublishing.com
Website: www.cavendishpublishing.com

Published in the United States by Cavendish Publishing
c/o International Specialized Book Services,
5824 NE Hassalo Street, Portland,
Oregon 97213-3644, USA

Published in Australia by Cavendish Publishing (Australia) Pty Ltd
45 Beach Street, Coogee, NSW 2034, Australia
Telephone: + 61 (2)9664 0909   Facsimile: + 61 (2)9664 5420

© Slapper, G and Kelly, D	2003
First edition	1994
Second edition	1995
Third edition	1997
Fourth edition	1999
Fifth edition	2001
Sixth edition	2003

British Library Cataloguing in Publication Data
Slapper, Gary
The English legal system – 6th ed
1 Law – England 2 Law – Wales
I Title II Kelly, David
349.4'2
Library of Congress Cataloguing in Publication Data
Data available

ISBN 1-85941-755-8

1 3 5 7 9 10 8 6 4 2

Printed and bound in Great Britain

PREFACE

A good comprehension of the English legal system requires knowledge and skill in a number of disciplines. The system itself is the result of developments in law, economy, politics, sociological change and the theories which feed all these bodies of knowledge. A detailed knowledge of several areas of law is indispensable, but students are also expected to appreciate the historical development of many legal institutions, and the social and political debates which surround legal issues.

It is also important to understand the legal theory underlying policies on matters as diverse as the law relating to arrest, search and seizure; the distribution of work among different types of court; the structure of legal services; judicial review of administrative discretion; the operation of the doctrines of precedent and statutory interpretation; plea bargaining, contingency fees and public funding. Being proficient in this subject also means being familiar with contemporary changes and proposed changes. This book aims to assist students of the English legal system in the achievement of a good understanding of the law, its institutions and processes. It is also our aim to help cultivate in students of the system a critical approach to current legal issues and problems.

Since the fifth edition of this book in 2001, the English legal system has, once again, undergone major and comprehensive changes.

The courts have now decided over 200 cases involving the Human Rights Act 1998, and important developments are digested in this text, including cases like *R v Benjafield*, *Mendoza v Ghaidan International Transport* and *Roth GmbH v Secretary of State for the Home Department*. The Court of Appeal's decision on entrapment in *R v Looseley* and cases involving civil liberties like *DPP v Avery* have also been digested in this edition.

The effects of the Anti-Terrorism, Crime and Security Act 2001, the Proceeds of Crime Act 2002 and the Nationality, Immigration and Asylum Act 2002 are also taken into account. Cases with an important constitutional and political element like *R v Secretary of State for the Home Department ex p Saadi* and *R (on the Application of Q) v Secretary of State for the Home Department* have been incorporated in the relevant chapters. The courts system has been undergoing change, and we examine the latest proposals of the Civil Justice Council for reforming the courts, and changes to the criminal court structure. We also look at the Coroners' Services Review Group 2002. Very significant changes have been made to the way the legal professions work since the 2001 edition of this work, including the issue of direct public access to barristers, and to the ways that the funding of the system operates.

A New Supreme Court for the UK?

An unusual development for the English legal system was announced by the government at 6.00 pm on Thursday 12 June 2003. The primary purpose of the announcement was to explain the details of the latest periodic reshuffle of the

Cabinet membership. However, although it had not previously published a White Paper on reforms to the judicial system, nor any other public discussion document, the government simply declared that it would be abolishing the historic position of the Lord Chancellor and the Lord Chancellor's Department. It also announced its intention to create a Supreme Court in which the most senior judges would sit outside the House of Lords. These changes are unlikely to be fully implemented before the end of 2004. Updates on any developments in this area can be found on the Companion Website for this book (see p ii for further details).

It is proposed that a Judicial Appointments Commission be established as an independent body to select new judges. It will take over responsibility for doing so from the Lord Chancellor. The head of the Commission is to be appointed by Lord Falconer of Thoroton, QC, the new Lord Chancellor (at least for the next year) and Secretary of State for Constitutional Affairs, in consultation with the Home Secretary. The three branches of government – the legislature, the executive and the judiciary – will be technically closer to being mutually exclusive than they are now because there will no longer be a government minister heading the judiciary, nor a Cabinet minister who sits as a judge in the highest court of the land.

As part of another proposed constitutional reform, the Lord Chancellor will no longer sit as Speaker of the House of Lords and there will be consultation on a new post which will be filled by someone other than a minister. Lord Falconer, however, is currently the Lord Chancellor and chairs the House of Lords in the customary way. He has stated, though, that he will not, unlike his predecessor, sit as a judge in House of Lords' cases.

Mark Littlewood, campaigns director of Liberty, the civil liberties campaign group, said ((2003) *The Times*, 13 June):

> At last there will [under the proposed system] be a clearer separation between judges and politicians. Some may lament the abolition of a position which has an even longer history than that of Prime Minister, but a modern democracy needs to be based on sensible and logical rules, not on anachronistic traditions. Making laws is a job for politicians, interpreting laws needs to be left to the courts. This marks an important and welcome step in securing and underlining the independent, non-political nature of our legal system.

How far, however, the process will be de-politicised by the proposed system is open to debate because the head of the Judicial Appointments Committee will be appointed by a government minister: the Secretary of State for Constitutional Affairs. Thus, the appointments will be made in the name of someone only one step removed from the Cabinet.

The redistribution of the functions of the Lord Chancellor has been debated since the Labour Party came to power in 1997. However, Lord Irvine was the biggest obstacle to the reform that would have ended his roles of Cabinet minister, head of the judiciary and Speaker of the House of Lords. The debates on these themes are covered in this book in Chapter 1.

Judges have become increasingly active on politically and socially sensitive issues and, it is often argued, should be removed from the political arena. Disquiet over the constitutional hybridity of the Lord Chancellor's role has been gradually increasing. In 2003, a report to the Council of Europe called for the role to be dismembered, arguing it was a breach of human rights' guarantees on judicial independence and impartiality. The House of Commons select committee on the Lord Chancellor's Department had also called into question the constitutional position of the Lord Chancellor.

The previous Lord Chancellor, Lord Irvine of Lairg, had, as we detail in this book, embarked on a far-reaching programme of reforms to legal aid, access to justice, human rights, Queen's Counsel and court dress, including wigs. He even promised to consult on a judicial appointments commission. He was, though, not going to abolish his own office.

Alan Beith MP, chairman of the Lord Chancellor's select committee, welcomed the proposals for reform but said: 'They do seem to have been rather drawn up on the back of an envelope. We have had the proposals before the consultation. For measures as far-reaching as this, there really does need to be proper consultation first' ((2003) *The Times*, 13 June).

The plans for change are in only the most simple and basic form in June 2003. So, much may change in 2004. The position of Lord Chancellor can only be abolished by legislation and that is unlikely to be passed and implemented before the end of 2004. In the appointment process for membership of the American Supreme Court, candidates are vetted by the Senate in respect of their political views. The judges have the power to declare legislation unconstitutional. Will the same apply in the UK? The answer is, apparently, no. Any Supreme Court in the UK would be staffed by judges who would perform the same judicial functions as the present members of the Judicial Committee of the House of Lords. They would not be able to invalidate legislation. There has been no published proposal on all sorts of other key matters such as whether any new Supreme Court would act, as in the USA, with all members presiding (there are nine members in the US Supreme Court) or whether it would, as now, sit in smaller panels of five. The role of any new Supreme Court in relation to the Commonwealth countries over which the existing Judicial Committee of the Privy Council now has appellate jurisdiction is also unaddressed by the proposals.

We are very grateful to all those who advanced suggestions for improvement of the book since the last edition; many of those suggestions have been implemented in this edition. We have aimed to state the law as of June 2003.

Gary Slapper
David Kelly
June 2003

ACKNOWLEDGMENTS

We are very grateful to many people for their assistance, counsel, expertise, good humour and patience, all of which have contributed to the writing of this book. We are especially indebted to Suzanne, Hannah, Emily, Charlotte, Jane and Michael.

Great thanks are due to Jon Lloyd at Cavendish Publishing from whose professionalism, diligence and vigilance we greatly benefited. We are also indebted for all the professional support given to earlier editions of this book by Jo Reddy, Sonny Leong and Cara Annett. We are very grateful to John Morris for excellent work on the updating of Chapters 3, 7, and 12, and to Dr Michael Watson for his marvellous work in the updating of Chapters 4, 9 and 10. For very helpful comments on earlier drafts, we are indebted to Marilyn Lannigan, Professor Hazel Genn, Liz Rodgers, Miceál Barden, Michael Fealy, Steve Greenfield, Janice Richardson and David Stott. Thanks also to Frances Gibb, Legal Editor at *The Times*, for her critical elucidation of the legal system. A great debt also to Doreen and Ivor Slapper, David and Julie Whight, Raie Schwartz, Emma Bland and Hugh McLaughlan.

CONTENTS

Contents

Contents

TABLE OF CASES

TABLE OF STATUTES

TABLE OF STATUTORY INSTRUMENTS

TABLE OF EC LEGISLATION

TABLE OF ABBREVIATIONS

AA	Arbitration Act
ABWOR	Assistance by way of representation
ACLEC	Advisory Committee on Legal Education and Conduct
ADR	Alternative dispute resolution
AJA	Administration of Justice Act 1985
BA	Bail Act
BIS	Bail Information Schemes
British J of Criminology	British Journal of Criminology
British JLS	British Journal of Law and Society
CAA	Criminal Appeal Act
CCR	County Court Rules
CCRC	Criminal Cases Review Commission
CDS	Criminal Defence Service
CEO	Civilian enforcement officers
CJA	Criminal Justice Act
CJPOA	Criminal Justice and Public Order Act
CJR	Civil Justice Review
CLC	Citizens' Law Centre
CLS	Community Legal Service
CLSP	Community Legal Service Partnership
CLSA	Courts and Legal Services Act
CPIA	Criminal Procedure and Investigations Act
CPR	Civil Procedure Rules
CPS	Crown Prosecution Service
Crim LR	Criminal Law Review
CSA	Child Support Agency
DCOA	Deregulation and Contracting Out Act
DGFT	Director General of Fair Trading
DPMCA	Domestic Proceedings and Magistrates' Courts Act
DPP	Director of Public Prosecutions
ECHR	European Court of Human Rights
ECJ	European Court of Justice
EEC	European Economic Community
EL Rev	European Law Review
EP(C)A	Employment Protection (Consolidation) Act
EU	European Union
Howard J	Howard Journal
HRA	Human Rights Act
JA	Juries Act
JCE	Justices' chief executive

JdA	Judicature Act
JLS	Journal of Law and Society
JP	Justice of the Peace
JPA	Justices of the Peace Act
JSB	Judicial Studies Board
JSPTL	Journal of Society of Public Teachers of Law
LAA	Legal Advice and Assistance
LAdA	Legal Aid Act
LAG	Legal Action Group
Law Soc Gazette	Law Society Gazette
LCD	Lord Chancellor's Department
LPC	Legal Practice Course
LQR	Law Quarterly Review
LSO	Legal Services Ombudsman
MCA	Magistrates' Courts Act
MCC	Magistrates' Courts Committee
MDP	Multi-disciplinary partnerships
MLR	Modern Law Review
MNP	Multi-national partnerships
NCC	National Consumer Council
NILQ	Northern Ireland Legal Quarterly
NLJ	New Law Journal
OSS	Office for the Supervision of Solicitors
PACE	Police and Criminal Evidence Act
PAP	Pre-action protocol
PCA	Parliamentary Commissioner for Administration
PCCC	Professional Conduct and Complaints Committee
POA	Prosecution of Offences Act
RSC	Rules of the Supreme Court
SJ	Solicitors Journal
SLR	Student Law Review
SFO	Serious Fraud Office
SEA	Single European Act

CHAPTER 1

LAW AND LEGAL STUDY

1.1 Introduction

There are a number of possible approaches to the study of law. One such is the traditional/formalistic approach. This approach to law is posited on the existence of a discrete legal universe as the object of study. It is concerned with establishing a knowledge of the specific rules, both substantive and procedural, which derive from statute and common law and which regulate social activity. The essential point in relation to this approach is that study is restricted to the sphere of the legal without reference to the social activity to which the legal rules are applied. In the past, most traditional law courses and the majority of law textbooks adopted this 'black letter' approach. Their object was the provision of information on what the current rules and principles of law were, and how to use those rules and principles to solve what were by definition legal problems. Traditionally, English legal system courses have focused attention on the institutions of the law, predominantly the courts, in which legal rules and principles are put into operation, and here too the underlying assumption has been as to the closed nature of the legal world; its distinctiveness and separateness from normal everyday activity. This book continues that tradition to a degree but also recognises, and has tried to accommodate, the dissatisfaction with such an approach that has been increasingly evident among law teachers and examiners in this area. To that end, the authors have tried not simply to produce a purely expository text, but have attempted to introduce an element of critical awareness and assessment into the areas considered. *Potential examination candidates should appreciate that it is just such critical, analytical thought that distinguishes the good student from the mundane one.*

Additionally, however, this book goes further than traditional texts on the English legal system by directly questioning the claims to distinctiveness made by, and on behalf of, the legal system and considering law as a socio-political institution. It is the view of the authors that the legal system cannot be studied without a consideration of the values that law reflects and supports, and again, students should be aware that it is in such areas that the truly first class students demonstrate their awareness and ability.

1.2 The nature of law

One of the most obvious and most central characteristics of all societies is that they must possess some degree of order to permit the members to interact over a sustained period of time. Different societies, however, have different forms of order. Some societies are highly regimented with strictly enforced social rules, whereas others continue to function in what outsiders might consider a very unstructured manner with apparently few strict rules being enforced.

Order is therefore necessary, but the form through which order is maintained is certainly not universal, as many anthropological studies have shown (see Mansell and Meteyard, *A Critical Introduction to Law*, 2nd edn, 1999).

In our society, law plays an important part in the creation and maintenance of social order. We must be aware, however, that law as we know it is not the only means of creating order. Even in our society, order is not solely dependent on law, but also involves questions of a more general moral and political character. This book is not concerned with providing a general explanation of the form of order. It is concerned more particularly with describing and explaining the key institutional aspects of that particular form of order that is *legal* order.

The most obvious way in which law contributes to the maintenance of social order is the way in which it deals with disorder or conflict. This book, therefore, is particularly concerned with the institutions and procedures, both civil and criminal, through which law operates to ensure a particular form of social order by dealing with various conflicts when they arise.

Law is a *formal* mechanism of social control and, as such, it is essential that the student of law be fully aware of the nature of that formal structure. There are, however, other aspects to law that are less immediately apparent, but of no less importance, such as the inescapable political nature of law. Some textbooks focus more on this particular aspect of law than others, and these differences become evident in the particular approach adopted by the authors. The approach favoured by this book is to recognise that studying the English legal system is not just about learning legal rules, but is also about considering a social institution of fundamental importance.

1.3   Categories of law

There are various ways of categorising law which initially tend to confuse the non-lawyer and the new student of law. What follows will set out these categorisations in their usual dual form whilst at the same time trying to overcome the confusion inherent in such duality. It is impossible to avoid the confusing repetition of the same terms to mean different things and, indeed, the purpose of this section is to make sure that students are aware of the fact that the same words can have different meanings depending upon the context in which they are used.

1.3.1 Common law and civil law

In this particular juxtaposition, these terms are used to distinguish two distinct legal systems and approaches to law. The use of the term 'common law' in this context refers to all those legal systems which have adopted the historic English legal system. Foremost amongst these is, of course, the United States, but many other Commonwealth and former Commonwealth countries retain a common law system. The term 'civil law' refers to those other jurisdictions which have adopted the European continental system of law derived essentially from ancient Roman law, but owing much to the Germanic tradition.

The usual distinction to be made between the two systems is that the common law system tends to be case-centred and hence judge-centred, allowing scope for a discretionary, *ad hoc*, pragmatic approach to the particular problems that appear before the courts, whereas the civil law system tends to be a codified body of general abstract principles which control the exercise of judicial discretion. In reality, both of these views are extremes, with the former over-emphasising the extent to which the common law judge can impose his discretion and the latter under-estimating the extent to which continental judges have the power to exercise judicial discretion. It is perhaps worth mentioning at this point that the European Court of Justice (ECJ), established, in theory, on civil law principles, is in practice increasingly recognising the benefits of establishing a body of case law.

It has to be recognised, and indeed the English courts do so, that, although the ECJ is not bound by the operation of the doctrine of *stare decisis* (see 2.3), it still does not decide individual cases on an *ad hoc* basis and, therefore, in the light of a perfectly clear decision of the European Court, national courts will be reluctant to refer similar cases to its jurisdiction. Thus, after the ECJ decided in *Grant v South West Trains Ltd* (1998) that Community law did not cover discrimination on grounds of sexual orientation, the High Court withdrew a similar reference in *R v Secretary of State for Defence ex p Perkins (No 2)* (1998) (see 13.3.6 for a detailed consideration of the ECJ).

1.3.2 Common law and equity

In this particular juxtaposition, the terms refer to a particular division within the English legal system.

The common law has been romantically and inaccurately described as the law of the common people of England. In fact, the common law emerged as the product of a particular struggle for political power. Prior to the Norman Conquest of England in 1066, there was no unitary, national legal system. The emergence of the common law represents the imposition of such a unitary system under the auspices and control of a centralised power in the form of a sovereign king; in that respect, it represented the assertion and affirmation of that central sovereign power.

Traditionally, much play is made about the circuit of judges travelling round the country establishing the 'King's peace' and, in so doing, selecting the best local customs and making them the basis of the law of England in a piecemeal but totally altruistic procedure. The reality of this process was that the judges were asserting the authority of the central State and its legal forms and institutions over the disparate and fragmented State and legal forms of the earlier feudal period. thus, the common law was common *to* all in application, but certainly was not common *from* all. (The contemporary meaning and relevance and operation of the common law will be considered in more detail later in this chapter and in Chapter 2.)

By the end of the 13th century, the central authority had established its precedence at least partly through the establishment of the common law. Originally, courts had been no more than an adjunct of the King's Council, the *Curia Regis*, but gradually the common law courts began to take on a distinct institutional existence in the form of the Courts of Exchequer, Common Pleas and King's Bench. With this institutional autonomy, however, there developed an institutional sclerosis, typified by a reluctance to deal with matters that were not or could not be processed in the proper *form of action*. Such a refusal to deal with substantive injustices because they did not fall within the particular parameters of procedural and formal constraints by necessity led to injustice and the need to remedy the perceived weaknesses in the common law system. The response was the development of *equity*.

Plaintiffs unable to gain access to the three common law courts might directly appeal to the sovereign, and such pleas would be passed for consideration and decision to the Lord Chancellor, who acted as the king's conscience. As the common law courts became more formalistic and more inaccessible, pleas to the Chancellor correspondingly increased and eventually this resulted in the emergence of a specific court constituted to deliver 'equitable' or 'fair' decisions in cases which the common law courts declined to deal with. As had happened with the common law, the decisions of the Courts of Equity established principles which were used to decide later cases, so it should not be thought that the use of equity meant that judges had discretion to decide cases on the basis of their personal idea of what was just in each case.

The division between the common law courts and the Courts of Equity continued until they were eventually combined by the Judicature Acts (JdA) 1873–75. Prior to this legislation, it was essential for a party to raise an action in the appropriate court – for example, the courts of law would not implement equitable principles; the Acts, however, provided that every court had the power and the duty to decide cases in line with common law and equity, with the latter being paramount in the final analysis.

Some would say that, as equity was never anything other than a gloss on common law, it is perhaps appropriate, if not ironic, that now both systems have been effectively subsumed under the one term: common law.

Common law remedies are available as of right. Remedies in equity are discretionary, in other words they are awarded at the will of the court and depend on the behaviour and situation of the party claiming such remedies. This means that, in effect, the court does not have to award an equitable remedy where it considers that the conduct of the party seeking such an award has been such that the party does not deserve it (*D & C Builders v Rees* (1965)).

1.3.3   Common law and statute law

This particular conjunction follows on from the immediately preceding section, in that the common law here refers to the substantive law and procedural rules that have been created by the judiciary through the decisions in the cases they have heard. Statute law, on the other hand, refers to law that has been created by Parliament in the form of legislation. Although there has been a significant increase in statute law in the 20th and 21st centuries, the courts still have an important role to play in creating and operating law generally and in determining the operation of legislation in particular. The relationship of this pair of concepts is of central importance and is considered in more detail in Chapters 2 and 5.

1.3.4   Private law and public law

There are two different ways of understanding the division between private and public law.

At one level, the division relates specifically to actions of the State and its functionaries vis à vis the individual citizen, and the legal manner in which, and form of law through which, such relationships are regulated: public law. In the 19th century, it was at least possible to claim, as AV Dicey did, that there was no such thing as public law in this distinct administrative sense and that the powers of the State with regard to individuals were governed by the ordinary law of the land, operating through the normal courts. Whether such a claim was accurate or not when it was made – and it is unlikely – there certainly can be no doubt now that public law constitutes a distinct and growing area of law in its own right. The growth of public law in this sense has mirrored the growth and increased activity of the contemporary State, and has seen its role as seeking to regulate such activity. The crucial role of judicial review in relation to public law will be considered in some detail in Chapter 6, and the content and impact of the Human Rights Act 1998 will be considered later in this chapter at 1.7.

There is, however, a second aspect to the division between private and public law. One corollary of the divide is that matters located within the private sphere are seen as purely a matter for individuals themselves to regulate, without the interference of the State, whose role is limited to the provision of the forum for deciding contentious issues and mechanisms for the enforcement of such decisions. Matters within the public sphere, however, are seen as issues relating to the interest of the State and general public, and as such are to be protected and prosecuted by the State. It can be seen, therefore, that the category to which any dispute is allocated is of crucial importance to how it is dealt with. Contract may be thought of as the classic example of private law, but the extent to which this purely private legal area has been subjected to the regulation of public law, in such areas as consumer protection, should not be under-estimated. Equally, the most obvious example of public law in this context would be criminal law. Feminists have argued, however, that the allocation of domestic matters to the sphere of private law has led to a denial of a general interest in the treatment and protection of women. By defining domestic matters as private, the State and its functionaries have denied women access to its power to protect themselves from abuse. In doing so, it is suggested that, in fact, such categorisation has reflected and maintained the social domination of men over women.

1.3.5 Civil law and criminal law

Civil law is a form of private law and involves the relationships between individual citizens. It is the legal mechanism through which individuals can assert claims against others and have those rights adjudicated and enforced. The purpose of civil law is to settle disputes between individuals and to provide remedies; it is not concerned with punishment as such. The role of the State in relation to civil law is to establish the general framework of legal rules and to provide the legal institutions to operate those rights, but the activation of the civil law is strictly a matter for the individuals concerned. Contract, tort and property law are generally aspects of civil law.

Criminal law, on the other hand, is an aspect of public law and relates to conduct which the State considers with disapproval and which it seeks to control and/or eradicate. Criminal law involves the *enforcement* of particular forms of behaviour, and the State, as the representative of society, acts positively to ensure compliance. Thus, criminal cases are brought by the State in the name of the Crown and cases are reported in the form of *Regina v …* (*Regina* is simply Latin for 'queen' and case references are usually abbreviated to *R v …*), whereas civil cases are referred to by the names of the parties involved in the dispute, for example, *Smith v Jones*. In criminal law, a prosecutor prosecutes a defendant (or 'the accused'). In civil law, a claimant sues (or 'brings a claim against') a defendant.

In distinguishing between criminal and civil actions, it has to be remembered that the same event may give rise to both. For example, where the driver of a car injures someone through their reckless driving, they will be liable to be prosecuted under the Road Traffic legislation, but at the same time, they will also be responsible to the injured party in the civil law relating to the tort of negligence.

A crucial distinction between criminal and civil law is the level of proof required in the different types of cases. In the criminal case, the prosecution is required to prove that the defendant is guilty beyond reasonable doubt, whereas in a civil case, the degree of proof is much lower and has only to be on the balance of probabilities. This difference in the level of proof raises the possibility of someone being able to succeed in a civil case, although there may not be sufficient evidence for a criminal prosecution. Indeed, this strategy has been used successfully in a number of cases against the police where the Crown Prosecution Service (CPS) has considered there to be insufficient evidence to support a criminal conviction for assault. A successful civil action may even put pressure on the CPS to reconsider its previous decision not to prosecute (see further 10.1 for an examination of the CPS).

It should also be noted that the distinction between civil and criminal responsibility is further blurred in cases involving what may be described as hybrid offences. These are situations where a court awards a civil order against an individual, on the balance of probabilities, but with the attached sanction that any breach of the order will be subject to punishment as a criminal offence. As examples of this procedure may be cited the Protection from Harassment Act 1997 and the provision for the making of Anti Social Behaviour Orders available under s 1(1) of the Crime and Disorder Act 1998. Both of these provisions are of considerable interest and deserve some attention in their own right. The Protection from Harassment Act was introduced as a measure to deal with 'stalking', the harassment of individuals by people continuously following them, and allowed the victim of harassment to get a court order to prevent the stalking. Whereas stalking may have been the high profile source of the Act, it is possible, however, that its most useful provision, if it is used appropriately, may actually lie in providing more protection for women who are subject to assault and harassment from their partners than is available under alternative criminal or civil law procedures. In March 2001, the Act was used successfully against *The Sun* newspaper in an action by a black clerk in a City of London police station. The newspaper had published three articles about the woman after she had reported four police officers in her station for making racist comments about a Somali asylum seeker and as a consequence she received hate mail. The paper admitted that the articles were 'strident, aggressive and inflammatory' and the judge held that they were also racist. In his view, the Protection from Harassment Act gave the claimant 'a right to protection from harassment by all the world including the press'. The Court of Appeal subsequently refused an application by the newspaper to strike out the action (*Thomas v News Group Newspapers* (2002)) and consequently it can be concluded that the Act potentially offers significant protection to the ordinary members of the public who have been the object of what many see as press harassment. Such protection is, of course, additional to any other protection provided under the Human Rights Act 1998. Anti Social Behaviour Orders, available against individuals aged 10 or over on the application of the police or local authority, may be made in situations where there has been intimidation through threats, violence and a mixture of unpleasant actions; persistent unruly behaviour by a small group on an estate; families who resort to abuse when complaints are made to them; vandalism; serious and persistent organised bullying of children; persistent racial or homophobic harassment; and persistent anti-social behaviour as a result of drug or alcohol abuse (Home Office Guidance Document 1999).

Whereas these Acts may seem initially to offer a welcome additional protection to the innocent individual, it has to be recognised that such advantage is achieved in effect by criminalising what was, and remains, in other circumstances non-criminal behaviour, and deciding its applicability on the basis of the lower civil law burden of proof. A further example of the relationship between criminal law and civil law may be seen in the courts' power to make an order for the confiscation of a person's property under the Drug Trafficking Act 1994 and the Criminal Justice Act (CJA) 1988. Under these Acts, the courts may assume that the assets of an individual convicted under them are the product of criminal activity and liable to confiscation unless that person can demonstrate otherwise. Thus, the usual balance of proof is reversed in relation to someone found guilty of a drug trafficking offence or two non-drug related offences under the CJA 1988. Although the criminal standard of proof applies to the original criminal conviction, the confiscation order is effected on the basis of the civil standard of proof. Where the individual fails to comply with the confiscation order, they are liable for a term of imprisonment. The impact of the Human Rights Act 1998 on these various Acts will be considered below at 1.7.1.2.

It should not be forgotten that although prosecution of criminal offences is usually the prerogative of the State, it remains open to the private individual to initiate a private prosecution in relation to a criminal offence. It has to be remembered, however, that even in the private prosecution, the test of the burden of proof remains the criminal one requiring the facts to be proved beyond reasonable doubt. An example of the problems inherent in such private actions can be seen in the case of Stephen Lawrence, the young black man who was gratuitously stabbed to death by a gang of white racists whilst standing at a bus stop in London. Although there was strong suspicion, and indeed evidence, against particular individuals, the CPS declined to press the charges against them on the basis of insufficiency of evidence. When the lawyers of the Lawrence family mounted a private prosecution against the suspects, the action failed for want of sufficient evidence to convict. As a consequence of the failure of the private prosecution, the rule against double jeopardy meant that the accused could not be re-tried for the same offence at any time in the future, even if the police subsequently acquired sufficient new evidence to support a conviction. The report of the Macpherson Inquiry into the manner in which the Metropolitan Police dealt with the Stephen Lawrence case gained much publicity for its finding of 'institutional racism' within the service, but it also made a clear recommendation that the removal of the rule against double jeopardy be considered. Subsequently, the Home Secretary invited the Law Commission to consider the matter, and it recommended, in spite of civil libertarian argument to the contrary, that in extremely limited circumstances the rule might be removed. The limited circumstances suggested by the Law Commission would only arise where any new evidence could not with due diligence have been produced at the first trial and there is a very high probability of the defendant being convicted of a serious offence. The Criminal Justice Bill produced at the end of 2002 embodies the recommendations of both Macpherson and the Law Commission, although it proposes to extend the number of offences that will be open to retrial.

In December 2000, the Lawrence family were reported to have accepted £320,000 in settlement of any claims against the Metropolitan Police Service, but, as yet, they have not initiated any civil action against the alleged perpetrators of their son's murder as they had been reported to be considering doing.

In considering the relationship between civil law and criminal law, it is sometimes thought that criminal law is the more important in maintaining social order, but it is at least arguable that, in reality, the reverse is the case. For the most part, people come into contact with the criminal law infrequently, whereas everyone is continuously involved with civil law, even if it is only the use of contract law to make some purchase. The criminal law of theft, for example, may be seen as simply the cutting edge of the wider and more fundamental rights established by general property law. In any case, there remains the fact that civil and criminal law each has its own distinct legal system. The nature of these systems will be considered in detail in later chapters. The structure of the civil courts is considered in Chapter 3 and that of the criminal courts in Chapter 4.

1.4   The separation of powers

Although the idea of the separation of powers can be traced back to ancient Greek philosophy, it was advocated in early modern times by the English philosopher Locke and the later French philosopher Montesquieu, and found its practical expression in the constitution of the United States. The idea of the separation of powers is posited on the existence of three distinct functions of government (the legislative, executive and judicial functions) and the conviction that these functions should be kept apart in order to prevent the centralisation of too much power. Establishing the appropriate relationship between the actions of the State and the legal control over those actions crucially involves a consideration of whether there is any absolute limit on the authority of the government of the day. Answering that question inevitably involves an examination of the general constitutional structure of the UK and, in particular, the inter-relationship of two doctrines: parliamentary sovereignty and judicial independence. It also requires an understanding of the role of judicial review and the effect of the Human Rights Act 1998, and has caused no little friction between the judiciary and the executive, especially in the form of the Home Secretary.

1.4.1 Parliamentary sovereignty

As a consequence of the victory of the parliamentary forces in the English revolutionary struggles of the 17th century, Parliament became the sovereign power in the land. The independence of the judiciary was secured, however, in the Act of Settlement 1701. The centrality of the independence of the judges and the legal system from direct control or interference from the State in the newly established constitution was emphasised in the writing of John Locke, who saw it as one of the essential reasons for, and justifications of, the social contract on which the social structure was assumed to be based. It is generally accepted that the inspiration for Montesquieu's *Spirit of Law* (*De L'Esprit des Lois*) was the English constitution, but if that is truly the case, then his doctrine of the separation of powers was based on a misunderstanding of that constitution, as it failed to take account of the express *superiority of Parliament* in all matters, including its relationship with the judiciary and the legal system.

It is interesting that some Conservative thinkers have recently suggested that the whole notion of parliamentary sovereignty is itself a product of the self-denying ordinance of the common law. Consequently, they have suggested that it is open to a subsequent, more robust, judiciary, confident in its own position and powers within the developing constitution, to re-assert its equality with the other two elements. When, however, it is recalled that when the Conservative Party was in power, it was to no little extent embarrassed by, and not too understanding of, the actions of recalcitrant judges, it is at least a moot point whether such a proposition reflects a real commitment to judicial equality with the executive, or merely represents the gall of a defeated executive, hoping to enlist the judges in their oppositional role. It does not require an uncritical commitment to the role of the judiciary to recognise that powerful executives, which exercise effective control over acquiescent legislatures, do not take too well to the interference of an active judiciary. At least somewhat paradoxically, the Conservative Party argued against the enactment of the Human Rights Act by the Labour government in 1998 on the grounds that it diminished the power of Parliament and gave too much power to the unelected judiciary.

Given the existence of the doctrine of parliamentary sovereignty, which effectively means that Parliament, as the ultimate source of law, can make such law as it determines, the exact extent to which the doctrine of the separation of powers operates in the UK is a matter of some debate. For example, the position of the Lord Chancellor, who is at the same time a member of the government and the most senior judge in the land with control over judicial appointments, is not unproblematic (this will be considered in detail in Chapter 6). There is, however, high judicial authority for claiming that the separation of powers is an essential element in the constitution of the UK (see *R v Hinds* (1979), in which Lord Diplock, whilst considering the nature of different Commonwealth constitutions in a Privy Council case, stated that 'It is taken for granted that the basic principle of the separation of powers will apply ...' at p 212). In any case, the point of considering the doctrine at this juncture is simply to highlight the distinction and relationship between the executive and the judiciary and to indicate the possibility of conflict between the two elements of the constitution. This relationship assumes crucial importance if one accepts, as some have suggested, that it is no longer possible to distinguish the executive from the legislature as, through its control of its majority in the House of Commons, the executive (that is, the government) can legislate as it wishes and, in so doing, can provide the most arbitrary of party political decisions with the form of legality. The question to be considered here is to what extent the judiciary can legitimately oppose the wishes of the government expressed in the form of legislation, or to what extent they can interfere with the pursuit of those wishes. As will be seen below at 1.7, the power of the judiciary in relation to legislative provisions has been greatly enhanced by the passage of the Human Rights Act 1998.

1.4.2 Judicial independence

The exact meaning of 'judicial independence' became a matter of debate when some members and ex-members of the senior judiciary suggested that the former Lord Chancellor, Lord Mackay of Clashfern, had adopted a too restrictive interpretation of the term which had reduced it to the mere absence of interference by the executive in the trial of individual cases. They asserted the right of the legal system to operate independently, as an autonomous system apart from the general control of the State, with the judiciary controlling its operation, or at least being free from the dictates and strictures of central control.

According to Lord Mackay, in the first of his series of Hamlyn lectures entitled 'The Administration of Justice' (1994):

> The fact that the executive and judiciary meet in the person of the Lord Chancellor should symbolise what I believe is necessary for the administration of justice in a country like ours, namely, a realisation that both the judiciary and the executive are parts of the total government of the country with functions that are distinct but which must work together in a proper relationship if the country is to be properly governed ... It seems more likely that the interests of

the judiciary in matters within the concerns covered by the Treasury are more likely to be advanced if they can be pursued within government by a person with a lifetime of work in law and an understanding of the needs and concerns of the judiciary and who has responsibility as Head of the Judiciary, than if they were to be left within government as the responsibility of a minister with no such connection with the judiciary.

There is, however, some concern within the judiciary as to whether the relationship between the executive and the judiciary is proper, and doubts have been raised as to the Lord Chancellor's positioning between the two institutions. Fears have been expressed that rather than representing the interests of the judiciary within the government, the current Lord Chancellor, Lord Irvine of Lairg, is actually pursuing and implementing policies that are driven by the economic dictates of the Treasury and which are having a severely detrimental impact on the operation of the whole justice system. Rather than being the voice of the judiciary in Cabinet, he is suspected by some, as was his predecessor, of being the voice of the Cabinet in the judiciary.

The tension inherent in the relationship between the courts and the executive government has taken on an even more fundamental constitutional aspect in relation to the development of the process of judicial review and the passing of the Human Rights Act 1998, by means of which the courts assert the right to subject the actions and operations of the executive and, indeed, all public authorities to the gaze and control of the law in such a way as to prevent the executive from abusing its power. In the United States, with its written constitution, the judiciary have the power to declare the Acts of the legislature to be unconstitutional and therefore unlawful, and some commentators see the Human Rights Act as eventually leading to a similar outcome in the UK.

1.4.3 Parliamentary Commissioner for Standards

Roger Smith observed in an article entitled 'Politics and the judiciary' in the New Law Journal ((1993) 143 NLJ 1486):

> Judicial review ... is pushing our political system towards a greater separation of powers. The judiciary is disengaging itself from its earlier subservience to the legislature and the executive. There are, doubtless, various strands to this which include the influence of the United States of Europe. However, another important element must be the failure in recent years of the usual checks and balance of democracy. Britain is in danger of becoming a one-party State ... Other parts of the constitution are forced into the opposition role, particularly when their interests and perceptions are offended.

It is of no little interest to note that Parliament, in the form of the House of Commons, re-asserted its ultimate authority in relation to the recommendations of the Committee on Standards in Public Life, which was established under the chairmanship of the senior judge, Lord Nolan. The Committee was set up to consider, amongst other things, ways in which either actual or perceived corruption within the legislative body could be controlled. The Committee's recommendation that an independent Parliamentary Commissioner for Public Standards should be appointed to enforce controls over the activities of MPs was resisted by some members of the Commons on the grounds that nobody outside of Parliament could be given the authority to regulate Parliament. The fact that such an assertion might be seen as protecting the right of particular members to engage in 'sleaze' was portrayed as being of secondary importance to the constitutional question as to the sovereignty of Parliament. The fact that this argument was almost completely spurious, in that any such Commissioner would be acting for Parliament and representing the authority of Parliament, was recognised and Sir Gordon Downey was appointed to fill the office of Commissioner for Public Standards, responsible to the Commons Committee on Standards and Privileges, in 1995.

Much of Sir Gordon's work related to what became known as the 'cash for questions' scandal. This affair referred to the fact that a number of Members of Parliament had been accused of, and some admitted to, being paid for asking questions in the House. The payment was made by Mohamed Al Fayed, the chairman of the House of Fraser group which owns Harrods, and was organised through the offices of the parliamentary lobbyist Ian Greer. In July 1997, Sir Gordon Downey issued a three volume report on the allegations of sleaze made against certain MPs. Five MPs were censured in the report with a severity which would have required them to be expelled from the House of Commons had they then still been MPs. In the event, however, all those condemned in the report had either not stood as candidates at the General Election on 1 May 1997 or were defeated on that occasion.

Geoffrey Robertson QC, who acted in the Downey Inquiry, stated after publication of the report:

> The real lesson of the Downey Report is that never again should MPs be regarded – or regard themselves – as above the law ... Self-regulation is not enough: it is time to follow the lead of Parliaments in the Commonwealth which have established an independent commission against corruption headed by a judge, to investigate and report allegations against ministers, MPs and public servants [(1997) *The Guardian*, 4 July].

The second Commissioner, Elizabeth Filkin, appointed in 1999 for a three year period, adopted a robust attitude to her duties and apparently upset some influential MPs by the rigour with which she pursued her investigation into their behaviour. It would appear that as a result, she was not re-appointed at the end of her period of office, Not only was her job re-advertised, but the terms in regards to time and pay were downgraded. As Ms Filkin stated at the time, in a letter to the Speaker of the House of Commons, 'Insuperable objects to independence have been created'. It was clear that many MPs saw her as usurping the role of the Parliamentary Committee on Standards and Privileges, whose employee she was. As *The Guardian* journalist Hugo Young stated at the time:

> She was not supposed to be the invigilator of MPs, merely their investigator, whose findings were to be left unrevealed, pending the judgment of other MPs.

A new Commissioner, Philip Mawer, was appointed in February 2002. It remains to be seen whether he is more amenable to the susceptibilities and privileges of his employers than was his predecessor.

The sensitive relationship between the judiciary and Parliament was highlighted in two cases. In *R v Parliamentary Commissioner for Standards ex p Al Fayed* (1997), it was held that the operation of the Parliamentary Commissioner for Public Standards was not open to judicial review, as he dealt with matters relating to the internal operation of Parliament. The operation of the Parliamentary Commissioner for Administration (the Ombudsman – see 8.4) is subject to judicial review, however, because his is an external, rather than an internal, parliamentary role (*R v Parliamentary Commissioner for Administration ex p Balchin* (1997)).

A consideration of the impact of the Human Rights Act 1998 on the relationship between the executive and the judiciary will be postponed until the provisions of that Act have been discussed below at 1.7. Judicial review and its political implications will be considered in detail in Chapter 6 but, at this point, it should be noted that any general treatment of the relationship of the judiciary and executive must take into account the particular meaning and scope of the doctrine known as the 'Rule of Law' and its relationship to human rights.

1.5   The Rule of Law

The Rule of Law represents a symbolic ideal against which proponents of widely divergent political persuasions measure and criticise the shortcomings of contemporary State practice. This varied recourse to the Rule of Law is, of course, only possible because of the lack of precision in the actual meaning of the concept; its meaning tends to change over time and, as will be seen below, to change in direct correspondence with the beliefs of those who claim its support and claim, in turn, to support it. It is undeniable that the form and content of law and legal procedure have changed substantially in the course of the 20th and 21st centuries. It is usual to explain such changes as being a consequence of the way in which, and the increased extent to which, the modern State intervenes in everyday life, be it economic or social. As the State increasingly took over the regulation of many areas of social activity, it delegated wide-ranging discretionary powers to various people and bodies in an attempt to ensure the successful implementation of its policies. The assumption and delegation of such power on the part of the State brought it into potential conflict with previous understandings of the Rule of Law which had entailed a strictly limited ambit of State activity. The impact of this on the understanding and operation of the principle of the Rule of Law and its implications in relation to the judiciary are traced out below and will be returned to in Chapter 6.

1.5.1 AV Dicey

According to AV Dicey in *Introduction to the Study of the Law of the Constitution* (1885), the UK had no such thing as administrative law as distinct from the ordinary law of the land. Whether he was correct or not when he expressed this opinion, and there are substantial grounds for doubting the accuracy of his claim even at the time he made it, it can no longer be denied that there is now a large area of law that can be properly called administrative, that is, related to the pursuit and application of particular State policies, usually within a framework of statutory powers.

According to the notoriously chauvinistic Dicey, the Rule of Law was one of the key features which distinguished the English constitution from its continental counterparts. Whereas foreigners were subject to the exercise of arbitrary power, the Englishman was secure within the protection of the Rule of Law. Dicey suggested the existence of three distinct elements which together created the Rule of Law as he understood it:

- *An absence of arbitrary power on the part of the State*: the extent of the State's power, and the way in which it exercises such power, is limited and controlled by law. Such control is aimed at preventing the State from acquiring and using wide discretionary powers, for, as Dicey correctly recognised, the problem with discretion is that it can be exercised in an arbitrary manner, and that above all else is to be feared, at least as Dicey would have us believe.

- *Equality before the law*: the fact that no person is above the law, irrespective of rank or class. This was linked with the fact that functionaries of the State are subject to the same law and legal procedures as private citizens.

- *Supremacy of ordinary law*: the fact that the English constitution was the outcome of the ordinary law of the land and was based on the provision of remedies by the courts rather than on the declaration of rights in the form of a written constitution.

It is essential to recognise that Dicey was writing at a particular historical period but, perhaps more importantly, he was writing from a particular political perspective that saw the maintenance of *individual* property and *individual* freedom to use that property as one chose as paramount. He was opposed to any increase in State activity in the pursuit of collective interests. In analysing Dicey's version of the Rule of Law, it can be seen that it venerated *formal* equality at the expense of *substantive* equality. In other words, he thought that the law and the State should be blind to the real concrete differences that exist between people, in terms of wealth or power or connection, and should treat them all the same, as possessors of *abstract* rights and duties.

There is an unaddressed, and certainly unresolved, tension in Dicey's work. The Rule of Law was only one of two fundamental elements of the English polity; the other was parliamentary sovereignty. Where, however, the government controls the legislative process, the sovereignty of Parliament is reduced to the undisputed supremacy of central government. The tension arises from the fact that, whereas the Rule of Law was aimed at controlling arbitrary power, Parliament could, within this constitutional structure, make provision for the granting of such arbitrary power by passing appropriate legislation.

This tension between the Rule of Law and parliamentary sovereignty is peculiar to the British version of liberal government. Where similar versions of government emerged on the continent, and particularly in Germany, the power of the legislature was itself subject to the Rule of Law. This subordinate relationship of State to law is encapsulated in the concept of the *Rechtsstaat*. This idea of the *Rechtsstaat* meant that the State itself was controlled by notions of law which limited its sphere of legitimate activity. Broadly speaking, the State was required to institute general law and could not make laws aimed at particular people.

The fact that this strong *Rechtsstaat* version of the Rule of Law never existed in England reflects its particular history. The revolutionary struggles of the 17th century had delivered effective control of the English State machinery to the bourgeois class who exercised that power through Parliament. After the 17th century, the English bourgeoisie was never faced with a threatening State against which it had to protect itself: it effectively was the State. On the continent, such was not the case and the emergent bourgeoisie had to assert its power against, and safeguard itself from, the power of a State machinery that it did not control. The development of *Rechtsstaat* theory as a means of limiting the power of the State can be seen as one of the ways in which the continental bourgeoisie attempted to safeguard its position. In England, however, there was not the same need in the 18th and 19th centuries for the bourgeoisie to protect itself behind a *Rechtsstaat* version of the Rule of Law. In England, those who benefited from the enactment and implementation of general laws as required by *Rechtsstaat* theory, the middle classes, also effectively controlled Parliament and could benefit just as well from its particular enactments. Thus, in terms of 19th century England, as Franz Neumann stated, the doctrines of parliamentary sovereignty and the Rule of Law were not antagonistic but complementary.

1.5.2 FA von Hayek

FA von Hayek followed Dicey in seeing the essential component of the Rule of Law as being the absence of arbitrary power in the hands of the State. As Hayek expressed it in his book *The Road to Serfdom* (1971):

> Stripped of all technicalities the Rule of Law means that government in all its actions is bound by rules fixed and announced beforehand.

Hayek, however, went further than Dicey in setting out the form and, at least in a negative way, the content that legal rules had to comply with in order for them to be considered as compatible with the Rule of Law. As Hayek expressed it:

> The Rule of Law implies limits on the scope of legislation, it restricts it to the kind of general rules known as formal law; and excludes legislation directly aimed at particular people.

This means that law should not be particular in content or application, but should be general in nature, applying to all and benefiting none in particular. Nor should law be aimed at achieving particular goals; its function is to set the boundaries of personal action, not to dictate the course of such action.

Hayek was a severe critic of the interventionist State in all its guises, from the fascist right wing to the authoritarian left wing and encompassing the contemporary welfare State in the middle. His criticism was founded on two bases:

- *Efficiency*. From the micro-economic perspective, and Hayek was an economist, only the person concerned can fully know all the circumstances of their situation. The State cannot wholly understand any individual's situation and should, therefore, as a matter of efficiency leave it to the individuals concerned to make their own decisions about what they want or how they choose to achieve what they want, so long as it is achieved in a legal way.

- *Morality*. From this perspective, to the extent that the State leaves the individual less room to make individual decisions, it reduces their freedom.

It is apparent, and not surprising considering his Austrian background, that Hayek adopted a *Rechtsstaat* view of the Rule of Law. He believed that the meaning of the Rule of Law, as it was currently understood in contemporary English jurisprudence, represented a narrowing from its original meaning which he believed had more in common with *Rechtsstaat* than it presently did. As he pointed out, the ultimate conclusion of the current weaker version of the Rule of Law was that, so long as the actions of the State were duly authorised by legislation, any such act was lawful, and thus a claim to the preservation of the Rule of Law could be maintained. It should be noted that Hayek did not suggest at any time that rules enacted in other than a general form are not laws;

they are legal, as long as they are enacted through the appropriate and proper mechanisms, they simply are not in accordance with the Rule of Law as he understood that principle.

Hayek disapproved of the change he claimed to have seen in the meaning of the Rule of Law. It is clear, however, that, as with Dicey, his views on law and the meaning of the Rule of Law were informed by a particular political perspective. It is equally clear that what he regretted most was the replacement of a free market economy by a planned economy, regulated by an interventionist State. The contemporary State no longer simply provided a legal framework for the conduct of economic activity, but was actively involved in the direct co-ordination and regulation of economic activity in the pursuit of the goals that it set. This had a profound effect on the form of law. Clearly stated and fixed general laws were replaced by open-textured discretionary legislation. Also, whereas the Diceyan version of the Rule of Law had operated in terms of abstract rights and duties, formal equality and formal justice, the new version addressed concrete issues and addressed questions of substantive equality and justice.

1.5.3   EP Thompson

The Rule of Law is a mixture of implied promise and convenient vagueness. It is vagueness at the core of the concept that permits the general idea of the Rule of Law to be appropriated by people with apparently irreconcilable political agendas in support of their particular political positions. So far, consideration has been given to Dicey and Hayek, two theorists on the right of the political spectrum who saw themselves as proponents and defenders of the Rule of Law; however, a similar claim can be made from the left. The case in point is EP Thompson, a Marxist historian, who also saw the Rule of Law as a protection against, and under attack from, the encroaching power of the modern State.

Thompson shared Hayek's distrust of the encroachments of the modern State and he was equally critical of the extent to which the contemporary State intervened in the day-to-day lives of its citizens. From Thompson's perspective, however, the problem arose not so much from the fact that the State was undermining the operation of the market economy, but from the way in which the State used its control over the legislative process to undermine civil liberties in the pursuit of its own concept of public interest.

In *Whigs and Hunters* (1975), a study of the manipulation of law by the landed classes in the 18th century, Thompson concluded that the Rule of Law is not just a necessary means of limiting the potential abuse of power, but that:

> ... the Rule of Law, itself, the imposing of effective inhibitions upon power and the defence of the citizen from power's all-intrusive claims, seems to me an unqualified human good.

In reaching such a conclusion, Thompson clearly concurs with Hayek's view that there is more to the Rule of Law than the requirement that law be processed through the appropriate legal institutions. He too argued that the core meaning of the Rule of Law involved more than mere procedural propriety and suggested that the other essential element is the way, and the extent to which, it places limits on the exercise of State power.

1.5.4 Joseph Raz

Some legal philosophers have recognised the need for State intervention in contemporary society and have provided ways of understanding the Rule of Law as a means of controlling discretion without attempting to eradicate it completely. Joseph Raz ('The Rule of Law and its virtue' (1977) 93 LQR 195), for example, recognised the need for the government of men as well as laws, and that the pursuit of social goals may require the enactment of particular as well as general laws. Indeed, he suggested that it would be impossible in practical terms for law to consist solely of general rules. Raz even criticised Hayek for disguising a political argument as a legal one in order to attack policies of which he did not approve. Yet at the same time, Raz also saw the Rule of Law as essentially a negative value, acting to minimise the danger that could follow the exercise of discretionary power in an arbitrary way. In that respect, of seeking to control the exercise of discretion, he shares common ground with Thompson, Hayek and Dicey.

Raz claimed that the basic requirement from which the wider idea of the Rule of Law emerged is the requirement that the law must be capable of guiding the individual's behaviour. He stated some of the most important principles that may be derived from this general idea:

- laws should be prospective rather than retroactive. People cannot be guided by or expected to obey laws which have not as yet been introduced. Laws should also be open and clear to enable people to understand them and guide their actions in line with them;
- laws should be stable and should not be changed too frequently as this might lead to confusion as to what was actually covered by the law;
- there should be clear rules and procedures for making laws;
- the independence of the judiciary has to be guaranteed to ensure that they are free to decide cases in line with the law and not in response to any external pressure;
- the principles of natural justice should be observed, requiring an open and fair hearing to be given to all parties to proceedings;
- the courts should have the power to review the way in which the other principles are implemented to ensure that they are being operated as demanded by the Rule of Law;

- the courts should be easily accessible as they remain at the heart of the idea of making discretion subject to legal control;
- the discretion of the crime preventing agencies should not be allowed to pervert the law.

It is evident that Raz saw the Rule of Law being complied with if the procedural rules of law-making were complied with, subject to a number of safeguards. It is of no little interest that Raz saw the courts as having an essential part to play in his version of the Rule of Law. This point will be considered further in Chapter 6 in relation to judicial review.

1.5.5 Roberto Unger

In *Law and Modern Society* (1976), the American critical legal theorist Roberto Unger set out a typology of social order, one category of which is essentially the Rule of Law system. Unger distinguished this form of social order from others on the basis of two particular and unique characteristics. The first of these is *autonomy*: the fact that law has its own sphere of authority and operates independently within that sphere without reference to any external controlling factor. Unger distinguished four distinct aspects of legal autonomy which may be enumerated as follows:

- *substantive autonomy*: this refers to the fact that law is not explicable in other, non-legal terms. To use the tautological cliché – the law is the law. In other words, law is self-referential, it is not about something else; it cannot be reduced to the level of a mere means to an end, it is an end in itself;
- *institutional autonomy*: this refers to the fact that the legal institutions such as the courts are separate from other State institutions and is highlighted in the fundamental principle of judicial independence;
- *methodological autonomy*: this refers to the fact that law has, or at least lays claim to having, its own distinct form of reasoning and justifications for its decisions;
- *occupational autonomy*: this refers to the fact that access to law is not immediate, but is gained through the legal professions, who act as gatekeepers and who exercise a large degree of independent control over the working of the legal system.

The second distinguishing feature of legal order, according to Unger, is its *generality*: the fact that it applies to all people without personal or class favouritism. Everyone is equal under the law and is treated in the same manner.

In putting forward this typology of social order, Unger recognised the advantages inherent in a Rule of Law system over a system that operates on the basis of arbitrary power, but he was ultimately sceptical as to the reality of the equality that such a system supports and questioned its future continuation.

The point of major interest for this book, however, is the way in which each of the four distinct areas of supposed autonomy is increasingly being challenged and undermined, as will be considered at the end of the next section.

1.5.6 Max Weber

Unger saw the development of the Rule of Law as a product of Western capitalist society and, in highlighting the distinct nature of the form of law under that system, he may be seen as following the German sociologist Max Weber. Weber's general goal was to examine and explain the structure and development of Western capitalist society. In so doing, he was concerned with those unique aspects of that society which distinguished it from other social formations. One such distinguishing characteristic was the form of law that he characterised as a formally rational system, which prefigured Unger's notion of legal autonomy. (See Weber, *Wirtschaft und Gesellschaft* (trans 1968).)

Weber's autonomous legal system was accompanied by a State which limited itself to establishing a clear framework of social order and left individuals to determine their own destinies in a free market system. In the course of the 20th century, however, the move from a free market to a basically planned economy, with the State playing an active part in economic activity, brought about a major change in both the form and function of law.

1.5.7 The Rule of Law and the contemporary form of law

While the State remained apart from civil society, its functions could be restricted within a limited sphere of activity circumscribed within the doctrine of the Rule of Law. However, as the State became increasingly involved in actually regulating economic activity, the form of law had by necessity to change. To deal with problems as and when they arose, the State had to assume discretionary powers rather than be governed by fixed pre-determined rules. Such discretion, however, is antithetical to the traditional idea of the Rule of Law which was posited on the fact of limiting the State's discretion. Thus emerged the tension between the Rule of Law and the requirements of regulating social activity that FA von Hayek, for one, saw as a fundamental change for the worse in our society.

With specific regard to the effect of this change on law's previous autonomy, there is clear agreement amongst academic writers that there has been a fundamental alteration in the nature of law. Whereas legislation previously took the form of fixed and precisely stated rules, now legislation tends be open-textured and to grant wide discretionary powers to particular State functionaries, resulting in a corresponding reduction in the power of the courts to control such activity. The courts have resisted this process to a degree, through the expansion of the procedure for judicial review, but their role in the area relating to administration remains at best questionable. The growth of delegated legislation, in which Parliament simply passes enabling Acts empowering ministers of State to make regulations as they consider necessary, is a prime example of this process (considered in detail in Chapter 2). In addition, once made, such regulations tend not to be general but highly particular, even technocratic in their detail.

The increased use of tribunals with the participation of non-legal experts rather than courts to decide disputes, with the underlying implication that the law is not capable of resolving the problem adequately, also represents a diminishment in law's previous power, as does the use of planning procedures as opposed to fixed rules of law in determining decisions. (Tribunals will be considered in Chapter 8.)

Legislation also increasingly pursues substantive justice rather than merely limiting itself to the provision of formal justice as required under the Rule of Law. As an example of this, consumer law may be cited; thus, in the Unfair Contract Terms Act 1977, contract terms are to be evaluated on the basis of reasonableness and, under the Consumer Credit Act 1974, agreements may be rejected on the basis of their being extortionate or unconscionable. Such provisions actually override the market assumptions as to formal equality in an endeavour to provide a measure of substantive justice.

All the foregoing examples of a change can be characterised as involving a change from 'law as end in itself' to 'law as means to an end'. In Weberian terms, this change in law represents a change from *formal rationality*, in which law determined outcomes to problems stated in the form of legal terms through the application of abstract legal concepts and principles, to a system of *substantive rationality*, where law is simply a mechanism to achieve a goal set outside of law.

In other words, law is no longer seen as completely autonomous as it once was. Increasingly, it is seen as merely instrumental in the achievement of some wider purpose which the State, acting as the embodiment of the general interest, sets. Paradoxically, as will be seen later, even when the law attempts to intervene in this process, as it does through judicial review, it does so in a way that undermines its autonomy and reveals it to be simply another aspect of political activity.

1.6 Human rights discourse and the Rule of Law

In an article published in the *London Review of Books* and *The Guardian* newspaper in May 1995, the High Court judge, as he then was, Sir Stephen Sedley made explicit the links and tensions between the doctrine of the Rule of Law and the relationship of the courts and the executive, and the implications for the use of judicial review as a means of controlling the exercise of executive power. In his view:

> Our agenda for the 21st century is not necessarily confined to choice between a 'rights instrument' interpreted by a judiciary with a long record of illiberal

adjudication, and rejection of any rights instrument in favour of Parliamentary government. The better government becomes, the less scope there will be for judicial review of it.

But, for the foreseeable future, we have a problem: how to ensure that as a society we are governed within a law which has internalised the notion of fundamental human rights. Although this means adopting the Rule of Law, like democracy, as a higher-order principle, we do have the social consensus which alone can accord it that primacy. And, if in our own society the Rule of Law is to mean much, *it must at least mean that it is the obligation of the courts to articulate and uphold the ground rules of ethical social existence which we dignify as fundamental human rights* ... There is a potential tension between the principle of democratic government and the principle of equality before the law ... The notion that the prime function of human rights and indeed the Rule of Law is to protect the weak against the strong is not mere sentimentality. It is the child of an era of history in which equality of treatment and opportunity has become perceived ... as an unqualified good, and of a significant recognition that you do not achieve equality merely by proclaiming it ... fundamental human rights to be real, have to steer towards outcomes which invert those inequalities of power that mock the principle of equality before the law.

Such talk of fundamental human rights denies the absolute sovereignty of Parliament in its recognition of areas that are beyond the legitimate exercise of State power. It also recognises, however, that notions of the Rule of Law cannot be satisfied by the provision of merely formal equality as Dicey and Hayek would have it and previous legal safeguards would have provided. For Sedley, the Rule of Law clearly imports, and is based on, ideas of substantive equality that market systems and legal formalism cannot provide and in fact undermine. His version of the Rule of Law clearly involves a reconsideration of the relationship of the executive and the judiciary, and involves the latter in a further reconsideration of their own previous beliefs and functions.

1.7   The Human Rights Act 1998

As is evident in the quotation from Sir Stephen Sedley above, some judges, at least, saw their role in maintaining the Rule of Law as providing protection for fundamental human rights. In attempting to achieve this end, they faced a particular problem in relation to the way in which the unwritten English constitution was understood, and was understood to operate. The freedom of individual action in English law was not based on ideas of positive human rights which could not be taken away, but on negative liberties: that is, individual subjects were entitled to do whatever was not forbidden by the law. This was particularly problematic when it was linked to the doctrine of the sovereignty of Parliament, which, in effect, meant that Parliament was free to restrict, or indeed remove, individual liberties at any time merely by passing the necessary legislation.

It is generally accepted that the courts developed the procedure of judicial review, as an aspect of the Rule of Law, in an attempt to protect individuals from the excesses of an over-powerful executive (see 6.10 for a detailed consideration). But, in so doing, they were limited in what they could achieve by the very nature of the procedure available to them. They could not directly question the laws produced by Parliament on the basis of substance, as constitutional courts in other systems could, but were restricted essentially to questioning the formal or procedural proprieties of such legislation. There was, however, an alternative forum capable of challenging the substance of English law, and one that was based on the assumption of positive rights rather than negative liberties. That forum was the European Court of Human Rights (ECtHR).

It has to be established and emphasised from the outset that the substance of this section has absolutely nothing to do with the European Union as such; the Council of Europe is a completely distinct organisation and, although membership of the two organisations overlap, they are not the same. The Council of Europe is concerned not with economic matters, but with the protection of civil rights and freedoms (the nature of these institutions and the operation of the ECtHR will be considered in detail in Chapter 13).

The UK was one of the initial signatories to the European Convention on Human Rights and Fundamental Freedoms (hereafter the ECHR) in 1950, which was instituted in post-war Europe as a means of establishing and enforcing essential human rights. In 1966, the UK recognised the power of the European Commission on Human Rights to hear complaints from individual UK citizens and, at the same time, recognised the authority of the European Court of Human Rights to adjudicate in such matters. It did not, however, at that time incorporate the ECHR into UK law.

The consequence of non-incorporation was that the Convention could not be directly enforced in English courts. In *R v Secretary of State for the Home Department ex p Brind* (1991), the Court of Appeal decided that ministerial directives did not have to be construed in line with the ECHR, as that would be tantamount to introducing the ECHR into English law without the necessary legislation. UK citizens were therefore in the position of having to pursue rights, which the State endorsed, in an external forum rather than through their own court system and, in addition, having to exhaust the domestic judicial procedure before they could gain access to that external forum. Such a situation was extremely unsatisfactory, and not just for complainants under the ECHR. Many members of the judiciary, including the then Lord Chief Justice Lord Bingham, were in favour of incorporation, not merely on general moral grounds, but equally on the ground that they resented having to make decisions in line with UK law which they knew full well would be overturned on appeal to the European Court. Equally, there was some discontent that the decisions in the European Court were being taken, and its general jurisprudence was being developed, without the direct input of the UK legal system. The courts, however, were not completely bound to decide cases in presumed ignorance of the ECHR, and did what they could to make decisions in line with it. For example, where domestic statutes were enacted to fulfil ECHR obligations, the courts could, of course, construe the meaning of the statute in the light of the ECHR. It was also possible that, due to the relationship of the ECHR with European Community law, the courts could find themselves applying the former in considering the latter. More indirectly, however, where the common law was uncertain, unclear or incomplete, the courts ruled, wherever possible, in a manner which conformed with the ECHR or, where statute was found to be ambiguous, they presumed that Parliament intended to legislate in conformity with the UK's international obligations under the ECHR. As Lord Bingham himself put it:

> In these ways, the Convention made a clandestine entry into British law by the back door, being forbidden to enter by the front [Earl Grey Memorial Lecture, http://webjcli.ncl.ac.uk/1998/issue1/bingham1.html].

Even allowing for this degree of judicial manoeuvring, the situation still remained unsatisfactory. Pressure groups did agitate for the incorporation of the ECHR into the UK legal system, but, when in 1995 a Private Member's Bill moving for incorporation was introduced in the House of Lords, the Home Office minister, Lady Blatch, expressed the then government's view that such incorporation was 'undesirable and unnecessary, both in principle and practice'. The Labour opposition, however, was committed to the incorporation of the ECHR into UK law and, when it gained office in 1997, it immediately set about the process of incorporation. This process resulted in the Human Rights Act (HRA) 1998.

Rights provided under the European Convention on Human Rights

The Articles incorporated into UK law, and listed in Sched 1 to the Act, cover the following matters:

- the right to life. Article 2 states that 'Everyone's right to life shall be protected by law';
- prohibition of torture. Article 3 actually provides that 'No one shall be subjected to torture or to inhuman or degrading treatment or punishment';
- prohibition of slavery and forced labour (Art 4);
- the right to liberty and security. After stating the general right, Art 5 is mainly concerned with the conditions under which individuals can lawfully be deprived of their liberty;
- the right to a fair trial. Article 6 provides that 'everyone is entitled to a fair and public hearing within a reasonable time by an independent and impartial tribunal established by law';

- the general prohibition of the enactment of retrospective criminal offences. Article 7 does, however, recognise the *post hoc* criminalisation of previous behaviour where it is 'criminal according to the general principles of law recognised by civilised nations';
- the right to respect for private and family life. Article 8 extends this right to cover a person's home and their correspondence;
- freedom of thought, conscience and religion (Art 9);
- freedom of expression. Article 10 extends the right to include 'freedom ... to receive and impart information and ideas without interference by public authority and regardless of frontiers';
- freedom of assembly and association. Article 11 specifically includes the right to form and join trade unions;
- the right to marry (Art 12);
- prohibition of discrimination (Art 14);
- the right to peaceful enjoyment of possessions and protection of property (Art 1 of Protocol 1);
- the right to education (subject to a UK reservation (Art 2 of Protocol 1));
- the right to free elections (Art 3 of Protocol 1);
- the right not to be subjected to the death penalty (Arts 1 and 2 of Protocol 6).

The rights listed can be relied on by any person, non-governmental organisation or group of individuals. Importantly, they also apply, where appropriate, to companies which are incorporated entities and hence legal persons. However, they cannot be relied on by governmental organisations, such as local authorities.

The nature of rights under the Act

The rights listed above are not all seen in the same way. Some are absolute and inalienable and cannot be interfered with by the State. Others are merely contingent and are subject to derogation, that is, signatory States can opt out of them in particular circumstances. The ECtHR also recognised the concept of 'a margin of appreciation', which allows for countries to deal with particular problems in the context of their own internal circumstances (see 13.4). The absolute rights are those provided for in Arts 2, 3, 4, 7 and 14. All the others are subject to potential limitations. In particular, the rights provided for under Arts 8, 9, 10 and 11 are subject to legal restrictions such as are:

> ... necessary in a democratic society in the interests of national security or public safety, for the prevention of crime, for the protection of health or morals or the protection of the rights and freedoms of others [Art 11(2)].

The UK entered such a derogation in relation to the extended detention of terrorist suspects without charge, under the Prevention of Terrorism (Temporary Provisions) Act 1989, subsequently replaced and extended by the Terrorism Act 2000. Those powers had been held to be contrary to Art 5 of the Convention by the ECtHR in *Brogan v UK* (1989). The UK also entered a derogation with regard to the Anti-Terrorism, Crime and Security Act 2001, which was enacted in response to the attack on the World Trade Center building in New York on 11 September of that year. The Act allows for the detention without trial of foreign citizens suspected of being involved in terrorist activity.

In deciding the legality of any derogation, courts are required not just to be convinced that there is a need for the derogation, but they must also be sure that the State's action has been proportionate to that need. In other words, the State must not overreact to a perceived problem by removing more rights than is necessary to effect the solution. With further regard to the possibility of derogation, s 19 of the 1998 Act requires a minister, responsible for the passage of any Bill through Parliament, either to make a written declaration that it is compatible with the Convention or, alternatively, to declare that although it may not be compatible, it is still the government's wish to proceed with it.

The structure of the Human Rights Act

The HRA has profound implications for the operation of the English legal system. However, to understand the structure of the HRA, it is essential to be to aware of the nature of the changes introduced by the Act, especially in the apparent passing of fundamental powers to the judiciary. Under the doctrine of parliamentary sovereignty, the legislature could pass such laws at it saw fit, even to the extent of removing the rights of its citizens. The 1998 Act reflects a move towards the entrenchment of rights recognised under the Convention but, given the sensitivity of the relationship between the elected Parliament and the unelected judiciary, it has been thought expedient to minimise the change in the constitutional relationship of Parliament and the judiciary.

Section 2 of the Act requires future courts to take into account any previous decision of the ECtHR. This provision impacts on the operation of the doctrine of precedent within the English legal system, as it effectively sanctions the overruling of any previous English authority that was in conflict with a decision of the ECtHR.

Section 3 requires all legislation to be read, so far as possible, to give effect to the rights provided under the Convention. As will be seen, this section provides the courts with new and extended powers of interpretation. It also has the potential to invalidate previously accepted interpretations of statutes which were made, by necessity, without recourse to the Convention (see *Mendoza v Ghaidan* (2002) at 1.7.1.3, below).

Section 4 empowers the courts to issue a declaration of incompatibility where any piece of primary legislation is found to conflict with the rights provided under the ECHR. This has the effect that the courts cannot invalidate primary legislation, essentially Acts of Parliament but also Orders in Council, which are found to be incompatible; they can only make a declaration of such incompatibility, and leave it to the legislature to remedy the situation through new legislation. Section 10 provides for the provision of remedial legislation through a fast track procedure, which gives a minister of the Crown the power to alter such primary legislation by way of statutory instrument.

Section 5 requires the Crown to be given notice where a court considers issuing a declaration of incompatibility and the appropriate government minister is entitled to be made a party to the case.

Section 6 declares it unlawful for any public authority to act in a way which is incompatible with the ECHR, and s 7 allows the 'victim of the unlawful act' to bring proceedings against the public authority in breach. Section 8 empowers the court to grant such relief or remedy against the public authority in breach of the Act as it considers just and appropriate.

Where a public authority is acting under the instructions of some primary legislation, which is itself incompatible with the ECHR, the public authority will not be liable under s 6.

Section 19 of the Act requires that the minister responsible for the passage of any Bill through Parliament must make a written statement that the provisions of the Bill are compatible with ECHR rights. Alternatively, the minister may make a statement that the Bill does not comply with ECHR rights, but that the government nonetheless intends to proceed with it.

Reactions to the introduction of the HRA have been broadly welcoming, but some important criticisms have been raised. First, the ECHR is a rather old document and does not address some of the issues that contemporary citizens might consider as equally fundamental to those rights actually contained in the document. For example, it is silent on the rights to substantive equality relating to such issues as welfare and access to resources. Also, the actual provisions of the ECHR are uncertain in the extent of their application, or perhaps more crucially in the area where they can be derogated from, and at least to a degree they are contradictory. The most obvious difficulty arises from the need to reconcile Art 8's right to respect for private and family life with Art 10's freedom of expression. Newspaper editors have expressed their concern in relation to this particular issue, and fear the development, at the hands of the court, of an overly limiting law of privacy which would prevent investigative journalism. This leads to a further difficulty – the potential politicisation, together with a significant enhancement in the power, of the judiciary.

Consideration of this issue will be postponed until some cases involving the HRA have been examined.

Perhaps the most serious criticism of the HRA is the fact that the government has not seen fit to establish a Human Rights Commission to publicise and facilitate the operation of its procedures. Many have seen the setting up of such a body as a necessary step in raising human rights awareness and assisting individuals, who might otherwise be unable to use the Act, to enforce their rights.

Although the HRA was enacted in 1998, it did not come into force generally until October 2000. The reason for the substantial delay was the need to train all members of the judiciary, from the highest Law Lord to the humblest magistrate, in the consequences and implications of the new Act. However, the Act was in force before that date in Scotland as a consequence of the devolution legislation, the Scotland Act, which specifically applied the provisions of the HRA to the Scottish Parliament and Executive. It is for that reason that the earliest cases under the Human Rights provisions were heard in the Scottish courts.

1.7.1 Cases decided under the Human Rights Act

Before and subsequent to the coming into effect in England of the HRA on 2 October 2000, the newspapers were full of dire warnings as to the damaging effect that the Act would have on accepted legal principles and practices. However, an examination of some of the earliest cases to reach the higher courts may serve to dispel such a view.

1.7.1.1 Road Traffic Act 1988

Brown v Stott (2001)

Brown had been arrested at a supermarket on suspicion of the theft of a bottle of gin. When the police officers noticed that she smelled of alcohol, they asked her how she had travelled to the store. Brown replied that she had driven and pointed out her car in the supermarket car park. Later, at the police station, the police used their powers under s 172(2)(a) of the Road Traffic Act 1988 to require her to say who had been driving her car at about 2.30 pm, that is, at the time when she would have travelled in it to the supermarket. Brown admitted that she had been driving. After a positive breath test Brown was charged with drink driving, but appealed to the Scottish High Court of Justiciary for a declaration that the case could not go ahead on the grounds that her admission, as required under s 172, was contrary to the right to a fair trial under Art 6 of the ECHR.

In February 2000, the High Court of Justiciary supported her claim on the basis that the right to silence and the right not to incriminate oneself at trial would be worthless if an accused person did not enjoy a right of silence in the course of the criminal investigation leading to the court proceedings. If this were not the case, then the police could require an accused person to provide an incriminating answer which subsequently could be used in evidence against them at their trial. Consequently, the use of evidence obtained under s 172 of the Road Traffic Act 1988 infringed Brown's rights under Art 6(1).

Even before the HRA was in operation in England, the Scottish case was followed by a similar ruling in Birmingham Crown Court in July 2000.

The implication of these decisions was extremely serious, not just in relation to drink driving offences, but also in relation to fines following the capture of speeding cars by speed cameras. As can be appreciated, the film merely identifies the car; it is s 172 of the Road Traffic Act that actually requires the compulsory identification of the driver. If *Brown v Stott* stated the law accurately, then the control of speeding cars and drink driving was in a parlous state.

However, on 5 December 2000, the Privy Council reversed the judgment of the Scottish appeal court in *Brown*. The Privy Council reached its decision on the grounds that the jurisprudence of the ECtHR, established through previous cases, had clearly established that whilst the overall fairness of a criminal trial could not be compromised, the constituent rights contained in Art 6 of the ECHR were not themselves absolute and could be restricted in certain limited conditions. Consequently, it was possible for individual States to introduce limited qualification of those rights, so long as they were aimed at 'a clear public objective' and were 'proportionate to the situation' under consideration. The ECHR had to be read as balancing community rights with individual rights. With specific regard to the Road Traffic Act, the objective to be attained was the prevention of injury and death from the misuse of cars, and s 172 was not a disproportionate response to that objective.

1.7.1.2 *Confiscation cases*

Prior to the Proceeds of Crime Act 2002, a number of Acts of Parliament allowed for the property of individuals to be confiscated where it was assumed that such assets were the result of criminal activity. That legislation included the Criminal Justice Act 1988, as amended by the Proceeds of Crime Act 1995, the Drug Trafficking Act 1994 and the Terrorism Act 2000.

In allowing the court to make such an assumption, the Acts reversed the usual burden of proof to the extent that the person against whom the powers are used is required to demonstrate, on the balance of probabilities, that their assets are not the product of criminal activity. Section 1(1) of the Proceeds of

Crime (Scotland) Act 1995 also allows for individual's assets to be confiscated on the basis of similar assumptions.

In October 2000, in *McIntosh v AG for Scotland*, it was argued that the assumption made under s 3(2) of the 1995 Act displaced the presumption of innocence in Art 6(2) of the ECHR and hence was unlawful. McIntosh had been convicted for supplying heroin and the Crown had applied for a confiscation order under the 1995 Act. The Crown submitted that, since confiscation orders did not constitute a separate criminal offence, Art 6(2) of the Convention could not grant him the presumption of innocence in respect of such an action.

The High Court of Justiciary, Lord Kirkwood dissenting, approved McIntosh's submission and issued a declaration to that effect and, in so doing, threatened the efficacy of the whole confiscation policy.

In December 2000, the Court of Appeal in England, sitting with Lord Chief Justice Woolf on the panel, had the opportunity to consider the effect of the HRA on the assumptions relating to confiscation powers in the case of *R v Benjafield and Others* (2001). In the Court of Appeal's opinion, the express reversal of the burden of proof in confiscation proceedings amounted to a substantial interference with the normal presumption of innocence. However, it held that Parliament had adequately balanced the defendant's interests against the public interest and cited the fact that the question of confiscation only arose after conviction and that the court should not make a confiscation order when there was a serious risk of injustice. It also considered that the court's role in the appeal procedure ensured that there was no unfairness to the individual concerned. As in the Privy Council's decision in *Brown*, the Court of Appeal held that where the discretion given to the court and prosecution was properly exercised, it was justifiable as a reasonable and proportionate response to a substantial public interest. In so doing, it declined to apply the High Court of Justiciary's decision in *McIntosh*, preferring the approach of the Privy Council in *Brown*.

When the further appeal in the *McIntosh* case came before the Privy Council in February 2001, the decision of the Scottish appeal court was unanimously overturned on two grounds:

- the confiscation order was not by way of a criminal action and therefore the assumptions were not in contravention of Art 6(2). An application for a confiscation order did not, of itself, lay a criminal charge against the convicted defendant. Although the court could assume that such a defendant had been involved in drug trafficking, there were no statutory assumptions as to a defendant's guilt for drug trafficking offences;

- in addition, and more generally, Art 6(2) was not an absolute right and therefore, following *Brown*, could justifiably be encroached upon by the proportionate enactment of a democratically elected Parliament in the pursuit of its anti-crime policy.

In reaching this decision, the Privy Council expressly approved the Court of Appeal's decision in *R v Benjafield*.

Subsequently, in *Phillips v UK*, decided in July 2001, the ECJ concurred with the decision of the Privy Council in *McIntosh* by holding, by a majority of 5:2, that the confiscation procedure under the Drug Trafficking Act 1994 was not contrary to European Convention rights and, unanimously, that in any event the provisions of the Act represented a proportionate response to the problem under consideration.

Finally, when *R v Benjafield* came on appeal to the House of Lords, it felt comfortable in following the decisions and reasoning in both *McIntosh* and *Phillips*. At the same time, the House of Lords also applied that reasoning to confiscation procedure under the Criminal Justice Act 1988 in *R v Rezvi* (2002).

The courts' power to make confiscation orders was extended under the Proceeds of Crime Act (PCA) 2002, which came into full effect in March 2003. The Act also consolidates provisions relating to money laundering. Amongst the 12 parts of the Act, the following are the most significant:

- Part 1 creates an Assets Recovery Agency (ARA) which became operational on 24 February 2003. The function of this agency is to carry out investigations into particular individuals which may lead to criminal confiscation or civil recovery proceedings. The former action relates to orders made consequent upon the conviction of a defendant in the Crown Court, whilst the latter refers to an action in the High Court to recover the proceeds of unlawful activity.

- Part 2 sets out the procedures relating to confiscation in England and Wales. Section 6 sets out the circumstances in which orders can be made. Confiscation orders may only be made in the Crown Court. However, where the conviction takes place in the magistrates' court, a confiscation order can still be made if the defendant is either committed to the Crown Court for sentence, or committed to the Crown Court for sentence and confiscation. Section 70 of the Act provides for this new form of committal from the magistrates' court. The confiscation procedures are mandatory and the courts must implement them where asked to do so by the prosecutor or the ARA. A confiscation order made under the Act is designed to ensure that the convicted person has to account for any benefit from criminal activity, and provides for confiscation of the defendant's benefit from either 'general criminal conduct' or 'particular criminal conduct'. General criminal conduct arises where the courts identify the person as having 'a criminal lifestyle'. This in turn is established by reference to the nature of the offence of which he has been convicted in the current proceedings, or certain previous offences set out in s 75 of and Sched 2 to the Act. Particular criminal conduct only involves the offences of which the defendant has been convicted in the current proceedings.

- Parts 3 and 4 extend the provision to Scotland and Northern Ireland respectively.

- Part 5 sets out new provisions for the recovery in the UK in civil proceedings of property or money which has been obtained through unlawful activity. It allows for the search, seizure and forfeiture of cash which has been obtained through unlawful activity or is intended for use in such activity.

- Part 6 empowers the Director of the ARA to exercise functions of the Inland Revenue in relation to income, gains and profits arising or accruing as a result of criminal conduct. That is to say, the ARA can actually tax individuals or companies on income generated by criminal activity.

- Part 7 consolidates, updates and reforms the criminal law in the UK with regard to money laundering.

- Part 8 sets out powers for use in criminal confiscation, civil recovery and money laundering investigations.

1.7.1.3 Cases applying s 3 of the HRA

R v A (2001)

It has long been a matter of concern that in cases where rape has been alleged, the common defence strategy employed by lawyers has been to attempt to attack the credibility of the woman making the accusation. Judges had the discretion to allow questioning of the woman as to her sexual history where this was felt to be relevant, and in all too many cases this discretion was exercised in a way that allowed defence counsel to abuse and humiliate women accusers. Section 41 of the Youth Justice and Criminal Evidence Act (YJCEA) 1999 placed the court under a restriction that seriously limited evidence that could be raised in cross-examination of a sexual relationship between a complainant and an accused. Under s 41(3) of the 1999 Act, such evidence was limited to sexual behaviour 'at or about the same time' as the event giving rise to the charge that was 'so similar' in nature that it could not be explained as a coincidence.

In *R v A*, the defendant in a case of alleged rape claimed that the provisions of the YJCEA were contrary to Art 6 of the ECHR to the extent that they prevented him from putting forward a full and complete defence. In reaching its decision, the House of Lords emphasised the need to protect women from humiliating cross-examination and prejudicial but valueless evidence in respect of their previous sex lives; it nonetheless held that the restrictions in s 41 of the 1999 Act were *prima facie* capable of preventing an accused from putting forward relevant evidence that could be crucial to his defence.

However, rather than make a declaration of incompatibility, the House of Lords preferred to make use of s 3 of the HRA to allow s 41 of the YJCEA to be read as permitting the admission of evidence or questioning relating to a relevant issue in the case where it was considered necessary by the trial judge to make the trial fair. The test of admissibility of evidence of previous sexual relations between an accused and a complainant under s 41(3) of the 1999 Act was whether the evidence was so relevant to the issue of consent that to exclude it would be to endanger the fairness of the trial under Art 6 of the ECHR. Where the line is to be drawn is left to the judgment of trial judges. In reaching its decision, the House of Lords was well aware that its interpretation of s 41 did a violence to its actual meaning, but it nonetheless felt it within its power so to do. The words of Lord Steyn are illustrative of this process:

> In my view section 3 requires the court to subordinate the niceties of the language of section 41(3)(c), and in particular the touchstone of coincidence, to broader considerations of relevance judged by logical and common sense criteria of time and circumstances. After all, it is realistic to proceed on the basis that the legislature would not, if alerted to the problem, have wished to deny the right to an accused to put forward a full and complete defence by advancing truly probative material. It is therefore possible under section 3 to read section 41, and in particular section 41(3)(c), as subject to the implied provision that evidence or questioning which is required to ensure a fair trial under Article 6 of the Convention should not be treated as inadmissible.

In this way, the House of Lords restored judicial discretion as to what can be raised in cross-examination in rape cases. It is to be hoped, sincerely but without much conviction on the basis of past history, that it is a discretion to be exercised sparingly and sympathetically.

Re S (2002)

In *Re S*, the Court of Appeal used s 3 of the HRA in such a way as to create new guidelines for the operation of the Children Act 1989, which increased the courts' powers to intervene in the interests of children taken into care under the Act. This extension of the courts' powers in the pursuit of the improved treatment of such children was achieved by reading the Act in such a way as to allow the courts increased discretion to make interim rather than final care orders, and to establish what were referred to as 'starred milestones' within a child's care plan. If such starred milestones were not achieved within a reasonable time, then the courts could be approached to deliver fresh directions. In effect, what the Court of Appeal was doing was setting up a new, and more active, regime of court supervision in care cases.

The House of Lords, however, although sympathetic to the aims of the Court of Appeal, felt that it had exceeded its powers of interpretation under s 3 of the HRA and, in its exercise of judicial creativity, it had usurped the function of Parliament.

Lord Nicholls explained the operation of s 3:

The Human Rights Act reserves the amendment of primary legislation to Parliament. By this means the Act seeks to preserve parliamentary sovereignty. The Act maintains the constitutional boundary. Interpretation of statutes is a matter for the courts; the enactment of statutes, are matters for Parliament ... [but that any interpretation which] departs substantially from a fundamental feature of an Act of Parliament is likely to have crossed the boundary between interpretation and amendment.

Unfortunately, the Court of Appeal had overstepped that boundary.

In *Mendoza v Ghaidan* (2002), the Court of Appeal used s 3 to extend the rights of same-sex partners to inherit a statutory tenancy under the Rent Act 1977. In *Fitzpatrick v Sterling Housing Association Ltd* (1999), the House of Lords had extended the rights of such individuals to inherit the lesser assured tenancy by including them within the deceased person's family. It declined to allow them to inherit statutory tenancies, however, on the grounds that they could not be considered to be the wife or husband of the deceased as the Act required. In *Mendoza*, the Court of Appeal held that the Rent Act, as it had been construed by the House of Lords in *Fitzpatrick*, was incompatible with Art 14 of the ECHR on the grounds of its discriminatory treatment of surviving same-sex partners. The court, however, decided that the failing could be remedied by reading the words 'as his or her wife or husband' in the Act as meaning 'as if they were his or her wife or husband'. *Mendoza* is of particular interest in the fact that it shows how the HRA can permit lower courts to avoid previous and otherwise binding decisions of the House of Lords. It also clearly shows the extent to which s 3 increases the powers of the judiciary in relation to statutory interpretation.

In spite of this potential increased power, the House of Lords found itself unable to use s 3 in *Bellinger v Bellinger* (2003). The case related to the rights of transsexuals and the court found itself unable, or at least unwilling, to interpret s 11(c) of the Matrimonial Causes Act 1973 in such a way as to allow a male to female transsexual to be treated in law as a female. Nonetheless, the court did issue a declaration of incompatibility (see below for explanation).

1.7.1.4 Declarations of incompatibility

As has been stated previously, the courts are not able to declare primary legislation invalid, but, as an alternative, they may make a declaration that the legislation in question is not compatible with the rights provided by the ECHR.

The first declaration of incompatibility was actually issued in *R v (1) Mental Health Review Tribunal, North & East London Region (2) Secretary of State for Health ex p H* in March 2001. In that case, the Court of Appeal held that ss 72 and 73 of the Mental Health Act 1983 were incompatible with Art 5(1) and (4) of the ECHR inasmuch as they reversed the normal burden of proof, by requiring the detained person to show that they should not be detained rather than the authorities to show that they should be detained.

Wilson v First County Trust (2000) was, however, the first case in which a court indicated the likelihood of its making a declaration of incompatibility under s 4 of the HRA 1998. The legislation in question was the Consumer Credit Act 1974 and, in particular, s 127(3) of that Act, which proscribed the enforcement of any consumer credit agreement which did not comply with the requirements of the 1974 Act. Wilson had borrowed £5,000 from First County Trust (FCT) and had pledged her car as security for the loan. Wilson was to be charged a fee of £250 for drawing up the loan documentation, but asked FCT to add it to the loan, which they agreed to do. The effect of this was that the loan document stated that the amount of the loan was £5,250. This, however, was inaccurate, as in reality, the extra £250 was not part of the loan as such; rather, it was part of the charge for the loan. The loan document had therefore been drawn up improperly and did not comply with the requirement of s 61 of the Consumer Credit Act 1974.

When Wilson subsequently failed to pay the loan at the end of the agreed period, FCT stated their intention of selling the car unless she paid £7,000. Wilson brought proceedings: (i) for a declaration that the agreement was unenforceable by reason of s 127(3) of the 1974 Act because of the misstatement of the amount of the loan; and (ii) for the agreement to be re-opened on the basis that it was an extortionate credit bargain. The judge rejected Wilson's first claim, but re-opened the agreement and substituted a lower rate of interest, and Wilson subsequently redeemed her car on payment of £6,900. However, she then successfully appealed against the judge's decision as to the enforceability of the agreement, the Court of Appeal holding that s 127(3) clearly and undoubtedly had the effect of preventing the enforcement of the original agreement, and that Wilson was entitled to the repayment of the money she had paid to redeem her car. Consequently, Wilson not only got her car back, but also the sum she paid to FCT, who lost their money completely. In reaching its decision, however, the Court of Appeal expressed the opinion that it was at least arguable that s 127(3) was incompatible with Art 6(1) and/or Art 1 of Protocol 1 to the ECHR. First, the absolute prohibition of enforcement of the agreement appeared to be a disproportionate restriction on the right of the lender to have the enforceability of its loan determined by the court, contrary to Art 6(1); and, secondly, to deprive FCT of its property, that is, the money which it had lent to Wilson, appeared to be contrary to Art 1 of Protocol 1.

Under those circumstances, the court considered it appropriate to give notice to the Crown under s 5 of the 1998 Act that it was considering making a declaration of incompatibility. On the continuation of the hearing, the Court of Appeal held that it was not possible to construe s 127(3) of the 1974 Act in such a way as to make it comply with the ECHR and, in May 2001, it issued a declaration of incompatibility.

A somewhat surprising factor in the *Wilson* case was that the human rights issue was raised by the court itself rather than by the parties to the action, thus indicating the judiciary's sensitivity to, and willingness to apply, the HRA. Also of interest and importance for the future impact of the Act was the fact that the issue was raised in an action between two private parties. Although s 7 of the HRA 1998 expressly applies it to the actions of public authorities, it can now clearly be seen that all legislation will be assessed for compatibility with the ECHR, even where public authorities are not concerned.

Similarly, in *Michael Douglas, Catherine Zeta-Jones, Northern and Shell plc v Hello! Ltd* (2001) and *Jon Venables and Robert Thompson v News Group Newspapers Ltd and Others* (2001), the courts used the HRA to extend common law doctrines into an unprecedented right to privacy and a right exercisable, not just vertically in relation to public authorities, but horizontally against other private individuals.

R v Secretary of State for the Environment, Transport and the Regions ex p Holding & Barnes plc and Others (2001)

In this case, the House of Lords overturned an earlier decision of the Administrative Court that had called into question the operation of the planning system under the Town and Country Planning Act 1990. Under the Act, the ultimate arbiter in relation to planning decisions was the Secretary of State. The Administrative Court held that, as a member of the executive, determining policy, the Secretary of State should not be involved in the quasi-judicial task of deciding applications. It followed, therefore, that the operation of the planning system was contrary to the right to a fair hearing by an independent tribunal as provided for under Art 6 of the ECHR.

In overturning that decision, the House of Lords unanimously decided that the planning process was human rights compatible. In their Lordships' view, the possibility of judicial review was sufficient to ensure compliance with Art 6(1) of the ECHR, even though it could only remedy procedural rather than substantive deficiencies.

Indeed, their Lordships showed some displeasure at the manner in which Art 6 had been deployed in an attempt to undermine the democratically elected Secretary of State by seeking to pass the power to make policy decisions from him to the courts. Both Lords Slynn and Hoffmann quoted the words of the European Commission in *ISKCON v UK* (1994) with approval:

> It is not the role of Article 6 of the Convention to give access to a level of jurisdiction which can substitute its opinion for that of the administrative authorities on questions of expediency and where the courts do not refuse to examine any of the points raised ...

Even more pointedly, Lord Hoffmann commented that:

> The Human Rights Act 1998 was no doubt intended to strengthen the rule of law but not to inaugurate the rule of lawyers.

1.7.1.5 Asylum and immigration

International Transport Roth GmbH v Secretary of State for the Home Department (2002)

As a means of trying to curtail illegal immigration into the UK, the Immigration and Asylum Act 1999 instituted a penalty regime to deter lorry drivers or haulage companies who, either intentionally or negligently, brought illegal entrants into the UK in their vehicles. The scheme allowed for imposition of a £2,000 penalty for every clandestine immigrant found in a vehicle. It also allowed for the detention of any vehicles involved in the carrying of the clandestine entrants if a senior immigration officer thought that the financial penalty would not be paid. The penalty was automatic unless the carrier showed that they had in place, and actually operated, an effective scheme to prevent the transport of clandestine entrants.

The penalty regime was struck down on two grounds at both first instance and in the Court of Appeal, by a majority decision. First, it was held that the reversal of the burden of proof was incompatible with Art 6 of the ECHR. Secondly, the power to detain vehicles to secure the payment of financial penalty, without allowing access to an independent tribunal to review the exercise of that power, was in conflict with Art 1 of Protocol 1 to the ECHR.

Whilst the courts recognised that the area of immigration control was quintessentially one where the State should have a wide discretion to pursue the general community interest, even at the expense of the rights of the individual, it was felt that in this instance, the State had exceeded that discretion. As Simon Brown LJ put it:

> There comes a point, however, when what is achieved is achieved only at the cost of basic fairness. The price in Convention terms becomes just too high. That is my judgment in the position here.

Rather than challenge the Court of Appeal's decision, the government announced in December 2002 a plan to introduce a more flexible system under the Nationality, Immigration and Asylum Act 2002. The new scheme will operate on the basis of variable penalties reflecting the degree of care taken by the hauliers to prevent the carriage of clandestine entrants. It will also introduce a statutory right of appeal against the penalty.

R v Secretary of State for the Home Department ex p Saadi (2001)

On 9 September 2001, Collins J in the Administrative Court held that the short term detention of asylum seekers in secure accommodation behind locked doors at the former RAF camp at Oakingham in Cambridgeshire, for what amounted to administrative convenience, was contrary to Art 5 of the ECHR. The Home Secretary, David Blunkett, immediately made known his anger at the decision and his intention to appeal against it. In October, the Court of Appeal overruled Collins J's decision, holding that the secure detention for a short period to allow for the expeditious processing of applicants' claims was not contrary to the ECHR.

A v Secretary of State for the Home Department (2002)

Following the terrorist attack on the World Trade Center on 11 September 2001, the UK Parliament introduced the Anti-Terrorism, Crime and Security Act 2001, which allowed for the detention, without charge, of non-UK citizens suspected of terrorist activities, who could not be repatriated to their own countries because of fear for their wellbeing. In July 2002, the Special Immigration Appeals Commission, instituted under the Act to hear appeals in relation to decisions taken under it, held that the Act was not in compliance with Art 14 of the ECHR to the extent that it treated non-nationals differently from UK nationals. Once again, the Home Secretary attacked the decision of the court, under the chairmanship of Collins J, and once again the Court of Appeal overruled the decision. In so doing, it emphasised that as the case related to matters of national security, it was self-evidently of a nature in which the courts should show considerable deference towards the executive. Consequently, as the Home Secretary was better qualified than the courts to decide what action had to be taken to safeguard national security, the courts should not intervene. This case represents an example of what has become known as the 'area of deference' within which the courts will 'defer on democratic grounds to the considered opinion of the elected body or person whose actual decision is said to be incompatible with the Convention'. (See Woolf LCJ's speech at the Oxford Lyceum in March 2003.)

R (on the Application of Q) v Secretary of State for the Home Department (2003)

In February 2003, Collins J once again antagonised the Home Secretary, this time by holding that the policy to refuse support to asylum seekers unless they claimed asylum at the port of entry under s 55 of the Nationality, Immigration and Asylum Act 2002 was unlawful. On this occasion, the Court of Appeal approved Collins J's decision, but in so doing, it provided the Home Secretary with advice on how to make the Act ECHR compliant, advice for which the Home Secretary thanked the court in his acceptance of the need to redraft the legislation.

1.7.2 The sentencing process

One area of criminal law that throws the relationship between the executive and the judiciary into particularly sharp focus is that of sentencing individuals who have been found guilty of particular offences. It is equally one that involves an interplay of judicial review, the ECHR and the HRA.

1.7.2.1 *Mandatory life sentences in relation to murder*

When the death penalty for murder was removed in 1965, it was replaced by a mandatory life sentence, that is, if an individual is found guilty of murder, the court has no alternative but to sentence them to a period of life imprisonment. By definition, a 'life sentence' is for an indeterminate period, but the procedure is for a period to be specified which the person must serve before they can be considered for release on parole. The problematic question of who sets this tariff is considered below. The judiciary have been consistently opposed to this fettering of their discretion; a number of leading judges, including the past Lord Chief Justices Bingham and Taylor, have spoken out against it and, in 1993, Lord Chief Justice Lane led a committee which recommended that the mandatory sentence be removed. As their Lordships correctly pointed out, there can be degrees of heinousness, even in regard to murder, and not all of those convicted deserve to be sentenced to life imprisonment. Mercy killers surely should not be treated in the same way as serial killers. This desire of the judges to remove the restriction in their sentencing power has, however, run up against the wish of politicians to be seen as tough on crime or at least not soft on crime.

The uncomfortable relationship between criminal justice and party politics can be seen in the conviction for murder of Norfolk farmer Tony Martin in April 2000. Martin had used a shotgun to shoot two people who had broken into his farmhouse. One was injured and the other, 16 year old Fred Barras, was killed. Martin was charged with murder and at his trial, evidence was led to show that he had lain in wait for his victims, had set traps in his house and had used an illegal pump-action shotgun to shoot Barras in the back as he was attempting to run away. By a majority of 10:2, the jury found him guilty of murder and, as required, the judge sentenced him to life imprisonment. Much of the press considered the sentence to be outrageously severe on a man whom they portrayed as merely protecting his property against the depredations of lawless louts (it has to be stated that Barras and his accomplice did have 114 previous convictions between them). In focusing attention on the right of individuals to use force to protect their property – which, in any case, they already had so long as they did not use more than reasonable force – the press displaced attention from where it could best be focused. Had the court not been required to pass a mandatory sentence, then it would have been able to pass a more suitable sentence, if that had been appropriate in the circumstances. The press, however, would not countenance the granting of such discretionary sentencing power to the courts which, in other circumstances, they persistently characterise as being out of touch and dangerously soft on criminals. The issue of mandatory life sentences for those convicted of murder has more recently come to prominence in relation to Sally Clark, a mother convicted and subsequently exonerated of the killing of her two infant children, one of whom died in 1996 and the other of whom died in 1998. Originally convicted on the spurious statistical evidence of an expert witness, she was released by the Court of Appeal when her husband discovered evidence that the second of their children had been suffering from a severe, and probably terminal, bacterial infection that had entered his cerebral and spinal fluid. Astonishingly, the existence of the infection had been known by the prosecution pathologist but was never revealed to the defence.

It may be claimed, as it has previously when other miscarriages of justice have come to light, that the outcome of the Sally Clark case demonstrates the essential validity of the English legal system. It should be emphasised, however, that the result only emerged due to the tenacity, skill and good luck of her husband. The conduct of the original case actually highlights problems in the reliance on the testimony of expert witnesses and the deficiency in the information provided to the defence by those involved in the prosecution.

The case also raises the general issue of women convicted of killing their babies. Under the Infanticide Act 1938, where a woman kills her child of under 12 months, what would ordinarily be murder is reduced to manslaughter if, at the time of the killing, 'the balance of her mind was disturbed by reason of her not having fully recovered from the effect of giving birth to the child or by reason of the effect of lactation'. As a result of this reduction in the severity of the charge, the judge, in the case of a conviction, will be in a position to exercise discretion in the sentence handed down. However, where women refuse to plead guilty to the lesser charge of manslaughter on the basis of their mental condition, they have on conviction to face the full force of the law in the form of the mandatory life sentence for murder. Following the Sally Clark appeal case, it is not unlikely that some of them have been convicted on doubtful evidence. Others may be serving life sentences for actions carried out in a state of *postpartum* depression, a well recognised and potentially severely debilitating medical condition. To sentence such women to life imprisonment is surely not to do justice, yet life imprisonment is the only sentence open to the judge where the accused is found guilty of murder. Thus, in the case of Angela Cannings, a woman convicted of smothering her two children, seven week old Jason in 1991 and four month old Matthew in 1999, Mrs Justice Hallett, the presiding judge, had no choice but to jail her for life, but clearly expressed her dissatisfaction with the situation:

> There was no evidence before the court that suggested there was anything wrong with you when you killed your children. I have no doubt that for a woman like you to suffocate these babies there must have been something seriously wrong with you. You wanted these babies and you cherished them. It's no coincidence, in my view, that you committed these acts in the weeks after their births. It is not my decision when you will be released, but I intend to make it known in my remarks that in my view you will never be a threat to anyone in future.

Such a situation resonates discordantly with the much less severe sentences received by men who kill their partners and plead guilty to the less severe crime of manslaughter, especially when it is supported by alleged, but unsubstantiated claims of provocation or temporary diminished responsibility.

1.7.2.2 Automatic life sentence under s 2 of the Crime (Sentences) Act 1997

In 1997, immediately prior to the election of that year, Parliament, in the guise of the former Conservative Home Secretary Michael Howard, required the provision of automatic life sentences for those found guilty of a second serious offence. Thus, s 2 of the Crime (Sentences) Act 1997 required judges to pass indeterminate life sentences for those found guilty of a range of offences including attempted murder, rape, manslaughter, wounding, causing grievous bodily harm with intent and robbery with a real or imitation firearm, where the guilty person had been previously convicted of another offence on the list. Given their discontent with the provisions for mandatory sentencing in relation to convictions for murder, it can be appreciated that many of the judiciary, led by the late Lord Justice Taylor, saw the Act as a dangerous party-politicisation of the criminal justice system and an unwarranted interference by the legislature with the scope of judicial power and discretion, and were vociferous in their opposition to it. However, even when the Act came into force, it still left a margin for judicial discretion where they could discover such 'exceptional circumstances' as could justify the non-application of the mandatory sentence. Until the implementation of the HRA, the question was as to what properly constituted such exceptional circumstances, and different courts tended to reach different conclusions of a more or less liberal nature. Thus, in *R v Stephens* (2000), the defendant, who already had a previous serious conviction, was found guilty of grievous bodily harm with intent and was consequently given an automatic life sentence. At his trial, the prosecution had offered, and Stephens had rejected, the opportunity to plead guilty to a lesser charge, which would not have led to the imposition of the automatic life sentence. When it emerged that his counsel had not advised him as to the possible consequences of his election to defend the more serious charge, the Court of Appeal held that that fact amounted to sufficient exceptional circumstances to quash the life sentence. However, in *R v Turner* (2000), where the defendant was also found guilty of causing grievous bodily harm with intent, the court felt obliged to impose the automatic life sentence, even though a period of some 30 years had elapsed since his previous conviction for manslaughter at the age of 22. The court could find no exceptional circumstances.

This unsatisfactory situation was resolved by reference to the HRA in *R v Offen and Others* (2000), in which the Court of Appeal considered five related claims that the imposition of automatic life sentences was contrary to the ECHR. The facts of Offen's case may provide a context for the decision.

Offen had robbed a building society using a toy gun. The cashiers thought the gun was real and placed £960 in his bag. During the robbery, he was nervous and shaking, and apologised to the staff as he left the building. A customer grabbed the bag with the money in it and gave it back to the building society. When he was arrested, Offen admitted the offence, but claimed he had not taken the medication he needed to deal with his schizophrenia. His previous conviction for robbery had been committed in similar circumstances. At his trial, he was subsequently sentenced automatically to life imprisonment.

In delivering its judgment, the Court of Appeal was extremely circumspect in considering its relationship with Parliament and its new powers under the HRA. It was equally firm, however, in its removal of the mandatory element from this aspect of the sentencing process.

As regards its relationship with Parliament, the court stressed that it was of the greatest importance to bear in mind Parliament's intention in establishing the automatic life sentences. In the present instance, it understood that intention as being to protect the public against a person who had committed two serious offences. The Court of Appeal went on, however, to draw the conclusion that, on the basis of that concentration on the importance of protecting the public, it could be assumed that the Act was not intended to apply to anyone who did not pose a future risk.

Focusing on the future danger posed by the offender to the public rather than on the mere fact of their having committed two offences would allow the court to decide each case on the basis of its own particular facts, and if the facts of any particular case showed that the statutory assumption was misplaced, then that would constitute exceptional circumstances for the purposes of s 2 of the 1997 Act. As examples, the committing of different offences, the age of the offender and the lapse of time between the offences could give rise to exceptional circumstances in the context of a particular case which could override the assumption as to the imposition of the mandatory life sentence.

The court's identification of Parliament's intention in passing the Act cannot be doubted. The supposed corollary of this intention is, however, much less certain. However, its process of logic allowed the Court of Appeal to interpret the Act in such a way as to support its own preferred approach, which was effectively to remove the automatic element in the sentencing process and to re-introduce an element of judicial discretion. The foregoing interpretation of the Act was supported by the court's marshalling of the HRA. In their judgments, the three members of the Court of Appeal stated that s 2 of the 1997 Act did not contravene Arts 3 and 5 of the ECHR so long as, and only to the extent that, exceptional circumstances were construed in such a way that it did not result in offenders being sentenced to life imprisonment when they did not constitute a significant risk to the public: that is, as the Court of Appeal had already decided it should be construed. In reaching this conclusion, the Court of Appeal can be seen as employing s 3 of the HRA, in that it was interpreting the primary legislation of the Crime (Sentences) Act 1997 in such a way as to make it compatible with the ECHR rights. In so doing, the judiciary achieved its preferred end without having to issue a declaration of incompatibility and without having to rely on the government introducing an amendment to its own Powers of Criminal Courts (Sentencing) Act 2000, s 109 of which had re-enacted s 2 of the 1997 Act.

1.7.2.3 Sentence tariffs

In relation to mandatory life sentences, the Home Secretary has had the power to set what is known as the tariff, whereas in relation to other, non-mandatory life sentences, it is for the trial judge to set the tariff. The tariff is that part of the sentence that must be served before the person serving the prison sentence can be considered for release, on licence, by the Parole Board. Release after the tariff period is not automatic and depends on the decision of the Parole Board, which in turn depends on the behaviour of the individual whilst in prison and the extent to which they pose a threat to the public. The justification of the tariff is that it serves to establish a minimum period of punishment and retribution. The question, however, is whether such a period should be determined by a member of the executive, the Home Secretary or by the judiciary and, as has been stated, the working out of this question involves an interplay of judicial review, the ECHR and the HRA, and demonstrates the way in which the HRA increases the powers of the courts in relation to the executive in a way that judicial review could never encompass.

There has been substantial criticism of the process of setting the tariff. In 1989, a Select Committee of the House of Lords, appointed to report on murder and life imprisonment, recommended the abolition of the mandatory life sentence. In 1996, the Home Affairs Select Committee of the House of Commons took evidence and deliberated on the same issues. Their report (*Murder: the Mandatory Life Sentence*) recommended that the tariff and release decisions be removed from the Home Secretary and left with the trial judge and Parole Board. Lord Lane, formerly Lord Chief Justice, chaired a Committee on the Penalty for Homicide, which also produced a critical report in 1993:

> (1) The mandatory life sentence for murder is founded on the assumption that murder is a crime of such unique heinousness that the offender forfeits for the rest of his existence his right to be set free. (2) That assumption is a fallacy. It arises from the divergence between the legal definition of murder and that which the lay public believes to be murder. (3) The common law definition of murder embraces a wide range of offences, some of which are truly heinous, some of which are not. (4) The majority of murder cases, though not those which receive the most publicity, fall into the latter category. (5) It is logically and jurisprudentially wrong to require judges to sentence all categories of murderer in the same way, regardless of the particular circumstances of the case before them. (6) It is logically and constitutionally wrong to require the distinction between the various types of murder to be decided (and decided behind the scenes) by the executive as is, generally speaking, the case at present ...

Before examining the situation in England, it should be noted that in Scotland, the Convention Rights (Compliance) (Scotland) Act 2001 now provides that in the case of mandatory life sentences, the trial judge fixes the 'punishment part' of the sentence, on the expiry of which the Parole Board decides on possible release on licence. The test applied to determine suitability for release is identical to that applied to discretionary life prisoners in England and Wales, namely, that the Parole Board is satisfied that the prisoner does not present a substantial risk of re-offending in a manner which is dangerous to life or limb or of committing serious sexual offences.

The situation is similar in Northern Ireland, where the Life Sentences (Northern Ireland) Order 2001 provides that the trial judge decides the tariff for a mandatory life prisoner and that release after serving the tariff is determined by Life Sentence Review Commissioners (with a status and functions very similar to those of the Parole Board operating in England and Wales). The test applied by the Commissioners is one of protection of the public from 'serious harm', this term meaning the risk of harm from violent or sexual offences.

There are in effect three distinct elements in a mandatory life sentence: the tariff, the period after the tariff has been served until the recommendation of the Parole Board to release the person on licence, and the overhanging possibility that the person might be recalled to prison if they breach the conditions of their release on licence at a later date. The first part, the tariff, is punitive. The other elements are preventative and intended for public protection. However, the question arises as to what should happen where there is no need for any preventative element to a sentence. Precisely such situations arose in the related cases of *R v Lichniak* (2002) and *R v Pyrah* (2002). The two individuals concerned had been found guilty of murder, but in both cases, the sentencing judges had clearly stated that neither of them represented a future danger to the community, nor was there any likelihood of their committing such offences in the future. Both were nonetheless subject to the mandatory life sentence for murder and appealed unsuccessfully to both the Court of Appeal and the House of Lords. Both courts held that the imposition of the mandatory life sentence did not violate Art 3 or 5 of the ECHR and that such sentences were neither arbitrary nor disproportionate. The decision of the House of Lords is, to say the least, somewhat surprising, especially when it is compared with the recent decision of the Privy Council in *Reyes v the Queen* (2002). In *Reyes*, it was held that a mandatory death sentence, operative in the jurisdiction of Belize, amounted to inhuman and degrading punishment. Amongst the grounds for that decision was the fact that the mandatory nature of the sentence precluded proper judicial consideration of the appropriate penalty. Although the Privy Council did expressly limit its reasoning to the Belize legal system in *Reyes*, and although the death penalty does stand on its own as the harshest of penalties, nonetheless, it is arguable that the mandatory life sentence in the UK achieves a similar, if less severe, consequence in limiting proper judicial consideration of the appropriate sentence to apply in different circumstances. It is apparent in both the *Lichniak* and *Pyrah* cases that the judges deciding the sentences did not really think that life sentences were appropriate, yet they had no choice but to pass such sentences. Can the imposition of an inappropriate sentence be anything other than arbitrary and disproportionate?

As will be considered below (see 1.7.2.3.2), perhaps Lichniak and Pyrah were unfortunate in the timing of their appeals, in that they followed a number of highly sensitive decisions in which the courts had used their powers under the HRA to remove the powers of the Home Secretary to set the punitive tariff in mandatory life sentences. Perhaps, given the highly charged, not to say antagonistic nature of the relationship between the courts and the current Home Secretary, removing the mandatory sentence altogether was a step too far for the courts, or at least a step further than they thought it wise to take under current political circumstances.

1.7.2.3.1 *Juveniles*

Just as in the cases of adults sentenced to a mandatory life sentence, so the Home Secretary used to have the power to set the tariff for juveniles sentenced to detention at Her Majesty's pleasure, that is, for an indeterminate period. However, in 1999, the ECtHR in Strasbourg held that the exercise of that power by the Home Secretary was in contravention of the ECHR. The Home Secretary subsequently relinquished the power. The path to such a resolution is traced below.

In 1993, Jon Venables and Robert Thompson, two 10 year old boys, were found guilty of the murder of two year old James Bulger. As juveniles, they were both sentenced, as required under s 53(1) of the Children and Young Persons Act (CYPA) 1933, to be detained at Her Majesty's pleasure. The trial judge recommended a tariff of eight years as an appropriate period for retribution and deterrence, although, on review, Lord Chief Justice Taylor recommended that the tariff should be increased to 10 years. However, the ultimate decision as to the length of the tariff lay with the then Conservative Home Secretary, Michael Howard. Given the particularly brutal manner of the killing, there was very considerable public interest in the case and the sentencing of the two boys. *The Sun* newspaper organised a public petition to the effect that they should be 'locked up for life' or serve at least 25 years. Some 306,000 people signed and submitted petitions to that effect to the Home Secretary, who ultimately decided that the tariff should be set at 15 years. Doubts were raised as to whether, in ignoring the recommendations of the judges in reaching his decision, the Home Secretary had taken a (party) political rather than quasi-judicial decision to assuage the concerns of potential voters by demonstrating a willingness to be tough on crime and criminals.

R v Secretary of State for the Home Department ex p Venables and Thompson (1997)

Lawyers for Venables and Thompson successfully sought judicial review of the Home Secretary's decision. On final appeal to the House of Lords (*Secretary of State for the Home Department v V (A Minor) and T (A Minor)* (1997)), the Home Secretary having lost all the previous cases, it was held that in setting the tariff at 15 years, he had not taken into account the welfare of the children as required by s 44 of the CYPA 1933. Additionally, the House of Lords stated that although the Home Secretary was entitled to take into account considerations of a public character, he must distinguish between legitimate public concern and mere public clamour. The Home Secretary had therefore misdirected himself and his decision was unlawful and should be quashed. The mechanism of judicial review therefore allowed the court to insist that, even if statute permitted the executive, in the form of the Home Secretary, to take sentencing decisions, in reaching any such decision, he must act in a judicial rather than a political manner. As Lord Steyn expressed it:

> In fixing a tariff the Home Secretary is carrying out, contrary to the constitutional principle of the separation of powers between the executive and the judiciary, a classic judicial function.

What judicial review could not achieve, however, was either the removal of the Home Secretary's general power or the substitution of the courts' decision for his particular decision. It would still have been for the Home Secretary to take the new decision as to the appropriate tariff, had the ECtHR not intervened before such a decision could be taken.

T v UK; V v UK (1999)

Lawyers for Thompson and Venables had appealed to the ECtHR, claiming that many aspects of their clients' cases had been conducted in a manner that was contrary to the ECHR. In December 1999, the ECtHR delivered its judgment and found that although many of the grounds for appeal were unfounded, the applicants had been denied a fair trial in accordance within Art 6 of the ECHR, as they had not been able to participate effectively in the proceedings. The reason for this finding was that the conduct of the case in the Crown Court must have been at times incomprehensible and frightening to the two boys, and it was not sufficient that they were represented by skilled and experienced lawyers. The Court also held that there had been a violation of Art 6 on the grounds that they had been denied a fair hearing by 'an independent and impartial tribunal'. The fixing of the tariff was tantamount to a sentencing procedure and therefore should have been exercised by an impartial judge, rather than a member of the executive, as the Home Secretary clearly was.

Subsequent to, and consequent upon, this decision, the Home Secretary, by this time the Labour politician Jack Straw, announced in March 2000 that legislation would be introduced to provide that tariffs for juveniles should be set by trial judges, in open court, in the same way as they are for adults sentenced to discretionary life sentences. Until that legislation was passed by Parliament, the Home Secretary undertook that in using his statutory power, he would follow the recommendations of the Lord Chief Justice. In July 2000, Lord Chief Justice Woolf issued a practice statement setting out the criteria to be applied in establishing the tariff for juvenile offenders, and in October of that year, in line with those criteria, he set the tariff for both Thompson and Venables at eight years, which meant that they were immediately open to the operation of the normal parole system. Lord Woolf's decision did not go without challenge both in the media and the courts, a subsequent application for judicial review being rejected, but perhaps the last words on the matter should remain with him:

> The one overriding mitigating feature of the offence is the age of the two boys when the crime was committed. However grave their crime, the fact remains that if that crime had been committed a few months earlier, when they were under 10, the boys could not have been tried or punished by the courts. In addition, account has to be taken of the fact that the last seven years, the period of their adolescence, has been passed in custody.

In January 2001, Dame Butler-Sloss, President of the Family Division, granted a permanent injunction banning the media in England from revealing any information about the new identities that Thompson and Venables would live under when they were eventually released from custody. In the light of the many threats that had been made against Thompson and Venables, the order, the first of its kind, was made on the basis of the HRA and Art 2 of the ECHR, in that the court held that it was necessary in order to protect their right to life.

In June 2001, the new Home Secretary, David Blunkett, announced that the Parole Board had agreed to the release on life licence of Thompson and Venables.

1.7.2.3.2 Adults

As has been pointed out above, the regime that once applied to juveniles sentenced to indeterminate sentences also applied to adults who were sentenced to mandatory, but indeterminate life sentences. Not only had the general power of the Home Secretary to determine a tariff been accepted by the courts, but, more contentiously, it had been accepted that the Home Secretary could set an 'all life' tariff in appropriate circumstances, such as those in *R v Secretary of State for the Home Department ex p Myra Hindley* (2000). Hindley had been convicted of murder in 1966 and was sentenced as required by the Murder (Abolition of Death Penalty) Act 1965 to life imprisonment. As the House of Lords later stated, she was subject to a mandatory life sentence, subject to a discretionary executive power, vested in the Home Secretary, at any time to direct her release on licence. The fact that the Home Secretary had such a discretion to release on licence led to the conclusion that he equally had the discretion not to release her, as long as he retained the duty to reconsider his decision at reasonable intervals.

Hindley's case was decided prior to the coming into effect of the HRA and, therefore, in deciding it, the courts were not at liberty to apply that Act. Subsequently, in an interview in the journal the *New Statesman*, Lord Chief Justice Woolf, who as the then Master of the Rolls had sat in the Court of Appeal in the *Hindley* case, expressed the view that, in reaching his decision in that case, he had been constrained by the law as it was then, but that the HRA had altered the situation. Consequently, it was likely that in the future domestic courts would follow the ECtHR in *T v UK* and *V v UK* and hold that it would be in breach of Art 6 for the Home Secretary to continue to determine the tariff in murder cases, on the grounds that such a procedure would be a denial of the right to a fair hearing by 'an independent and impartial tribunal'. Lord Woolf's interview was widely reported in the news media, with the strong implication that the courts in the future might sanction the release of Myra Hindley.

Subsequent to his interview in the *New Statesman*, however, the Lord Chief Justice seemed to have a re-think as to the wisdom of a direct challenge to the Home Secretary's power to set the tariff in mandatory life sentences.

R v Secretary of State for the Home Department ex p Anderson and Taylor (2001)

In November 2001, two convicted murderers complained that the Home Secretary had fixed their tariffs higher than had been recommended by the judges at their trial: 20 years instead of 15 years for the first and 30 years instead of 16 years for the second. They argued that it was incompatible with Art 6(1) of the ECHR for a member of the executive to carry out what was in fact a sentencing exercise. The Court of Appeal, made up of Lord Woolf and Simon Brown and Buxton LJJ, rejected their arguments. In doing so, the Court of Appeal's disapproving views on mandatory life sentences in general were expressed by Simon Brown LJ, who stated that:

> ... I accept of course that the mandatory life sentence is unique. But not all the offences for which it is imposed can be regarded as uniquely grave. Rather the spectrum is a wide one with multiple sadistic murders at one end and mercy killings at the other. Lifelong punitive detention will be appropriate only exceptionally.

Nonetheless, the Court of Appeal felt itself constrained by case law from the ECtHR and, in particular, the authority of *Wynne v UK* decided in 1994 and *T v UK* and *V v UK*. In *Wynne*, the ECtHR decided that no violation arose under Art 5(4) in relation to the continued detention after release, and recall to prison, of a mandatory life prisoner convicted of an intervening offence of manslaughter, the tariff element of which had expired. The ECtHR held that the sentence constituted a *punishment* for life. In *T v UK* and *V v UK*, whilst citing the *Wynne* judgment, the ECtHR reiterated that an adult mandatory life sentence constituted punishment for life. On the face of those authorities, the Court of Appeal in *Anderson and Taylor* declined to challenge the Home Secretary's power in relation to mandatory life sentences.

Perhaps the Court of Appeal's reluctance to challenge the executive's power head-on was based on the realisation that, as the court noted, a decision on the same point was expected within the following year in the ECtHR (*Stafford v UK* (2002)). It is perhaps not overly cynical to suggest that the Court of Appeal adopted its conservative approach in the realisation that, in the context of the prevailing tense relationship between the Home Secretary and the courts, it was perhaps politic to leave the final decision to remove the Home Secretary's power to the ECtHR, which decision their Lordships clearly expected.

Stafford v UK (2002)

Derek Stafford was convicted of murder in 1967 and released on licence in April 1979. His licence required him to remain in the UK, but he left to live in South Africa. In April 1989, he was arrested in the UK having returned from South Africa on a false passport. Although the possession of a false passport only led to a fine, he remained in custody due to the revocation of his life licence. He was released in March 1991, once again on a life licence. In 1994, he was convicted of conspiracy to forge travellers' cheques and passports and sentenced to six years' imprisonment. In 1996, the Parole Board recommended his release on life licence, having reached the conclusion that he did not present a danger of violent re-offending. The Secretary of State rejected the Board's recommendation. But for the revocation of his life licence, the applicant would have been released from prison on the expiry of the sentence for fraud in July 1997, and in June 1997, he sought judicial review of the Secretary of State's decision to reject the Board's recommendation for immediate release. He was successful at first instance, but both the Court of Appeal and the House of Lords denied his claim and upheld the power of the Home Secretary to revoke his licence and thus effectively detain him under ss 39(1) and 35(2) of the Criminal Justice Act 1991 (the latter subsequently replaced by s 29 of the Crime (Sentences) Act 1997), even though there was no prospect of his committing any violent crime in the future. Both courts, however, expressed unease at their decisions. As Lord Bingham CJ stated in the Court of Appeal:

> The imposition of what is in effect a substantial term of imprisonment by the exercise of executive discretion, without trial, lies uneasily with ordinary concepts of the Rule of Law. I hope that the Secretary of State may, even now, think it right to give further consideration to the case.

When the case came before the ECtHR in May 2002, it decided in grand chamber, indicating the importance of the case, and as the Court of Appeal in

Anderson had expected, that it was no longer in the interest of justice to follow its previous decision in *Wynne*. The ECtHR stated that although it was not formally bound to follow any of its previous judgments, it was 'in the interests of legal certainty, foreseeability and equality before the law that it should not depart, without cogent reason, from precedents laid down in previous cases'. However, it felt that the fixing of the tariff for mandatory life sentences was clearly a sentencing exercise, and that it was no longer possible to distinguish between mandatory life prisoners, discretionary life prisoners and juvenile murderers as regards the nature of that sentencing process. The ECtHR also held that the finding in *Wynne* that the mandatory life sentence constituted punishment for life could no longer be maintained. It was therefore open to the court to decide that the Secretary of State's role in fixing the tariff was a sentencing exercise and not merely a matter relating to the administrative implementation of the sentence. As a result, it concluded that the exercise of such power by the Home Secretary was contrary to Art 5(1) and (4) of the ECHR.

When the decision of the ECtHR in *Stafford* was delivered, the UK press immediately returned to the possibility of the imminent release of the child killer Myra Hindley. What they failed to indicate was that the ECtHR itself, in line with previous statements of the UK courts, had actually recognised the validity of 'whole life' tariffs in exceptional circumstances. Its decision was merely that it was for the courts rather than the executive to make such recommendations. In any event, Hindley died in prison in November 2002.

The first person actually to benefit from the *Stafford* decision was Satpal Ram, who was released from prison in June 2002 after having served more than 15 years for a murder he claimed was committed in self-defence in a racial attack. The previous Home Secretary had overturned a Parole Board recommendation to release Mr Ram in 2000, but the present Home Secretary preferred to release him rather than to contest an action for judicial review of his predecessor's decision, recognising that *Stafford* made any argument to the contrary untenable.

R v Secretary of State for the Home Department ex p Anderson and Taylor (2002)

By November 2002, the appeals in the *Anderson and Taylor* cases had reached the House of Lords and were considered by a seven member panel, indicating their importance. The essential issue under consideration was the effect that the *Stafford* decision in the ECtHR would have on English law, s 35(2) and (3) of the Criminal Justice Act 1991 having been replaced by similar provisions under s 29 of the Crime (Sentences) Act 1997. In the event, the House of Lords followed the decision of the ECtHR and held that the fixing of the tariff for a convicted murderer was legally indistinguishable from the imposition of sentence. Consequently, to ensure compatibility with Art 6(1), any such tariff should be set by an independent and impartial tribunal and not the Home Secretary, who was part of the executive. It was therefore incompatible with Art 6 for the Home Secretary to fix the tariff of a convicted murderer. However, the House of Lords went on to decide that it was not possible to interpret s 29 of the Crime (Sentences) Act 1997 in such a way as to make it compatible with the rights provided under the ECHR. As a result, the House of Lords issued a declaration of incompatibility to the effect that s 29 was contrary to the right under Art 6 to have a sentence imposed by an independent and impartial tribunal.

The above series of cases demonstrates how the implied wishes of the Court of Appeal in *Anderson* could be given express effect in the later House of Lords decision, without the possibility of any direct accusation of political interference on the part of the judiciary.

The political sensitivity of the preceding cases, and the extent to which they challenge executive power, may go some way to explain the apparent conservatism of the decision of the House of Lords in the *Lichniak* and *Pyrah* cases, considered previously. A close reading of the cases certainly reveals grounds for the House of Lords to overturn those decisions and to remove mandatory life sentences all together.

Although the foregoing analysis has used the term 'tariff' to refer to the period which a person sentenced to a life term must serve for the purposes of punishment, it should be noted that in a Practice Statement issued in May 2002, the Lord Chief Justice accepted the recommendation of the Sentencing Advisory Panel that it should be replaced by the clearer expression 'minimum term'.

The political tension around the issue of sentencing was further heightened when in May 2003, the Home Secretary, David Blunkett, announced his intention to introduce proposals into the current Criminal Justice Bill which would introduce a new statutory system in relation to sentencing in murder cases. For further details, see the Companion Website for this book (www.cavendishpublishing.com/els).

LAW AND LEGAL STUDY

Studying law

The study of law is not just a matter of learning rules. It is a general misconception that learning the law is about learning a mass of legal rules. Critical, analytical thought should inform the work of the good student.

The nature of law

Legal systems are particular ways of establishing and maintaining social order. Law is a formal mechanism of social control. Studying the English legal system involves considering a fundamental institution in our society.

Categories of law

Law may be categorised in a number of ways, although the various categories are not mutually exclusive.

Common law and civil law relate to distinct legal systems. The English legal system is a common law one as opposed to continental systems, which are based on civil law.

Common law and equity distinguish the two historical sources and systems of English law. Common law emerged in the process of establishing a single legal system throughout the country. Equity was developed later to soften the formal rigour of the common law. The two systems are now united, but in the final analysis, equity should prevail.

Common law and statute relate to the source of law. Common law is judge-made; statute law is produced by Parliament.

Private law and public law relate to whom the law is addressed. Private law relates to individual citizens, whereas public law relates to institutions of government.

Civil law and criminal law distinguish between law the purpose of which is to facilitate the interaction of individuals and law that is aimed at enforcing particular standards of behaviour.

Separation of powers

The judges and the executive in the separation of powers have distinct but interrelated roles in the constitution. The question arises as to the extent to which the courts can act to control the activities of the executive through the operation of judicial review. The position of the present Lord Chancellor as judge and member of the government has been questioned by some.

The Rule of Law

Various writers have different understandings of what the concept actually means, but see it essentially as involving a control of arbitrary power – Dicey, Hayek, Thompson, Raz, Unger and Weber.

The essential question is whether the UK is still governed under the Rule of Law, and of course the conclusion depends on the original understanding of the Rule of Law: Hayek and Thompson would have said not; Raz would say it was. Sir Stephen Sedley has a view as to the continued operation of the Rule of Law which is based on substantive equality and challenges previous legal thought.

The Human Rights Act 1998

The HRA incorporates the ECHR into domestic UK law. The Articles of the ECHR cover the following matters:

- the right to life (Art 2);
- prohibition of torture (Art 3);
- prohibition of slavery and forced labour (Art 4);
- the right to liberty and security (Art 5);
- the right to a fair trial (Art 6);
- the general prohibition of the enactment of retrospective criminal offences (Art 7);
- the right to respect for private and family life (Art 8);
- freedom of thought, conscience and religion (Art 9);
- freedom of expression (Art 10);
- freedom of assembly and association (Art 11);
- the right to marry (Art 12);
- prohibition of discrimination (Art 14).

The incorporation of the ECHR into UK law means that UK courts must decide cases in line with the above Articles. This has the potential to create friction between the judiciary and the executive/legislature.

CHAPTER 2

SOURCES OF LAW

2.1 European Community

Ever since the UK joined the European Economic Community, now the European Community ('Union' in some legal contexts), it has progressively but effectively passed the power to create laws which have effect in this country to the wider European institutions. In effect, as regards Community matters, the UK's legislative, executive and judicial powers are now controlled by, and can only be operated within, the framework of European Community (EC) law. It is essential, therefore, even in a text that is primarily concerned with the English legal system, that the contemporary law student is aware of the operation of the legislative processes of the EC. Chapter 13 of this book will consider the EC and its institutions in some detail; the remainder of this chapter will concentrate on internal sources of law.

2.2 Legislation

If the institutions of the EC are sovereign within its boundaries, then within the more limited boundaries of the UK, the sovereign power to make law lies with Parliament. Under UK constitutional law, it is recognised that Parliament has the power to enact, revoke or alter such, and any, law as it sees fit. Even the Human Rights Act (HRA) 1998 re-affirms this fact in its recognition of the power of Parliament to make primary legislation that is incompatible with the rights provided under the European Convention on Human Rights (ECHR). Whether this will remain the case in the future is, however, a moot point. Coupled to this wide power is the convention that no one Parliament can bind its successors in such a way as to limit their absolute legislative powers.

This absolute power is a consequence of the historical struggle between Parliament and the Stuart monarchy in the 17th century. In its conflict with the Crown, Parliament claimed the power of making law as its sole right. In so doing, Parliament curtailed the royal prerogative and limited the monarchy to a purely formal role in the legislative procedure. Prerogative powers still exist and remain important, but are now exercised by the government in the name of the Crown, rather than by the Crown itself. In this struggle for ultimate power, the courts sided with Parliament and, in return, Parliament recognised the independence of the courts from its control.

Although we still refer to our legal system as a common law system and although the courts still have an important role to play in the interpretation of statutes, it has to be recognised that legislation is the predominant method of law-making in contemporary times. It is necessary, therefore, to have some knowledge of the workings of the legislative process.

2.2.1 The pre-parliamentary process

Any consideration of the legislative process must be placed in the context of the political nature of Parliament. Most statutes are the outcome of the policy decisions taken by government, and the actual policies pursued will of course depend upon the political persuasion and imperatives of the government of the day. Thus, a great deal of law creation and reform can be seen as the implementation of party political policies. Examples of this type of legal reform are the changes in trade union law, education law or the financing of local services introduced by the previous Conservative administrations.

It also has to be recognised that the previous Labour government, elected in May 1997, introduced considerable constitutional reform as proposed in its manifesto. Thus, the Scottish Parliament and the Welsh Assembly have been instituted and many hereditary peers have been removed from the House of Lords.

As, by convention, the government is drawn from the party controlling a majority in the House of Commons, it can effectively decide what policies it wishes to implement and trust to its majority to ensure that its proposals become law. Accusations have been made that when governments have substantial majorities, they are able to operate without taking into account the consideration of their own party members, let alone the views of opposition members. It is claimed that their control over the day-to-day procedure of the House of Commons, backed with their majority voting power, effectively reduces the role of Parliament to that of merely rubber-stamping their proposals.

It is certainly true, as the experience of the previous Conservative administration in the UK demonstrated, that governments with small majorities, if not actually in a minority, have to be circumspect in the policies they pursue through Parliament. The fact that the elections of 1997 and 2001 returned the Labour Party to power, with much larger majorities than even they expected, has raised once again the prospect of an over-powerful executive forcing its will through a politically quiescent Parliament. Even the large vote against the war with Iraq in March 2003 was not sufficient to derail the will of the executive.

The government generates most of the legislation that finds its way into the statute book, but individual Members of Parliament may also propose legislation in the form of Private Members' Bills.

There are in fact three ways in which an individual Member of Parliament can propose legislation:

- through the ballot procedure, by means of which 20 backbench Members get the right to propose legislation on the 10 or so Fridays in each parliamentary Session specifically set aside to consider such proposals;
- under Standing Order 39, which permits any Member to present a Bill after the 20 balloted Bills have been presented;
- under Standing Rule 13, the 10-minute rule procedure, which allows a Member to make a speech of up to 10 minutes in length in favour of introducing a particular piece of legislation.

Of these procedures, however, only the first has any real chance of success and even then success will depend on securing a high place in the ballot and on the actual proposal not being too contentious. Examples of this include the Abortion Act 1967, which was introduced as a Private Member's Bill to liberalise the provision of abortion, and the various attempts that have subsequently been made by Private Members' Bills to restrict the original provision. In relation to particular reforms, external pressure groups or interested parties may very often be the original moving force behind them. When individual Members of Parliament are fortunate enough to find themselves at the top of the ballot for Private Members' Bills, they may well also find themselves the focus of attention from such pressure groups proffering pre-packaged law reform proposals in their own particular areas of interest.

The decision as to which government Bills are to be placed before Parliament in any Session is under the effective control of two Cabinet committees:

- the *Future Legislation Committee* determines which Bills will be presented to Parliament in the *following* parliamentary Session;
- the *Legislation Committee* is responsible for the legislative programme conducted in the *immediate* parliamentary Session. It is the responsibility of this committee to draw up the legislative programme announced in the Queen's Speech, delivered at the opening of the parliamentary Session.

Green Papers are consultation documents issued by the government which set out and invite comments from interested parties on particular proposals for legislation. After considering any response, the government may publish a second document in the form of a White Paper, in which it sets out its firm proposals for legislation.

2.2.2 The legislative process

Parliament consists of three distinct elements: the House of Commons; the House of Lords; and the monarch. Before any legislative proposal, known at that stage as a Bill, can become an Act of Parliament, it must proceed through and be approved by both Houses of Parliament and must receive the Royal

Assent. The ultimate location of power, however, is the House of Commons, which has the authority of being a democratically elected institution.

A Bill must be given three readings in both the House of Commons and the House of Lords before it can be presented for the Royal Assent. It is possible to commence the procedure in either House, although Money Bills must be placed before the Commons in the first instance.

When a Bill is introduced in the Commons, it undergoes five distinct procedures:

- *First reading*. This is purely a formal procedure in which its title is read and a date set for its second reading.

- *Second reading*. At this stage, the general principles of the Bill are subject to extensive debate. The second reading is the critical point in the process of a Bill. At the end, a vote may be taken on its merits and, if it is approved, it is likely that it will eventually find a place in the statute book.

- *Committee stage*. After its second reading, the Bill is passed to a standing committee whose job it is to consider the provisions of the Bill in detail, clause by clause. The committee has the power to amend it in such a way as to ensure that it conforms with the general approval given by the House at its second reading. Very occasionally, a Bill may be passed to a special standing committee which considers the issues involved before going through the Bill in the usual way as a normal standing committee. Also, the whole House may consider certain Bills at committee stage. In general, these are Bills of constitutional importance, such as the *House of Lords Bill*, which proposed the reformation of the upper House in 1999. Other Bills which need to be passed very quickly and certain financial measures, including at least part of each year's Finance Bill, are also considered by the committee of the whole House.

- *Report stage*. At this point, the standing committee reports the Bill back to the House for consideration of any amendments made during the committee stage.

- *Third reading*. Further debate may take place during this stage, but it is restricted to matters relating to the content of the Bill; questions relating to the general principles of the Bill cannot be raised.

When a Bill has completed all these stages, it is passed to the House of Lords for its consideration. After consideration by the Lords, the Bill is passed back to the Commons, which must then consider any amendments to the Bill that might have been introduced by the Lords. Where one House refuses to agree to the amendments made by the other, Bills can be repeatedly passed between them but, as Bills must usually complete their process within the life of a particular parliamentary Session, a failure to reach agreement within that period might lead to the total loss of the Bill. However, in 1998, the House of Commons Modernisation Committee agreed that, in defined circumstances and subject to certain safeguards, government Bills should be able to be carried over from one Session to the next, in the same way that Private and Hybrid Bills may be. The first Bill to be treated in this way was the Financial Services and Markets Bill 1998–99, which the House agreed to carry over into the 1999–2000 Session after a debate on 25 October 1999. The effect was to stay proceedings on the Bill in standing committee at the end of the 1998–99 Session and to carry it over into the next Session, when the committee resumed at the point in the Bill it had previously reached. Later in 2002, the committee recommended, amongst a raft of proposals relating to the conduct of House of Commons matters, that the carry-over provisions should be used more frequently.

Since the Parliament Acts of 1911 and 1949, the blocking power of the House of Lords has been restricted as follows:

- a 'Money Bill', that is, one containing only financial provisions, can be enacted without the approval of the House of Lords after a delay of one month;
- any other Bill can be delayed by one year by the House of Lords.

The House of Lords, no doubt, has used its reforming and delaying powers to good effect, but its inbuilt Conservative/conservative majority has also been deployed for less than totally praiseworthy campaigns. One such involved the procedure of equalising the age of sexual consent between homosexuals at 16, as it is between heterosexuals. In 1998, the House of Lords managed to avoid an equalisation of the age of consent by threatening the government's major Criminal Justice Bill, subsequently the Crime and Disorder Act 1998. In order to get the Bill through Parliament before the end of the Session, the Home Secretary removed the provision. The Lords maintained its resistance, but gave way when the government stated that it would use the Parliament Acts to ensure that the necessary legislation would be passed. The age of consent was equalised by the Sexual Offences (Amendment) Act 2000. However, the House of Lords was not finished with resisting the liberalisation of homosexual rights and forced the government to drop its promise to remove s 28 of the Local Government Act 1988. That section had introduced the requirement that local authorities shall not:

(a) intentionally promote homosexuality or publish material with the intention of promoting homosexuality;

(b) promote the teaching in any maintained school of the acceptability of homosexuality as a pretended family relationship.

The section was much resented within the gay and lesbian community and was seen by many as signally illiberal. That it remains on the statute book is due to the efforts of the newly reformed House of Lords. Although, as this edition is being written, there is a renewed attempt to remove it from the statute book, the effectiveness of any Lords' attempt to block its removal remains to be seen.

The Royal Assent is required before any Bill can become law. There is no constitutional rule requiring the monarch to assent to any Act passed by Parliament. There is, however, a convention to that effect, and refusal to grant the Royal Assent to legislation passed by Parliament would place the constitutional position of the monarchy in jeopardy. The procedural nature of the Royal Assent was highlighted by the Royal Assent Act 1967, which reduced the process of acquiring Royal Assent to a formal reading out of the short title of any Act in both Houses of Parliament.

An Act of Parliament comes into effect on the date of the Royal Assent, unless there is any provision to the contrary in the Act itself. It is quite common either for the Act to contain a commencement date for some time in the future, or for it to give the appropriate Secretary of State the power to give effect to its provisions at some future time by issuing statutory instruments. The Secretary of State is not required to bring the provisions into effect and it is not uncommon for some parts of Acts to be repealed before they are ever in force.

2.2.3 The drafting of legislation

In 1975, in response to criticisms of the language and style of legislation, the Renton Committee on the Preparation of Legislation (1975, Cmnd 6053) examined the form in which legislation was presented. Representations were made to the Committee by a variety of people ranging from the judiciary to the lay public. The Committee divided complaints about statutes into four main headings relating to:

- obscurity of language used;
- over-elaboration of provisions;
- illogicality of structure;
- confusion arising from the amendment of existing provisions.

It was suggested that the drafters of legislation tended to adopt a stylised archaic legalism in their language and employed a grammatical structure that was too complex and convoluted to be clear, certainly to the lay person and even, on occasion, to legal experts. These criticisms, however, have to be considered in the context of the whole process of drafting legislation and weighed against the various other purposes to be achieved by statutes.

The actual drafting of legislation is the work of parliamentary counsel to the Treasury, who specialise in this task. The first duty of the drafters must be to give effect to the intention of the department instructing them, and to do so in as clear and precise a manner as is possible. These aims, however, have to be achieved under pressure, and sometimes extreme pressure, of time. An insight into the various difficulties faced in drafting legislation was provided by a former parliamentary draftsman, Francis Bennion, in an article entitled 'Statute law obscurity and drafting parameters' ((1978) British JLS 235). He listed nine specific parameters which the drafter of legislation had to take into account. These parameters are as follows:

- *Legal effectiveness*. This is the need for the drafters to translate the political wishes of those instructing them into appropriate legal language and form.

- *Procedural legitimacy*. This refers to the fact that the legislation must conform with certain formal requirements if it is to be enacted. For example, it is a requirement that Acts be divided into clauses, and Bills not assuming this form would not be considered by Parliament.

- *Timeliness*. This refers to the requirement for legislation to be drawn up within particularly pressing time constraints. The effect of such pressure can be poorly drafted and defective provisions.

- *Certainty*. It is of the utmost importance that the law be clearly set down so that individuals can know its scope and effect and can guide their actions within its provisions. The very nature of language, however, tends to act against this desire for certainty. In pursuit of certainty, the temptation for the person drafting the legislation is to produce extremely long and complex sentences consisting of a series of limiting and refining sub-clauses. This process in turn, however, tends merely to increase the obscurity of meaning.

- *Comprehensibility*. Ideally, legislation should be comprehensible to the lay person, but given the complex nature of the situation that the legislature is dealing with, such an ideal is probably beyond attainment in practice. Nonetheless, legislative provisions certainly should be open to the comprehension of the Members of Parliament who are asked to vote on them, and they certainly should not be beyond the comprehension of the legal profession who have to construe them for their clients. Unfortunately, some legislation fails on both these counts.

- *Acceptability*. This refers to the fact that legislation is expected to be couched in uncontentious language and using a traditional prose style.

- *Brevity*. This refers to the fact that legislative provisions should be as short as is compatible with the attainment of the legislative purpose. The search for brevity in legislation can run counter to the wish for certainty in, and acceptability of, the language used.

- *Debatability*. This refers to the fact that legislation is supposed to be structured in such a way as to permit it, and the policies that lie behind it, to be debated in Parliament.

- *Legal compatibility*. This refers to the need for any new provision to fit in with already existing provisions. Where the new provision alters or repeals existing provisions, it is expected that such effect should be clearly indicated.

A consideration of these various desired characteristics shows that they are not necessarily compatible; indeed, some of them, such as the desire for clarity and brevity, may well be contradictory. The point remains that those people charged with the responsibility for drafting legislation should always bear the above factors in mind when producing draft legislation, but if one principle is to be pursued above others, it is surely the need for clarity of expression and meaning.

2.2.4   Types of legislation

Legislation can be categorised in a number of ways. For example, distinctions can be drawn between the following:

- *Public Acts*, which relate to matters affecting the general public. These can be further subdivided into either government Bills or Private Members' Bills.

- *Private Acts*, on the other hand, relate to the powers and interests of particular individuals or institutions, although the provision of statutory powers to particular institutions can have a major effect on the general public. For example, companies may be given the power to appropriate private property through compulsory purchase orders.

- *Enabling legislation* gives power to a particular person or body to oversee the production of the specific details required for the implementation of the general purposes stated in the parent Act. These specifics are achieved through the enactment of statutory instruments. (See 2.2.5 below for a consideration of delegated legislation.)

Acts of Parliament can also be distinguished on the basis of the function they are designed to carry out. Some are *unprecedented* and cover new areas of activity previously not governed by legal rules, but other Acts are aimed at *rationalising* or *amending* existing legislative provisions:

- *Consolidating legislation* is designed to bring together provisions previously contained in a number of different Acts, without actually altering them. The Companies Act of 1985 is an example of a consolidating Act. It brought together provisions contained in numerous amending Acts which had been introduced since the previous consolidation Act of 1948.

- *Codifying legislation* seeks not just to bring existing statutory provisions under one Act, but also looks to give statutory expression to common law rules. The classic examples of such legislation are the Partnership Act of 1890 and the Sale of Goods Act 1893 (now 1979).

- *Amending legislation* is designed to alter some existing legal provision. Amendment of an existing legislative provision can take two forms:
  (i) a *textual amendment* is one where the new provision substitutes new words for existing ones in a legislative text or introduces completely new words into that text. Altering legislation by means of textual amendment has one major drawback, in that the new provisions make very little sense on their own, without the contextual reference of the original provision they are designed to alter;
  (ii) *non-textual amendments* do not alter the actual wording of the existing text, but alter the operation or effect of those words. Non-textual amendments may have more immediate meaning than textual alterations, but they too suffer from the problem that, because they do not alter the original provisions, the two provisions have to be read together to establish the legislative intention.

Neither method of amendment is completely satisfactory, but the Renton Committee on the Preparation of Legislation favoured textual amendments over non-textual amendments.

2.2.5 Delegated or subordinate legislation

Delegated legislation is of particular importance. Generally speaking, delegated legislation is law made by some person or body to whom Parliament has delegated its general law-making power. A validly enacted piece of delegated legislation has the same legal force and effect as the Act of Parliament under which it is enacted but, equally, it only has effect to the extent that its enabling Act authorises it.

The Deregulation and Contracting Out Act (DCOA) 1994 is an example of the wide-ranging power that enabling legislation can extend to ministers. The Act gave ministers the authority to amend legislation by means of statutory instruments, where they considered such legislation to impose unnecessary burdens on any trade, business, or profession. Although the DCOA 1994 imposed the requirement that ministers should consult with interested parties to any proposed alteration, it nonetheless gave them extremely wide powers to alter primary legislation without the necessity of having to follow the same procedure as was required to enact that legislation in the first place. For that reason, deregulation orders were subject to a far more rigorous procedure (sometimes referred to as 'super-affirmative') than ordinary statutory instruments.

The order-making power under the DCOA 1994 was limited in its scope and was mostly used for small items. The powers under the DCOA 1994 were extended in the Regulatory Reform Act (RRA) 2001. Orders under the new Act, called regulatory reform orders, will be capable of:

- making and re-enacting statutory provision;
- imposing additional burdens where necessary, provided they are proportionate and they strike a fair balance between the public interest and the interests of those affected by the new burden;
- removing inconsistencies and anomalies in legislation;
- dealing with burdensome situations caused by a lack of statutory provision to do something;
- applying to legislation passed after the Bill if it is at least two years old when the order is made and has not been amended in substance during the last two years;
- relieving burdens from anyone, including ministers and government departments, but not where only they would benefit; and
- allowing administrative and minor detail to be further amended by subordinate provisions orders, subject to negative resolution procedure.

The super-affirmative procedure of the DCOA 1994 is maintained and supplemented by an additional test that no order should prevent anyone from exercising an existing right or freedom which they might reasonably expect to continue to exercise (the 'reasonable expectations' test). Two further stringent tests, proportionality and fair balance, will be applied if an order would impose or increase a burden. Finally, ministers bringing forward regulatory reform orders will be required to present more explanatory information to Parliament than they did with deregulation orders, to reflect the wider powers provided under the RRA 2001.

An example of the effect of the DCOA 1994 may be seen in the Deregulation (Resolutions of Private Companies) Order 1996, which simplifies the procedures which private companies have to comply with in passing resolutions. The effect of this statutory instrument was to introduce new sections into the Companies Act 1985, relaxing the previous provisions in the area in question. A second example is the Deregulation (Model Appeal Provisions) Order 1996, which sets out a model structure for appeals against enforcement actions in business disputes.

The output of delegated legislation in any year greatly exceeds the output of Acts of Parliament, as may be seen from the 2002 statistics, which reveal that although only 44 general public Acts were passed, no fewer than 3,299 statutory instruments were made.

In statistical terms, therefore, it is at least arguable that delegated legislation is actually more significant than primary Acts of Parliament.

There are various types of delegated legislation:

- *Orders in Council* permit the government through the Privy Council to make law. The Privy Council is nominally a non-party political body of eminent parliamentarians, but in effect it is simply a means through which the government, in the form of a committee of ministers, can introduce legislation without the need to go through the full parliamentary process. Although it is usual to cite situations of State emergency as exemplifying occasions when the government will resort to the use of Orders in Council, in fact, a great number of Acts are brought into operation through Orders in Council. Perhaps the widest scope for Orders in Council is to be found in relation to EC law, for under s 2(2) of the European Communities Act 1972, ministers can give effect to provisions of the Community which do not have direct effect (see further 13.2, below).

- *Statutory instruments* are the means through which government ministers introduce particular regulations under powers delegated to them by Parliament in enabling legislation. Examples have already been considered in relation to the DCOA 1994.

- *Bylaws* are the means through which local authorities and other public bodies can make legally binding rules. Bylaws may be made by local authorities under such enabling legislation as the Local Government Act 1972.

- *Court Rule Committees* are empowered to make the rules which govern procedure in the particular courts over which they have delegated authority, under such Acts as the Supreme Court Act 1981, the County Courts Act 1984 and the Magistrates' Courts Act 1980.

- *Professional regulations* governing particular occupations may be given the force of law under provisions delegating legislative authority to certain professional bodies who are empowered to regulate the conduct of their members. An example is the power given to The Law Society, under the Solicitors' Act 1974, to control the conduct of practising solicitors.

2.2.6   Advantages in the use of delegated legislation

The advantages of delegated legislation include the following:

- *Time saving*
  Delegated legislation can be introduced quickly, where necessary in particular cases, and can permit rules to be changed in response to emergencies or unforeseen problems.
  The use of delegated legislation, however, also saves parliamentary time generally. Given the pressure on debating time in Parliament and the highly detailed nature of typical delegated legislation, not to mention its sheer volume, Parliament would not have time to consider each individual piece of law that is enacted in the form of delegated legislation. It is considered of more benefit for Parliament to spend its time in a thorough consideration of the principles of the enabling Act, leaving the appropriate minister or body to establish the working detail under its authority.

- *Access to particular expertise*

  Related to the first advantage is the fact that the majority of Members of Parliament simply do not have sufficient expertise to consider such provisions effectively. Given the highly specialised and extremely technical nature of many of the regulations that are introduced through delegated legislation, it is necessary that those authorised to introduce the legislation should have access to the necessary external expertise required to formulate such regulations. With regard to bylaws, it practically goes without saying that local and specialist knowledge should give rise to more appropriate rules than reliance on the general enactments of Parliament.

- *Flexibility*

  The use of delegated legislation permits ministers to respond on an *ad hoc* basis to particular problems, as and when they arise, and provides greater flexibility in the regulation of activity subject to the minister's overview.

2.2.7 Disadvantages in the prevalence of delegated legislation

The disadvantages in the use of delegated legislation include the following:

- *Accountability*

  A key issue involved in the use of delegated legislation concerns the question of accountability and erosion of the constitutional role of Parliament.

  Parliament is presumed to be the source of legislation, but with respect to delegated legislation, the individual members are not the source of the law. Certain people, notably government ministers and the civil servants who work under them to produce the detailed provisions of delegated legislation, are the real source of such regulations. Even allowing for the fact that they are, in effect, operating on powers delegated to them from Parliament, it is not beyond questioning whether this procedure does not give them more power than might be thought appropriate, or indeed constitutionally correct, whilst at the same time disempowering and discrediting Parliament as a body.

- *Scrutiny*

  The question of general accountability raises the need for effective scrutiny, but the very form of delegated legislation makes it extremely difficult for ordinary Members of Parliament to fully understand what is being enacted and to monitor it effectively. This difficulty arises in part from the tendency for such regulations to be highly specific, detailed and technical. This problem of comprehension and control is compounded by the fact that regulations appear outside the context of their enabling legislation, but only have any real meaning within that context.

- *Bulk*

  The problem faced by ordinary Members of Parliament in effectively keeping abreast of delegated legislation is further increased by the sheer mass of such legislation. If parliamentarians cannot keep up with the flow of delegated legislation, how can the general public be expected to do so?

These difficulties and potential shortcomings in the use of delegated legislation are, at least to a degree, mitigated by the fact that specific controls have been established to oversee it:

- *Parliamentary control over delegated legislation*

  Power to make delegated legislation is ultimately dependent upon the authority of Parliament and Parliament retains general control over the procedure for enacting such law.

  New regulations in the form of delegated legislation are required to be laid before Parliament. This procedure takes two forms depending on the provision of the enabling legislation. Some regulations require a positive resolution of one or both of the Houses of Parliament before they become law. Most Acts, however, simply require that regulations made under their auspices be placed before Parliament. They automatically become law after a period of 40 days unless a resolution to annul them is passed.

  The problem with the negative resolution procedure is that it relies on Members of Parliament being sufficiently aware of the content, meaning and effect of the detailed provisions laid before them. Given the nature of such statutory legislation, such reliance is unlikely to prove secure.

  Since 1973, there has been a Joint Select Committee on Statutory Instruments whose function it is to consider statutory instruments. This Committee scrutinises statutory instruments from a technical point of view as regards drafting and has no power to question the substantive content or the policy implications of the regulation. Its effectiveness as a general control is therefore limited. EC legislation is overseen by a specific committee and local authority bylaws are usually subject to the approval of the Department to the Deputy Prime Minister.

- *Judicial control of delegated legislation*

  It is possible for delegated legislation to be challenged through the procedure of judicial review, on the basis that the person or body to whom Parliament has delegated its authority has acted in a way that exceeds the limited powers delegated to them. Any provision outside this authority is *ultra vires* and is void. Additionally, there is a presumption that any power delegated by Parliament is to be used in a reasonable manner, and the courts may on occasion hold particular delegated legislation to be void on the basis that it is unreasonable. The process of judicial review will be considered in more detail in Chapter 6. However, an interesting example of this procedure may illuminate the point. In January 1997, the Lord

Chancellor raised court fees and, at the same time, restricted the circumstances in which a litigant could be exempted from paying such fees. In March, a Mr John Witham, who previously would have been exempted from paying court fees, successfully challenged the Lord Chancellor's action. In a judicial review, it was held that Lord Mackay had exceeded the statutory powers given to him by Parliament. One of the judges, Rose LJ, stated that there was nothing to suggest that Parliament ever intended 'a power for the Lord Chancellor to prescribe fees so as to preclude the poor from access to the courts'.

The power of the courts in relation to delegated legislation has been considerably increased by the enactment of the HRA 1998. As has been seen, the courts cannot directly declare primary legislation invalid, but can only issue a declaration of incompatibility. However, no such limitation applies in regard to subordinate legislation, which consequently may be declared invalid as being in conflict with the rights provided under the ECHR. This provision significantly extends the power of the courts in relation to the control of subordinate legislation, in that they are no longer merely restricted to questioning such legislation on the grounds of procedure, but can now assess it on the basis of content, as measured against the rights provided in the ECHR. It should be noted that Orders in Council as expressions of the exercise of the royal prerogative are not open to challenge and control in the same way as other subordinate legislation.

2.3 Case law

Case law refers to the creation and refinement of law in the course of judicial decisions. The foregoing has highlighted the increased importance of legislation in its various guises in today's society but, even allowing for this and the fact that case law can be overturned by legislation, the UK is still a common law system and the importance and effectiveness of judicial creativity and common law principles and practices cannot be discounted.

2.3.1 Precedent

The doctrine of binding precedent, or *stare decisis*, lies at the heart of the English legal system. The doctrine refers to the fact that, within the hierarchical structure of the English courts, a decision of a higher court will be binding on a court lower than it in that hierarchy. In general terms, this means that when judges try cases, they will check to see if a similar situation has come before a court previously. If the precedent was set by a court of equal or higher status to the court deciding the new case, then the judge in the present case should follow the rule of law established in the earlier case. Where the precedent is from a lower court in the hierarchy, the judge in the new case may not follow, but will certainly consider it. (The structure of the civil courts will be considered in detail in Chapter 3 and that of the criminal courts in Chapter 4.)

2.3.2 Law reporting

It is apparent that the operation of binding precedent is reliant upon the existence of an extensive reporting service to provide access to previous judicial decisions. This section briefly sets out where one might locate case reports on particular areas of the law. This is of particular importance to counsel, who are under a duty to bring all relevant case authority to the attention of the court, whether it advances their case or not. Consequently, they are expected to make themselves thoroughly aware of the current reports.

The Year Books

The earliest reports of particular cases appeared between 1275 and 1535 in what are known as *The Year Books*. These reports are really of historical interest as they were originally written in that peculiar language that was, and to a degree still is, the bane of law students and to the incomprehension of French students, Legal French. As with the common law generally, the focus was on procedural matters and forms of pleading. Those who are engaged in the study of legal history will find the most important cases translated and collected together in the Seldon Society series or the Rolls series but, for the main part, they represent a backwater little navigated by those whose concern is modern law.

Private reports (1535–1865)

These reports bear the name they do because they were produced by private individuals and cited by the name of the person who collected them. They were, however, published commercially for public reference. The ongoing problem with the private reports relates to their accuracy. At best it can be said that some were better, that is, more accurate than others. Of particular importance amongst the earlier reports were those of Plowden, Coke and Burrows, but there are many other reports that are of equal standing in their own right, with full and accurate reports of the cases submitted by counsel, together with the reason for the decisions in the particular case. A substantial number of the private reports have been collated and published as the *English Reports*. The series comprises 178 large volumes – 176 volumes being reports and the last two volumes providing an index of all the cases reported. In addition, the reports are accompanied by a useful wall chart to assist location of individual reports.

Modern reports (1865 to present)

As has been seen, the private reports were not without their problems. In addition to at least occasional inaccuracy, their publication could be both dilatory and expensive. This situation was at last remedied by the establishment of the Council for Law Reporting in 1865, subsequently registered as a corporate body in 1870 under the name of The Incorporated Council of Law Reporting for England and Wales. The Council was established under the auspices of the Inns of Court and The Law Society with the aim of producing quicker, cheaper and more accurate reports than had been available previously.

The Law Reports

These are the case reports produced by the Council. They have the distinct advantage of containing summaries of counsels' arguments and, perhaps even more importantly, they are subject to revision by the judges in the case before they are published. Not surprisingly, the *Law Reports* are seen as the most authoritative of reports, and it is usual for them to be cited in court cases in preference to any other report.

The current series of Law Reports from 1891 is issued annually in four parts:

Appeal Cases	(AC)
Chancery Division	(Ch)
Family Division	(Fam)
King's/Queen's Bench	(KB/QB)

Delays in reporting can obviously mean that cases decided in one year are not reported till the following year. Since the start of the current series, individual volumes of reports carry the year of publication in square brackets together with a volume number if there is a need for more than one. Cases are cited, therefore, in relation to the year and volume in which they are published, rather than the year they were decided.

Weekly Law Reports (citation WLR)

These have also been published by the Council since 1953 and, although they are not reports of cases decided in the current week as the name might suggest, they are produced much more quickly than the Law Reports. The need for speed means that these reports do not contain counsels' arguments, nor do they enjoy the benefit of judicial correction before printing. There are three volumes of reported cases, the last two containing the cases that will also appear in the Law Reports.

All England Law Reports (citation All ER)

These reports are produced by the legal publishers Butterworths and, although they do enjoy judicial revision, they do not contain counsels' arguments. They are published weekly and are then collated annually in volumes.

Legal periodicals and newspapers

The *Solicitors Journal* (Sol Jo or SJ) has been reporting cases since 1851 and some cases are only to be found in its reports. In such circumstances, the reports may be cited in court. The same is also true for cases reported in other journals such as the *New Law Journal* or the other specialist legal journals.

The reports in the broadsheet newspapers, *The Times*, *The Guardian* and *The Independent*, may also be cited in such circumstances, as long as they have been produced by appropriately qualified individuals (the Courts and Legal Services Act 1990 extended the right to solicitors as well as barristers). It has to be recognised, however, that some of these reports are rather insubstantial in nature.

Specialist reports

There are a number of specialist reports. Indeed, there are more than can be mentioned here, but amongst the most important of these are:

Industrial Relations Law Reports	(IRLR)
Knight's Local Government Reports	(LGR)
Lloyd's Law Reports	(Lloyd's Rep)
Report on Tax Cases	(TC or Tax Cas)
Criminal Appeal Reports	(Cr App R)

European Community reports

Although European cases may appear in the reports considered above, there are two specialist reports relating to EC cases:

- *European Court Reports (ECR)*

These are the official reports produced by the European Court of Justice (ECJ). As such, they are produced in all the official languages of the Community and consequently suffer from delay in reporting.

- *Common Market Law Reports (CMLR)*

These are unofficial reports published weekly in English by the European Law Centre.

Reports of the European Court of Human Rights in Strasbourg are provided in the European Human Rights Reports (EHRR).

CD-ROMs and Internet facilities

As in most other fields, the growth of information technology has revolutionised law reporting and law finding. Many of the law reports mentioned above are both available on CD-ROM and on the Internet. See, for example, Justis, Lawtel, Lexis-Nexis and Westlaw UK amongst others. Indeed, members of the public can now access law reports directly from their sources in the courts, both domestically and in Europe. The first major electronic cases database was the Lexis system, which gave immediate access to a huge range of case authorities, some unreported elsewhere. The problem for the courts was that lawyers with access to the system could simply cite lists of cases from the database, without the courts having access to paper copies of the decisions. The courts soon expressed their displeasure at this indiscriminate citation of unreported cases trawled from the Lexis database (see *Stanley v International Harvester Co of Great Britain Ltd* (1983)).

Neutral citation

In line with the ongoing modernisation of the whole legal system, the way in which cases are to be cited has been changed. Thus, from January 2001, following *Practice Direction (Judgments: Form and Citation)* [2001] 1 WLR 194, a new neutral system was introduced and extended in the following year in a further Practice Direction in April 2002. Cases in the various courts are now cited as follows:

House of Lords	[year]	UKHL case no
Court of Appeal (Civil Division)	[year]	EWCA Civ case no
Court of Appeal (Criminal Division)	[year]	EWCA Crim case no
High Court		
Queen's Bench Division	[year]	EWHC case no (QB)
Chancery Division	[year]	EWHC case no (Ch)
Patents Court	[year]	EWHC case no (Pat)
Administrative Court	[year]	EWHC case no (Admin)
Commercial Court	[year]	EWHC case no (Comm)
Admiralty Court	[year]	EWHC case no (Admlty)
Technology & Construction Court	[year]	EWHC case no (TCC)
Family Division	[year]	EWHC case no (Fam)

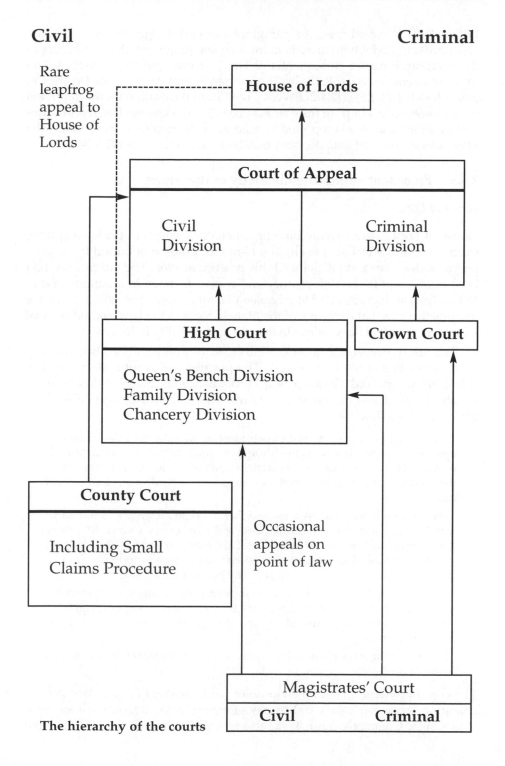

Civil   **Criminal**

Rare leapfrog appeal to House of Lords

House of Lords

Court of Appeal

Civil Division

Criminal Division

High Court

Queen's Bench Division
Family Division
Chancery Division

Crown Court

County Court

Including Small Claims Procedure

Occasional appeals on point of law

Magistrates' Court

Civil   Criminal

The hierarchy of the courts

Within the individual case, the paragraphs of each judgment are numbered consecutively, and where there is more than one judgment, the numbering of the paragraphs carries on sequentially. Thus, for example, the neutral citation for *International Transport Roth GmbH v Secretary of State for the Home Department* (considered at 1.7.1.5) is [2002] EWCA Civ 158 and the citation for the quotation from Simon Brown LJ from the case is at para 53. The specific law report series within which the case is reported is cited after the neutral citation: thus, the *International Transport Roth* decision may be found at [2002] 3 WLR 344.

2.3.3 Precedent within the hierarchy of the courts

House of Lords

House of Lords' decisions are binding on all other courts in the legal system, except the House of Lords itself. The House of Lords was bound by its own previous decisions until it changed this practice in 1966. The old practice had been established in the 19th century and was re-affirmed in a famous case in 1898 – *London Tramways Co Ltd v London County Council*. The rationale for the old practice was that decisions of the highest court in the land should be final so that there would be certainty in the law and a finality in litigation.

The rule, however, did not appear to create certainty and had become very rigid by the end of the 19th century. The practice was eventually changed in July 1966 when Lord Gardiner, the Lord Chancellor, made a statement on behalf of himself and his fellow Law Lords. This *Practice Statement* [1966] 3 All ER 77 runs as follows:

> Their Lordships regard the use of precedent as an indispensable foundation upon which to decide what is the law and its application to individual cases. It provides at least some degree of certainty upon which individuals can rely in the conduct of their affairs as well as a basis for orderly development of legal rules.

> Their Lordships nevertheless recognise that too rigid adherence to precedent may lead to injustice in a particular case and also unduly restrict the proper development of the law. They propose, therefore, to modify their present practice and, while treating former decisions of this House as normally binding, to depart from a previous decision when it appears right to do so.

> In this connection they will bear in mind the danger of disturbing retrospectively the basis on which contracts, settlements of property, and fiscal arrangements have been entered into and also the special need for certainty as to the criminal law.

> This announcement is not intended to affect the use of precedent elsewhere than in this house.

The current practice enables the House of Lords to adapt English law to meet changing social conditions and to pay attention to the decisions of superior courts in the Commonwealth. It was also regarded as important at the time that the House of Lords' practice be brought into line with that of superior courts in other countries, like the United States Supreme Court and State supreme courts elsewhere which are not bound by their own previous decisions. It also has the effect of bringing the practice of the UK's highest domestic court into line with the practice of both the ECJ and the European Court of Human Rights (ECtHR), neither of which is bound by a rigid doctrine of precedent, although in practice, they do not wilfully ignore previous decisions they have made. The possibility of the House of Lords changing its previous decisions is a recognition that law, whether expressed in statutes or cases, is a living, and therefore changing, institution which must adapt to the circumstances in which and to which it applies if it is to retain practical relevance.

Any appellant who intends to ask the House of Lords to depart from its own previous decision must draw special attention to this in the appeal documents (*Practice Direction (House of Lords: Preparation of Case)* [1971] 1 WLR 534). Since 1966, the House has used this power quite sparingly. It will not refuse to follow its earlier decision merely because that decision was wrong. A material change of circumstances will usually have to be shown.

In *Conway v Rimmer* (1968), the House of Lords unanimously overruled *Duncan v Cammell Laird and Co* (1942) on a question of the discovery of documents. *Duncan v Cammell Laird and Co* concerned the question of whether a plaintiff could get the defendant to disclose documents during war time which related to the design of a submarine. *Conway v Rimmer* concerned whether a probationary police officer could insist on getting disclosure of reports written about him by his superintendent. In the earlier case, the House of Lords held that an affidavit sworn by a government minister was sufficient to enable the Crown to claim privilege not to disclose documents in civil litigation, without those documents being inspected by the court. In the later case, their Lordships held that the minister's affidavit was not binding on the court. The second decision held that it is for the court to decide whether or not to order disclosure. This involves balancing the possible prejudice to the State if disclosure is ordered against any injustice that might affect the individual litigant if disclosure is withheld. Today, the minister's affidavit will be considered by the court, but it is no longer the sole determinant of the issue.

In *Herrington v British Railway Board* (1972), the House of Lords overruled *Addy and Sons v Dumbreck* (1929). In the earlier case, the House of Lords had decided that an occupier of premises was only liable to a trespassing child if that child was injured by the occupier intentionally or recklessly. In its later decision, the House of Lords changed the law in line with the changed social and physical conditions since 1929. Their Lordships felt that even a trespasser was entitled to some degree of care, which they propounded as a test of 'common humanity'.

In *R v United Railways of the Havana and Regla Warehouses Ltd* (1961), the House of Lords decided that damages awarded in an English civil case could only be awarded in sterling. The issue came up for reconsideration in 1976, by which time there had been significant changes in foreign exchange conditions, and the instability of sterling at the later date was of much greater concern than it had been in 1961. In the second case, *Miliangos v George Frank (Textiles) Ltd* (1976), the House of Lords overruled the earlier decision, stating that damages could be awarded in other currencies.

In *R v Secretary of State for the Home Department ex p Khawaja* (1983), the House of Lords departed from its own previous decision made two years earlier – *R v Secretary of State for the Home Department ex p Zamir* (1980). The earlier case had put the main burden of proof on an alleged illegal immigrant to show that his detention was not justified. In its decision two years later, the House of Lords expressed the view that the power of the courts to review the detention and summary removal of an alleged illegal immigrant had been too narrowly defined in the 1980 decision. It held that continued adherence to the precedent would involve the risk of injustice and would obstruct the proper development of law.

In *Murphy v Brentwood District Council* (1990), the House of Lords overruled its earlier decision in *Anns v Merton London Borough Council* (1978) on the law governing the liability of local authorities for the inspection of building foundations. In the earlier decision, the House of Lords held that a local authority was under a legal duty to take reasonable care to ensure that the foundations of a building complied with building regulations. The duty was owed to the owner and occupier of the building who had a legal action if the duty was broken. This created a very wide and extensive duty of care for local authorities, which was out of kilter with the development of this area of law (negligence) in relation to other property-like goods. There was considerable academic and judicial resistance to the decision in *Anns*. In overruling it, the House of Lords in *Murphy* cited the reluctance of English law to provide a remedy for pure economic loss, that is, loss which is not consequential upon bodily injury or physical damage.

If a person commits a murder or assists someone to do so under duress, that is, while under threat that unless he kills or helps, he himself will be murdered, should this afford him a legal defence? In *DPP for Northern Ireland v Lynch* (1975), the House of Lords decided that duress was available as a defence to a person who had participated in a murder as an aider and abettor. Twelve years later, the House of Lords overruled that decision. It held in *R v Howe* (1987) that the defence of duress is not available to a person charged with murder or as an aider and abettor to murder. Some people might regard it as unjust that a person who kills, or assists in a killing, whilst under duress should be so severely punished under the criminal law, but in taking away the defence of duress from murderers and those who assist them, the House of Lords founded its decision partly upon considerations of social policy (it made references to a rising tide of crimes of violence and terrorism which needed a strict response from the law) and a recognition that, where people killed others or assisted in such events while under duress, their conviction could be addressed by other mechanisms, such as the availability of parole and the royal prerogative of mercy.

Another significant example of the House of Lords recognising and accommodating changed circumstances can be seen in *Hall v Simons* (2000), in which it declined to follow the previous authority of *Rondel v Worsley* (1969), which had recognised the immunity of barristers against claims for negligence in their presentation of cases (see 11.5.1 for an extended analysis of this case).

The final cases to consider at this point relate to the effect of the HRA 1998 and they reveal an extremely unsatisfactory and confusing legal situation. In *R v Lambert*, in July 2001, the House of Lords, with Lords Slynn, Steyn, Hope, Hutton and Clyde presiding, decided that the HRA was not retrospective in relation to appeals from cases decided before it came into effect. Lord Clyde, in a minority of one, held that the Act did have retrospective effect in such circumstances.

However, only four months later, in November 2001, in *R v Kansal*, the House of Lords, with Lords Slynn, Steyn, Hope, Hutton and Lloyd presiding (only one difference from *Lambert*), decided by a 3:2 majority that the decision in *R v Lambert* could no longer be supported. However, the court also held, by a 4:1 majority, that *R v Lambert* should be followed nonetheless. Comparing the two cases reveals that only Lords Slynn and Sutton were consistent, although wrong according to the later majority, in their view that the HRA was not retrospective. Although *R v Lambert* was followed in *R v Benjafield* (2001), it still remains a matter of deep concern that the House of Lords could reveal itself to be so inconsistent, not to say uncertain, as to the precise effect of the HRA.

The Court of Appeal

In civil cases, the Court of Appeal is generally bound by previous decisions of the House of Lords. Although the Court of Appeal, notably under the aegis of Lord Denning, attempted on a number of occasions to escape from the constraints of *stare decisis*, the House of Lords repeatedly re-asserted the binding nature of its decisions on the Court of Appeal. The House of Lords emphasised the balance between the need for certainty in the law against the need to permit scope for the law to develop, and in so doing, it asserted its function, as the court of last resort at the head of the hierarchy, to undertake necessary reform. The relationship between and functions of the House of Lords and the Court of Appeal was clearly stated by Lord Diplock in *Davis v Johnson* (1979):

> In an appellate court of last resort a balance must be struck between the need on the one side for legal certainty resulting from the binding effect of previous decisions and on the other side the avoidance of undue restriction on the proper development of law. In the case of an intermediate appellate court, however, the second desideratum can be taken care of by an appeal to a superior court, if

reasonable means of access to it are available; while the risk to the first desideratum, legal certainty, if the court is not bound by its own previous decisions grows ever greater with increasing membership and the number of three-judge divisions in which it sits ... So the balance does not lie in the same place as the court of last resort.

However, as has been seen in 1.7.1.3, the Court of Appeal in *Mendoza v Ghaidan* (2002) used s 3 of the HRA to extend the rights of same-sex partners to inherit a statutory tenancy under the Rent Act 1977. In so doing, it went against the earlier decision of the House of Lords in *Fitzpatrick v Sterling Housing Association Ltd* (1999), which had been decided before the HRA came into force. Thus, it can be seen that the HRA gives the Court of Appeal latitude to effectively overrule decisions of the House of Lords which were decided before the HRA came into effect and in conflict with the ECHR.

Similarly, decisions of the ECJ which effectively overrule previous decisions of the House of Lords will also be followed by the Court of Appeal.

The Court of Appeal generally is also bound by its own previous decisions in civil cases. There are, however, a number of exceptions to this general rule. Lord Greene MR listed these exceptions in *Young v Bristol Aeroplane Co Ltd* (1944):

- Where there is a conflict between two previous decisions of the Court of Appeal. In this situation, the later court must decide which decision to follow and, as a corollary, which to overrule. Such a situation arose in *Tiverton Estates Ltd v Wearwell Ltd* (1974). In that case, which dealt with the meaning of s 40 of the Law of Property Act 1925 (subsequently repealed), the court elected to follow older precedents rather than follow the inconsistent decision in *Law v Jones* (1974). The decision in *Tiverton Estates Ltd v Wearwell Ltd* can be justified as the mere working out of the rules of precedent. As *Law v Jones* must have been made in ignorance of, or based on a failure to properly understand, the earlier decisions (see *per incuriam*, below), it could have been ignored on that ground alone. However, this particular exception is wider than that, in that it allows the current Court of Appeal to choose between the previous conflicting authorities. Hence, the Court of Appeal could have decided to follow *Law v Jones* if it preferred.

- Where a previous decision of the Court of Appeal has been overruled, either expressly or impliedly, by the House of Lords. An express overruling would obviously occur where the House of Lords actually considered the Court of Appeal precedent, but it is equally possible that the *ratio* in a precedent from the Court of Appeal could be overruled without the actual case being cited and considered. In this situation, the Court of Appeal, in line with the normal rules of precedent, is required to follow the decision of the House of Lords. Thus, in *Family Housing Association v Jones* (1990), the Court of Appeal felt obliged to ignore its own precedents on the distinction between a licence and a tenancy in property law where, although they had not been expressly overruled, they were implicitly in conflict with later decisions of the House of Lords in *AG Securities Ltd v Vaughan* (1988) and *Street v Mountford* (1985).

- Where the previous decision was given *per incuriam* or, in other words, that previous decision was taken in ignorance of some authority, either statutory or case law, that would have led to a different conclusion. In this situation, the later court can ignore the previous decision in question. It is important to emphasise, however, that the missing authority must be such that it must have led to a different conclusion; the mere possibility is not enough. There are so many case authorities that it is simply not possible to cite all of them. However, the essential authorities, those that lead to a particular decision, must be considered. It is the absence of any such of these authorities that renders a decision *per incuriam*. As will be appreciated, the instances of decisions being ignored on the basis of a ruling of *per incuriam* are 'of the rarest occurrence' (*Morelle Ltd v Wakeling* (1952)). One example, however, may be seen in *Williams v Fawcett* (1985), in which the Court of Appeal did find such exceptional circumstances as would permit it to treat its previous decisions as having been made *per incuriam*. The facts of the case involved an appeal against a decision to commit a person to prison for contempt of court in breaching a non-molestation order. Previous decisions of the Court of Appeal had held that any such committal order had to be signed by the court officer who issued it. However, the present court found that the law as stated in the Criminal Court Rules did not allow for appeal simply on the grounds that the order was not signed by a proper officer as long as the seal of the court was applied. Of crucial importance amongst the circumstances that led to the finding of *per incuriam* in relation to the earlier decisions was the fact that, given the expense involved, the case would be unlikely to go to the House of Lords for its final determination of the legal situation. It should be noted that this justification can be seen to fit with the previous quotation from Lord Diplock in *Davis v Johnson*, to the extent that the Court of Appeal decided that, in this instance, there was no 'reasonable means of access to' the court of last resort. A similar justification for another finding of *per incuriam* can be found in *Rickards v Rickards* (1989), in which the Court of Appeal held that its previous decision in *Podberry v Peak* (1981) had misunderstood and wrongly applied the House of Lords' decision in *Laine v Eskdale* (1891). In overruling *Podberry*, the court held that it had the power to hear an appeal against a refusal to extend the time limit within which a person could appeal against the award of a lump sum in a clean-break divorce settlement. The court once again held that as the issue involved was so serious, and as it was unlikely to go to the House of Lords, then the Court of Appeal should itself remedy the earlier misunderstanding stated in its own previous decision. An interesting example of the principle can be found in *R (on the Application of W) v Lambeth LBC* (2002), in which the Court of Appeal overruled its earlier judgment of only six months previously in *R (A) v Lambeth LBC* (2001) as regards the interpretation and effect of s 17 of the Children Act 1989. The matter of interest is not so much that the later court held that the earlier one would have reached a different conclusion had the law been fully explained to it, but that one of the judges in the unanimous decision in *R (W) v Lambeth LBC* was Laws LJ, who had delivered a minority judgment to the same effect in *R (A) v Lambeth LBC*.

The foregoing list deals with all the exceptions set out in *Young v Bristol Aeroplane Co Ltd*, but the following additional exceptions to the rule have become apparent since that decision:

- there is also the possibility/likelihood that, as a consequence of s 3 of the European Communities Act 1972, the Court of Appeal can ignore a previous decision of its own which is inconsistent with EC law or with a later decision of the ECJ. As s 3 requires courts either to refer cases dealing with Community law to the ECJ, or alternatively to decide the cases themselves in the light of the previous decision of the ECJ, it would appear that the section gives the Appeal Court grounds for ignoring any of its previous decisions which conflict with subsequent decisions of the ECJ. This effectively fits the ECJ into the traditional hierarchical structure of precedence as the court of last resort in relation to Community law matters;

- the precise effect of the HRA 1998 remains to be seen, but it can be noted that s 2 of the Act requires all courts and tribunals to take into account any judgment, decision, declaration or advisory opinion of the ECtHR. As previously the decisions of the ECtHR were not directly binding on the UK courts, this means that the decisions and jurisprudence of the ECtHR will affect the way in which the UK courts reach decisions in cases involving the rights provided under the European Convention. In *Director General of Fair Trading v Proprietary Association of Great Britain* (2001) (see 6.1.3), the Court of Appeal felt able to refine the decision of the House of Lords in *R v Gough* (1993) to bring it into line with ECtHR jurisprudence, and it is almost without doubt that it will overrule its own decisions where those are in conflict with the provisions of the ECHR.

There used to be a further exception to the general rule that the Court of Appeal was bound by its own earlier decisions and that was in relation to an interlocutory or interim decision made by a panel of only two judges (*Boys v Chaplin* (1968)); even interim decisions by a full panel of three judges were still binding. However, as a consequence of the Woolf reforms and under the Civil Procedure Rules 1998, the distinction between interlocutory and final appeals was removed. Consequently, it was held in *Cave v Robinson, Jarvis and Rolf* (2002) that the decision in *Boys v Chaplin* was no longer sustainable, although the Court of Appeal stated that it might be possible to adjust the reasoning in

Boys v Chaplin where the later court was satisfied that the earlier decision of the two-person court was 'manifestly wrong'.

Although on the basis of *R v Spencer* (1985) it would appear that there is no difference in principle between the operation of the doctrine of *stare decisis* between the criminal and civil divisions of the Court of Appeal, it is generally accepted that in practice, precedent is not followed as strictly in the former as it is in the latter. Courts in the criminal division are not bound to follow their own previous decisions that they subsequently consider to have been based on either a misunderstanding or a misapplication of the law. The reason for this is that the criminal courts deal with matters involving individual liberty and therefore require greater discretion to prevent injustice.

Divisional Courts

The Divisional Courts, each located within the three divisions of the High Court, hear appeals from courts and tribunals below them in the hierarchy. They are bound by the doctrine of *stare decisis* in the normal way and must follow decisions of the House of Lords and the Court of Appeal. In turn, they bind the courts below them in the hierarchy, including the ordinary High Court cases. The Divisional Courts are also normally bound by their own previous decisions, although in civil cases, they may make use of the exceptions open to the Court of Appeal in *Young v Bristol Aeroplane Co Ltd* (1944) and, in criminal appeal cases and cases relating to judicial review, the Queen's Bench Divisional Court may refuse to follow its own earlier decisions where it feels the decision to have been made wrongly.

In *R v Greater Manchester Coroner ex p Tal* (1984), the Divisional Court held that it had supervisory jurisdiction in relation to coroners' courts, although this was contrary to its previous decision in *R v Surrey Coroner ex p Campbell* (1982). In so doing, the court stated that its power to depart from its previous decisions was conferred under the Supreme Court Act 1981, but it also held, on the basis of the House of Lords decision in *O'Reilly v Mackman* (1982), that *Campbell* had wrongly applied *Anisminic v Foreign Compensation Commission* (1969). *Tal*, therefore, may also be seen as an example of the normal exceptions in *Young v Bristol Aeroplane Co Ltd*.

In *R v Stafford Justices ex p Commissioners of Customs and Excise* (1990), the Queen's Bench Divisional Court held that its previous decision in *R v Ealing Justices ex p Dixon* (1990) had been wrongly decided. Both cases related to the rights to undertake prosecutions where individuals had been charged, as required under s 37 of the Police and Criminal Evidence Act (PACE) 1984, by the police. Contrary to the *Ealing Justices* case, the Divisional Court in the *Stafford Justices* case held that merely being charged by the police did not require that the police should pursue the prosecution and that the Customs and

Excise could undertake the prosecution. In a similar case, although this time relating to the powers of the Inland Revenue to undertake prosecutions on indictment without the consent of the Attorney General, the Divisional Court approved the *Stafford Justices* decision and stated clearly that the *Ealing Justices* case should no longer be followed (*R v Criminal Cases Review Commission ex p Hunt* (2001)).

The House of Lords implicitly approved the Divisional Court's power to overrule its own previous decisions in *DPP v Butterworth* (1994). This case was the culmination of a number of cases relating to the refusal to provide a breath specimen contrary to s 7(6) of the Road Traffic Act 1988. In *DPP v Corcorran* (1993), a Divisional Court held that where a person was not informed for which of two potential offences he was being required to provide a specimen, any prosecution was undermined for duplicity. However, in *DPP v Shaw* (1993), a differently constituted Divisional Court subsequently held that *Corcorran* was wrongly decided and was an example of a *per incuriam* decision. *Shaw* rather than *Corcorran* was followed in the later Divisional Court decision in *DPP v Butterworth*. That decision was expressly approved by the House of Lords.

High Court

The High Court is also bound by the decisions of superior courts. Decisions by individual High Court judges are binding on courts inferior in the hierarchy, but such decisions are not binding on other High Court judges, although they are of strong persuasive authority and tend to be followed in practice. The simple reason for this is that different judgments would lead to confusion in relation to exactly how the particular law in question was to be understood. It is possible, however, for High Court judges to disagree and for them to reach different conclusions as to the law in a particular area. The question then becomes, how is a later High Court judge to select which precedent to follow? It is usually accepted, although it is not a rule of law, that where the later decision has actually considered the previous one and has provided cause for not following it, then that is the judgment which later High Court judges should follow (*Colchester Estates v Carlton Industries plc* (1984)).

Conflicting decisions at the level of the High Court can, of course, be authoritatively decided by reference upwards to the Court of Appeal and then, if necessary, to the House of Lords, but when the cost of such appeals is borne in mind, it is apparent why, even on economic grounds alone, it is important for High Court judges not to treat their discretion as a licence to destabilise the law in a given area.

In relation to conflicting judgments at the level of the Court of Appeal, the High Court judge is required to follow the later decision.

Crown Courts cannot create precedent and their decisions can never amount to more than persuasive authority.

County courts and magistrates' courts do not create precedents.

It has to be particularly noted that the HRA now requires courts in the UK to take into consideration all previous decisions of the ECtHR, which now become precedents for the UK courts to follow. This is the case even where the ECtHR decision was in conflict with previous UK law. Equally, any English precedent which was in conflict with a decision of the ECtHR is now invalidated.

2.3.4   Binding precedent

Not everything in a case report sets a precedent. The contents of a report can be divided into two categories:

- *Ratio decidendi*

  It is important to establish that it is not the actual decision in a case that sets the precedent; that is set by the rule of law on which the decision is founded. This rule, which is an abstraction from the facts of the case, is known as the *ratio decidendi* of the case. The *ratio decidendi* of a case may be understood as the statement of the law applied in deciding the legal problem raised by the concrete facts of the case.

- *Obiter dictum*

  Any statement of law that is not an essential part of the *ratio decidendi* is, strictly speaking, superfluous, and any such statement is referred to as an *obiter dictum* (*obiter dicta* in the plural), that is, said 'by the way'. Although *obiter dicta* do not form part of the binding precedent, they are persuasive authority and can be taken into consideration in later cases if the judge in the later case considers it appropriate to do so.

The division of cases into these two distinct parts is a theoretical procedure. Unfortunately, judges do not actually separate their judgments into the two clearly defined categories, and it is for the person reading the case to determine what the *ratio* is. In some cases, this is no easy matter, and it may be made even more difficult in appellate cases where each of the judges may deliver their own lengthy judgments with no clear single *ratio*. (The potential implications of the way in which later courts effectively determine the *ratio* in any particular case will be considered below and in Chapter 5.) Students should always read cases fully; although it is tempting to rely on the headnote at the start of the case report, it should be remembered that this is a summary provided by the case reporter and merely reflects what that person thinks the *ratio* is. It is not unknown for headnotes to miss an essential point in a case.

Example 1

Carlill v Carbolic Smoke Ball Co Ltd (1892)

Facts

Mrs Carlill made a retail purchase of one of the defendant's medicinal products: the 'Carbolic Smoke Ball'. It was supposed to prevent people who used it in a specified way (three times a day for at least two weeks) from catching influenza. The company was very confident about its product and placed an advertisement in a paper, *The Pall Mall Gazette*, which praised the effectiveness of the smoke ball and promised to pay £100 (a huge sum of money at that time) to:

> ... any person who contracts the increasing epidemic influenza, colds, or any disease caused by taking cold, having used the ball three times daily for two weeks according to the printed directions supplied with each ball.

The advertisement went on to explain that the company had deposited £1,000 with the Alliance Bank, Regent Street, London as a sign of its sincerity in the matter. Any proper plaintiffs could get their payment from that sum. On the faith of the advertisement, Mrs Carlill bought one of the balls at the chemists and used it as directed, but still caught the 'flu. She claimed £100 from the company, but was refused it, so she sued for breach of contract. The company said there was no contract for several reasons, but mainly because:

(a) the advert was too vague to amount to the basis of a contract – there was no time limit and no way of checking the way the customer used the ball;

(b) the plaintiff did not give any legally recognised value to the company;

(c) one cannot legally make an offer to the whole world, so the advert was not a proper offer;

(d) even if the advert could be seen as an offer, Mrs Carlill had not given a legal acceptance of that offer because she had not notified the company that she was accepting;

(e) the advert was a 'mere puff', that is, a piece of insincere sales talk not meant to be taken seriously.

Decision

The Court of Appeal found that there was a legally enforceable agreement, a contract, between Mrs Carlill and the company. The company would have to pay damages to the plaintiff.

Ratio decidendi

The three Lord Justices of Appeal who gave judgments in this case all decided in favour of Mrs Carlill. Each, however, used slightly different reasoning, arguments and examples. The process, therefore, of distilling the 'reason for the decision' of the court is quite a delicate art. The *ratio* of the case can be put as follows.

Offers must be sufficiently clear to allow the courts to enforce agreements that follow from them. The offer here was 'a distinct promise expressed in language which is perfectly unmistakable'. It could not be a 'mere puff' in view of the £1,000 deposited specially to show good faith. An offer may be made to the world at large and the advert was such an offer. It was accepted by any person, like Mrs Carlill, who bought the product and used it in the prescribed manner. Mrs Carlill had accepted the offer by her conduct when she did as she was invited to do, and started to use the smoke ball. She had not been asked to let the company know that she was using it.

Obiter dictum

In the course of his reasoning, Bowen LJ gave the legal answer to a set of facts which were not in issue in this case. This answer was thus an *obiter dictum*. He did this because it assisted him in clarifying the answer to Mrs Carlill's case. He said:

> If I advertise to the world that my dog is lost, and that anybody who brings the dog to a particular place will be paid some money, are all the police or other persons whose business it is to find lost dogs to be expected to sit down and write me a note saying that they have accepted my proposal? Why, of course, they at once look [for] the dog, and as soon as they find the dog they have performed the condition.

If such facts were ever subsequently in issue in a court case, then the words of Bowen LJ could be used by counsel as persuasive precedent.

This decision has affected the outcome of many cases. The information system LEXIS, for example, lists 70 cases in which *Carlill* is cited. It was *applied* in *Peck v Lateu* (1973) and distinguished in *AM Satterthwaite & Co v New Zealand Shipping Co* (1972).

Example 2

Psychiatric harm

In what circumstances can someone who has suffered psychiatric injury as a result of having witnessed a terrible accident successfully sue the person whose negligence has caused the accident?

The leading case on recovery of compensation in such circumstances is *Alcock v Chief Constable of South Yorkshire Police* (1992), which arose from the

Hillsborough Stadium disaster. At the FA Cup semi-final match at Hillsborough Stadium in Sheffield between Nottingham Forest and Liverpool in April 1989, 96 people were killed and over 400 physically injured in a crush which developed owing to poor crowd control by the police. The Chief Constable admitted liability towards those physically harmed. Many more people variously related to, or connected with, the dead and injured suffered psychiatric illness resulting from the shock of witnessing the event, seeing it on television or identifying the bodies. Sixteen claims were heard at first instance, of which 10 succeeded in 1991. Hidden J held: (1) that brothers and sisters, as well as parents and spouses, could sue, but that grandfathers, uncles, brothers-in-law, fiancées and friends could not; and (2) that seeing the scene on television was equivalent to being at the scene itself. The Court of Appeal (1991) dismissed all the claims on the ground that, apart from rescuers, only parents and spouses could claim and that 'a perception through the broadcast of selective images accompanied by a commentary is not such as to satisfy the proximity test'. Ten plaintiffs then appealed unsuccessfully to the House of Lords.

Where was the line to be drawn between sufferers of psychiatric harm who could sue those responsible for the disaster and those who could not? The House of Lords refused to prescribe rigid categories of the potential claimants in nervous shock claims. It ruled that there must generally be a close and intimate relationship between the plaintiff and the primary victim (for example, in the Hillsborough setting, someone who was crushed or asphyxiated) of the sort generally enjoyed by spouses and parents and children. The House of Lords ruled that siblings and other more remote relatives would normally fall outside such a relationship in the absence of special factors. But, for example, a grandmother who had brought up a grandchild since infancy might qualify. Therefore, claims by brothers, sisters and brothers-in-laws failed in *Alcock*, while the claim on the part of a fiancée was allowed. One of the judges, Lord Ackner, suggested that in cases of exceptional horror where even a reasonably strong-nerved individual might suffer shock-induced psychiatric injury, a bystander unrelated to the victim might recover damages.

Their Lordships went on to rule that a degree of proximity in time and space between the plaintiff and the accident is required. The plaintiff must therefore either actually be at the accident itself and witness it, or come upon the aftermath in a very short period of time. Identifying a relation several hours after death was not sufficient to pass the legal test. Witnessing the accident via the medium of television will not generally be enough either.

Parents who watched the Hillsborough disaster on television had their claims rejected. This is because television pictures would not normally be equated with actual sight or hearing at the event or its aftermath. Lords Keith and Oliver, did, however, recognise that there might be exceptional cases where simultaneous broadcasts of a disaster were equivalent to a personal presence at the accident. In the Court of Appeal, Nolan LJ gave the example of a balloon carrying children at some live broadcast event suddenly bursting into flames.

The harm for which the person sues, the psychiatric illness, must be shown to result from the trauma of the event or its immediate aftermath. Psychiatric illness resulting from being informed of a loved one's death, however shocking the circumstances, is not recoverable. The approach taken by the House of Lords in *Alcock* is a very pragmatic one. It rejected the simple approach based on strict categories of those who could and could not recover and in what circumstances. In his judgment, Lord Keith said:

> ... as regards the class of person to whom a duty may be owed to take reasonable care to avoid inflicting psychiatric illness through nervous shock sustained by reason of physical injury or peril to another, I think it is sufficient that reasonable foreseeability should be the guide. I would not seek to limit the class by reference to particular relationships such as husband and wife or parent and child. The kinds of relationship which may involve close ties of love and affection are numerous, and it is the existence of such ties which lead to mental disturbance when the loved one suffers a catastrophe. They may be present in family relationships or those of close friendship, and may be stronger in the case of engaged couples than in that of persons have been married to each other for many years. It is common knowledge that such ties exist, and reasonably foreseeable that those bound by them may in certain circumstances be at real risk of psychiatric illness if the loved one is injured or put in peril. The closeness of the tie would, however, require to be proved by a plaintiff, though no doubt being capable of being presumed in appropriate cases. The case of a bystander unconnected with the victim of an accident is difficult. Psychiatric injury to him would not, ordinarily, in my view, be within the range of reasonable foreseeability, but could not perhaps be entirely excluded from it if the circumstances of a catastrophe occurring very close to him were particularly horrific.

Thus, the *ratio decidendi* of this case, while being one which is reasonably clear, is one nevertheless whose precise application in future cases is difficult to predict. In a subsequent case, *McFarlane v EE Caledonia Ltd* (1994), the Court of Appeal had to apply the general principle expounded by the Lords in *Alcock*. In this case, the plaintiff witnessed the destruction of an oil rig (the Piper Alpha) from aboard a support vessel which had been involved in attempts to rescue survivors of the explosion which tore apart the rig. The plaintiff was not himself involved directly in the rescue effort, and was far enough away from the burning rig to avoid any personal danger to himself. Even so, the events which he witnessed were horrific almost beyond imagining. He had to watch people in agony, burning to death, as the rig was devastated by fire and explosions. Although technically a 'bystander' to the incident because he was neither a relative of any of the primary victims nor a rescuer, he does seem to fit within the last category of possible claimants described above by Lord Keith.

His case, though, was rejected by the Court of Appeal, which suggested that practical and policy reasons militated against allowing him to recover.

Evaluation

The foregoing has set out the doctrine of binding precedent as it operates in theory to control and indeed limit the ambit of judicial discretion. It has to be recognised, however, that the doctrine does not operate as stringently as it appears at first sight and that there are particular shortcomings in the system that have to be addressed in weighing up the undoubted advantages with the equally undoubted disadvantages.

Nonetheless, the practical importance of the doctrine of precedent can be seen in the history of three conjoined cases, *Fairchild v Glenhaven Funeral Services Ltd and Others* (2002).

The cases related to claims for compensation for injury – mesothelioma – a terminal lung disease caused by the exposure of workers to asbestos fibre during the course of their working lives with more than one employer. Both the High Court and the Court of Appeal held that the claimants' cases could not succeed, as they could not prove which exposure to asbestos fibre had actually caused the resultant disease. As they could not prove which employer was at fault, no employer could be held liable.

Only a matter of days before the House of Lords was due to hear the appeal, a consortium of insurance companies, which would have had to provide any recompense in the final analysis, offered to settle the present cases on a voluntary basis and set up a compensation scheme for the hundreds of other claimants who were waiting for the outcome of those cases. The point, however, was that the payments to be made would have been significantly less than would have been awarded if the claimants won their case in the House of Lords. The insurers decided that they would rather not risk an adverse decision in the House of Lords, and actually told the Lords' judicial office that the settlement had been reached, thus removing the need to hear the final appeal. In reality, no such settlement had been reached.

The representative of the claimants stated that the settlement scheme was a 'sordid attempt to manipulate the judicial process. The whole objective [being] to ensure that the Court of Appeal's decision remains intact'. The representative of the insurers stated that it was 'not cynical – it was practical'. Lord Bingham, the senior judge in the House of Lords, stated that the episode had been 'entirely regrettable'.

When the cases subsequently came before the House of Lords, the fears of the insurance companies were proved justified by that court overruling the decision of the Court of Appeal, thus laying the insurers open to significantly more liability than they would have had to meet under their voluntary scheme.

It has to be admitted, however, that this sort of manoeuvring also occurs in relation to trade union and other civil rights cases, where the specialist lawyers who deal with such issues attempt to ensure that potentially ground-breaking issues are argued in relation to relatively stronger cases rather than very weak ones. The practicality is that once a positive precedent, the legal rule, is established in the strong case, it can be extended into a wider area. It would, however, be much more difficult to overturn a contrary precedent handed down in a weak case.

2.3.5 Advantages of case law

There are numerous perceived advantages of the doctrine of *stare decisis*, amongst which are the following:

- *Consistency*. This refers to the fact that like cases are decided on a like basis and are not apparently subject to the whim of the individual judge deciding the case in question. This aspect of formal justice is important in justifying the decisions taken in particular cases.

- *Certainty*. This follows from, and indeed is presupposed by, the previous item. Lawyers and their clients are able to predict what the outcome of a particular legal question is likely to be in the light of previous judicial decisions. Also, once the legal rule has been established in one case, individuals can orientate their behaviour with regard to that rule, relatively secure in the knowledge that it will not be changed by some later court.

- *Efficiency*. This refers to the fact that it saves the time of the judiciary, lawyers and their clients for the reason that cases do not have to be re-argued. In respect of potential litigants, it saves them money in court expenses because they can apply to their solicitor/barrister for guidance as to how their particular case is likely to be decided in the light of previous cases on the same or similar points. (It should of course be recognised that the vast bulk of cases are argued and decided on their facts rather than on principles of law, but that does not detract from the relevance of this issue and is a point that will be taken up later in Chapter 4.)

- *Flexibility*. This refers to the fact that the various mechanisms by means of which the judges can manipulate the common law provide them with an opportunity to develop law in particular areas without waiting for Parliament to enact legislation.

  In practice, flexibility is achieved through the possibility of previous decisions being either overruled or distinguished, or the possibility of a later court extending or modifying the effective ambit of a precedent. (It should be re-emphasised that it is not the decision in any case which is binding, but the *ratio decidendi*. It is correspondingly and equally incorrect to refer to a decision being overruled.)

This apparently small measure of discretion, in relation to whether later judges are minded to accept the validity of *obiter* statements in precedent cases, opens up the possibility that judges in later cases have a much wider degree of discretion than is originally apparent in the traditional view of *stare decisis*. It is important in this respect to realise that it is the judges in the later cases who actually determine the *ratio decidendi* of previous cases.

Judges, as has been noted previously, in delivering judgments in cases do not separate and highlight the *ratio decidendi* from the rest of their judgment, which can lead to a lack of certainty in determining the *ratio decidendi*. This uncertainty is compounded by the fact that reports of decisions in cases may run to considerable length, and where there are a number of separate judgments, although the judges involved may agree on the decision of a case, they may not agree on the legal basis of the decision reached. This difficulty is further compounded where there are a number of dissenting judgments. In the final analysis, it is for the judge deciding the case in which a precedent has been cited to determine the *ratio* of the authority and thus to determine whether he or she is bound by the case or not. This factor provides later courts with a considerable degree of discretion in electing whether to be bound or not by a particular authority.

The main mechanisms through which judges alter or avoid precedents are as follows:

• *Overruling*

This is the procedure whereby a court higher up in the hierarchy sets aside a legal ruling established in a previous case.

It is somewhat anomalous that, within the system of *stare decisis*, precedents gain increased authority with the passage of time. As a consequence, courts tend to be reluctant to overrule long standing authorities even though they may no longer accurately reflect contemporary practices or morals. In addition to the wish to maintain a high degree of certainty in the law, the main reason for judicial reluctance to overrule old decisions would appear to be the fact that overruling operates retrospectively, with the effect that the principle of law being overruled is held never to have been law. Overruling a precedent might, therefore, have the consequence of disturbing important financial arrangements made in line with what were thought to be settled rules of law. It might even, in certain circumstances, lead to the imposition of criminal liability on previously lawful behaviour. It has to be emphasised, however, that the courts will not shrink from overruling authorities where they see them as no longer representing an appropriate statement of law.

The decision in *R v R* (1992) to recognise the possibility of rape within marriage may be seen as an example of this, although, even here, the House of Lords felt constrained to state that it was not actually altering the law, but was merely removing a misconception as to the true meaning and effect of the law (see 5.5 for an extended analysis of this case). As this demonstrates, the courts are rarely ready to challenge the legislative prerogative of Parliament in an overt way. For example, in *Curry v DPP* (1994), the Divisional Court attempted to remove the presumption that children between the ages of 10 and 14, who were charged with a criminal offence, did not know that what they did was seriously wrong and the prosecution had to provide evidence to rebut that presumption. Mann LJ justified reversing the presumption by claiming that although it had often been assumed to be the law, it had never actually been specifically considered by earlier courts. On such reasoning, he felt justified in departing from previous decisions of the Court of Appeal which otherwise would have bound him. The House of Lords subsequently restored the previous presumption. Although their Lordships recognised the problem, and indeed appeared to sympathise with Mann LJ's view, they nonetheless thought that such a significant change was a matter for parliamentary action rather than judicial intervention. The doctrine of *doli incapax* was finally removed by s 34 of the Crime and Disorder Act 1998. Of perhaps even greater concern is the fact that s 35 extended s 35 of the Criminal Justice and Public Order Act 1994 to cover all persons aged 10 or over. Thus, courts are now entitled to draw (adverse) inferences from the failure of such children to either give evidence or answer questions at their trial. *Bellinger v Bellinger* (2003), considered at 1.7.1.3, provides a contemporary example of the courts' reluctance to overrule cases and change the law where Parliament is the appropriate forum for such change.

Overruling should not be confused with *reversing*, which is the procedure whereby a superior court in the hierarchy reverses the decision of a lower court in the same case.

- *Distinguishing*

  In comparison to the mechanism of overruling which is rarely used, the main device for avoiding binding precedents is that of distinguishing. As was previously stated, the *ratio decidendi* of any case is an abstraction from, and is based upon, the material facts of the case. This opens up the possibility that a court may regard the facts of the case before it as significantly different from the facts of a cited precedent and thus, consequentially, it will not find itself bound to follow that precedent. Judges use the device of distinguishing where, for some reason, they are unwilling to follow a particular precedent and the law reports provide many examples of strained distinctions where a court has quite evidently not wanted to follow an authority that it would otherwise have been bound by.

2.3.6 Disadvantages of case law

It should be noted that the advantage of flexibility at least potentially contradicts the alternative advantage of certainty, but there are other disadvantages in the doctrine which have to be considered. Amongst these are the following:

- *Uncertainty*

  This refers to the fact that the degree of certainty provided by the doctrine of *stare decisis* is undermined by the absolute number of cases that have been reported and can be cited as authorities. This uncertainty is increased by the ability of the judiciary to select which authority to follow through use of the mechanism of distinguishing cases on their facts. A further element leading to uncertainty was highlighted by James Richardson, the editor of *Archbold* (1995), the leading practitioners' text on criminal law, who has claimed that the lack of practical experience of some judges in the Criminal Appeal Court is:

  ... compounded by an apparent willingness, on occasion, to set aside principle in order to do what the court feels to be right (either way) in the individual case.

  As Richardson suggests:

  In the long run, this can only undermine a system which claims to operate on the basis of a hierarchy of binding precedent.

- *Fixity*

  This refers to the possibility that the law in relation to any particular area may become ossified on the basis of an unjust precedent, with the consequence that previous injustices are perpetuated. An example of this is the possibility of rape within marriage, which has only relatively recently, given its long history, been recognised (*R v R* (1992)).

- *Unconstitutionality*

  This is a fundamental question that refers to the fact that the judiciary are overstepping their theoretical constitutional role by actually *making law* rather than restricting themselves to the role of simply applying it. This possibility requires a close examination of the role of the courts in the process of law-making.

  The traditional *declaratory theory of law* claims that judges do not make law, they simply state what it is. This view, however, gives rise to two particular conceptual difficulties:

  (a) *Innovation*: legal rules, as social institutions and creations, cannot be subject to infinite regression; they must have had a beginning at some time in the past when some person or group of people made or recognised them. Every common law rule must have had an origin. To put this in a simpler way, if a particular law was not created by statute, it must have been created by a judge; even if the level of creative activity was no more than recognising the legitimacy, or otherwise, of the practice in question, as was the role of the original circuit judges. Where an issue arises before a court for the first time, it follows, as a matter of course, that there can be no precedent for the court to follow and, given the rapid change in contemporary society, it can only be suggested that such innovations and potentially innovatory court cases are increasingly likely. In such novel circumstances, courts are faced with the choice of either refusing to decide a case, or stating what the law should be. In earlier times, judges did not shirk from this task and, even in modern times, courts are required on occasion to consider situations for the first time. Such cases are described as cases of first impression and inevitably involve judges in the creation of new law.

(b) *Reform*: the question arises as to how the law is to develop and change to cater for changed circumstances if cases are always to be decided according to precedent.

These considerations raise the question that if the law, as represented in either common law or statute law, is out of line with current social beliefs and practices, then should it not be incumbent upon the judiciary to decide cases in line with the currently prevailing standards, even if this means ignoring previous decisions and interpretations? Not to do so leaves the judges open to the charge of being out of touch with social reality. To overtly change the law, however, opens them up to the alternative charge of acting beyond their powers and of usurping the role and function of the legislature. Opinions on this matter range from those that would deny completely the right of judges to make or change the law, to those that would grant the judges the right to mould the law in line with their conception of justice. Others would recognise the fact that the common law was judge-made and restrict judicial creativity to the development of established common law principles. There is an important corollary to this latter position which links it with those who limit judicial creativity, for the implicit assertion is that judges have no place in reforming statutory provisions. They may signal the ineffectiveness of such provisions and call for their repeal or reform, but it would be a usurpation of the legislature's function and power for the courts to engage in such general reform.

In any case, this question unavoidably raises the issue of the actual extent of judicial creativity (compare and contrast *R v R* (1992) and *DPP v C* (1995) in this light). The previous consideration of distinguishing has demonstrated how the doctrine of *stare decisis* can be avoided by the judiciary. A further way in which judges have a creative impact on the law is in the way in which they adapt and extend precedent in instant cases. In addition, judicial reasoning, which will be considered in detail in Chapter 5, tends to be carried out on the basis of analogy, and judges have a large degree of discretion in selecting what are to be considered as analogous cases. They also have a tendency to extend, continuously, existing precedents to fit new situations, as the evolution of the tort of negligence will show.

It is now probably a commonplace of legal theory that judges do make law. Perhaps the more interesting question is not whether judges make law, but why they deny that they do so. In spite of the protestations of the judiciary, law and judicial decision-making is a political process to the extent that it is deciding which values are to be given priority within society. Through their choice of values, the judiciary sanction or prohibit particular forms of behaviour. Due to their position in the constitution, however, judges have to be circumspect in the way in which, and the extent to which, they use their powers to create law and impose values. To overtly assert or exercise the power would be to challenge the power of the legislature. For an unelected body to challenge a politically supreme Parliament would be unwise to say the least. It is for that reason that the courts on occasion take refuge behind the cloak of a naïve declaratory theory of law. (The political nature of judicial action will be considered further in Chapter 7.)

2.4 Books of authority

When a court is unable to locate a precise or analogous precedent, it may refer to legal textbooks for guidance. Such books are subdivided, depending on when they were written. In strict terms, only certain works are actually treated as authoritative sources of law. Amongst the most important of these works are those by Glanvill from the 12th century, Bracton from the 13th century, Coke from the 17th century and Blackstone from the 18th century. When cases such as *R v R* are borne in mind, it might be claimed, with justification, that the authority of such ancient texts may be respected more in the breach than in the performance. Given the societal change that has occurred in the intervening time, one can only say that such a refusal to fetishise ancient texts is a positive, and indeed necessary, recognition of the need for law to change in order to keep up with its contemporary sphere of operation. Legal works produced after Blackstone's *Commentaries* of 1765 are considered to be of recent origin, and they cannot be treated as authoritative sources. The courts, however, will look at the most eminent works by accepted experts in particular fields in order to help determine what the law is or should be. For example, in the sphere of company law, the work of Professor LCB Gower has been referred to by the courts in order to help to elucidate some abstruse legal principles, as has Sir William Wade and Anthony Bradley's work in the sphere of public law. For a more recent example, see the citation of Shetreet's *Judges on Trial*, and De Smith, Wolf and Jowell, *Judicial Review of Administrative Action*, in Lord Browne-Wilkinson's decision in *Re Pinochet* (1999).

2.5 Custom

There is some academic debate about the exact relationship of custom and law. Some claim that law is simply the extension of custom and that with the passage of time, customs develop into laws. From this point of view, law may be seen as the redefinition of custom for the purposes of clarity and enforcement by the legal institutions. The State institutions are seen as merely refining the existing customary behaviour of society. Others deny this evolutionary link and claim that law and custom are in fact contradictory, with law emerging in opposition to, and replacing, customary forms of behaviour. From this perspective, law is seen as being a new form of regulation handed down by the State rather than as emerging from society as a whole.

The traditional view of the development of the common law tends to adopt the first of these views. This overly romantic notion of the common law represents its emergence as no more than the crystallisation of common customs. This distillation is accomplished by the judiciary in the course of their historic travels around the land. This view, however, tends to play down the political process that gave rise to the procedure. The imposition of a common system of law represented the political victory of a State that had fought to establish and assert its central authority. Viewed in that light, the emergence of the common law can be seen actually to support the second of the two approaches suggested above.

Although some of the common law may have had its basis in general custom, a large proportion of these so called customs were invented by the judges themselves and represented what they wanted the law to be, rather than what people generally thought it was.

One source of customary practice that undoubtedly did find expression in the form of law was business and commercial practice. These customs and practices originally were constituted in the distinct form of the Law Merchant, but gradually this became subsumed under the control of the common law courts and ceased to exist apart from the common law.

Notwithstanding the foregoing, it is still possible for specific local customs to operate as a source of law. In certain circumstances, parties may assert the existence of customary practices in order to support their case. Such local customs may run counter to the strict application of the common law and, where they are found to be legitimate, they will effectively replace the common law. Even in this respect, however, reliance on customary law as opposed to common law, although not impossible, is made unlikely by the stringent tests that have to be satisfied. The requirements that a local custom must satisfy in order to be recognised are that:

- it must have existed from 'time immemorial', that is, 1189;
- it must have been exercised continuously within that period;
- it must have been exercised peaceably without opposition;

- it must also have been felt to be obligatory;
- it must be capable of precise definition;
- it must have been consistent with other customs;
- it must be reasonable.

Given this list of requirements, it can be seen why local custom is not an important source of law. However, the courts will have recourse to custom where they see it as appropriate, as may be seen in *Egerton v Harding* (1974), in which the courts upheld a customary duty to fence land against cattle straying from an area of common land.

2.6 Law reform

At one level, law reform is either a product of parliamentary or judicial activity as has been considered previously. Parliament tends, however, to be concerned with particularities of law reform, and the judiciary are constitutionally and practically disbarred from reforming the law in anything other than an opportunistic and piecemeal way. Therefore, there remains a need for the question of law reform to be considered generally and a requirement that such consideration be conducted in an informed but disinterested manner.

Reference has already been made to the use of consultative Green Papers by the government as a mechanism for gauging the opinions of interested parties to particular reforms. More formal advice may be provided through various advisory standing committees. Amongst these is the *Law Reform Committee*. The function of this Committee is to consider the desirability of changes to the civil law which the Lord Chancellor may refer to it. The *Criminal Law Revision Committee* performs similar functions in relation to criminal law.

Royal Commissions may be constituted to consider the need for law reform in specific areas. The Commission on Criminal Procedure (1980) led to the enactment of the Police and Criminal Evidence Act 1984, and the recommendation of the 1993 Royal Commission on Criminal Justice (Runciman Commission) informed subsequent reform of the criminal law system.

Committees may be set up in order to review the operation of particular areas of law, the most significant of these being the Woolf review of the operation of the civil justice system. Similarly, Sir Robin Auld conducted a review of the whole criminal justice system and Sir Andrew Leggatt reviewed the tribunal system. Detailed analysis of the consequences flowing from the implementation of the recommendations of these reviews will be considered subsequently.

If a criticism is to be levelled at these Committees and Commissions, it is that they are all *ad hoc* bodies. Their remit is limited and they do not have the power either to widen the ambit of their investigation or to initiate reform proposals.

The *Law Commission* fulfils the need for some institution to concern itself more generally with the question of law reform. Its general function is to keep the law as a whole under review and to make recommendations for its systematic reform. The Commission continuously keeps under review the need to remove antiquated and/or anachronistic laws from the statute book, the continued existence of which make it subject to derision even if they do not bring it into disrepute. To that end, 14 Statute Law Repeal Acts have been enacted since 1969, and following a 1995 Law Commission Report (No 230), the Law Reform (Year and a Day Rule) Act was introduced in 1996. This Act removed the ancient rule which prevented killers being convicted of murder or manslaughter if their victim survived for a year and a day after the original offence.

The Commission is a purely advisory body and its scope is limited to those areas set out in its current programme of law reform. It recommends reform after it has undertaken an extensive process of consultation with informed and/or interested parties. At the conclusion of a project, a report is submitted to the Lord Chancellor and Parliament for their consideration and action.

Although the scope of the Commission is limited to those areas set out in its programme of law reform, its ambit is not unduly restricted, as may be seen from the range of matters covered in its eighth programme set out in October 2001 which includes: damages; limitation of actions; property law; housing law; the law of trusts; partnership law; unfair terms in contracts; compulsory purchase; and the codification of criminal law. In addition, ministers may refer matters of particular importance to the Commission for its consideration. As was noted in Chapter 1, it was just such a referral by the Home Secretary, after the Macpherson Inquiry into the Stephen Lawrence case, that gave rise to the Law Commission's recommendation that the rule against double jeopardy be removed in particular circumstances. An extended version of that recommendation was included in the Criminal Justice Bill 2002.

Annual reports list all Commission publications. The Law Commission claims that, in the period since its establishment in 1965 until the end of 2001, over 100 of its law reports have been implemented. The 2001 annual report, however, expresses concern about the delay in implementing its reports due to the lack of parliamentary time, and has considered the possibility of some reforms being introduced under the Regulatory Reform Act 2001 (see 2.2.5). Examples of legislation following from Law Commission reports are: the Contracts (Rights of Third Parties) Act 1999, based on the recommendations of the Commission's Report No 180, *Privity of Contract*; and the Trustee Act 2000, based on the Commission's Report No 260. In February 2002, the Land Registration Act was passed. That Act, which will have a major impact on the land registration procedure, implemented the draft Bill which was the outcome of the Commission's largest single project.

Current judicial review procedures are very much the consequence of a 1976 Law Commission report, and a review of their operation and proposals for reform was issued in October 1994. This report and its recommendations will be considered in detail in Chapter 6.

However, at the end of 2001, 27 reports containing recommendations for law reform remained to be implemented. According to the previous Chairman of the Commission, Robert Carnwath, the most serious failing in implementation is in the criminal law area where, as yet, none of the Commission's reports has been implemented, although the recommendations in the report on double jeopardy were included in the Criminal Justice Bill 2002. Nor has there been any significant move towards the codification of the criminal law as the Commission supports. The current Chairman, appointed in 2002, is Mr Justice Roger Coulson.

Mention should also be made of the relatively new Civil Justice Council, established under the Civil Procedure Act 1997. The remit of this Council, which is made up of a variety of judges, lawyers, academics and those representing the interests of consumers and others, under the chair of Lord Woolf, is to:

- keep the civil justice system under review;
- consider how to make the civil justice system more accessible, fair and efficient;
- advise the Lord Chancellor and the judiciary on the development of the civil justice system;
- refer proposals for change to the civil justice system to the Lord Chancellor and the Civil Procedure Rule Committee;
- make proposals for research.

Given the massive upheaval that has resulted from the implementation of Lord Woolf's recent review of the civil justice system, it is to be hoped that this new Council will function effectively to bring about smaller alterations in the system as soon as they become necessary.

SOURCES OF LAW

The EC is increasingly a source of law for the UK.

Legislation

Legislation is law produced through the parliamentary system. The government is responsible for most Acts, but individual Members of Parliament do have a chance to sponsor Private Members' Bills. The passage of a Bill through each House of Parliament involves five distinct stages: first reading; second reading; committee stage; report stage; and third reading. It is then given Royal Assent. The House of Lords only has limited scope to delay legislation.

Amongst the problems of drafting Acts is the need to reconcile such contradictory demands as brevity and precision. Legislation can be split into different categories: public Acts affect the general public; private Acts relate to particular individuals; consolidation Acts bring various provisions together; codification Acts give statutory form to common law principles; amending Acts alter existing laws and amendments may be textual, which alters the actual wording of a statute, or non-textual, in which case, the operation rather than the wording of the existing law is changed.

Delegated legislation

Delegated legislation appears in the form of: Orders in Council; statutory instruments; bylaws; and professional regulations.

The main advantages of delegated legislation relate to: speed of implementation; the saving of parliamentary time; access to expertise; and flexibility.

The main disadvantages relate to: the lack of accountability of those making such law; the lack of scrutiny of proposals for such legislation; and the sheer amount of delegated legislation.

Controls over delegated legislation are: in Parliament, the Joint Select Committee on Statutory Instruments; and, in the courts, *ultra vires* provisions may be challenged through judicial review.

Case law

Case law is that law created by judges in the course of deciding cases. The doctrine of *stare decisis* or binding precedent refers to the fact that courts are bound by previous decisions of courts equal to or above them in the court hierarchy. The House of Lords can now overrule its own previous rules; the Court of Appeal cannot.

It is the reason for a decision, the *ratio decidendi*, that binds. Everything else is *obiter* and not bound to be followed.

Judges avoid precedents through either overruling or distinguishing them.

The advantages of the doctrine relate to: saving the time of all parties concerned; certainty; flexibility; and the meeting of the requirements of formal justice.

The disadvantages relate to: uncertainty; fixity; and unconstitutionality.

Custom

Custom is of arguable historic importance as a source of law and is of very limited importance as a contemporary source.

Law reform

Law reform in particular areas is considered by various standing committees particularly established for that purpose and Royal Commissions may also be established for such purposes. The Law Commission, however, exists to consider the need for the general and systematic reform of the law.

CHAPTER 3

THE CIVIL COURT STRUCTURE

This chapter looks at which type of cases are heard in which trial courts, the rules relating to transfer of cases from one level of court to another, the system of appeals and the criticisms which have been made of the various aspects of these systems.

What is the difference between a criminal and civil case? There are several key distinctions:

- Criminal cases are brought by the State against individual or corporate defendants, whereas civil cases are brought by one citizen or body against another such party. The State here involves the police (or possibly Customs and Excise officers or tax inspectors), who investigate the crime and collect the evidence, and the Crown Prosecution Service, which prepares the Crown's case. In civil cases, the State is not involved here, except in so far as it provides the courts and personnel so that the litigation can be judged. If a party refuses, for example, to be bound by the order a court makes in a civil case, then that party may be found in contempt of court and punished, that is, imprisoned or fined.

- The outcomes of civil and criminal cases are different. If a criminal case is successful from the point of view of the person bringing it (*the prosecutor*) because the magistrate or jury finds *the defendant* (sometimes called *the accused*) guilty as charged, then the result will be a sentence. There is a wide range of sentences available, from absolute or conditional discharges (where the convicted defendant is free to go without any conditions or with some requirement, for example, that the defendant undertakes never to visit a particular place) to life imprisonment. Criminal sentences, or 'sanctions', are imposed to mark the State's disapproval of the defendant's crime. Sometimes the State loses financially in imposing a punishment. For example, in 1999, the prison population rose to over 63,000, with very high costs to the State – £34,000 to keep a convicted offender in Brixton prison for one year and £32,000 to keep a woman offender in Holloway for one year. On the other hand, fines (the most common sentence or 'disposal') can often bring revenue to the State. In any event, however, the victim of a crime never gains from the sanction imposed on the criminal. A criminal court can order a convicted person to pay the victim compensation, but this will be in addition to and separate from the sentence for the crime.

- If a civil case is successful from the point of view of the person bringing the claim (the *claimant*), the outcome will be one of a number of civil remedies which are designed to benefit the *claimant* and in which the State, or wider community, has no direct interest. Civil remedies include damages, court orders like injunctions, orders of prohibition and specific performance. So, in civil proceedings, the *claimant* will sue the *defendant* and a successful claim will result in *judgment for* the *claimant*. In matrimonial cases, the party who brings an action is called the *petitioner* and the other party is known as the *respondent*.

- Civil and criminal cases are processed differently by the English legal system. They use different procedures and vocabulary, and they are dealt with, on the whole, by different courts. It is very important not to confuse the vocabularies of the different systems and speak, for example, about a claimant 'prosecuting' a company for breach of contract. The law of contract is civil law, so the defendant would be 'sued' or 'litigated against' or have 'a claim brought' taken against it by the claimant.

The following question then arises: 'what is the difference between a crime and a civil wrong; how am I to tell into which category a particular wrong falls?' The answer will be found simply by building up a general legal knowledge. There is nothing inherent in any particular conduct which makes it criminal. One cannot say, for example, that serious wrongs are crimes and that lesser transgressions will be civil wrongs: some crimes are comparatively trivial, like some parking offences, whilst some civil wrongs can have enormously harmful consequences, as where a company in breach of a contract causes financial harm to hundreds or thousands of people.

Sometimes a single event can be both a crime and a civil wrong. If you drive at 50 mph in a 30 mph zone and crash into another vehicle, killing a passenger, you may be prosecuted by the State for causing death by dangerous driving and, if convicted, imprisoned or fined. Additionally, you may be sued for negligence (a tortious civil wrong) by a dependant of the killed passenger and the driver.

The organisation of the civil courts is currently undergoing a period of relatively rapid change. A highly detailed study of the business of the civil courts was undertaken by the Civil Justice Review which was instituted by Lord Hailsham, the then Lord Chancellor, in 1985. The purpose of the Review was to improve the machinery of civil justice by means of reforms in jurisdiction, procedure and court administration. In particular, the Review was concerned with ways of reducing delays, costs and complexity of process. The subsequent report was based on a study of five areas of civil action: personal injury, small claims, the commercial court, the process of debt enforcement and housing cases. In each area, a fact finding research project was commissioned mostly from management consultants. The Lord Chancellor's Department (LCD) then published five discussion papers on these areas. A *General Issues Paper* was published in 1987, in which problems common to civil process were discussed. The Review's final report was published a year later and largely implemented in the Courts and Legal Services Act (CLSA) 1990.

'High quality justice' had been identified in the *General Issues Paper* as the main objective in all parts of the civil court process. This included fair procedures, methods of adjudication so that each party was given a proper opportunity to present their case and to have it judged impartially within a setting of consistency of judicial decisions. The primary aim was not, however, to be paramount. It had to be balanced against the aim of keeping parties' costs, delay and the cost to the State in proportion to the subject matter in dispute. This aim of efficiency included time targets for the handling of cases by the courts; effective deployment of judges, court staff and court facilities; the appropriate matching of the complexity of the case to the level of experience of the judge; the adoption of streamlined procedures for simple cases; and limiting the costs to the parties and to the Court Service.

An additional aim was expressed as the need for the courts to be 'effective', that is, court locations and hours that were convenient to litigants, and the use of simple rules regarding jurisdiction and procedure.

Generally, the Review recommended that much of the case work previously dealt with by the High Court should be moved to the county courts, as they were more numerous, relatively cheap and used simpler procedure. This has been carried out by the CLSA and by statutory instruments, as we shall see later in this chapter.

Since the introduction of the Civil Procedure Act 1997 and the new Civil Procedure Rules (CPR) 1998, the operation of the civil courts has undergone yet another series of major changes. The implications of these changes are dealt with in Chapter 7.

3.1 The Court Service

From April 1995, a new executive agency was established to run all the courts except the magistrates' courts and the coroners' courts, both of which remain under the control of local authorities. The Court Service, which was previously controlled by the LCD, now has overall management responsibility for the law courts. Statements from the agency that it aims at 'reducing the unit cost of production per court hour' have attracted criticism that judges may thus be put under pressure to wind up cases more quickly. The agency is introducing court fees for litigants (for example, £200 per day for the county courts), and its longer term aim is to move to recovering the full costs of the civil courts, including the judges, from fees charged to litigants.

3.2 Magistrates' courts

Magistrates' courts have a significant civil jurisdiction. They hear family proceedings under the Domestic Proceedings and Magistrates' Courts Act (DPMCA) 1978 and the Children Act (CA) 1989. Here, the court is termed a 'family proceedings court'. A family proceedings court must normally be composed of not more than three justices, including, as far as is practicable, both a man and a woman. Justices who sit on such benches must be members of the 'family panel' which comprises people specially appointed to deal with family matters. The magistrates' court deals with adoption proceedings, applications for residence and contact orders (CA 1989), and maintenance relating to spouses and children. Under the DPMCA 1978, these courts also have the power to make personal protection orders and exclusion orders in cases of matrimonial violence. They have powers of recovery in relation to council tax and charges for water, gas and electricity. Magistrates grant, renew and revoke licences for selling liquor.

3.3 County courts

The county courts were introduced in 1846 to provide local, accessible fora for the adjudication of relatively small scale litigation. There are 220 county courts. These courts are served by circuit judges and District Judges, the latter appointed by the Lord Chancellor from persons who have a seven year qualification (s 71 of the CLSA 1990).

The new CPR, which we examine in Chapter 7, operate the same process irrespective of whether the case forum is the High Court or the county court. Broadly speaking, county courts will hear small claims and fast track cases, while the more challenging multi-track cases will be heard in the High Court.

Over the past 10 years, the numbers of cases being resolved by the county court has increased as the financial limit of cases within its jurisdiction has increased. Also during this period, the profile of county court work has changed. Whereas the number of full trials has been relatively constant during recent years, the number of small claims arbitrations has risen sharply. In 1989, there were 22,267 trials and 49,829 arbitrations, whereas in 1994, the comparable figures were 24,219 and 87,885. This reflects the doubling of the small claims limit from £500 to £1,000 in 1989. The trebling of this limit to £3,000 in 1996 and from £3,000 to £5,000 in April 1999 resulted in the numbers of small claims totalling over 88,000 in 1999. These increases have put a substantial strain upon the court system. The following complaints by practitioners working in the county courts are cited in Smith (ed), *Achieving Civil Justice* (1996):

- inconsistent practice between different courts;
- too many judges without specialist knowledge of relevant areas of law, like housing;
- inadequate use of new technology, lost files and judges without access to computer assistance;
- overloading of case lists, for example, 40–50 housing possession cases listed for hearing within one hour.

Therefore, it might have been expected that the civil reforms would continue the pressure on the courts, if not increase it. However, the figures for 2001 show a decrease in the number of claims by 7%, with 58,000 being disposed of as small claims and 13,430 being disposed of by trial. The decrease in cases is thought to be attributable to a number of causes including: improvements introduced by the civil reforms which encourage the settlement of claims without trial; changes to legal aid (see Chapter 12) which have received a more mixed response; and increases in certain civil court fees which are considered by many to be detrimental to the administration of justice.

A *Practice Direction* ([1991] 3 All ER 722) states that certain types of actions set down for trial in the High Court are considered too important for transfer to a county court. These are cases involving:

- professional negligence;
- fatal accidents;
- allegations of fraud or undue influence;
- defamation;
- malicious prosecution or false imprisonment;
- claims against the police.

The county court jurisdiction also involves probate, property cases, tort, contract, bankruptcy, insolvency and relations. Regarding remedies, the county court cannot grant the prerogative remedies (see 6.9.2); that is, they cannot grant search orders (an interim mandatory injunction obtained without notice to prevent the defendant from removing, concealing or destroying evidence in the form of documents or moveable property, formerly know as the Anton Piller order) and neither, generally, can they grant freezing orders (formerly *Mareva* injunctions) to prevent the defendant from removing his assets out of the jurisdiction of the English courts or dissipating them. For recent authoritative guidance of both of these orders, see *Practice Direction ex p Mareva Injunctions and Anton Piller Orders* (1994).

The small claims limit is £5,000, except for personal injury claims which are limited to £1,000. The small claims procedure has been seen by many as a major success of the civil justice system. Currently, 58,000 cases are disposed of this way (known as 'arbitration') by small claims courts annually. The procedure's speed, simplicity and relative inexpensiveness make it attractive to many users. Unfortunately, its popularity has reduced the speed with which cases are dealt with. In 1999, the average time between the issue of summons and the start of the hearing was 21 weeks; however, this period increased to 28 weeks in 2001.

The government believes that extension of the small claims regime to a wider band of cases will enable more people to benefit from this quick and effective means of securing their rights.

One problem with the system, however, is that a significant proportion of successful small claimants are unable to recover the monies awarded them by the court.

The main advantage to litigants using the small claims process is the fact that, if sued, they can defend without fear of incurring huge legal costs, since the costs that the winning party can claim are strictly limited. Although successful claimants are unable to recover costs of legal representation, the small claims procedure does not exclude litigants from seeking legal advice or engaging such legal representation. If a litigant is unrepresented, the District Judge may assist him or her by putting questions to witnesses or to the other party, and by explaining any legal terms or expressions.

A litigant simply needs to complete a claim form, available from any county court, and send it to the court with the issue fee appropriate to the amount claimed (ranging from £80 to £230, depending on the value of the claim). If the case is defended, it will be dealt with at an informal hearing, sitting around a table in the District Judge's office. This avoids the need for a trial in open court, which many litigants find daunting.

The working of the small claims system is looked at in greater detail in Chapter 8.

3.4 The High Court of Justice

The High Court was created in 1873 as a part of the Supreme Court of Judicature. It now has three administrative divisions: the Court of Chancery, the Queen's Bench Division (QBD) and the Family Division (Divorce and Admiralty and Exchequer and Common Pleas were merged with the QBD in 1880 and 1970). High Court Judges sit mainly in the Courts of Justice in the Strand, London, although it is possible for the High Court to sit anywhere in

England or Wales. Current directions from the Lord Chancellor mean that the court sits in 27 provincial cities and towns.

The High Court judiciary comprises the Lord Chancellor (who is technically president of the Chancery Division but never sits); the Vice Chancellor, who usually sits; the Lord Chief Justice who presides over the QBD; the President, who presides over the Family Division; the Senior Presiding Judge (s 72 of the CLSA 1990); and 101 High Court Judges or *'puisne* judges' (pronounced 'pewnee' and meaning 'lesser').

To be qualified for appointment as a *puisne* judge, a person must have 10 years' qualification within the meaning of s 71 of the CLSA 1990 – essentially, someone who has had a general right of audience on all matters in that court for at least 10 years. These judges are appointed by the Queen on the advice of the Lord Chancellor. There is particular controversy about these appointments as they are made by invitation without any advertisement. The Lord Chancellor consults opinion he thinks relevant and reads a secret dossier on each possible appointee. Although the Lord Chancellor agreed in 1993 to appoint District Judges using advertisements and conventional appointment procedures, he declined to use such methods in the appointment of High Court Judges. High Court Judges are appointed to a particular division, although they can, if required by the Lord Chancellor, be asked to sit in another division when the volume of work dictates such transfer.

3.4.1 The Queen's Bench Division

The Queen's Bench Division, the main common law court, takes its name from the original judicial part of the general royal court which used to sit on a bench in the Palace of Westminster. It is the division with the largest workload and has some criminal jurisdiction (see 4.5.1 and 4.5.2, on criminal courts) and appellate jurisdiction. The main civil work of this court is in contract and tort cases. The Commercial Court is part of this division, being served by up to 10 judges with specialist experience in commercial law and presiding over cases concerning banking and insurance matters. The formal rules of evidence can be abandoned here, with the consent of the parties, to allow testimony and documentation which would normally be inadmissible. This informality can be of considerable benefit to the business keen to settle its dispute as quickly and easily as possible. The QBD also includes an Admiralty Court to deal with the often esoteric issues of law relating to shipping. Commercial Court Judges are sometimes appointed as arbitrators.

The Enterprise Act 2002 provides that the Office of Fair Trading (OFT), which investigates markets where it has reasonable grounds to suspect that competition is being prevented, restricted or distorted, may refer cases to the Competition Commission (CC). Decisions of the OFT and the CC can be reviewed by the Competition Appeal Tribunal.

The Employment Appeal Tribunal is presided over by a High Court Judge and either two or four lay persons, and hears appeals from employment tribunals. It is not part of the High Court, but is termed a superior court of record.

It is important to remember that most civil claims are settled out of court; only about 1% of cases where claim forms are issued result in civil trials.

3.4.2 The Queen's Bench Divisional Court

The nomenclature can be puzzling here. This court, as distinct from the QBD, exercises appellate jurisdiction. Here, two or sometimes three judges sit to hear appeals in the following circumstances:

- appeals on a point of law by way of case stated from magistrates' courts, tribunals and the Crown Court;
- by exercising judicial review of the decisions made by governmental and public authorities, inferior courts and tribunals. Leave to apply for judicial review is granted or refused by a single judge. Civil judicial reviews can be heard by a single judge;
- applications for the writ of habeas corpus from persons who claim they are being unlawfully detained.

3.4.3 The Chancery Division

The Chancery Division is the modern successor to the old Court of Chancery, the Lord Chancellor's court from which equity was developed. Its jurisdiction includes matters relating to:

- the sale or partition of land and the raising of charges on land;
- the redemption or foreclosure of mortgages;
- the execution or declaration of trusts;
- the administration of the estates of the dead;
- bankruptcy;
- contentious probate business, for example, the validity and interpretation of wills;
- company law;
- partnerships;
- revenue law.

Like the QBD, the Chancery Division contains specialist courts; these are the Patents Court and the Companies Court. The Chancery Division hears its cases in London or in one of eight designated provincial High Court centres. The work is very specialised and there is a Chancery Bar for barristers who practise in this area. Chancery Judges are normally appointed from this Bar.

3.4.4 The Chancery Divisional Court

Comprising one or two Chancery Judges, this appellate court hears appeals from the Commissioners of Inland Revenue on income tax cases, and from county courts on certain matters like bankruptcy.

3.4.5 The Family Division

The Family Division of the High Court was created by the Administration of Justice Act 1970. It deals with:

- all matrimonial matters, both at first instance and on appeal;
- matters relating to minors, proceedings under the CA 1989;
- legitimacy;
- adoption;
- proceedings under the Domestic Violence and Matrimonial Proceedings Act 1976 and s 30 of the Human Fertilisation and Embryology Act 1990.

3.4.6 The Family Divisional Court

The Family Divisional Court, consisting of two High Court Judges, hears appeals from decisions of magistrates' courts and county courts in family matters. Commonly these involve appeals against orders made about financial provision under the DPMCA 1978.

3.5 Appeals from the High Court

Appeals from decisions made by a judge in one of the three High Court Divisions will go to the Court of Appeal (Civil Division). An exception to this rule allows an appeal to miss out or 'leapfrog' a visit to the Court of Appeal and go straight to the House of Lords (ss 12–15 of the Administration of Justice Act 1969). In order for this to happen, the trial judge must grant a 'certificate of satisfaction' and the House of Lords must give leave to appeal. For the judge to grant a certificate, he or she must be satisfied that the case involves a point of law of general public importance, either concerned mainly with statutory interpretation or one where he or she was bound by a Court of Appeal or House of Lords' decision. Also, both parties must consent to the procedure. There are very few leapfrog procedures each year (there was only one during 1999, but eight in 2001).

3.6 The Court of Appeal (Civil Division)

The Court of Appeal was established by the Judicature Act (JdA) 1873. Together with the High Court of Justice, the Court of Appeal forms the Supreme Court of Judicature. Why is it called 'Supreme' if the House of Lords is a superior court? The answer is that the JdA 1873 abolished the House of Lords in its appellate capacity, hence the Court of Appeal became part of the Supreme Court but, after a change of government, the House of Lords was reinstated as the final court of appeal by the Appellate Jurisdiction Act 1876.

The Court of Appeal is served by senior judges, currently 35, termed Lord Justices of Appeal. Additionally, the Lord Chancellor, the President of the Family Division of the High Court, the Vice Chancellor of the Chancery Division and High Court Judges can sit. The court hears appeals from the three divisions of the High Court, the divisional courts, the county courts, the Employment Appeal Tribunal, the Lands Tribunal and the Transport Tribunal. The most senior judge is the Master of the Rolls. Usually, three judges will sit to hear an appeal, although for very important cases, five may sit. In the interests of business efficiency, some matters can be heard by two judges. These include:

- applications for leave to appeal;
- an appeal where all parties have consented to the matter being heard by just two judges;
- any appeal against an interim order or judgment (that is, one which is provisional).

Where such a court is evenly divided, the case must be reheard by three or five judges before it can be further appealed to the House of Lords.

There may be four or five divisions of the court sitting on any given day. The court has a heavy workload, although there has been a substantial drop since the introduction of the requirement that leave to appeal must be obtained in all cases. In 1999, the court dealt with 611 appeals to the full court and 1,150 to a single judge, whereas in 2001, the full court dealt with 288 appeals and 335 were dealt with by a single judge. In cases of great urgency, this court is often *de facto* the final court of appeal, so that a party can act in reliance on its decision without waiting to see the outcome of any possible appeal to the Lords. In *C v S and Others* (1987), a case concerning a putative father's right to prevent a prospective mother from having an abortion, the woman was between 18 and 21 weeks' pregnant and her termination, if it was to be carried out, had to be performed within days of the Court of Appeal's decision. The hospital concerned was reluctant to carry out the operation in case the father appealed to the Lords and won. To have earlier terminated the pregnancy might then, the hospital believed, have been the crime of infanticide. Leave to appeal to the Lords was refused and the termination was performed but, in the Court of Appeal, Sir John Donaldson MR said:

> It is a fact that some thousand appeals are heard by this court every year, of which about 50 go to the House of Lords ... So, in practical terms, in the every day life of this country, this court is the final court of appeal and it must always

be the final court of appeal in cases of real urgency. In those circumstances, no one could be blamed in any way, *a fortiori* could they as a practical matter be prosecuted, for acting on a judgment of this court. If that be wrong, which it is not, the life of the country in many respects would grind to a halt. The purpose of any supreme court, including the House of Lords, is to review historically and on a broad front; it is not to decide matters of great urgency which have to be decided once and for all.

3.7 Reforms to the appeal process

3.7.1 Background

In his 1994–95 Annual Report on the Court of Appeal, the then Master of the Rolls, Lord Bingham, stated that 'the delay in hearing certain categories of appeal in the Civil Division of the Court of Appeal has reached a level which is inconsistent with the due administration of justice'.

Lord Woolf addressed this issue in his report, *Access to Justice* (July 1996), which set out his proposals for the reform of the civil justice system. At the heart of his proposals was the allocation of civil cases to 'tracks', which would determine the degree of judicial case management. Broadly speaking, cases would be allocated to the small claims track, the fast track or to the multi-track, depending upon the value and complexity of the claim. Those proposals have now been implemented in the Civil Procedure Act 1997 and the Civil Procedure Rules 1998 (see Chapter 7). The principle that underlies this system of tracks is the need to ensure that resources devoted to managing and hearing a case are proportional to the weight and substance of that case. In order that the benefits arising from these reforms should not be weakened on appeal, Lord Woolf recommended that an effective system of appeals should be based on similar principles.

In 1996, Sir Jeffrey Bowman chaired a Review of the Civil Division of the Court of Appeal (*Review of the Court of Appeal (Civil Division) –* Report to the Lord Chancellor, September 1997). He identified a number of problems besetting the Court of Appeal. In particular, he noted that the court was being asked to consider numerous appeals which were not of sufficient weight or complexity for two or three of the country's most senior judges, and which had sometimes already been through one or more levels of appeal. Additionally, he concluded that existing provisions concerning the constitution of the court were too inflexible to deal appropriately with its workload. To redress this situation, Bowman's Report included recommendations to alter the jurisdiction and constitution of the Court of Appeal. The Lord Chancellor consulted on proposals to effect certain of these changes (*Reform of the Court of Appeal (Civil Division): Proposals for Change to Constitution and Jurisdiction*, LCD, July 1998).

Due to the complex nature of routes of appeal in family matters, the Bowman Report recommended that a specialist committee should examine this area, with a view to rationalising the arrangements for appeals in family cases and bringing them in line with the underlying principles for civil appeals. The Family Appeal Review Group, chaired by Lord Justice Thorpe, published recommendations in July 1998 aimed at simplifying the current appeals procedure in family cases, applying the principles outlined in Sir Jeffrey Bowman's Report.

The provisions enabling certain matters to be heard by a single High Court Judge have the same objective of ensuring that the most appropriate use is made of judicial resources.

3.7.2   Changes made by the Access to Justice Act 1999 (Part IV)

In relation to civil appeals, the Access to Justice Act (AJA) 1999 makes several changes, which came into effect on 2 May 2000. The changes:

- provide for permission to appeal to be obtained at all levels in the system (s 54);

- provide that, in normal circumstances, there will be only one level of appeal to the courts (s 55);

- introduce an order-making power to enable the Lord Chancellor to vary appeal routes in secondary legislation, with a view to ensuring that appeals generally go to the lowest appropriate level of judge (s 56);

- ensure that cases which merit the consideration of the Court of Appeal reach that court (s 57);

- give the Civil Division of the Court of Appeal flexibility to exercise its jurisdiction in courts of one, two or more judges (s 59).

Together, these measures are intended to ensure that appeals are heard at the right level, and dealt with in a way which is proportionate to their weight and complexity; that the appeals system can adapt quickly to other developments in the civil justice system; and that existing resources are used efficiently, enabling the Court of Appeal (Civil Division) to tackle its workload more expeditiously. The provisions relating to the High Court (ss 61–65) allow judicial review applications.

3.7.3   Right to appeal

The AJA 1999 provides for rights of appeal to be exercised only with the permission of the court, as prescribed by rules of court. Previously, permission was required for most cases going to the Civil Division of the Court of Appeal, but not elsewhere. Under the Act, with three exceptions, permission to appeal must be obtained in all appeals to the county courts, High Court or Civil Division of the Court of Appeal. The exceptions are appeals against committal to prison, appeals against a refusal to grant habeas corpus and appeals against the making of secure accommodation orders under s 25 of the Children Act 1989 (a form of custodial 'sentence' for recalcitrant children). There is no appeal against a decision of the court to give or refuse permission, but this does not affect any right under rules of court to make a further application for permission to the same or another court.

The Act provides that, where the county court or High Court has already reached a decision in a case brought on appeal, there is no further possibility of an appeal of that decision to the Court of Appeal, unless (s 55) the Court of Appeal considers that the appeal would raise an important point of principle or practice, or there is some other compelling reason for the court to hear it.

3.7.4 Destination of appeals

Section 56 of the AJA 1999 enables the Lord Chancellor to vary, by order, the routes of appeal for appeals to and within the county courts, the High Court, and the Civil Division of the Court of Appeal. Before making an order, the Lord Chancellor will be required to consult the Heads of Division, and any order will be subject to the affirmative resolution procedure. The following appeal routes are specified by order:

- In fast track cases heard by a District Judge, appeals will be to a circuit judge.
- In fast track cases heard by a circuit judge, appeals will be to a High Court Judge.
- In multi-track cases, appeals of interim decisions made at first instance by a District Judge will be to a circuit judge, by a master or circuit judge to a High Court Judge, and by a High Court Judge to the Court of Appeal.
- In multi-track cases, appeals of final orders, regardless of the court of first instance, will be to the Court of Appeal.
- The Heads of Division are the Lord Chief Justice, the Master of the Rolls, the President of the Family Division and the Vice Chancellor.
- A decision is interim where it does not determine the final outcome of the case.

The legislation provides for the Master of the Rolls or a lower court to direct that an appeal that would normally be heard by a lower court be heard instead by the Court of Appeal. This power would be used where the appeal raises an important point of principle or practice, or is a case which, for some other compelling reason, should be considered by the Court of Appeal.

3.7.5 Civil Division of Court of Appeal

The Act makes flexible provision for the number of judges of which a court must be constituted in order for the Court of Appeal to be able to hear appeals. Section 54 of the Supreme Court Act 1981 provided that the Court of Appeal was constituted to exercise any of its jurisdiction if it consisted of an uneven number of judges not less than three. In limited circumstances, it provided that a court could be properly constituted with two judges. The 1999 Act allows the Master of the Rolls, with the concurrence of the Lord Chancellor, to give directions about the minimum number of judges of which a court must consist for given types of proceedings. Subject to any directions, the Act also allows the Master of the Rolls, or a Lord Justice of Appeal designated by him for the purpose, to determine the number of judges who will sit to hear any particular appeal.

3.7.6 Jurisdiction of single judge of High Court

The 1999 Act allows certain applications to be routinely heard by a single judge of the High Court. It does this by removing an obstacle that exists in the current legislation by which the route of appeal for these cases is to the House of Lords, but the Administration of Justice Act 1960 provides that the House of Lords will only hear appeals in these matters from a Divisional Court (that is, more than one judge) of the High Court. The 1999 Act amends the 1960 Act so that the House of Lords can hear appeals from a single High Court Judge. It will then be possible to make rules of court to provide for these cases to be heard by a single judge, while enabling the judge to refer particularly complex cases to a Divisional Court. The cases in question are judicial reviews and some appeals from inferior civil courts.

3.7.7 The Civil Procedure Rules

Under Part 52 of the CPR, since 2 May 2000, the general rule is that permission to appeal in virtually all cases is mandatory. It should be obtained immediately following the judgment from the lower court or appellate court. Permission will only be given where the court considers that the appellant shows a real prospect of success or there is some other compelling reason.

All appeals will now be limited to a review rather than a complete rehearing and the appeal will only be allowed if the decision of the lower court was wrong or unjust due to a serious procedural or other irregularity.

The rule now is that there should be only one appeal. Lord Justice Brooke emphasised in the leading case of *Tanfern v Cameron MacDonald and Another* (2000), 'The decision of the first appeal court is now to be given primacy'. An application for a second or subsequent appeal (from High Court or county court) must be made to the Court of Appeal, which will not accede unless the appeal would raise an important point of principle or practice, or there is some other compelling reason.

The route of appeal has been altered. The general rule is that the appeal lies to the next level of judge in the court hierarchy, that is, District Judge to county court judge to High Court Judge. The main exception relates to an appeal against a final decision in a multi-track claim, which will go straight to the Court of Appeal.

Great emphasis is placed on ensuring that cases are dealt with promptly and efficiently, and on weeding out and deterring unjustified appeals. The result is that the opportunity to appeal a decision at first instance in a lower court is much more restricted. It is vital, therefore, that practitioners be properly prepared at the initial hearing. For more on this, see Richard Harrison ((2000) 150 NLJ, pp 1175–76).

3.8   The House of Lords

Acting in its judicial capacity, as opposed to its legislative one, the House of Lords is the final court of appeal in civil as well as criminal law. Its judgments govern the courts in England, Wales and Northern Ireland. They can also govern civil law in Scotland. Most appeals reaching the House of Lords come from English civil cases. During 2001, there was a total of 84 appeals presented and disposed of by the House of Lords. In England and Wales, 57 were from the Civil Division of the Court of Appeal and only one from the Criminal Division. There is also a 'leapfrog' procedure, introduced by ss 12–15 of the Administration of Justice Act 1969, by which an appeal may go to the Lords direct from the High Court if the High Court Judge certificates the case as being suitable for the Lords to hear and the House of Lords gives leave to appeal. All the parties must consent and the case must be one which involves a point of general public importance about a matter of statutory interpretation (sometimes called statutory 'construction' from the verb *to construe*, meaning to interpret), or where the contentious issue is one on which the trial judge is bound by a precedent of the Court of Appeal or House of Lords.

The appeals are heard by Lords of Appeal in Ordinary, of whom there are currently 12. Two of these must be from Scotland and one from Northern Ireland. Other senior judges like the Lord Chancellor sometimes sit to hear appeals. It is customary only for peers with distinguished legal and judicial careers to become Lords of Appeal in Ordinary. These judges are known as 'Law Lords'.

For most cases, five Law Lords will sit to hear the appeal, but seven are sometimes convened to hear very important cases. The House of Lords' decision which abolished the 250 year old rule against convicting a husband for rape of his wife (*R v R* (1991)) is such a case. Cases are heard in relative informality in a committee room in the Palace of Westminster. The Appellate

Committee of the House of Lords, as it is technically termed, sits with its members in suits, not judicial robes. Counsel, however, do wear wigs and robes. Unlike criminal cases (s 33 of the Criminal Appeal Act (CAA) 1968), there is no requirement that the appeal is on a point of law of general public importance. An appeal from the Court of Appeal to the House of Lords must have 'leave' (that is, permission) of either court.

The judges may deliver their judgments, termed 'opinions', as speeches in the parliamentary chamber. A majority decides the case. Sometimes, however, where a case has been heard at three levels of the civil process, the final outcome is not determined, overall, by a majority of what could be described as senior judges. Consider the case of *Gillick v West Norfolk and Wisbech Area Health Authority* (1985), a case in which the plaintiff, Mrs Gillick, sought a ruling that the defendant's policy to allow contraceptive advice to be given to girls under 16 in some circumstances was illegal. Her argument was rejected by the judge hearing the case in the High Court, accepted unanimously by the three Lord Justices in the Court of Appeal and then rejected in the House of Lords by three votes to two. Thus, overall, a majority of the eight senior judges who heard her case accepted it (five out of eight), but she lost her case because she was unsuccessful in the final court.

3.9   The European Court of Justice

As we shall see in detail in Chapter 13, the Treaty of Amsterdam 1997 introduced a completely new system for numbering the Articles of the European Community treaties. In order to try to avoid confusion when readers consult other, already existing authorities, which will refer to the old numbering, this book will refer to both the new and the previous numbering.

The function of the European Court of Justice (ECJ), which sits in Luxembourg, is to 'ensure that in the interpretation and application of this Treaty [the EEC Treaty 1957] the law is observed' (Art 220, formerly 164). The Court is the ultimate authority on European law. As the Treaty is often composed in general terms, the Court is often called upon to provide the necessary detail for European law to operate. By virtue of the European Communities Act 1972, European law has been enacted into English law, so the decisions of the Court have direct authority in the English jurisdiction.

The Court hears disputes between nations and between nations and European institutions like the European Commission. An individual, however, can only bring an action if he is challenging a decision which affects him.

The Treaty states in Art 234 (formerly 177) that any judicial or quasi-judicial body, however low ranking, may refer a question to the ECJ if it considers that 'a decision on that question is necessary to enable it to give judgment', and that such a reference must be made where any such question is raised in a case before a national court from which there is no further appeal. So, the High

Court would have a discretion as to whether to refer a point, but the House of Lords would not. The system was installed to try to ensure uniformity of interpretation of European law across all the Member States. Without such a mechanism, it would be possible for the English courts to be interpreting a point of European law one way while the Spanish courts were treating it as meaning something different.

Lord Denning MR formulated guidelines in *Bulmer v Bollinger* (1974) as to when an inferior court should refer a case to the ECJ for a preliminary ruling. He offered four guidelines to determine whether the reference was 'necessary' within the meaning of Art 234 (formerly 177):

- The decision on the point of European law must be conclusive of the case.
- The national court may choose to follow a previous ruling of the ECJ on the same point of Community law, but it may choose to refer the same point of law to the court again in the hope that it will give a different ruling.
- The national court may not make a reference on the grounds of *acte clair* where the point is reasonably clear and free from doubt.
- 'In general, it is best to decide the facts first' before determining whether it is necessary to refer the point of Community law.

If a national court decides that a reference is necessary, it still has the discretion (unlike the highest court) as to whether to refer the point. Lord Denning MR then listed some factors to help courts decide whether to refer; for example: bear in mind the expense to parties of a reference and do not send points unless they are difficult and important.

These guidelines have been influential in a number of subsequent cases. It is possible, however, for an appeal to be made against a decision of a court of first instance to refer a case to the ECJ for a preliminary ruling under Art 234 (formerly 177). The appellate court will interfere with the discretion of the trial judge who referred the case, but only if the decision was 'plainly wrong': see *Bulmer v Bollinger*, above.

The language of Art 234 (formerly 177) is imperative, saying that courts or tribunals against whose judgments there is no appeal *must* refer a point of Community law. This does not apply where the point has already been ruled on by the ECJ. Equally, it does not apply where the national court has ruled that the issue in question is not one which requires the application of Community law. In *R v London Boroughs Transport Committee* (1992), the House of Lords decided that the case did not involve any Community law issues because it concerned the regulation of local traffic, even though the Court of Appeal had held unanimously that UK legislation was in breach of certain Community directives.

The ECJ is a court of reference: the ruling the Court makes is preliminary, in the sense that the case is then remitted to the national court for it to apply the law to the facts. The Court only addresses itself to points arising from actual cases; it will not consider hypothetical problems.

Lord Diplock (*R v Henn* (1981)) has characterised the Court's work in the following way:

> The European Court, in contrast to English courts, applies teleological rather than historical methods to the interpretation of the Treaties and other Community legislation. It seeks to give effect to what it conceives to be the spirit rather than the letter of the Treaties; sometimes, indeed, to an English judge, it may seem to the exclusion of the letter. It views the Communities as living and expanding organisms and the interpretation of the provisions of the Treaties as changing to match their growth.

The Court is made up from senior judges from each Member State (15) and a President of the Court, assisted by nine Advocates General. The latter are 'persons whose independence is beyond doubt' (Art 223, formerly 167) and their task is to give to the Court a detailed analysis of all the relevant legal and factual issues along with recommendations. The recommendations are not necessarily followed by the Court, but they can be used on later occasions as persuasive precedent. The Court attempts to ensure consistency in its decisions, but is not bound by precedent to the same extent as a court in England.

The Court of First Instance was set up to ease the mounting workload of the ECJ. It began work in 1989 and has a jurisdiction which is limited to hearing disputes between the Community and its staff, cases involving EU competition law (excluding Art 234, formerly 177, references) and some matters involving the European Coal and Steel Community.

3.10   The European Court of Human Rights

The European Court of Human Rights (ECtHR) does not arise from the EU, but arises from the 1950 European Convention on Human Rights, signed by 21 European States including the UK. It deals with matters relating to human and political rights. The ECtHR sits in Strasbourg and consists of judges from each Member State. The signatory States undertook to guarantee a range of human and political rights to the citizens within their jurisdictions.

See 13.4 for further treatment of the ECtHR.

3.11   Judicial Committee of the Privy Council

The Judicial Committee of the Privy Council was created by the Judicial Committee Act 1833. Under the Act, a special committee of the Privy Council was set up to hear appeals from the Dominions. The cases are heard by the judges (without wigs or robes) in a committee room in London. The

Committee's decision is not a judgment but an 'advice' to the monarch, who is counselled that the appeal be allowed or dismissed.

The Committee is the final court of appeal for certain Commonwealth countries which have retained this option, and from some independent members and associate members of the Commonwealth. The Committee comprises Privy Councillors who hold (or have held) high judicial office. In most cases, which come from places such as the Cayman Islands and Jamaica, the Committee comprises five Lords of Appeal in Ordinary, sometimes assisted by a judge from the country concerned. The decisions of the Privy Council are very influential in English courts because they concern points of law that are applicable in this jurisdiction and they are pronounced upon by Lords of Appeal in Ordinary in a way which is thus tantamount to a House of Lords' ruling. These decisions, however, are technically of persuasive precedent only, although they are normally followed by English courts; see, for example, *The Wagon Mound* (1963), a tort case in which the Privy Council ruled, on an appeal from Australia, that in negligence claims, a defendant is liable only for the reasonably foreseeable consequences of his tortious conduct. A total of 64 appeals were registered in 1999. The Committee is also the final appeal court for the Professional Conduct and Health Committees of the General Medical Council and the General Dental Council.

3.12 Civil court fees

In May 2000, the government introduced a policy to make the civil courts self-financing, and a new scale of increased court fees, some as high as 35% more, came into effect. It has continued to pursue this policy and, following consultation, a new scale of fees was introduced in February 2003. The fee for starting a claim in the county court is £30 for claims up to £300, £50 for claims up to £500, £80 for claims up to £1,000, and £120 for claims up to £5,000, which is the maximum for small claims. Fees now rise quite steeply for claims over this amount and are the same whether pursued in the county court or High Court. Prior to the recent increase, a fee of £500 was charged for any claim over £50,000. Now the fees are £250, £400, £600 and £700 for claims of up to £15,000, £50,000, £100,000 and £150,000 respectively. For claims over £150,000, a fee of £800 is charged. Additional fees are then charged as the claim proceeds through the court process, that is, £120 is charged in the High Court when the claim is allocated to a track, and a further sum of £600 is charged when the matter is set down for trial. Thus, the full court fees for pursuing a court case could be substantial. If the claimant does not pay these fees, then the claim will automatically be struck out to stop claims being issued and lying dormant in the court process only to be re-instigated at a future date.

However, the principle of running the civil courts according to business principles was, and still is, highly controversial. When the innovation was announced by the Lord Chancellor, it was denounced by Sir Richard Scott, Head of the Chancery Division of the High Court. He warned that justice should be reasonably accessible and without excessive cost. He stated that:

> The policy fails to recognise that the civil justice system is, like the criminal justice system, the bulwark of a civilised State and the maintenance of order within that State. People have to use the civil courts. They can't engage in self-help in a way which would lead to chaos.

Although people who receive public funding still have their court fees paid, many unaided people can only just afford to litigate, and the raised fees may be turning a difficult hurdle into an insurmountable barrier. The policy of making litigants pay for judges and courtrooms – for that is the essence of this new court fee structure – is highly controversial. Many litigants would believe that they and others, as taxpayers, have already contributed to the funding of the legal system.

In a debate in the House of Lords (*Hansard*, 1997, Vol 581, coll 863–81), the Lord Chancellor revisited the theme of at what rate, if at all, citizens should be charged fees for using the civil courts. He stated that he did not accept that all citizens had a constitutional right to go to law in the civil courts freely at the point of use. To do that, he observed, it would be necessary to find the money currently supporting the system from court fees (£257 million paid by citizens) from somewhere else, that is, he would have to cut that amount from somewhere else in his budget. He raised the possibilities of ending Criminal Legal Aid, or ending legal aid for family proceedings. The Lord Chancellor said:

> Those who argue for free access to courts for all are really arguing that the government should charge taxpayers an additional £257 m and then increase my budget by that amount. The Secretary of State for Health might argue that with that money he could provide several new acute hospitals. The Secretary of State for Education might argue that with that money he could provide 30 extra secondary schools.

Many theoretical questions about 'justice' and the legal system quickly reduce to matters of political economy. The issue of court fees is a good illustration. Is the provision of free access to court services for all (including many who could easily afford to pay court fees) more important than the provision of schools and hospitals?

The principal idea here is that where people can afford to pay the costs involved in their bringing a legal action, the taxpayer should not be expected to pay for them.

There is a subsidy for costs associated with some family proceedings. This is intended to put as few barriers as possible in the way of people using the courts to protect themselves from violence or harassment, or trying to resolve disputes on the care of children.

Under the new proposals, people on low incomes will continue to be exempted from all court fees. Automatic exemptions to the fees will apply to people in receipt of Income Support, Family Credit, Disability Working Allowance, and income-based Job Seeker's Allowance.

Should fees be payable by those wishing to use the courts? Some observers point out that payments are not made by members of the public at the point of use in the education and health systems, and that justice can be seen as being just as important as those services. On the other hand, the Lord Chancellor has pointed out that were the courts to become free at the point of use, the money needed to pay for this would have to come from closing down large parts of the Civil Legal Aid or shutting schools or hospitals. Thus, legal policy is inextricably bound up with social policy in general.

THE CIVIL COURT STRUCTURE

The differences between civil and criminal law

There is no such thing as inherently criminal conduct. A crime is whatever the State has forbidden on pain of legal punishment. The conduct that attracts criminal sanctions changes over time and according to different social systems. The terminology and outcomes of the two systems are different. In criminal cases, the *prosecutor prosecutes the defendant* (or *accused*); in civil cases, the *claimant sues the defendant*.

The Court Service

The courts (except for the magistrates' courts and coroners' courts) are now run by the Court Service, an executive agency, formerly part of the Lord Chancellor's Department.

Magistrates' courts

Magistrates' courts have a significant civil jurisdiction, especially under the Children Act 1989 as 'family proceedings courts'.

County courts

There are about 220 county courts in England and Wales. They are presided over by District Judges and circuit judges. County courts hear small claims, that is, those whose value is £5,000 or under, and fast track cases. The civil justice reforms are likely to put a considerable burden of work on the county courts under the new system. The main advantage to litigants using the small claims process is the fact that, if sued, they can defend without fear of incurring huge legal costs, since the costs the winning party can claim are strictly limited.

The High Court

The High Court's judicial composition should be noted, as should the meaning of the 10 year qualification according to s 71 of the Courts and Legal Services Act (CLSA) 1990. The High Court is under considerable pressure of work, hence the CLSA 1990 provisions to ease its workload. The Queen's Bench Division deals with contract and tort, etc; its Divisional Court deals with judicial review and criminal appeals from magistrates' courts and Crown Courts. Chancery deals with cases involving land, mortgages, bankruptcy and probate, etc; its Divisional Court hears taxation appeals. The Family Division hears matrimonial and child related matters and its Divisional Court hears appeals from magistrates' courts and county courts on these issues.

The Court of Appeal (Civil Division)

The Court of Appeal (Civil Division) usually has three judges whose decision is by majority. For many purposes, it is the *de facto* final appeal court (*C v S and Others* (1987)).

Reform of the appeal process

Certain appeals which previously reached the Court of Appeal (Civil Division) are now heard at a lower level, and the requirement for leave to appeal has been extended to all cases coming to the Court of Appeal except for adoption cases, child abduction cases and appeals against committal orders or refusal to grant habeas corpus. The Access to Justice Act 1999 reformed the appeal process by establishing the principle that there is the need for permission to appeal at all levels in the system. The Act provides that, in normal circumstances, there will be only one level of appeal to the courts and it gives to the Civil Division of the Court of Appeal flexibility to exercise its jurisdiction in courts of one, two or more judges. Taken together, these reforms are intended to ensure that appeals are heard at the right level and in a way which is proportionate to their weight and complexity.

The House of Lords

In most of its cases, five Law Lords sit. They hear cases of general public importance concerning points of law, for example, *R v R* (1991), changing a 250 year old rule and allowing prosecutions for marital rape.

The European Court of Justice

The European Court of Justice (ECJ) sits in Luxembourg. Its remit is to ensure that the interpretation and application of the EEC 'Treaty of Rome' is observed consistently by all Member States. Note the importance of Art 234 (formerly 177) and the guidance provided by *Bulmer v Bollinger* (1974).

The European Court of Human Rights

The European Court of Human Rights (ECtHR) sits in Strasbourg and arose from the 1950 European Convention on Human Rights. It has no mechanism for enforcement other than of a political nature. Its effect can be illustrated by cases like *Malone v UK* (1984).

As a consequence of the Human Rights Act 1998, the decisions of the ECtHR are now precedents for, and binding on, domestic UK courts. In terms of human rights issues, therefore, it is superior to the House of Lords.

The Judicial Committee of the Privy Council

The Judicial Committee of the Privy Council acts as a final appeal court for some Commonwealth countries. Because it comprises senior judges from the English legal system, it gives decisions which are persuasive precedent in English law.

Civil court fees

A new scale of court fees for people using the civil courts came into effect in 1997, with a further increase introduced in 2003. The aim of the new fees is to make the civil court self-financing. This change raises matters of importance in legal, social and economic debates. There are those who argue, for example, that the courts should, like the National Health Service, be free to people at the point of use, and financed by general taxation. There are others who argue that some payments should be made at the point of use. The Lord Chancellor has pointed out that, were the courts to become free in this way, the money needed to pay for this would have to come from closing down large parts of the Civil Legal Aid system or closing schools or hospitals.

CHAPTER 4

THE CRIMINAL COURT STRUCTURE

This chapter looks at the structure of the criminal courts. You need to know which type of cases are heard in which trial courts; the procedures of summary hearings, either way offences, transfers for trial, Crown Court trials and the rules governing the transfer of proceedings; the system of appeals; and the criticisms which have been made of the various aspects of these systems.

4.1   Coroners' courts

The coroners' courts are one of the most ancient parts of the English legal system, dating back to at least 1194. They are not, in modern function, part of the criminal courts, but because of historical associations, it makes more sense to classify them with the courts in this chapter rather than that dealing with civil courts. Coroners were originally appointed as *custos placitorum coronae*, keepers of the pleas of the Crown. They had responsibility for criminal cases in which the Crown had an interest, particularly a financial interest.

Today, there are 157 coroners' courts, of which 21 sit full time. These are presided over by 138 full time coroners and 240 deputy and assistant coroners. Coroners are usually lawyers (with at least a five year qualification within s 71 of the Courts and Legal Services Act (CLSA) 1990), although about 25% are medical doctors with a legal qualification. The main jurisdiction of the coroner today concerns unnatural and violent deaths, although treasure trove is also something occasionally dealt with in these courts.

The classifying of types of death is clearly of critical importance, not just to the State, politicians and policy makers, but also to the sort of campaign groups that exist in a constitutional democracy to monitor suicides, drug-related deaths, deaths in police custody and prison, accidental deaths, deaths in hospitals and deaths through industrial diseases.

In 2001, there were 532,000 registered deaths in England and Wales. Deaths must be reported to a coroner if they seem unnatural or violent; the coroner will order a postmortem and this may reveal a natural cause of death which can be duly registered. If not, or in certain other circumstances, such as where the death occurred in prison or police custody or if the cause is unknown, there will be an inquest. There were 201,000 deaths reported to coroners in 2001 resulting in 121,100 postmortem examinations and 25,800 inquests ('Statistics of deaths reported to coroners', *Home Office Statistical Bulletin*, 2 May 2002).

Most inquests (96%) are held without juries, but the State has been insistent that certain types of case must be heard by a jury in order to promote public faith in government. When, in 1926, legislation for the first time permitted inquests to be held without juries, certain types of death were deliberately marked off as still requiring jury scrutiny and these included deaths in police custody, deaths resulting from the actions of a police officer on duty and deaths in prison. This was seen as a very important way of fostering public trust in potentially oppressive aspects of the State. In 1971, the Brodrick Committee Report on the coronial system saw the coroner's jury as having a symbolic significance and thought that it was a useful way to legitimate the decision of the coroner.

The coroner's court is unique in using an inquisitorial process. There are no 'sides' in an inquest. There may be representation for people such as the relatives of the deceased, insurance companies, prison officers, car drivers, companies (whose policies are possibly implicated in the death) and train drivers, etc, but all the witnesses are the coroner's witnesses. It is the coroner who decides who shall be summoned as witnesses and in what order they shall be called.

Historically, an inquest jury could decide that a deceased had been unlawfully killed and then commit a suspect for trial at the local assizes. When this power was taken away in 1926, the main bridge over to the criminal justice system was removed. There then followed, in stages, an attempt to prevent inquest verdicts from impinging on the jurisdictions of the ordinary civil and criminal courts. Now, an inquest jury is exclusively concerned with determining who the deceased was and 'how, when and where he came by his death'. The court is forbidden to make any wider comment on the death and must not determine or appear to determine criminal liability 'on the part of a named person'.

Nevertheless, the jury may still now properly decide that a death was unlawful (that is, a crime). The verdict 'unlawful killing' is on a list of options (including 'suicide', 'accidental death' and 'open verdict') made under legislation and approved by the Home Office.

In July 2001, a Coroner Services Review Group was appointed by the Home Office to conduct a fundamental review of the coronial system. In 2002, it proposed a new court structure to deal with coroners' judicial inquests, with higher courts available to deal with complex cases and appeals against coroners' decisions.

4.2 The criminal trial courts

There are over 7,000 different criminal offences in English law. These offences can be classified in different ways. You could, for example, classify them according to whether they are offences against people or property; again, you could classify them according to the type of mental element (*mens rea*) required for the offence, for example, 'intention' or 'recklessness'. One other type of classification, and the one to concern us here, is whether the offence is triable *summarily* in a magistrates' court (for relatively trivial offences like traffic offences) or is an *indictable* offence (the more serious offences like murder and rape) triable in front of a judge and jury in a Crown Court.

From the mid-19th century, magistrates were empowered to hear some indictable cases in certain circumstances. Today, there is still a class of offence which is triable 'either way', that is, summarily or in a jury trial. A typical example would be a potentially serious offence such as theft, but one which has been committed in a minor way, as in the theft of a milk bottle. These offences now account for about 80% of those tried in Crown Courts. Most defendants, however, opt for summary trial. Where several defendants are charged together with either way offences, each defendant's choice can be exercised separately. So, if one elects for trial in the Crown Court, the others may still be tried summarily if the magistrates agree (*R v Brentwood Justices ex p Nicholls* (1991)).

Which types of case should be dealt with in which courts? This question was investigated by the James Committee, which reported in 1975 on *The Distribution of Business Between the Crown Court and Magistrates' Courts*. It found that for similar cases, Crown Court trials were three times more expensive than summary hearings. It concluded that the division of work between the different levels of court should reflect the public view as to what are the more serious offences justifying full trials, and those which should be dealt with by magistrates. The Committee also proposed a category of cases triable either way.

In all offences triable either way, the defendant has the right of trial by jury. If the defendant elects for summary trial, the magistrates (and, in some cases, the prosecution) still have the right to remit the case for trial at the Crown Court if they think trial there would be more suitable.

4.3   Magistrates' courts

The office of magistrate or Justice of the Peace (JP) dates from 1195, when Richard I first appointed 'keepers of the peace' to deal with those who were accused of breaking 'the King's peace'. The JPs originally acted as local administrators for the king in addition to their judicial responsibilities. Apart from the 30,000 lay justices who sit in some 700 courts, there are also 98 District Judges (Magistrates' Courts) (formerly known as stipendiary magistrates) and 171 Deputy District Judges (Magistrates' Courts) who sit in cities and larger towns. They are qualified, experienced lawyers who are salaried justices. Where a magistrates' court commits a person for trial of offences in classes 1 to 3 (see 4.4, below), the most convenient location of the Crown Court, where a High Court Judge regularly sits, should be specified (save for some offences in class 2, such as rape, where a presiding judge has specified that such offences may be sent to a specified location where a High Court Judge does not regularly sit). For offences in class 4, the most convenient location of the Crown Court should be chosen. These matters are confirmed in the *Practice Directions on the Allocation of Crown Court Business* (1995), as amended in 1998 and 2000.

4.3.1 Summary trial

Summary offences are created and defined by statute. There are thousands of different summary offences. They include traffic offences, common assault, taking a motor vehicle without consent and driving whilst disqualified: 98% of all criminal cases are dealt with by the courts summarily.

Cases are heard in the court for the district in which the offence is alleged to have been committed. In most cases, the defendant will be in court, but it is possible for the accused in road traffic offences to plead guilty by post and not to attend court.

The cases will be heard by two or three magistrates whose powers of sentencing are limited by the Acts which govern the offences in question. A District Judge (Magistrates' Courts) may sit without lay magistrates. The maximum sentence that magistrates can impose on a private individual, however, is a £5,000 fine and/or a six month prison sentence. Businesses may be fined up to £20,000 for certain offences. The maximum sentences for many summary offences are much less than these limits. Where a defendant is convicted of two or more offences at the same hearing, consecutive sentences amounting to more than six months are not permitted, although this can rise to 12 months in cases involving offences triable 'either way' (s 133 of the Magistrates' Courts Act (MCA) 1980). Many statutory offences are now given particular 'levels' according to their seriousness. This means that if a government minister wishes to raise fines (say to be in line with inflation), he does not have to go through hundreds of different offences, altering the maximum fine in relation to each one separately; the maxima for each level are simply altered. The current figures (last adjusted in 1991) are as follows: Level 5 up to £5,000; Level 4 up to £2,500; Level 3 up to £1,000; Level 2 up to £500; and Level 1 up to £200.

The Criminal Justice Act (CJA) 1991 (the framework statute for many of the sentencing powers of the courts in recent times until the enactment of a consolidating statute, the Powers of the Criminal Courts (Sentencing) Act 2000) provided for a new system of fining in magistrates' courts: the 'unit fine' system. Under this system, fines were linked to the offender's income. The idea was that the rich should pay more than the poor for the same offence. Crimes were graded from one to 10 and the level of crime was then multiplied by the offender's weekly disposable income. The system's figures, however, resulted in many anomalies and it was eventually abolished. Nevertheless, in fixing the appropriate amount for a convicted defendant's fine, the magistrates will still take into account his income. Other sentences that the court may use include absolute discharge, conditional discharge, community rehabilitation orders (formerly known as probation), community punishment orders (formerly known as community service) and compensation orders. The sentencing powers of magistrates are likely to be substantially increased when the Criminal Justice Bill 2002 is enacted by Parliament.

After a conviction, the magistrates will hear whether the defendant has a criminal record and, if so, for what offences. This is to enable them to pass an appropriate sentence. If, after hearing that record, they feel that their powers of sanction are insufficient to deal with the defendant, then he may be sent to the Crown Court for sentencing.

A bench of lay magistrates is legally advised by a justices' clerk who is legally qualified and guides the justices on matters of law, sentencing and procedure. The justices' clerk may give advice even when not specifically invited to do so. It is an established principle of English law that 'justice should not only be done but manifestly and undoubtedly be seen to be done' (*R v Sussex Justices ex p McCarthy* (1924), *per* Lord Hewart CJ). The magistrates are independent of the clerks and, according to the principle, the clerks should not *instruct* the magistrates what decision to make on any point, nor should they appear to be doing so. The clerk should not, therefore, normally retire with the justices when they go to consider their verdict in any case, although he may be called by them to give advice on any point. The clerk should not give any judgment on matters of fact.

The court is required in certain cases to consider a compensation order and to give reasons if it decides not to make such an order. Compensation orders are now governed by the provisions of ss 130–34 of the Powers of the Criminal Courts (Sentencing) Act (PCC(S)A) 2000. Section 130 states that a court before which a person is convicted, in addition to dealing with him in any other way, may make a compensation order. The order is to compensate personal injury, loss or damage resulting from the offence in question or any other offence 'taken into consideration' (that is, admitted by the defendant) by the court. The defendant can also be ordered to make payments for funeral expenses or bereavement in respect of a death resulting from an offence committed by the defendant (other than a death due to a motor accident). The court, s 130(3) states, 'shall give reasons, on passing sentence, if it does not make such a compensation order in a case where this section empowers it to do so'. Unlike a fine, the compensation will go to the victim rather than to the State, so these orders save victims of crime from having to claim damages against defendants in the civil courts. They are not intended as an alternative to punishment, enabling the defendant to buy his way out of the penalties for the crime. Even so, s 130(12) gives priority to the issue of a compensation order over a fine. In 1994, the Crown Court issued compensation orders in 9% of cases where the accused was sentenced – a total of 6,600 orders. The magistrates' courts issued over 88,000 orders.

A new system of funding the magistrates' courts was introduced in 1991. The system links the amount of money given to a court to the number of cases it processes. One survey (for *File on Four*) found that 74% of clerks felt these changes put justice at risk. Clerks have reported that the changes have put pressure on the courts to give priority to 'quick' cases such as television licence prosecutions and traffic offences. Courts are allocated points for each case processed, but a complex case may attract the same points as a simple one. The government has contended that, under good management, 'efficiency is the handmaiden of justice'. Anthony Scrivener QC, Chairman of the Bar Council when the system was introduced, stated that courts were not 'canning factories, their most important function is to dispense justice and this cannot be measured statistically'. Cost-conscious courts could be pressured into making poor decisions.

4.3.2 Offences triable 'either way'

Where the defendant is charged with an offence triable 'either way', two preliminary decisions have to be made: first, should he be tried summarily (by magistrates) or on indictment (in the Crown Court by a judge and jury)? The procedure by which this matter is resolved is known as a mode of trial hearing. Secondly, if the determination is in favour of trial on indictment, is there a sufficient *prima facie* case to go before the Crown Court? This question is answered at a hearing known as *committal proceedings*.

At present, the defendant can always insist on trial on indictment, but cannot insist on being tried summarily if the magistrates decline jurisdiction. Similarly, the magistrates can always decide that the defendant should be tried on indictment, but cannot insist that he be tried summarily. Most defendants charged with 'either way' offences are tried by magistrates: 9% of cases go to the Crown Court because the magistrates consider their current sentencing powers to be inadequate; 4% of cases go to the Crown Court because the defendants elect trial by jury.

Prosecutions conducted by the Attorney General, the Solicitor General or the Director of Public Prosecutions must be tried on indictment if so requested by the prosecutor.

So, when the defendant comes before the justices (there are usually two for these purposes, though there can be only one), the procedure is:

- the defendant is asked to indicate whether he would plead guilty or not guilty at trial;
- if he indicates a guilty plea, the court will proceed as if the defendant had pleaded guilty at summary trial;
- if he indicates a not guilty plea, the defence and prosecution will make any representations they wish about mode of trial;

- the court will consider whether summary trial or trial on indictment appears more suitable;
- if the court favours summary trial, the defendant will be asked whether he consents. If he does, the court will proceed to summary trial. If he does not, the court will proceed to committal;
- if the court favours trial on indictment, it will proceed to committal.

The mode of trial hearing

If the court favours summary trial, it must point out to the accused that, even if they consent, if they are convicted, they may still be committed to the Crown Court for sentence. The power to commit for sentence is given by s 3 of the PCC(S)A 2000 where the court is of the opinion that either the offence or the combination of the offence, and one or more offences associated with it, was so serious that greater punishment should be inflicted than the court has power to impose or, in the case of a violent or sexual offence, that a custodial sentence longer than the court has power to impose is necessary to protect the public from serious harm from the accused. By s 151 of the PCC(S)A 2000, a court may take into account any previous convictions or any failure to respond to previous sentences when considering the seriousness of an offence, whilst s 153 identifies racial aggravation as a factor increasing seriousness. The power to commit for sentence raises important issues both for the magistrates and for the accused when they make their respective decisions about mode of trial. Though magistrates may effectively take a different view about their powers of sentencing once the case has been tried summarily, they should be careful about accepting jurisdiction and then committing for sentence where no new facts have emerged. The accused may accept summary trial and then find themselves exposed to a range of penalties far beyond the power of the magistrates to impose. The power of magistrates to commit a case to the Crown Court is likely to be restricted (or perhaps abolished) when the Criminal Justice Bill 2002 is enacted.

The procedure for determining the mode of trial is set out in ss 18–26 of the MCA 1980. The court must consider: (a) the nature of the case; (b) whether the circumstances make the offence one of a serious character; (c) whether the punishment that the magistrates' court could impose would be adequate; and (d) any representations about the mode of trial made by the prosecution and defence. Further guidelines appear in a *Practice Note* (1990). The gist of this guidance is that 'either way' offences should be tried summarily unless a case has one or more aggravating features *and* the court considers that its sentencing powers are inadequate. In 1995, these guidelines (the *National Mode of Trial Guidelines*) were revised by the Secretariat of the Criminal Justice Consultative Committee. The guidelines set out general principles. They explain features, for example, which would make trial on indictment appropriate for certain offences like burglary, criminal damage, dangerous driving, drugs offences, indecent assault, fraud and offences of violence. The guidelines say, for instance, that trial in the Crown Court is appropriate in the case of burglary where it was committed in the daytime when the occupier or another person was at home; or where entry was at night into a house normally occupied; or where the offence has professional hallmarks.

In the case of either way offences, it is possible for:

- summary trial to be converted into committal proceedings at any time before the conclusion of the evidence for the prosecution (s 25(2) of the MCA 1980);

- committal proceedings to be converted into summary trial where, at any time during the proceedings, the court hears representations from the prosecution and/or accused and, in view of the nature of the case, decides that it is after all more suitable for summary trial (s 25(3) of the MCA 1980).

In the first case, the accused's consent is not required. In the second case, of course, his consent must be obtained. For recent developments, see 4.7.

Committal proceedings

A defendant charged with an 'either way' offence who has elected for trial at the Crown Court will first have his case subject to committal proceedings (a person charged with an indictable only offence now goes direct to the Crown Court: see 4.3.4). These proceedings used to take the form of 'old style' committals (small trials) or 'new style' committals (or 'paper trials' where the evidence was just documentary). Following a recommendation by the Royal Commission on Criminal Justice (1993, Cmnd 2263), committal proceedings were abolished by s 44 of the Criminal Justice and Public Order Act (CJPOA) 1994. The new system, however, of 'transfers for trial', which would have expedited the process of deciding whether a defendant should stand trial, encountered great difficulties in being implemented and was never brought into force. Section 44 of the Criminal Procedure and Investigations Act (CPIA) 1996 repeals s 44 of the CJPOA 1994 and, in effect, introduces a new, streamlined version of committal proceedings in which no oral evidence can be given.

The new system of committals is governed by s 47 of and Sched 1 to the CPIA 1996. The effect of the new law is to abolish the 'old style' mini-trial committals and the right of the defendant to have witnesses called and cross-examined at the magistrates' court. Now, defendants may only use written evidence at committal stage, such as witness statements and depositions from the prosecution. Exhibits may also be considered. Both sides can make oral representations to the magistrates as to whether the defendant should be sent for trial or discharged.

The system thus remains largely unchanged, with the exception of the exclusion of witness testimony. This will save witnesses from having to go through the ordeal of giving evidence twice. Time and money will also be saved. There can no longer be any unmeritorious requests for 'old style' committals, made in the hope that witnesses will not turn up. Nevertheless, the new system also means that the defence will be deprived of the opportunity of testing the evidence and having the defendant discharged early during the proceedings if the witnesses do not come up to proof.

In a few limited circumstances, a case can reach the Crown Court without having passed through committal proceedings. This applies to serious fraud cases (s 4 of the CJA 1987) where the complexity of the case demands that it be managed from the outset by a Crown Court. The bypass procedure also exists for certain cases involving children where there has been alleged violence, cruelty or a sexual element (s 53 of the CJA 1991).

Old style committal proceedings were expensive, and the proportion of all committals that they occupied rose from 8% in 1981 to 13% in 1986. The effectiveness of the sifting procedure designed to weed out very weak cases was called into doubt by the high acquittal rate in jury trials. How far the new system will be an improvement upon the old remains to be seen.

4.3.3 Youth Courts

The procedures previously discussed apply only to those aged at least 18. Defendants who are aged less than 18 will normally be tried by a Youth Court, no matter what the classification of the offence (summary, either way, indictable only). However, a defendant under 18 must be tried on indictment where the charge is homicide, and may be tried on indictment where:

- the offence charged is punishable with at least 14 years' imprisonment, or is indecent assault, or (if the defendant is at least 14 years of age) is causing death by dangerous driving or causing death by careless driving whilst under the influence of drink or drugs;

- the defendant is jointly charged with an adult who is going to be tried on indictment and the court considers that it is in the interests of justice that both should be tried on indictment.

A defendant under 18 may be tried summarily in an adult magistrates' court where:

- he is to be tried jointly with an adult. This is subject to the power to commit both for trial on indictment, and also subject to a power to remit the defendant under 18 for trial to a Youth Court where the adult pleads guilty, or is discharged or committed for trial on indictment, but the defendant is not;

- he is charged as a principal offender and an adult is charged with aiding, abetting, etc;

- he is charged separately from, but at the same time as, an adult, and the charges against each arise out of the same or connected circumstances;

- it appears during summary trial that, contrary to the initial belief, he is under the age of 18.

There is likely to be a significant reduction in the number of defendants under the age of 18 tried at the Crown Court following the enactment of the Criminal Justice Bill 2002.

When defendants under 18 are tried by magistrates in the Youth Court, there will generally be three justices to hear the case, of whom at least one must be a man and one a woman. These justices will have had special training to deal with such cases. There are special provisions relating to punishments for this age group. The current maximum fine for a child (under 14 years of age) is £250, and for a young person (under 18) £1,000. Members of both groups may be made the subject of supervision orders and compensation orders. A sentence of imprisonment may be imposed only on a defendant who is at least 21 years old. A sentence of detention in a young offenders institution may be imposed only on a defendant who is at least 18 years old (the intention is to bring all those aged at least 18 within the imprisonment regime). For those under 18, the custodial sentence is a detention and training order, which may be imposed only where an adult could have been sentenced to imprisonment. Where the defendant is under 15, a detention and training order can be imposed only if he is a 'persistent' offender. In measures under Part III of the PCC(S)A 2000, the Youth Court will on some occasions be obliged, and on others will have the discretion, to refer the young offender to a youth offender panel, the members of which will agree with the young offender and his family a course of action designed to tackle the offending behaviour and its causes. This could involve actions such as making apologies, carrying out reparation, doing community work and taking part in family counselling.

Traditionally, the aim of the Youth Court system has been to take the young offender out of the normal criminal court environment, and this has involved strict rules about public access to the court. In general, members of the public have not been permitted to attend and reporting restrictions have been very tight. Parents can be required to attend, and must attend in the case of any person under the age of 16, unless such a requirement would be unreasonable in the circumstances. The name or photograph of any person under 18 appearing in a case must not be printed in any newspaper or broadcast without the authority of the court or the Home Secretary. However, more recently, the view has developed that there needs to be a greater degree of involvement of offenders in the process and that maintaining the private nature of the proceedings may not be the best way to bring home to young offenders their responsibility for their actions. An evaluation of two pilot projects conducted in Youth Courts in Rotherham and Leicestershire and Rutland between October 1998 and March 2000 concluded that Youth Courts could enhance their effectiveness in dealing with juvenile offending by becoming more accessible to offenders, their families and victims (*Evaluation of the Youth Court Demonstration Project*, Home Office Research Study, 2000). Techniques adopted in the courts carrying out the experiment included:

- using clear language to explain to defendants what was happening in court, examining their circumstances and encouraging them to take responsibility for their behaviour and plans for change;

- a more informal court layout to aid communication, such as seating the magistrate at the same level or slightly higher than the defendant, no dock and seating defendants next to their solicitor;

- greater provision to accommodate victims either at court, if they wished to attend, or through providing timely information to them about the case;

- developing feedback to magistrates on reconviction rates, breaches and completion of sentences;

- considering the lifting of reporting restrictions, where appropriate.

All Youth Courts are now encouraged to take similar measures in a 'Good Practice Guide', issued jointly by the Home Office and the Lord Chancellor's Department in March 2001.

4.3.4   Indictable offences – committal proceedings

Where the magistrates decide that an offence triable either way should be tried in the Crown Court, they hold committal proceedings (as described at 4.3.2, above):

- *Section 51 of the Crime and Disorder Act 1998*

  These proceedings were also held where the defendant was charged with an indictable-only offence (for example, murder). If, having read the papers, the magistrates took the view that there was a *prima facie* case to answer, they had to commit the defendant to the Crown Court for trial; if not, they had to discharge the defendant. Now, however, s 51 of the Crime and Disorder Act (CDA) 1998 states that, where an adult is charged with an offence triable only on indictment, the court shall send him directly to the Crown Court for trial. Where he is also charged with an either way offence or a summary offence, he may be sent directly to trial for that as well, provided the magistrates believe that it is related to the indictable offence and, in the case of a summary offence, it is punishable with imprisonment or involves obligatory or discretionary disqualification from driving. Under this procedure, the accused may apply to a Crown Court judge for the charge(s) to be dismissed, and the judge should so direct if it appears that the evidence would be insufficient to convict the accused (Sched 3 to the CDA 1998).

- *Reporting committal proceedings*

In the old style committal proceedings, it was generally only the prosecution that would give evidence, with the defence reserving its arguments. Until 1967, this prosecution case was frequently reported on in the press so that it was virtually impossible to find an unbiased jury for the trial. A notorious instance of this was the case of Dr John Bodkin Adams in 1957. During the committal, deaths of patients other than the one for which he was to stand trial were referred to, but were not afterwards part of the evidence at the trial. The law on reporting was eventually changed in the CJA 1967 and is now in the MCA 1980. There are restrictions now on any application for dismissal put in by the defence. It is thus an offence to report on any aspect of the case if reporting restrictions have not been lifted by the bench. The bare matters which may as a matter of course be reported are:

(a) the identity of the court and the names of the examining magistrates;

(b) the names, ages, addresses and occupations of the accused and witnesses;

(c) the offence charged;

(d) the names of the lawyers engaged in the case;

(e) the decision of the court whether to commit or not and, if so, details of the committal, for example, to which court;

(f) any arrangements for bail;

(g) whether public funding was granted.

These restrictions, however, must be lifted by the magistrates if requested to do so by the accused. Where there are two or more accused and one objects to the reporting restrictions being lifted, then the magistrates must not lift them unless they regard it to be in the interests of justice to do so.

- *Effectiveness*

Full committal proceedings were protracted and expensive. A government research project in 1987 found that their average duration was one hour and 15 minutes as opposed to six minutes for new style 'paper' committals. The overall cost for committals was about £4 million a year (excluding the costs of the Crown Prosecution Service (CPS) and public funding) of which £2.7 million was spent on full committals. That this system does not effectively achieve what it aims to do – to act as a filter against cases with insufficient evidence – is testified to by the high acquittal rate on the direction of the judge in the High Court: of all those acquitted in Crown Court trials after pleading not guilty in 1990, for example, 16% were acquitted on the direction of the judge (mainly because the prosecution case was inadequate) and 42% of those acquitted were discharged by the judge because, for instance, the prosecution offered no evidence. In 1999, the comparable figures were 15% and 52%. So, whether the new system of committals will ultimately prove to be any significant improvement on the old in this respect remains to be seen.

- *Consistency of sentencing*

  Concern is often expressed at the sometimes quite notable discrepancies in sentencing practices employed by different benches of magistrates. It might be that these variations are unavoidable in circumstances where the rigidity of fixed penalties is unacceptable for most offences and regional differences in types of prevalent crime prompt justices to have certain attitudes to particular offences. There are several research surveys which demonstrate the discrepancies in magistrates' sentencing. Tarling, for example (*Sentencing and Practice in Magistrates' Courts*, 1979, Home Office Study 98), showed that in the 30 courts he surveyed, the use of probation varied between 1% and 12%, suspended sentences between 4% and 16%, and fines between 46% and 76%.

- *Independence*

  Magistrates' courts were often called 'police courts' from the time when they were situated in the same building as, or adjacent to, the local police station. There is criticism that as the magistrates still hear local police officers giving evidence so regularly, they become too credulous and trusting of the officers' evidence. There is also criticism that many magistrates are too suggestible under the influence of their clerks.

- *The future*

  The current system has the twin advantages of being relatively inexpensive to run (as the 30,000 lay justices are unsalaried) and allowing for lay participation (albeit from a narrow social band) in a crucially important part of the criminal justice system. Any change to a system involving fully paid, legally qualified inferior judges or inquisitors would entail great expense for the Exchequer.

4.3.5 The Access to Justice Act 1999 – magistrates' courts

Important changes to the magistrates' court system were made by Part V of the Access to Justice Act 1999.

Part V contains a range of provisions relating to magistrates and magistrates' courts:

- it provides for various changes to the organisation and management of magistrates' courts;

- it unifies the provincial and metropolitan stipendiary magistrates into a single bench;

- it removes the requirement for magistrates to sit on cases committed to the Crown Court for sentence, and enables the Crown Court, rather than a magistrates' court, to deal with breaches of community sentences imposed by the Crown Court;

- it extends and clarifies the powers of civilians to execute warrants; this is intended to enable this function to be transferred from the police to the magistrates' courts.

The government's objective is to develop a magistrates' court service which is effectively and efficiently managed, at a local level by local people, within a consistent national framework. The government announced its plans for developing this new framework in statements to both Houses of Parliament on 29 October 1997 (*Hansard*: House of Lords coll 1057–67; House of Commons, coll 901–14). As part of this programme of reform, the Act includes provisions to:

- reform the organisation and management of the magistrates' courts by:
  (a) creating more flexible powers to alter the various territorial units that make up the magistrates' court service, and to allow summary cases to be heard outside the commission area in which they arose;

  (b) expanding the potential membership of magistrates' courts committees by removing the limit on co-opted members;

  (c) establishing a single authority to manage the magistrates' courts service in London;

  (d) removing the requirement for justices' chief executives to be qualified lawyers, and transferring responsibility for certain administrative functions from justices' clerks to justices' chief executives; and

  (e) giving the Lord Chancellor power to require all magistrates' courts committees (MCCs) to procure common goods and services, where he considers this will lead to more effective or efficient administration;

- unify the provincial and metropolitan stipendiary benches into a single bench of District Judge (Magistrates' Courts), able to sit in any magistrates' court in the country;

- remove the requirement for lay magistrates to sit as judges in the Crown Court on committals for sentence;

- extend and clarify the powers of civilians to execute warrants.

The new powers to change organisational units reflect the government's intention to develop a more coherent geographical structure for the criminal justice system as a whole. Common boundaries should enable the various criminal justice agencies to co-operate more effectively.

The administration of the magistrates' courts service is based on three organisational units – the MCC area, the commission area and the petty sessions area. The MCC area is the unit on which the administration and organisation of the courts is based. MCCs are the bodies responsible for the administration of the magistrates' courts service. There are currently 96 MCCs in England and Wales. Each MCC appoints a justices' chief executive to manage the courts in its area.

The Justices of the Peace Act 1997 already provides power to change the boundaries of MCC areas. The government believes that a structure with fewer and larger areas would be more efficient and effective. The number of MCCs has been reduced in recent years by a series of amalgamations; this trend is likely to continue in future, as part of the policy of a greater alignment of boundaries between criminal justice agencies. The commission area is the unit on which the appointment of magistrates and the jurisdiction of the magistrates' courts to hear summary cases is based. Magistrates are appointed to a particular commission area, on the basis of where they reside; and most summary offences must be tried in the commission area where the alleged offence took place.

Historically, MCC and commission areas have aligned with one another and with county and metropolitan county borders. However, most commission areas are defined in primary legislation and can be changed by secondary legislation only to reflect changes in local government boundaries. Increasingly, there are MCCs which cover two or more commission areas. These MCCs cannot transfer magistrates or cases between areas. The ability to change commission area boundaries is intended to enable MCCs to allocate cases and deploy magistrates between the courts in their MCC area more effectively and efficiently.

Most MCC areas are broken down into smaller areas, called petty sessions areas. These are the benches, the basic unit of local court organisation. Petty sessions areas are defined in terms of local authority boundaries. This can limit an MCC's ability to organise its structure effectively, particularly where amalgamation has occurred. As a result, the full benefits of amalgamation may not be realised.

The Act redefines the basis of these units to allow MCCs to decide the most appropriate and efficient structure for their area. The Act also removes the artificial distinction between a petty sessions area and a 'petty sessional division' – a distinction which currently exists solely for the purposes of geographical identification.

Constitution of MCCs

Each MCC comprises up to 12 members and is composed primarily of lay magistrates, appointed by their peers, who undertake the task in addition to their magisterial duties. Individuals are appointed to the MCC on the basis of their skills and experience.

Where an MCC believes that additional skills are required which cannot be found amongst the applicants for membership of the MCC, they may co-opt individuals who need not be magistrates. The Act removes the limit on the number of co-opted and appointed members, and provides power for MCCs to remunerate those members.

MCCs are the bodies responsible for the administration of the magistrates' court service. Local authorities are responsible for providing the accommodation needed by an MCC and for paying the expenses it incurs. Local authorities recoup 80% of the net cost from the Lord Chancellor's Department in the form of a specific grant. In cases where an MCC area encompasses two or more authorities, the costs and accommodation are divided equitably between the authorities, but a 'lead' authority is appointed to receive the grant and pay the expenses.

A single authority for London

The Greater London area comprises a significantly larger number of MCCs (22) and local authorities (33) than any other area. The consequences of this, for issues such as funding and accommodation, are such that amalgamation under the provisions of the Justices of the Peace Act 1997 is not practical. The Act provides for the establishment of a Greater London Magistrates' Courts Authority, with special provision for its funding, accommodation, constitution and other necessary powers to enable the existing MCCs to be amalgamated effectively. MCCs are likely to be abolished when the Criminal Justice Bill 2002 is enacted by Parliament (see 4.7, below).

Justices' clerks and justices' chief executives

Most cases in magistrates' courts are heard by magistrates who are not qualified lawyers. They rely heavily on the legal advice of justices' clerks and their deputies, acting as court clerks. All justices' clerks are legally qualified and may have certain powers of a single magistrate delegated to them.

The post of justices' chief executive (JCE) was introduced in 1994, and every MCC has appointed a JCE. The JCE supports the MCC in planning and managing the efficient and effective administration of the courts within the area of the MCC. At present, however, justices' clerks continue to be responsible in statute for many administrative matters. In practice, many of these tasks are delegated to administrators. In 1998, the government published a Consultation Paper which considered the functions of justices' clerks (*The Future Role of Justices' Clerks*, Lord Chancellor's Department, September 1998).

The provisions in the Act relating to the qualifications and functions of JCEs are intended to clarify the role of the JCE and the lines of responsibility and accountability between the JCE, the MCC and the other staff of the MCC, and to achieve a clearer distinction between the roles of JCEs and justices' clerks.

The primary function of justices' clerks will continue to be the giving of legal advice to lay magistrates. Under the new management structure, JCEs will be able to delegate any administrative function to any staff, including the justices' clerks, depending on local needs.

Unification of the stipendiary bench

The Act unifies the stipendiary bench, establishing the stipendiary magistrates as a unified bench of professional judges with a new judicial title – District Judge (Magistrates' Courts). In April 1998, the government published a Consultation Paper about creating a unified stipendiary bench with national jurisdiction (*Unification of the Stipendiary Bench: Consultation Paper*, Lord Chancellor's Department, April 1998), with the intention of increasing the efficiency of the administration of justice at summary level. There are now 98 such judges.

The effect of this provision is to create a unified national bench, headed by a single judge, which can be deployed anywhere in the country to deal with fluctuations in workload, as and when they occur, or with particularly complex cases that arise. The new District Judges (Magistrates' Courts) are able to exercise jurisdiction in every commission area of England and Wales. The new title is intended to recognise more fully the status of stipendiaries as members of the professional judiciary. The new law has amended ss 11–22 of the Justices of the Peace Act 1997.

The main differences from the old law are as follows:

- Appointments are to be made without reference to any specific Commission area within England and Wales. A District Judge (Magistrates' Courts) has jurisdiction for every commission area.

- A Senior District Judge (Chief Magistrate) will be appointed as a national head of all District Judges (Magistrates' Courts). Previously, there was a Chief Metropolitan Stipendiary Magistrate, but no equivalent head of the provincial stipendiary bench.

- The Lord Chancellor will be able to remove one of these judges from office on the grounds of 'incapacity or misbehaviour'. Previously, the Lord Chancellor could remove a metropolitan stipendiary from office on the grounds of 'inability or misbehaviour'. Provincial stipendiaries could only be removed from office on the Lord Chancellor's recommendation, but no criteria were specified in statute (s 11(3)(b) of the Justices of the Peace Act 1997).

The test and procedure for removal have been unified to remove the inconsistency. 'Incapacity' has replaced 'inability' to reflect a similar change relating to circuit judges under the Courts Act 1971. The change of language brings these judicial posts into line.

- The Lord Chancellor may appoint Deputy District Judges (Magistrates' Courts) (new s 10B(1) of the Justices of the Peace Act 1997). In 2002, there were 171 Deputy District Judges in post. Unlike the appointment of acting stipendiary magistrates under the previous provisions, these appointments are not limited to three months' duration, or solely permitted for the purpose of avoiding delays in the administration of justice:

  (a) s 10A(1): the 'seven year general qualification' is defined in the CLSA 1990 as 'a right of audience in any class of proceedings in the county courts or magistrates' courts';

  (b) s 10D(2): this provision maintains specific exclusions of the rule codified under the Stipendiary Magistrates Act 1858, which allowed a single stipendiary to exercise the jurisdiction of two lay justices. Any express provision to the contrary made after that Act came into force survives by virtue of this section.

Although most cases heard in magistrates' courts are dealt with by lay magistrates, the use of professional judges in these courts has been increasing for some time. Between 1970 and 2000, the number of full time provincial stipendiaries rose from 11 to 47. There were 66 acting stipendiaries in 1991; by 2000, there were 148.

Committals for sentence

Currently, cases committed to the Crown Court for sentence must be heard in the Crown Court by a bench composed of a High Court Judge, circuit judge or recorder sitting with between two and four JPs. In October 1997, a new procedure was implemented by which defendants are required to indicate whether they intend to plead guilty or not guilty before the decision is made about whether the case should be heard in the magistrates' court or the Crown Court (s 17A of the MCA 1980, as amended by s 49 of the CPIA 1996). This has led to a significant increase in the number of cases committed to the Crown Court solely for sentence, and an increase in the seriousness of the cases being committed for sentence (previously, all more serious cases were committed for trial, although many defendants subsequently pleaded guilty).

The change in procedure has meant that magistrates are dealing in the Crown Court with cases which are outside their normal range of experience. In August 1998, the government issued a Consultation Paper (*Magistrates Sitting as Judges in the Crown Court*, Lord Chancellor's Department) which examined the role of magistrates in the Crown Court. The majority of responses agreed that the requirement for magistrates to sit on committals for sentence should be removed. As stated above, committals for sentencing are likely to be restricted or abolished in the near future.

Warrant execution

Until now, the police have been primarily responsible for arresting fine defaulters and those in breach of community sentences. Increasingly, however, some police forces have given this work a low priority. The government therefore intends to transfer responsibility for the execution of warrants from the police to the magistrates' courts. The intention is to ensure that fines and community sentences are seen as credible and effective punishments by ensuring that they can be effectively enforced.

A number of MCCs employed civilian enforcement officers (CEOs), who worked with the police under local arrangements. However, under previous legislation, the powers of CEOs were unclear in a number of respects. In order to enable the courts to take on this new function effectively, the Act contains provisions to clarify and extend the powers of appropriate civilians to execute certain kinds of warrant issued by a magistrates' court.

The provisions relating to warrants are intended to enhance the credibility of fines and community sentences by improving the effectiveness of their enforcement. This involves a transfer of resources from the police to magistrates' courts. The government has stated its intention to consult individual MCCs about the additional resources they require to implement the transfer, but no significant change in overall public expenditure on this function is expected. Over time, it is hoped to achieve an increase in the proportion of fines collected of at least 5%. In November 2002, the Public Accounts Committee reported that 40% of fines go unpaid. This amounts to £148 million *per annum*. Criminal sanctions seem to be taken more seriously in some areas than others. In Dorset, 89% are paid; in Liverpool, the figure is a mere 34%.

Sections 92–97 of the Access to Justice Act 1999 extends and clarifies the range of warrants issued by a magistrates' court which may be executed by CEOs employed by MCCs, local authorities or police authorities.

The warrants include warrants of distress, commitment, arrest or detention in connection with the payment of any sum, and also warrants of arrest issued in connection with breaches of a range of non-financial penalties. The list includes warrants made under the Child Support Act 1991 and the Council Tax (Administration and Enforcement) Regulations 1992.

The Act allows MCCs to approve and appoint private enforcement agencies to execute certain kinds of warrant. Some MCCs were using private enforcement agencies or bailiffs to execute distress warrants. However, there was some uncertainty about whether a warrant could be 'directed' to such a person within the meaning of s 125(2) of the MCA 1980 unless it referred to him by name. The Act clarifies the law, so that warrants can be addressed to approved agencies for the area concerned, rather than just to an individual, named bailiff. In future, the authorised employees of approved enforcement agencies will be able to execute the same range of warrants as CEOs anywhere in England and Wales.

These provisions significantly enlarge the use of private commercial agencies to perform what many would see as proper matters for only properly trained and accountable police officers or officials to perform. Is this enlargement of the private and for-profit sector within the criminal justice system a desirable development? It can be argued that without it, the criminal justice system would come under unnecessary and severe strain as police officers, much needed on patrol and responding to dangerous crime, would be occupied in chasing debtors. On the other hand, the entry of private commercial companies into the criminal justice system has been marked by periodic crises. In November 1998, for example, there was public scandal at the extent of injury to prison officers and trainers, and criminal damage at Britain's first private penal institution for young offenders. Riots at the Medway Secure Training Centre in Kent caused £100,000 of damage and the police were called in to deal with the rampaging 12–14 year olds ((1998) *The Times*, 13 November).

4.4 The Crown Court

Until 1971, the main criminal courts were the Assizes and the Quarter Sessions. These courts did not sit continuously and were not held in locations which corresponded with centres of population, as had been the case when they developed. The system was very inefficient as circuit judges wasted much time simply travelling from one town on the circuit to the next, and many defendants spent long periods in gaol awaiting trial.

Change was made following the *Report of the Beeching Royal Commission on Assizes and Quarter Sessions* (1969). The Courts Act 1971 abolished the Assizes and Quarter Sessions. These were replaced by a single Crown Court, a part of the Supreme Court of Judicature. The Crown Court is not a local court like the magistrates' court but a single court which sits in over 90 centres. England and Wales are divided into six circuits, each with its own headquarters and staff. The centres are divided into three tiers. In first-tier centres, High Court Judges hear civil and criminal cases, whereas circuit judges and recorders hear only criminal cases. Second-tier centres are served by the same types of judge, but hear criminal cases only. At third-tier centres, recorders and circuit judges hear just criminal cases.

Criminal offences are divided into four classes according to their gravity. Class 1 offences are the most serious, including treason and murder, and are usually tried by a High Court Judge; exceptionally he may transfer a murder case (including attempts) to be heard by a circuit judge approved for this purpose by the Lord Chief Justice. Class 2 offences include manslaughter and rape and are subject to similar provisions. Class 3 offences include all remaining offences triable only on indictment and are usually tried by a High

Court Judge, although releases of cases to circuit judges are more common here. Class 4 offences include robbery, grievous bodily harm and all offences triable 'either way', and are not normally tried by a High Court Judge.

4.4.1 The judges

The High Court Judges are usually from the Queen's Bench Division (QBD). Circuit judges are full time appointments made by the Queen on the advice of the Lord Chancellor. They are drawn from advocates with at least 10 years' experience of Crown Court practice (s 71 of the CLSA 1990) or lawyers who have been recorders. Appointment is also possible for someone who has had three years' experience in a number of other quasi-judicial offices like that of the stipendiary magistrate. Circuit judges retire at the age of 72, or 75 if the Lord Chancellor thinks it in the public interest.

A circuit judge may be removed from office by the Lord Chancellor on the grounds of incapacity or misbehaviour (s 17(4) of the Courts Act 1971). This right has not been exercised since 1983 when Judge Bruce Campbell, an Old Bailey judge, was removed from office a week after being convicted of two charges of smuggling.

To qualify for appointment as a recorder, a person must have 10 years' experience of advocacy in the Crown Court or county courts. JPs may also sit in the Crown Court, provided they are with one of the types of judge mentioned above. It is mandatory for between two and four JPs to sit when the Crown Court is hearing an appeal or dealing with persons committed for sentence by a magistrates' court.

In March 2001, the Lord Chancellor, Lord Irvine of Lairg, established a Commission for Judicial Appointments to review appointment processes and investigate complaints. The Commission's first report, published at the end of 2002, was critical of the Lord Chancellor's Department's failure to keep adequate records regarding judicial appointments.

4.4.2 Jurisdiction

The Crown Court hears all cases involving trial on indictment. It also hears appeals from those convicted summarily in the magistrates' courts. At the conclusion of the hearing, it has the power to confirm, reverse or vary any part of the decision under appeal (s 48(2) of the Supreme Court Act 1981). If the appeal is decided against the accused, the Crown Court has the power to impose any sentence which the magistrates could have imposed, including one which is harsher than the one originally imposed on the defendant.

4.4.3 Delay

Defendants committed to the Crown Court to be tried will have to wait an average of three months for their case to come to trial. This wait is sometimes in custody. Ever since the Streatfield Committee Report recommended in 1961 that the maximum time a defendant should have to wait after committal for trial should be eight weeks, there have been many schemes to help achieve this aim, but none has been particularly successful. Since 1985, for example, a person charged with an offence triable 'either way' can request the prosecution to furnish him with information (in the form of witness statements, a summary of the case, etc) of the case against him. This was aimed at increasing the number of guilty pleas by showing to the defendant at an early stage the strength of the prosecution's case.

According to the Crown Court's 2001 annual report, the average waiting time across court centres in England and Wales is 14.68 weeks. The average delay at the Central Criminal Court (the 'Old Bailey') is 24.46 weeks. The targets for defendants in custody and on bail are eight and 12 weeks respectively. There are approximately 1,900 circuit judges and recorders. When one remembers that the average time to try a case on a plea of not guilty is about seven hours (one and a half court days), the burden of work on the courts becomes clear. The consequent delay has very serious repercussions on the criminal justice system: justice delayed is justice denied. The accuracy of testimony becomes less reliable the longer the gap between the original reception of the data by a witness and his account of it in court. Also important is the stress and pain for those innocent defendants who have to wait so long before their case can be put to a jury.

The largest ever study of Crown Court cases, undertaken by Zander and Henderson for the Runciman Commission, made some worrying findings. Their research was based on responses to questionnaires by more than 22,000 people involved in 3,000 Crown Court cases. The views of lawyers, judges, clerks, jurors, police and defendants were all canvassed. There were convictions in 8% of cases that defence lawyers thought weak, 6% that prosecution barristers thought weak and 4% that judges thought weak, suggesting that innocent people were still being convicted in significant numbers. Further, 31 defendants said that they had pleaded guilty to offences they had not committed. Their reasons were varied: to avoid a trial; to gain a less severe sentence; or because they had been advised to do so by their lawyers.

Another worrying discovery, since poor defence lawyers have recently been cited as contributing to miscarriages of justice, is the large number of Crown Court cases (about one-third) that were being dealt with by clerks rather than by trained, qualified solicitors. Some defendants met with their barrister for the first time on the morning of their trial, and for about one-third of these cases, the conference lasted for just 15 minutes. In about one-third of all cases, the barristers only received their instructions the day before the trial.

4.4.4   Magistrates' courts v Crown Courts

For offences triable 'either way', there has been much debate about the merits of each venue. The introduction of the 'plea before venue' procedure previously described has significantly reduced the number of cases committed for trial to the Crown Court and significantly increased the number committed for sentence. At the same time, the proportion of cases disposed of on a not guilty plea has risen. Even so, of approximately 65,000 cases disposed of by the Crown Court in 1999, 59% were decided on a guilty plea (which actually represented a fall of almost 10% from 1998). Obviously, this means that the CPS incurs considerable costs in wasted preparation. One of the reasons defendants do this is that prosecution cases often fall apart during the delay before a Crown Court hearing, allowing the defendant to go free (see 10.1, below). Another is that juries cannot be compelled to give reasons for convicting, unlike magistrates, who can be required to justify their reasons in writing for review in the High Court which can overturn convictions or acquittals. Thus, there is a greater chance with jury convictions that an appeal court will regard a conviction (should there be one) as unsafe and unsatisfactory because the jury's reasons for having convicted will not be known. Thus, a defendant who suspects that he might be convicted can reasonably prefer to be convicted by a jury than by a magistrate because the former do not and cannot give reasons for their verdicts and are therefore perhaps easier to appeal. Jury verdicts are arguably more likely to be regarded as unsafe on appeal because it will not be known whether some improper factor (like a judge's misdirection) had entered their deliberation. The reports of the Court of Appeal (Criminal Division) contain many cases where the court states that a conviction should be quashed because the jury might have been influenced by a misleading statement from the judge. It might be said that a defendant should prefer the magistrates' court as the sentencing is generally lower, but when the defendant's antecedents are known (after a conviction), he can still be committed to the Crown Court for sentence, so the magistrates' courts are not really preferable to a defendant with a criminal record who fears another conviction is likely.

4.5   Criminal appeals

The process of appeal depends upon how a case was originally tried, whether summarily or on indictment.

4.5.1 Appeals from magistrates' courts

Two routes of appeal are possible. The first route allows only a defendant to appeal. The appeal is to a judge and between two and four magistrates sitting in the Crown Court and can be: (a) against conviction (only if the defendant pleaded not guilty) on points of fact or law; or (b) against sentence. Such an appeal will take the form of a new trial (a trial *de novo*).

Alternatively, the defendant can appeal 'by way of case stated' to the High Court (the Divisional Court of the QBD). This court consists of two or more judges (usually two), of whom one will be a Lord Justice of Appeal. Here, either the defence or the prosecution may appeal, but the grounds are limited to: (a) a point of law; or (b) that the magistrates acted beyond their jurisdiction. If the prosecution succeeds on appeal, the court can direct the magistrates to convict and pass the appropriate sentence. There is also an appeal by way of case stated from the Crown Court to the Divisional Court when the Crown Court has heard an appeal from the magistrates' court.

Appeal from the Divisional Court is to the House of Lords. Either side may appeal, but only on a point of law and only if the Divisional Court certifies the point to be one of general public importance. Leave to appeal must also be granted either by the Divisional Court or the House of Lords.

The Criminal Justice Bill 2002 proposes to give magistrates information regarding defendants' criminal records at mode of trial hearings. If magistrates decide that summary trial is appropriate, the defendant will gain the right to request an indication of sentence (following an admission of guilt) before deciding on mode of trial. At present, more than half of the 'either way' cases that go to the Crown Court result in sentences that could have been imposed by magistrates. In the future, more defendants may elect trial by jury.

4.5.2 Appeals from the Crown Court

Appeals from the Crown Court lie to the Court of Appeal (Criminal Division), which hears appeals against conviction and sentence. This court, replacing the Court of Criminal Appeal, was established in 1966. The Division usually sits in at least two courts: one composed of the Lord Chief Justice sitting with two judges of the QBD and the other of a Lord Justice of Appeal and two Queen's Bench judges. The court hears about 8,000 criminal appeals and applications each year. In 1999, it heard 8,274 applications, 2,104 of which were appeals against conviction and 6,170 of which concerned sentence.

Until 1996, s 2 of the Criminal Appeal Act (CAA) 1968 read:

2(1) Except as provided by this Act, the Court of Appeal shall allow an appeal against conviction if they think:

    (a) that the verdict of the jury should be set aside on the ground that, under all the circumstances of the case, it is unsatisfactory or unsafe; or

(b) that the judgment of the court of trial should be set aside on the ground of a wrong decision of any question of law; or

(c) that there was a material irregularity in the course of the trial,

and in any other case shall dismiss the appeal:

provided that the court may, notwithstanding that they are of opinion that the point raised in the appeal might be decided in favour of the appellant, dismiss the appeal if they consider that no miscarriage of justice has actually occurred.

January 1996 saw the introduction of the Criminal Appeal Act (CAA) 1995. The introduction of ss 1, 2 and 4 of the Act brought particularly significant changes to the criminal appeal system.

Section 1 amended the CAA 1968 so as to bring an appeal against conviction, an appeal against a verdict of not guilty by reason of insanity and an appeal against a finding of disability, *on a question of law alone*, into line with other appeals against conviction and sentence (that is, those involving questions of fact, or mixtures of law and fact). Now, all appeals against conviction and sentence must first have leave of the Court of Appeal or a certificate of fitness for appeal from the trial judge before the appeal can be taken. Before the 1995 Act came into force, it was possible to appeal without the consent of the trial judge or Court of Appeal on a point of law alone. In Parliament, the reason for this change was given as the need to 'provide a filter mechanism for appeals on a ground of law alone which are wholly without merit' (HC Official Report, SC B (Criminal Appeal Bill) Col 6, 21 March 1995).

Section 2 changed the grounds for allowing an appeal under the CAA 1968. Under the old law, the Court of Appeal was required to allow an appeal where: (1) the conviction, verdict or finding should have been set aside on the ground that, under all the circumstances, it was unsafe or unsatisfactory; or (2) that the judgment of the court of trial or the order of the court giving effect to the verdict or finding should be set aside on the ground of a wrong decision of law; or (3) that there was a material irregularity in the course of the trial. In all three situations, the Court of Appeal was allowed to dismiss the appeal if it considered that no miscarriage of justice had actually occurred. The law now requires the Court of Appeal to allow an appeal against conviction under s 1 of the CAA 1968, an appeal against verdict under s 12 (insanity) or an appeal against a finding of disability if it thinks that the conviction, verdict or finding is 'unsafe' (as opposed to the old law, which used the 'unsafe or *unsatisfactory*' formula).

During the parliamentary passage of the Act, there was much heated debate about whether the new provisions were designed to narrow the grounds of appeal. That would amount to a tilt in favour of the State in that it would make it harder for (wrongly) convicted people to appeal. Government ministers insisted that the effect of the new law was simply to re-state or consolidate the practice of the Court of Appeal. One government spokesman said that:

> In dispensing with the word 'unsatisfactory', we agree with the Royal Commission on criminal justice that there is no real difference between 'unsafe' and 'unsatisfactory'; the Court of Appeal does not distinguish between the two. Retaining the word 'unsatisfactory' would imply that we thought there was a real difference and would only lead to confusion.

There were many attempts during the legislation's passage to insert the words 'or may be unsafe' after the word 'unsafe'. The Law Society, the Bar, Liberty and JUSTICE called on the government to make such a change. Also opposed to the use of the single word 'unsafe' was the eminent criminal law expert Professor JC Smith. He has argued cogently that there are many cases where a conviction has been seen as 'unsatisfactory' rather than 'unsafe', so there is a need for both words. Sometimes, the Court of Appeal might be convinced that the defendant is guilty (so the conviction is 'safe') but still wishes to allow the appeal because fair play, according to the rules, must be seen to be done. Accepting improperly extracted confessions (violating s 76 of the Police and Criminal Evidence Act (PACE) 1984) simply because it might seem obvious that the confessor is guilty will promote undesirable interrogation practices, because police officers will think that even if they break the rules, any resulting confession will nevertheless be allowed as evidence.

Professor Smith has given the example ((1995) 145 NLJ 534) of where there has been a serious breach of the rules of evidence. In *Algar* (1954), the former wife of the defendant testified against him about matters during the marriage. The Court of Appeal allowed his appeal against conviction, but Lord Goddard said: 'Do not think that we are doing this because we think that you are an innocent man. We do not. We think that you are a scoundrel.' The idea behind such remarks is that rules are rules, and the rules of evidence must be obeyed in order to ensure justice. Once you start to accept breaches of the rules as being justified by the outcome (ends justifying means), then the whole law of evidence could begin to collapse.

The proposal to include 'or might be unsafe' was rejected for the reason probably best summarised by Lord Taylor, the then Lord Chief Justice, who argued in the Lords that there was no merit in including the words 'or may be unsafe', as the implication of such doubt is already inherent in the word 'unsafe'.

Cases decided since the new formula was introduced have tended to indicate that the Court of Appeal has not adopted a restrictive interpretation. Thus, a conviction was quashed as unsafe in *Smith (Patrick Joseph)* (1999) because of irregularities at trial, even though the accused had admitted his guilt during cross-examination. The Human Rights Act (HRA) 1998 has now introduced a further significant element into the consideration of this issue, to which the Court of Appeal is currently struggling to develop the correct approach. Article 6 of the European Convention on Human Rights (ECHR), to which English courts must give effect unless incompatible with an Act of Parliament, gives the defendant a right to a fair trial. Irregularities in a trial, including misdirections by the judge, admission of improperly obtained evidence and so on, might cast doubt on the fairness of the trial without necessarily making the conviction unsafe on a narrow view of that word. In *Davis* (2001), the Court of Appeal suggested that since a conviction might be unsafe even where there was no doubt about guilt, but there were serious irregularities at the trial, English rules on appeals were compatible with Art 6. However, it went on to argue that a violation of Art 6 did not necessarily imply that the conviction must be quashed. Subsequently, Lord Woolf CJ argued in *Togher* (2000) that obligations under the ECHR meant that it was almost inevitable that if the accused had been denied a fair trial, his conviction would have to be regarded as unsafe.

Section 4 provides a unified test for the receipt of fresh evidence in the Court of Appeal. Under the old law, the Court of Appeal had a discretion under s 23(1)(c) of the CAA 1968 to receive fresh evidence of any witness if it was thought necessary or expedient in the interests of justice. Section 23(2) added a duty to receive new evidence which was relevant, credible and admissible, and which could not reasonably have been adduced at the original trial. There was often much argument about whether new evidence should be received under the court's discretion or its duty. Gradually, the 'duty' principles came to be merged into the 'discretion' principles. The aim of the latest amendment is to reflect the current practice of the court. The general discretion under s 23(1) has been retained, but the 'duty' principle has been replaced with a set of criteria which the court must consider. They are:

- whether the evidence appears to the court to be capable of belief;
- whether it appears to the court that the evidence may afford any ground for allowing the appeal;
- whether the evidence would have been admissible at the trial on the issue under appeal; and
- whether there is a reasonable explanation for the failure to adduce the evidence at trial.

Only the accused may appeal. No leave to appeal is required if the appeal is against conviction on a point of law, but it is needed for appeals on points of fact or mixed fact and law. Leave is also required for appeals against sentence.

Under s 36 of the CJA 1972, the Attorney General can refer a case which has resulted in an acquittal to the Court of Appeal where he believes the decision to have been questionably lenient on a point of law. The Court of Appeal deals just with the point of law and the defendant's acquittal is not affected even if the court decides the point against the defendant. It merely clarifies the law for future cases.

Sections 35–36 of the CJA 1988 allow the Attorney General to refer indictable-only cases to the Court of Appeal where the sentence at trial is regarded as unduly lenient. The court can impose a harsher sentence.

Following the determination of an appeal by the Court of Appeal or by the Divisional Court, either the prosecution or the defence may appeal to the House of Lords. Leave from the court below or the House of Lords must be obtained and two other conditions fulfilled according to s 33 of the CAA 1968:

- the court below must certify that a point of law of general public importance is involved; and
- either the court below or the House of Lords must be satisfied that the point of law is one which ought to be considered by the House of Lords.

The High Court can quash tainted acquittals under s 54 of the CPIA 1996. An acquittal is 'tainted' where someone has since been convicted of conspiring to pervert the course of justice in the case by interfering with the jury.

4.5.3   The Access to Justice Act 1999 – jurisdiction

Section 61 of the Access to Justice Act 1999 establishes the jurisdiction of the High Court to hear cases stated by the Crown Court for an opinion of the High Court. This part of the Act (Part IV) enables these and certain other applications to the High Court to be listed before a single judge. It provides for the appointment of a Vice President of the QBD. It also prohibits the publication of material likely to identify a child involved in proceedings under the Children Act 1989, before the High Court or a county court, and allows for those under 14 years old to attend criminal trials.

Jurisdiction of a single judge of the High Court

The Act allows certain applications to be routinely heard by a single judge of the High Court. It does this by removing an obstacle that exists in the current legislation by which the route of appeal for these cases is to the House of Lords, but the Administration of Justice Act 1960 provides that the House of Lords will only hear appeals in these matters from a Divisional Court (that is, more than one judge) of the High Court. The 1999 Act (ss 63–65) amends the 1960 Act so that the House of Lords can hear appeals from a single High Court judge. It will then be possible to make rules of court to provide for these cases to be heard by a single judge, while enabling the judge to refer particularly complex cases to a Divisional Court.

The cases in question include:

- appeals by way of case stated in criminal causes and matters;
- appeals from inferior (civil and criminal) courts and tribunals in contempt of court cases;
- criminal applications for habeas corpus.

4.5.4 Judicial Committee of the Privy Council

The Judicial Committee of the Privy Council was created by the Judicial Committee Act 1833. Under the Act, a special committee of the Privy Council was set up to hear appeals from the Dominions. The cases are heard by the judges (without wigs or robes) in a committee room in London. The Committee's decision is not a judgment but an 'advice' to the monarch, who is counselled that the appeal be allowed or dismissed.

The Committee is the final court of appeal for certain Commonwealth countries which have retained this option, and from some independent members and associate members of the Commonwealth. The Committee comprises Privy Councillors who hold (or have held) high judicial office. In most cases, the Committee comprises five Lords of Appeal in Ordinary, sometimes assisted by a judge from the country concerned.

Most of the appeals heard by the Committee are civil cases (see 3.11, above). In the rare criminal cases, it is only on matters involving legal questions that appeals are heard. The Committee does not hear appeals against criminal sentence.

The decisions of the Privy Council are very influential in English courts because they concern points of law that are applicable in this jurisdiction and they are pronounced upon by Lords of Appeal in Ordinary in a way which is thus tantamount to a House of Lords' ruling. These decisions, however, are technically of persuasive precedent only, although they are normally followed by English courts; see, for example, the criminal appeal case *Abbot v R* (1977). This was an appeal from Trinidad and Tobago. The Privy Council ruled that duress is no defence to the perpetrator of murder.

4.5.5 Royal Commission on Criminal Justice

Research undertaken for the Royal Commission by Kate Malleson of the London School of Economics found that judges' mistakes are by far the most common ground for successful appeals against conviction. The research discovered that in about 80% of cases where convictions were quashed, there had been an error at the trial; in most instances, it was judicial error.

Of 300 appeals in 1990, just over one-third were successful. Of those appealing, almost two-thirds of defendants appealed against conviction on the ground that the trial judge had made a crucial mistake and, of those, 43% succeeded in having their convictions quashed. Sixteen defendants were vindicated by the Court of Appeal in claims that the judge's summing up to the jury was biased or poor; a further 42 convictions were quashed because the judge was wrong about the law or evidence.

This research was critical of the way the Court of Appeal failed to consider cases where fresh evidence had emerged since the trial or where there was a 'lurking doubt' about the conviction. The Report urged that the court be given a new role allowing it to investigate the events leading up to a conviction.

The Royal Commission was set up, under the chairmanship of Viscount Runciman, in March 1991, after the release of the Birmingham Six (an important case in a series of notorious miscarriages of justice in which people were found to have been wrongly convicted and sentenced for serious crimes). It reported in July 1993, with 352 recommendations largely designed to prevent wrongful conviction. Several of the recommendations are relevant to discussion of the criminal courts. The numbers here refer to those of the recommendations in the Report.

The Commission recommended (331) that the Home Secretary's power to refer cases to the Court of Appeal under s 17 of the CAA 1968 should be removed and a new body, the Criminal Cases Review Authority, should be set up to consider allegations (332) that a miscarriage of justice might have occurred. The Authority should have 'operational independence' (333), with a chairman appointed by the Queen on the advice of the Prime Minister. The Authority should be independent of the court structure (336) and should refer meritorious cases directly to the Court of Appeal. There should be neither a right of appeal nor a right to judicial review (340) in relation to decisions reached by the authority. The Authority should consist of both lawyers and lay people, should be supported by a staff of lawyers (344) and should devise its own rules and procedures. It should be able to discuss cases directly with applicants (345) and should have powers (347) to direct its own investigations. These recommendations were largely met by the terms of the CAA 1995.

4.5.6 Criminal Cases Review Commission

The Criminal Cases Review Commission (CCRC) is an independent body set up under the CAA 1995. The CCRC came into being on 1 January 1997. There are 14 members from a wide variety of backgrounds. It is responsible for investigating suspected miscarriages of criminal justice in England, Wales and Northern Ireland. This function was previously carried out through the office of the Home Secretary. He would make occasional referrals of cases back to the Court of Appeal when a unit of civil servants in the Home Office evaluated a case (which had otherwise exhausted the formal court appeal system) as warranting further consideration. Over 250 cases were transferred from the Home Office around 31 March 1997, when the Commission took over responsibility for casework.

The CCRC cannot overturn convictions or sentences itself. Instead, it may refer to the Court of Appeal a conviction for an offence tried on indictment, or a finding of not guilty by reason of insanity, or a finding that a person was under a disability when he did the act or made the omission, and may also refer cases in respect of sentence where they were tried on indictment (s 9 of the CAA 1995). Additionally, the CCRC may refer to the Crown Court convictions and sentences imposed by magistrates' courts, though the Crown Court may not impose any punishment more severe than that of the court from which the decision is referred (s 11 of the CAA 1995). The Court of Appeal itself may direct the CCRC to carry out an investigation and it must report to the court when finished or as required to do so by the court. Once the reference has been made, it will be treated as an appeal for the purposes of the CAA 1968.

The Commission is given power by ss 17–21 of the CAA 1995 to obtain information and carry out investigations, including appointing investigating officers (who are likely to be police officers where there have been previous police investigations).

Any decision to refer a case to the relevant appellate court has to be taken by a committee of at least three members. The CCRC considers whether or not there is a real possibility that the conviction, finding, verdict or sentence would not be upheld were a reference to be made.

In order to establish that there is a real possibility of an appeal succeeding regarding a conviction, there has to be:

- an argument or evidence which has not been raised during the trial or at appeal; or
- exceptional circumstances.

In order to establish that there is a real possibility of an appeal succeeding against a sentence, there has to be a legal argument or information about the individual or the offence which was not raised in court during the trial or at appeal.

Other than in exceptional circumstances, the Commission can only consider cases in which an appeal through the ordinary judicial appeal process has failed and, once a decision is taken to refer a case to the relevant court of appeal, the Commission has no other involvement.

The CCRC referred the notorious case of Derek William Bentley to the Court of Appeal. Mr Bentley was convicted at the Central Criminal Court on 11 December 1952 of the murder of PC Sidney Miles. Mr Bentley did not actually shoot the officer. The gun was fired by his accomplice in a failed burglary attempt, but Mr Bentley was convicted under the principles of 'joint enterprise', even though he was being held under arrest by a police officer metres away from where his accomplice fired the pistol. An appeal against conviction was heard by the Court of Criminal Appeal on 13 January 1953 and dismissed. Mr Bentley was hanged on 28 January 1953.

Bentley's conviction and sentence were the subject of numerous representations to the Home Office. In July 1993, on the recommendation of the Home Secretary, Her Majesty The Queen, in the exercise of the Royal Prerogative of Mercy, granted to Mr Bentley a posthumous pardon limited to sentence.

Following submissions from the applicants' solicitors and the completion of its own inquiries, the CCRC concluded that Mr Bentley's conviction should be reconsidered by the Court of Appeal. The trial was seen as unfair in a number of respects, for example, the fact that, although 18, Bentley had a mental age of 11 was kept a secret from the jury, and the judge's summing up to the jury was astonishingly biased in favour of the police. In August 1998, on a momentous day in legal history, the Court of Appeal cleared Bentley of the murder for which he was hanged 46 years earlier. In giving judgment, the Lord Chief Justice, Lord Bingham, said: '... the summing up in this case was such as to deny the appellant that fair trial which is the birthright of every British citizen.'

By March 2001, the total number of applications dealt with by the CCRC was 3,994. Of these, 2,926 had been dealt with, including 124 referrals. Of 65 referrals heard by the Court of Appeal, 48 had resulted in convictions being quashed, 15 in convictions being upheld and two were currently reserved.

Assessing the success of the CCRC thus far is difficult. Ultimately, the test of success for the CCRC will be the same one as that which was apparently failed by its predecessor – carrying the confidence of the general public and of politicians – that it represents a safe, quick and impartial method of dealing with cases not given justice in the ordinary courts.

4.6   A miscarriage of justice

One of the English legal system's worst miscarriages of justice cases in recent history was exposed in the Court of Appeal in February 1998. In 1979, Vincent Hickey, Michael Hickey, Jimmy Robertson and Pat Molloy, who became known as the Bridgewater Four, were convicted of the murder of a 13 year old boy, Carl Bridgewater. Although the men were not angelic characters (and two had serious criminal records), they strenuously protested that they were not guilty of the horrific child murder.

Eighteen years later, and after two earlier failed visits to the Court of Appeal and seven police investigations, three of the men were released on 21 February on unconditional bail in anticipation of an appeal hearing in April. The fourth defendant, Mr Molloy, died in jail in 1981. The appeal was eventually allowed.

The Crown has conceded that the case against the men was 'flawed' by evidence falsified and fabricated by police officers. There has also come to light significant fingerprint evidence, tending to exonerate the four, which was not disclosed to the defence by the prosecution. Mr Molloy was questioned for 10 days without access to a solicitor, and a fabricated statement from Vincent Hickey was used to persuade Mr Molloy to confess to the crime. Before he died, Mr Molloy claimed he had been beaten by police officers in the course of his interrogation. The former police officers alleged to have falsified the evidence are now under investigation.

The case was given extensive coverage in the print and broadcast media in February 1997 and made a significant impact upon public consciousness. How far it will negatively affect public confidence in the criminal justice system remains to be judged. This major case raises many points germane to the operation of the criminal justice system. The following are of particular importance:

- The case was originally investigated in 1978, before PACE 1984 had been passed. The requirements under PACE 1984 for suspects to be given access to legal advice (s 58, Code C) and for interviews to be recorded (s 60, Code E) may have reduced or eliminated the opportunity for police malpractice of the sort which occurred in the *Bridgewater* case.

- Although the criminal justice system ultimately corrected an injustice, this result was achieved primarily through the indefatigable efforts of a few dedicated family members, campaigning journalists and Members of Parliament who would not let the issue disappear from the public forum. The case attracted attention because of the terrible nature of the crime – a child murder. It is quite possible that many other unjust convictions in cases with more mundane facts are never propelled into public discussion or overturned.

- Miscarriages of justice cases involve two types of insult to notions of legal fairness: (a) the wrongly imprisoned endure years of incarceration; (b) the real culprits (a child killer in the *Bridgewater* case) are never identified and could well go on to commit other offences.

- The men were released due to the discovery of evidence which had been fabricated and falsified, yet the CPIA 1996 restricts defence access to prosecution evidence.

- The CCRC has been established to re-evaluate alleged cases of miscarriages of justice. One criticism of it has been that it does not have its own independent investigators, but will rely on police officers to re-examine cases. How far this new body will be able to succeed in its mission statement, and carry public confidence, remains to be seen.

- The jury is only as good as the information and arguments put before it allow it to be. After the prosecution's case had been devastated by the discovery of new scientific evidence in 1993 (a forensic psychiatrist showed that Molloy's 'confession' used language the suspect would not have used), the foreman of the jury from the 1979 trial risked prosecution for contempt of court by issuing a statement to say that he thought that the men were not guilty. He, along with another juror, said they regretted that they had not been given all the evidence that was available at the time of the trial.

4.7 Reform of the criminal courts

It is evident from the earlier discussion in this chapter that there is continuing debate about the need for reform. The latest impetus for proposals for reform comes from the desire on the part of the government to subject the criminal courts to a process of review which parallels that undertaken by Lord Justice Woolf in relation to the civil courts. In December 1999, the Lord Chancellor appointed Lord Justice Auld to conduct on his own an independent review of the working of the criminal courts. His terms of reference required him to inquire into and report on:

> ... the practices and procedures of the criminal courts at every level, with a view to ensuring that they deliver justice fairly, by streamlining all their processes, increasing their efficiency and strengthening the effectiveness of their relationships with others across the whole of the criminal justice system, and having regard to the interests of all parties including victims and witnesses, thereby promoting confidence in the rule of law.

Lord Justice Auld's review of the criminal courts was published in September 2001. It contained a number of controversial proposals. These included restrictions on the right to elect trial by jury for 'either way' offences, legislation against perverse jury verdicts, and the establishment of an intermediate court presided over by a professional judge and two magistrates. In July 2002, the government published its own proposals in a White Paper called *Justice for All* (Cmnd 5563).

On 21 November 2002, a new Criminal Justice Bill was introduced to Parliament. It consists of 293 pages, 273 clauses and 26 schedules. The main features include the following:

- Magistrates should be told of defendants' prior convictions when allocation decisions are made (Sched 3).
- If magistrates decide that summary trial is appropriate, the defendant should be able to ask for an indication of sentence (Sched 3).
- Committal for sentencing to be abolished except for serious cases (Sched 3).
- Crown Court defendants to have right to trial by judge alone (cl 36).
- Judges to be given the power to order trial without jury in exceptional cases (cll 37–38).
- Prosecution to gain a right of appeal against a ruling by a Crown Court judge that leads to the premature termination of a trial (cll 49–61).
- Magistrates' sentencing powers to be increased to one year for a single offence (cl 137(1)). The Home Secretary will have the right to increase this to 18 months (cl 139).
- Abolition of the categories of ineligibility for and excusal 'as of right' from jury service (cl 258 and Sched 22).

On 28 November 2002, a Courts Bill was introduced to Parliament. This was intended to implement the main courts-related recommendations found in Lord Justice Auld's review and *Justice for All*. Its central aim is the establishment of a unified criminal court system. Key main features include:

- the creation of a new arrangements to replace the MCCs (cll 1–6);

- the establishment of advisory Court Administration Councils (CACs) (cll 3–5);

- the appointment of fines officers and the creation of new sanctions to improve the effectiveness of fine enforcement (cl 31 and Sched 2);

- the appointment of magistrates to be national, not local (cl 17);

- the creation of local justice areas to replace Commission and Petty Sessions areas (cl 8);

- permitting District Judges (Magistrates' Courts) to sit as Crown Court judges (cl 60);

- amending the procedures for appeals to the Court of Appeal and the House of Lords (cll 87–88).

Although the Bills currently before Parliament appear to allow a greater role for lay justice than was proposed by Lord Justice Auld, it is likely that their enactment will lead to a decline in the number of jury trials. It may also be questioned whether it is appropriate for lay magistrates to have their sentencing powers doubled (or trebled). One possibility would be to increase the number of District Judges (Magistrates' Courts) and Deputy District Judges (Magistrates' Courts). If this were to happen, lay magistrates might find themselves increasingly relegated to dealing with routine cases. The Courts Bill threatens the local management functions currently exercised by lay magistrates. The response of the Magistrates' Association has been less than enthusiastic:

> The most important feature of the current magistrates' courts system is local justice – dispensed by local magistrates, managed by local Magistrates' Courts Committees … Many of the proposals contained within the Bill, if enacted, would sever or substantially curtail the currently strong connections between magistrates, their staff, their courts and the managers and users of those courts, to the general detriment of the quality of the service provided [*Magistrates' Association Briefing* Paper, 20 January 2003].

In essence, the debate is about whether (or how far) there should be a centrally administered national court system or a system that reflects local needs and traditions.

THE CRIMINAL COURT STRUCTURE

The main courts

The trial courts are the magistrates' courts and Crown Courts. In serious offences, known as *indictable offences*, the defendant is tried by a jury in a Crown Court; for *summary offences*, he is tried by magistrates; and for 'either way' offences, the defendant can be tried by magistrates if they agree, but he may elect for jury trial.

The main issues here concern the distribution of business between the magistrates' court and Crown Courts: what are the advantages of trial in the magistrates' court: (a) for the State; and (b) for the defendant? Conversely, what are the disadvantages?

Reforms

In 1999, the government announced its intention to introduce a change concerning the way decisions are made about where a defendant is to be tried. Under the new system proposed by the government, a defendant charged with an 'either way' offence would be able to make representations to magistrates that he wished to be tried in the Crown Court before a judge and jury, but the magistrates would have power to override the desire of the defendant and try the case themselves if they thought they were properly suited to this task, even against the wishes of the defendant. These plans were thwarted by the House of Lords, which rejected two different Mode of Trial Bills. A review of the criminal courts by Lord Justice Auld proposed the establishment of a new middle-tier court which would hear cases of intermediate seriousness. This suggestion aroused considerable hostility and failed to gain government support. The powers of magistrates are likely to be increased when the Criminal Justice Bill 2002 is enacted. This will probably lead to a significant reduction in the number of jury trials.

Reformed court management

Certain changes concerning the magistrates' courts have been made by the Access to Justice Act 1999. The 1999 Act provides for various changes to the organisation and management of the magistrates' courts. For example, the Act redefines the basis of the unit of magistrates' courts committees (MCCs). The Act also unifies the provincial and metropolitan stipendiary magistrates into a single bench, and it removes the requirement for magistrates to sit on cases committed to the county court for sentence. The Act also makes some controversial changes in relation to warrant execution by allowing MCCs to approve and appoint private enforcement agencies to execute certain kinds of warrant. More radical reforms (including the abolition of MCCs) are likely to follow the enactment of the Courts Bill.

Appeals

Criminal appeals from the magistrates go to the Crown Court or to the QBD Divisional Court 'by way of case stated' on a point of law or that the JPs went beyond their proper powers. If the prosecution succeeds on appeal, the court can direct the magistrates to convict and pass the appropriate sentence. There is also an appeal by way of case stated from the Crown Court to the Divisional Court when the Crown Court has heard an appeal from the magistrates' court. From the Crown Court, appeals against conviction and sentence lie to the Court of Appeal (Criminal Division). Note the powers of the Attorney General under s 36 of the CJA 1972 and his powers under ss 35 and 36 of the CJA 1988.

Part IV of the Access to Justice Act 1999 establishes the High Court's jurisdiction to hear cases stated by the Crown Court for an opinion. It enables these cases stated to be heard by a single judge.

The Judicial Committee of the Privy Council hears final appeals from some Commonwealth countries and its decisions are of persuasive precedent in English law.

Review after appeal

In an attempt to deal with possible miscarriages of justice, and following the recommendations of the Royal Commission on Criminal Justice in 1993 (Runciman), the Criminal Appeal Act 1995 established the Criminal Cases Review Commission (CCRC). The CCRC has power to investigate and to refer cases to the Court of Appeal (or, where appropriate, the Crown Court) where it considers that there is a real possibility of an appeal succeeding.

CHAPTER 5

JUDICIAL REASONING

5.1 Introduction

The popular perception of the judicial process is described by David Kairys as government by law, not people; together with the understanding that law is separate from, and superior to, politics, economics, culture and the values and preferences of judges. This ruling perception is based on particular attributes of the decision making process itself, which Kairys suggests comprises, amongst other things: the judicial recognition of their subservient role in constitutional theory; their passive role in the operation of the doctrine of precedent; their subordinate role in the determination and interpretation of legislation; and the *'quasi-scientific*, objective nature of legal analysis, and *technical* expertise of judges and lawyers' (*The Politics of Law: A Progressive Critique* (1982)). To the extent that law is generally portrayed as quasi-scientific, the operation of objective, technical and hence supposedly neutral rules, to that degree, the decisions that judges make are accepted as legitimate by the public. It is necessary, therefore, to consider the nature of reasoning in general and the extent to which judges make use of such reasoning, before considering the social location of the judges. It is only on the basis of the *non-existence* of distinct and strictly applied principles of legal reasoning that the *existence* of judicial creativity and the *possibility* of judicial bias come into consideration.

5.1.1 Law and logic

There is a long-running controversy as to the relationship of law and logic and the actual extent to which legal decisions are the outcome of, and limited by, logical processes. At times, lawyers have sought to reject what is seen as the rigid inflexibility inherent in logical reasoning in favour of flexibility and discretion. As the American Supreme Court Judge, eminent legal writer and proponent of *Legal Realism*, Oliver Wendel Holmes expressed it: 'The life of the law has not been logic, it has been experience' (*The Common Law* (1881)).

The implication of this position is that the law is no more than a mechanism for solving particular problems and that judges should operate in such a way as to ensure the best possible result, even if this means ignoring previously established legal rules.

At other times, however, the courts have appeared to base and justify their decisions on the working out of deterministic formal rules of law, categorised in such phrases as 'The Law is the Law' and 'The Law must run its course'. The suggestion behind such expressions of the *Declaratory Theory of Law* is that the judge is no more than the voice of an autonomous legal system that he, through his legal training, is able to gain access to but is in no way able to influence. If, as the declaratory theory of law maintains, judges do no more than give expression to already existing legal principles and rules, then the particular views, opinions or prejudices of the judiciary are of absolutely no consequence. If such a representation were accurate, then the logical conclusion would be that judges could be replaced by a computerised *expert system*, which could be programmed to make decisions on the basis of a strict application of general rules. It is doubtful, however, if anyone would actually accept such a suggestion. It cannot be denied that the bulk of cases are decided on the simple application of the legal rules to the particular facts of the case with little or no consideration of the legal principles. In other cases, however, the straightforward and automatic application of a legal rule might lead to the possibility of injustice.

(For those particularly interested in the possibility of developing computer models of judicial reasoning and decision making, see Allen, Aikenhead and Widdison, 'Computer simulation of judicial behaviour', http://webjcli.ncl.ac.uk/1998/issue3/allen3.html.)

Hard cases are decided on the basis of judicial reaction to the immediate facts of the case. Such a situation, however, is clearly antithetical to the declaratory theory of law.

These *hard cases* demand a consideration of the legal principles involved in order to achieve a just result. They may therefore be decided other than on the strict application of the law as it had been previously expressed. It should be pointed out that such cases are usually the province of the higher courts and of particularly active judges within those courts. The old maxim/cliché that '*hard cases make bad law*' should also be borne in mind. (The career of Lord Denning might be cited as an example of this procedure and its shortcomings. Reference should be made to material covered previously in Chapters 1 and 2 of this book for a more detailed consideration of the problems inherent in judicial law making and reform.)

5.2 Reasoning in general

In order to assess this apparent tension, if not divergence, of approach to the question whether legal reasoning is logical or not, it is necessary first of all to engage, at least minimally, in a consideration of what is to be understood by reasoning generally and logical reasoning in particular.

5.2.1 Deductive reasoning

As regards reasoning in general, there is a division between deductive and inductive reasoning. *Deductive reasoning* may be categorised as reasoning from the whole to the part; from the general to the particular. Deductive reasoning finds its simplest and yet most powerful expression in the Aristotelian syllogism. The syllogism takes the following form:

Major premise:	A = B	for example, Socrates is a man.
Minor premise:	B = C	for example, All men are mortal.
Conclusion: therefore	A = C	that is, Socrates is mortal.

The power of the syllogism lies in its certainty. If the premises are true, then the conclusion cannot be false. The reason for this is that the conclusion is actually contained in the premises and amounts to no more than a restatement of those premises.

With regard to syllogisms, however, it is important to distinguish between *validity* of form and *truth* of content. It is quite possible for a syllogism to be logically valid but false. An example of this would be:

Major premise:	A = B	for example, Socrates is a man.
Minor premise:	B = C	for example, All men are pigs.
Conclusion: therefore	A = C	that is, Socrates is a pig.

The logical form of this argument, as represented in alphabetical terms is valid, but the conclusion is not true. The reason for this is obviously that the minor premise is false: the statement that all men are pigs is simply not true.

It is also possible for a syllogism to be both true and valid yet still be based on a false premise. An example of this would be:

Major premise:	A = B	for example, Socrates is a man.
Minor premise:	B = C	for example, All men are Greek.
Conclusion: therefore	A = C	that is, Socrates is Greek.

Once again, the logical form expressed in alphabetical terms is valid, and once again the minor premise is false. On this occasion, however, the conclusion is true.

To reiterate the essential point, all that the syllogistic form of reasoning maintains is that *if the premises are true then the conclusion cannot be false*; in itself, it states nothing as to the truth of those premises or the truth of the conclusion derived from them. As will be considered below, much legal argument is about the truth of particular premises rather than the validity of the logical form being operated.

Deductive reasoning can take another form as follows:

If X then Y: If it rains, you will get wet.

X: It is raining.

Therefore, Y: You will get wet.

Again, the conclusion is contained in the premises, but equally again, if the premises are false, the conclusion may also be false.

5.2.2   Inductive reasoning

The second classic form of reasoning, *inductive reasoning*, may be described as arguing from the part to the whole; from the particular to the general. Inductive reasoning differs from deductive reasoning in two major respects:

- It reaches a conclusion which is *not* simply a restatement of what is already contained in the basic premises.

- It is *less certain* in its conclusions than deductive logic.

An example of this type of reasoning would be:

The sun has always risen in the east.

Therefore, the sun will rise in the east tomorrow.

If the premise is true, then the conclusion is probably true, but not 100% necessarily so because the conclusion is not contained in the premise, but is a projection from it. On the basis of past experience, we can reasonably expect the sun to rise in the east tomorrow, but there is the possibility, no matter how remote it might be, that something might happen to the sun, or indeed the earth, to prevent its appearance tomorrow. The point is that we cannot predict with 100% accuracy what will happen in the future just because it happened in the past. Because the inductive argument goes beyond the content of its premises, it provides the power to predict events, but it gives predictive power at the expense of certainty in its conclusion.

An alternative example of this type of inductive reasoning would be:

John is lying dead with a bullet in his head.

Jane is standing over him with a smoking gun in her hand.

Therefore, it can be concluded that Jane shot John.

Now, the conclusion may be reasonable under the circumstances, but there are other possible explanations for the scene. Jane may have simply picked up the gun after someone else had shot John. We cannot actually tell who killed John, but we may reasonably suspect Jane of the crime and she would be the first person to be questioned to confirm either her guilt or innocence. The investigation of this event would use a form of reasoning equivalent to scientific reasoning. From available data, a hypothesis would be formed; in this case, that Jane killed John. Investigations would then be undertaken to test the validity of the hypothesis. Depending on the outcome of the investigation, the original hypothesis would be either accepted, rejected or refined.

5.2.3　Reasoning by analogy

A third type of reasoning is *reasoning by example or analogy*. If deductive reasoning involves reasoning from the whole to the part, and inductive reasoning involves reasoning from the part to the whole, then reasoning by analogy involves reasoning from part to part.

An example of this type of reasoning would be:

Wood floats on water.

Plastic is like wood.

Therefore, plastic floats on water.

Or similarly:

Wood floats on water.

Stone is like wood.

Therefore, stone floats on water.

It can be seen that the truth of the conclusion depends completely on the accuracy of the analogy. The connection between the two objects that are being compared depends on weighing up and assessing their similarities and their differences. Only some characteristics are similar, and the question is whether those are more important than the differences between the two objects. If the analogy is valid, then the conclusion may very well be equally valid, although not necessarily correct, but, if it is not valid, then the conclusion will certainly be wrong, as the above examples demonstrate.

5.3　Judicial reasoning

It is now appropriate to determine whether, or to what extent, judges use logical reasoning in reaching their decisions in particular cases and to determine which forms, if any, they make use of.

5.3.1　The syllogism in law

Some statutory provisions and also some common law rules can be expressed in the form of a syllogism. For example, the offence of theft may be reduced into such a formulation:

If A dishonestly appropriates B's property with the intention of permanently depriving B of it, *then* A is guilty of theft.

A has done this.

Therefore, A is guilty of theft.

This, however, represents an over-simplification of the structure of statute but, more importantly, the effect of concentrating on the logical form of the offence tends to marginalise the key issues in relation to its actual application. As has been stated previously, the great majority of cases are decided on the *truth* of the premises rather than the formal *validity* of the argument used. In other words, argument will concentrate primarily on whether A actually did the act or not and, secondly, on whether A appropriated the property either 'dishonestly' or 'with the intention of permanently depriving' B of it. Those are questions of fact, not logic.

5.3.2   The logical form of precedent

The operation of the rules of precedent appears, at first sight, to involve a similar operation of deductive logic to that applied in statute law: the judge merely applies the legal principle established in the precedent to the facts in hand to determine the outcome of the case. Thus:

> *Precedent*: in case X involving particular circumstances, legal principle Y was applied leading to conclusion Z.

> *Instant case*: in case W similar circumstances to those in X have occurred.

> *Therefore*: principle Y must be applied to reach a conclusion similar to Z.

A closer consideration of the actual procedure involved in precedent, however, will reveal that it is not totally accurate to categorise precedent as a form of deductive reasoning.

In looking for a precedent on which to base a decision, judges are faced with a large number of cases from which to select. It is extremely unlikely that judges will find an authority which corresponds precisely to the facts of the case before them. What they have to do is to find an analogous case and use its reasoning to decide the case before them. This use of analogy to decide cases is prone to the same shortcomings as were revealed in the previous consideration of reasoning from analogy in general. The major difficulty is the need to ensure the validity of the analogy made, if the conclusion drawn is to be valid. There is, no doubt, considerable merit in the wish for similar cases to be treated similarly, but given the lack of precision that is inherent in the process of reasoning by analogy, it is not altogether certain that such a wish will be met.

A further reason why the operation of precedent cannot simply be considered as an example of deductive reasoning relates to the process through which the precedent is actually determined once an analogous case has been selected. The binding element in any precedent is the *ratio decidendi* of the decision. In delivering his decision, the judge does not separate the *ratio* of the case from other *obiter* comments. As has been considered previously, the *ratio* is a legal abstraction from the concrete facts of the case in which it appears, and in practice, it is for judges in subsequent cases to determine the *ratio* of any authority. The determination of the *ratio* and thus the precedent in a previous case may be seen as a process of *inductive reasoning*, in that the judge in the present case derives the *general* principle of the *ratio* from the *particular* facts of the previous case. This move from the particular to the general is by its nature inductive. The point to be remembered here is that, as was considered in relation to reasoning in general, the use of inductive reasoning cannot claim the certainty inherent in the use of deductive reasoning. The introduction of this increased element of uncertainty is inescapable and unconscious, but it is also appropriate to note that the determination of precedent by later courts gives the later judges scope to *consciously* manipulate precedents. This is achieved by the later judges formulating the *ratio* of a previous case in the light of their opinion as to what it *should* have been, rather than what it might actually have been. In other words, they have the scope to substitute their version of the *ratio*, even if it contradicts what the original judge thought the *ratio* was.

Thus, the apparent deductive certainty of the use of precedent is revealed to be based on the much less certain use of inductive reasoning and reasoning by analogy, with even the possibility of personal views of the judges playing some part in deciding cases. This latter factor introduces the possibility that judges do not in fact use any form of logical reasoning to decide their cases, but simply deliver decisions on the basis of an intuitive response to the facts of the case and the situation of the parties involved. The suggestion has been made that judges decide the outcome of the case first of all and only then seek some *post hoc* legal justification for their decision; and given the huge number of precedents from which they are able to choose, they have no great difficulty in finding such support as they require. The process of logical reasoning can be compared to the links in a chain, one following the other, but a more fitting metaphor for judicial reasoning would be to compare it with the legs of a chair: forced into place to support the weight of a conclusion reached *a priori*. Some critics have even gone so far as to deny the existence of legal reasoning altogether as a method of determining decisions, and have suggested that references to such are no more than a means of justifying the social and political decisions that judges are called upon to make.

In conclusion, however, it is not suggested that legal reasoning does not employ the use of logic, but neither can it be asserted that it is only a matter of logic. Perhaps the only conclusion that can be reached is that legal reasoning as exercised by the judiciary is an amalgam; part deductive, part inductive, part reasoning by analogy, with an added mixture of personal intuition, not to say personal prejudice.

5.4   Statutory interpretation

A particular aspect of legal reasoning, and one which also raises questions as to the political persuasion of judges and the scope they have to exercise that persuasion in their decisions, relates specifically to the manner in which the judges interpret statutes when they are called upon to do so.

5.4.1 Problems in interpreting legislation

The accepted view is that the constitutional role of the judiciary is simply to *apply* the law. The function of creating law is the prerogative of Parliament. As has already been seen, such a view is simplistic to the extent that it ignores the potential for judicial creativity in relation to the operation of the common law and the doctrine of judicial precedent. Equally, however, it ignores the extent to which the judiciary have a measure of discretion and creative power in the manner in which they interpret the legislation that comes before them.

Chapter 2 has already considered the general difficulties involved in drafting legislation from the point of view of the person carrying out the drafting; but equally, it has to be recognised that determining the actual meaning of legislation presents judges with a practical difficulty. In order to *apply* legislation, judges must ascertain the meaning of the legislation, and in order to ascertain the meaning, they are faced with the difficulty of interpreting the legislation.

Before considering the way in which judges interpret legislation, it is pertinent to emphasise that, in spite of the best endeavours of those who draft legislation to be precise in communicating the meaning of what they produce, the process of interpretation is inescapable and arises from the nature of language itself. Legislation can be seen as a form of linguistic communication. It represents and passes on to the judiciary what Parliament has determined the law should be in relation to a particular situation. Legislation, therefore, shares the general problem of uncertainty inherent in any mode of communication. One of the essential attributes of language is its fluidity; the fact that words can have more than one meaning and that the meaning of a word can change depending on its context. In such circumstances, it is immediately apparent that understanding is an active process. Faced with ambiguity, the recipient of information has to decide which of various meanings to assign to specific words, depending upon the context in which they are used.

Legislation gives rise to additional problems in terms of communication. One of the essential requirements of legislation is generality of application, the need for it to be written in such a way as to ensure that it can be effectively applied in various circumstances, without the need to detail those situations individually. This requirement, however, gives rise to particular problems of interpretation, for, as has been pointed out in Chapter 2, the need for generality can only really be achieved at the expense of clarity and precision of language. A further possibility, that is not as uncommon as it should be is that the legislation under consideration is obscure, ambiguous, or indeed meaningless, or fails to achieve the end at which it is aimed simply through being badly drafted. The task facing the judge in such circumstances is to provide the legislation with some effective meaning.

Legislation therefore involves an inescapable measure of uncertainty that can only be made certain through judicial interpretation. To the extent, however, that the interpretation of legislative provisions is an active process, it is equally a creative process, and inevitably it involves the judiciary in creating law through determining the meaning and effect to be given to any particular piece of legislation. There is a further possibility that has to be considered: that judges might actually abuse their role as necessary interpreters of legislation in such a way as to insinuate their own particular personal views and prejudices into their interpretations, and in so doing misapply the legislation and subvert the wishes of the legislature.

5.4.2 Approaches to statutory interpretation

Having considered the problems of interpreting language generally and the difficulties in interpreting legislation in particular, it is appropriate to consider in detail the methods and mechanisms which judges bring to bear on legislation in order to determine its meaning. There are, essentially, two contrasting views as to how judges should go about determining the meaning of a statute – the restrictive, literal approach and the more permissive, purposive approach:

- *The literal approach*

  The literal approach is dominant in the English legal system, although it is not without critics, and devices do exist for circumventing it when it is seen as too restrictive. This view of judicial interpretation holds that the judge should look primarily to the words of the legislation in order to construe its meaning and, except in the very limited circumstances considered below, should not look outside of, or behind, the legislation in an attempt to find its meaning.

- *The purposive approach*

  The purposive approach rejects the limitation of the judges' search for meaning to a literal construction of the words of legislation itself. It suggests that the interpretative role of the judge should include, where necessary, the power to look beyond the words of statute in pursuit of the reason for its enactment, and that meaning should be construed in the light of that purpose and so as to give it effect. This purposive approach is typical of civil law systems. In these jurisdictions, legislation tends to set out general principles and leaves the fine details to be filled in later by the judges who are expected to make decisions in the furtherance of those general principles.

European Community (EC) legislation tends to be drafted in the continental manner. Its detailed effect, therefore, can only be determined on the basis of a purposive approach to its interpretation. This requirement, however, runs counter to the literal approach that is the dominant approach in the English system. The need to interpret such legislation, however, has forced a change in that approach in relation to Community legislation and even with respect to domestic legislation designed to implement Community legislation. Thus, in *Pickstone v Freemans plc* (1988), the House of Lords held that it was permissible, and indeed necessary, for the court to read words into inadequate domestic legislation in order to give effect to Community law in relation to provisions relating to equal pay for work of equal value. (For a similar approach, see also the House of Lords' decision in *Litster v Forth Dry Dock* (1989) and the decision in *Three Rivers DC v Bank of England (No 2)* (1996), considered below at 5.4.5.)

The advent of purposive interpretation for Community law has not dislodged the primacy of literal interpretation for non-Community domestic legislation. It should be pointed out, however, that the traditional restrictive approach has not gone unchallenged, and it should not be surprising to find that Lord Denning was involved in the attack. As in other areas, his unorthodox approach was rejected by the House of Lords (see *Nothman v London Borough of Barnet* (1988)). In advocating the adoption of a purposive approach, Lord Denning was in fact merely expressing the earlier view of the Law Commission which, as early as 1969, had recommended such a change without success.

It is now clearly established that judges can only adopt the purposive approach where they can discover a clear statement of the purpose of the legislation expressed either in the statute itself, or in extrinsic material to which they may legitimately refer for guidance as to meaning (*Shah v Barnet LBC* (1983)). The effect of *Pepper v Hart* (1993), permitting access to *Hansard*, will be considered at 5.4.5, below, but for the moment, it is still the case that the judges remain subject to the established rules of interpretation of which there are three primary rules of statutory interpretation, together with a variety of other secondary aids to construction.

5.4.3 Rules of interpretation

What follows in this and the following two sections should be read within the context of the Human Right Act (HRA) 1998, which requires all legislation to be construed in such a way as, if at all possible, to bring it within the ambit of the European Convention on Human Rights (ECHR). The effect of this requirement is to provide the judiciary with powers of interpretation much wider than those afforded to them by the more traditional rules of interpretation, as can be seen from *R v A* (2001), considered above at 1.7.1.3. However, to quote Lord Steyn further in this particular context:

> ... the interpretative obligation under section 3 of the 1998 Act is a strong one. It applies even if there is no ambiguity in the language in the sense of the language being capable of two different meanings ... [s]ection 3 places a duty on the court to strive to find a possible interpretation compatible with Convention rights. Under ordinary methods of interpretation a court may depart from the language of the statute to avoid absurd consequences: section 3 goes much further. Undoubtedly, a court must always look for a contextual and

purposive interpretation: section 3 is more radical in its effect ... In accordance with the will of Parliament as reflected in section 3 it will sometimes be necessary to adopt an interpretation which linguistically may appear strained. The techniques to be used will not only involve the reading down of express language in a statute but also the implication of provisions. A declaration of incompatibility is a measure of last resort. It must be avoided unless it is plainly impossible to do so.

The three rules of statutory interpretation are as follows:

* *The literal rule*

  Under this rule, the judge is required to consider what the legislation actually says rather than considering what it might mean. In order to achieve this end, the judge should give words in legislation their literal meaning – that is, their plain, ordinary, everyday meaning – even if the effect of this is to produce what might be considered an otherwise unjust or undesirable outcome. The literal rule appears at first sight to be the least problematic method of interpreting legislation. Under this rule, the courts most obviously appear to be recognising their limitations by following the wishes of Parliament as expressed in the words of the legislation under consideration. When, however, the difficulties of assigning a fixed and unchallengeable meaning to any word is recalled, the use of the literal rule becomes less uncontroversial. A consideration of the cases reveals examples where the literal rule has been used as a justification for what otherwise might appear as partial judgments on the part of the court concerned in the case.

  Inland Revenue Commissioners v Hinchy (1960) concerned s 25(3) of the Income Tax Act 1952, which stated that any taxpayer who did not complete their tax return was subject to a fixed penalty of £20 plus *treble the tax which he ought to be charged under the Act*. The question that had to be decided was whether the additional element of the penalty should be based on the total amount that should have been paid, or merely the unpaid portion of that total. The House of Lords adopted a literal interpretation of the statute and held that any taxpayer in default should have to pay triple their original tax bill.

  In *Fisher v Bell* (1961), the court, in line with general contract principles, decided that the placing of an article in a window did not amount to offering but was merely an invitation to treat, and thus the shopkeeper could not be charged with 'offering the goods for sale'. In this case, the court chose to follow the contract law literal interpretation of the meaning of offer in the Act in question, and declined to consider the usual non-legal literal interpretation of the word offer. (The executive's attitude to the courts' legal-literal interpretation in *Fisher v Bell*, and the related case of *Partridge v Crittenden* (1968), can be surmised from the fact that later legislation, such as the Trade Descriptions Act 1968, has effectively legislated that invitations to treat are to be treated in the same way as offers for sale.)

A further problem with regard to the literal rule, relating to the difficulty judges face in determining the literal meaning of even the commonest of terms, can be seen in *R v Maginnis* (1987). The defendant had been charged under the Misuse of Drugs Act 1971, with having drugs in his possession and *with intent to supply them*. He claimed that, as he had intended to return the drugs to a friend who had left them in his car, he could not be guilty of *supplying* as charged. In this case, the judges, from first instance, through the Court of Appeal to the House of Lords, disagreed as to the literal meaning of the common word 'supply'. Even in the House of Lords, Lord Goff, in his dissenting judgment, was able to cite a dictionary definition to support his interpretation of the word. It is tempting to suggest that the majority of judges in the House of Lords operated in a totally disingenuous way by justifying their decision on the literal interpretation of the law whilst, at the same time, fixing on a non-literal meaning for the word under consideration. In actual fact, in *R v Maginnis*, each of the meanings for 'supply' proposed by the various judges could be supported by dictionary entries. That fact, however, only highlights the essential weakness of the literal rule, which is that it wrongly assumes that there is such a thing as a single, uncontentious, literal understanding of words. Whilst *R v Maginnis* concerned the meaning of 'supply', *Attorney General's Reference (No 1 of 1988)* (1989) concerned the meaning of 'obtained' in s 1(3) of the Company Securities (Insider Dealing) Act 1985, since replaced by the Criminal Justice Act 1993, and led to similar disagreement as to the precise meaning of an everyday word. *Bromley LBC v GLC* (1983) may be cited as an instance where the courts arguably took a covert politic decision under the guise of applying the literal meaning of a particular word in a piece of legislation.

- *The golden rule*

This rule is generally considered to be an extension of the literal rule. In its general expression, it is applied in circumstances where the application of the literal rule is likely to result in what appears to the court to be an obviously absurd result. The golden rule was first stated by Lord Wensleydale in *Grey v Pearson* (1857), but its operation is better defined by the words of Lord Blackburn in *River Wear Commissioners v Adamson* (1877) as follows:

> [W]e are to take the whole statute and construe it all together, giving the words their ordinary signification, unless when so applied they produce an inconsistency, or an absurdity or inconvenience so great as to convince the Court that the intention could not have been to use them in their ordinary signification, and to justify the Court in putting them in some other signification, which, though less proper, is one which the Court thinks the words will bear.

It should be emphasised, however, that the court is not at liberty to use the golden rule to ignore, or replace, legislative provisions simply on the basis that it does not agree with them; it must find genuine difficulties before it declines to use the literal rule in favour of the golden one. How one determines or defines genuine difficulty is of course a matter of discretion and, therefore, dispute. As Lord Blackburn's definition makes clear, the use of the rule actually involves the judges in finding what they consider the statute should have said or provided, rather than what it actually did state or provide. As will be seen below, the justification for this judicial activity is based on that extremely wide, amorphous, not to say spurious, legal concept: public policy. However, such a justification immediately raises the questions of the judges' understanding of, and right to determine, public policy, which will be considered later in the next section of this chapter.

It is sometimes stated that there are two versions of the golden rule:

(a) *The narrow meaning*

This is used where there are two apparently contradictory meanings to a particular word used in a legislative provision or the provision is simply ambiguous in its effect. In such a situation, the golden rule operates to ensure that preference is given to the meaning that does not result in the provision being an absurdity. An example of the application of the golden rule in this narrow sense is *Adler v George* (1964). The defendant had been charged, under the Official Secrets Act 1920, with obstruction in the vicinity of a prohibited area, whereas she had actually carried out the obstruction inside the area. The court preferred not to restrict itself to the literal wording of the Act and found the defendant guilty as charged.

(b) *The wider meaning*

This version of the golden rule is resorted to where, although there is only one possible meaning to a provision, the court is of the opinion that to adopt such a literal interpretation will result in Lord Blackburn's 'inconsistency, absurdity or inconvenience'. The classic example of this approach is to be found in *Re Sigsworth* (1935), in which the court introduced common law rules into legislative provisions, which were silent on the matter, to prevent the estate of a murderer from benefiting from the property of the party he had murdered. Just as it was contrary to public policy to allow a murderer to benefit directly from the proceeds of his offence, so it would equally be contrary to public policy to allow the estate of a murderer to benefit from his offence. However, the public policy issue becomes less certain when one realises that there was actually no question of the murderer benefiting directly in this case, as he had committed suicide. In that light, the decision can be seen as punishing those who would have benefited on his death for an offence that they had nothing to do with – effectively cutting them out from what had been a legitimate expectation before the murder.

Another example of this approach is found in *R v National Insurance Commissioner ex p Connor* (1981), in which the court held, in spite of silence in the actual legislation, that Connor was not entitled to a widow's pension on the grounds that she had been the actual cause of her widowed status by killing her husband. Once again, when taken at face value, the decision in *Connor* appears perfectly justifiable on the grounds of public policy as the court stated, but appears less so when it is pointed out that Connor was actually found guilty of manslaughter and sentenced merely to a two year period of probation.

Subsequent to the *Connor* case, the Forfeiture Act 1982 was passed, giving courts the discretionary power to ignore the rule of public policy that precludes a person who has unlawfully killed another from acquiring a benefit as a consequence of the killing. The Act does not apply in relation to murder, but nonetheless it does give the courts discretion to mitigate the effects of the rule applied in *Connor* where they are of the opinion that the circumstances of the case merit it. Thus, in *Dunbar v Plant* (1997), the Court of Appeal held that the forfeiture rule applied to the survivor of a suicide pact who had abetted the death of her partner. The court, however, applied the Forfeiture Act to permit her to benefit from his share in their jointly owned house and to claim against his life insurance policy.

In deciding whether or not to make use of the Forfeiture Act, the courts will look at the behaviour of both the killer and the person killed, so it might be expected that it would be used in relation to cases where the killing has been as a result of long term abuse or some other mitigating circumstances. However, as the introduction of the public policy rule was itself a product of the common law, so the courts have felt free to distinguish and restrict the strict application of the rule in *Connor* (see, for example, *Re K (Deceased)* (1985)).

- *The mischief rule*

At one level, the mischief rule is clearly the most flexible rule of interpretation, but in its traditional expression it is limited by being restricted to using previous common law rules in order to decide the operation of contemporary legislation. It is also, at least somewhat, paradoxical that this most venerable rule, originally set out in *Heydon's Case* (1584), is also the one which most obviously reveals the socio-political nature of judicial decisions.

In *Heydon's Case*, it was stated that in making use of the mischief rule, the court should consider the following four things:

(a) What was the common law before the passing of the statute?

(b) What was the mischief in the law which the common law did not adequately deal with?

(c) What remedy for that mischief had Parliament intended to provide?

(d) What was the reason for Parliament adopting that remedy?

It has to be remembered that, when *Heydon's Case* was decided, it was the practice to cite in the preamble of legislation the purpose for its enactment, including the mischief at which it was aimed. (An example where the preamble made more sense than the actual body of the legislation is the infamous Bubble Act of 1720.) Judges in this earlier time did not, therefore, have to go beyond the legislative provision itself to implement the mischief rule. With the disappearance of such explanatory preambles, the question arises as to the extent to which judges can make use of the rule in *Heydon's Case* to justify their examination of the policy issues that underlie particular legislative provisions. Contemporary practice is to go beyond the actual body of the legislation. This, however, raises the question as to what courts can legitimately consider in their endeavour to determine the purpose and meaning of legislation, which will be considered separately below.

The example usually cited of the use of the mischief rule is *Corkery v Carpenter* (1950), in which a man was found guilty of being drunk in charge of a 'carriage', although he was in fact only in charge of a bicycle. A much more controversial application of the rule is to be found in *Royal College of Nursing v DHSS* (1981), where the courts had to decide whether the medical induction of premature labour to effect abortion, under the supervision of nursing staff, was lawful. In this particularly sensitive area, whether one agrees with the ultimate majority decision of the House of Lords in favour of the legality of the procedure or not probably depends on one's view of abortion. This fact simply serves to highlight the socio-political nature of the question that was finally determined by the House of Lords under the guise of merely determining the legal meaning of a piece of legislation.

5.4.4 Legal reasoning and the regulation of abortion: a case study

A related issue was raised in *R (Smeaton) v Secretary of State for Health* (2002), in which the applicant sought a declaration that the unsupervised use of the 'morning after' contraceptive pill was unlawful because its purpose was 'to procure a miscarriage', contrary to ss 58 and 59 of the Offences Against the Person Act 1861. On this occasion, the issue was decided by reference to the literal rule, although in a manner which highlights its inherent uncertainty. In refusing to grant the declaration, the judge held that the pill acted only to prevent the implantation of a fertilised egg, and that such an action did not amount to a miscarriage as the word is generally used nowadays. As

Parliament in 1861 had not chosen to define the word, it should be understood according to its accepted modern meaning.

When the Abortion Act 1967 had been introduced, the termination procedure had been surgical in nature, but in the 1970s, the surgical procedure was replaced by the chemical induction of labour. This latter process was twofold in nature: first, a catheter was surgically inserted into the woman and later, a chemical, prostaglandin, was introduced through it. The prostaglandin induced premature labour, which occurred some time, certainly a matter of hours, later. In practice, the first part of the procedure was carried out by doctors. The second part, the introduction of the prostaglandin, was carried out by nursing staff.

Section 1(1) of the Abortion Act 1967 provided that: '... a person shall not be guilty of an offence under the law relating to abortion when a pregnancy is terminated by a registered medical practitioner.'

In a letter dated 21 February 1980, sent to regional and area medical officers and regional, area and district nursing officers, the Department of Health and Social Security purported to explain the law relating to abortion in connection with the termination of pregnancy by medical induction. The Department's advice was that termination using the prostaglandin method could properly be said to be termination by a registered medical practitioner, provided that it was decided on and initiated by him (*sic*) and provided he remained throughout responsible for its overall conduct and control. This was the case even if the acts needed to bring the termination to its conclusion were done by staff acting on the specific instructions of the registered medical practitioner, but not necessarily in his presence. Consequently, the Department stated that the first stage of the procedure, the insertion of an extra-amniotic catheter, must be carried out by a registered medical practitioner, but that the second stage, connection of labour inducing drugs to the catheter, could be carried out by an appropriately skilled nurse or midwife acting in accordance with precise instructions given by the registered medical practitioner.

The Royal College of Nursing, seeking to clarify the legal position as regards its members, sought a declaration that the circular was wrong in law.

At first instance, Woolf J, as he was then, refused the application and granted the Department a declaration that their advice did not involve the performance of any unlawful acts by members of the College. On appeal, the Court of Appeal unanimously reversed his decision, but on further appeal, the House of Lords, Lord Wilberforce and Lord Edmund-Davies dissenting, re-instated the decision of Woolf J. In reaching their various decisions, the judges made use of different approaches to statutory interpretation, some preferring the literal rule, whilst others preferred to make use of the mischief rule. In the first camp can be placed the three Court of Appeal judges, who saw no reason for reading s 1(1) in any other way than in the limited manner that would preclude the current practice. As Lord Denning MR expressed it:

> Stress was laid by the Solicitor-General on the effect of this ruling. The process of medical induction can take from 18 to 30 hours. No doctor can be expected to be present all that time. He must leave it to the nurses or not use the method at all. If he is not allowed to leave it to the nurses, the result will be either that there will be fewer abortions or that the doctor will have to use the surgical method *with its extra hazards*. This may be so. But I do not think this warrants us departing from the statute [emphasis added].

There is a double irony in this particular judgment – Lord Denning, the great iconoclast and pusher forward of the legal boundaries, appears as a proponent of the essentially conservative literal rule. However, a reading of the rhetorical nature of his judgment also reveals how his reliance on the literal rule allows him to give support to his own personal, and certainly unliberal, views on abortion. Of equal, if not greater, concern is the almost malicious way in which he recognises, only to dismiss, the additional safety to women in the non-surgical procedure (see emphasis added in quotation).

In the House of Lords, the preferred approach, although only by the narrow majority of 3:2, was to adopt the mischief rule and to examine the purpose of the legislation and to read its provisions in line with that purpose. The minority followed the Court of Appeal and preferred to use the literal rule.

Speaking of the Act, Lord Diplock stated:

> … its purpose in my view becomes clear if one starts by considering what was the state of the law relating to abortion before the passing of the Act, what was the mischief that required amendment, and in what respect was the existing law unclear … My Lords, the wording and structure of the section are far from elegant, but the policy of the Act, it seems to me, is clear. There are two aspects to it: the first is to broaden the grounds upon which abortions may be lawfully obtained; the second is to ensure that the abortion is carried out with all proper skill and in hygienic conditions …

As has been stated previously, one's reaction to this case will almost certainly be determined by one's approach to abortion. For those who disagree with the extension of termination, the case may represent a black day and the Court of Appeal, especially Lord Denning MR, and the minority in the House of Lords can be seen as attempting to hold back the tide of liberalism. For those who approve of the decision, the House of Lords will be seen as having got it right and deserving of congratulation. But surely this begs the much wider question as to whether such overtly political questions should be in the hands of the courts.

From one point of view, the mischief rule serves a very positive purpose by providing courts with the authority to go behind the actual wording of statutes in order to consider the problems that those statutes are aimed at remedying. Alternatively, it is possible to see the mischief rule as justifying the courts' interference in the areas of public policy that are, strictly speaking, beyond the realm of their powers and competence. It is equally relevant to point out that in cases such as *Royal College of Nursing v DHSS*, such decisions are forced on the courts whether they like it or not. It is only to be hoped that they make proper and socially acceptable decisions, but such questions remain to be considered below.

It is sometimes suggested that the rules of interpretation form a hierarchical order. On that basis, the first rule that should be applied is the literal rule, and that rule only cedes to the golden rule in particular circumstances where ambiguity arises from the application of the literal rule. The third rule, the mischief rule, it is suggested, is only brought into use where there is a perceived failure of the other two rules to deliver an appropriate result. On consideration, however, it becomes obvious that no such hierarchy exists. The literal rule is supposed to be used unless it leads to a manifest absurdity, in which case it will give way to the golden rule. The immediate question this supposition gives rise to is what is to be considered as an absurdity in any particular case, other than the view of the judge deciding the case. The three rules are contradictory, at least to a degree, and there is no way in which the outsider can determine in advance which of them the courts will make use of to decide the meaning of a particular statute. Perhaps it would be better if the 1969 recommendation of the Law Commission was given effect and judges were expressly permitted to adopt a purposive approach to statutory interpretation (Law Comm 21). At least then judicial creativity in this regard would be out in the open.

5.4.5 Aids to construction

In addition to the three main rules of interpretation, there are a number of secondary aids to construction. These can be categorised as either intrinsic or extrinsic in nature:

- *Intrinsic assistance*

  Intrinsic assistance is derived from the statute which is the object of interpretation; the judge uses the full statute to understand the meaning of a particular part of it.

  The *title*, either long or short, of the Act under consideration may be referred to for guidance (*Royal College of Nursing v DHSS* (1981)).

  It should be noted, however, that a general intention derived from the title cannot overrule a clear statement to the contrary in the text of the Act.

  It was a feature of older statutes that they contained a *preamble*, which was a statement, preceding the actual provisions of the Act, setting out its purposes in some detail and to which reference could be made for purposes of interpretation. Again, however, any general intention derived from the preamble could not stand in the face of express provision to the contrary within the Act.

  Whereas preambles preceded the main body of an Act, schedules appear as additions at the end of the main body of the legislation. They are, however, an essential part of the Act and may be referred to in order to make sense of the main text.

Some statutes contain section headings and yet others contain marginal notes relating to particular sections. The extent to which either of these may be used is uncertain, although *DPP v Schildkamp* (1969) does provide authority for the use of the former as an aid to interpretation.

Finally, in regard to intrinsic aids to interpretation, it is now recognised that punctuation has an effect on the meaning of words and can be taken into account in determining the meaning of a provision.

- *Extrinsic assistance*

Extrinsic assistance, that is, reference to sources outside of the Act itself, may on occasion be resorted to in determining the meaning of legislation; but which sources? Some external sources are unproblematic. For example, judges have always been entitled to refer to *dictionaries* in order to find the meaning of non-legal words. They also have been able to look into *textbooks* for guidance in relation to particular points of law, and in using the mischief rule, they have been able to refer to *earlier statutes* to determine the precise mischief at which the statute they are trying to construe is aimed. The Interpretation Act 1978 is also available for consultation with regard to particular difficulties. Unfortunately, its title is somewhat misleading, in that it does not give general instructions for interpreting legislation, but simply defines particular terms that are found in various statutes.

Other extrinsic sources, however, are more controversial. In Chapter 2, the various processes involved in the production of legislation were considered. As was seen, there are many distinct stages in the preparation of legislation. Statutes may arise as a result of reports submitted by a variety of commissions. In addition, the preparation of the precise structure of legislation is subject to consideration in working papers, known as *travaux préparatoires*. Nor should it be forgotten that in its progress through Parliament, a Bill is the object of discussion and debate, both on the floor of the Houses of Parliament and in committee. Verbatim accounts of debates are recorded and published in *Hansard*.

Each of these procedures provides a potential source from which a judge might discover the specific purpose of a piece of legislation or the real meaning of any provision within it. The question is, to which of these sources are the courts entitled to have access?

Historically, English courts have adopted a restrictive approach to what they are entitled to take into consideration. This restrictive approach has been gradually relaxed, however, to the extent that judges are allowed to use extrinsic sources to determine the mischief at which particular legislation is aimed. Thus, they have been entitled to look at Law Commission reports, Royal Commission reports and the reports of other official commissions. Until fairly recently, however, *Hansard* literally remained a closed book to the courts, but in the landmark decision in *Pepper v Hart* (1993), the House of Lords decided to overturn the previous rule. The issue in the case was the tax liability owed by teachers at Malvern College, a fee-paying school. Employees were entitled to have their sons educated at the school whilst paying only 20% of the usual fees. The question was as to the precise level at which this benefit in kind was to be taxed. In a majority decision, it was held that where the precise meaning of legislation was uncertain or ambiguous or where the literal meaning of an Act would lead to a manifest absurdity, the courts could refer to *Hansard*'s reports of parliamentary debates and proceedings as an aid to construing the meaning of the legislation.

The operation of the principle in *Pepper v Hart* was extended in *Three Rivers DC v Bank of England (No 2)* (1996) to cover situations where the legislation under question was not in itself ambiguous but might be ineffective in its intention to give effect to some particular EC directive. Applying the wider purposive powers of interpretation open to it in such circumstances (see 5.4.2), the court held that it was permissible to refer to *Hansard* in order to determine the actual purpose of the statute.

The *Pepper v Hart* principle only applies to statements made by ministers at the time of the passage of legislation, and the courts have declined to extend it to cover situations where ministers subsequently make some statement as to what they consider the effect of a particular Act to be (*Melluish (Inspector of Taxes) v BMI (No 3) Ltd* (1995)).

It is essential to bear in mind that *Pepper v Hart* was not intended to introduce a general purposive approach to the interpretation of non-European Community legislation. Recourse to *Hansard* is to be made only in the context of the mischief rule, as a further method of finding out the mischief at which the particular legislation is aimed.

An additional restriction is that only statements made by a government minister, or some other sponsor, responsible for the legislation will be considered as authoritative in setting out the mischief.

5.4.6 Presumptions

In addition to the rules of interpretation, the courts may also make use of certain presumptions. As with all presumptions, they are rebuttable. The presumptions operate:

- *Against the alteration of the common law.* Parliament is sovereign and can alter the common law whenever it decides to do so. In order to do this, however, Parliament must expressly enact legislation to that end. If there is no express intention to that effect, it is assumed that statute does not make any fundamental change to the common law. With regard to particular provisions, if there are alternative interpretations, one of which will maintain the existing common law situation, then that interpretation will be preferred. In *R (Rottman) v Commissioner of Police* (2002), the claimant was arrested on a warrant issued under the Extradition Act 1989, and the police searched his house and seized various items which they believed to be evidence. The House of Lords affirmed the legality of this search and seizure. The common law power to search an arrested person's premises was not extinguished in relation to extradition offences by the Police and Criminal Evidence Act (PACE) 1984. According to Lord Hutton, whilst that Act clearly replaced the pre-existing common law in relation to domestic offences, it made no reference to extradition offences and so must be supposed to have left the common law intact in relation to them.

- *That a mental element is required for criminal offences.* It is a general requirement of the criminal law that, in order for a person to be convicted of a crime, he is proved not only to have committed the relevant act or conduct (or sometimes to have failed to do something), but also to have done this with a blameworthy state of mind. This state of mind is known by the Latin tag *mens rea* (the mental element).

The necessary mental element can include: (a) intention; (b) gross negligence; (c) recklessness; (d) inadvertence; or (e) simple knowledge of a state of affairs. Because the consequences of being convicted of a criminal offence are very serious and include a possible custodial sentence and a life-ruining conviction, there was always the assumption in the common law (judge made law) that criminal law offences require some form of *mens rea* before a person can be convicted.

Today, more criminal law offences have been created through parliamentary legislation than those which existed by virtue of the common law. When interpreting statutes, the court will presume that Parliament intended that no criminal liability should arise without a requirement that *mens rea* be proven.

In some areas of social concern, however, like traffic accidents or underage drinking, Parliament has seen fit to pass what are known as 'strict liability' offences. These are criminal offences for which it is *not* necessary for the prosecution to prove that the defendant had a particular attitude towards the crime in question, for example, that he intended to commit it, but merely that the relevant conduct took place. The thinking behind such criminalisation of conduct is that because defendants will not be able to escape liability by pleading that they did not intend to produce a particular result or that they did not have relevant knowledge, everyone will be encouraged to be that much more vigilant that they do not offend that particular law.

Sometimes, someone comes before the criminal law courts accused of an offence created by statute, and the courts must decide whether the words of the statute imply that it is necessary for the prosecution to prove the defendant had a mental element. The general rule here is that Parliament will be presumed not to have wanted to create a strict liability criminal offence unless it has been explicit about wanting to do so. There are, though, a number of factors to be taken into account in answering this question, including the nature of the language used, the subject matter of the activity and the overall framework of the Act. In *Sweet v Parsley* (1970), the accused had a house just outside of Oxford, which she rented out and visited only occasionally. She was convicted of being concerned in the management of premises used for the purpose of smoking cannabis, contrary to s 5(b) of the Dangerous Drugs Act 1965; however, she had had no knowledge that the house was being used in this way. The House of Lords held that her conviction should be quashed, since it had to be proved that it was the accused's 'purpose' that the premises were used for smoking cannabis (that is, that she intended the premises to be so used). In the case, Lord Reid said that:

> ... whenever a section is silent as to *mens rea* there is a presumption that ... we must read in words appropriate to require *mens rea*.

In *R v Hussain* (1981), the Court of Appeal decided that possessing a firearm without a certificate is, under s 1 of the Firearms Act 1968, an offence of strict liability, so that the prosecution is not required to prove that the accused knew the article he had was a firearm. Similarly, the Court of Appeal decided in *R v Bradish* (1990) that, under s 5(1) of the Firearms Act 1968, the offence of being in possession of a prohibited weapon (a spray canister containing CS gas) is a crime of strict liability. It was therefore not a defence for the accused to argue that because the gas was concealed within the canister, he did not know, and could not reasonably have been expected to know, that the article in his possession was a prohibited weapon. The court's choice in these cases to impose strict liability is in furtherance of the general purpose of the firearms legislation, that is, to put everyone on their guard that so wrong is the possession of firearms that those who have them without the appropriate licence will effectively be deemed automatically to be guilty of an offence.

In another case, the Court of Appeal decided that the offence created by s 11 of the Company Directors (Disqualification) Act 1986 of acting as a director of a company while an undischarged bankrupt, except with the leave of the court, was one of strict liability. Thus, a mistaken but genuinely held belief that the bankruptcy had been discharged was no defence to the crime (*R v Brockley* (1994)). The court took the view that the mischief sought to be tackled by s 11 of the Act was of wide social concern and that, therefore, the creation of strict liability would promote the object of the Act by obliging bankrupts themselves to ensure that their bankruptcy was in fact discharged before they acted again as company directors.

In *R v K* (2001), the defendant was charged with indecently assaulting a 14 year old girl, who had in fact consented and who had told him she was over 16. Section 14(1) of the Sexual Offences Act 1956 was silent as to *mens rea* so far as knowledge of the girl's age was concerned. On the other hand, s 14(4) expressly stated that genuine belief was to be a defence where the woman lacked the mental capacity to consent. Consequently, the court could legitimately infer that Parliament had not intended genuine belief to be a defence in that situation. The House of Lords reversed the finding of the Court of Appeal holding that, as the 1956 Act was a consolidating Act, drawing together provisions from several previous Acts without making any substantive changes to them, the inference suggested by the Court of Appeal was not appropriate and the common law presumption against strict liability should prevail.

- *Against retrospective effect of new law.* The courts operate a presumption of interpretation that statutes will not operate retrospectively. It is one thing for Parliament to legislate that, for example, as from next year all foxhunting is illegal. It would be quite another thing for Parliament to legislate that not only will foxhunting be illegal if carried on in future, but that anyone who participated in such an event during the last five years is open to prosecution today. Such a presumption against retrospective effect is important in relation to crimes, but is relevant in other areas too, such as contractual arrangements and taxation.

This principle operates not only to stop people whose conduct was innocent at the time from being convicted by a backward looking Act, but also to stop people whose conduct was guilty at any given time from being free from blame just because an Act decriminalises certain conduct. So, if an Act abolishes an offence by repealing a statutory provision, then the repeal will not affect the punishment of someone who has been convicted of this crime at an earlier stage, nor the continuation of legal proceedings in respect of crimes that were committed before the law was changed. The presumption against retrospective effect was considered by the Court of Appeal in *Home Secretary v Wainwright* (2002). Two relatives visiting a prisoner were strip-searched as a condition of entry to the prison, and subsequently claimed a violation of their right to respect for private life. The court held that since the events in question had happened before the HRA 1998 came into force, s 3 of that Act could not be relied on. As Parliament had expressly made s 22(4) of the Act retroactive, its failure to do the same for s 3 must be taken to have been intentional. See also *R v Lambert* (2001) and *R v Kansal* (2001)).

As Parliament is supreme, there being no body with higher constitutional powers, it can pass retrospective legislation if it wishes, but it must do so using express words to achieve this end. The War Damage Act 1965 was passed specifically to overrule the decision of the House of Lords in *Burmah Oil Co Ltd v The Lord Advocate* (1965), and to deprive Burmah Oil of the results of having won that case. The oil company's installations in Burma, which was then a British colony, had been destroyed by the British Forces in 1942 in order to prevent them being captured by Japanese forces. The company, which was registered in Scotland, sued the Crown for compensation. The Crown contended that no compensation was payable when property was destroyed under the Royal Prerogative. The House of Lords decided that compensation was payable. The Act of Parliament was then passed to override the House of Lords' decision and to prevent the burden of compensation having to be met by the taxpayer. An example of modern legislation which has been made expressly retrospective is the War Crimes Act 1991. This Act allows the Attorney General to authorise criminal proceedings for homicide committed in Germany or German occupied territory during World War II. The prosecution can be against a person in the UK regardless of his nationality at the time of the alleged offence. The proposed relaxation of the 'double jeopardy' rule under the Criminal Justice Bill 2002 will by its very nature be retrospective.

- *Presumption against deprivation of liberty.* The law courts work on the assumption that Parliament does not intend to deprive a person of his liberty unless it is explicitly making provision for such a punishment. Thus, Lord Scarman has stated that:

  > ... if Parliament intends to exclude effective judicial review of the exercise of a power in restraint of liberty, it must make its meaning crystal clear [*R v Secretary of State for the Home Department ex p Khawaja* (1983)].

The House of Lords ruled that an immigration Act which it was examining did not have the effect of placing the burden of proof on an immigrant to show that the decision of the Home Office to detain him was unjustified. In other words, one could not read the Act in a way which allowed someone to be deprived of their liberty unless and until they proved that such imprisonment was unjustified.

- *Against application to the Crown.* Unless the legislation contains a clear statement to the contrary, it is presumed not to apply to the Crown.

- *Against breaking international law.* Where possible, legislation should be interpreted in such a way as to give effect to existing international legal obligations.

- *In favour of words taking their meaning from the context in which they are used.* This final presumption refers back to, and operates in conjunction with, the major rules for interpreting legislation considered previously. The general presumption appears as three distinct sub-rules, each of which carries a Latin tag. The *noscitur a sociis* rule is applied where statutory provisions include a list of examples of what is covered by the legislation. It is presumed that the words used have a related meaning and are to be interpreted in relation to each other. (See *IRC v Frere* (1969), in which the House of Lords decided which of two possible meanings of the word 'interest' was to be preferred by reference to the word's location within a statute.) The *ejusdem generis* rule applies in situations where general words are appended to the end of a list of specific examples. The presumption is that the general words have to be interpreted in line with the prior restrictive examples. Thus, a provision which referred to a list that included 'horses, cattle, sheep and other animals' would be unlikely to apply to domestic animals such as cats and dogs. (See *Powell v Kempton Park Racecourse* (1899), in which it was held that, because a statute prohibited betting in a specified number of *indoor* places, it could not cover an *outdoor* location.) The *expressio unius exclusio alterius* rule simply means that where a statute seeks to establish a list of what is covered by its provisions, then anything not expressly included in that list is specifically excluded. (See *R v Inhabitants of Sedgley* (1831), where rates expressly stated to be payable on *coal* mines were held not to be payable in relation to *limestone* mines.)

5.5 Legal reasoning and the possibility of rape within marriage: a case study

[T]hough it would be inconvenient to change the words ... it would not be inconvenient to change in a quiet way the meaning which we put upon those words. This ... was the way it was done in the case law; this had been the law's mode of growth and adaptation, and had in all ages been found a righteous and convenient method of affecting change [Samuel Butler, *The Way of All Flesh*, 1993].

This case study examines the way in which the common law develops over time through cases. It also involves an analysis of the ways in which the courts apply the rules of statutory interpretation. The subject matter of the study relates to the once generally accepted legal doctrine that men could not commit the crime of rape against their wives. As will be seen, whilst the common law had been able to conduct piecemeal reform and to reduce the ambit of the rule by limiting its sphere of operation, by the late 20th century, social circumstances and attitudes had so changed that the law had reached a state of crisis that required the total rejection of the doctrine. If the law were not to be reconstructed, then it would be brought into disrepute. The question was whether, and if so how, the common law could achieve such a radical alteration.

In his *History of the Pleas of the Crown* (1736), Sir Matthew Hale made the following pronouncement:

> But the husband cannot be guilty of a rape committed by himself upon his lawful wife, for by their mutual matrimonial consent and contract the wife hath given up herself in this kind unto her husband which she cannot retract.

As Hale had held the office of Chief Justice for five years, there can be little doubt that what he wrote was an accurate expression of the common law as it then stood, even though he had died some 60 years before the publication of the work. Hale's justification for his statement was that, on marriage, the wife gave up her body to her husband and gave her irrevocable consent to sexual intercourse.

That Hale's pronouncement was accepted as an enduring principle of the common law is evidenced by the first edition of Archbold, *A Summary of the Law Relative to Pleading and Evidence in Criminal Cases* (1822), which simply stated: 'A husband also cannot be guilty of a rape upon his wife.'

Although some doubts were raised about the doctrine in *R v Clarence* (1888), it was not until in *R v Clarke* (1949) that Byrne J held that the husband's immunity was lost where the justices had made an order providing that the wife should no longer be bound to cohabit with the defendant. But even Byrne J had to recognise that:

> As a general proposition it can be stated that a husband cannot be guilty of rape on his wife. No doubt, the reason for that is that on marriage the wife consents to the husband's exercising the marital right of intercourse during such time as the ordinary relations created by the marriage contract subsist between them.

However, in *R v Miller* (1954), Lynskey J ruled that Hale's proposition was correct and that the husband had no case to answer on a charge of rape, although the wife had before the act of intercourse presented a petition for divorce, which had not reached the stage of a *decree nisi*. This was followed by *R v O'Brien* (1974), in which Park J ruled that a *decree nisi* effectively terminated a marriage and revoked the consent to marital intercourse given by a wife at the time of marriage. And in *R v Steele* (1976), it was held that where a husband and wife are living apart and the husband has made an undertaking to the court not to molest the wife, that is in effect equivalent to the granting of an injunction and eliminates the wife's implied consent to sexual intercourse.

The courts had thus developed the doctrine of implied consent as a means of mitigating the stark harshness of Hale's original doctrine, but as the 20th century drew towards its final decade, it became increasingly apparent that such tinkering with the doctrine was not sufficient. Thus, in Scotland, whose legal system had also harboured a similar doctrine since 1797, the courts in *S v HM Advocate General* (1989) held that the whole concept of a marital exemption in rape was misconceived. Then, in *R v R* (1990), at first instance, Owen J clearly expressed his reluctant acquiescence with Hale's general pronouncement, and the need to extend the exceptions to the doctrine of implied consent as follows:

> I accept that it is not for me to make the law. However, it is for me to state the common law as I believe it to be. If that requires me to indicate a set of circumstances which have not so far been considered as sufficient to negative consent as in fact so doing, then I must do so. I cannot believe that it is a part of the common law of this country that where there has been withdrawal of either party from cohabitation, accompanied by a clear indication that consent to sexual intercourse has been terminated, that that does not amount to a revocation of that implicit consent. In those circumstances, it seems to me that there is ample here, both on the second exception and the third exception, which would enable the prosecution to prove a charge of rape or attempted rape against this husband.

That ruling was followed by two other conflicting decisions, both at first instance.

In *R v C (Rape: Marital Exemption)* (1991), Simon Brown J, concentrating on the common law, took the radical step of holding that Hale's proposition was no longer the law. As he stated:

> Were it not for the deeply unsatisfactory consequences of reaching any other conclusion upon the point, I would shrink, if sadly, from adopting this radical view of the true position in law. But adopt it I do. Logically, I regard it as the only defensible stance, certainly now as the law has developed and arrived in the late 20th century. In my judgment, the position in law today is, as already declared in Scotland, that there is no marital exemption to the law of rape.

However, in *R v J (Rape: Marital Exemption)* (1991), the argument was based on statutory interpretation. The wording of s 1(1) of the Sexual Offences (Amendment) Act 1976 provided that:

> For the purposes of section 1 of the Sexual Offences Act 1956 a man commits rape if – (a) he has *unlawful* sexual intercourse with a woman who at the time of the intercourse does not consent to it ...

The contention was that the Act of 1976 provided a statutory definition of rape and that the only possible meaning which could be ascribed to the word *'unlawful'* was 'illicit', effectively meaning outside the bounds of matrimony. Consequently, Parliament's intention must have been to preserve the husband's immunity.

Rougier J not only accepted this argument, but went on to try to constrain further attempts to limit Hale's doctrine beyond what had already been achieved. Thus, he stated that:

> Once Parliament has transferred the offence from the realm of common law to that of statute and, as I believe, had defined the common law position as it stood at the time of the passing of the Act, then I have very grave doubt whether it is open to judges to continue to discover exceptions to the general rule of marital

immunity by purporting to extend the common law any further. The position is crystallised as at the making of the Act and only Parliament can alter it.

Thus stood the authorities when *R v R* was heard by the Court of Appeal, also in 1991. The court was clearly of the view that the ancient rule had to be removed, but how was that desideratum to be achieved? According to Lord Lane CJ, who delivered the decision of the court:

> The ... radical solution is said to disregard the statutory provisions of the Act of 1976 and, even if it does not do that, it is said that it goes beyond the legitimate bounds of judge-made law and trespasses on the province of Parliament. In other words the abolition of a rule of such long standing, despite its emasculation by later decisions, is a task for the legislature and not the courts ... Ever since the decision of Byrne J in *R v Clarke*, courts have been paying lip service to the Hale proposition, whilst at the same time increasing the number of exceptions, the number of situations to which it does not apply. This is a legitimate use of the flexibility of the common law which can and should adapt itself to changing social attitudes. There comes a time when the changes are so great that it is no longer enough to create further exceptions restricting the effect of the proposition, a time when the proposition itself requires examination to see whether its terms are in accord with what is generally regarded today as acceptable behaviour ... It seems to us that where the common law rule no longer even remotely represents what is the true position of a wife in present day society, the duty of the court is to take steps to alter the rule if it can legitimately do so in the light of any relevant parliamentary enactment.

Nonetheless, the Court of Appeal obviously felt constrained by its constitutional position and its position within the operation of *stare decisis* for, rather than just dismissing Hale as wrong law, it had to say that it never was law. Thus:

> [It] can never have been other than a fiction, and fiction is a poor basis for the criminal law.

That dealt with the common law, but the statutory provision remained and was dealt with as follows:

> ... in the end [it] comes down to consideration of the word 'unlawful' in the Act of 1976 ... The only realistic explanations seem to us to be that the draftsman either intended to leave the matter open for the common law to develop in that way ... or, perhaps more likely, that no satisfactory meaning at all can be ascribed to the word and that it is indeed surplusage. In either event, we do not consider that we are inhibited by the Act of 1976 from declaring that the husband's immunity as expounded by Hale no longer exists. We take the view that the time has now arrived when the law should declare that a rapist remains a rapist subject to the criminal law, irrespective of his relationship with his victim.

Such a radical decision could not but go to the House of Lords, which unanimously followed the decision and reasoning of the Court of Appeal. Their Lordships agreed that Hale's pronouncement never was law; it was always a fiction that had infiltrated the common law. What the present case did was merely to put the common law back on its correct tracks. As for the interpretation of the Sexual Offences (Amendment) Act 1976, the appearance of 'unlawful' in s 1(1) was mere surplusage.

Subsequently, the word 'unlawful' was removed from the definition of rape under the Criminal Justice and Public Order Act 1994. Thus was the fiction of marital consent removed forever: reality remains a more intractable matter.

5.6   Legal reasoning and rhetoric

Following on from the previous questioning of the logical nature of legal reasoning, it might be valuable to consider further the claim that legal decisions are not the outcome of a process of logical reasoning, but are in fact the products of a completely different form of communication. According to Peter Goodrich (*Reading the Law* (1986)):

> ... the legal art is an art of interpretation; it is concerned not with a necessary or scientific logic, but with probable arguments, with evaluative reasoning and not with absolute certainty. Rhetoric is the discipline which most explicitly studies the techniques relevant to presenting and evaluating, affirming or refuting, such probable arguments ... rhetoric, here, is defined as the reading of legal texts as acts of communication, as discourse designed to influence, to persuade and to induce action.

Goodrich analysed the use of rhetoric in law, from ancient Greece until the present time, in Chapter 6 of his book. In so doing, he revealed the specific rhetorical devices which judges bring to bear in their decisions in order to persuade their audience as to the objective validity of their decisions.

The question, however, is as to who constitutes the audience that the judiciary addresses. In the case of summings up to juries, the answer is obvious, but there is still an audience being addressed when the judge delivers a judgment in any case. That audience, it is suggested, is the community at large, but with the community not as an active participant in the legal process, but as a passive body that merely has to be persuaded of the inherent and unquestionable validity of the judge's decision in any particular case.

As Goodrich points out:

> The language of the legal decision strives for the appearance of objectivity and the exclusion of dialogue in favour of monologue. Its principal aim and function is that of achieving an image of incontestable authority and of correct legal meanings. Such a task is, essentially, a rhetorical one: the monologue is the language-usage of authority, it precludes dialogue or any questioning of the meanings given, and it closes legal discourse by privileging the voice of the judicial author as the supreme arbiter of meanings.

Rather than being presented as a particular individual's opinion, the legal text is typically expressed as in the language of objectivity. The use of such terms as 'thus', 'because', 'for the reason that', 'in spite of' indicates the voice of necessity, not of choice. When this is combined with the use of terms such as 'therefore' or 'consequently', the outcome is to reinforce the impression that the judge is merely engaged in a working out and presentation of the formal operation of the objective system that is law. In this fashion, the language of apparently objective, and logically determined, legal categories is revealed to be a mere rhetorical device marshalled by judges to provide their particular decisions with the justification of pseudo-objectivity. This process is complemented by the use of axioms; unquestioned and apparently unquestionable self-evident truths, to which the judiciary frequently have recourse in order to validate, without justifying, their own assumptions and presumptions. One should be on one's guard when one reads judges referring to principles that are 'so fundamental that they need not be debated', or where conclusions follow 'as a matter of course' on the basis of 'well settled principle'. The question is whether such claims merely appeal to uncorroborated precedents and unsubstantiated prejudices.

One further aspect of the rhetorical nature of the judicial presentation directly relates to the inherently political nature of judicial decision making. It is almost a commonplace in the most politically sensitive cases that the judges involved will ritually intone the mantra to the effect that, 'it is fortunate that the court does not have to consider the political aspects of this case ...' before going on to make what cannot but be a political decision. As this book maintains, all judicial decisions are political in that they reflect a disposition as to where power should be located in any particular situation.

Judgments, and judicial presentations to juries, therefore, are not merely statements of law; they are equally, if not more fundamentally, exercises in rhetoric. To read a judgment in this way is to see it in a new revelatory light which shows the justificatory, if not manipulative, use of language and linguistic devices that are an essential element of the judgment. It has to be pointed out, however, that the nature and use of rhetoric has changed over time. The difference between the operation of rhetoric in the ancient world and its use by the judiciary today is that, whereas in the ancient world it was used as a means of *persuading* an audience to reach a particular decision, its contemporary role is that of justifying the decision that the judge has taken. The judge speaks, the audience listens and is persuaded: the role of the audience as a participant has been removed and it now merely exists as the passive receiver of the court's decision.

JUDICIAL REASONING

Reasoning in general

Deductive reasoning is reasoning from the whole to the part; from the general to the particular. The syllogism is a form of deductive reasoning.

Inductive reasoning is reasoning from the part to the whole; from the particular to the general.

Reasoning by analogy is reasoning from part to part.

Judicial reasoning

Laws can be presented in the form of syllogisms but do not actually focus on questions of deductive reasoning.

The doctrine of judicial precedent appears at first sight to involve deductive reasoning, but is in fact based on the much less certain use of inductive reasoning and reasoning by analogy.

Statutory interpretation

Communication is inherently uncertain, but legislation has particular problems that arise from the contradictory nature of the various ends it tries to achieve.

Judges have to interpret legislation to give it effect – the question is whether they give it the effect that Parliament intended.

Approaches to statutory interpretation

The literal approach, theoretically at least, limits judges to simply deciding the meaning of the words of the statute. It is the main approach in the English legal system, apart from cases involving European Community law.

The purposive approach allows judges to go behind the words of the statute to seek to give effect to its purpose, but it is only recognised in relation to Community law.

The rules of interpretation

The literal rule gives words in legislation their plain, ordinary, everyday meaning, even if this leads to an apparent injustice.

The golden rule is used in circumstances where the application of the literal rule is likely to result in an obviously absurd result. In such circumstances, the court will not apply the literal meaning, but will instead interpret the provision in such a way as to avoid the absurdity.

The mischief rule permits the court to go beyond the words of the statute in question to consider the mischief at which it was aimed. This is the nearest the English system comes to openly acknowledging the purposive approach to statutory interpretation, but its ambit of operation is not nearly so wide.

Aids to construction

Intrinsic assistance relies on such internal evidence as the statute under consideration can provide through reference to the following: the title of the Act, any preamble, or any schedules to it.

Extrinsic assistance permits the judge to go beyond the Act in question in order to ascertain its meaning. Amongst possible sources are dictionaries, textbooks, other statutes (including the Interpretation Act 1978), reports, other parliamentary papers and, since *Pepper v Hart* (1993), *Hansard* may also be consulted.

Presumptions

In addition to the rules of interpretation, there are also various presumptions that will be applied unless rebutted. The most important of these are presumptions against the alteration of the common law; against retrospective application; against the deprivation of an individual's liberty, property or rights; and against application to the Crown. In addition, there are presumptions in favour of the requirement for *mens rea* in relation to criminal offences; and deriving the meaning of words from their contexts.

Rhetoric

Judgments and judicial submissions to juries are not merely statements of law; they are also exercises in persuasion and justification through the use of language and linguistic devices.

CHAPTER 6

THE JUDICIARY

6.1 The constitutional role of the judiciary

Central to the general idea of the Rule of Law is the specific proposition that it involves the rule of *law* rather than the rule of *people*. Judges hold a position of central importance in relation to the concept of the Rule of Law. They are expected to deliver judgment in a completely impartial manner through a strict application of the law, without allowing their personal preference, or fear or favour of any of the parties to the action, to affect their decision in any way.

This desire for impartiality is reflected in the constitutional position of the judges. In line with Montesquieu's classical exposition of the separation of powers, the judiciary occupy a situation apart from the legislative and executive arms of the State, and operate independently of them. Prior to the English revolutionary struggles of the 17th century between Parliament and the monarch, judges held office at the king's pleasure. Not only did this mean that judges could be dismissed when the monarch so decided, but it highlighted the lack of independence of the law from the State in the form, and person, of the monarch. With the victory of Parliament and the establishment of a State based on popular sovereignty, and limited in its powers, the independence of the judiciary was confirmed in the Act of Settlement 1701. The centrality of the independence of the judges and the legal system from direct control or interference from the State in the newly established constitution was emphasised in the writing of the English philosopher John Locke, who saw it as one of the essential reasons for, and justifications of, the social contract on which the social structure was assumed to be based.

In order to buttress the independence of the judiciary and remove them from the danger of being subjected to political pressure, it has been made particularly difficult to remove senior judges once they have been appointed. Their independence of thought and opinion is also protected by the doctrine of judicial immunity. Both of these principles will be considered in more detail below.

6.1.1 The constitutional role of the Lord Chancellor

It should be noted that the Lord Chancellor holds an anomalous position in respect of the separation of powers in the contemporary State, in that the holder of that position plays a key role in each of the three elements of the State. The Lord Chancellor is the most senior judge in the English court structure, sitting as he does in the House of Lords. At the same time, however, the Lord Chancellorship is a party political appointment, and the occupant of the office owes his preferment to the Prime Minister of the day. Not only is the incumbent a member of the executive, having a seat in the Cabinet, but he is also responsible for the operation of his own government department. In addition to these roles, it should not be overlooked that the Chancellor is also the Speaker of the House of Lords in its general role as a legislative forum. The peculiar situation of the Lord Chancellor is also reflected in the fact that the incumbent can be dismissed or persuaded to resign by the Prime Minster and may cease to hold office on the election of a new government.

The present Lord Chancellor, Lord Irvine of Lairg, and his immediate predecessor, Lord Mackay, have not gone without criticism from within the legal profession generally and the judiciary in particular. The suggestion has been made that these Lord Chancellors have represented the interests of their political masters at the expense of the interests of their legal colleagues. For some time, the legal professions have argued that economic imperatives have driven the machinery of the justice system, rather than the wish to provide the best possible service. Lord Mackay's motives and actions were continuously open to such suspicions. As Lord Steyn, one the Lords of Appeal in Ordinary in the House of Lords, was quoted as saying: 'The Lord Chancellor is always a spokesman for the government in furtherance of its party political agenda' ([1997] PL 84).

However, for the moment at least, a truce appears to have been declared between the judges and the current Lord Chancellor, as is evident from the words of the then Master of the Rolls, Lord Woolf:

> I do not forget that there was a period of confrontation between some of the judiciary and the former Lord Chancellor, Lord Mackay, but that was primarily concerned with reforms relating to the professions, including rights of audience for solicitors, and not the role of the judiciary in the administration of the courts. There was also the concern over the shortage of judges in 1994–95. However, after powerful and frank speeches by the then Lord Chief Justice and Master of the Rolls, a much needed injection of additional judges was provided. The present Lord Chancellor, Lord Irvine of Lairg, is also proposing far reaching changes to the rights of audience, but these are unlikely to meet with the same hostility [(1998) 114 LQR 579, p 585].

The party political role of the Lord Chancellor gave rise to a furore when, in February 2001, Lord Irvine personally wrote to lawyers who were known sympathisers of the Labour Party, asking them to donate at least £200 to the party at a fundraising dinner he was to host. His political critics made much of the fact that, as the person ultimately responsible for appointing the judiciary, his soliciting of party funds from those who might apply for such positions in the future could be represented as improper. As such, the press immediately entitled it the 'cash for wigs' affair, echoing the previous 'cash for questions' scandal in the House of Commons mentioned above at 1.4.3. The Lord

Chancellor, however, refused to apologise for his action. In a statement to the House of Lords, delivered in his political persona and therefore two paces apart from the woolsack on which he sits when acting as the Speaker of the House of Lords, he stated that:

> I do not believe I have done anything wrong nor do I believe that I have broken any current rules. If I did I would be the first to apologise.

According to Lord Irvine, it was misconceived to claim that the Lord Chancellor was not a party political post, and that every minister from the Prime Minister down was involved in fundraising. The best that could be said for the Lord Chancellor was that, although he had done nothing unlawful, he had acted in an unwise, politically naïve and injudicious manner, and one which once again brought the anomalous constitutional role of his office to the political foreground and renewed calls for its reformation, if not removal.

In addition to difficulties arising directly from his responsibility for implementing political policies in relation to the legal system, the Lord Chancellor's judicial role has also come into question. As a consequence of the fact that the appointment of the Lord Chancellor is a purely political one, there is no requirement that the incumbent should have held any prior judicial office. Indeed, in the case of Lord Irvine, he has never served in any judicial capacity, making his reputation as a highly successful barrister, at one time having both the present Prime Minister and the Prime Minister's wife in his chambers. Nonetheless, as Lord Chancellor, he is the most senior judge and is entitled to sit, as he deems appropriate (see 6.3.2 for further observations about the Lord Chancellor's residual powers).

There is, however, a much more fundamental issue relating to the manner in which the Lord Chancellor's multi-functional role may be seen as breaching the doctrine of the separation of powers. There cannot but be doubts as to the suitability, not to say propriety, of a member of the executive functioning as a member of the judiciary. Given the heightened sensitivity in relation to impartiality generated by Lord Hoffmann's participation in the *Pinochet* case (see 6.1.3, below), the Lord Chancellor himself withdrew from sitting in a case in March 1999 in which he recognised the possibility of a conflict of interest. That case involved an action by the family of a man who had died in police custody. The suggestion was made that the Lord Chancellor's participation in the judicial panel raised doubts as to whether the case would be decided by an independent and impartial tribunal. Given his recent guidelines warning the judiciary about the need to be sensitive to issues of conflict of interest, the Lord Chancellor clearly felt himself required to stand down from hearing the case.

In *McGonnell v UK* (2000), the European Court of Human Rights (ECtHR) confirmed the previous decision of the Commission in relation to the judicial function of the Bailiff of the island of Guernsey. It was held that the that fact that the Bailiff had acted as the judge in a case in which he had also played an administrative role was in breach of Art 6 of the European Convention on Human Rights (ECHR). In the words of the Commission decision:

> It is incompatible with the requisite appearance of independence and impartiality for a judge to have legislative and executive functions as substantial as those carried out by the Bailiff.

Although those words could apply equally to the Lord Chancellor, the actual court decision was limited to the situation of the Bailiff, and the Lord Chancellor has made it clear that its application is limited to the particular facts of the Guernsey situation. Nonetheless, the Lord Chancellor has continued not to sit on cases where there may appear to be a conflict between his judicial and other roles. In February 2003, the Lord Chancellor's dual role as judge and member of the executive came under attack in the parliamentary assembly of the Council of Europe, which oversees the operation of the ECHR (see 13.4). A Dutch member, Erik Jurgens, a vice president of the assembly, tabled a motion which stated that:

> The assembly ... has repeatedly stressed that judges should be a completely independent branch of government. It is undeniable that combining the function of judge with functions in other branches of government calls that independence seriously into question.

Mr Jurgens was quoted as saying that he was advising eastern European countries seeking entry to the Council of Europe that they would not be admitted unless their judges were totally independent; so it was an anomaly that one of the original members had a figure like the Lord Chancellor, and further that:

> Sooner or later a case is going to come to the European Court of Human Rights at Strasbourg, and I think they will certainly say that this is an unacceptable combination.

In April 2003, Lord Irvine defended the unique position of the Lord Chancellor in an appearance before the parliamentary select committee with oversight of the Lord Chancellor's Department. Questioned on the conflict inherent in his power to make law and still sit as a judge, he responded that he had 'difficulty seeing why this issue is so important', and argued against changing a legal system that had an enviable international reputation, simply for the sake of constitutional purity. As he put it:

> The basic point is that the higher judiciary accept this role – they believe profoundly that it is a superior system to any other.

It is possible that, under the Human Rights Act (HRA) 1998, the Lord Chancellor's judicial position will be invalidated by the other judges. It should of course be recognised, perhaps with no little degree of irony, that it was Lord Irvine who was instrumental in bringing the ECHR into UK law, through the HRA 1998.

It might be preferable if the position of the Lord Chancellor were considered afresh. To do so would require a complete reassessment of the present structure of the English legal system, but this possibility is not without merit, as will be considered below.

6.1.2 The constitution and the role of the House of Lords

A number of issues have come together to raise questions about the operation of the House of Lords as the final court of appeal in the English legal system and the role of the Privy Council. Amongst these are: the devolution of parliamentary power to the new Scottish Parliament and Welsh Assembly; the previous and proposed further reform of the House of Lords; the enactment of the HRA 1998; and the role of the House of Lords itself in the *Pinochet* case (see below).

It is almost incontrovertible that changes will be required in the future – perhaps this time large constitutional change – and that this presents the best opportunity for a considered revision of the operation of the senior judiciary and their courts.

In other constitutional systems, whether civil, as in France, or common law, as in the USA, not only is there a clear separation of powers between the judiciary, the executive and the legislature, but there is also a distinct Constitutional Court, which deals with such issues. The English constitution provides for neither of these. The anomalous position of the Lord Chancellor has already been commented on, as has the doctrine of the supremacy of Parliament (see 1.4), but it remains to be considered whether either of these can continue to exist as they have, under the changed circumstances of the contemporary constitution. Equally, the potential role of the courts as Constitutional Courts, and the existing position of the House of Lords as a court within the legislative body, must come into issue.

It is a commonplace of politics that the devolution of power from the UK Parliament in London, particularly to the Scottish Parliament in Edinburgh, will give rise to disputes as to the relationship between the two bodies. Eventually, such issues will have to be resolved in the courts, and the Privy Council has been given that role.

Equally, the HRA 1998 has, for the first time, given the courts clear power to declare the UK Parliament's legislative provision to be contrary to essential human rights (see 1.7). Even allowing for the fact that the HRA has been introduced in such a way as to maintain the theory of parliamentary sovereignty, in practice, the courts will inevitably become involved in political/constitutional issues. Once the courts are required to act in constitutional matters, it is surely a mere matter of time before they become Constitutional Courts, as distinct from ordinary courts, with specialist judges with particular expertise in such matters. Once a Constitutional Court develops, the position of the Lord Chancellor will become untenable as a judge, as his political roles would automatically place him in a position of conflict of interest. He would have to give up his position as head of the judiciary, probably, as some have already proposed, to the Lord Chief Justice.

A further problematic consequence of such a development would be the continued location of the Constitutional Court within the House of Lords. The 1997 Labour government was elected on the promise of the fundamental reform of the House of Lords, which it saw as undemocratic and unrepresentative. After establishing a Royal Commission, the government embarked on a two-stage process of reform. The first stage of reform was achieved through the House of Lords Act 1999, which removed the right of the majority of hereditary peers to sit in the House of Lords. The second stage of reform was set out, towards the end of 2001, in a White Paper entitled *Completing the Reform*. Amongst the most significant measures contained in the consultation document were the proposals that:

- the membership of the House of Lords should be 600, a cut of more than 100;
- all remaining hereditary peers should be abolished;
- an independent Appointments Commission should be established;
- no more than 332 seats should be held by political members *nominated* by the political parties in proportion to their performance in General Elections, as determined by the Appointments Committee;
- a fifth, 120 members, should have no political affiliation and should be appointed by the Appointments Committee;
- a fifth, 120 members, representing the nations and regions should be *directly elected*; and
- although no changes were proposed to the powers of the second chamber over Bills, the House of Lords' powers over subordinate legislation should be changed to one of delay only.

The most controversial aspect of the White Paper was the relatively small proportion of directly elected members it proposed, especially when compared with the large proportion of members who would be nominated rather than elected. The government faced much criticism, even from its own MPs, with regard to this suggestion and set up a joint committee of both Houses of Parliament to consider the course of future reform. Somewhat surprisingly, that committee made no recommendation and merely listed seven possible options for determining the membership of a reformed House of Lords. The options were:

- A fully appointed house.
- A fully elected house.
- 80% appointed, 20% elected.

- 80% elected, 20% appointed.
- 60% appointed, 40% elected.
- 60% elected, 40% appointed.
- 50% appointed, 50% elected.

Even more surprisingly, in February 2003, the House of Commons voted against all of the options and thus failed to approve any of them. The closest vote, for an 80% elected house, fell narrowly by 284 votes against to 281 in favour.

The consequences of these votes remain uncertain, but it would appear that any further reform of the House of Lords may be postponed until after the next election. Nonetheless, it remains clear that even the current level of reform undergone by the House of Lords raises issues as to the position of the most senior judiciary in that institution.

If the existing House of Lords were to be replaced by an elected body, then questions would have to be asked about the situation of unelected members such as bishops and judges, but even if it were replaced by an appointed second chamber, the separation of powers would surely demand that the Constitutional Court be separate from it.

Membership of a new Constitutional Court could also be an issue. The present situation, where panels of five Law Lords, or seven as in the third *Pinochet* hearing, are selected from the full complement of 12, has been criticised as introducing an element of lottery into the judicial procedure. The question arises: would the decision in any case have been different, had a different body of judges been empanelled? In the *Pinochet* case, the second panel of seven reached the same decision as the previous five member court, but for different reasons. The *Pinochet* proceedings brought the House of Lords no doubt unwelcome publicity, and may have revealed the need for its internal reform. Already suggestions have been made that the court should sit as a full court, involving all its members, but that in turn must bring into question the actual appointment procedures of these most senior judges, especially if it were to develop into a Constitutional Court. For the question has to be asked as to what expertise in constitutional matters generally, and human rights in particular, do the commercial lawyers who make up a significant number of the highest judicial posts have? And if expertise in such issues is to be seen as the criterion for appointment to the Constitutional Court, should not membership of the court be open to non-practitioners, such as academics? For the moment, such issues remain purely hypothetical, but for how much longer can this remain the case?

It is worth noting that the case set out in the above two sections, for the reform of the Lord Chancellor's position and against the location of the most senior judges in the House of Lords, was presented in essence to the commission examining the reform of the House of Lords, by Justice, the civil rights organisation. Both aspects of the challenges were strongly rejected by Lord Chancellor Irvine in a speech to the Third Worldwide Common Law Judiciary Conference in Edinburgh, delivered in July 1999. Nonetheless, spring 2002 saw a spate of speeches and interviews highlighting disagreement, if not actual tension, between the Lord Chancellor and some of the most senior members of the judiciary. In March of that year Lord Steyn, the second longest serving current Law Lord, expressed the view that Lord Irvine's insistence on sitting as a judge in the House of Lords was a major obstacle to the creation of a Supreme Court to replace the House of Lords. In April, the Lord Chancellor's response was reported in the *Financial Times* newspaper. The article stated that that, 'Lord Irvine may have an impressive intellect, but his lack of diplomacy means he will seldom be short of enemies'. The point of that comment was supported by the Lord Chancellor's reaction to Lord Steyn's previous comments, dismissing them in a tone of effete arrogance, as 'rather wearisome … he's not a political scientist, he knows nothing about the internal workings of government – or very little'. As reported, he reduced Lord Steyn's argument to a demand for 'a grand new architectural venture', stating that the argument that, 'the Lord Chancellor, because of his desire to continue sitting is preventing the judges from having a new building – that's just nonsense'.

Lord Irvine's views should, however, be contrasted with those of the current senior Law Lord, Lord Bingham, expressed in the Spring Lecture given at the Constitution Unit at University College London in May 2002. In a paper entitled *A New Supreme Court for the UK*, Lord Bingham directly addressed all of the issues raised above, except for the role of the Lord Chancellor, before stating his preference for:

> … a supreme court severed from the legislature, established as a court in its own right, re-named and appropriately re-housed, properly equipped and resourced and affording facilities for litigants, judges and staff such as, in most countries of the world, are taken for granted.

As to the views and future role of the Lord Chancellor, the reduction of his direct judicial powers is implicit in the speech. As Lord Bingham concludes: '… inertia … is not an option.'

6.1.3 Judicial impartiality

Re Bow Street Metropolitan Stipendiary Magistrate ex p Pinochet Ugarte (1999)

No consideration of the operation of the judiciary generally, and the House of Lords in particular, can be complete without a detailed consideration of what can only be called the *Pinochet* case (the various cases are actually cited as *R v Bartle* and *R v Evans* (House of Lords' first hearing); *Re Pinochet* (House of Lords' appeal against Lord Hoffmann); *R v Bartle* and *R v Evans* (final House of Lords' decision)).

In September 1973, the democratically elected government of Chile was overthrown in a violent army coup led by the then General, Augusto Pinochet Ugarte; the president, Salvador Allende, and many others were killed in the fighting. Subsequently, in the words of Lord Browne-Wilkinson, in the final House of Lords' hearing:

> There is no doubt that, during the period of the Senator Pinochet regime, appalling acts of barbarism were committed in Chile and elsewhere in the world: torture, murder and the unexplained disappearance of individuals on a large scale.

Although it was not suggested that Pinochet had committed these acts personally, it was claimed that he was fully aware of them and conspired to have them undertaken.

In 1998, General Pinochet, by now Senator for life and recipient of a Chilean amnesty for his actions (extracted as the price for his returning his country to democracy), came to England for medical treatment. Although he was initially welcomed, he was subsequently arrested on an extradition warrant issued in Spain, for the crimes of torture, murder and conspiracy to murder allegedly orchestrated by him in Chile during the 1970s. Spain issued the international warrants, but Pinochet was actually arrested on warrants issued by the metropolitan stipendiary magistrate under s 8(1)(b) of the Extradition Act 1989. The legal question for the English courts was whether General Pinochet, as Head of State at the time when the crimes were committed, enjoyed diplomatic immunity. In November 1998, the House of Lords rejected Pinochet's claim by a 3:2 majority, Lord Hoffmann voting with the majority but declining to submit a reasoned judgment.

Prior to the hearing in the House of Lords, Amnesty International, which campaigns against such things as State mass murder, torture and political imprisonment, and in favour of general civil and political liberties, had been granted leave to intervene in the proceedings, and had made representations through its counsel, Geoffrey Bindman QC. After the *Pinochet* decision, it was revealed, although it was hardly a secret, that Lord Hoffmann was an unpaid director of the Amnesty International Charitable Trust, and that his wife also worked for Amnesty. On that basis, Pinochet's lawyers initiated a very peculiar action: they petitioned the House of Lords about a House of Lords' decision; for the first time, the highest court in the land was to be subject to review, but to itself, only itself differently constituted. So, in January 1999, another panel of Law Lords set aside the decision of the earlier hearing on the basis that Lord Hoffmann's involvement had invalidated the previous hearing. The decision as to whether Pinochet had immunity or not would have to be heard by a new, and differently constituted, committee of Law Lords.

It has to be stated in favour of this decision that the English legal system is famously rigorous in controlling conflicts of interest which might be seen to affect what should be a neutral decision making process. The rule, which applies across the board to trustees, company directors and other fiduciaries as well as to judges, is so strict that the mere possibility of a conflict of interest is sufficient to invalidate any decision so made, even if in reality the individual concerned was completely unaffected by their own interest in coming to the decision. In the words of the famous *dictum* of Lord Hewart, it is of fundamental importance that 'justice must not only be done but should manifestly and undoubtedly be seen to be done' (*R v Sussex Justices ex p McCarthy* (1924)). With regard to the judicial process, it has been a long established rule that no one may be a judge in his or her own cause, that is, they cannot judge a case in which they have an interest. This is sometimes known by the phrase *nemo judex in causa sua*. Thus, for example, judges who are shareholders in a company appearing before the court as a litigant must decline to hear the case (*Dimes v Grand Junction Canal* (1852)). It is therefore astonishing that Lord Hoffmann did not withdraw from the case, or at least declare his interest in Amnesty when it was joined to the proceedings. The only possible justification is that Lord Hoffmann assumed that all of those involved in the case, including the Pinochet team of lawyers, were aware of the connection. Alternatively, he might have thought that his support for a charitable body aimed at promoting civil and political liberties was so worthy in itself as to be unimpeachable: could not, and indeed should not, every English judge subscribe, for example, to cl 3(c) of the Amnesty International Charitable Trust memorandum, which provides that one of its objects is 'to procure the abolition of torture, extra-judicial execution and disappearance'?

In either case, Lord Hoffmann was wrong.

Once it was shown that Lord Hoffmann had a relevant interest in its subject matter, he was disqualified without any investigation into whether there was a likelihood or suspicion of bias. The mere fact of his interest was sufficient to disqualify him unless he had made sufficient disclosure. Hitherto, only pecuniary or proprietary interests had led to automatic disqualification. But, as Lord Browne-Wilkinson stated, Amnesty, and hence Lord Hoffmann, plainly had a non-pecuniary interest sufficient to give rise to an automatic disqualification for those involved with it.

The House of Lords therefore decided that Lord Hoffmann had been wrong, but it remained for the House of Lords to extricate itself, with whatever dignity it could manage, from the situation it had, through Lord Hoffmann, got itself into. This it endeavoured to do by reconstituting the original hearing with a specially extended committee of seven members. Political and legal speculation was rife before the decision of that court. It was suggested that the new committee could hardly go against the decision of the previous one without bringing the whole procedure into disrepute, yet the earlier court had actually contained the most liberal, and civil liberties minded, of the Lords. It was assumed that the new hearing would endorse the earlier decision, if with reluctance, but what was not expected was the way in which it would actually do so.

In reaching the decision that General Pinochet could be extradited, the House of Lords relied on, and established, Pinochet's potential responsibility for the alleged crimes from the date on which the UK incorporated the United Nations Convention on Torture into its domestic law through the Criminal Justice Act 1988 – 29 September 1988. Consequently, he could not be held responsible for any crimes committed before then, but was potentially liable for any offences after that date. Thus, although the later House of Lords' committee provided the same decision as the first one, it did so on significantly different, and much more limited, grounds to those on which Lords Steyn and Nicholls, with the support of Lord Hoffmann, relied. Such a conclusion is neither satisfactory in law nor political practice, and did nothing to deflect the unflattering glare of unwanted publicity that had been visited on the House of Lords.

It is important not to overstate what was decided in *Re Pinochet*. The facts of that case were exceptional and it is unlikely that it will lead to a mass withdrawal of judges from cases; however, there might well be other cases in which the judge would be well advised to disclose a possible interest. Finally, with regard to *Re Pinochet*, whatever one's views about the merits, sagacity or neutrality of the current judiciary, there is considerable evidence to support the proposition that, historically, judges have often been biased towards certain causes and social classes. For example, JAG Griffith's book, *The Politics of the Judiciary* (1997) (see 6.11.1, below), is brimming with concrete examples of judges who have shown distinctly conservative and illiberal opinions in cases involving workers, trade unions, civil liberties, Northern Ireland, police powers, religion and other matters. Lord Hoffmann was wrong, but it is nonetheless ironic that the first senior judge to have action taken against him for possible political bias was someone whose agenda was nothing more than being against torture and unjudicial killings.

Locabail (UK) Ltd v Bayfield Properties Ltd (1999)

Following a number of other cases in which lawyers sought to challenge a judgment on the grounds that through a social interest or remote financial connection the judge was potentially biased, the Court of Appeal delivered authoritative guidance on the matter in *Locabail (UK) Ltd v Bayfield Properties Ltd and Another* (1999).

The Court of Appeal ruled that all legal arbiters were bound to apply the law as they understood it to the facts of individual cases as they found them without fear or favour, affection or ill will: that is, without partiality or prejudice. Any judge, that term embracing every judicial decision maker, whether judge, lay justice or juror, who allowed any judicial decision to be influenced by partiality or prejudice deprived the litigant of his important right and violated one of the most fundamental principles underlying the administration of justice. The law was settled in England and Wales by the House of Lords in *R v Gough* (1993), and in consequence, the relevant test was whether there was in relation to any given judge a real danger or possibility of bias. When applying the real danger test, it would often be appropriate to inquire whether the judge knew of the matter relied on as appearing to undermine his impartiality. If it were shown that he did not, the danger of its having influenced his judgment was eliminated and the appearance of possible bias dispelled. It was for the reviewing court, not the judge concerned, to assess the risk that some illegitimate extraneous consideration might have influenced his decision.

There was one situation where, on proof of the requisite facts, the existence of bias was effectively presumed and in such cases, it gave rise to automatic disqualification, namely, where the judge was shown to have an interest in the outcome of the case which he was to decide or had decided: see *Dimes v Proprietors of the Grand Junction Canal* (1852), *R v Rand* (1866) and *R v Camborne Justices ex p Pearce* (1955). However, it would be dangerous and futile to attempt to define or list factors which might, or alternatively might not, give rise to a real danger of bias, since everything would depend on the particular facts. Nonetheless, the court could not conceive of circumstances in which an objection could be soundly based on the religion, ethnic or national origin, gender, age, class, means or sexual orientation of the judge. Nor, at any rate ordinarily, could an objection be soundly based on his social, educational, service or employment background or history; nor that of any member of his family; nor previous political associations, membership of social, sporting or charitable bodies; nor Masonic associations; nor previous judicial decisions; nor extra-curricular utterances, whether in textbooks, lectures, speeches, articles, interviews, reports or responses to consultation papers; nor previous receipt of instructions to act for or against any party, solicitor or advocate engaged in a case before him; nor membership of the same Inn, circuit, local Law Society or chambers.

By contrast, a real danger of bias might well be thought to arise if there existed personal friendship or animosity between the judge and any member of the public involved in the case; or if the judge were closely acquainted with any such member of the public, particularly if that individual's credibility could be significant in the decision of the case; or if in a case where the credibility of any individual were an issue to be decided by the judge, he had in a previous case rejected that person's evidence in such outspoken terms as to throw doubt on his ability to approach such a person's evidence with an open mind on any later occasion.

It might well be thought that the Court of Appeal was bound to come to this conclusion. Had it ruled that membership of certain societies, or a particular social background, or the previous political associations of a trial judge were grounds for appeal, two consequences would follow. First, there would be a rapid expansion of the use by law firms of special units that monitor and keep files on all aspects of judges' lives. Secondly, there would be a proliferation of appeals in all departments of the court structure at the very time when there is such a concerted effort to reduce the backlog of appeals. The decision in *Locabail* leaves the question of profound jurisprudential importance: how far can judges judge in an entirely neutral and socially detached manner?

R v Gough (1993)

Locabail was decided before the HRA 1998 came into force, but the Court of Appeal soon had the opportunity to assess the rules in *R v Gough* against the requirements of the European Court's approach to bias in relation to Art 6 of the ECHR. *Director General of Fair Trading v Proprietary Association of Great Britain* (2001) related to a case before the Restrictive Practices Court. Six weeks into the trial, one of the lay members of the panel hearing the case, an economist, disclosed that, since the start of the case, she had applied for a job with one of the main witnesses employed by one of the parties to the case. On learning this, the respondents argued that such behaviour must imply bias on her part and that consequently, the whole panel should stand down, or at least the member in question should stand down. The Restrictive Practices Court rejected the argument. On appeal, the Court of Appeal took the opportunity to refine the common law test as established in *R v Gough*. Previously, the court determining the issue had itself decided whether there had been a real danger of bias in the inferior tribunal. Now, in line with the jurisprudence of the ECtHR, the test was whether a fair-minded observer would conclude that there was a real possibility of bias. In other words, the test moved from being a subjective test on the part of the court to an objective test from the perspective of the fair-minded observer. In the case in question, the Court of Appeal held that there was sufficient evidence for a fair-minded observer to conclude bias on the part of one member of the panel and that consequently, at the stage the trial had reached, her discussions would have contaminated the other two members, who should also have been stood down.

6.2 Judicial offices

Although not required to know the names of present incumbents, students should at least be aware of the various titles of judges and equally know which courts they operate in:

- *Lord Chancellor*. The peculiar nature of this office has already been commented on, but it should be pointed out that, as well as being the senior judge in the House of Lords, the Lord Chancellor is formally the most senior judge in the Court of Appeal, and holds the position of President of the Chancery Division. The present Lord Chancellor is Lord Irvine of Lairg and he is referred to in reports as Lord Irvine LC.

- *Lord Chief Justice*. The holder of this position is second only to the Lord Chancellor in eminence. The Lord Chief Justice is the President of the Criminal Division of the Court of Appeal and is formally the senior judge in the Queen's Bench Division of the High Court. The present incumbent is Lord Woolf CJ.

- *Master of the Rolls*. The holder of this office is President of the Civil Division of the Court of Appeal. At present, this position is held by Lord Phillips MR.

- *President of the Family Division of the High Court of Justice*. This person is the senior judge in the Family Division and is responsible for organising the operation of the court. The current president is Dame Elizabeth Butler-Sloss P.

- *Vice Chancellor*. Although the Lord Chancellor is nominally the head of the Chancery Division of the High Court, the actual function of organising the Chancery Division falls to the Vice Chancellor. The current incumbent is Sir Robert Morritt VC.

- *Senior Presiding Judge for England and Wales*. The Courts and Legal Services Act (CLSA) 1990 recognised the existing system and required that each of the six separate Crown Court circuits should operate under the administration of two Presiding Judges appointed from the High Court. In addition, a Senior Presiding Judge is appointed from the Lords Justices of Appeal (see below).

6.2.1 Judicial hierarchy

The foregoing are specific judicial offices. In addition, the various judges who function at the various levels within the judicial hierarchy are referred to in the following terms:

- *Lords of Appeal in Ordinary*. These are the people who are normally referred to as the Law Lords for the simple reason that they sit in the House of Lords and are ennobled when they are appointed to their positions. There can be between seven and 12 Law Lords, although the maximum number is subject to alteration by Order in Council. The House of Lords is the highest domestic court in the UK. The qualifications for the position of Lord of Appeal in Ordinary will be considered later. They are referred to by their specific titles.

- *Lords Justices of Appeal*. This category, of which there may be up to 36 individuals, constitutes the majority of the judges in the Court of Appeal, although the other specific office holders considered previously may also sit in that court, as may High Court Judges specifically requested so to do. They all used to be known as Lord Justice, even if they were female. The first female member of the Court of Appeal, Elizabeth Butler-Sloss, had to be referred to by the male title because the Supreme Court Act 1981 had not considered the possibility of a woman holding such high judicial office. The rules were changed subsequently to allow female judges in the Court of Appeal to be referred to as Lady Justices, and whereas their male counterparts receive knighthoods on their elevation, the women become Dames.

- *High Court Judges*. These are sometimes referred to as *'puisne'* (pronounced 'pewnee') judges, in reference to their junior status in relation to those of superior status in the Supreme Court. There may be up to 98 such judges appointed. Judges are appointed to particular divisions depending on the amount of work needing to be conducted by that division, although they may be required to hear cases in different divisions and may be transferred from one division to another by the Lord Chancellor. Others, such as former High Court and Court of Appeal judges, or former circuit judges or recorders, may be requested to sit as judges in the High Court. High Court Judges are referred to by their name followed by the initial 'J'.

- The Lord Chancellor may also appoint *deputy judges* of the High Court on a purely temporary basis, in order to speed up the hearing of cases and to reduce any backlog that may have built up. The Heilbron Report on the operation of the civil justice system was critical of the use of deputy judges and recommended that more permanent High Court Judges should be appointed if necessary. The maximum numbers were subsequently increased to their present level, but the use of deputy judges has continued to provide grounds for criticism of the operation of the legal system, and has led to suggestions that the use of 'second rate' judges might eventually debase the whole judicial currency.

- *Circuit judges*. Although there is only one Crown Court, it is divided into six distinct circuits which are serviced, in the main, by circuit judges who also sit as county court judges to hear civil cases. There are currently 622 circuit judges, each being addressed as 'Your Honour'.

- *Recorders* are part time judges appointed to assist circuit judges in their functions in relation to criminal and civil law cases.

- *District Judges*. This category of judge, previously referred to as registrars, is appointed on a full time and part time basis to hear civil cases in the county court.

- The situation of *magistrates* will be considered separately at 6.8, below and the situation of *chairmen of tribunals* will be considered in Chapter 8.

6.2.2   Legal offices

In addition to these judicial positions, there are three legal offices which should be noted:

- The *Attorney General*, like the Lord Chancellor, is a political appointee whose role is to act as the legal adviser to the government. For example, in March 2003, the current Attorney General, Lord Goldsmith, advised the government that there was a legal basis for its use of military force against Iraq. The Attorney General alone has the authority to prosecute in certain circumstances and appears for the Crown in important cases. As may be recalled from 4.5.2, the Attorney General also has powers to appeal against points of law in relation to acquittals under the Criminal Justice Act (CJA) 1972 and can also appeal against unduly lenient sentences under the CJA 1988. The crucially important decision of the House of Lords that DNA evidence, acquired in regard to another investigation and which should have been destroyed under s 64 of the Police and Criminal Evidence Act (PACE) 1984, could nonetheless be used, was taken as the result of a reference by the Attorney General (*Attorney General's Reference (No 3 of 1999)*). The *Solicitor General* is the Attorney General's deputy.

- The *Director of Public Prosecutions* (DPP) is the head of the national independent Crown Prosecution Service (CPS) established under the Prosecution of Offences Act 1985 to oversee the prosecution of criminal offences. The decision of the DPP whether to prosecute or not in any particular case is subject to judicial review in the courts. In *R v DPP ex p C* (1994), it was stated that such powers should be used sparingly and only on grounds of unlawful policy, failure to act in accordance with policy and perversity. Nonetheless, successful actions have been taken against the DPP in relation to decisions not to prosecute in *R v DPP ex p Jones* (2000) and in *R v DPP ex p Manning* (2000) (see 10.1 for an examination of the CPS).

6.3   Appointment of judiciary

In the first of his Hamlyn Lectures of 1993, the then Lord Chancellor, Lord Mackay, stated that the pre-eminent qualities required by a judge are:

> ... good sound judgment based upon knowledge of the law, a willingness to study all sides of an argument with an acceptable degree of openness, and an ability to reach a firm conclusion and to articulate clearly the reasons for the conclusion.

Although the principal qualification for judicial office was experience of advocacy, Lord Mackay recognised that some people who have not practised advocacy may well have these necessary qualities to a great degree. This was reflected in the appointment of an academic and member of the Law Commission, Professor Brenda Hoggett, to the High Court in December 1993. Professor Hoggett, who sat as Mrs Justice Hale, was the first High Court Judge not to have had a career as a practising barrister, although she qualified as a barrister in 1969 and was made a QC in 1989. As Dame Brenda Hale, she now sits in the Court of Appeal.

The CLSA 1990 introduced major changes into the qualifications required for filling the positions of judges. Judicial appointment is still essentially dependent upon the rights of audience in the higher courts, but at the same time as the CLSA 1990 effectively demolished the monopoly of the Bar to rights of audience in such courts, it opened up the possibility of achieving judicial office to legal practitioners other than barristers.

Lawrence Collins became the first solicitor to be appointed directly to the High Court.

6.3.1 Qualifications

The main qualifications for appointment are as follows (the CLSA 1990 is dealt with in detail at 11.7, below):

- *Lord of Appeal in Ordinary*
  (a) the holding of high judicial office for two years; or
  (b) possession of a 15 year Supreme Court qualification under the CLSA 1990.

- *Lord Justice of Appeal*
  (a) the holding of a post as a High Court Judge; or
  (b) possession of a 10 year High Court qualification under the CLSA 1990.

- *High Court Judges*
  (a) the holding of a post as a circuit judge for two years;
  (b) possession of a 10 year High Court qualification under the CLSA 1990.

- *Deputy judges* must be qualified in the same way as permanent High Court Judges.

- *Circuit judges*
  (a) the holding of a post as a recorder;
  (b) possession of a either 10 year Crown Court qualification or a 10 year county court qualification under the CLSA 1990;
  (c) the holding of certain offices, such as District Judge, Social Security Commissioner, chairman of an industrial tribunal, stipendiary magistrate for three years.

- *Recorders* must possess a 10 year Crown Court or county court qualification under the CLSA 1990.

- *District Judges* require a seven year general qualification under the CLSA 1990.

6.3.2 Selection of judges

The foregoing has concentrated on the specific requirements for those wishing to fulfil the role of judge, but it remains to consider the more general question relating to the general process whereby people are deemed suitable and selected for such office. All judicial appointments remain, theoretically, at the hands of the Crown. The Crown, however, is guided, if not actually dictated to, in regard to its appointment by the government of the day. Thus, as has been seen, the Lord Chancellor is a direct political appointment. The Prime Minister also advises the Crown on the appointment of other senior judicial office holders and the Law Lords and Appeal Court judges. Such apparent scope for patronage in the hands of the Prime Minister has not gone without criticism.

Judges at the level of the High Court and Circuit Bench are appointed by the Crown on the advice of the Lord Chancellor, and the Lord Chancellor personally appoints District Judges, lay magistrates and the members of some tribunals. This system has not gone without challenge either, the question being raised as to how the Lord Chancellor actually reaches his decision to recommend or appoint individuals to judicial offices.

Circuit judges and below

All appointments up to and including circuit judges are made on the basis of open competition and the Lord Chancellor's Department (LCD) publishes a guidance booklet entitled *Judicial Appointments*, also available on the LCD's website (www.lcd.gov.uk). The guidance information sets out the criteria against which candidates are assessed as follows:

- legal knowledge;
- intellectual and analytical ability;
- sound judgment;
- decisiveness;
- communication and listening skills;
- authority and case management skills;
- integrity and independence;
- fairness and impartiality;
- understanding of people and society;
- maturity and sound temperament;
- courtesy;
- commitment, conscientiousness and diligence.

The first stage in the open competition selection procedure is an advertisement for a particular judicial vacancy which appears in the national press and/or legal journals. The candidates are required to provide the names of three members of the judiciary or the legal profession as referees.

Written assessments of candidates are then sought from those people whose names are given by the candidates themselves and 'a wide range of other judges and lawyers who are approached for assessments on the Lord Chancellor's behalf'.

The LCD, and indeed the Lord Chancellor himself, is adamant that there is no secrecy about those who are consulted, as lists detailing this latter group are given in the application packs and every person on this list will be invited to comment on each applicant.

All assessments are made against the criteria set out above and it is felt, not without some justification, that judges and members of the legal profession are in a good position to assess the merits of candidates, as they are familiar with the role of the judge and with the skills and qualities required to do the job well. All assessments are provided in confidence, which the LCD points out, with equal justification, is a common practice where references are sought by prospective employers.

Shortlisting of candidates is carried out by a panel of three, a judge, a lay person and one of the Lord Chancellor's senior officials, which conducts formal interviews, although the Lord Chancellor personally considers the situation of those interviewed before reaching a final decision.

The LCD provides feedback and advice to unsuccessful candidates, including, on a non-attributed basis, information about matters contained in the assessments received.

Relying on the recommendations and opinions of the existing judiciary as to the suitability of the potential candidates may appear sensible at first sight. However, it brings with it the allegation, if not the fact, that the system is over-secretive and leads to a highly conservative appointment policy. Judges are suspected, perhaps not unnaturally, of favouring those candidates who have not been troublesome in their previous cases and who have shown themselves to share the views and approaches of the existing office holders. In his 1993 Hamlyn Lecture, Lord Mackay stated that the arrangements in the UK for the collection of data about candidates for the judiciary are comparatively well developed, and provide those who have to take the decisions, essentially the Lord Chancellor himself, with fuller information than would otherwise be available to them. The reasoning behind this claim would appear to be that, because the procedure is secret and limited, people commenting on the suitability of candidates are willing to be more frank and open than would otherwise be the case were the references open to wider inspection. Such spurious justification is worrying in its complacency and its refusal to recognise that the secretive nature of the process might permit referees to make unsubstantiated derogatory comments that they would otherwise not feel free to make.

High Court Bench

In the past, appointment to the High Court Bench was by way of invitation from the Lord Chancellor. However, in 1998 the LCD issued an advertisement inviting applicants to apply for such positions. However, the Lord Chancellor retained his right to invite individuals to become High Court Judges, and since 1998, of the 46 High Court Judges who have been appointed, only 21 came through the application procedure, the other 25 being invited to accept appointment. As regards the system of invitation, the question immediately raised is as to exactly how the Lord Chancellor selects the recipients of his favour; there being no system as such, there can be no transparency and without transparency there must be doubts as to the fairness of the process. Even where a candidate applies for the post of High Court Judge, the procedure is different from applications at a lower level, for the reason that the candidate is not interviewed after the usual consultation process with the senior judiciary and the candidate's own referees. The Lord Chancellor simply decides whom to appoint on the basis of that consultation process. Thus are the doubts about the secretive nature of the consultancy procedure compounded as regards applicants for the High Court Bench.

Lord Irvine's repeated insistence on the objectivity of the judicial appointments process has done little to remove the suspicion that, because it still relies on the sounding of the senior members of the judiciary and professions, it remains in the final analysis restrictive, conservative and unfair, especially to minority groups. Suspicions about the system are shared by both the Bar and The Law Society. In 1999, The Law Society expressed its discontent by withdrawing its co-operation with the present system. The publication of the Judicial Appointments Annual Report for the year 1999–2000 brought the comment from Lord Irvine that The Law Society's action was a:

> ... disservice to its members, creating obstacles for solicitors who want to be appointed to the judiciary by failing to provide them with the supporting testimonials they deserve.

In his introduction to the Report, the Lord Chancellor re-affirmed his denial of the myth that the appointment system operated on the basis of 'secret soundings'. Nonetheless, the view, whether mythical or not, persists and that negative perception cannot but damage confidence in the whole appointment system.

The current procedure of appointment to the High Court was subject to some sharp criticism in a review conducted for the Bar Council under the chairmanship of the former Appeal Court Judge, Sir Iain Glidewell. The main review concluded that the current system of appointment was not sufficiently transparent. More contentiously, however, it suggested that, given the increased role of the judiciary in matters relating to the review of administrative decisions, devolution issues and human rights, it was no longer constitutionally acceptable for judges to be appointed by the government of the day, a member of which is the Lord Chancellor. Consequently, the review recommended that:

- the Lord Chancellor should cease to be responsible for the selection and appointment of High Court Judges;

- the responsibility for such appointments should be transferred to a newly created independent body, a High Court Appointments Board; and

- the appointments to the High Court should only be made from amongst people who have made application for the position.

As a least favoured option, the review recommended that, if the Lord Chancellor continues to be responsible for appointments to the High Court, he should reach his decisions only after receiving the report and advice of a panel which should have the task of shortlisting and interviewing candidates, as is done for other judicial offices.

It is perhaps of relevance that since May 2002, the system of judicial appointments in Scotland has come under the control of a 10 member Judicial Appointments Board, consisting of five lawyers and five lay members, with the chair being one of the lay members. All judicial posts are advertised, suitable candidates are interviewed, and a short-list of appropriate candidates is drawn up and submitted to the Scottish First Minister, who, after consultation with the Lord President, makes a recommendation to the Queen. If Scotland recognises the need for transparency and to remove perceptions of political patronage, can England and the Lord Chancellor continue to hold out for much longer?

One of Lord Irvine's earliest actions as Lord Chancellor had been to declare the government's intention to inquire into the merits of establishing a Judicial Appointments Commission. However, rather than carry out that intention, he announced in 1999 that Sir Leonard Peach, the former Commissioner for Public Appointments, would be conducting an independent scrutiny of the way in which the current appointment processes for judges operated. In December of that year, Sir Leonard reported that he had been:

> ... impressed by the quality of work, the professionalism and the depth of experience of the civil servants involved [LCD Press Release, 3 December 1999].

Sir Leonard did recommend that a Commission for Judicial Appointments be established, with a Commissioner and Deputy Commissioners, whose role would be to monitor the procedures and act as an Ombudsman for disappointed applicants. It was recommended that the Commission should not have any role in the actual appointments, but should merely maintain an independent oversight of the procedure.

Not surprisingly, Lord Irvine was most happy to accept such findings and Sir Leonard's proposals, and the system of appointing the judiciary remains essentially unchanged. The appointment of Sir Colin Campbell, Vice Chancellor of Nottingham University, as the first Commissioner was announced in March 2001. The first report of the Judicial Appointments Commission for the period up to April 2002 was reassuringly robust. It concluded that there was no reason to believe that the present system results in the appointment of people who do not have the required qualities, either for judicial office or for silk. However, it also recognised that perhaps a more important issue might be whether others, who also have the required qualities, are not being fairly considered or selected due to flaws in the processes and systems. It was also clearly aware of the potential damage that a lack of confidence in the judicial appointments system could have on the whole legal process, and found a number of significant respects in which the current judicial appointments system should be improved.

Of the six complaints covered in the report, three were substantially upheld, one was partially upheld and two were not upheld. It has to be recognised that the four complaints upheld were on the basis of procedural and administrative failings, rather than the merits of any particular decision. Of more potential significance, however, was the fact that the Commission also identified a number of other issues on which it was not yet in a position to form a considered view, but which it stated warranted further investigation and debate. These were:

- the role to be played by consultation, in particular automatic consultation, in the judicial appointments system;
- what constitutes merit, in the context of judicial appointments and silk, and how best merit can be measured;
- how fairness in the appointment of the High Court Bench can be ensured whilst continuing to attract high quality candidates. As the Commission pointed out, the current judiciary and silks are overwhelmingly white, male and from a narrow social and educational background; and
- what the role of the government in the appointment of the judiciary and silks should be.

The Commission stated that it intended to consider these issues further in its future work and to promote a wide-ranging debate around them amongst the legal profession and the public at large. One can only surmise that such a statement of intentions was not met with enthusiasm by the Lord Chancellor, in spite of his public welcoming of the report.

Somewhat surprisingly, Lord Irvine announced in April 2003, before the select committee with oversight of his department, that he intended to issue three separate consultation documents relating to:

- whether judges and lawyers should continue to wear wigs and gowns in court;
- whether the status of Queen's Counsel should be retained and the related appointment process; and
- the role of the Judicial Appointments Commission.

Gender and racial constitution of the judiciary

Advertisements were used for the first time in 1994 to recruit likely candidates from the professions for the positions of assistant recorder, Deputy District Judge and circuit judge and, as has been seen above, advertising was extended to appointments to the High Court Bench in 1998.

The first of such advertisements stated:

> The Lord Chancellor will recommend for appointment the candidates who appear to him to be best qualified regardless of ethnic origin, gender, marital status, sexual orientation, political affiliation, religion or (subject to the physical requirements of the office) disability.

By 2000, the Lord Chancellor had slightly changed the emphasis. Whilst retaining his emphasis on appointment purely on merit, he stated that:

> I am particularly keen that eligible women and ethnic minority lawyers and judges should give this opportunity serious thought.

Advertising was seen as a practical step to address the matter of gender and race imbalance amongst the present judicial body. Currently, there are no women in the House of Lords and only three in the Court of Appeal. In the High Court, the number is 6 out of 107 and, of 622 circuit judges, 60 are women. At the level of recorders, there are 167 women from a total of 1,342; and at District Judge level, the number is 80 from 428 (March 2003).

The LCD has collated statistics on ethnic origin of the judiciary, but it warns that the information they provide may be inaccurate as it is only supplied on a voluntary basis. However, using the statistics provided, it is apparent that if one restricts analysis to the black and Asian ethnic communities, for which groups statistics are available, then there are no members of those groups above the level of circuit judge and at that level, the ethnic minority representation is 1%. At the level of recorder, the percentage is 3%, at District Judge level, it is 3%, and at Deputy District Judge level, it is 2%. In the magistrates' courts, black and Asian people make up 3% of the complement of full time District Judges, as the old stipendiary magistrates are now called. The highest rate of ethnic representation is to be found at the level of Deputy District Judges in the magistrates' courts, where it stands at almost 6%.

Lord Irvine has consistently encouraged women and people from ethnic backgrounds or other minorities to apply for judicial positions, as encapsulated in his sound bite, 'Don't be shy! Apply!'. As he admitted:

> Yes, it is true that many judges today are white, Oxbridge educated men. But, it is also true that they were appointed on merit, from the then available pool, at the time the vacancies arose ... It does not mean that the social composition of the judiciary is immutably fixed. For too long barristers were drawn from a narrow social background. As this changes over time, I would expect the composition of the Bench to change too. That is inherent in the merit principle [Speech to the Association of Women Barristers, February 1998].

A 1997 Labour Research survey, although admittedly carried out when Lord Irvine had only been in his new job for two months, found that, in fact:

> ... even greater proportions of the judiciary attended Oxbridge universities than a decade earlier ... [Labour Research, July 1997].

In April 2003, the Labour MP Keith Vaz, a member of the select committee on the LCD, claimed that 78% of senior judges in England and Wales achieved the full house of being white, male, public school and Oxbridge educated. Such a situation, he claimed, represented 'a complete failure for a Labour government'.

Still, Lord Irvine remained optimistic, not to say bullish, about the way things are changing. As he pointed out:

> ... things are already on the move. In December 1994, 7.6% of the main tiers of the judiciary ... were women. It is now a little over 9%. Not a meteoric rise, true, but a steady one.

Accepting Lord Irvine's statistics, one certainly would have to agree that the change is not meteoric; in fact, at the rate he quotes it would take 90 years for women to hold 50% of judicial offices. According to the latest annual report on judicial appointments for the year 2001–02: 'There has been a steady increase in the percentage of women appointed ... the proportion of minority ethnic appointments ... dropped in 1999–2000, but there has since been a rise in the level of appointments.'

For a time in 1999, it looked as if the secrecy surrounding the way in which judicial and other legal offices are filled was about to be opened up to scrutiny, to the dismay and discomfort of all of those involved. When the government appointed a new Treasury Devil in 1998, that is, their chief advocate in the civil courts, senior members of the judiciary were consulted about the suitability of the candidates on the usual secret basis. However, when the appointment went to a male member of the Lord Chancellor's ex-chambers, a woman candidate, Josephine Hayes, registered a claim for sex discrimination in relation to the appointment. As a result of this action, the then Attorney General, John Morris, who made the appointment, would have been required to disclose details of the process leading to the decision, which included representations made by senior judges. The soundings were actually taken by the Attorney General's deputy, the Solicitor General, Lord Falconer at the time. Lord Falconer, however, was himself a close personal friend of the Prime Minister, Tony Blair, and his wife, Cherie, who were both once members of the Lord Chancellor's chambers. It would at least appear, therefore, that there was a measure of legitimate dubiety about the procedure, especially when it is alleged that all of the people sounded out were men, including the Lord Chancellor, and at least two others were intimates of the Blairs and the Lord Chancellor. Fortunately for all those involved, although not for those who wished to see the appointment procedures opened up to scrutiny, the matter was resolved and the case dropped when the Attorney General agreed to pay £5,000 to a charity promoting the rights of women.

The above case merely compounded the Lord Chancellor's misfortune in his and/or his department's appointment policy, in that he had already been found to have appointed a member of staff in breach of the sex discrimination legislation. In this instance, the person appointed as Lord Irvine's adviser was Gary Hart, who had been a partner in the solicitors' firm Herbert Smith. Hart was a friend of both Lord Irvine and the Blairs; in fact, he was the godfather one of the Blairs' children, and his wife had acted for Mrs Blair when she sought an injunction to prevent the publication of photographs in the possession of her ex-nanny. When Hart was appointed without the job being advertised, a woman lawyer, Jane Coker, brought a sex discrimination action against the Lord Chancellor. The employment tribunal unanimously decided that Lord Irvine has acted unlawfully in not advertising the job but, by a majority of 2:1, the Employment Appeal Tribunal overturned that decision, a decision which was approved by the Court of Appeal in *Coker v The Lord Chancellor* (2001).

Even the appointment of Lawrence Collins, the first solicitor to be appointed directly to the High Court, was not without controversy when it was revealed that he was a personal friend of the Lord Chancellor and was a former partner for the Herbert Smith firm.

Alternative approaches to appointing judges

A different approach, following the example of the USA, might be for the holders of the higher judicial offices to be subjected to confirmation hearings by, for example, a select committee of the House of Commons. Lord Mackay dismissed any such possibility as follows:

> The tendency of prior examination ... is to discover and analyse the previous opinions of the individual in detail. *I question whether the standing of the judiciary in our country, or the public's confidence in it, would be enhanced by such an inquiry,* or whether any wider public interest would be served by it [emphasis added].

It is perhaps unfortunate that the italicised words in the above passage can be interpreted in a way that no doubt Lord Mackay did not intend but which, nonetheless, could suggest a cover up of the dubious opinions of those appointed to judicial office.

An even more radical alternative would be to open judicial office holding to election as they also do in the USA, although in this case, one might well agree with Lord Mackay that:

> The British people would not feel that this was a very satisfactory method of appointing the professional judiciary.

Alternatively, and following Lord Mackay's emphasis on the professional nature of the judiciary, the UK could follow continental examples and provide the judiciary with a distinct professional career structure as an alternative to legal practice. (For a consideration of the way in which other jurisdictions appoint their judges, readers are referred to a 1991 Law Society Research Study No 5 entitled *Judicial Appointments* by Eleni Skordaki.)

Such alternative suggestions would not eradicate all questions of the judge's impartiality, but they would certainly be an improvement on the existing system. For, as things stand at present, the lack of transparency in the appointment procedure merely clouds a more fundamental question which can be posed in two forms: first, whether the best people are being selected from the available pool of talent; or, alternatively and more radically, whether the present procedure ensures the appointment of the wrong type of judge generally.

6.4   Training of the judiciary

All judicial training, from the induction of new magistrates (see 6.8, below) to the honing of the skills of the judges in the House of Lords, is overseen by the Judicial Studies Board (JSB). Prior to the establishment of the JSB, the training of judges in the UK was almost minimal, especially when considered in the light of the continental practice where being a judge, rather than practising as an advocate, is a specific and early career choice which leads to specialist and extensive training.

The Magisterial Committee of the JSB organises the training of newly elected chairmen of Magistrates' Benches and induction and continuation training for Deputy District Judges (Magistrates' Courts) and District Judges (Magistrates' Courts). It is also responsible for advising on, developing and monitoring the training of lay magistrates, which is delivered locally by Magistrates' Courts Committees.

The JSB provides training and instruction to all part time and full time judges in judicial skills. An essential element of the philosophy of the JSB is that the training is provided by judges for judges. The training requirements of the different jurisdictions are the responsibility of five committees (Criminal, Civil, Tribunals, Family and Magisterial). Another Committee, the Equal Treatment Advisory Committee, provides advice and support for all five committees. The JSB membership is drawn mainly from the judiciary, but also includes some leading academics and other professionals. The Board enjoys considerable autonomy from its parent department, the LCD, in deciding the need for and nature of judicial training

Assistant recorders are required to attend seminars on procedure and sentencing before they can sit on their own in the Crown Court. Later, training takes the form of further, intermittent seminars focusing primarily on sentencing. Those sitting in the Crown Court benefit specifically from the advice contained in the *Crown Court Bench Book of Specimen Directions*. In the foreword to the latest edition, produced in 1999, Mr Justice Kay, the Chair of the JSB Criminal Committee, explained its function thus:

> This is the sixth edition of the Specimen Directions, which has become one of the most useful tools available to judges, experienced and inexperienced, in preparing a summing up. They are increasingly referred to by the Court of Appeal, Criminal Division as a starting point for a correct direction on matters of law and it is important that they are understood in that context and not simply repeated without being adapted to the facts and circumstances of a particular case. The Judicial Studies Board does not seek to lay down legal principles or to resolve difficult questions of law. It attempts to do no more than reflect the law and interpretation of the law as laid down by the courts and to that end every decision of the Court of Appeal, Criminal Division referring to these directions is studied to see if change is necessary.

The specific nature of the Specimen Directions is a delicate matter, as they do not, and indeed cannot, represent an unconditional statement of what the law and judicial practice is. They always have to be adapted by the judges to fit particular circumstances. Such a fact has to be recognised, and indeed it is enforced by an injunction not to reproduce the Directions as a part of any commercial activity. A civil law Bench Book has also been produced, and there are other Bench Books for reference in family law proceedings, Youth Court proceedings, and for the guidance of District Judges (Magistrates' Courts). There is also an *Equal Treatment Bench Book* for use by all members of the judiciary (see 6.4.1, below).

Judicial training has probably never been of greater public concern or been executed with such rigour since the JSB was established in 1979. For example, the judiciary were subject to thorough re-training in the new civil procedure (see Chapter 7). This training included residential seminars for all full time and part time judges dealing with civil work, local training, and conferences held at various national locations. Similarly, following the incorporation of the ECHR into English law by the HRA, the government set aside £4.5 million for human rights judicial training during 1999–2000. The budget for this enormous project included £1.6 million for the JSB, and £1 million for the Court Service to provide cover for judges who were in training.

6.4.1   Equal treatment training

Law is supposed to operate on the basis of formal equality: everyone is assumed to be equal before the law and to be treated equally, regardless of their personal attributes or situation (see 1.5). In the past, however, accusations have been levelled at the judiciary that allege that, at the very least, they themselves are insensitive to the sensitivities of others, particularly in matters of race, gender, sexual orientation and in relation to people with disabilities. Not only have they been accused of lacking understanding and sympathy towards others with different values or practices from their own, but it has also been claimed that many of them have been resistant to changing their attitudes.

As regards attitudes towards race, such a situation was highlighted in an article by Lincoln Crawford, a barrister, part time judge, Bar Council member and former member of the Commission for Racial Equality in *Counsel*, the journal of the Bar (February 1994).

In his article, he listed a number of reasons why judges were opposed to the race training. First, there was the belief that judges apply the law fairly and do not need to be trained in race awareness for the simple reason that they are not racist in their outlook or practice. Such an assertion sits uncomfortably, however, with the documented research that reveals that black defendants found guilty of offences are treated more harshly than equivalent white defendants. Secondly, this initial approach was supported by an attitude that considered it to be an affront to the independence of their judgments to require judges to try to take account of the different cultural backgrounds of those black and Asian people who came before them. (One white judge actually remarked that he had been called 'nigger' at his school and that it had not caused him any harm.) Thirdly, Crawford claimed that there was a bloody-mindedness amongst the judiciary, representing the view that they operated the British legal system and that anyone within the jurisdiction should take the law as they found it, even if it was partial and discriminatory in its lack of sympathy for other cultural values. The fourth justification for resistance to race awareness training was the view that it smacked of interference with the impartiality and independence of the judiciary, the implication being that judges should not be held to account even when they were operating in a questionable, if not a patently discriminatory, manner.

All of the foregoing supposed justifications are completely spurious and represent a denial of the cultural existence of a large section of British society. As Crawford put it:

> A judiciary which fears and feels nervous about plurality and diversity runs the danger of becoming closed, narrow and brittle.

It also runs the danger of completely alienating large sections of the population over which it exercises its power and, when law is reduced to the level of mere power rather than legitimate authority, its effectiveness is correspondingly reduced. In the light of the recognition that something had to be done to forestall such potential damage, the JSB instituted seminars for training part time and circuit judges in racial awareness, for example, reminding them that, in a multi-cultural/multi-faith society, it is offensive to ask for people's 'Christian' names, as well as warning them as to the dangers of even more crassly offensive language and racial stereotyping that appears to be so much a part of the English use of metaphor.

In 1999, for the first time, JSB training included new guidance for all judges on equal treatment issues such as disability, gender and sexual orientation, and litigants-in-person. In announcing that equal treatment training was to be integral to all induction courses, Lord Justice Waller (chairman of the JSB) stated:

> There is absolutely no room for complacency in these areas. And I am not going to say – just because someone has been on our course, they will be perfect, but I hope that, as result, judges are better equipped to do their jobs [(1999) *The Times*, 13 July].

A key component in the JSB's strategy of overcoming the appearance of insensitivity and related perception of prejudice was the production of the *Equal Treatment Bench Book*, which it has to be said provides a truly comprehensive first class guide for the judiciary in ensuring awareness of the need to treat all those who come before them equally and with sensitivity and civility.

Ethnic minorities in the criminal court

An opportunity to assess the success of the JSB's policy in assuring equality of treatment was provided in March 2003 by the publication of a research report entitled *Ethnic Minorities in the Criminal Court: Perceptions of Fairness and Equality of Treatment*.

The research project investigated the extent to which ethnic minority defendants and witnesses in Crown Courts and magistrates' courts perceived their treatment to have been unfair and whether those who did perceive unfairness attributed it to racial bias. The experience of the ethnic minority group was compared with that of white defendants. The study also took into account the views of court staff, judges, magistrates and lawyers. Altogether, 1,252 people were interviewed in Manchester, Birmingham and London, and the proceedings in more than 500 cases were observed.

As regards defendants:

- The proportion who said their treatment had been unfair in court was about one-third in the Crown Court and about a quarter in the magistrates' courts.

- There was little difference between ethnic minority and white defendants (33% of black, 27% of Asian and 29% of white defendants).

- One in five black defendants in the Crown Court and one in 10 in the magistrates' courts, and one in eight Asian defendants in both types of court, thought that their unfair treatment in court related to their ethnicity.

- Very few perceived racial bias in the conduct or attitude of judges or magistrates (only 3% in the Crown Court and 1% in the magistrates' courts).

- There were no complaints about racist remarks from the bench.
- Most complaints about racial bias concerned sentences perceived to be more severe than those imposed on a similar white defendant.
- 31% of ethnic minority defendants in the Crown Court and 48% in the magistrates' courts said they would like more people from ethnic minorities sitting in judgment and amongst the staff of the courts.

As regards witnesses:

- None complained of racial bias in the Crown Court.
- 7% perceived racial bias in the magistrates' courts.

As regards the judges and magistrates:

- All the judges and two-thirds of the magistrates had received training in ethnic awareness.
- Only two judges and three magistrates said that it had 'added nothing' or been 'unhelpful'.

As regards court officials and lawyers:

- 98% of white clerks and ushers thought there was equal treatment of ethnic minorities by the courts; compared with
- 71% of Asian staff; and
- 28% of black staff.

- 69% of white lawyers thought there was equal treatment of ethnic minorities by the courts; compared with
- 63% of Asian lawyers; and
- 43% of black lawyers.

- 30% of black lawyers said they had personally witnessed incidents in court that they regarded as 'racist'; as opposed to
- 13% of white lawyers; and
- 11% of Asian lawyers.

The conclusion of the research project was that there had been:

> ... a substantial change for the better in perceptions of ethnic minorities of racial impartiality in the criminal courts. Several judges mentioned that attitudes had altered markedly in recent years and magistrates reported a substantial decline in the frequency of racially inappropriate remarks. Many lawyers also reported that racial bias or inappropriate language was becoming 'a thing of the past'. These positive findings, taken together with the much lower than expected proportion of defendants complaining of racial bias, may be a reflection of both general social improvements in the treatment of ethnic minorities and the specific efforts begun by the Lord Chancellor's Department in the early 1990s to heighten the awareness of all involved in the system of the need to guard against racial bias.

Nonetheless, the report warned against complacency and emphasised that the fact that one in five black and one in eight Asian defendants definitely perceived racial bias in the Crown Court, and at least one in 10 in the magistrates' courts, combined with the fact that black lawyers and staff were more likely to perceive racial bias than others, was sufficient cause to continue the efforts towards eliminating the vestiges of perceived unequal treatment.

Perceptions of racial bias, more frequently held by black defendants in the Crown Court, may well arise from a belief that the disproportionately large number of black people caught up by the criminal justice and prison systems must, at least to some extent, be a reflection of racism. Every effort therefore should be made when passing sentence to demonstrate and convince defendants that no element of racial stereotyping or bias has entered into the decision.

Among black defendants and lawyers in particular, there was a belief that the authority and legitimacy of the courts, and confidence in them, would be strengthened if more personnel from ethnic minorities were seen to be playing a part in the administration of criminal justice. Indeed, in the Crown Court, many judges agreed that more could be done to avoid the impression of the courts as 'white dominated institutions'.

However, there is an undercurrent in the report which supports a more critical reading. Whilst it was concerned with '*perceptions* of racial bias', such perceptions may not wholly comprehend the underlying reality. Eliminating inappropriate language may well be a good thing in itself, but if it merely provides camouflage for a system that remains fundamentally biased in terms of its outcomes, then doubts have to be raised about its fundamental worth. The difference in perception of the black lawyers and court staff as to the true nature of the system would seem to provide grounds to support such a possibility. Given that differential sentencing remains the major ground of complaint relating to allegations of ethnic bias, that surely remains the most pressing issue in relation to equality. As the report states:

> The findings of this study may go some way to dispelling the view that most minority ethnic defendants believe that their treatment by the courts has been racially biased. But *if it could be shown that the 'cultural change' which this study has identified has had a real impact on eliminating differential sentencing of white and ethnic minority defendants*, this would further encourage the confidence of ethnic minorities in the criminal courts [emphasis added].

6.5 Retirement of judges

All judges are now required to retire at 70, although they may continue in office at the discretion of the Lord Chancellor. The Judicial Pensions and Retirement Act 1993 reduced the retirement age from the previous 75 years for High Court Judges and 72 years for other judges.

The reduction of the retirement age may have been designed to reduce the average age of the judiciary, but of perhaps even more significance in this respect is the change that was introduced at the same time in judicial pensions. The new provision requires judges to have served for 20 years, rather than the previous 15, before they qualify for full pension rights. This effectively means that if judges are to benefit from full pension rights, they will have to take up their appointments by the time they are 50. Given that judges are predominantly appointed from the ranks of high earning QCs, this will either reduce their potential earnings at the Bar or reduce their pay package as judges by approximately 7.5%. This measure led to a great deal of resentment within both the Bar and the judiciary, Lord Chief Justice Taylor referring to its unfairness and meanness, and was one of the issues that fuelled the antagonism between Lord Mackay and the other members of the judiciary.

In any event, according to the statistics provided by the LCD, the average age for the Law Lords is almost 68, with Lord Hutton being the oldest at 71, and Lord Rodger the youngest at 58. In the Court of Appeal, the average age is 62, with the youngest being Dame Mary Arden at 56 and the oldest Sir Peter Gibson at 69.

6.6   Removal of judges

Reference has already been made to the need, with of course the exception of the Lord Chancellorship, to protect the independence of the judiciary by making it difficult for a discomforted government to remove judges from their positions on merely political grounds. The actual provision is that judges of the House of Lords, the Court of Appeal and the High Court hold their office during good behaviour, subject to the proviso that they can be removed by the Crown on the presentation of an address by both Houses of Parliament. In actual fact, this procedure has never been used in relation to an English judge, although it was once used in 1830 to remove an Irish judge who was found guilty of misappropriating funds.

Judges below the level of the High Court do not share the same degree of security of tenure as their more senior colleagues, and can be removed, on grounds of misbehaviour or incapacity, by the action of the Lord Chancellor who does not require the sanction of Parliament. However, even the infamous Judge Richard Gee was never actually dismissed. He was appointed as a circuit judge in February 1991 and in November 1995 was arrested and charged with conspiracy to commit offences under the Theft Act 1978 in relation to his previous solicitor's practice. He pleaded not guilty and at his trial in March 1998, the jury failed to reach a verdict. Before a retrial could be held, the Attorney General entered a *nolle prosequi* on the grounds that Gee was not fit to face another trial. This effectively meant that no further action could be taken against him. Gee had been, and remained, suspended on full pay since his original arrest in 1995. When asked in the House of Lords what was to be done about the matter, Lord Irvine answered that:

> I am considering whether the evidence disclosed in Judge Gee's criminal trial would justify me in concluding, on the standard of civil proof, that Judge Gee has been guilty of misbehaviour sufficient to allow me to remove him from office under my statutory powers to dismiss a circuit judge for misbehaviour.

The Lord Chancellor's considerations were cut short and any action pre-empted by Gee's resignation in November 1999. The Lord Chancellor had no power to prevent the payment of a judicial pension of £23,000, together with a lump sum of £46,000, both inflation proofed, when Gee reached the age of 65.

As yet, the only judge to be removed for misbehaviour remains the circuit judge who, in 1983, was found guilty of smuggling cigarettes and alcohol.

In a letter circulated in July 1994, Lord Mackay asked that judges inform him immediately if they are ever charged with any criminal offence other than parking or speeding violations. The Lord Chancellor stated that he wished to make it clear that a conviction for drink driving would amount, *prima facie*, to misbehaviour. Causing offence on racial or religious grounds could also be seen as misbehaviour, as could sexual harassment.

The discretionary power of the Lord Chancellor not to extend the appointment of a recorder, without the need to explain or justify his action, has previously provided grounds for criticism and accusations of political interference on the part of the Lord Chancellor.

Stipendiary magistrates are subject to removal by the Crown on the recommendation of the Lord Chancellor and lay magistrates are subject to removal by the Lord Chancellor without cause or explanation.

6.7 Judicial immunity from suit

A fundamental measure to ensure the independence of the judiciary is the rule that they cannot be sued in relation to things said or acts done in their judicial capacity in good faith. The effect of this may be seen in *Sirros v Moore* (1975), in which a judge wrongly ordered someone's detention. It was subsequently held by the Court of Appeal that, although the detention had been unlawful, no action could be taken against the judge as he had acted in good faith in his judicial capacity. Although some judges on occasion may be accused of abusing this privilege, it is nonetheless essential if judges are to operate as independent representatives of the law, for it is unlikely that judges would be able to express their honest opinions of the law, and the situations in which it is being applied, if they were to be subject to suits from disgruntled participants.

Given the increased use of the doctrine of *ultra vires* to justify legal action by way of judicial review against members of the executive, it is satisfyingly ironic that at least one judge, Stephen Sedley, who now sits in the Court of

Appeal, sees the possibility of a similar *ultra vires* action providing grounds for an action against judges in spite of their previously assumed legal immunity. As he expressed the point in the *London Review of Books* of April 1994:

> Judges have no authority to act maliciously or corruptly. It would be rational to hold that such acts take them outside their jurisdiction and so do not attract judicial immunity.

No doubt such a suggestion would be anathema to the great majority of the judiciary, but the point remains: why should judges be at liberty to abuse their position of authority in a way that no other public servant can?

Before 1991, magistrates could be liable for damages for actions done in excess of their actual authority, but the CLSA 1990 extended the existing immunity from the superior courts to cover the inferior courts, so magistrates now share the same protection as other judges.

It is worth stating at this point that this immunity during court proceedings also extends as far as advocates and witnesses, and of course jurors, although the controls of *perjury* and *contempt of court* are always available to cover what is said or done in the course of court proceedings.

Related to, although distinct from, the principle of immunity from suit is the convention that individual judges should not be subject to criticism in parliamentary debate, unless subject to an address for their removal: legal principles and the law in general can be criticised, but not judges.

In the course of 2000, it was announced that public money was to be made available to allow judges to sue for libel. Such a proposal is surprising to say the least. Surely those who benefit from immunity should not be assisted to take actions against those who do not enjoy such a benefit. And who would hear such a case? A fellow judge; hardly the stuff of transparent impartiality. It has to be reported that as yet no judge has availed himself of this opportunity.

6.8 Magistrates

The foregoing has concentrated attention on the professional and legally qualified judges. It should not be forgotten, however, that there are some 30,000 unpaid part time lay magistrates, 105 full time professional stipendiary magistrates (known as District Judges (Magistrates' Courts)) and 152 Deputy District Judges (Magistrates' Courts) operating within some 700 or so magistrates' courts in England. These magistrates are empowered to hear and decide a wide variety of legal matters and the amount and importance of the work they do should not be underestimated: 97% of all criminal cases are dealt with by the magistrates' courts. The operation of the magistrates' courts and the powers of magistrates have been considered in detail above at 4.3. It remains, however, to examine the manner in which they are appointed to their positions.

There is no requirement for lay magistrates to have any legal qualifications. On being accepted onto the bench, however, magistrates undertake a training process, under the auspices of the JSB. Magistrates are required to attend training courses, with a special emphasis being placed on Equal Treatment Training. The way in which the training programme seeks to overcome conceptions as to the politically narrow nature of the magistracy is evident in the content of the extensive training materials produced for the magistrates. These include modules on: raising awareness and challenging discrimination; discretion and decision making; prejudice and stereotype; so the overall emphasis may be seen to be on equality of people, and equality of treatment. There is, however, a new emphasis on the practical skills involved in performing the duties placed on magistrates, and consequently much of the training will actually be based on sitting as magistrates with the input of specially trained monitors to give guidance and advice on how the new magistrates perform their tasks and fulfil their roles.

The training course is designed to give new magistrates an understanding of the functions and powers of the bench generally, and to locate that understanding within the context of national practice, particularly with regard to sentencing. On the topic of discretion and sentencing, Lord Irvine provided the magistrates with the following strong advice, not to say warning:

> You ... must exercise your discretion in individual cases with great care within a system that needs to secure continuing public confidence. This is what makes the sentencing guidelines produced by the Magistrates' Association so important. They are guidelines – they do not curtail your independent discretion to impose sentences you think are right, case by case. But the guidelines exist to help you in that process, to give you more information in reaching your decision. And they help to assist the magistracy, to maintain an overall consistency of approach ... I urge you to follow the guidelines, which are drawn up for your benefit and the magistracy as a whole [Speech to the Council of Magistrates' Association, March 1999].

Although particular key legal issues may be considered in the course of the training, it is not the intention to provide the magistrate with a complete grasp of substantive law and legal practice. Indeed, to expect such would be to misunderstand both the role of the magistrates and the division of responsibility within the magistrates' court. Every bench of magistrates has a legally qualified justices' clerk, whose function it is to advise the bench on questions of law, practice, and procedure, leaving matters of fact to magistrates to decide upon (see 4.3.1). This division of powers raises a further possible area of contention with regard to the operation of magistrates' courts, for in the case of some particularly acquiescent benches, the justices' clerks appear to run the court, and this leads to the suspicion that they actually direct the magistrates as to what decisions they should make. This perception is compounded by the fact that the bench is entitled to invite their clerk to accompany them when they retire to consider their verdicts. A *Practice Direction (Justices: Clerks to the Court)*

(2000)) set out the role and functions of the clerk to the court. Thus, the clerk, or legal adviser who stands in for the clerk, is stated to be responsible for providing the justices with any advice they require to properly perform their functions, whether or not the justices have requested that advice, on the following matters:

- questions of law (including ECHR jurisprudence and those matters set out in s 2(1) of the HRA 1998);
- questions of mixed law and fact;
- matters of practice and procedure;
- the range of penalties available;
- any relevant decisions of the superior courts or other guidelines;
- other issues relevant to the matter before the court;
- the appropriate decision making structure to be applied in any given case; and
- in addition to advising the justices, it shall be the legal adviser's responsibility to assist the court, where appropriate, as to the formulation of reasons and the recording of those reasons.

As regards when and where this advice should be given, the *Practice Direction* states that:

> At any time, justices are entitled to receive advice to assist them in discharging their responsibilities. If they are in any doubt as to the evidence which has been given, they should seek the aid of their legal adviser, referring to his/her notes as appropriate. This should ordinarily be done in open court. Where the justices request their adviser to join them in the retiring room, this request should be made in the presence of the parties in court. Any legal advice given to the justices other than in open court should be clearly stated to be provisional and the adviser should subsequently repeat the substance of the advice in open court and give the parties an opportunity to make any representations they wish on that provisional advice.

6.8.1 Appointment

Under the Justices of the Peace Act 1997, magistrates are appointed to, and indeed removed from, office by the Lord Chancellor on behalf of the Queen, after consultation with local advisory committees. There are currently 111 such advisory committees and 134 sub-committees within the UK. Section 50 of the Employment Rights Act 1996 provides that employers are obliged to release their employees, for such time as is reasonable, to permit them to serve as magistrates. In the event of an employer refusing to sanction absence from work to perform magistrate's duties, the employee can take the matter before an employment tribunal. Understandably, there is no statutory requirement for the employer to pay their employees in their absence, but magistrates are entitled to claim expenses for loss of earnings in the exercise of their office.

Proposals for office tend to be generated by local interest groups, such as political parties, trade unions, chambers of commerce and such like bodies, and this limited constituency may give rise to the view that the magistracy only represents the attitudes of a limited section of society. In a multi-cultural, multi-racial society, it is essential that the magistrates' court should reflect the composition of the wider society, and the rules relating to the appointment and training of magistrates do, at least in theory, support this conclusion.

Once candidates of a suitable quality have been identified, the local advisory committee is placed under the injunction to have regard to the need to ensure that the composition of the bench broadly reflects the community which it serves in terms of gender, ethnic origin, geographical spread, occupation and political affiliation. It may even be that individuals who are otherwise suitably qualified may not be appointed if their presence would exacerbate a perceived imbalance in the existing bench. Nonetheless, there remains a lingering doubt, at least in the minds of particular constituencies, that the magistracy still represents the values, both moral and political, of a limited section of society. A further significant step towards opening up the whole procedure of appointing magistrates was taken when local advisory committees were granted the power to advertise for people to put themselves forward for selection. As the chairman of the Mid-Staffordshire Magistrates' Bench stated in a local newspaper, although previously rank and social position were the main qualifications, nowadays:

> ... it is important a bench has a balance of sexes, professions and political allegiances.

In March 1999, the LCD launched a campaign to attract a wider section of candidates to apply to be magistrates. In announcing the campaign, Lord Irvine stated that:

> Magistrates come from a wide range of backgrounds and occupations. We have magistrates who are dinner ladies and scientists, bus drivers and teachers, plumbers and housewives. They have different faiths and come from different ethnic backgrounds, some have disabilities. All are serving their communities, ensuring that local justice is dispensed by local people. The magistracy should reflect the diversity of the community it serves ... Rest assured appointments are made on the merit, regardless of educational background, social class or ethnic background.

The campaign was supported by adverts in some 36 newspapers and magazines, from broadsheets to tabloids, from TV listings to women's magazines. The campaign was particularly aimed at ethnic minorities, its adverts being carried in such publications as the *Caribbean Times*, the *Asian Times* and *Muslim News*. The 1999 campaign was followed in 2001 by a *Judiciary for All* scheme, which aimed to encourage more people from ethnic minority groups to apply to become magistrates. Within the scheme, the main initiative was the Magistrates' Shadowing Project, which had ordinary people following magistrates. It was hoped that the participants would act as ambassadors for the lay magistracy within their communities. The success of these campaigns may be judged by the fact that in the year 2000/2001, the proportion of new appointments drawn from ethnic minority communities rose to 9.3%, up from 8.6% in the previous year.

The statistics demonstrate that the gender balance and ethnic mix of the magistracy does not appear to pose a problem, but the same cannot be said in terms of its class mix. However, in 1998, the LCD issued a Consultation Paper relating to the political balance in the lay magistracy, which suggested that political affiliation was no longer a major issue, and therefore did not have to be controlled in relation to the make up of benches of magistrates. As support for its suggestion, the consultancy document made three points. First, that actually ensuring a political balance on the bench raises:

> ... the danger of creating a perception that politics do play a part in the administration of justice, notwithstanding that it is agreed on all sides that, in a mature democracy, politics have no place in the court room.

Secondly, that advisory committees:

> ... have increasingly found that many magistrates have declined to provide the information [relating to their political allegiance] or classed themselves as 'uncommitted'.

Thirdly, it claimed that in any case, 'geodemographic classification schemes', based on an analysis of particular personal attributes such as ethnicity, gender, marital status, occupation, home ownership and car owning status, are much more sensitive indicators for achieving social balance on benches than stated political allegiance.

Such 'geodemographics' might well represent the emergence of the truly classless society. Alternatively, they might represent a worrying denial of the importance of political attitudes within law generally, and the magistrates' bench in particular.

In any case, in March 2001, Jane Kennedy MP, Parliamentary Secretary to the LCD, announced that, at least for the moment, the Lord Chancellor had reluctantly decided that political balance would have to remain an issue. This statement was made in response to the disclosure that the Magistrates' Advisory Committee in Stoke-on-Trent had sent out a letter to several local organisations, which stated that:

> ... whilst the overriding criterion for appointment is always the suitability of the candidate, the Advisory Committee is particularly keen to receive applications from members of ethnic minorities, shop floor workers, the unemployed and Labour Party supporters.

In answering charges that such a letter was politicising the magistracy, Ms Kennedy pointed out that:

Public confidence in lay magistrates is vital. This is achieved, first and foremost, by individual magistrates discharging their duties effectively. It is also achieved when Benches reflect the diversity of the communities which they serve. In Stoke-on-Trent the Labour vote is significantly under-reflected on the magistrates' Bench. Of those who expressed political affiliation 40% were Labour, compared to 60% who voted Labour in the area at the last General Election. This compares to 47% of the Bench being acknowledged Conservative voters, compared to 27% in the area.

The Advisory Committee was simply and correctly trying to attract more Labour voters to apply to become magistrates, in order that the composition of the Bench more broadly reflected the local voting pattern.

6.8.2 The future of the magistrates' courts

In December 2000, the results of a report, *The Judiciary in the Magistrates' Courts*, were published. The extensive report was jointly commissioned by the Home Office and the LCD and provided an extremely valuable comparison between the lay magistracy and stipendiaries. It found as follows.

As regards the lay magistracy:

- they are drawn overwhelmingly from professional and managerial ranks;
- 40% of them are retired from full time employment;
- the cost of an appearance before lay magistrates is £52.10 per hour.

As regards the stipendiaries

- they are younger, but are mostly male and white;
- they hear cases more quickly;
- they are more likely to refuse bail and to make use of immediate custodial sentences;
- they are less likely to need legal advisers;
- the cost of an appearance before stipendiary magistrates is £61.78 per hour.

In the following January, 2001, a report entitled *Community Justice* by Professor Andrew Sanders for the Institute for Public Policy Research called for the replacement of panels of lay justices by panels composed of District Judges, the former stipendiary magistrates, assisted by two lay magistrates. According to Professor Sanders:

These proposals would increase public confidence, and they would enhance the contribution ordinary members of the public make to our justice system.

The Magistrates' Association took a rather different view and saw the proposals as an attack on what was already an extremely representative system of justice. According to its then Chair, Harry Mawdsley, the proposed scheme would cost around £30 million annually in salaries alone, but apart from costs:

> Lay magistrates provide community justice: they are ordinary people who live and work in the local community and who have an intimate knowledge of that community.

Although praising the magistracy's gender and ethnic make up, Mr Mawdsley nevertheless recognised the need to recruit more magistrates from working class backgrounds.

When the Auld Report into the criminal court system was issued later that year, it suggested a compromise between these two positions: the retention of the magistrates' courts as one division in a unified criminal court, with the creation of a new District Division, made up of a District Judge and two magistrates, to hear mid-range either way offences (the third division, the Crown Division, retained the role of the current Crown Court). In the event, the government declined to adopt the Auld recommendations in this regard, but proposed to increase the sentencing powers of the magistrates to 12 months in detention in the Criminal Justice Bill 2002. As Lord Irvine told the Magistrates' Association in October 2002:

> What the Government's proposals cement and enhance is your position at the heart of a reformed and more joined-up Criminal Justice System; one in which we have better pre-trial preparation; a more efficient trial process; and effective and appropriate sentencing.

Nonetheless, he felt required to re-emphasise how the magistrates should use their new sentencing power:

> I cannot emphasise this to you too strongly: your greater sentencing powers are to be exercised with restraint and in accordance with these principles: 'imprisonment only when necessary and for no longer than necessary'. The proposed new Sentencing Framework aims to encourage you to make full use of community sentences; and to reserve custodial sentences for serious, dangerous and persistent offenders.

6.9   Judicial review

The effect of the HRA on the interface between the judiciary and the executive has been considered previously at 1.7 and in this chapter, but that Act merely heightened the potential for conflict in a relationship that was already subject to some tension as a consequence of the operation of judicial review. If the interface between judiciary and executive tends now to be most sharply defined in human rights actions, the previous and continued role of judicial review in that relationship should not be underestimated.

The growth in applications for judicial review prior to the HRA was truly startling, as individuals and the judiciary recognised its potential utility as a means of challenging administrative decisions. The records show that in 1980, there were only 525 applications for judicial review; in 1996, 4,586; in 1997, 4,636 such applications; and by 1998, applications had passed the 5,000 mark and continued to rise.

At the outset, it should be noted that although this section focuses on those instances where the judiciary have decided against the exercise of executive power in a particular way, it has to be emphasised that the vast majority of judicial review cases are decided in favour of the executive. This may be significant when the views of Professor Griffith are examined at 6.11.1.

The remedies open to anyone challenging the decisions or actions of administrative institutions or public authorities can be divided into *private* or *public* law remedies.

6.9.1 Private law remedies

There are three private law remedies:

- *Declaration*

  This is a definitive statement, by the High Court or county court, of what the law is in a particular area. The procedure may be used by an individual or body to clarify a particularly contentious situation. It is a common remedy in private law, but it also has an important part to play in regard to individuals' relations with administrative institutions. This can be seen, for example, in *Congreve v Home Office* (1976), where the Court of Appeal stated that it would be unlawful for the Home Office to revoke annual television licences after only eight months because they had been bought in anticipation of an announced price rise but before the expiry of existing licences.

  Declarations, however, cannot be enforced either directly or indirectly through the contempt of court procedure. Public authorities are, as a matter of course, expected to abide by them.

- *Injunctions*

  Usually, an injunction seeks to restrain a person from breaking the law; alternatively, however, a mandatory injunction may instruct someone to undo what they have previously done, or alternatively to stop doing what they are doing. Both types of injunction may be sought against a public authority. See *Attorney General v Fulham Corp* (1921), in which a local authority was ordered to stop running a laundry service where it only had the power to establish laundries for people to wash their own clothes.

- *Damages*

  Damages cannot be awarded on their own in relation to administrative misconduct, but may be claimed in addition where one of the other remedies considered above is sought, as, for example, in *Cooper v Wandsworth Board of Works* (1863). In this case, a builder had put up a building without informing the Board of Works as he was required to do. When the Board demolished the building, he nonetheless recovered damages against them on the basis that the Board had exceeded its powers by not allowing him to defend or explain his actions.

In order to seek one of these private law remedies, an individual merely had to issue a writ against a public authority in their own name. They did not require the approval of the court.

6.9.2 The prerogative orders

The prerogative orders are so called because they were originally the means whereby sovereigns controlled the operation of their officials. As a consequence, the prerogative orders cannot be used against the Crown, but they can be used against individual ministers of State and, since *R v Secretary of State for the Home Department ex p Fire Brigades Union* (1995), considered at 6.10.2 below, it is clear that ministers cannot avoid judicial review by hiding behind the cloak of prerogative powers. The prerogative orders are as follows:

- *A quashing order*, formerly known as *certiorari*, is the mechanism by means of which decisions of inferior courts, tribunals and other authoritative bodies are brought before the High Court to have their validity examined. Where any such decision is found to be invalid, it may be set aside. An example of this can be seen in *Ridge v Baldwin* (1964). Here, the plaintiff had been dismissed from his position as Chief Constable without having had the opportunity to present any case for his defence. The House of Lords held that the committee which had taken the decision had acted in breach of the requirements of natural justice and granted a declaration that his dismissal was null and void.

- *A prohibiting order*, formerly known as *prohibition*, is similar to certiorari in that it relates to invalid acts of public authorities, but it is different to the extent that it is pre-emptive and prescriptive in regard to any such activity and operates to prevent the authority from taking invalid decisions in the first place. An example of the use of the order arose in *R v Telford Justices ex p Badham* (1991). In this case, an order was issued to stop committal proceedings in relation to an alleged rape that had not been reported until some 14 years after the alleged incident. The delay meant that the defendant would have been unable to prepare a proper defence against the charge.

- *A mandatory order*, formerly known as *mandamus*, may be seen as the obverse of a prohibiting order, in that it is an order issued by the High Court instructing an inferior court or some other public authority to carry out a duty laid on them. Such an order is frequently issued in conjunction with an order of certiorari, to the effect that a public body is held to be using its powers improperly and is instructed to use them in a proper fashion. In *R v Poplar BC (Nos 1 and 2)* (1922), the court ordered the borough council to pay over money due to the county council and to levy a rate to raise the money if necessary. Failure to comply with the order led to the imprisonment of some of the borough councillors.

In *O'Reilly v Mackman* (1982), however, the House of Lords decided that issues relating to *public* rights could *only* be enforced by means of the judicial review procedure, and that it would be an abuse of process for an applicant to seek a declaration by writ in relation to an alleged breach of a public duty or responsibility by a public authority. In deciding the case in this way, the House of Lords did much to demarcate and emphasise the role of judicial review as the method of challenging public authorities in their performance of their powers and duties in public law.

6.9.3 Grounds for application for judicial review

Judicial review allows people with a sufficient interest in a decision or action by a public body to ask a judge to review the lawfulness of:

(a) an enactment; or

(b) a decision, action or failure to act in relation to the exercise of a public function.

However, it is not an appeal on the merits of a decision.

The grounds of application can be considered under two heads: *procedural ultra vires* and *substantive ultra vires*:

- *Procedural ultra vires*, as its name suggests, relates to the failure of a person or body, provided with specific authority, to follow the procedure established for using that power. It also covers instances where a body exercising a judicial function fails to follow the requirements of natural justice by acting as prosecutor and judge in the same case or not permitting the accused person to make representations to the panel deciding the case.

- *Substantive ultra vires* occurs where someone does something that is not actually authorised by the enabling legislation. And, in *Associated Provincial Picture House v Wednesbury Corp* (1947), Lord Greene MR established the possibility of challenging discretionary decisions on the basis of unreasonableness.

Lord Greene's approach was endorsed and refined by Lord Diplock in *Council of Civil Service Unions v Minister for the Civil Service* (1984), in which he set out the three recognised grounds for judicial review, namely:

- illegality;
- irrationality;
- procedural impropriety.

Lord Diplock, however, introduced the possibility of a much more wide-ranging reason for challenging administrative decisions: namely, the doctrine of *proportionality*. Behind this doctrine is the requirement that there should be a reasonable relation between a decision and its objectives. It requires the achievement of particular ends by means that are not more oppressive than they need be to attain those ends. The potentially innovative aspect of this doctrine is the extent to which it looks to the substance of the decisions rather than simply focusing on the way in which they are reached.

Lord Diplock's listing of proportionality within the grounds for judicial review was controversial, if not at the very least arguably mistaken. Proportionality, however, is a key principle within the jurisdiction of the ECtHR, and is used frequently to assess the validity of State action which interferes with individual rights protected under the Convention. Consequently, as the HRA has incorporated the European Convention into UK law, proportionality will be a part of UK jurisprudence and legal practice, at least in cases which fall within the scope of the HRA. Although HRA cases and judicial review are different and distinct procedures, nonetheless, it is surely a mere matter of time before the doctrine of proportionality is applied by the judges in judicial review cases unrelated to the Convention.

Indeed such an approach was supported by Lord Slynn in *R v Secretary of State for the Environment, Transport and the Regions ex p Holding and Barnes* (2001), in which he stated:

> The European Court of Justice does of course apply the principle of proportionality when examining such acts and national judges must apply the same principle when dealing with Community law issues. There is a difference between that principle and the approach of the English courts in *Associated Provincial Picture Houses Ltd v Wednesbury Corporation* [1948] 1 KB 223. But the difference in practice is not as great as is sometimes supposed. The cautious approach of the European Court of Justice in applying the principle is shown *inter alia* by the margin of appreciation it accords to the institutions of the Community in making economic assessments. I consider that even without reference to the Human Rights Act the time has come to recognise that this principle is part of English administrative law, not only when judges are dealing with Community acts but also when they are dealing with acts subject to domestic law. Trying to keep the *Wednesbury* principle and proportionality in separate compartments seems to me to be unnecessary and confusing. Reference to the Human Rights Act however makes it necessary that the court

should ask whether what is done is compatible with Convention rights. That will often require that the question should be asked whether the principle of proportionality has been satisfied ...

6.9.4 The exclusion of judicial review

As will be considered in Chapter 8, one of the reasons for the setting up of extensive systems of administrative tribunals was precisely the wish to curb the power of the judges. It was felt that judges, and indeed the common law itself, tended to be more supportive of *individual* rights and freedoms as opposed to *collective* notions of welfare pursued by post-war governments, and that they would not administer such policies sympathetically. The judges, however, asserted their ultimate control over such tribunals generally through the use of judicial review. There have been various attempts by parliamentary drafters to exclude the judiciary from certain areas by wording provisions in such a way as to deny the possibility of judicial review. These attempts, however, have mainly proved to be in vain and have been rendered ineffective by the refusal of the courts to recognise their declared effect. Examples are:

- *'Finality' or 'ouster' clauses*

  There is a variety of possible wordings for these clauses. For example, the legislation might provide that 'the minister's [or the tribunal's] decision shall be final', or alternatively it might attempt to emphasise the point by stating that the decision in question 'shall be final and conclusive', or it might even provide that 'it shall be final, conclusive and shall not be questioned in any legal proceedings whatsoever'. Unfortunately for the drafter of the legislation and the minister or tribunal in question, all three formulations are equally likely to be ineffective. The courts have tended to interpret such phrases in a narrow way, so as to recognise the exclusion of an appeal procedure but to introduce the possibility of judicial review, as distinct from appeal. The classic case on this point is *R v Medical Appeal Tribunal ex p Gilmore* (1957), in which Lord Denning stated that, 'The word "final" ... does not mean without recourse to certiorari'. This, however, raised the point of provisions which expressly sought to exclude certiorari.

  In *South East Asia Fire Bricks Sdn Bhd v Non-Metallic Mineral Products Manufacturing Employees Union* (1980), the Privy Council decided that a Malaysian statute was sufficiently detailed in its wording to effectively exclude certiorari *for an error of law on the face of the record*. The Privy Council pointed out, however, that the exclusion could not be effective to prevent judicial review where the institution in question had acted *ultra vires* or in breach of natural justice.

- *Partial exclusion clauses*

  Where legislation has provided for a limited time period within which parties have to apply for judicial review, then applications outside of the period will not be successful. In *Smith v East Elloe Rural DC* (1956), the House of Lords, although only by 3:2 majority, recognised the effectiveness of a six week limitation clause in the Acquisition of Land (Authorisation Procedure) Act 1946. Although that case was subject to criticism in *Anisminic Ltd v Foreign Compensation Commission* (1969), it was explained and followed in *R v Secretary of State for the Environment ex p Ostler* (1976).

In response to the Franks Committee's recommendation that judicial review should not be subject to exclusion, s 14(1) of the Tribunals and Inquiries Act 1971 was enacted to that end. Unfortunately, it only applies to pre-1958 legislation.

6.10 Politics and the judiciary

Law is an inherently and inescapably political process. Even assertions as to the substantive autonomy of law (see Chapter 1) merely disguise the fact that, in making legal decisions, judges decide where the weight of public approval is to be placed and which forms of behaviour are to be sanctioned (see, for example, *R v Brown* (1993), where the House of Lords criminalised the sexual activities of consenting sado-masochists, arguably without fully comprehending some aspects of what was going on).

There is, however, an increasingly apparent tendency for contemporary judges to become actively, directly and openly engaged in more overtly political activity. The 1955 Kilmuir rules, named after the Lord Chancellor who introduced them, were designed to control the instances when the judiciary could express opinion in the media. The rules were abrogated in 1987 by Lord Mackay and since then, the judiciary have been more forthcoming in expressing their views, not just on matters strictly related to their judicial functions but also on wider political matters.

6.10.1 Sentencing policy

It is surely only correct that judges should be free to express views in areas where they have particular experience and expertise. However, even there, the judges can come into direct political confrontation with the policies of elected representatives. An example of this process can be cited in the concerted action of the judiciary in response to the pronouncements of the then Home Secretary, Michael Howard, at the Conservative Party Conference in Autumn 1993, in which he asserted the success of prison as a means of dealing with crime and declared his commitment to sending more offenders to prison. First of all, Lord Woolf, architect of the government's prison reform programme and who was conducting an investigation into the operation of the whole civil law process, responded by making reference to:

... a fashion, not confined to the totally uninformed, to indulge in rhetoric advocating increased sentences across the board in a way which will be counter productive ...

He was quoted in *The Guardian* newspaper as stating that such talk was 'shortsighted and irresponsible'.

Perhaps the really surprising aspect of this difference of opinion was not that Lord Woolf disagreed with the Home Secretary, but that he was supported in his views by seven other judges in a series of interviews in *The Observer*, 17 October 1993, including the then Law Lord, Lord Ackner, and the chairman of the JSB, Lord Justice Farquharson.

A similar scenario was replayed in February 2001, following a speech to the Social Market Foundation by the then new Labour Home Secretary, Jack Straw, in which he announced the need to target the 100,000 most persistent criminal offenders and to punish them by imprisonment. As he put it:

Almost without exception, every persistent offender sentenced to custody has been through the mill of community sentences and has still reoffended ... If we are to get on top of this problem of persistent criminality and to process more through the system prison numbers may well have to rise.

Within hours, Lord Woolf, by now the Lord Chief Justice but still as committed to prison reform as he ever was, had responded extremely strongly. In a lecture to the Prison Reform Trust, he stated that overcrowding was the 'AIDS virus of the prison system' and went on to express his view, totally at odds with that of the Home Secretary, that:

The judiciary must play their part in reducing the use of custody to what is the acceptable and appropriate minimum. When a custodial sentence is necessary the shortest sentence ... should be imposed. Frequently one month will achieve everything that can be achieved by three months and three months will achieve everything that can be by six months and so on ... What has to be realised, and I include the government here, is that a short custodial sentence is a very poor alternative to a sentence to be served in the community. It is far more expensive. It will do nothing to tackle the offender's behavioural problems. It should be regarded as being no more than a necessary evil whose primary purpose is to obtain compliance with court orders.

Another instance of Lord Woolf's continued and controversial influence over sentencing policy arose towards the end of 2002. In November of that year, the government announced its Criminal Justice Bill, which it claimed would 'rebalance the system in favour of victims, witnesses and communities and deliver justice for all, by building greater trust and credibility while protecting the rights of the innocent'. Or, in the Prime Minister's sound bite, it was designed to create a 'victim justice system' rather than the present 'criminal justice system'. However in December, in *R v McInerney* (2002), Lord Woolf took the opportunity to restate sentencing policy in relation to burglary. Sitting with Mr Justice Silber and Mr Justice Grigson, he ruled that the average first time, non-professional and non-violent domestic burglar should receive a community punishment rather than be sentenced to a period of imprisonment. Consequently, the previous sentencing 'starting point' of up to 18 months in prison should no longer apply.

Lord Woolf recommended that the initial approach of the courts should be to impose a community sentence, so long as it was an effective punishment that would tackle the offender's underlying problems such as drug addiction. If, and only if, the court was satisfied that the offender had demonstrated by their behaviour that punishment in the community was not practicable should the court resort to a custodial sentence.

The new approach, and its subsequent support by the Lord Chancellor, was severely attacked in the tabloid press and by some politicians as being soft on crime and out of touch with the views of ordinary people. One Labour MP, Graham Allen, was quoted as saying that:

> We should not let burglars think that the first one is free ... I am rather surprised that the Lord Chief Justice has issued this ruling ahead of consideration of the House of Commons for sentencing in general. Is it appropriate that he can make this sort of decision, which is completely disengaged from the reality of people's lives on council estates and other parts of the country?

In the light of the attack, and some allegations that he had tried to slip it out unnoticed in the run up to Christmas, Lord Woolf took the unusual step of emailing all circuit judges and Chairmen of Magistrates' Benches in England and Wales on 23 December 2002. In his message, he stated that the new approach:

> ...is consistent with the repeated advice you have received only to resort to imprisonment when necessary and then to make the punishment as short as possible. The guidance makes clear that if the court is satisfied that the offender has demonstrated by his behaviour, that punishment in the community is not practical then there is to be a custodial sentence. As to when a community sentence is not practical the judgment recognises that the only guidance that the court can give is to say that a community sentence may not be appropriate because of the effect of the offence on the victim, the nature of the offence or the offender's record. The guidance is intended to reduce the use of imprisonment but only if this is consistent with the protection of the public. It also makes clear that if appropriate, heavy sentences are to be imposed.

6.10.2 The politics of judicial review and the Human Rights Act

As has been stated, the HRA merely heightened the potential for conflict between the judges and the executive and Parliament, but the relationship was already subject to some tension as a consequence of the operation of judicial review, as can be seen in a number of cases.

In *M v Home Office* (1993), the House of Lords decided that the court has jurisdiction in judicial review proceedings to grant interim and final injunctions against officers of the Crown, and to make a finding of contempt of court against a government department or a minister of the Crown in either his personal *or his official capacity.*

M v Home Office is of signal importance in establishing the powers of the courts in relation to the executive. It is also interesting to note that in delivering the leading speech, Lord Woolf quoted extensively from, and clearly supported, Dicey's view of the Rule of Law as involving the subjection of all, including State officials, to the ordinary law of the land (see Chapter 1).

In November 1994, the government suffered two damaging blows from the judiciary. In *R v Secretary of State for Foreign Affairs ex p World Development Movement Ltd* (1995), the Queen's Bench Divisional Court held that the Secretary of State had acted beyond his powers in granting aid to the Malaysian Government in relation to the Pergau Dam project. The financial assistance was given, not for the promotion of development *per se*, as authorised by s 1 of the Overseas Development and Cooperation Act 1980, but in order to facilitate certain arms' sales. As Rose LJ stated:

> Whatever the Secretary of State's intention or purpose may have been, it is, as it seems to me, a matter for the courts and not for the Secretary of State to determine whether, on the evidence before the court, the particular conduct was, or was not, within the statutory purpose.

In *R v Secretary of State for the Home Department ex p Fire Brigades Union* (1995), the Court of Appeal held that the Home Secretary had committed an abuse of power in implementing a scheme designed to cut the level of payments made to the subjects of criminal injuries. The court held that he was under an obligation, under the CJA 1988, to put the previous non-statutory scheme on a statutory basis. It was not open for the Secretary of State to use his prerogative powers to introduce a completely new tariff scheme contrary to the intention of Parliament as expressed in the CJA 1988. The decision of the Court of Appeal was confirmed by a 3:2 majority in the House of Lords in April 1995, the majority holding that the Secretary of State had exceeded or abused powers granted to him by Parliament. It is of interest to note that in his minority judgment Lord Keith warned that to dismiss the Home Secretary's appeal would be:

> ... an unwarrantable intrusion into the political field and a usurpation of the function of Parliament.

In 1997, in *R v Secretary of State for the Home Department ex p Venables and Thompson*, the House of Lords decided that the Home Secretary had misused his powers in relation to two juveniles who had been sentenced to detention during Her Majesty's pleasure (see 1.7.2.3.1).

Even Lord Chancellors have not escaped the unwanted control of judicial review, and in March 1997, John Witham successfully argued that the Lord Chancellor had exceeded his statutory powers in removing exemptions from court fees for those in receipt of State income support. The exemptions had been removed as part of a wider measure to increase court income by raising fee levels, but Lord Justice Rose and Mr Justice Laws held that Lord Mackay had exceeded the statutory powers given to him by Parliament. Rose LJ stated that there was nothing to suggest that Parliament ever intended 'a power for the Lord Chancellor to prescribe fees so as to preclude the poor from access to the courts'. Laws J on the other hand stated that: 'Access to the courts is a constitutional right; it can only be denied by the government if it persuades Parliament to pass legislation which specifically permits the executive to turn people away. That has not been done in this case' (*R v Lord Chancellor ex p Witham* (1997)).

The change of government in 1997 did nothing to stem the flow of judicial review cases, with the occasional embarrassing defeat for the executive. Thus, in *R v Secretary of State for Education and Employment ex p National Union of Teachers* (2000), the Divisional Court held that the Secretary of State for Education had exceeded his statutory powers in seeking to alter teachers' contracts of employment, particularly by introducing threshold standards in relation to a new scheme of performance related pay. He had sought to introduce the changes in the Education (School Teachers' Pay and Conditions) (No 2) Order 2000 after only four days' consultation with the trade union. The court held that although the Secretary of State had the statutory powers to alter the contracts of employment under the Teachers' Pay and Conditions Act 1991, he had not adopted the correct procedure for doing so as set out in that Act. Consequently, the Education (School Teachers' Pay and Conditions) (No 2) Order was quashed. Although this decision represented a victory for the Union and an embarrassment for the Secretary of State, it was only temporary in nature and the new contracts were subsequently introduced following the proper statutory procedure.

Given his centrality in the operation of the criminal justice system and immigration, it is hardly surprising that the Home Secretary is subject to more claims for judicial review than any other minister, nor is it surprising that some of them go against him. In relation to his role in the criminal justice system, *R v Secretary of State for the Home Department ex p Tawfick* (2000) is of particular interest, in that it involved issues relating to judicial summing up and compensation for imprisonment following wrongful conviction.

The CJA 1988 introduced compensation as of right, in particular and limited instances where people have been wrongly imprisoned. Prior to that, the Home Secretary had a discretionary power to make *ex gratia* payments to such people and he retained that power in relation to cases that do not come under the CJA 1988. These discretionary payments may be made to the victim, or their family where appropriate, in 'exceptional circumstances'. The question is what amounts to 'exceptional circumstances'? An *ex gratia* payment was made to the family of Derek Bentley, who had been hanged for murder in 1953. Bentley's conviction had been referred to the Court of Appeal by the Criminal Cases Review Commission (CCRC), and his conviction was quashed as unsafe on the basis that the judge in his trial had given a summing up 'such as to deny Bentley that fair trial which is the right of every British citizen' (Lord Bingham, *R v Bentley* (1998)).

In *R v Secretary of State for the Home Department ex p Tawfick*, the Divisional Court was asked to review the Home Secretary's refusal to make a discretionary payment to the claimant. Tawfick had been found guilty of conspiracy to steal and handling stolen goods. He had already served five months in prison before the Court of Appeal quashed his conviction on the grounds that the trial judge had:

> ... allowed himself to be drawn into making observations which would in all probability have led the jury to regard the appellant as a liar.

Tawfick applied for compensation and was refused. He then successfully sought judicial review of the Home Secretary's decision but, again on reconsideration, the Home Secretary refused to make a compensation award. Subsequent to the decision to award compensation to Bentley's family, Tawfick sought a further judicial review and this time the court held that the circumstances of his case were of such an exceptional nature as to warrant payment, and that the Home Secretary had fallen into error by using the extreme circumstances of the *Bentley* case as the benchmark for making discretionary awards.

R v Secretary of State for the Home Department ex p Adan and Others (2001) considered the Home Secretary's role in relation to asylum applications. These cases concerned three applicants, two of whom had previously been refused asylum in Germany and one of whom had previously been refused asylum in France. On being refused asylum in those countries, the three had made their way to the UK and had applied for, and been refused, asylum there. The question at issue was whether the three could be returned to the countries in which they had first applied for asylum, as the Home Office had ordered. The argument for the claimants was that, whereas both Germany and France only considered those who fled 'State' persecution as coming within the definition of refugees under the Geneva Convention for the Protection of Refugees 1951, the UK recognised that persecution by 'non-State' agents could provide grounds for refugee status. All three claimed to have been subjected to 'non-State' persecution and that to return them to Germany and France would lead to their being sent back to their own States, contrary to the principles of the Geneva Convention and s 2(2) of the Asylum and Immigration Act 1996, which required that they be returned to 'safe' third countries.

The Divisional Court originally held that the applicants could be returned to Germany and France, as these were both safe countries within the meaning of the Asylum and Immigration Act. However, both the Court of Appeal and later the House of Lords held that Germany and France were not to be considered 'safe third countries' for the purposes of s 2(2) of the Asylum and Immigration Act 1996; consequently, the applicants could not be deported to either of those countries.

It can be seen from the foregoing that judicial review provided the judiciary with the means for addressing the potential for abuse that followed on from the growth of discretionary power in the hands of the modern State, particularly if it was operated on the basis of the doctrine of proportionality. Alongside the growth in the number of applications, there were also indications that at least some of the higher judiciary saw it as part of their function to exercise such control over the executive. For example, the former Master of the Rolls and former Lord Chief Justice, Lord Bingham, was quoted in *The Observer* newspaper of 9 May 1993 as saying that:

> Slowly, the constitutional balance is tilting towards the judiciary. The courts have reacted to the increase in powers claimed by the government by being more active themselves.

Judicial review is a delicate exercise and by necessity draws the judiciary into the political arena, using the word 'political' in its widest, non-party sense. That the judges were aware of this is evident from the words of Lord Woolf in the same article. As he recognised:

> Judicial review is all about balance: between the rights of the individual and his need to be treated fairly, and the rights of government at local and national level to do what it has been elected to do. There is a very sensitive and political decision to be made.

However, another former Law Lord, Lord Browne-Wilkinson, observed on a BBC radio programme, admittedly before his elevation to the House of Lords, that a great void was apparent in the political system, deriving from the fact that no government had a true popular majority and yet all governments were able to carry Parliament in support of anything they wanted. He went on to express the view that Parliament was not a place where it was easy to get accountability for abuse or misuse of powers. According to Lord Browne-Wilkinson, while judicial review could not overcome the will of Parliament, judges had a special role because *democracy was defective*. He then asked a rhetorical question as to who else but the judges could ensure that executive action is taken in accordance with law, *and not abused by increasingly polarised political stances*.

Such thinking is also evident in an article by Mr Justice Stephen Sedley (as he was then) in the May 1995 edition of the *London Review of Books*, in which he asserted that after decades of passivity, there is a new 'culture of judicial assertiveness to compensate for, and in places repair, dysfunctions in the democratic process', and that the last three decades of the 20th century may have seen the British constitution being re-fashioned by judges 'with sufficient popular support to mute political opposition'.

As has been seen at 1.7, the introduction of the HRA greatly increased judicial power in relation to the other two branches of the constitution, and it might have been thought that the judges would not have been reluctant to use their new powers. However, as was also seen in that section, the courts, and the Court of Appeal and the House of Lords in particular, have been reluctant to use their new powers in a radical manner. As the Lord Chancellor expressed it in his inaugural Human Rights Lecture at the University of Durham:

> It is all about balance. The balance between intense judicial scrutiny and reasonable deference to elected decision-makers is a delicate one to strike. But the judiciary have struck it well: and I welcome that. Whilst scrutiny is undoubtedly an important aid to better governance, there are areas in which decisions are best taken by the decision-makers entrusted by Parliament to make them. This may be for reasons of democratic accountability, expertise or complexity.

The Lord Chancellor may well be of the view that the judges have got it right, but his views do not sound in harmony with those of his colleague, the current Home Secretary, David Blunkett, who has been a consistent source of attack on the judiciary. Perhaps his most severe attack came after Collins J's decision in *R (on the Application of Q) v Secretary of State for the Home Department* (2003) (see 1.7.1.5), which declared unlawful his power under s 55 of the Nationality, Immigration and Asylum Act 2002 to refuse to provide assistance to those who had not immediately declared their intention to claim asylum when they arrived in the UK. In the press, the Home Secretary was quoted as saying: 'Frankly, I am fed up with having to deal with a situation where Parliament debates issues and judges then overturn them. We were aware of the circumstances, we did mean what we said and, on behalf of the British people, we are going to implement it.'

Of even more concern were the reports that the Prime Minister was 'prepared for a showdown with the judiciary to stop the courts thwarting government's attempts to curb the record flow of asylum seekers into Britain', and that he was looking into the possibility of enacting legislation to limit the role of judges in the interpretation of international human rights obligations and re-assert the primacy of Parliament. There were even reports that the Prime Minister was considering withdrawing completely from the ECHR, rather than merely issuing derogations where it was thought necessary.

Given such pressure, it is perhaps not surprising that when the Court of Appeal heard the *Q* case, whilst it supported Collins J's decision, it went out of its way to provide the Home Secretary with advice on how to make the Act, and the procedures under it, compatible with ECHR rights. It is suggested that those who celebrated the decision as leaving the government's asylum policy 'in tatters' failed to fully appreciate its consequences. Certainly for once, the Home Secretary did not react with antagonism to the Court of Appeal's decision; rather he welcomed it as 'helpfully clarifying the law' and stated that he would not be taking the case to the House of Lords.

In an article in *The Guardian* newspaper in November 2001, the commentator Hugo Young expressed his puzzlement about the Home Secretary's behaviour as follows:

> The judges have not been immune to the demands of the security state. Given what they are sometimes prepared to do to assist the executive, it is not easy to understand why Blunkett has marked his tenure by regularly casting aspersions on them.

It might not be too cynical to suggest that the continued favourable outcome is the justification for the continued attack. It might even not be overly cynical to suggest that the senior judiciary have been extremely circumspect in actually using their new powers, and have not been willing to use them to the extent they might have under other circumstances, when they have been generally accepted by both Parliament and the public. In April 2003, Lord Irvine entered the dispute when he offered an implicit, if no doubt stinging, criticism of the Home Secretary in his appearance before the select committee on the LCD. As he stated:

> When the judiciary gives decisions that the executive does not like, as in all governments, some ministers have spoken out against … [them] … I disapprove of that. I think it undermines the rule of law.

Still, as Lord Woolf recognised in a speech to the Royal Academy, which linked the HRA, judicial review and the rule of law, the possibility of a major confrontation between the judges and the executive still remains:

> Just as the development of judicial review in the final quarter of last century improved administration in our increasingly complex society, so will the existence of the [HRA] protect our individual interests, which are so easily lost sight of in meeting the demands of the global economy. The real test of the [HRA] arises when individuals or minorities attract the antagonism of the majority of the public. When the tabloids are in full cry. Then, the courts must, without regard for their own interests, make the difficult decisions that ensure that those under attack have the benefit of the rule of law. At the heart of the [HRA] is the need to respect the dignity of every individual by ensuring he or she is not subject to discrimination.

The fact that the judges increasingly see it as incumbent upon them to use judicial review and the HRA as the means of questioning and controlling what they see as the abuse of executive power does, at the very least, raise very serious questions in relation to their suitability for such a role. These doubts can be set out in terms of:

- *Competence*

  This refers to the question whether the judges are sufficiently competent to participate in deciding the substantive issues that they have been invited to consider under the guise of judicial review, and may be entitled to consider under the HRA. Judges are experts in law; they are not experts in the various and highly specialised areas of policy that by definition tend to be involved in judicial review cases. They may disagree with particular decisions, but it has to be at least doubted that they are qualified to take such policy decisions. A classic example of this difficulty was the 'fares' fair' cases (*Bromley London BC v GLC* (1983) and later, *R v London Transport Executive ex p GLC* (1983)), in which the courts got involved in deciding issues relating to transport policy for London on the pretext that they were judicially defining the meaning of particular words in a statute. As was considered in Chapter 5, the apparently technocratic, and hence neutral, application of rules of interpretation simply serves to disguise a political procedure and, in these cases, the policy issue concerned was certainly beyond the scope of the judges to determine. In *Bellinger v Bellinger* (2003), the House of Lords, although obviously sympathetic to the case, admitted their incompetence as regards deciding issues relating to the rights of transsexuals. For that reason, they issued a declaration of incompatibility under the HRA 1998 and thus passed the matter to Parliament for review and appropriate reform.

- *Constitutionality*

  This refers to the wider point that the separation of powers applies equally to the judiciary as it does to the executive. In interfering with substantive decisions and involving themselves in political matters, albeit on the pretence of merely deciding points of law, the judiciary may be seen to be exceeding their constitutional powers. It has to be remembered that judges are unelected and unaccountable.

- *Partiality*

  This refers to the possibility of individual, and indeed corporate, bias within the judiciary, as will be considered at 6.11, below.

The foregoing has indicated that the relationship between the State and the courts may, on occasion, involve a measure of tension, with the courts attempting to rein in the activities of the State. The relationship between the judiciary and the executive is well summed up in the words of Lord Justice Farquharson, again taken from an *Observer* article:

> We have to be very careful: the executive is elected. We have a role in the Constitution but, if we go too far, there will be a reaction. The Constitution only works if the different organs trust each other. If the judges start getting too frisky, there would be retaliation, renewed attempts to curb the judiciary.

Although no longer in force, the Kilmuir rules did have a valid point to make:

... the overriding consideration ... is the importance of keeping the judiciary in this country isolated from the controversies of the day. So long as a judge keeps silent, his reputation for wisdom and impartiality remains unassailable; but every utterance which he makes in public ... must necessarily bring him within the focus of criticism.

6.11 Politics of the judiciary

When considering the role which the judiciary play in the process of applying the law, or indeed the process already adverted to in Chapter 2, whereby they actually make the law, criticism is usually levelled at the particular race, class and gender position of the majority of the judges. It is an objective and well documented fact that the majority of judges are 'white, middle class, middle aged to elderly men', but the question that has to be considered is whether this *necessarily* leads to the conclusion that judges reach inherently biased decisions. It is always possible, indeed the newspapers make it relatively easy, to provide anecdotal evidence which apparently confirms either the bias or the lack of social awareness of the judiciary; but the fundamental question remains as to whether these cases are exceptional or whether they represent the norm.

Why should judges' class/race/gender placement make them less objective arbiters of the law? It is worth considering the fact that *unsupported* general assertions as to the inherently partial approach of the judiciary is itself partial. Simon Lee, not totally fatuously, has highlighted the logical flaw in what he refers to as the 'Tony Benn thesis' (Benn, the former left wing, Labour Party Member of Parliament who created history by being the first hereditary peer to renounce his peerage in order to remain in the House of Commons). Just because judges are old, white, rich, upper middle class, educated at public school and Oxbridge does not mean that they all necessarily think the same way; after all, Benn was a product of the same social circumstances. There is, of course, the point that people from that particular background *generally* tend to be conservative in outlook, and the apparent validity of Lee's argument is clearly the product of logic-chopping that reverses the accepted relationship and uses the exception as the rule, rather than seeing the exception as proving/testing the rule. Nevertheless, Lee's point remains true: that proof of judicial bias is needed.

As the previous chapter of this book pointed out, if law were completely beyond the scope of judges to manipulate to their own ends, then the race, class and gender placement of individual judges would be immaterial, as they would not be in any position to influence the operation of the law. That chapter also demonstrated, however, the way in which the doctrines which set the limits within which the judiciary operate are by no means as rigid and restrictive as they might at first appear. It was seen that, although judges are supposed merely to apply rather than create law, they possess a large measure of discretion in determining which laws to apply, what those laws mean, and how they should be applied. In the light of this potential capacity to create law, it is essential to ensure that the judiciary satisfactorily represent society at large in relation to which they have so much power, and to ensure further that they do not merely represent the views and attitudes of a self-perpetuating elite.

The limited class background of the judiciary was confirmed in figures issued by the Lord Chancellor's office on 17 May 1995, which revealed that 80% of Lords of Appeal, Heads of Division, Lord Justices of Appeal and High Court Justices were educated at Oxford or Cambridge. In justifying the figures, the Lord Chancellor's Permanent Secretary, Sir Thomas Legg, showing insouciance to the level of arrogance, simply stated that, 'It is not the function of the professional judiciary to be representative of the community'. Such a response, even if it is true, let alone acceptable, must surely undermine the right of such an unrepresentative body to take action in the name of the majority, as the courts do in their use of judicial review.

Unfortunately, the continuing social imbalance amongst the senior judiciary was further confirmed in a report on judicial appointments by the Commons Home Affairs Committee, presented in June 1996. It revealed that four-fifths of judges went to both public schools and Oxbridge colleges, that only seven out of 96 High Court Judges were women, and that only five out of the 517 circuit judges were black or Asian. Nevertheless, the Committee rejected proposals for positive discrimination or even for the establishment of a judicial appointments committee to replace the present informal system under the control of the Lord Chancellor.

Instead of things improving, if one actually has the temerity to consider it an improvement to have fewer Oxbridge men on the bench, a Labour Research investigation found that things were actually getting worse in terms of the wider representational make up of the judiciary (as has been considered above at 6.3.2). Still, Lord Irvine holds fast to appointment solely on merit, which appears wholly commendable, but, as has been stated before, who decides on merit, and what qualities are they actually measuring?

A Nuffield Foundation funded report produced in November 1999 by Professor Hazel Genn in conjunction with the National Centre for Social Research, entitled *Paths to Justice*, revealed a truly remarkable lack of general confidence in the judiciary. The research surveyed a random selection of 4,125 people, from which total 1,248 people who had had experience of legal problems were selected for more detailed interview, with a smaller group of 48 being extensively interviewed. The results suggest that two out of three people think that judges are out of touch with ordinary people's lives, but more worryingly, only 53% thought that they would get a fair hearing if they ever went to court. Disappointingly, at the launch of the report, Lord Woolf claimed that this 'misconception' was due to 'irresponsible media reporting' and stated that:

> It behoves the media to learn from this and recognise the dangers posed to confidence in the judicial system.

Surely, it more behoves the judiciary and the LCD to do more to redress this negative perception than simply blame the media for focusing on silly judge stories of which, unfortunately, there are still too many.

One of the findings of the report was that judges could improve their image by getting rid of their wigs and gowns. Perish the thought: there are standards and distinctions to be maintained. Thus, in *Practice Direction (Court Dress) (No 3)* (1998), the Lord High Chancellor, Lord Irvine of Lairg, provides:

> Queens' Counsel wear a short wig and silk (or stuff) gown over a court coat; junior counsel wear a short wig and stuff gown with bands; solicitors and other advocates authorised under the Courts and Legal Services Act 1990 wear a black stuff gown, *but no wig* [emphasis added].

6.11.1 Criticisms

The treatment of some aspects of potential bias within the judiciary has already been dealt with at 6.1.3, but this section addresses a more amorphous form of prejudice, and therefore one that is correspondingly more difficult to recognise or deal with. Given the central position of judges in the operation of law and the legal system, particularly with regard to the growth in judicial review and their new role in relation to giving effect to the HRA, the question these reports raise is whether the social placement of the judiciary leads to any perceptible shortfall in the provision of justice. The pre-eminent critic of the way in which the judiciary permit their shared background, attitudes and prejudices to influence their understanding and statement of the law is Professor JAG Griffith. According to Griffith, bias can occur at two levels:

- *Personal bias*

    Personal bias occurs where individual judges permit their own personal prejudices to influence their judgment and thus the effective application of the law. It is relatively easy to cite cases where judges give expression to their own attitudes and in so doing exhibit their own prejudices. As examples of this process, two cases can be cited which consider the rule of natural justice, that a person should not be both the accuser and judge in the same case. In *Hannam v Bradford Corp* (1970), the court held that it was contrary to natural justice for three school governors to sit as members of a local authority education disciplinary committee, charged with deciding whether or not to uphold a previous decision of the governors to dismiss a teacher. This was so even though the three governors had not been present at the meeting where it was decided to dismiss the teacher. On the other hand, in *Ward v Bradford Corp* (1971), the Court of Appeal refused to interfere with a decision by governors of a teacher training college to confirm the expulsion of a student, although they had instituted the disciplinary proceedings and three members of the governors sat on the original disciplinary committee. What possible explanation can there be for this discrepancy? The only tenable explanation is to be found in the latter court's disapproval of the plaintiff's behaviour in that case. The truly reprehensible judgment of Lord Denning concludes that the student lost nothing, as she was not a fit person to teach children in any case. Can such a conclusion be justified on purely legal grounds or is it based on individual morality? Lord Denning did his best to buttress his judgment with spurious legal reasoning, but it could be suggested that, in so doing, he merely brought the process of legal reasoning into disrepute and revealed its fallaciousness.

Courts have also been notoriously unsympathetic to victims of rape and have been guilty of making the most obtuse of sexist comments in relation to such victims. Nor can it be claimed that depreciatory racist remarks have been totally lacking in court cases.

Such cases of bias are serious and reprehensible, but the very fact that the prejudice they demonstrate appears as no more than the outcome of particular judges, who are simply out of touch with current standards of morality or acceptable behaviour, suggests that it might be eradicated by the Lord Chancellor exercising stricter control over such mavericks and appointing more appropriate judges in the first place. Professor Griffith, however, suggests that there is a further type of bias that is actually beyond such relatively easy control.

• *Corporate bias*

Corporate bias involves the assertion that the judges *as a body* decide certain types of cases in a biased way. This accusation of corporate bias is much more serious than that of personal bias, for the reason that it asserts that the problem of bias is *systematic* rather than merely limited to particular maverick judges. As a consequence, if such a claim is justified, it has to be concluded that the problem is not susceptible to treatment at the level of the individual judge, but requires a complete alteration of the whole judicial system.

Griffith claims that, as a consequence of their shared educational experience, their shared training and practical experience at the Bar and their shared social situation as members of the Establishment, judges have developed a common outlook. He maintains that they share homogeneous values, attitudes and beliefs as to how the law should operate and be administered. He further suggests that this shared outlook is inherently conservative, if not Conservative in a party political sense.

Griffith's argument is that the highest judges in the judicial hierarchy are frequently called upon to decide cases on the basis of a determination of what constitutes the public interest and that, in making that determination, they express their own corporate values which are in turn a product of their position in society as part of the ruling Establishment. Griffith maintains that judges can be seen to operate in such a way as to maintain the status quo and resist challenges to the established authority. Underlying this argument is the implication that the celebrated independence of the judiciary is, in fact, a myth and that the courts will tend to decide cases in such a way as to buttress the position of the State, especially if it is under the control of a Conservative government.

In an attempt to substantiate his claims, Griffith examines cases relating to trade union law, personal rights, property rights and matters of national security, where he claims to find judges consistently acting to support the interests of the State over the rights of the individual. Some of the concrete examples he cites are the withdrawal of trade union rights from GCHQ at Cheltenham (*Council of Civil Service Unions v Minister for Civil Service* (1984)); the banning of publishing any extracts from the *Spycatcher* book (*AG v Guardian Newspapers Ltd* (1987)); and the treatment of suspected terrorists.

There certainly have been some overtly right wing decisions taken by the courts, and the history of trade union cases is replete with them even at the highest level. The greater strength of Griffith's argument, however, would appear to be in the way that the courts have understood and expressed what is to be meant by 'public interest' in such a way as to reflect conservative, but not necessarily illiberal, values. It is surely only from that perspective that the higher judiciary's antagonistic response to some of the electorally driven policy decisions in relation to the legal system by *both* Conservative and New Labour administrations can be reconciled.

As would be expected, Griffith, and other academics associated with the left, have expressed their reservations about the extent to which the HRA will hand power to an unelected, unaccountable, inherently conservative and unreformed body, as they claim the judiciary is.

A notable, if somewhat complacent, response to Griffith's book was provided by Lord Devlin, who pointed out that, in most cases and on most issues, there tended to be plurality rather than unanimity of opinion and decision amongst judges. He also claimed that it would be just as possible for a more conservatively minded person than Griffith to go through the casebooks to provide a list of examples where the courts had operated in an over-liberal manner. Lord Devlin also adopted a different explanation of the judiciary's perceived reluctance to abandon the status quo. For him, any conservatism on the part of judges was to be seen as a product of age rather than class. In conclusion, he asserted that even if the judiciary were biased, their bias was well known and allowances could be made for it.

The issue of the way in which the criminal appeal procedure dealt with suspected terrorist cases is of particular relevance in the light of the Runciman Commission Report. General dissatisfaction with the trials and appeals involving suspected terrorists such as the Maguire Seven, the Birmingham Six, the Guildford Four, the Tottenham Three, Stefan Kiszko and Judith Ward helped to give rise to the widespread impression that the UK criminal justice system, and in particular the British appeal system, needed to be considered for reform.

In the light of the fact that the appeal system did not seem to be willing to consider the possibility of the accused's innocence once they had been convicted, the Runciman Commission's recommendation that a Criminal Case Review Authority be established, independent of the Home Office, was widely welcomed and resulted in the establishment of the CCRC in the Criminal Appeal Act 1995 (see 4.5.6, above). The question still remains, however, whether those earlier cases reflect an inherently and inescapably conservative judiciary, or were they simply unfortunate instances of more general errors of the system which the implementation of the CCRC can overcome? And perhaps more importantly, will the Court of Appeal give a fair hearing to the cases referred to it by the CCRC?

It is apparent from the statistics produced by the LCD cited previously that senior judges are still being appointed from the same limited social and educational elite as they always have been. This gives rise to the suspicion, if not the reality, that the decisions that this elite make merely represent values and interests of a limited and privileged segment of society rather than society as a whole. Even if the accusations levelled by Professor Griffith are inaccurate, it is surely still necessary to remove even the possibility of those accusations.

THE JUDICIARY

The constitutional role of the judiciary

Judges play a central role in the English constitution. The doctrine of the separation of powers maintains that the judicial function be kept distinct from the legislative and executive functions of the State. The Lord Chancellor occupies an anomalous situation in this respect.

The constitutional role of the Lord Chancellor

The Lord Chancellor holds an anomalous position in respect of the separation of powers within the UK constitution, in that he is at one and the same time: the most senior member of the judiciary and can hear cases in the House of Lords as a court; a member of the legislature as Speaker of the House of Lords as a legislative assembly; and a member of the executive holding a position in the government. Although doubts have been raised about this situation, the present incumbent shows no desire to alter it, and indeed has gone on record as supporting the status quo.

The effect of the *Pinochet* case on the House of Lords

The recent case involving the previous dictator of Chile, General Augusto Pinochet, has brought the House of Lords into the glare of unwanted publicity. It has raised questions as to its current role within the present constitution and even more concern has been expressed about its role under a reformed constitution with devolution and a non-hereditary House of Lords.

Judicial offices

The main judicial offices are the Lord Chancellor, the Lord Chief Justice, the Master of the Rolls, the President of the Family Division, the Vice Chancellor and the Senior Presiding Judge. Law Lords are referred to as Lords of Appeal in Ordinary. Court of Appeal judges are referred to as Lords Justices of Appeal.

Appointment of the judiciary

The Courts and Legal Services Act 1990 has opened the possibility of judicial office, even in the higher courts, to non-barristers.

All judicial appointments remain, theoretically, in the hands of the Crown. The Prime Minister advises the Crown on the appointment of senior judicial office holders and the Law Lords and Appeal Court judges. Judges at the level of High Court Judges and below, including lay magistrates, are appointed on the advice of the Lord Chancellor.

Lord Chancellor Mackay's limited steps to open up appointment procedure have been followed up by Lord Irvine, but as yet the system remains open to accusations of secrecy, and although a Commission on Judicial Appointments has been established, it does not play an active part in the appointment process.

Training of the judiciary

Training of English judges is undertaken under the auspices of the Judicial Studies Board. Judges from the highest Law Lord to the lowest magistrate are subject to training. It is gratifying to note that anti-discriminatory training is a priority, although some have continued to express doubt about judicial attitudes in this regard. General training focuses on various aspects of discrimination and special training was undertaken in relation to the Woolf reforms and the introduction of the Human Rights Act. This being said, it remains arguable that the training undergone by UK judges is not as rigorous as the training of judges on the continent.

Removal of judges

Senior judges hold office subject to good behaviour. They can be removed by an address by the two Houses of Parliament.

Judges below High Court status can be removed by the Lord Chancellor on grounds of misbehaviour or incapacity and he can remove magistrates without the need to show cause.

Judicial immunity

To ensure judicial integrity, it is provided that judges cannot be sued for actions done or words said in the course of their judicial function.

This immunity extends to trial lawyers, witnesses and juries.

Magistrates

Magistrates have powers in relation to both criminal and civil law.

Stipendiary magistrates are professional and are legally qualified.

Lay magistrates are not paid and they are not legally qualified.

Magistrates are appointed by the Lord Chancellor.

Important issues relate to the representative nature of the magistracy.

Judicial review

Under the constitution of the UK, and within the doctrine of the separation of powers, judges and the executive have distinct but interrelated roles.

Judicial review remedies are the prerogative remedies of *quashing orders*, *mandatory orders* and *prohibiting orders*, together with the private law remedies of declaration, injunction and damages. Private law remedies cannot be used in relation to public law complaints.

Increased judicial activity in relation to State programmes raises questions about the competence and authority of judges to act, as well as raising doubts as to their political views.

Politics of the judiciary

Judges have a capacity to make law – the question is, do they exercise this power in a biased way?

Bias can take two forms: personal and corporate.

Accusations of corporate bias suggest that, as a group, judges represent the interest of the status quo and decide certain political cases in line with that interest.

CHAPTER 7

THE CIVIL PROCESS

Jarndyce [v] Jarndyce drones on. This scarecrow of a suit has, in the course of time, become so complicated that no man alive knows what it means. The parties to it understand it least; but it has been observed that no two Chancery lawyers can talk about it for five minutes without coming to a total disagreement as to all the premises. Innumerable children have been born into the cause; innumerable young people have married into it; innumerable old people have died out of it. Scores of persons have deliriously found themselves made parties in Jarndyce [v] Jarndyce, without knowing how or why; whole families have inherited legendary hatreds with the suit. The little plaintiff or defendant, who was promised a new rocking horse when Jarndyce [v] Jarndyce should be settled, has grown up, possessed himself of a real horse, and trotted away into the other world. Fair wards of court have faded into grandmothers; a long procession of Chancellors has come in and gone out ... there are not three Jarndyces left upon the earth perhaps, since old Tom Jarndyce in despair blew his brains out at a coffee-house in Chancery Lane; but Jarndyce [v] Jarndyce still drags its dreary length before the Court, perennially hopeless [*Bleak House*, Charles Dickens].

Many critics believe that the adversarial system has run into the sand, in that, today, delay and costs are too often disproportionate to the difficulty of the issue and the amount at stake. The solution now being followed to that problem requires a more interventionist judiciary: the trial judge as the trial manager [Henry LJ, *Thermawear v Linton* (1995) CA].

The extent of delay, complication and therefore expense of civil litigation may have changed since the time of Dickens' observations about the old Court of Chancery, but how far the civil process is as efficient as it might be is a matter of some debate.

7.1 The need for reform

A survey by the National Consumer Council in 1995 found that three out of four people in serious legal disputes were dissatisfied with the civil justice system (*Seeking Civil Justice: A Survey of People's Needs and Experiences*, 1995, NCC). Of the 1,019 respondents, 77% claimed the system was too slow, 74% said it was too complicated and 73% said that it was unwelcoming and outdated.

According to the Civil Justice Review (CJR) 1988, delay in litigation 'causes continuing personal stress, anxiety and financial hardship to ordinary people and their families. It may induce economically weaker parties to accept unfair settlements. It also frustrates the efficient conduct of commerce and industry'. Despite some of the innovations in the five years following that CJR, the problems continued.

The Heilbron Hodge Report, *Civil Justice on Trial: The Case for Change* (1993), recommended many changes in civil procedure. The Report resulted from an independent working party set up in 1992 by the Bar Council and the Law Society. The 39 member working party was chaired by Hilary Heilbron QC; its vice chair was solicitor Henry Hodge OBE. The Report called for a 'radical reappraisal of the approach to litigation from all its participants'.

The Report painted a depressing picture of the civil justice system, where delays are endemic and often contrived and procedures are inflexible, rule ridden and often incomprehensible to the client. It noted that, incongruously for a multi-million pound operation, technology scarcely featured. All High Court and county court records, for example, were kept manually. The main plank of the Report was concerned with making the operation of the courts more 'litigant-friendly'. It said that judges, lawyers and administrators should develop a culture of service to the litigant. The report made 72 recommendations for change.

Historically, change has come very slowly and gradually to the legal system. The report of the CJR was largely ignored and, with the exception of a shift in the balance of work from the High Court to the county court (under the Courts and Legal Services Act (CLSA) 1990), no major changes came from its recommendations. The whole process began again with the Woolf Review of the civil justice system. In March 1994, the Lord Chancellor set up the Woolf Inquiry to look at ways of improving the speed and accessibility of civil proceedings, and of reducing their cost. Lord Woolf was invited by the government to review the work of the civil courts in England and Wales. He began from the proposition that the system was 'in a state of crisis … a crisis for the government, the judiciary and the profession'. The recommendations he formulated – after extensive consultation in the UK and in many other jurisdictions – form the basis of major changes to the system that came into effect in April 1999. David Gladwell, head of the Civil Justice Division of the Lord Chancellor's Department (LCD), stated (*Civil Litigation Reform*, 1999, LCD, p 1) that these changes represent 'the greatest change the civil courts have seen in over a century'.

In the system that Lord Woolf examined, the main responsibility for the initiation and conduct of proceedings rested with the parties to each individual case, and it was normally the plaintiff (now claimant) who set the pace. Thus, Lord Woolf also noted:

> Without effective judicial control ... the adversarial process is likely to encourage an adversarial cultural and to degenerate into an environment in which the litigation process is too often seen as a battlefield where no rules apply. In this environment, questions of expense, delay, compromise and fairness have only a low priority. The consequence is that the expense is often excessive, disproportionate and unpredictable; and delay is frequently unreasonable [*Access to Justice*, Interim Report, 1995, p 7].

The system has degenerated in a number of other respects. Witness statements, a sensible innovation aimed at 'cards on the table', began after a very short time to follow the same route as pleadings, with the drafter's skill often used to obscure the original words of the witness. In addition, the use of expert evidence under the old system left a lot to be desired:

> The approach to expert evidence also shows the characteristic range of difficulties: instead of the expert assisting the court to resolve technical problems, delay is caused by the unreasonable insistence on going to unduly eminent members of the profession and evidence is undermined by the partisan pressure to which party experts are subjected.

When Lord Woolf began his examination of the civil law process, the problems facing those who used the system were many and varied. His Interim Report published in June 1995 identified these problems. He noted, for example, that:

> ... the key problems facing civil justice today are cost, delay and complexity. These three are interrelated and stem from the uncontrolled nature of the litigation process. In particular, there is no clear judicial responsibility for managing individual cases or for the overall administration of the civil courts. Just as the problems are interrelated, so too the solutions, which I propose, are interdependent. In many instances, the failure of previous attempts to address the problem stems not from the solutions proposed but from their partial rather than their complete implementation [*Access to Justice*, Interim Report of Lord Woolf, 1995].

Many potential litigants are deterred from taking action by the high costs. It is also relevant to remember that whichever party loses the claim must pay for his own expenses and those of the other side; a combined sum which will, in many cases, be more than the sum in issue. An appeal to the Court of Appeal will increase the costs even further (in effect, fees and expenses for another claim) and the same may be true again if the case is taken to the House of Lords. There is in such a system a great pressure for parties to settle their claims. The CJR found that 90–95% of cases were settled by the parties before the trial.

The cost of taking legal action in the civil courts has been gigantic. Two cases cited by Adrian Zuckerman in an address to Lord Woolf's Inquiry illustrate the point. In one, a successful claim by a supplier of fitted kitchens to stop a £10,000 a year employee from taking up a job with a competitor cost the employer £100,000, even though judgment was obtained in under five weeks from the start of the proceedings. The expense of this case was in fact double the stated amount when the cost of the Legal Aid Fund's bill for the employee's defence was added to the total. In another case, a divorced wife had to pay £34,000 in costs for a judgment which awarded her £52,000 of the value of the family home.

It was the spiralling costs of civil litigation, to a large extent borne by the taxpayer through legal aid, which prompted the Lord Chancellor to move to cap the Legal Aid Fund. The legal aid budget rose from £426 million in 1987–88 to £1,526 million in 1997–98.

The system of civil procedure entails a variety of devices. Very complex cases may require the full use of many of these devices, but most cases could be tried without parties utilising all the procedures. Exorbitant costs and long delays often resulted from unduly complicated procedures being used by lawyers acting for parties to litigation. Zuckerman has argued that this problem arose from the fact that the legal system was evolved principally by lawyers with no concern for cost efficiency. In both the High Court and the county court, the system allowed parties to quarrel as much over procedural matters as the actual merits of the substantive dispute. In one case, for example, the issue of whether a writ had been properly served on the other side had to be considered by a Master (the High Court judicial officer empowered to deal with procedural matters) and then on appeal, by a judge, and then on another appeal, by the Court of Appeal. Thus, cost and delay could build up before the parties even arrived at the stage of having their real argument heard. If a claim or defence was amended, the fate of the amendment could take two appeal hearings to finally resolve. The pre-trial proceedings often degenerated into an intricate legal contest separate from the substantive issue.

The CJR 1988 recommended unification of the county courts and the High Court. It accepted the need for different levels of judiciary, but argued that having different levels of courts was inefficient. This recommendation carried what Roger Smith, then director of the Legal Action Group, called an 'unspoken sting', namely, that a divided legal profession could hardly survive a unified court. The Bar rebelled and the judiciary were solidly opposed to such change. The recommendation was not legislated.

The CLSA 1990, following other recommendations in the CJR, legislated for large numbers of cases in the High Court being sent down to the county courts to expedite their progress. No extra resources were given to the county courts to cope with the influx of cases and so, not surprisingly, there has been a growing backlog of cases and a poorer quality of service in the county courts. This problem may well have worsened rather than been helped by the introduction of the Civil Procedure Rules (CPR), as more cases are now heard in the county courts.

There were tactical reasons why parties were tempted to use the full panoply of procedural rules. The rule that 'costs follow success' (that is, the losing side usually has to pay the legal costs of the other side) can operate to encourage the building up of expense. Wealthy litigants could employ protracted procedures in an effort to worry poorer opponents to settle on terms determined by the former. Conditional fee arrangements (see 12.9) have made very little impact on the system, so lawyers who are paid by the hour regardless of success are unlikely to be especially anxious about the speed and efficiency of their work.

Zuckerman has argued for the introduction of a more efficient system like the one used in Germany. There, legal fees are determined by law. A lawyer is paid for litigation in units that represent a small proportion of the value of the claim. Payment is in three stages. The first is made at the commencement of the claim; the second when representation begins at a hearing where the judge will attempt to procure a settlement. If this fails, he will give directions for the preparation of evidence. The third payment will be made if the case goes to a full hearing. Since lawyers earn only a fixed fee, there is no systemic incentive for them to prolong any stage of the litigation; on the contrary, they have an incentive to work as expeditiously as possible so as to maximise their rate of pay at any given stage (that is, to get a reasonable return per hour). There was evidence, however, that this system encourages some lawyers to go to the final stage even where there might have been a reasonable chance of settlement at the second stage. To overcome that difficulty, it has now been regulated that a lawyer can get a full three-part fee even if the case is settled at the second stage.

In January 1995, instructions to judges from Lord Taylor, the then Lord Chief Justice, and Sir Nicholas Scott, the Vice Chancellor, have had an effect on the length and therefore cost of High Court cases. Judges were instructed to use their discretion to set strict time limits to lawyers' speeches and cross-examination, to limit the issues in cases and the documents to be disclosed ahead of trial and to curb reading aloud from documents and case reports (*Practice Direction, Civil Litigation: Case Management* (1995)). Lawyers who violated these instructions would stand to lose some of their fees as the direction states that failure by practitioners to conduct cases economically would be visited by appropriate orders for costs, including wasted costs orders (that is, some of the costs incurred would not be recoverable). Now, lawyers are no longer allowed to examine their own witnesses in court (examination-in-chief) without the express permission of the judge. These rules apply to actions in the Queen's Bench Division (QBD) and Chancery Division of the High Court and the county courts, and are modelled on those which have been used for some time in the Commercial Court where cases are dealt with most expeditiously.

In a statement to launch the rules (24 January 1995), the Lord Chief Justice said that:

> The aim is to try and change the whole culture, the ethos, applying in the field of civil litigation. We have over the years been too ready to allow those who are litigating to dictate the pace at which cases proceed. Time is money, and wasted

time in court means higher charges for litigants and for the taxpayer. It also means that everyone else in the queue has to wait longer for justice.

For this system to operate well, however, there is a need for judges to be better assisted by researchers and assistant lawyers, so that they can be properly briefed on the contents and significance of witness statements, and so forth. So far, there has been little improvement in the provision of such services for judges.

The CJR recommended that more cases should be devolved from the county court to arbitration in the small claims procedure. Such a policy was facilitated by changes to the rule in 1992 and 1996, which raised the limit of the value of claims on which the county court small claims procedure can adjudicate to £1,000 and £3,000, respectively (now, the limit is £5,000; see 7.4, below). Cases in the small claims procedure are heard without the ordinary formal rules of evidence and procedure, the consequential informality being seen as conducive to quicker settlement of issues. The full width of jurisdiction of the court has been confirmed by the Court of Appeal's decision in *Afzal and Others v Ford Motor Company Ltd* (1994). The court gave guidance on the approach to be adopted by county court judges when deciding whether small claims involving amounts below £1,000 should be tried in court instead of being automatically referred to arbitration under Ord 19, r 3 of the County Court (Amendment No 2) Rules 1992 (SI 1992/1965). The court allowed an appeal by Ford against the decision of a judge who had declined to refer to arbitration 16 employees' claims for damages for personal injuries sustained in the workplace. The employees were supported by their trade union and the employer's case was handled by its insurer.

The employees had argued that compulsory arbitration was unsuitable for their claims and that the issues of liability involved were too complex for summary resolution. Moreover, it was argued that the denial of the right to recover the cost of legal advice and representation at arbitration would deter trade unions from assisting claimants, who would be at a disadvantage in negotiating compensation settlements out of court. In a submission to the Woolf Inquiry in 1995, Marlene Winfield of the National Consumer Council argued that companies and insurance firms are the real beneficiaries of this law. As neither public funding nor costs are generally available for arbitrated disputes, many people who suffer relatively minor injuries now no longer go to law because they cannot afford the assistance of a lawyer. How far the new system for small claims (see 7.4.1) is able to ensure greater fairness remains to be judged, but the limited costs regime in the new system and absence of public funding do not provide for much optimism.

When Lord Woolf came to examine the system, small claims hearings played a very important part in the resolution of disputes. He noted that:

> ... in 1994, 24,219 cases where disposed of by full trial [in the county courts] while the number of small claims hearings was 87,885 [*Access to Justice*, Interim Report, 1995, p 102].

What had begun life in 1973 as a new system, designed to facilitate ordinary individuals using the law, had degenerated by 1995 into a system in which business and organisations played the major part. Lord Woolf noted:

> ... in a sample [by RDA Bowles] of 134 county court cases, in one court including a hundred small claims, only 12% of the cases were brought by private individuals, although individuals formed a large proportion of defendants. More recently, Professor John Baldwin of the University of Birmingham found that some 40% of the 109 plaintiffs in his 1994 research for the Office of Fair Trading were individuals [*Access to Justice*, Interim Report, 1995, p 106].

Professor Baldwin's research also identified some fundamental differences among District Judges in the way in which they dealt with evidence and applied the substantive law to small claims. Additionally, Lord Woolf found a real problem in the way that ordinary citizens were expected to present their cases in court (see *Access to Justice*, Interim Report, 1995, pp 102–10).

7.2   The new civil process

Following the Civil Procedure Act 1997, the changes have been effected through the new Civil Procedure Rules (CPR) 1998. These have been supplemented by new practice directions and pre-action protocols. The principal parts of all of these new rules and guidelines are examined below. The rules are divided into 75 parts, each dealing with a particular aspect of procedure. Within each part is a set of rules laying down the procedure relating to that aspect. Also, under most parts can be found new practice directions which give guidance on how the rules are to be interpreted. In addition, the rules are kept under constant review and there are regular updates; between 1999 and March 2003, there have been some 31 amendments. Of major importance has been the accessibility of the CPR, which can be found on the LCD website, including practice directions and updates. A further method of improving the civil process has been the introduction of pre-action protocols for certain types of case, which are designed to increase the opportunity for settling cases as early in the proceedings as possible by improving communication between the parties and their advisers. The rules are quoted as, for example, 'rule 4.1', which refers to Part 4, r 1 of the CPR.

The reforms work towards conflict resolution as the main purpose for civil legal proceedings, rather than a case being a prolonged opportunity for lawyers to demonstrate a range of legalistic skills.

The main features of the new civil process are as follows.

The case control

The progress of cases is monitored by using a computerised diary monitoring system. Parties are encouraged to co-operate with each other in the conduct of the proceedings; which issues need full investigation and trial are decided promptly and others disposed of summarily.

Court allocation and tracking

The county courts retain an unlimited jurisdiction for handling contract and tort claims, but issuing proceedings in the High Court is now limited to personal injury claims with a value of £50,000 or more; other claims with a value of more than £15,000; claims where an Act of Parliament requires a claim to start in the High Court; or specialist High Court claims.

Cases are allocated to one of three tracks for a hearing, that is, small claims, fast track or multi-track, depending on the value and complexity of the claim.

The documentation and procedures

Most claims will be begun by a multi-purpose form and the provision of a response pack, and the requirement that an allocation questionnaire is completed is intended to simplify and expedite matters.

7.2.1   The Civil Procedure Rules

The CPR are the same for the county court and the High Court. The vocabulary is more user-friendly, so, for example, what used to be called a 'writ' will be a 'claim form' and a *guardian ad litem* will be a 'litigation friend'.

Although in some ways all the fuss about the new CPR being so far reaching creates the impression that the future will see a sharp rise in litigation, the truth may be different. It seems likely that a fall off in litigation in the 1990s will continue. Judge John Frenkel ('On the road to reform' (1998) Law Soc Gazette, 16 December) has pointed to the data. QBD writs were down from 50,295 in 1993–94 to 22,483 in 1997–98 and county court summonses from 2,577,704 to 1,959,958. During the same period, the number of District Judges increased from 289 to 337. In 2001, claims continued to decrease, with 21,613 in the QBD and 1,739,090 being issued in the county court, which was a 7% decrease on 2000.

7.2.2   The overriding objective (CPR Part 1)

The overriding objective of the CPR is to enable the court to deal justly with cases. The first rule reads:

1.1(1) These rules are a new procedural code with the overriding objective of enabling the court to deal with cases justly.

This objective includes ensuring that the parties are on an equal footing and saving expense. When exercising any discretion given by the CPR, the court must, according to r 1.2, have regard to the overriding objective and a checklist of factors, including the amount of money involved, the complexity of the issue, the parties' financial positions, how the case can be dealt with expeditiously and by allotting an appropriate share of the court's resources while taking into account the needs of others. In future, as Judge John Frenkel observes ('On the road to reform' (1998)), 'the decisions of the Court of Appeal are more likely to illustrate the application of the new rules to the facts of a particular case as opposed to being interpretative authorities that define the meaning of the rules'.

7.2.3 Practice directions

Practice directions (official statements of interpretative guidance) play an important role in the new civil process. In general, they supplement the CPR, giving the latter fine detail. They tell parties and their representatives what the court will expect of them in respect of documents to be filed in court for a particular purpose, and how they must co-operate with the other parties to their action. They also tell the parties what they can expect of the court, for example, they explain what sort of sanction a court is likely to impose if a particular court order or request is not complied with. Almost every part of the new rules has a corresponding practice direction. They supersede all previous . practice directions in relation to civil process.

7.2.4 Pre-action protocols

The pre-action protocols (PAPs) are an important feature of the reforms. They exist for cases of *clinical negligence* (formerly called medical negligence, but now extended to cover claims against dentists, radiologists *et al*) and *personal injury, construction and engineering disputes, defamation, professional negligence and judicial review*. Further protocols are likely to follow.

In the *Final Report on Access to Justice* (1996), Lord Woolf stated (Chapter 10) that PAPs are intended to 'build on and increase the benefits of early but well informed settlements'. The purposes of the PAPs, he said, are:

(a) to focus the attention of litigants on the desirability of resolving disputes without litigation;

(b) to enable them to obtain the information they reasonably need in order to enter into an appropriate settlement;

...

(d) if a pre-action settlement is not achievable, to lay the ground for expeditious conduct of proceedings.

The protocols were drafted with the assistance of The Law Society, the Clinical Disputes Forum, the Association of Personal Injury Lawyers and the Forum of Insurance Lawyers. Most clients in personal injury and medical negligence claims want their cases settled as quickly and as economically as possible. The new spirit of co-operation fostered by the Woolf reforms should mean that fewer cases are pushed through the courts. The PAPs are intended to improve pre-action contact between the parties and to facilitate better exchange of information and fuller investigation of a claim at an earlier stage. Both clinical negligence and personal injury PAPs recommend:

- the claimant sending a reasonably detailed letter of claim to the proposed defendant, including details of the accident/medical treatment, a brief explanation of why the defendant is being held responsible, a description of the injury and an outline of the defendant's losses. Unlike a 'pleading' in the old system (which could not be moved away from by the claimant), there will be no sanctions applied if the proceedings differ from the letter of claim. However, as Gordon Exall has observed ('Civil litigation brief' (1999) SJ 32, 15 January), letters of claim should be drafted with care because any variance between them and the claim made in court will give the defendant's lawyers a fruitful opportunity for cross-examination;

- the defendant should acknowledge the letter within 21 days, identifying insurers if applicable. The defendant then has a maximum of three months to investigate and tell the claimant whether liability is admitted. If it is denied, reasons must be given;

- within that three month period or on denial of liability, the parties should organise disclosure of key documents. For personal injury cases, the protocol lists the main types of defendant's documents for different types of cases. If the defendant denies liability, then he should disclose all the relevant documents in his possession which are likely to be ordered to be disclosed by the court. In clinical negligence claims, the key documents will usually be the claimant's medical records, and the protocol includes a *pro-forma* application to obtain these;

- the personal injury PAP also includes a framework for the parties to agree on the use of expert evidence, particularly in respect of a condition and prognosis report from a medical expert. Before any prospective party instructs an expert, he should give the other party a list of names of one or more experts in the relevant specialty which he considers are suitable to instruct. Within 14 days, the other party may indicate an objection to one or more of the experts; the first party should then instruct a mutually acceptable expert. Only if all suggested experts are objected to can the sides instruct experts of their own. The aim here is to allow the claimant to get the defendant to agree to one report being prepared by a mutually agreeable non-partisan expert. The clinical negligence PAP encourages the parties to consider sharing expert evidence, especially with regard to quantum (that is, the amount of damages payable);

- both PAPs encourage the parties to use alternative dispute resolution (ADR) or negotiation to settle the dispute during the pre-action period.

At the early stage of proceedings, when a case is being allocated to a track (that is, small claims, fast track), after the defence has been filed, parties will be asked whether they have complied with a relevant protocol, and if not, why not. The court will then be able to take the answers into account when deciding whether, for example, an extension of time should be granted. The court will also be able to penalise poor conduct by one side through costs sanctions – an order that the party at fault pay the costs of the proceedings or part of them.

7.3   Case control (CPR Part 3)

Case control by the judiciary, rather than leaving the conduct of the case to the parties, is a key element in the reforms resulting from the Woolf Review. The court's case management powers are found in Part 3 of the CPR, although there is a variety of ways in which a judge may control the progress of the case. A judge may make a number of orders to give opportunities to the parties to take stock of their case by case management conferences, check they have all the information they need to proceed or settle by pre-trial reviews, or halt the proceedings to give the parties an opportunity to consider a settlement. When any application is made to the court, there is an obligation on the judge to deal with as many outstanding matters as possible. The court is also under an obligation to ensure that witness statements are limited to the evidence that is to be given if there is a hearing, and expert evidence is restricted to what is required to resolve the proceedings. Judges receive support from court staff in carrying out their case management role. The court monitors case progress by using a computerised diary monitoring system which:

- records certain requests, or orders made by the court;
- identifies the particular case or cases to which these orders/requests refer, and the dates by which a response should be made; and
- checks on the due date whether the request or order has been complied with.

Whether there has been compliance or not, the court staff will pass the relevant files to a procedural judge (a Master in the Royal Courts of Justice, a District Judge in the county court) who will decide if either side should have a sanction imposed on them.

In the new system, the litigants have much less control over the pace of the case than in the past. They will not be able to draw out proceedings, or delay in the way that they once could have done, because the case is subject to a timetable. Once a defence is filed, the parties get a timetable order that includes the prospective trial date. The need for pre-issue preparation is increased, and this benefits litigants because, as Professor Hazel Genn's research has shown

(*Hard Bargaining: Out of Court Settlement in Personal Injury Claims* (1987)), in settled personal injury actions, 60% of costs were incurred before proceedings. The court now has a positive duty to manage cases. Rule 1.4(1) states that 'The court must further the overriding objective by actively managing cases'. The rule goes on to explain what this management involves:

1.4(2) Active case management includes–

(a) encouraging the parties to co-operate with each other in the conduct of the proceedings;

(b) identifying the issues at an early stage;

(c) deciding promptly which issues need full investigation and trial and accordingly disposing summarily of the others;

(d) deciding the order in which issues are to be resolved;

(e) encouraging the parties to use an alternative dispute resolution procedure if the court considers that appropriate ...;

(f) helping the parties to settle the whole or part of the case;

(g) fixing timetables or otherwise controlling the progress of the case;

(h) considering whether the likely benefits of taking a particular step justify the cost of taking it;

(i) dealing with as many aspects of the case as it can on the same occasion;

(j) dealing with the case without the parties needing to attend court;

(k) making use of technology; and

(l) giving directions to ensure that the trial of a case proceeds quickly and efficiently.

It is worth noting here that District Judges and Deputy District Judges have had extensive training to promote a common approach (see 6.4). Training is being taken very seriously by the judiciary. District Judges now occupy a pivotal position in the civil process.

Part 3 of the CPR gives the court a wide range of substantial powers. The court can, for instance, extend or shorten the time for compliance with any rule, practice direction or court order, even if an application for an extension is made after the time for compliance has expired. It can also hold a hearing and receive evidence by telephone or 'by using any other method of direct oral communication'.

The Association of District Judges, the Association of Personal Injury Lawyers and the Forum of Insurance Lawyers, who meet at six-monthly intervals to discuss how the operation of the CPR might be improved ((2000) 13 Law Soc Gazette 11), agreed that telephone hearings are now working very well (on the whole), but contested interim applications are often not suitable for telephone hearings and should not be disguised as case management conferences. Furthermore, not all courts have yet received the right equipment to be able to conduct a telephone hearing. The District Judge cannot be put in the role of a go-between, which happens in some judges' rooms where there is no conference facility but one party has attended in person and the opponent is on the other end of a standard telephone.

Part 3 of the CPR also gives the court powers to:

- strike out a statement of case;
- impose sanctions for non-payment of certain fees;
- impose sanctions for non-compliance with rules and practice directions;
- give relief from sanctions.

There is, though, a certain flexibility built into the rules. A failure to comply with a rule or practice direction will not necessarily be fatal to a case. Rule 3.10 of the CPR states:

> Where there has been an error of procedure such as a failure to comply with a rule or practice direction:
>
> (a) the error does not invalidate any step taken in the proceedings unless the court so orders; and
>
> (b) the court may make an order to remedy the error.

The intention of imposing a sanction will always be to put the parties back into the position they would have been in if one of them had not failed to meet a deadline. For example, the court could order that a party carries out a task (like producing some sort of documentary evidence) within a very short time (for example, two days) in order that the existing trial dates can be met.

7.3.1 Case management conferences

Case management conferences may be regarded as an opportunity to 'take stock'. Many of these are now conducted by telephone. There is no limit to the number of case management conferences which may be held during the life of a case, although the cost of attendance at such hearings against the benefits obtained will always be a consideration in making the decision. They will be used, among other things, to consider:

- giving directions, including a specific date for the return of a listing questionnaire;
- whether the claim or defence is sufficiently clear for the other party to understand the claim they have to meet;
- whether any amendments should be made to statements of case;
- what documents, if any, each party needs to show the other;
- what factual evidence should be given;
- what expert evidence should be sought and how it should be sought and disclosed; and
- whether it would save costs to order a separate trial of one or more issues.

7.3.2   Pre-trial reviews

Pre-trial reviews will normally take place after the filing of listing questionnaires and before the start of the trial. Their main purpose is to decide a timetable for the trial itself, including the evidence to be allowed and whether this should be given orally; instructions about the content of any trial bundles (bundles of documents including evidence, such as written statements, for the judge to read) and confirming a realistic time estimate for the trial itself.

Rules require that, where a party is represented, a representative 'familiar with the case and with sufficient authority to deal with any issues likely to arise must attend every case management conference or pre-trial review'.

7.3.3   Stays for settlement (CPR Part 26) and settlements (CPR Part 36)

Under the new CPR, there is a greater incentive for parties to settle their differences.

The court will take into account any pre-action offers to settle when making an order for costs. Thus, a side which has refused a reasonable offer to settle will be treated less generously in the issue of how far the court will order their costs to be paid by the other side. For this to happen, the offer must be one which is made to be open to the other side for at least 21 days after receipt (to stop any undue pressure being put on someone with the phrase 'take it or leave it, it is only open for one day then I shall withdraw the offer'). Also, if the offer is made by the defendant, it must be an offer to pay compensation and to pay the claimant's costs.

Several aspects of the new rules encourage litigants to settle rather than take risks in order (as a claimant) to hold out for unreasonably large sums of compensation, or try to get away (as a defendant) with paying nothing rather than some compensation. The system of Part 36 payments or offers does not apply to small claims but, for other cases, it seems bound to have a significant effect. Thus, if at the trial, a claimant does not get more damages than a sum offered by the defendant in what is called a 'Part 36' payment (that is, an offer to settle or a payment into the court), or obtain a judgment more favourable than a Part 36 offer, the court will order the claimant to pay any costs incurred by the defendant after the latest date for accepting the payment or offer. The court now has a discretion to make a different order for costs than the normal order. District Judge Frenkel has given the following example:

> Claim, £150,000 – judgment, £51,000 – £50,000 paid into court. The without prejudice correspondence shows that the claimant would consider nothing short of £150,000. The claimant may be in trouble. The defendant will ask the judge to consider overriding principles of Part 1 'Was it proportional to incur the further costs of trial to secure an additional £1,000?'. Part 44.3 confirms the general rule that the loser pays but allows the court to make a different order to

take into account offers to settle, payment into court, the parties' conduct including pre-action conduct and exaggeration of the claim [(1999) 149 NLJ 458].

Similarly, where at trial, a defendant is held liable to the claimant for more money than the proposals contained in a claimant's Part 36 offer (that is, where the claimant has made an offer to settle), the court may order the defendant to pay interest on the award at a rate not exceeding 10% above the base rate for some or all of the period, starting with the date on which the defendant could have accepted the offer.

Active case management imposes a duty on the courts to help parties settle their disputes. A 'stay' is a temporary halt in proceedings, and an opportunity for the court to order such a pause arises at the stage when the defence to a claim has been filed. Parties can indicate that they have agreed on a stay to attempt to settle the case and, provided the court agrees, can have an initial period of one month to try to settle the case. In order to avoid the stay being used as a delaying tactic, the order granting the stay will require the parties to report back to the court within 14 days of the end of the period of the stay.

The court will always give the final decision about whether to grant the parties more time to use a mediator or arbitrator or expert to settle, even if the parties are agreed they wish to have more time. A stay will never be granted for an indefinite period.

7.3.4 Applications to be made when claims come before a judge (CPR Part 1)

The overriding objective in Part 1 requires the court to deal with as many aspects of the case as possible on the same occasion. The filing of an allocation questionnaire, which is to enable the court to judge in which track the case should be heard, is one such occasion. Parties should, wherever possible, issue any application they may wish to make, such as an application for summary judgment (CPR Part 24), or to add a third party (CPR Part 20), at the same time as they file their questionnaire. Any hearing set to deal with the application will also serve as an allocation hearing if allocation remains appropriate.

7.3.5 Witness statements (CPR Part 34)

In the *Final Report on Access to Justice*, Lord Woolf recognised the importance of witness statements in cases, but observed that they had become problematic because lawyers had made them excessively long and detailed in order to protect against leaving out something which later proved to be relevant. He said 'witness statements have ceased to be the authentic account of the lay witness; instead they have become an elaborate, costly branch of legal drafting' (para 55).

Under the new rules, witness statements must contain the evidence that the witness will give at trial, but they should be briefer than those drafted under the previous rules: they should be drafted in lay language and should not discuss legal propositions. Witnesses will be allowed to amplify on the statement or deal with matters that have arisen since the report was served, although this is not an automatic right and a 'good reason' for the admission of new evidence will have to be established.

7.3.6   Experts (CPR Part 35)

The rules place a clear duty on the court to ensure that 'expert evidence is restricted to that which is reasonably required to resolve the proceedings'. That is to say that expert evidence will only be allowed either by way of written report, or orally, where the court gives permission. Equally important is the rules' statement about experts' duties. Rule 35.3 states that it is the clear duty of experts to help the *court* on matters within their expertise, bearing in mind that this duty overrides any obligation to the person from whom they have received instructions or by whom they are paid.

There is greater emphasis on using the opinion of a single expert. Experts are only to be called to give oral evidence at a trial or hearing if the court gives permission. Experts' written reports must contain a statement that they understand and have complied with their duty to the court. Instructions to experts are no longer privileged and their substance, whether written or oral, must be set out in the expert's report. Thus, either side can insist, through the court, on seeing how the other side phrased its request to an expert.

7.4   Court and track allocation (CPR Part 26)

Part 7 of the CPR sets out the rules for starting proceedings. A new restriction is placed on which cases may be begun in the High Court. The county courts retain an unlimited jurisdiction for handling contract and tort claims (that is, negligence cases, nuisance cases). Issuing proceedings in the High Court is now limited to:

* personal injury claims with a value of £50,000 or more;
* other claims with a value of more than £15,000;
* claims where an Act of Parliament requires proceedings to start in the High Court; or
* specialist High Court claims which need to go to one of the specialist 'lists', like the Commercial List, the Technology and Construction List.

The new civil system works on the basis that the court, upon receipt of the defence, requires the parties to complete 'allocation questionnaires' (giving all the relevant details of the claim, including how much it is for and an indication of its factual and legal complexity). Under Part 26 of the CPR, the case will then be allocated to one of three tracks for a hearing. These are: (a) small claims track; (b) fast track; and (c) multi-track. Each of the tracks offers a different degree of case management.

The new small claims limit will be £5,000, although personal injury and housing disrepair claims for over £1,000, illegal eviction and harassment claims will be excluded from the small claims procedure. The limit for cases going into the fast track system will be £15,000, and only claims for over £15,000 can be issued in the Royal Courts of Justice. Applications to move cases 'up' a track on grounds of complexity will have to be made on the new allocation questionnaire (see below).

Directions (instructions about what to do to prepare the case for trial or hearing) will be proportionate to the value of the claim, its importance, complexity and so on. Each track requires a different degree of case monitoring, that is, the more complex the claim, the more milestone events there are likely to be (that is, important points in the process, like the date by which the allocation questionnaire should be returned). Time for carrying out directions, no matter which track, may be extended or shortened by agreement between parties, but must not, as a result, affect any of the milestones relevant to that track. The time for carrying out directions will be expressed as calendar dates rather than periods of days or weeks. Directions will include the court's directions concerning the use of expert evidence.

7.4.1 The small claims track (CPR Part 27)

There is no longer any 'automatic reference' to the small claims track. Claims are allocated to this track in exactly the same way as to the fast track or multi-track. The concept of an *'arbitration'* therefore disappears and is replaced by a *small claims hearing*. Aspects of the old small claims procedure which are retained include their informality, the interventionist approach adopted by the judiciary, the limited costs regime and the limited grounds for appeal (misconduct of the District Judge or an error of law made by the court).

Changes to the handling of small claims are:

- *an increase in the jurisdiction from £3,000 to no more than £5,000* (with the exception of claims for personal injury where the damages claimed for pain and suffering and loss of amenity do not exceed £1,000 and the financial value of the whole claim does not exceed £5,000; and for housing disrepair where the claim for repairs and other work does not exceed £1,000 and the financial value of any other claim for damages is not more than £1,000);

- *hearings to be generally public hearings* – but subject to some exceptions (CPR Part 39);

- *paper adjudication, if parties consent* – where a judge thinks that paper adjudication may be appropriate, parties will be asked to say whether or not they have any objections within a given time period. If a party does object, the matter will be given a hearing in the normal way;

- *parties need not attend the hearing* – a party not wishing to attend a hearing will be able to give the court and the other party, or parties, written notice that they will not be attending. The notice must be filed with the court seven days before the start of the hearing. This will guarantee that the court will take into account any written evidence that the party has sent to the court. A consequence of this is that the judge must give reasons for the decision reached which will be included in the judgment;

- *use of experts* – expert witnesses will only be allowed to give evidence with the permission of the court;

- *costs* – these are not generally awarded, but a small award may be made to cover costs in issuing the claim, court fees, and expenses incurred by the successful party, witnesses and experts. Under r 27.14 of the CPR, additional costs may be awarded against any party who has behaved unreasonably;

- *preliminary hearings* – these may be called:
  (a) where the judge considers that special directions are needed to ensure a fair hearing;
  (b) to enable the judge to dispose of the claim where he is of the view that either of the parties has no real prospect of success at a full hearing;
  (c) to enable the judge to strike out either the whole or part of a statement of case on the basis that it provides no reasonable grounds for bringing such a claim;

- *the introduction of tailored directions* – to be given for some of the most common small claims, for example, spoiled holidays or wedding videos, road traffic accidents, building disputes.

Parties can consent to use the small claims track even if the value of their claim exceeds the normal value for that track, but subject to the court's approval. The limited cost regime will not apply to these claims, but costs will be limited to the costs that might have been awarded if the claim had been dealt with in the fast track. Parties will also be restricted to a maximum one day hearing.

The milestone events for the small claims track are the date for the return of the allocation questionnaire and the date of the hearing.

The right to appeal under the CPR is governed by new principles. Parties can appeal on the basis that:

(a) there was a serious irregularity affecting the proceedings; or

(b) the court made a mistake of law.

An example of (a) (see Paul McGrath in (1999) 149 NLJ 748) would be where an arbitrator fails to allow submissions on any crucial point upon which he bases his judgment.

7.4.2   The fast track (CPR Part 28)

In accordance with one of the main principles of the Woolf reforms, the purpose of the fast track is to provide a streamlined procedure for the handling of moderately valued cases – *those with a value of more than £5,000 but less than £15,000* – in a way which will ensure that the costs remain proportionate to the amount in dispute. The features of the procedure which aim to achieve this are:

- standard directions for trial preparation which avoid complex procedures and multiple experts, with minimum case management intervention by the court;
- a limited period between directions and the start of the trial, or trial period, of around 30 weeks;
- a maximum of one day (five hours) for trial;
- trial period must not exceed three weeks and parties must be given 21 days' notice of the date fixed for trial;
- normally, no oral expert evidence is to be given at trial; and
- costs allowed for the trial are fixed depending on the level of advocacy.

Directions given to the parties by the judge will normally include a date by which parties must file a listing questionnaire. As with allocation questionnaires, the procedural judge may impose a sanction where a listing questionnaire is not returned by the due date. Listing questionnaires will include information about witnesses, confirm the time needed for trial, parties' availability and the level of advocate for the trial.

The milestone events for the fast track are *the date for the return of allocation* and *listing questionnaires* and the *date for the start of the trial or trial period*.

7.4.3   The multi-track (CPR Part 29)

The multi-track is intended to provide a flexible regime for the handling of the higher value, more complex claims, that is, those with a *value of over £15,000*.

This track does not provide any standard procedure, such as those for small claims or claims in the fast track. Instead, it offers a range of case management tools – *standard directions, case management conferences* and *pre-trial reviews* – which can be used in a 'mix and match' way to suit the needs of individual cases. Whichever of these is used to manage the case, the principle of setting a date for trial, or a trial period at the earliest possible time, no matter that it is some way away, will remain paramount.

Where a trial period is given for a multi-track case, this will be one week. Parties will be told initially that their trial will begin on a day within the given week. The rules and practice direction do not set any time period for giving notice to the parties of the date fixed for trial.

7.5 Documentation and procedures

One of the main aims of the Woolf reforms is to simplify court forms. Under the old system, there were various forms that needed to be completed at the outset of a claim – different types including summonses, originating applications, writs and petitions. Under the new system, most claims will be begun by using a 'Part 7' claim form.

7.5.1 How to start proceedings – the claim form (CPR Part 7)

A Part 7 claim form has been designed for multi-purpose use. It can be used if the claim is for a *specified* amount of money (the old term was *liquidated* damages) or an *unspecified* amount (replacing the term *unliquidated* damages). The form can also be used for non-monetary claims, for example, where the claimant just wants a court order, not money. The person issuing the claim form is called a claimant (plaintiff in old vocabulary) and the person at whom it is directed will continue to be known as a defendant.

Under the new rules, the court can grant any remedy to which the claimant is entitled, even if the claimant does not specify which one he wants. It is, though, as Gordon Exall has observed ((1999) SJ 162, 19 February), dangerous to start a claim without having a clear idea of the remedy you want. The defendant might be able to persuade the court not to allow the claimant a certain part of his costs if he (the defendant) finds himself having to consider a remedy which had not been mentioned prior to the trial.

In the longer term, it seems clear that a plain set of language forms designed all at one time as a part of one coherent system will provide a more efficient system than that afforded by a collection of outdated forms which have been generated reactively over a long period. The most important change to come out of the 21st CPR update was the new allocation questionnaire. All the questions were revised in the light of experience since April 1999.

7.5.2 Alternative procedure for claims (CPR Part 8)

Part 8 of the rules introduced the *alternative procedure for claims*. This procedure is commenced by the issue of a Part 8 claim form. It is intended to provide a speedy resolution of claims which are not likely to involve a substantial dispute of fact, for example, applications for approval of infant settlements, or for orders enforcing a statutory right such as a right to have access to medical records (under the Access to Health Records Act 1990).

The main differences between this and the Part 7 procedure are as follows:

- a hearing may be given on issue or at some later stage if required;
- only an acknowledgment of service is served with the claim form by way of a response document;
- a defendant must file an acknowledgment of service to be able to take part in any hearing;
- a defendant must serve a copy of the acknowledgment on the other parties, as well as filing it with the court;
- no defence is required;
- default judgment is not available to the claimant; the court must hear the case;
- there are automatic directions for the exchange of evidence (in this case, in the form of witness statements);
- Part 8 claims are not formally allocated to a track; they are automatically multi-track cases.

7.5.3 Statement of case – value (CPR Part 16)

The 'value' of a claim is the amount a claimant reasonably expects to recover. Unless the amount being claimed is a specified amount, a claimant will be expected (Part 16) to state the value band into which the claim is likely to fall. The value bands reflect the values for the different tracks (for example, £1 to £5,000 for small claims). Value is calculated as the amount a claimant expects to recover, ignoring any interest, costs, contributory negligence, or the fact that a defendant may make a counterclaim or include a set-off in the defence. If a claimant is not able to put a value on the claim, the reasons for this must be given.

7.5.4 Statement of case – particulars of claim (CPR Part 16)

Particulars of claim may be included in the claim form, attached to it, or may be served (that is, given or sent to a party by a method allowed by the rules) separately from it. Where they are served separately, they must be served within 14 days of the claim form being served. The time for a defendant to respond begins to run from the time the particulars of claim are served.

Part 16 is entitled *Statements of case* (replacing the term *pleadings*). Statements of case include documents from both sides: claim forms, particulars of claims, defences, counterclaims, replies to defences and counterclaims, Part 20 (third party) claims and any *further information* provided under CPR Part 18 (replacing the term *further and better particulars*). Part 16 also sets out what both particulars of claim and defences should contain.

The particulars of claim must contain:

- a concise statement of facts on which the claimant relies;
- details of any interest claimed;
- specific details if exemplary, provisional or aggravated damages are claimed.

The Woolf Report was against obliging the claimant to state the legal nature of the claim as this would prejudice unrepresented defendants. If the nature of the claim is uncertain, then the court can take its own steps to clarify the matter.

Where a claimant is going to rely on the fact that the defendant has been convicted for a crime arising out of the same circumstances for which the claimant is now suing, then the particulars of claim must contain details of the conviction, the court which made it, and exactly how it is relevant to the claimant's arguments.

It is optional for the claimant also to mention any point of law on which the claim is based and the names of any witnesses which he proposes to call.

All statements of case must also contain a statement of truth.

7.5.5   Statements of truth (CPR Part 22)

A statement of truth is a statement that a party believes that the facts or allegations set out in a document, which they put forward, are true. It is required in statements of case, witness statements and expert reports. Any document which contains a statement of truth may be used in evidence. This will avoid the previous need to swear affidavits in support of various statements made as part of the claim.

Any document with a signed statement of truth which contains false information given deliberately, that is, without an honest belief in its truth, will constitute a contempt of court (a punishable criminal offence) by the person who provided the information. Solicitors may sign statements of truth on behalf of clients, but on the understanding that it is done with the clients' authority, and with clients knowing that the consequences of any false statement will be personal to them.

7.5.6 Response to particulars of claim (CPR Part 9)

When a claim form is served, it will be served with a response pack. The response pack will contain an acknowledgment of service, a form of admission and a form of defence and counterclaim. The response pack will be served with a claim form containing the particulars of claim, which are attached to it or, where particulars of claim are served after the claim form, with the particulars. A defendant must respond within 14 days of service of the particulars of claim. If a defendant ignores the claim, the claimant may obtain judgment for the defendant to pay the amount claimed. A defendant may:

- pay the claim;
- admit the claim, or partly admit it;
- file an acknowledgment of service; or
- file a defence.

Requirements have also been introduced regarding the content of a defence. A defence which is a simple denial is no longer acceptable and runs the risk of being struck out by the court (that is, deleted so that it may no longer be relied upon). A defendant must state in any defence:

- which of the allegations in the particulars of claim are denied, giving reasons for doing so;
- which allegations the defendant is not able to admit or deny but which the claimant is required to prove;
- which allegations are admitted; and
- if the defendant disputes the claimant's statement of value, the reasons for doing so and, if possible, stating an alternate value.

These rules mark a significant change of culture from the old civil procedure rules. Under the old rules, a defendant could, in his defence, raise a 'non-admission' or a 'denial'. The first meant that the defendant was putting the plaintiff (now claimant) to proof, that is, challenging him to prove his case on the balance of probabilities. The second meant that the defendant was raising a specific defence, for example, a 'development risks defence' under the Product Liability Act 1987. Defendants were allowed under the old rules to keep as many avenues of defence available for as long as possible. Under the new rules, the defendant must respond according to the choices in the four options above. According to r 16.5(5), if the defendant does not deal specifically with an allegation, then it will be deemed to be admitted.

7.5.7 Service (CPR Part 6)

Where the court is to serve any document (not just claim forms), it is for the court to decide the method of service. This will generally be by first class post.

The deemed date of service is two days after the day of posting for all defendants, including limited companies. Where a claim form originally served by post is returned by the Post Office, the court will send a notice of non-service to the claimant. The notice will tell the claimant that the court will not make any further attempts at service. Service, therefore, becomes a matter for claimants. The court will return the copies of the claim form, response pack, etc, for claimants to amend as necessary and re-serve.

Claimants may serve claim forms, having told the court in writing that they wish to do so, either personally, by post, by fax, by document exchange (a private courier service operated between law firms) or by email or other electronic means. A claimant who serves a document must file a certificate of service within seven days of service with a copy of the document served attached.

7.5.8 Admissions and part admissions (CPR Part 14)

The possibility of admitting liability for a claim for a specific amount and making an offer to pay by instalments, or at a later date, applies to both county court and High Court cases. Where the claim is for a specific amount, the admission will be sent direct to the claimant. However, if a claimant objects to the rate of payment offered, there are changes which affect the determination process, that is, the process by which a member of a court's staff or a judge decides the rate of payment.

Cases involving a specific amount where the balance outstanding, including any costs, is less than £50,000, will be determined by a court officer. Those where the balance is £50,000 or more, or for an unspecified amount of any value, must be determined by a Master or District Judge. The Master or Judge has the option of dealing with the determination on the papers without a hearing or at a hearing.

A defendant in a claim for an unspecified amount of money (damages) will be able to make an offer of a specific sum of money in satisfaction of a claim, which does not have to be supported by a payment into court. A claimant can accept the admission and rate of payment offered as if the claim had originally been for a specific amount. The determination procedure described above will apply where a claimant accepts the amount offered, but not the rate of payment proposed.

If a claimant does not accept the amount offered, a request that judgment be entered for liability on the strength of the defendant's admission may be made to the court. This is referred to as *judgment for an amount and costs to be decided by the court* (replacing *interlocutory judgment for damages to be assessed*). Where judgment is entered in this way, the court will at the same time give case management directions for dealing with the case.

Where a request for such a judgment is received, the court file will be passed to a procedural judge. The judge may allocate the case to the small claims track and give directions if it is of appropriate value; ask that the case be set down for a *disposal* hearing; or where the amount is likely to be heavily disputed, order a trial. Directions will be given as appropriate. A disposal hearing in these circumstances may be a hearing either at which the court gives directions, or at which the amount and costs are decided.

7.5.9 Defence and automatic transfer (CPR Part 26)

Claims for specified amounts will be transferred automatically to the defendant's 'home court' where the defendant is an individual who has filed a defence. The defendant's home court will be the court or district registry, including the Royal Courts of Justice, for the district in which the defendant's address for service as shown on the defence is situated. This means that, where the defendant is represented by a solicitor, this will be the defendant's solicitor's business address.

Where there is more than one defendant, it is the first defendant to file a defence who dictates whether or not automatic transfer will take place. For example, if there were two defendants to a claim, one an individual and one a limited company, there would be no automatic transfer if the limited company was the first defendant to file a defence.

7.5.10 Allocation questionnaire (Form N150)

The purpose of this document is to enable the judge to allocate in which track the case should be heard. When a defence is filed, the issuing court will send out a copy of the defence to all other parties to the claim, together with an allocation questionnaire, a notice setting out the date for returning it, and the name and address of the court (or district registry or the Royal Courts of Justice (that is, High Court), as appropriate) to which the completed allocation questionnaire must be returned. A notice of transfer will also be sent if the case is being automatically transferred.

When the allocation questionnaire is returned, or at the end of the period for returning it, and whether or not only some or none of the questionnaires (if there is more than one defendant) have been filed, the court file will be passed to a procedural judge for directions and allocation to track. If there is sufficient information, the judge will allocate the case to a track and a notice of allocation and directions will be sent out to each party. In particularly complex cases, for those allocated to the multi-track, the judge may first list the matter for a case management conference to formulate directions.

Where only one party has filed a questionnaire or there is insufficient information, the judge may make an order requesting further information, or order an allocation hearing. Where none of the parties has filed a questionnaire, the judge may also decide to impose a sanction, for example, ordering that a statement, or statements, of case be struck out unless a completed questionnaire is filed within three days of service of the order.

The questionnaire asks a number of questions, for example:

- Do you wish there to be a one month stay to attempt to settle this case?
- Which track do you consider most suitable for your case (small claims, fast track or multi-track)? A party wishing a case to be dealt with on a track which is not the obviously suitable track must give reasons.
- At this stage, you are asked whether you have complied with any relevant protocols, and if not, why not and the extent of the non-compliance.
- You are asked for an estimate of costs to date and the overall costs up to trial.
- You are asked if you wish to use expert evidence at the trial, whether expert reports have been copied to the other side, who the expert is and, if the parties have not agreed upon a common expert, why not.

The purpose of this questionnaire is to make both sides have a clear overview of the case at an early stage, so it becomes very difficult for lawyers to bumble along buffeted by developments in a case. To reduce delays and therefore costs, it is desirable that a lawyer should be able to purposefully stride through a case along a planned route.

7.5.11 Default judgment (CPR Part 12)

If a defendant (to a Part 7 claim) files an acknowledgment stating an intention to defend the claim, this extends the period for filing a defence from 14 to 28 days from the date of service of the particulars. Failure to file an acknowledgment, or later, failure to file a defence, can result in default judgment, that is, the court will find for the claimant, so the defendant will lose the case.

If the defendant does not to reply to the claim, a claimant may apply for default judgment for the amount claimed if the amount claimed is a specified amount, or on liability if the amount claimed is unspecified, after the 14 day period from service has elapsed.

There are a number of cases in which it is not possible to obtain judgment in default, notably in claims for delivery of goods subject to an agreement controlled by the Consumer Credit Act 1974.

7.5.12 Summary judgment (CPR Part 24)

Summary judgment is available to both claimants and defendants. Where either party feels that the other does not have a valid claim or defence, they can apply to the court for the claim or defence to be struck out and for judgment to be entered in their favour. The applicant, either claimant or defendant, must prove to the court's satisfaction that the other party has no real prospect of success and that there is no other reason why the case or issue should be dealt with at trial.

Application for summary judgment cannot be made without the court's permission (replacing the term 'leave'), before an acknowledgment of service has been filed. Where an application is made by the claimant before a defendant files a defence, the defendant against whom it is made need not file a defence. If a claimant's application is unsuccessful, the court will give directions for the filing of a defence.

7.6 Public and private hearings (CPR Part 39)

In the new rules, the distinction between 'public' and 'private' hearings is not whether a claim or application is heard in a court room or the *judge's room* (formerly called *chambers*), but whether members of the public are allowed to sit in on the hearing wherever it takes place.

Courts are not required to make any special arrangements to accommodate members of the public, for example, if the judge's room is too small to accommodate more than those directly concerned with the claim. However, where a hearing is 'public', anyone may obtain a copy of the order made upon payment of the appropriate fee.

7.7 Appeals (CPR Part 52)

The appeal system is covered in Chapter 3 above. The important procedural points are as follows.

From the county court, appeal lies to the Court of Appeal (Civil Division). In almost all cases, permission is needed in order to appeal.

Appeals from the three Divisions of the High Court and from the Divisional Courts also go to the Court of Appeal (Civil Division). Appeals are not retrials with witnesses being called again. The appellant is limited to arguing only the narrow points of law, or law and fact, on which the appeal has been granted. The parties have four weeks from the judge's judgment in which to give notice of appeal. There are usually eight or nine courts sitting during term.

Appeals from the Court of Appeal lie to the House of Lords, but the appellant must be granted leave either by the Court of Appeal or by the House of Lords. Only cases involving points of public importance reach the House of Lords and there are usually fewer than 50 civil appeals heard by the Lords each year. It is possible, under the Administration of Justice Act 1969, for the House of Lords to hear an appeal direct from the High Court, 'leapfrogging' the Court of Appeal. The agreement of both parties and the High Court judge is required. Such cases must concern a point of statutory interpretation (including the construction of a statutory instrument) which has been fully explored by the High Court judge, or concern a point which he was bound by precedent to follow.

7.8 Remedies

The preceding sections of this chapter have examined the institutional and procedural framework within which individuals pursue civil claims. What it has not addressed is the question why people pursue such claims. Taking a claim to court can be expensive, time consuming and very stressful, but people accept these costs, both financial and personal, because they have a grievance that they require to be settled. In other words, they are seeking a remedy for some wrong they have suffered, or at least that they believe they have suffered. In practice, it is the actual remedy available that the litigant focuses on, rather than the finer points of law or procedure involved in attaining that remedy; those are matters for the legal professionals. It is appropriate, therefore, to offer a brief explanation of remedies, although students of the law will engage with the details of remedies in the substantive legal subjects, such as contract and tort. As will be seen, it is essential to distinguish between the common law remedy of damages, available as of right, and equitable remedies, which are awarded at the discretion of the court (see 1.3.2, above).

7.9 Damages

As has been said, the whole point of damages is compensatory: to recompense someone for the wrong they have suffered. There are, however, different ways in which someone can be compensated. For example, in contract law, the object of awarding damages is to put the wronged person in the situation they would have been in had the contract been completed as agreed; that is, it places them in the position they would have been after the event. In tort, however, the object is to compensate the wronged person, to the extent that a monetary award can do so, for injury sustained; that is, to return them to the situation they were in before the event.

7.9.1 Types of damages

(a) *Compensatory damages*: these are the standard awards considered above, intended to achieve no more than to recompense the injured party to the extent of the injury suffered. Damages in contract can only be compensatory.

(b) *Aggravated damages*: these are compensatory in nature, but are additional to ordinary compensatory awards and are awarded in relation to damage suffered to the injured party's dignity and pride. They are, therefore, akin to damages being paid in relation to mental distress. In *Khodaparast v Shad* (2000), the claimant was awarded aggravated damages after the defendant had been found liable for the malicious falsehood of distributing fake pictures of her in a state of undress, which resulted in her losing her job.

(c) *Exemplary damages*: these are awarded in tort in addition to compensatory damages. They may be awarded where the person who committed the tort intended to make a profit from their tortious action. The most obvious area in which such awards might be made is in libel cases, where the publisher issues the libel to increase sales. Libel awards are considered in more detail at 10.7.1, but an example of exemplary awards can be seen in the award of £50,000 (originally £275,000) to Elton John as a result of his action against *The Mirror* newspaper (*John v MGN Ltd* (1996)).

(d) *Nominal damages*: these are awarded in the few cases which really do involve 'a matter of principle', but where no loss or injury to reputation is involved. There is no set figure in relation to nominal damages; it is merely a very small amount.

(e) *Contemptuous damages*: these are extremely small awards made where the claimant wins their case, but has suffered no loss and has failed to impress the court with the standard of their own behaviour or character. In *Reynolds v Times Newspaper Ltd* (1999), the former Prime Minister of Ireland was awarded one penny in his libel action against *The Times* newspaper; this award was actually made by the judge after the jury had awarded Reynolds no damages at all. Such an award can be considered nothing if not contemptuous.

7.9.2　Damages in contract

The estimation of what damages are to be paid by a party in breach of contract can be divided into two parts: remoteness and measure.

Remoteness of damage

What kind of damage can the innocent party claim? This involves a consideration of causation, and the remoteness of cause from effect, in order to determine how far down a chain of events a defendant is liable. The rule in *Hadley v Baxendale* (1845) states that damages will only be awarded in respect of losses that arise naturally, that is, in the natural course of things, or which both parties may reasonably be supposed to have contemplated, when the contract was made, as a probable result of its breach.

The effect of the first part of the rule in *Hadley v Baxendale* is that the party in breach is deemed to expect the normal consequences of the breach, whether they actually expected them or not.

Under the second part of the rule, however, the party in breach can only be held liable for abnormal consequences where they have actual knowledge that the abnormal consequences might follow. In *Victoria Laundry Ltd v Newham Industries Ltd* (1949), the defendants contracted to deliver a new boiler to the plaintiffs, but delayed in delivery. The plaintiffs claimed for normal loss of profit during the period of delay, and also for the loss of abnormal profits from a highly lucrative contract which they could have undertaken had the boiler been delivered on time. In this case, it was decided that damages could be recovered in regard to the normal profits, as that loss was a natural consequence of the delay. The second claim failed, however, on the grounds that the loss was not a normal one, but was a consequence of an especially lucrative contract, about which the defendant knew nothing.

As a result of the test for remoteness, a party may be liable for consequences which, although within the reasonable contemplation of the parties, are much more serious in effect than would be expected.

In *H Parsons (Livestock) Ltd v Uttley Ingham and Co* (1978), the plaintiffs, who were pig farmers, bought a large food hopper from the defendants. While erecting it, the plaintiffs failed to unseal a ventilator on the top of the hopper. Because of lack of ventilation, the pig food stored in the hopper became mouldy. The pigs that ate the mouldy food contracted a rare intestinal disease and died. It was held that the defendants were liable for the loss of the pigs. The food affected by bad storage caused the illness as a natural consequence of the breach, and the death from such illness was not too remote.

Measure of damages

Damages in contract are intended to compensate an injured party for any financial loss sustained as a consequence of another party's breach. The object is not to punish the party in breach, so the amount of damages awarded can never be greater than the actual loss suffered. The aim is to put the injured party in the same position they would have been in had the contract been properly performed. Where the breach relates to a contract for the sale of goods, damages are usually assessed in line with the market rule. This means that, if goods are not delivered under a contract, the buyer is entitled to go into the market and buy similar goods, and pay the market price prevailing at the time. They can then claim the difference in price between what they paid and the original contract price as damages. Conversely, if a buyer refuses to accept goods under a contract, the seller can sell the goods in the market and accept the prevailing market price. Any difference between the price they receive and the contract price can be claimed in damages.

Non-pecuniary loss

At one time, damages could not be recovered where the loss sustained through breach of contract was of a non-financial nature. The modern position is that such non-pecuniary damages can be recovered. In *Jarvis v Swan Tours Ltd* (1973), the defendant's brochure stated that various facilities were available at a particular ski resort. The facilities available were in fact much inferior to those advertised. The plaintiff sued for breach of contract. The court decided that Jarvis was entitled to recover not just the financial loss he suffered, which was not substantial, but also for loss of entertainment and enjoyment. The Court of Appeal stated that damages could be recovered for mental distress in appropriate cases, and this was one of them.

7.9.3 Damages in tort

Remoteness of damage

Even where causation is established, the defendant will not necessarily be liable for all of the damage resulting from the breach. The question to be asked in determining the extent of liability is whether the damage is of such a kind as the reasonable person should have foreseen, but this does not mean that the defendant should have foreseen precisely the sequence or nature of the events. The test for remoteness of damage in tort was set out in *The Wagon Mound (No 1)* (1961). The defendants negligently allowed furnace oil to spill from a ship into Sydney harbour. The oil spread and came to lie beneath a wharf owned by the plaintiffs. The plaintiffs had been carrying out welding operations and, on seeing the oil, they stopped welding in order to find out whether it was safe to continue. They were assured that the oil would not catch fire and resumed welding. However, cotton waste that had fallen into the oil caught fire, which in turn ignited the oil, and the resultant fire spread to the plaintiff's wharf. It was held that the defendants were liable in tort, as they had breached their duty of care. However, they were only held liable for the damage caused to the wharf and slipway through the fouling of the oil. They were not liable for the damage caused by fire because that damage was unforeseeable due to the high ignition point of the oil.

Economic loss

There are two categories of economic loss that may form the basis of a claim in negligence. First, there is economic loss arising out of physical injury or damage to property and, secondly, there is what is known as 'pure economic loss', which is unconnected with physical damage. Following recent developments, only the former is recoverable unless the claimant can show that there was 'a special relationship' between them and the defendant (*Williams v Natural Life Health Foods Ltd* (1998)).

7.10 Equitable remedies

Equitable remedies are not available as of right and are only awarded at the discretion of the court. They will not be granted where the claimant has not acted properly. There are a number of maxims that relate to the awarding of equitable remedies. Thus, for example, it is frequently stated that *'He who comes to equity must come with clean hands'*, which simply means that persons looking for the remedy must have behaved properly themselves (*D & C Builders v Rees* (1966)). The actual remedies are as follows.

Specific performance

It will sometimes suit a party to break their contractual obligations and pay damages; however, through an order for specific performance, the party in breach may be instructed to complete their part of the contract. An order of specific performance will only be granted in cases where the common law remedy of damages is inadequate. It is not usually applied to contracts concerning the sale of goods where replacements are readily available. It is most commonly granted in cases involving the sale of land, where the subject matter of the contract is unique.

Specific performance will not be granted where the court cannot supervise its enforcement. For this reason, it will not be available in respect of contracts of employment or personal service. In *Ryan v Mutual Tontine Westminster Chambers Association* (1893), the landlords of a flat undertook to provide a porter, who was to be constantly in attendance to provide services such as cleaning the common passages and stairs, and delivering letters. The person appointed spent much of his time working as a chef at a nearby club. During his absence, his duties were performed by a cleaner or by various boys. The plaintiff sought to enforce the contractual undertaking. It was held that, although the landlords were in breach of their contract, the court would not award an order of specific performance. The only remedy available was an action for damages.

Injunction

This is the term used in relation to the courts' powers to order someone to either do something or, alternatively, to refrain from doing something. Injunctions are governed by s 37 of the Supreme Court Act 1981 and they may be granted on an interim or a permanent basis. Breach of an injunction is a contempt of court. Examples of specific injunctions are 'freezing orders', formerly known as Mareva injunctions, which are interim orders which prevent defendants from moving their assets out of the jurisdiction of the English courts before their case can be heard. Another well known order is the search order, formerly known as an Anton Piller order, which prevents the concealment or disposal of documents which might be required in evidence at a later time. It can also authorise the searching of premises for such evidence.

In contract, an injunction directs a person not to break their contract. It can have the effect of indirectly enforcing contracts for personal service. In *Warner Bros v Nelson* (1937), the defendant, the actress Bette Davis, had entered a contract that stipulated that she was to work exclusively for the plaintiffs for a period of one year. When she came to England, the plaintiffs applied for an injunction to prevent her from working for someone else. The court granted the order to Warner Bros. In doing so, the court rejected Nelson's argument that granting it would force her either to work for the defendants or not to work at all. An injunction will only be granted to enforce negative covenants within the agreement, and cannot be used to enforce positive obligations (*Whitwood Chemical Co v Hardman* (1891)).

Rectification

This award allows for the alteration of contractual documents. It is generally assumed that written contractual documents accurately express the parties' terms, especially where the document has been signed. There are occasions, however, when the court will allow the written statement to be altered where it does not represent the true agreement (*Joscelyne v Nissen* (1970)).

Rescission

This action sets aside the terms of a contractual agreement and returns the parties to the situation they were in before the contract was entered into. The right to rescind a contact may be available as a result of fraud, misrepresentation of any type or the exercise of undue influence. The right can be lost, however, for a number of reasons, such as it being impossible to return the parties to their original position, affirmation, delay or the intervention of third party rights.

7.11 Court fees

The fee structure is designed so that fees become payable as various stages of a claim are reached (a 'pay as you go' regime).

Courts are proactive in collecting fees, in particular those which are payable at allocation and listing stages, but *without interrupting* a case's progress. There are sanctions for non-payment of allocation and listing questionnaire fees, which could lead to a party's statement of case being struck out.

7.12 Costs (CPR Parts 44–48)

Fixed costs (CPR Part 45)

There are rates for the fixed costs allowed on issue of a claim and on entry of judgment where a party is represented by a solicitor.

Assessment (CPR Part 47)

The terms *taxed* costs and *taxation* are now redundant and have been replaced by assessment. Costs will either be assessed summarily, that is, there and then, or there will be a *detailed assessment* at some later stage where one party has been ordered to pay another's costs.

Summary assessment

Judges will normally summarily assess costs at the end of hearings, both interim and final, and particularly at the end of fast track trials. Parties will be expected to bring any necessary documentation to the hearing for this purpose. In this way, the need for detailed assessment of costs is avoided so far as possible.

7.13 What has the new system achieved?

The new CPR, the most fundamental changes in civil process for over 100 years, have radically altered the operation of civil justice. Since the new rules came into force (26 April 1999), they have been regularly reformed. The 31st update came into force on 24 March 2003.

Part of the rationale of the new rules was to expedite the way cases were dealt with and to allow more cases to be settled early through negotiation between the parties or ADR. In this respect, there is some evidence of success. During the May to August period in 1999, there was a 25% reduction in the number of cases issued in the county courts compared with the same period the previous year. By the end of January 2000, there was a further fall to 23%. There is also evidence (speech by David Lock MP, Parliamentary Secretary to the LCD, 15 October 1999) that changes to pre-action behaviour as a result of the pre-action protocols have been partly responsible for the reduction in the number of cases going all the way through to trial.

An interesting assessment of the new rules was presented by Mr Justice Burton of the QBD. Speaking at the City law firm, Kennedys, he outlined five benefits of the reforms, five problems, and what he referred to as 'one big question mark' ((2000) Law Soc Gazette, 10 February).

The five problems with the reforms were: the courts' inflexibility in not allowing parties to agree extensions of time between themselves; the danger of the judiciary pushing time guillotines onto parties; the risk that lawyers and clients could exploit 'standard' disclosure to conceal important documents; single joint experts possibly usurping the role of judges; and summary assessments of costs leading to judges making assumptions replacing detailed costs analysis. The benefits were listed as: pre-action protocols; emphasis on encouraging settlement; judicial intervention; Part 24 strike-out provisions; and Part 36 offers to settle.

Mr Justice Burton said there had been three options for reforming appeals: (1) to extend the present system in order to discourage more than one appeal; (2) to refuse appeals without leave; or (3) to abolish the present system, giving no right to rehearings, only appeals. He said he regretted that all three had been adopted (in the Access to Justice Act 1999). The consequence will be pressure on judges 'to get it right first time' and higher costs for parties.

Richard Burns, a barrister and recorder sitting in the county court, and thus someone who has experienced the new rules from both sides of the Bench, has made some interesting observations about the new system ('A view from the ranks' (2000) 150 NLJ, pp 1829–30). On the positive side, Burns says that 'the transition has been far smoother than many had anticipated and there have been a number of very worthwhile gains'. He notes, however, that set against the ambitious aims Lord Woolf had for the reforms, they were a 'relative failure'. Among the gains, the judge lists: the unified system of procedure in all civil courts; awareness that the costs of litigation should bear a 'passing resemblance to the value of the claim'; vastly improved pre-action co-operation; more sensible and open pleadings which force the parties to define the issues at an early stage; the wider use of jointly instructed (and therefore impartial) experts; and, in CPR Part 36, rules cunningly devised to encourage the parties to settle.

One way in which the system is not working properly, according to Richard Burns, is in relation to costs. He argues that the system is in fact proving more expensive than the old system for many litigants, as the timetable imposed usually compels the parties 'to spend time and money progressing claims to trial whether or not they expect to settle. Paradoxically the procedures, encouraging as they do the front end loading of expenditure on cases, may lead to more trials – certainly this appears to have been happening in some of the court centres where I appear'.

Another difficulty concerns the system of case management, which Lord Woolf envisaged would be the engine to drive forward the litigation cheaply and expeditiously. Burns regards this as a system which is 'excessively bureaucratic and makes too many demands on the parties'. It is also, he argues, very poorly resourced, as the Court Service received very little extra money to finance the sort of increases in judicial staffing and information technology Woolf had seen as essential.

Concealed delays are also blighting the system, according to Judge Burns. While recognising that, on the whole, cases come to trial more quickly than they did, he notes that:

> ... the overall delay experienced by litigants is much the same as it ever was. This is because solicitors, feeling daunted by the demands made on them by the CPR and lacking the time and resources to manage more than a certain quota of cases through the system, are delaying the issue of proceedings. The delay frequently runs into years.

Eversheds, the corporate law claims firm, has conducted an 'access to justice' survey for five years. It canvasses the opinions and experiences of lawyers and those using the legal system. Results published in 2000, after one year of the Woolf reforms, showed that of its respondents, 54% said that the civil litigation process had improved in the past year, a big increase on 1998's 15%. Some 52% of respondents believed that litigation was quicker, but only 22% thought costs were lower.

John Heaps, head of litigation at Eversheds, has stated ((2000) *The Times*, 2 May) that: 'The UK legal system historically has been plagued by unsatisfactory delays and expense. The style of dispute resolution is changing as a result of the Woolf reforms; people no longer seek aggressive uncompromising lawyers, but those who look for commercial solutions'.

The survey sought the views of heads of legal departments of UK companies and public sector bodies: 70% of respondents were in the private sector, with 30% in London. The replies suggested that a change in culture is emerging. Nearly two-thirds of respondents did not think the reforms would make them less likely to start proceedings, but 43% said they were settling cases earlier and almost half said their lawyers were handling disputes differently. Mediation, or ADR, is also becoming more popular: 41% had used it, compared with 30% in 1998.

There is, however, concern that while judges are managing cases more effectively, the courts do not have adequate resources (this was expressed by 50% of respondents). Only 24% believed that litigants were now getting better justice; 44% said they were not.

On the matter of costs, opinions were sharply divided. Nearly half did not believe costs to have been affected by the introduction of the new rules. Disturbingly, however, 19% said costs had risen, particularly in the regions. But a conference on the Woolf reforms held by the Centre for Dispute Resolution (CEDR) found that although costs had increased at the start of litigation (front loading), overall they were down, as settlements came sooner.

Conditional, or 'no win, no fee', work is attractive in principle but little used: 48% of respondents said they would pay lawyers a higher fee for winning if they could pay a lower fee, or none, if the case was lost. However, only 24% had discussed such a deal.

Litigation may be quicker and less likely to go to court, but 52% of respondents expected to have the same number of business disputes in the following year, with as many being resolved through litigation. One in five was more optimistic and thought fewer disputes would be resolved in court.

John Heaps argues that, overall, the findings are positive. He has said: 'Over half the respondents feel the speed of resolving disputes has improved. But there are concerns that the aims and aspirations are not matched by court resources'.

A survey carried out by the City Research Group of the firm Wragge & Co obtained similar findings ((2000) *The Times*, 2 May). It suggests that among in-house lawyers from FTSE 100 companies, a lack of resources has become 'a major stumbling block'. Some 81% of respondents thought courts did not have the resources to process claims quickly enough, and some complained of 'inconsistent interpretation' between courts. But 89% of respondents backed the changes and said litigation was quicker with fewer 'frivolous claims'. Some 41% thought costs had been cut, and there was strong backing for ADR, with 80% saying it had proved popular. Nine out of 10 lawyers thought clients were more involved in the management of the dispute, but 38% believed that the reforms had compromised justice at the expense of cost cutting. As with the CEDR survey, the change singled out for the biggest impact is that which allows either party to make a formal settlement offer at any stage – or potentially face cost penalties.

A senior litigation partner at Wragge & Co, Andrew Manning Cox, observed that the survey mirrored the firm's experiences. Among surprise findings was the low awareness of the Woolf reforms among businesses. Their lawyers were apparently not using the new rules to the best tactical advantage of their companies.

Another City law firm, Lovells, found 71% of respondents now treating litigation as a last resort, with 72% willing voluntarily to exchange documents with the other side. Where litigation was unavoidable it was quicker, with 66% saying that judges now set tighter timetables. Two-thirds found the court 'rubber stamped' joint requests by the parties to move back dates in the timetable, but this flexibility did not extend to trial dates.

One of the findings that will be very disappointing for many involved with the project of the Woolf reforms is the apparently low use of a jointly appointed expert. According to the survey, only 7% of respondents were involved in cases with such an expert.

The survey also highlights a low level of case management. Only 9% found that the court monitored case progress and chased lawyers to meet deadlines; 42% found the court had sought to narrow the issues as early as it could. The Commercial Court, Lovells found, was managing cases better than other High Court divisions. Courts did not penalise parties who failed to comply with the new rules. This certainly ties in with the experience of the barrister and county court judge, Richard Burns. He has noted that the burden of work on many civil judges is so heavy that they cannot properly manage each case:

> Their burden in the busier courts is so huge that all they can do is skim the surface of files that cross their desks. It is rare, in my experience, for the same judge to be able to deal with all the interlocutory stages of even the bigger cases and so there is little or no continuity [(2000) 150 NLJ, 8 December, p 1830].

Asked for the worst aspect of the reforms, respondents chose the rule on summary assessment of costs in preliminary hearings, criticised as a lottery. In fact, the main deficiency in the new system seems to be one of variable application according to the style or interpretation of them favoured in any given court or region. This, though, may well become more uniform over time and if that occurs, then the new rules really can claim to have radically and successfully altered the civil process in England and Wales.

7.14 The division of work between the High Court and county courts after the Woolf reforms

In *A Programme for the Future*, the LCD's strategic plan for 1993/94–1995/96, a number of aims were set out in relation to the civil process. One of the plan's objectives was stated to be the need 'To match fora [that is, each type of court being a different forum] and resources to different types and levels of cases'. The problem of allocating the right sort and volume of cases to the appropriate courts is a long running challenge. It is a matter of debate how far the problems highlighted by the CJR and tackled by the CLSA 1990 have been significantly reduced.

The differences in procedure between the High Court and the county court were considerable and applied from the inception of litigation until the enforcement of court judgments. The arguments for a single court were rehearsed over many years, beginning not long after the establishment of the county courts (1846) when the Judicature Commission considered the proposal in 1869. The Law Society supported the idea in 1980, arguing that: 'A one court system would lead to the expedition, standardisation and simplification of proceedings and to a saving in judicial time.'

A merger of the High Court and county court was considered by the Beeching Royal Commission in 1969, but was rejected. Instead, it recommended a more flexible use of the judiciary. Some judges are more experienced and expert than others. Clearly, it makes sense for the judges with greater expertise to preside in the more important cases, but how is 'importance' to be judged? The sum involved may not be very large, but the legal point in issue may be of enormous significance. Conversely, a case where the sum claimed is very great may not raise any particularly difficult or consequential point of law. Beeching recommended that the allocation of cases to the different tiers of judges should be determined to some extent by judges, rather than by simply looking at the sum claimed. Now, because there is just one set of rules (the CPR) governing both the High Court and the county courts, the courts in one sense have been unified. We now have a single procedural system.

7.15 Do we need two sorts of court after Woolf?

The introduction of the Woolf reforms in 1999 added new impetus to the case for having only one type of civil court. With a unified set of forms and procedures applicable to both the High Court and the county courts, the question is raised as to why we need to have two sorts of venue. In an article entitled 'Why have two types of civil court?' ((1999) 149 NLJ 65), Richard Harrison has argued for unification.

Lord Woolf came close to recommending that the two sorts of court be merged, but stopped short of that because such a suggested merger would have involved him in dealing with matters beyond his remit. There are three main issues:

- the need to preserve the special status of High Court judges;
- the existence of inherently specialist jurisdictions in each court;
- the problem with rights of audience.

Harrison presents cogent arguments against all three points being raised as obstacles to change. He argues:

- under the new system, cases could be allocated simply to judges 'at the right level', without levels being characterised by special conditions of service and the trappings of prestige. Now, a High Court Judge is given a knighthood or a damehood and his tenure is under letters patent, with removal from office being only theoretically possible under address by both Houses of Parliament. Her Majesty's judges are the fount of the common law, as opposed to being creatures of statute like circuit judges and District Judges. Harrison states that: 'I do not think it is possible to argue sensibly that there should be a distinction between levels of the judiciary with increased prestige, respect and remuneration being afforded to an elite band';

- resistance to change relies on the view that High Court Judges should not have to deal with small claims and that county court judges should not be able to judge in cases like those involving judicial review. Harrison says that specialist judges (from the High Court) could carry on, as at present, dealing with highly complex or sensitive cases without having a separate rank;

- in future, rights of audience will depend upon fitness and qualification, not on whether one is a solicitor or barrister or practising in the High

Court or county court. In these circumstances, it does not appear, argues Harrison, that this will present any problem for a unified court.

Harrison recognises that unification of the civil court structure may be some time away. He therefore proposes an interim practical solution – ignoring the distinction in procedural terms. Cases could be headed 'Before the Civil Courts …' without worrying the claimant about through which type of court his case is going. Case management decisions on allocation could then be made in accordance with the spirit of the Woolf reforms.

7.16 Enforcement of civil remedies

It is one thing to be awarded a remedy by the court against another party, but it is another thing to actually enforce that remedy. Consequently, an effective enforcement system is essential to providing access to justice. Statistics in the 2001 Green Paper, *Towards Effective Enforcement*, reveal that as regards warrants of execution, which account for about 85% of all enforcement effort, only 35% of all warrants issued are paid (see also 4.3.5). It was also estimated that the value of unpaid post-judgment debt is more than £600 million per year. With specific regard to small claims, once again 35% of successful claimants had received no part of the sum awarded to them, several months after judgment.

In March 2003, the LCD issued the White Paper, *Effective Enforcement*, in which it claimed to set out a strategy for reforming the current system by:

- improving methods of recovering civil debt; and
- establishing a more rigorous system of controls for enforcement agents, previously known as bailiffs.

In announcing the White Paper, Baroness Scotland, Civil Justice Minister, said:

> Society wants those who owe money judgments to pay their dues but also wants to protect the vulnerable. It's about getting the balance right in a system that is firm but fair in enforcing decisions of the court. So the system we propose will utilise the full weight of the law on those who won't pay while at the same time safeguarding vulnerable individuals who simply can't pay.

The response of a significant number of individuals and organisations which specialise in the provision of debt advice has, however, been less than enthusiastic about the approach set out in the White Paper, seeing it as being far from balanced and as favouring the interest of debt recovery at the expense of those who genuinely cannot pay.

To enforce court decisions, the White Paper proposes:

- giving the courts the power to issue data disclosure orders which will require parties to disclose information about their financial circumstances;

- making attachment of earnings faster, more effective and, it is suggested, fairer;
- streamlining the system for charging orders which allow creditors to gain security against the debtor's house.

To safeguard those who are genuinely unable to repay their debt, the White Paper proposes:

- an adequate regulatory system, unified law and fairer fee structure for all enforcement agents. The Security Industry Authority (SIA) will license all enforcement agents and would aim to ensure that their work is carried out appropriately, effectively and fairly in relation to both debtors and creditors;
- a complete overhaul of distress for rent (taking legal control of goods as security for payment of, or in satisfaction of, rent arrears) laws. In the future, it is proposed that these rules will not be used for residential properties, but solely as a commercial rent arrears recovery system.

When the White Paper was issued, some commentators appeared to be more interested in the fact that the ancient title of 'bailiff' was to be replaced by the modern usage 'enforcement agent'. It would have been better had the commentators actually focused more carefully on the details of the proposals it contained. Currently, 'bailiffs' are not entitled to use force to enter debtors' homes in order to effect warrants. They can seize goods outside the home, but they can only gain access to goods inside after being invited to enter. Under the White Paper proposals, 'enforcement agents', subject to the requirement to obtain a warrant from a judge, will be able to use force to gain entry into domestic premises. It is unlikely that those who suffer the forced invasion of their homes will be particularly concerned as to the lineage of the title borne by the invaders. The proposals, which extend the rights of forced entry in all cases, are set out in paras 165–67 as follows:

165 We seek to establish the principle that refusing to open a door or unlock a gate will not stop legitimate enforcement action, nor should superior technology to protect the entrance to a property prevent enforcement from taking place. For example, currently there is little scope for entering private homes that are protected by video cameras and electronic gates. *Forcible entry in domestic premises will be permitted – but only with prior judicial authority.*

166 Forcible entry in commercial premises is currently allowed for those enforcement agents who undertake civil enforcement on behalf of the High Court and County Court. It will continue to be permitted for those who presently have this power. *Forcible entry to commercial premises will also be permitted for other enforcement agents with prior judicial authority.* Having failed to gain normal entry, enforcement agents, save for those who are currently officers of the court, may apply to the court for permission to undertake forcible entry in commercial premises with or without notice.

167 Normal entry to third party premises will be appropriate. However, the agent should be certain that the goods are on the premises before attempting to gain entry. *Forcible entry to third party premises will require prior judicial authority in all cases* [emphasis added in all cases].

Of equal concern is the White Paper's approval of the continuation of the pernicious charging order mechanism as a means of securing debts. This permits creditors to apply to the courts, where debtors are in default, to have existing unsecured debts charged against the interest debtors might have in their houses. Consequently, the debtors risk losing their houses if they subsequently fail to pay off their debts. Thus, the debt is effectively transformed into a second mortgage, but of course the interest rate on the debt remains at the level of the original unsecured debt and at a much higher level than would be charged by a genuine mortgage lender.

When the review of civil enforcement procedures was first announced, it was felt by many that it would lead to the reduction in the powers of bailiffs, if only to bring them into compliance with the debtors' rights under the European Convention on Human Rights (ECHR). It would appear, however, that the government has decided that not only are existing bailiffs' powers ECHR compliant, but that they can safely be extended, subject to the safeguard of improved regulation of the area. Many debt advisers and civil liberties lawyers would disagree and if the White Paper ever becomes an Act of Parliament, it will undoubtedly face challenge in the courts on that issue.

THE CIVIL PROCESS

The need for reform

The Woolf Inquiry into the civil justice system was set up by the government in 1994 to examine why civil litigation was generally very costly, protracted, complicated and subject to long delays.

The Inquiry published its final report in 1996 and its proposals resulted in the Civil Procedure Act 1997 and the Civil Procedure Rules 1998. The new Civil Procedure Rules (CPR) are the same for the county court and the High Court. They apply to all cases except (Part 2) to insolvency proceedings, family proceedings, and non-contentious probate proceedings.

The new civil process

The changes are effected through the Civil Procedure Act 1997 and CPR 1998. These have been supplemented by new practice directions and pre-action protocols.

The overriding objective (CPR Part 1)

The overriding objective of the new CPR is to enable the court to deal justly with cases. The first rule reads:

> 1.1(1) These rules are a new procedural code with the overriding objective of enabling the court to deal with cases justly.

Practice directions

Practice directions (official statements of interpretative guidance) play an important role in the new civil process. In general, they supplement the CPR, giving the latter fine detail. They tell parties and their representatives what the court will expect of them in respect of documents to be filed in court for a particular purpose, and how they must co-operate with the other parties to their action. They also tell the parties what they can expect of the court.

The pre-action protocols

The pre-action protocols (PAPs) are an important feature of the reforms. They exist for cases of clinical negligence, personal injury, construction and engineering, defamation, professional negligence and defamation. They are likely to be followed, over time, with similar protocols for cases involving other specialisms like debt.

Case control (CPR Part 3)

Judges will receive support from court staff in carrying out their case management role. The court will monitor case progress by using a computerised diary monitoring system.

Active case management includes:

(a) encouraging the parties to co-operate with each other in the conduct of the proceedings;

(b) identifying the issues at an early stage;

(c) deciding promptly which issues need full investigation and trial and, accordingly, disposing summarily of the others;

(d) deciding the order in which issues are to be resolved.

Case management conferences

Case management conferences may be regarded as an opportunity to 'take stock'. There is no limit to the number of case management conferences which may be held during the life of a case, although the cost of attendance at such hearings measured against the benefits obtained will always be a consideration in making the decision.

Pre-trial reviews

Pre-trial reviews will normally take place after the filing of listing questionnaires and before the start of the trial. Their main purpose is to decide a timetable for the trial itself (including the evidence to be allowed and whether this should be given orally), instructions about the content of any trial bundles (bundles of documents including evidence such as written statements, for the judge to read) and confirming a realistic time estimate for the trial itself.

Rules require that where a party is represented, a representative 'familiar with the case and with sufficient authority to deal with any issues likely to arise must attend every case management conference or pre-trial review'.

Stays for settlement (CPR Part 26) and settlements (Part 36)

Under the new CPR, there is a greater incentive for parties to settle their differences.

The court will take into account any pre-action offers to settle when making an order for costs. Thus, a side which has refused a reasonable offer to settle will be treated less generously in the issue of how far the court will order their costs to be paid by the other side. For this to happen, the offer, though, must be one which is made open to the other side for at least 21 days after receipt (to stop any undue pressure being put on someone with the phrase: 'take it or leave it; it is only open for one day, then I shall withdraw the offer'). Also, if the offer is made by the defendant, it must be an offer to pay compensation and to pay the claimant's costs.

Witness statements (CPR Part 34)

Under the new rules, witness statements must contain the evidence that the witness will give at trial, but they should be briefer than those drafted under the previous rules; they should be drafted in lay language and should not discuss legal propositions. Witnesses will be allowed to amplify on the statement or deal with matters that have arisen since the report was served, although this is not an automatic right and a 'good reason' for the admission of new evidence will have to be established.

Experts (CPR Part 35)

New rules place a clear duty on the court to ensure that 'expert evidence is restricted to that which is reasonably required to resolve the proceedings'. That is to say, expert evidence will only be allowed either by way of written report or orally, where the court gives permission. Equally important is the rules' statement about experts' duties. They state that it is the clear duty of experts to help the court on matters within their expertise, bearing in mind that this duty overrides any obligation to the person from whom they have received instructions or by whom they are paid.

Court and track allocation (CPR Part 26)

Part 7 of the CPR sets out the rules for starting proceedings. A new restriction is placed on which cases may be begun in the High Court. The county courts retain an unlimited jurisdiction for handling contract and tort claims (that is, negligence cases, nuisance cases). Issuing proceedings in the High Court is now limited to:

- personal injury claims with a value of £50,000 or more;
- other claims with a value of more than £15,000;
- claims where an Act of Parliament requires an action to start in the High Court; or
- specialist High Court claims which need to go to one of the specialist 'lists', like the Commercial List, the Technology and Construction List.

The new civil system works on the basis of the court, upon receipt of the claim (accompanied by duly filled in forms giving all the relevant details of the claim, including how much it is for and an indication of its factual and legal complexity), allocating the case to one of three tracks for a hearing. These are:

- small claims;
- fast track;
- multi-track.

The new small claims limit will be £5,000, although personal injury and housing disrepair claims for over £1,000, illegal eviction and harassment claims will be excluded from the small claims court. The limit for cases going into the fast track system will be £15,000, and only claims for over £15,000 can be issued in the Royal Courts of Justice. Applications to move cases 'up' a track on grounds of complexity will have to be made on the new allocation questionnaire.

Documentation and procedures

How to start proceedings – the claim form (CPR Part 7)

Under the new system, most claims will be begun by using a 'Part 7' claim form – a form which has been designed for multi-purpose use. It can be used if the claim is for a *specified* amount of money (the old term was *liquidated* damages) or an *unspecified* amount (replacing the term *unliquidated* damages) and for non-monetary claims.

Under the new rules, the court can grant any remedy to which the claimant is entitled, even if the claimant does not specify which one he wants.

Alternative procedure for claims (CPR Part 8)

Part 8 of the new rules introduces the alternative procedure for claims. This procedure is commenced by the issue of a Part 8 claim form. It is intended to provide a speedy resolution of claims which are not likely to involve a substantial dispute of fact, for example, applications for approval of infant settlements, or for orders enforcing a statutory right such as a right to have access to medical records (under the Access to Health Records Act 1990).

Statement of case – particulars of claim (CPR Part 16)

Particulars of claim may be included in the claim form, attached to it, or may be served (that is, given or sent to a party by a method allowed by the rules) separately from it. Where they are served separately, they must be served within 14 days of the claim form being served. The time for a defendant to respond begins to run from the time the particulars of claim are served.

Part 16 of the CPR is entitled 'statements of case' (replacing the word 'pleadings'). Statements of case include documents from both sides: claim forms, particulars of claims, defences, counterclaims, replies to defences and counterclaims, Part 20 (third party) claims and any further information provided under Part 18 of the CPR (replacing the term 'further and better particulars'). Part 16 of the rules also sets out what both particulars of claim and defences should contain.

Statements of truth (CPR Part 22)

A statement of truth is a statement that a party believes that the facts or allegations set out in a document, which they put forward, are true. It is required in statements of case, witness statements and expert reports. Any document which contains a statement of truth may be used in evidence. This will avoid the previous need to swear affidavits in support of various statements made as part of the claim.

Defence and automatic transfer (CPR Part 26)

Claims for specified amounts will be transferred automatically to the defendant's 'home court' where the defendant is an individual who has filed a defence. The defendant's home court will be the court or district registry, including the Royal Courts of Justice, for the district in which the defendant's address for service as shown on the defence is situated. This means that where the defendant is represented by a solicitor, this will be the defendant's solicitor's business address.

Where there is more than one defendant, it is the first defendant to file a defence who dictates whether or not automatic transfer will take place. For example, if there were two defendants to a claim, one an individual and one a limited company, there would be no automatic transfer if the limited company was the first defendant to file a defence.

Allocation questionnaire (Form N150)

The purpose of this document is to enable the judge to allocate in which track the case should be heard. When a defence is filed, the issuing court will send out a copy of the defence to all other parties to the claim together with an allocation questionnaire, a notice setting out the date for returning it and the name and address of the court (or district registry or the Royal Courts of Justice – that is, High Court – as appropriate) to which the completed allocation questionnaire must be returned. A notice of transfer will also be sent if the case is being automatically transferred.

When the allocation questionnaire is returned, or at the end of the period for returning it, and whether or not only some, or none, of the questionnaires (if there is more than one defendant) have been filed, the court file will be passed to a procedural judge for directions and allocation to track. If there is sufficient information, the judge will allocate the case to a track and a notice of allocation and directions will be sent out to each party. Where only one party has filed a questionnaire or there is insufficient information, the judge may make an order requesting further information, or order an allocation hearing. Where none of the parties has filed a questionnaire, the judge may also decide to impose a sanction, for example, ordering that a statement, or statements, of case be struck out unless a completed questionnaire is filed within three days of service of the order.

Default judgment (CPR Part 12)

If a defendant (to a Part 7 claim) files an acknowledgment stating an intention to defend the claim, this extends the period for filing a defence from 14 to 28 days from the date of service of the particulars. Failure to file an acknowledgment or, later, failure to file a defence can result in default judgment, that is, the court will find for the claimant, so the defendant will lose the case.

Remedies

It is essential to distinguish between the common law remedy of damages, available as of right, and equitable remedies, which are awarded at the discretion of the court.

Damages

Damages are compensatory, to recompense someone for the wrong they have suffered. There are, however, different ways in which someone can be compensated.

In contract law, the object of awarding damages is to put the wronged person in the situation they would have been in had the contract been completed as agreed: that is, it places them in the position they would have been after the event. In tort, however, the object is to compensate the wronged person, to the extent that a monetary award can do so, for injury sustained: that is, to return them to the situation they were in before the event.

Types of damages

(i) Compensatory damages.

(ii) Aggravated damages.

(iii) Exemplary damages.

(iv) Nominal damages.

(v) Contemptuous damages.

Equitable remedies

Specific performance

This remedy will only be granted in cases where the common law remedy of damages is inadequate. It is not usually applied to contracts concerning the sale of goods where replacements are readily available. It is most commonly granted in cases involving the sale of land, where the subject matter of the contract is unique.

Injunction

This is the term used in relation to the courts' powers to order someone either to do something or alternatively to refrain from doing something.

Rectification

This award allows for the alteration of contractual documents.

Rescission

This action sets aside the terms of a contractual agreement and returns the parties to the situation they were in before the contract was entered into.

Court fees

A new fee structure takes account of the different procedures, a movement towards a 'pay as you go' fees regime and the need for full cost recovery. 'Pay as you go' means that parties will be expected to contribute more in fees, the more court and judicial time they use, for example, if they do not settle and carry on to trial.

CHAPTER 8

ARBITRATION, TRIBUNAL ADJUDICATION AND ALTERNATIVE DISPUTE RESOLUTION

8.1 Introduction

Law is one method of resolving disputes when, as is inevitable, they emerge. All societies have mechanisms for dealing with such problems, but the forms of dispute resolution tend to differ from society to society. In small scale societies, based on mutual co-operation and interdependency, the means of solving disputes tend to be informal and focus on the need for mutual concessions and compromise to maintain social stability. In some such societies, the whole of the social group may become involved in settling a problem, whereas in others, particular individuals may be recognised as intermediaries, whose function it is to act as a go-between to bring the parties to a mutually recognised solution. The common factor remains the emphasis on solidarity and the need to maintain social cohesion. With social as well as geographical distance, disputes become more difficult to deal with.

It should not be thought that this reference to anthropological material is out of place in a book of this nature. It is sometimes suggested that law itself is a function of the increase in social complexity and the corresponding decrease in social solidarity; the oppositional, adversarial nature of law being seen as a reflection of the atomistic structure of contemporary society. Law as a *formal* dispute resolution mechanism is seen to emerge because *informal* mechanisms no longer exist or no longer have the power to deal with the problems that arise in a highly individualistic and competitive society. That is not to suggest that the types of mechanisms mentioned previously do not have their place in our own society: the bulk of family disputes, for example, are resolved through internal informal mechanisms without recourse to legal formality. It is generally recognised, however, that the very form of law makes it inappropriate to deal adequately with certain areas, family matters being the most obvious example. Equally, it is recognised that the formal and rather intimidatory atmosphere of the ordinary courts is not necessarily the most appropriate one in which to decide such matters, even where the dispute cannot be resolved internally. In recognition of this fact, various alternatives have been developed specifically to avoid the perceived shortcomings of the formal structure of law and court procedure.

The increased importance of alternative dispute resolution mechanisms has been signalled in both legislation and court procedures. For example, the Commercial Court issued a practice statement in 1993, stating that it wished to encourage alternative dispute resolution (ADR), and followed this in 1996 with a further direction allowing judges to consider whether a case is suitable for ADR at its outset, and to invite the parties to attempt a neutral non-court settlement of their dispute. In cases in the Court of Appeal, the Master of the Rolls now writes to the parties, urging them to consider ADR and asking them for their reasons for declining to use it. Also, as part of the civil justice reforms, the general requirement placed on courts to actively manage cases includes 'encouraging the parties to use an alternative dispute resolution procedure if the Court considers that to be appropriate and facilitating the use of such procedure'. Rule 26.4 of the Civil Procedure Rules (CPR) 1998 enables judges, either on their own account or at the agreement of both parties, to stop court proceedings where they consider the dispute to be better suited to solution by some alternative procedure, such as arbitration or mediation. If, subsequently, a court is of the opinion that an action it has been required to decide could have been settled more effectively through ADR, then under r 45.5 of the CPR, it may penalise the party who insisted on the court hearing by awarding them reduced or no damages should they win the case.

In *Cowl v Plymouth City Council* (2001), the Court of Appeal, with Lord Woolf as a member of the panel, made it perfectly clear that lawyers for both parties are under a heavy duty only to resort to litigation if it is unavoidable and the dispute cannot be settled by some other non-court based mechanism. In *Kinstreet Ltd v Belmargo Corp Ltd* (1999), the court actually ordered ADR against the wishes of one of the parties to the action, requiring that:

> [T]he parties shall take such serious steps as they may be advised to resolve their disputes by ADR procedures before the independent mediator … [and] if the actions are not finally settled by 30 October 1999 the parties are to inform the court by letter within three working days what steps towards ADR have been taken and why such steps have failed.

The potential consequences of not abiding by a recommendation to use ADR may be seen in *Dunnett v Railtrack plc* (2002). When Dunnett won a right to appeal against a previous court decision, the court granting the appeal recommended that the dispute should be put to arbitration. Railtrack, however, refused Dunnett's offer of arbitration and insisted on the dispute going back to a full court hearing. In the subsequent hearing in the Court of Appeal, Railtrack proved successful. The Court of Appeal, however, held that if a party rejected ADR out of hand when it had been suggested by the court, they would suffer the consequences when costs came to be decided. In the instant case, Railtrack had refused to even contemplate ADR at a stage prior to the costs of the appeal beginning to flow. In his judgment, Brooke LJ set out the modern approach to ADR:

> Skilled mediators are now able to achieve results satisfactory to both parties in many cases which are quite beyond the power of lawyers and courts to achieve. This court has knowledge of cases where intense feelings have arisen, for instance in relation to clinical negligence claims. But when the parties are brought together on neutral soil with a skilled mediator to help them resolve their differences, it may very well be that the mediator is able to achieve a result by which the parties shake hands at the end and feel that they have gone away

having settled the dispute on terms with which they are happy to live. A mediator may be able to provide solutions which are beyond the powers of the court to provide ... It is to be hoped that any publicity given to this part of the judgment of the court will draw the attention of lawyers to their duties to further the overriding objective in the way that is set out in Part 1 of the Rules and to the possibility that, if they turn down out of hand the chance of alternative dispute resolution when suggested by the court, as happened on this occasion, they may have to face uncomfortable costs consequence.

The Court of Appeal subsequently applied *Dunnett* in *Leicester Circuits Ltd v Coates Brothers plc* (2003) where, although it found for Coates, it did not award it full costs on the grounds that it had withdrawn from a mediation process. The Court of Appeal also dismissed Coates' claim that there was no realistic prospect of success in the mediation. As Judge LJ stated:

> We do not for one moment assume that the mediation process would have succeeded, but certainly there is a prospect that it would have done if it had been allowed to proceed. That therefore bears on the issue of costs.

It is possible to refuse to engage in mediation without subsequently suffering in the awards of costs. The test, however, is an objective rather than a subjective one, and a difficult one to sustain, as was shown in *Hurst v Leeming* (2002). Hurst, a solicitor, started legal proceedings against his former partners and instructed Leeming, a barrister, to represent him. When the claim proved unsuccessful, Hurst sued Leeming in professional negligence. When that claim failed, Hurst argued that Leeming should not be awarded costs, as he, Hurst, had offered to mediate the dispute, but Leeming had rejected the offer. Leeming cited five separate justifications for his refusal to mediate. These were:

- the heavy costs he had already incurred in meeting the allegations;
- the seriousness of the allegation made against him;
- the lack of substance in the claim;
- the fact that he had already provided Hurst with a full refutation of his allegation;
- the fact that, given Hurst's obsessive character, there was no real prospect of a successful outcome to the litigation.

Only the fifth justification was accepted by the court, although even in that case it was emphasised that the conclusion had to be supported by an objective evaluation of the situation. However, in the circumstances, given Hurst's behaviour and character, the conclusion that mediation would not have resolved the complaint could be sustained objectively.

The Family Law Act 1996, which aimed to reform the operation of divorce law, places particular emphasis on the importance of mediation in this area and provides for the possibility of public finding to finance it in appropriate instances. This will be considered further in 8.5.

More generally, Lord Mackay, the former Lord Chancellor, considered various ADR mechanisms in the fourth of his Hamlyn Lectures, expressing the view that:

> ... the need seems to be not for further law based processes outside the courts ... but ... for processes which broaden the issues and available outcomes beyond those based in law.

The current Lord Chancellor has continued to look favourably on ADR, as is evident in his inaugural lecture to the Faculty of Mediation and ADR, in which he said:

> ADR has many supporters. But they, too, have a responsibility to proceed with care. ADR is not a panacea, nor is it cost free. But, I do believe that it can play a vital part in the opening of access to justice.

And in its 1999 Consultation Paper, *Alternative Dispute Resolution*, the Lord Chancellor's Department (LCD) redefined 'access to justice' as meaning:

> [W]here people need help there are effective solutions that are proportionate to the issues at stake. In some circumstances, this will involve going to court, but in others, that will not be necessary. *For most people most of the time, litigation in the civil courts, and often in tribunals too, should be the method of dispute resolution of last resort.*

That extremely useful Consultation Paper also set out the following list of types of alternative dispute resolution mechanisms:

- *Arbitration* is a procedure whereby both sides to a dispute agree to let a third party, the arbitrator, decide. In some instances, there may be a panel. The arbitrator may be a lawyer or may be an expert in the field of the dispute. He will make a decision according to the law. The arbitrator's decision, known as an award, is legally binding and can be enforced through the courts.

- *Early neutral evaluation* is a process in which a neutral professional, commonly a lawyer, hears a summary of each party's case and gives a non-binding assessment of the merits. This can then be used as a basis for settlement or for further negotiation.

- *Expert determination* is a process where an independent third party who is an expert in the subject matter is appointed to decide the dispute. The expert's decision is binding on the parties.

- *Mediation* is a way of settling disputes in which a third party, known as a mediator, helps both sides to come to an agreement which each considers acceptable. Mediation can be 'evaluative', where the mediator gives an assessment of the legal strength of a case, or 'facilitative', where the mediator concentrates on assisting the parties to define the issues. When mediation is successful and an agreement is reached, it is written down and forms a legally binding contract unless the parties state otherwise.

- *Conciliation* is a procedure like mediation but where the third party, the conciliator, takes a more interventionist role in bringing the two parties together and in suggesting possible solutions to help achieve an agreed settlement. The term 'conciliation' is gradually falling into disuse and the process is regarded as a form of mediation.

- *Med-arb* is a combination of mediation and arbitration where the parties agree to mediate, but if that fails to achieve a settlement, the dispute is referred to arbitration. The same person may act as mediator and arbitrator in this type of arrangement.

- *Neutral fact finding* is a non-binding procedure used in cases involving complex technical issues. A neutral expert in the subject matter is appointed to investigate the facts of the dispute and make an evaluation of the merits of the case. This can form the basis of a settlement or a starting point for further negotiation.

- *Ombudsmen* are independent office holders who investigate and rule on complaints from members of the public about maladministration in government and, in particular, services in both the public and private sectors. Some Ombudsmen use mediation as part of their dispute resolution procedures. The powers of Ombudsmen vary. Most Ombudsmen are able to make recommendations; only a few can make decisions which are enforceable through the courts.

- *Utility regulators* are watchdogs appointed to oversee the privatised utilities such as water or gas. They handle complaints from customers who are dissatisfied by the way a complaint has been dealt with by their supplier.

Whilst ADR is usually regarded as referring to arbitration and mediation and the operation of the Ombudsman scheme, this chapter will extend this meaning to allow an examination of the role of the various administrative tribunals which exercise so much power in contemporary society. In addition, although located within the formal court structure and so strictly speaking not a part of ADR, the small claims track will also be considered.

8.2   Arbitration

The first and oldest of these alternative procedures is arbitration. This is the procedure whereby parties in dispute refer the issue to a third party for resolution, rather than take the case to the ordinary law courts. Studies have shown a reluctance on the part of commercial undertakings to have recourse to the law to resolve their disputes. At first sight, this appears paradoxical. The development of contract law can, to a great extent, be explained as the law's response to the need for regulation in relation to business activity, yet business declines to make use of its procedures. To some degree, questions of speed and cost explain this peculiar phenomenon, but it can be explained more fully by reference to the introduction to this chapter. It was stated there that informal procedures tend to be most effective where there is a high degree of mutuality and interdependency, and that is precisely the case in most business relationships. Businesses seek to establish and maintain long term relationships with other concerns. The problem with the law is that the court case tends to terminally rupture such relationships. It is not suggested that, in the final analysis, where the stakes are sufficiently high, recourse will not be had to law, but such action does not represent the first or indeed the preferred option. In contemporary business practice, it is common, if not standard, practice for commercial contracts to contain express clauses referring any future disputes to arbitration. This practice is well established and its legal effectiveness has long been recognised by the law.

8.2.1 Procedure

The Arbitration Act (AA) 1996 repeals Part I of the Arbitration Act 1950 and the whole of the Arbitration Acts of 1975 and 1979. As the Act is a relatively new piece of legislation, it is necessary to consider it in some detail.

Section 1 of the 1996 Act states that it is founded on the following principles:

(a) the object of arbitration is to obtain the fair resolution of disputes by an impartial tribunal without necessary delay or expense;

(b) the parties should be free to agree how their disputes are resolved, subject only to such safeguards as are necessary in the public interest;

(c) in matters governed by this part of the Act, the court should not intervene except as provided by this part.

This provision of general principles, which should inform the reading of the later detailed provisions of the Act, is unusual for UK legislation, but may be seen as reflecting the purposes behind the Act, one major purpose of which was the wish to ensure that London did not lose its place as a leading centre for international arbitration. As a consequence of the demand-driven nature of the legislation, it would seem that court interference in the arbitration process has had to be reduced to a minimum and replaced by party autonomy. Under the 1996 Act, the role of the arbitrator has been increased and that of the court has been reduced to the residual level of intervention where the arbitration process either requires legal assistance or else is seen to be failing to provide a just settlement.

The Act follows the Model Arbitration Law adopted in 1985 by the United Nations Commission on International Trade Law (UNCITRAL).

Whilst it is possible for there to be an oral arbitration agreement at common law, s 5 provides that Part I of the 1996 Act only applies to agreements in writing. What this means in practice, however, has been extended by s 5(3) which provides that, where the parties agree to an arbitration procedure which is in writing, that procedure will be operative, even though the agreement between the parties is not itself in writing. An example of such a situation would be where a salvage operation was negotiated between two vessels on the basis of Lloyd's standard salvage terms. It would be unlikely that the actual agreement would be reduced to written form, but nonetheless, the arbitration element in those terms would be effective.

In analysing the AA 1996, it is useful to consider it in three distinct parts: autonomy of the parties; powers of the arbitrator and the court; and appellate rights:

- *Autonomy*

  It is significant that most of the provisions set out in the AA 1996 are not compulsory. As is clearly stated in s 1, it is for the parties to an arbitration agreement to agree what procedures to adopt. The main purpose of the Act is to empower the parties to the dispute and to allow them to choose how it is to be decided. In pursuit of this aim, the mandatory parts of the Act only take effect where the parties involved do not agree otherwise. It is actually possible for the parties to agree that the dispute should not be decided in line with the strict legal rules, but rather in line with commercial fairness, which might be a completely different thing altogether.

- *Powers of the arbitrator*

  Section 30 provides that, unless the parties agree otherwise, the arbitrator can rule on questions relating to jurisdiction, that is, in relation to:

  (a) whether there actually is a valid arbitration agreement;

  (b) whether the arbitration tribunal is properly constituted;

  (c) what matters have been submitted to arbitration in accordance with the agreement.

  Section 32 allows any of the parties to raise preliminary objections to the substantive jurisdiction of the arbitration tribunal in court, but provides that they may only do so on limited grounds which require either: the agreement of the parties concerned; the permission of the arbitration tribunal; or the agreement of the court. Leave to appeal will only be granted where the court is satisfied that the question involves a point of law of general importance.

  Section 28 expressly provides that the parties to the proceedings are jointly and severally liable to pay the arbitrators such reasonable fees and expenses as appropriate. Previously, this was only an implied term.

  Section 29 provides that arbitrators are not liable for anything done or omitted in the discharge of their functions unless the act or omission was done in bad faith.

319

Section 33 provides that the tribunal has a general duty:

(a) to act fairly and impartially between the parties, giving each a reasonable opportunity to state their case; and

(b) to adopt procedures suitable for the circumstance of the case, avoiding unnecessary delay or expense.

Section 35 provides that, subject to the parties agreeing to the contrary, the tribunal shall have the following powers:

(a) to order parties to provide security for costs (previously a power reserved to the courts);

(b) to give directions in relation to property subject to the arbitration;

(c) to direct that a party or witness be examined on oath, and to administer the oath.

The parties may also empower the arbitrator to make provisional orders (s 39).

- *Powers of the court*

Where one party seeks to start a court action, contrary to a valid arbitration agreement, then the other party may request the court to stay the litigation in favour of the arbitration agreement under ss 9–11 of the AA 1996. Where, however, both parties agree to ignore the arbitration agreement and seek recourse to litigation then, following the party consensual nature of the Act, the agreement may be ignored.

The courts may order a party to comply with an order of the tribunal and may also order parties and witnesses to attend and to give oral evidence before tribunals (s 43).

The court has power to revoke the appointment of an arbitrator on application of any of the parties where there has been a failure in the appointment procedure under s 18, but it also has powers to revoke authority under s 24. This power comes into play on the application of one of the parties in circumstances where the arbitrator:

(a) has not acted impartially;

(b) does not possess the required qualifications;

(c) does not have either the physical or mental capacity to deal with the proceedings;

(d) has refused or failed to properly conduct the proceedings, or has been dilatory in dealing with the proceedings or in making an award, to the extent that it will cause substantial injustice to the party applying for their removal.

Under s 45, the court may, on application by one of the parties, decide any preliminary question of law arising in the course of the proceedings.

- *Arbitrators*

  The arbitration tribunal may consist of a single arbitrator or a panel, as the parties decide (s 15). If one party fails to appoint an arbitrator, then the other party's nominee may act as sole arbitrator (s 17). Under s 20(4), where there is a panel and it fails to reach a majority decision, the decision of the chair shall prevail.

  The tribunal is required to adopt procedures fairly and impartially, which are suitable to the circumstances of each case. It is also for the tribunal to decide all procedural and evidential matters. Parties may be represented by a lawyer or any other person and the tribunal may appoint experts or legal advisers to report to it.

  Arbitrators will be immune from action being taken against them except in situations where they have acted in bad faith.

- *Appeal*

  Once the decision has been made, there are limited grounds for appeal. The first ground arises under s 67 of the AA 1996 in relation to the substantive jurisdiction of the arbitral panel, although the right to appeal on this ground may be lost if the party attempting to make use of it took part in the arbitration proceedings without objecting to the alleged lack of jurisdiction. The second ground for appeal to the courts is on procedural grounds, under s 68, on the basis that some serious irregularity affected the operation of the tribunal. By serious irregularity is meant:

  (a) failure to comply with the general duty set out in s 33;

  (b) failure to conduct the tribunal as agreed by the parties;

  (c) uncertainty or ambiguity as to the effect of the award;

  (d) failure to comply with the requirement as to the form of the award.

  Parties may also appeal on a point of law arising from the award under s 69. However, the parties can agree beforehand to preclude such a possibility, and where they agree to the arbitral panel making a decision without providing a reasoned justification for it, they will also lose the right to appeal.

8.2.2 Relationship to ordinary courts

In general terms, the courts have no objection to individuals settling their disputes on a voluntary basis, but at the same time, they are careful to maintain their supervisory role in such procedures. Arbitration agreements are no different from other terms of a contract, and in line with the normal rules of contract law, courts will strike out any attempt to oust their ultimate jurisdiction as being contrary to public policy. Thus, as has been stated previously, arbitration proceedings are open to challenge through judicial review on the grounds that they were not conducted in a judicial manner.

The AA 1950 allowed for either party to the proceedings to have questions of law authoritatively determined by the High Court through the procedure of *'case stated'*. The High Court could also set aside the decision of the arbitrator on grounds of fact, law or procedure. Whereas the arbitration process was supposed to provide a quick and relatively cheap method of deciding disputes, the availability of the appeals procedures meant that parties could delay the final decision and in so doing increase the costs. In such circumstances, arbitration became the precursor to a court case rather than replacing it. The AA 1979 abolished the 'case stated' procedure and curtailed the right to appeal and, as has been seen, the AA 1996 has reduced the grounds for appeal to the court system even further.

8.2.3 Advantages

There are numerous advantages to be gained from using arbitration rather than the court system:

- *Privacy*

  Arbitration tends to be a private procedure. This has the twofold advantage that outsiders do not get access to any potentially sensitive information and the parties to the arbitration do not run the risk of any damaging publicity arising out of reports of the proceedings.

- *Informality*

  The proceedings are less formal than a court case and they can be scheduled more flexibly than court proceedings.

- *Speed*

  Arbitration is generally much quicker than taking a case through the courts. Where, however, one of the parties makes use of the available grounds to challenge an arbitration award, the prior costs of the arbitration will have been largely wasted.

- *Cost*

  Arbitration is generally a much cheaper procedure than taking a case to the normal courts. Nonetheless, the costs of arbitration and the use of specialist arbitrators should not be under-estimated.

- *Expertise*

  The use of a specialist arbitrator ensures that the person deciding the case has expert knowledge of the actual practice within the area under consideration, and can form their conclusion in line with accepted practice.

It can be argued that arbitration represents a privatisation of the judicial process. It may be assumed, therefore, that of all its virtues, perhaps the greatest, at least as far as the government is concerned, is the potential reduction in costs for the State in providing the legal framework within which disputes are resolved.

8.2.4 Small claims procedure in the county court

Since 1973, an arbitration service had been available within the county court specifically for the settlement of relatively small claims. This small claims procedure, known as arbitration, was operated by county court District Judges.

This procedure has been replaced following Part 27 of the CPR 1998. Under the rules, the concept of arbitration disappears and is replaced by a small claims hearing. The details of the new procedure are examined at 7.4.1, above, and it only remains to offer a valuation of the procedure.

Problems had become evident in the operation of the arbitration procedure, particularly in cases where one party was represented whilst the other was not. In spite of the clear intention to facilitate the resolution of disputes cheaply, and without the need for legal practitioners, some individuals, particularly large business enterprises, insisted on their right of legal representation. As public funding was never available in respect of such claims, most individuals could not afford to be legally represented and therefore found themselves at a distinct disadvantage when opposed by professional lawyers.

One solution to this difficulty would have been to make public funding available in the case of arbitration. Such a proposal was never likely to come to fruition, first on economic grounds, but also on the grounds that the use of professional lawyers in such cases would contradict the spirit and the whole purpose of the procedure.

Alternatively, it might have been provided that no party could be legally represented in arbitration procedures. Such a proposal was canvassed in the LCD's Consultation Paper, *Access to Justice – the Small Claims Procedure* (1997), but to introduce such a measure would have been a denial of an important civil right.

The actual method chosen to deal with the problem was to lift the restrictions on the rights of audience in small debt proceedings. Parties to the proceedings were entitled to be accompanied by a *McKenzie* friend to give them advice, but such people had no right of audience and thus had no right actually to represent their friend in any arbitration (see *McKenzie v McKenzie* (1970)). In October 1992, under the Courts and Legal Services Act (CLSA) 1990, the Lord Chancellor extended the right of audience to lay representatives in small claims courts. This decision had the effect of allowing individuals access to non-professional, but expert, advice and advocacy. Members of such organisations as Citizens Advice Bureaux and Legal Advice Centres are permitted to represent their clients, although they are still not permitted to issue proceedings. In cases involving claims of more than £1,000, they may even charge a fee.

The increase in the maximum amount to be claimed to £5,000 introduces two particular difficulties with regard to representation. The first, and by far the more serious, is the fact that the raising of the ceiling to what is a not an inconsiderable sum of money means that individuals lost public funding to fund their claims in such cases and, therefore, might not have had access to the best possible legal advice with respect to their case. The second and apparently contradictory point is that the number of lawyers appearing in small claims proceedings may actually increase as a result of the rise in the limit. Whereas it might not have been worth paying for legal representation in a £3,000 claim, it might make more economic sense to pay for professional help if the sum being claimed is that much higher. Which alternative actually happens remains to be seen.

In evaluating the small claims procedure, regard has to be had to the Civil Justice Review of 1996, which specifically considered the arbitration procedure and concluded that it generally works in a satisfactory way to produce a relatively quick, cheap and informal mechanism for resolving many smaller cases without the need to overburden the county courts.

In March 2003, the LCD issued the recommendations that followed from its Civil Enforcement Review. Unsurprisingly, its conclusion was that creditors who have established a legitimate claim should be able to pursue it through a straightforward and accessible system and, if necessary, enforce a judgment by the most appropriate means. As it stated:

> ... without effective means of enforcement people ordered to pay a court judgment or criminal penalty would have little or no incentive to do so and the authority of the courts, the effectiveness of penalties, and confidence in the justice system would all be undermined.

This has been considered in some detail at 7.16.

8.2.5 Arbitration under Codes of Conduct

When it was first established in 1973, the small claims procedure was seen as a mechanism through which consumers could enforce their rights against recalcitrant traders. In reality, the arbitration procedure has proved to be just as useful for, and to have been used just as much by, traders and businesses as consumers. There remains one area of arbitration, however, that is specifically focused on the consumer: arbitration schemes run under the auspices of particular trade associations. As part of the regulation of trade practices and in the pursuit of effective measures of consumer protection, the Office of Fair Trading has encouraged the establishment of voluntary codes of practice within particular areas. It is usual to find that such codes of practice provide arbitration schemes to resolve particularly intractable problems between individual consumers and particular members of the association. Such schemes are never compulsory and do not seek to replace the consumer's legal rights, but they do provide a relatively inexpensive mechanism for dealing with problems without the need even to bother the county court. Such schemes are numerous; the most famous one is probably the travel industry scheme operated under the auspices of the Association of British Travel Agents, but other associations run similar schemes in such areas as car sales, shoe retailing and dry cleaning. Again, the point of such schemes is to provide a quick, cheap means of dealing with problems without running the risk of completely alienating the consumer from the trade in question.

Although many of the trade arbitration schemes offered consumers distinct advantages, some did not, and in order to remedy any abuses, the Consumer Arbitration Act 1988 was introduced. This statute provides that, in the case of consumer contracts, no prior agreement between the parties that subsequent disputes have to be referred to arbitration can be enforced. However, consumers will be bound by arbitration procedures where they have already entered into them as a consequence of a prior agreement, or have agreed to them subsequently.

8.3   Administrative tribunals

Although attention tends to be focused on the operation of the courts as the forum within which legal decisions are taken, it is no longer the case that the bulk of legal and quasi-legal questions are determined within that court structure. There are, as an alternative to the court system, a large number of tribunals which have been set up under various Acts of Parliament to rule on the operation of the particular schemes established under those Acts. There are almost 70 different types of administrative tribunal, and within each type there may well be hundreds of individual tribunals operating locally all over the country to hear particular cases. Almost one million cases are dealt with by tribunals each year, and as the Royal Commission on Legal Services (Cmnd 7648) pointed out in 1979, the number of cases then being heard by tribunals was six times greater than the number of contested civil cases dealt with by the High Court and county court combined. It is evident, therefore, that tribunals are of major significance as alternatives to traditional courts in dealing with disputes.

The generally accepted explanation for the establishment and growth of tribunals in Britain since 1945 was the need to provide a specialist forum to deal with cases involving conflicts between an increasingly interventionist Welfare State, its functionaries and the rights of private citizens. It is certainly true that, since 1945, the Welfare State has intervened more and more in every aspect of people's lives. The intention may have been to extend various social benefits to a wider constituency, but in so doing, the machinery of the Welfare State, and in reality those who operate that machinery, have been granted powers to control access to its benefits, and as a consequence have been given the power to interfere in and control the lives of individual subjects of the State. By its nature, welfare provision tends to be discretionary and dependent upon the particular circumstance of a given case. As a consequence, State functionaries were extended discretionary power over the supply/withdrawal of welfare benefits. As the interventionist State replaced the completely free market as the source of welfare for many people, so access to the provisions made by the State became a matter of fundamental importance, and a focus for potential contention, especially given the discretionary nature of its provision. At the same time as Welfare State provisions were being extended, the view was articulated that such provisions and projects should not be under the purview and control of the ordinary courts. It was felt that the judiciary reflected a culture which tended to favour a more market-centred, individualistic approach to the provision of rights and welfare and that their essentially formalistic approach to the resolution of disputes would not fit with the operation of the new projects.

8.3.1   Tribunals and courts

There is some debate as to whether tribunals are merely part of the machinery of administration of particular projects or whether their function is the distinct one of adjudication. The Franks Committee (Cmnd 218, 1957) favoured the latter view, but others have disagreed and have emphasised the administrative role of such bodies. Parliament initiated various projects and schemes, and included within those projects specialist tribunals to deal with the problems that they inevitably generated. On that basis, it is suggested that tribunals are merely adjuncts to the parent project and that this therefore defines their role as more administrative than adjudicatory.

If the foregoing has suggested the theoretical possibility of distinguishing courts and tribunals in relation to their administrative or adjudicatory role, in practice it is difficult to implement such a distinction for the reason that the members of tribunals may be, and usually are, acting in a judicial capacity. Thus, in *Pickering v Liverpool Daily Post and Echo Newspapers* (1991), it was held that a mental health review tribunal was a court whose proceedings were subject to the law of contempt. Although a newspaper was entitled to publish the fact that a named person had made an application to the tribunal, together with the date of the hearing and its decision, it was not allowed to publish the reasons for the decision or any conditions applied.

If the precise distinction between tribunals and courts is a matter of uncertainty, what is certain is that tribunals are inferior to the normal courts. One of the main purposes of the tribunal system is to prevent the ordinary courts of law from being overburdened by cases, but a tribunal is still subject to judicial review on the basis of breach of natural justice, or where it acts in an *ultra vires* manner, or indeed where it goes wrong in relation to the application of the law when deciding cases.

In addition to the control of the courts, tribunals are also subject to the supervision of the Council on Tribunals originally established under the Tribunals and Inquiries Act 1958, as subsequently amended by the Tribunals and Inquiries Acts 1971 and 1992, which is the current legislation. Members of the Council are appointed by the Lord Chancellor and its role is to keep the general operation of the system under review.

In May 2000, Lord Irvine appointed Sir Andrew Leggatt to review the current operation of the tribunal system, and the attendant Consultation Paper stated that:

> There are signs ... that the complexity of the system (if indeed it amounts to a system at all), its diversity, and the separateness within it of most tribunals, may be creating problems for the user and an overall lack of coherence.

Sir Andrew's task was to review the delivery of justice through tribunals other than ordinary courts of law. See 8.3.8 for a fuller consideration of the Leggatt Review.

8.3.2 Composition of tribunals

Tribunals are usually made up of three members, only one of whom, the chair, is expected to be legally qualified. The other two members are lay representatives. The lack of legal training is not considered a drawback, given the technical, administrative, as opposed to specifically legal, nature of the provisions the members have to consider. Indeed, the fact of there being two lay representatives on tribunals provides them with one of their perceived advantages over courts. The non-legal members may provide specialist knowledge and thus they may enable the tribunal to base its decision on actual practice as opposed to abstract legal theory or mere legal formalism. An example of this can be seen with regard to the tribunals having responsibility for determining issues relating to employment, which usually have a trade union representative and an employers' representative sitting on the panel and are therefore able to consider the immediate problem from both sides of the employment relationship.

The procedure for nominating tribunal members is set out in the parent statute, but generally it is the minister of State with responsibility for the operation of the statute in question who ultimately decides the membership of the tribunal. As tribunals are established to deal largely with conflicts between the general public and government departments, this raises at least the possibility of suspicion that the members of tribunals are not truly neutral. In response to such doubts, the 1957 Franks Committee recommended that the appointment of the chairmen of tribunals should become the prerogative of the Lord Chancellor and that the appointment of the other members should become the responsibility of a Council on Tribunals. This recommendation was not implemented and ministers by and large still retain the power to appoint tribunal members. As a compromise, however, the minister selects the chairperson from a panel appointed by the Lord Chancellor.

8.3.3 Statutory tribunals

There are a number of tribunals which have considerable power in their areas of operation, and it is necessary to have some detailed knowledge of a selection of the most important of these. Examples of such tribunals are:

- *Employment tribunals*

  These are governed by the Employment Tribunals Act 1996 which sets out their composition, major areas of competence and procedure. In practice, such tribunals are normally made up of a legally qualified chairperson, a representative chosen from a panel representing employers and another representative chosen from a panel representing the interests of employees.

  Employment tribunals have jurisdiction in relation to a number of statutory provisions relating to employment issues. The majority of issues arise in relation to such matters as disputes over the meaning and operation of particular terms of employment, disputes relating to redundancy payments, disputes involving issues of unfair dismissal, and disputes as to the provision of maternity pay.

  They also have authority in other areas under different legislation. Thus, they deal with complaints about racial discrimination in the employment field under the Race Relations Act 1976; complaints about sexual discrimination in employment under the Sex Discrimination Act 1975; complaints about equal pay under the Equal Pay Act 1970, as amended by the Sex Discrimination Act; complaints under the Disability Discrimination Act 1995; complaints about unlawful deductions from wages under the Wages Act 1986; and appeals against the imposition of improvement notices under the Health and Safety at Work Act 1974. There are, in addition, various ancillary matters relating to trade union membership and activities that employment tribunals have to deal with.

  The tribunal hearing is relatively informal. As in arbitration hearings, the normal rules of evidence are not applied and parties can represent themselves or be represented by solicitors or barristers. And, as appropriate in an employment context, they may also be represented by trade union officials or representatives, or indeed by any other person they wish to represent them.

  Appeal, on a point of law only, is to the Employment Appeal Tribunal, which also sits with lay representatives (see 3.4.1, above).

  Although less formal than ordinary courts, the process of taking a case to, or defending a case in, an employment tribunal can be time consuming and expensive, and employers' representatives have complained about the increased use of tribunals. In an attempt to remedy these alleged shortcomings, the Advisory, Conciliation and Arbitration Service (ACAS) initiated a new voluntary arbitration process for dealing with unfair dismissal claims as an alternative to using the employment tribunals. In the guide to the new scheme, ACAS state that:

> The intention is that the resolution of disputes under the Scheme will be confidential, relatively fast and cost efficient. Procedures under the Scheme are non-legalistic and far more informal and flexible than the employment tribunal. The process is inquisitorial rather than adversarial with no formal pleadings or cross-examination by parties or representatives. Instead of applying strict law or legal tests the arbitrator will have regard to general principles of fairness and good conduct in employment relations including, for example, principles referred to in the ACAS Code of Practice Disciplinary and Grievance Procedures and the ACAS Handbook *Discipline at Work* which were current at the time of the dismissal. In addition, as it is only possible to appeal or otherwise challenge an arbitrator's award (decision) in very limited circumstances, the Scheme should also provide quicker finality of outcome for the parties to an unfair dismissal dispute.

However, even before it was introduced, the scheme came under attack from the Industrial Society. In a pamphlet entitled *Courts or Compromise? Routes to Resolving Disputes*, it argued that the new alternative to employment tribunals could well become as rigid, formal and almost as expensive as current tribunal and court processes, and claimed that in any event, the impact on the tribunal system was likely to be slight. Whilst it recognised the advantages in such schemes, that they were faster, cheaper, more informal and flexible than tribunals, it also foresaw inherent risks. The pamphlet argued that ADR does not guarantee fairness or consistency in outcomes. In particular, it highlighted dangers where there is no appeal process, in lack of precedent, and where confidentiality is unjustifiable. It also pointed out the risk that compensation awarded through ADR might be less than in a tribunal or court. In conclusion, the report warned that people who opt for ADR need to make sure that they understand the implications, for example, where the decision is binding and leaves no route to appeal.

- *Social security appeal tribunal*

Various Social Security Acts have provided for safety-net provisions for the disadvantaged in society to ensure that they at least enjoy a basic standard of living. In the pursuit of this general goal, various State functionaries have been delegated the task of implementing the very complex provisions contained in the legislation, and have been granted considerable discretionary power in the implementation of those provisions. The function of the social security tribunals is to ensure that such discretion is not abused and that the aims of the legislation are being met generally. The tribunals, of which there are some 200 in England and

Wales, are charged with the duty of hearing and deciding upon the correctness of decisions made by adjudication officers, who are the people who actually determine the level of benefit individuals are entitled to receive.

- *Mental health review tribunals*

  These operate under the Mental Health Act 1983. The tribunals have wide powers to decide whether individuals should be detained for the purposes of compulsory treatment. They can also dispose of the property of such individuals. Given the particular area within which the mental health review tribunal operates, it is essential that there are medical experts present to decide on medical issues. This latter requirement also applies in respect of social security issues relating to the state of the individual claimant's health.

- *The Lands Tribunal*

  Established under the Lands Tribunal Act 1949, its essential function is to determine the legality of, and the levels of compensation in relation to, compulsory purchase orders over land. It also considers matters relating to planning applications.

- *Rent Assessment Committee*

  This Committee deals with matters specifically relating to the rent charged for property. It resolves disputes between landlords and tenants of private accommodation, hears appeals from decisions of rent officers and has the power to fix rent in relation to furnished and unfurnished residential tenancies.

The importance and sheer power of tribunals can be appreciated even from the truncated treatment of the short list of tribunals considered above.

8.3.4 Immigration and asylum appeals procedure

Given the publicity currently afforded to asylum issues, it is advantageous to have an awareness of how the asylum system actually operates. Decisions as to rights of entry into and rights to remain in the UK are initially made by Immigration Officers, Entry Clearance Officers or the Home Secretary. Thereafter, appeals against those decisions take the following course:

- *The Immigration Appellate Authority*

  The Immigration Appellate Authority (IAA) is a tribunal which hears appeals against decisions made by the Home Secretary and his officials in asylum and immigration matters. The IAA has two tiers: the Immigration Adjudicators and the Immigration Appeal Tribunal.

- *Immigration Adjudicators*

  All refused asylum applicants are entitled to a right of appeal on asylum grounds to an independent, legally qualified special adjudicator appointed by the Lord Chancellor. They form the first tier in considering appeals against decisions made by Immigration Officers, Entry Clearance Officers and the Home Secretary. Public funding is not available for representation at appeal hearings, but free representation can be obtained from the Refugee Legal Centre and the Immigration Advisory Service. Some appeals are 'certified', where the Home Secretary decides to refuse asylum. If the special adjudicator agrees with this decision, there is no further right of appeal to the Immigration Appeal Tribunal. If the special adjudicator does not agree with the certification of the appeal by the Home Secretary, there is a right of leave to appeal further to the Immigration Appeal Tribunal.

- *The Immigration Appeal Tribunal*

  The Immigration Appeal Tribunal (IAT) is an independent judicial body, which is constituted under the Immigration Act 1971 and the Immigration and Asylum Act 1999. It deals with applications for leave to appeal and appeals against decisions made by an Immigration Adjudicator. The chair of the Immigration Appellate Authority considers the grounds of appeal and decides whether or not to grant leave to appeal to the Tribunal. If leave is granted, the appeal will be heard by a legally qualified chairman as head of a three person panel (one legal and two lay members), appointed by the Lord Chancellor.

- *The Special Immigration Appeals Commission*

  The Special Immigration Appeals Commission (SIAC) is an independent Commission established by the Special Immigration Appeals Commission Act 1997, and it is responsible for dealing with appeals against decisions made by the Secretary of State under the terms of Part 4 of the Anti-Terrorism, Crime and Security Act 2001.

- *The Court of Appeal*

  From the IAT or SIAC, the route of appeal is into the ordinary court structure at the level of the Court of Appeal. Such appeals are only available in relation to a point of law.

- *Judicial review*

  Asylum seekers are also entitled like anyone else to apply to the High Court for leave to move for judicial review of any decision taken during the process, so long as they have exhausted their statutory rights.

8.3.5 Domestic tribunals

The foregoing has focused on public administrative tribunals set up under particular legislative provisions to deal with matters of public relevance. The term 'tribunal', however, is also used in relation to the internal, disciplinary procedures of particular institutions. Whether these institutions are created under legislation or not is immaterial; the point is that domestic tribunals relate mainly to matters of private rather than public concern, although at times the two can overlap. Examples of domestic tribunals are the disciplinary committees of professional institutions such as the Bar, The Law Society or the British Medical Association; trade unions; and universities. The power that each of these tribunals has is very great and it is controlled by the ordinary courts through ensuring that the rules of natural justice are complied with and that the tribunal does not act *ultra vires*, that is, beyond its powers. Matters relating to trade union membership and discipline are additionally regulated by the Employment Rights Act 1996.

8.3.6   Advantages of tribunals

Advantages of tribunals over courts relate to such matters as:

- *Speed*

  The ordinary court system is notoriously dilatory in hearing and deciding cases. Tribunals are much quicker to hear cases. A related advantage of the tribunal system is the certainty that it will be heard on a specific date and not subject to the vagaries of the court system. This being said, there have been reports that the tribunal system is coming under increased pressure and is falling behind in relation to its caseload. Thus, in 1993, in relation to the employment tribunal, Fraser Youlson, the Vice Chair of the Employment Lawyers Association, complained that cases which had previously taken three to five months to be heard could now take over 18 months.

- *Cost*

  Tribunals are a much cheaper way of deciding cases than using the ordinary court system. One factor that leads to a reduction in cost is the fact that no specialised court building is required to hear the cases. Also, the fact that those deciding the cases are less expensive to employ than judges, together with the fact that complainants do not have to rely on legal representation, makes the tribunal procedure considerably less expensive than using the traditional court system. These reductions are further enhanced by the additional facts that there are no court fees involved in relation to tribunal proceedings and that costs are not normally awarded against the loser.

- *Informality*

  Tribunals are supposed to be informal in order to make them less intimidating than full-blown court cases. The strict rules relating to evidence, pleading and procedure which apply in courts are not binding in tribunal proceedings. The lack of formality is strengthened by the fact that proceedings tend not to be inquisitorial or accusatorial, but are intended to try to encourage and help participants to express their views of the situation before the tribunal. Informality should not, however, be mistaken for a lack of order, and the Franks Committee Report itself emphasised the need for clear rules of procedure. The provision of this informal situation and procedure tends to suggest that complainants do not need to be represented by a lawyer in order to present their grievance. They may represent themselves or be represented by a more knowledgeable associate such as a trade union representative or some other friend. This contentious point will be considered further below.

- *Flexibility*

  Tribunals are not bound by the strict rules of precedent, although some pay more regard to previous decisions than others. It should be remembered that, as tribunals are inferior and subject to the courts, they are governed by the precedents made in the courts.

- *Expertise*

  Reference has already been made to the advantages to be gained from the particular expertise that is provided by the lay members of tribunals, as against the more general legal expertise of the chairperson.

- *Accessibility*

  The aim of tribunals is to provide individuals with a readily accessible forum in which to air their grievances, and gaining access to tribunals is certainly not as difficult as getting a case into the ordinary courts.

- *Privacy*

  The final advantage is the fact that proceedings can be taken before a tribunal without triggering the publicity that might follow from a court case.

8.3.7 Disadvantages of tribunals

It is important that the supposed advantages of tribunals are not simply taken at face value. They represent significant improvements over the operation of the ordinary court system, but it is at least arguable that some of them are not as advantageous as they appear at first sight, and that others represent potential, if not actual, weaknesses in the tribunal system.

Tribunals are cheap, quick, flexible and informal, but their operation should not be viewed with complacency. These so called advantages could be seen as representing an attack on general legal standards, and the tribunal system could be portrayed as providing a second-rate system of justice for those who cannot afford to pay to gain access to 'real law' in the court system. Vigilance is required on the part of the general community to ensure that such does not become an accurate representation of the tribunal system.

In addition to this general point, there are particular weaknesses in the system of tribunal adjudication. Some of these relate to the following:

- *Appeals procedures*

Confusion can arise from lack of uniformity in relation to appeals from tribunals. Rights of appeal from decisions of tribunals and the route of such appeals depend on the provision of the statute under which a particular tribunal operates. Where such rights exist, they may be exercised variously to a further tribunal, a minister or a court of law. A measure of coherence would not come amiss in this procedure.

Prior to the Franks Committee Report, tribunals were not required to provide reasons for their decisions and this prevented appeals in most cases. Subsequent to the Franks Report, however, most tribunals, although still not all of them, are required to provide reasons for their decisions under s 10 of the Tribunals and Inquiries Act 1992. The importance of this provision is that in cases where a tribunal has erred in its application of the law, the claimant can appeal to the High Court for an application for judicial review to have the decision of the tribunal set aside for error of law on the face of the record. All tribunals should be required to provide reasons for their decisions.

- *Publicity*

It was stated above that lack of publicity in relation to tribunal proceedings was a potential advantage of the system. A lack of publicity, however, may be a distinct disadvantage because it has the effect that cases involving issues of general public importance are not given the publicity and consideration that they might merit.

- *The provision of public funding*

It was claimed previously that one of the major advantages of the tribunal system is its lack of formality and non-legal atmosphere. Research has shown, however, that individual complainants fare better where they are represented by lawyers. Additionally, as a consequence of the Franks recommendations, the fact that chairpersons have to be legally qualified has led to an increase in the formality of tribunal proceedings. As a result, non-law experts find it increasingly difficult in practice to represent themselves effectively. This difficulty is compounded when the body which is the object of the complaint is itself legally represented; although the parties to hearings do not have to be legally represented, there is nothing to prevent them from being so represented. The full effect of the replacement of public funding by the Community Legal Service Fund, under the Access to Justice Act 1999, remains to be seen. It is probably accurate to say, however, that in this particular area, it certainly cannot make matters worse, and that the establishment of Community Legal Service Partnerships may well improve the availability of quality advice for those with problems to be decided by tribunals.

8.3.8 The Leggatt Review of Tribunals

In May 2000, Sir Andrew Leggatt was appointed by the Lord Chancellor to undertake a review of the tribunal system as a whole. As Sir Andrew found, there are 70 different administrative tribunals in England and Wales, leaving aside regulatory bodies, and between them they deal with nearly one million cases a year. However, of those 70 tribunals, only 20 hear more than 500 cases a year and many are in fact defunct. Sir Andrew's task was to rationalise and modernise the tribunals structure, and to that end, he made a number of proposals, including the following:

- *making the 70 tribunals into one tribunals system*

  He suggested that the existing 'system' did not really merit that title and that combining the administration of the different tribunals was necessary to generate a collective standing to match that of the court system, together with the collective power to fulfil the needs of users in the way that was originally intended. Within the new constituted 'system', he recommended that the tribunals should be grouped by subject matter into Divisions, in a structure that made sense to the user.

- *ensuring that the tribunals were independent of their sponsoring departments by having them administered by one Tribunals Service*

  He thought that, as currently happens, where a Department of State may provide the administrative support for a tribunal, pay its fees and expenses, appoint some of its members, provide its IT support and possibly promote legislation prescribing the procedure which the tribunal is to follow, the tribunal neither appears to be independent, nor is it independent in fact.

- *improving the training of chairpersons and members in the interpersonal skills peculiarly required by tribunals*

  He saw the prime necessity for improved training in the interpersonal skills peculiar to tribunals so as to enable the users of the tribunals to cope on their own without the need for legal representation.

- *ensuring that unrepresented users could participate effectively and without apprehension in tribunal proceedings*

  Following on from the previous finding, he felt that every effort should be made to reduce the number of cases in which legal representation is needed. He recognised, however, that there would always be a residual category of complex cases in which legal representation was necessary. Voluntary and community bodies should be funded so that they could provide such representation and only as a last resort should it be provided by public funding.

- *providing a coherent appeal system*

  He found the current system to be confusing and some tribunals to have too many appeal stages, leading to long delays in reaching finality. He suggested that there should be a right of appeal on a point of law, by permission, on the generic ground that the decision of the tribunal was unlawful:

  (i) from the first-tier tribunals in each Division to its corresponding appellate tribunal;

  (ii) from appellate tribunals to the Court of Appeal; and

  (iii) where there is no corresponding appellate tribunal, to any such court as may be prescribed by statute, or in default to such appellate tribunal as may be appointed by the Senior President.

- *reconsidering the position of lay members*

  He considered that there was no justification for any members to sit, whether expert or lay, unless they have a particular function to fulfil, as they do in the employment tribunal. In all other situations, the President of the Division (or Regional or District Chairmen) should be given discretion as to whether lay members should sit in any particular case or category of cases.

Subsequently, in March 2003, the Lord Chancellor's Office revealed the government's intention to follow Sir Andrew Leggatt's recommendations and to institute a new unified Tribunals Service. The detail of the proposals would appear in a White Paper, but according to Lord Irvine:

> A unified tribunal service will have at its core the top 10 non-devolved tribunals which currently exist throughout departments in Whitehall. By combining the administration we will deliver a more efficient and effective service to the users of tribunals. The new Service will be established as a distinct part of the justice system, *accountable to the Lord Chancellor*. The Service will bring together the 10 largest tribunals from across central Government, with smaller tribunals joining as appropriate.

The 10 tribunals concerned are:

- The Appeals Service.
- The Immigration Appellate Authority.
- The employment tribunals service.
- The Criminal Injuries Compensation Appeals Panel.
- The mental health review tribunal.
- The Office for Social Security and Child Support Commissioners.
- The Tax Tribunals.
- The Special Education Needs and Disability Tribunal.

- The Pensions Appeal Tribunal.
- The Lands Tribunal.

8.4   Ombudsman

As with tribunals, so the institution of the Ombudsman reflects the increased activity of the contemporary State. As the State became more engaged in everyday social activity, it increasingly impinged on, and on occasion conflicted with, the individual citizen. Courts and tribunals were available to deal with substantive breaches of particular rules and procedures, but there remained some disquiet as to the possibility of the adverse effect of the implementation of general State policy on individuals. If tribunals may be categorised as an ADR procedure to the ordinary court system in relation to *decisions taken in breach of rules*, the institution of Ombudsman represents a procedure for the redress of complaints about *the way in which those decisions have been taken*. It has to be admitted, however, that the two categories overlap to a considerable degree. The Ombudsman procedure, however, is not just an alternative to the court and tribunal system; it is based upon a distinctly different approach to dealing with disputes. Indeed, the Parliamentary Commissioner Act 1967, which established the position of the first Ombudsman, provides that complainants with rights to pursue their complaints in either of those forums will be precluded from making use of the Ombudsman procedure. (Such a prohibition is subject to the discretion of the Ombudsman who tends to interpret it in a generous manner in favour of the complainant.)

The concept of the Ombudsman is Scandinavian in origin, and the function of the office holder is to investigate complaints of *maladministration*; that is, situations where the performance of a government department has fallen below acceptable standards of administration. The first Ombudsman, appointed under the 1967 legislation, operated, and the present Ombudsman still operates, under the title of the Parliamentary Commissioner for Administration (PCA), and was empowered to consider central government processes only. The PCA also serves as Health Service Ombudsman, in which capacity they investigate complaints that hardship or injustice has been caused by the National Health Service's failure to provide a service, by a failure in service provided or by maladministration. Since that date, a number of other Ombudsmen have been appointed to oversee the administration of local government in England and Wales, under the Local Government Act 1974. Scotland and Northern Ireland have their own local government Ombudsmen fulfilling the same task. There are also Health Service Commissioners for England, Wales and Scotland, whose duty it is to investigate the administration and provision of services in the health service, and in October 1994, Sir Peter Woodhead was appointed as the first Prisons Ombudsman. This proliferation of Ombudsmen has led to some confusion as to which one any particular complaint should be taken to. This can be especially problematic where the complaint concerns more than one public body. In order to remedy this potential difficulty, a Cabinet Office review recommended in April 2000 that access be made easier through the establishment of one new Commission, bringing together the Ombudsmen for central government, local government and the health service.

The Ombudsman system has also spread beyond the realm of government administration and there are Ombudsmen overseeing the operation of, amongst other things, legal services (see 11.7.7 for details), banking and insurance. Some schemes, such as the legal services scheme, have been established by statute, but many others have been established by industry as a means of self-regulation. The Legal Services Ombudsman deals with complaints about solicitors, barristers and other legal practitioners. The Ombudsman is appointed by the Lord Chancellor in accordance with s 21 of the CLSA 1990 and is completely independent of the legal profession. In reflection of this, they cannot be a qualified lawyer. Complaints must first be to the relevant professional body of the member who is being complained about, and only if the complainants are not satisfied with the way the professional body deals with their complaint may they refer the matter to the Legal Services Ombudsman. The Ombudsman has powers to recommend that the professional body reconsider the complaint and may also recommend that the professional body and/or the person complained about pay compensation for loss, distress or inconvenience. Where necessary, any recommendation may be backed by a binding order for the payment of compensation.

It is a peculiarity of the system that reference is always made to the Ombuds*man*, irrespective of the gender of the office holder. The present Parliamentary Ombudsman is in fact Ann Abraham; however, as she was the previous Legal Services Ombudsman, she is no doubt used to the strange gender-specific title.

The European Parliament appointed an Ombudsman under the powers extended to it by the Treaty Establishing the European Community (EC Treaty) (Art 195, formerly 138(e)). The European Ombudsman has the function of investigating maladministration in all of the Community institutions, including the non-judicial operation of the European Court of Justice.

Before going on to consider the work of the Parliamentary Commissioner in some detail, mention should also be made of the various regulatory authorities which were established to control the operation of the recently privatised former State monopolies such as the water, gas, telephone and railway industries. Thus were OFWAT, OFGAS and OFTEL, etc, set up, with part of their remit being to deal with particular consumer complaints, as well as the general regulation of the various sectors.

8.4.1 Procedure

Although maladministration is not defined in the Parliamentary Commissioner Act 1967, it has been taken to refer to an error in the way a decision was reached rather than an error in the actual decision itself. Indeed, s 12(3) of the Parliamentary Commissioner Act 1967 expressly precludes the PCA from questioning the merits of particular decisions taken without maladministration. Maladministration therefore can be seen to refer to procedure used to reach a result rather than the result itself. In an illuminating and much quoted speech introducing the Act, Richard Crossman, the then leader of the House of Commons, gave an indicative, if non-definitive, list of what might be included within the term maladministration, and included within it: bias, neglect, inattention, delay, incompetence, ineptitude, perversity, turpitude and arbitrariness.

Members of the public do not have the right to complain directly to the PCA, but must channel any such complaint through a Member of Parliament. Complainants do not have to provide precise details of any maladministration. They simply have to indicate the difficulties they have experienced as a result of dealing with an agency of central government. It is the function of the PCA to discover whether the problem arose as a result of maladministration. There is a 12 month time limit for raising complaints, but the PCA has discretion to ignore this.

The powers of the PCA to investigate complaints are similar to those of a High Court Judge to require the attendance of witnesses and the production of documents; wilful obstruction of the investigation is treated as contempt of court.

On conclusion of an investigation, the PCA submits reports to the Member of Parliament who raised the complaint, and to the principal of the government office which was subject to the investigation. The Ombudsman has no enforcement powers, but if their recommendations are ignored, and existing practices involving maladministration are not altered, they may submit a further report to both Houses of Parliament in order to highlight the continued bad practice. The assumption is that on the submission of such a report, Members of Parliament will exert pressure on the appropriate Minister of State to ensure that any changes needed in procedure are made.

Annual reports are laid before Parliament and a Parliamentary Select Committee exists to oversee the operation of the PCA. The operation of the PCA is subject to judicial review (*R v Parliamentary Commissioner for Administration ex p Balchin* (1997)); however, the Parliamentary Commissioner for Public Standards, established after the Nolan Inquiry into cash for questions in Parliament, is not open to judicial review (*R v Parliamentary Commissioner for Standards ex p Al Fayed* (1997)) (see 1.4.3, above).

The relationship between the PCA and the government is highlighted by three case studies:

(a) *Barlow Clowes*

The first of these concerned the Barlow Clowes group of companies. In 1988, Peter Clowes and three others were arrested and charged with offences in connection with the Prevention of Fraud (Investments) Act 1958 and theft. The prosecution alleged an investment fraud said to have been over £115 million. The main allegation was that members of the public were induced to deposit their moneys in the belief that they would be invested in gilt-edged securities, but that only £1.9 million was in fact so invested. The rest was misappropriated by the defendants. Clowes alone faced charges of theft totalling some £62 million. The PCA received hundreds of complaints from investors who had lost their money in relation to the Barlow Clowes affair, all alleging maladministration on the part of the Department of Trade and Industry (DTI), which had responsibility for licensing such investment companies. The PCA made five findings of maladministration against the DTI and recommended that compensation should be paid to those who had suffered as a result of it. Surprisingly, the government initially denied any responsibility for providing compensation. Subsequently, after the PCA had expressed his regret at the government's initial stance, the government agreed to pay the recommended compensation payments, amounting to £150 million, but with the rider that it still accepted no legal liability.

(b) *Child Support Agency*

The much-criticised Child Support Agency (CSA) had been established in an endeavour to ensure that absent parents, essentially fathers, would have to accept financial responsibility for the maintenance of their children as determined by the Agency. The PCA's report followed complaints referred to him by 95 Members of Parliament covering the time from when the Agency started its operations in April 1994 until the end of 1995. Although the PCA investigated 70 complaints, the report focused on seven of those as being representative of the whole. These complaints highlighted a number of failures on the part of the CSA: mistakes as to the identity of individuals subject to the determinations of the CSA; failure to answer correspondence; delay in assessing and reviewing maintenance assessments and delays in actually securing payments due; and the provision of incorrect or misleading advice. The conclusion of the PCA was that the CSA was liable for maladministration, inexcusable delays and slipshod service. In response to the report, the chief executive of the CSA wrote to the PCA informing him that steps were being taken to deal with the problems highlighted in the report. Such changes in the way the CSA operated have not staved off its proposed replacement by a more sympathetic and efficient organisation.

(c) *Channel Tunnel Rail Link*

As a consequence of the four year delay on the part of the Department of Transport in deciding on a route for the Channel Tunnel Rail Link, the owners of properties along the various possible routes found the value of their properties blighted, not to say unsaleable. The situation was not finalised until the Department announced its final selection in 1994.

According to the PCA:

> The effect of the Department of Transport's policy was to put the project in limbo, keeping it alive when it could not be funded.

As a consequence, he held that the Department:

> ... had a responsibility to consider the position of such persons suffering exceptional or extreme hardship and to provide redress where appropriate. They undertook no such considerations. That merits my criticism.

The unusual thing about this case, however, was the reaction of the Department of Transport, which rejected the findings of the PCA and refused to provide any compensation. The refusal of the Department of Transport led the PCA to lay a special report before Parliament, consequent upon a situation where an 'injustice has been found which has not or will not be remedied' (s 10(3) of the Parliamentary Commissioner Act 1967). Even in the face of the implementation of this extremely rare form of censure, the government maintained its original policy that it was not liable for the consequences of either general or particular blight. The matter was then taken up by the Select Committee on the Parliamentary Commissioner for Administration, which supported the conclusions of the PCA and recommended that:

> ... the Department of Transport reconsider its response to the Ombudsman's findings, accept his conclusions that maladministration had occurred ... It would be most regrettable if the department were to remain obdurate. In such an event, we recommend that as a matter of urgency a debate on this matter be held on the floor of the House on a substantive motion in government time [*Sixth Report of PCA*].

Such a demonstration of solidarity between the PCA and the Committee had the desired effect, leading to the government's climbdown and payments of £5,000 to those property owners who had suffered as a consequence of the housing blight.

8.4.2   Freedom of information

The Parliamentary Ombudsman also has responsibility for investigating complaints as to government secrecy under the Code of Practice on Access to Government Information (the Code). The non-statutory Code came into being in 1994 and will continue in force until the Freedom of Information Act 2000 comes fully into effect in 2005. The Code requires that information in the hands of government departments should not be withheld without justification, whilst itself providing a number of such justifications. The effect of the Code is that any government department which withholds information from those requesting it must cite the Code exemptions on which it is relying to justify its stance. The function of the Ombudsman, on receiving a complaint about the withholding of information, is to investigate whether or not the alleged justification is legitimate and, as with his other functions, to recommend any necessary remedial action.

The Ombudsman undertakes a number of such enquiries every year and usually departments follow any recommendations made. However, in November 2001, for the first time, the government rejected the recommendation of the then Ombudsman, Sir Michael Buckley, that information should be released under the Code. The situation arose following a series of questions from Andrew Robathan MP to the Home Secretary, relating to ministers' declarations of interest under the Ministerial Code of Conduct. The Home Secretary refused to provide the information, citing exemption 2 and exemption 12 of the Code. The Ombudsman found that neither of the two exemptions applied to the particular information sought by Mr Robathan and recommended that the information be released to him. The Home Office would not agree to its release.

Subsequently, in his 2001/02 annual report, Sir Michael was highly critical of the approach of the government, stating:

> I hope … that the Government will in future accept the Ombudsman's recommendations, as they and their predecessors have in the overwhelming majority of earlier cases. However, I cannot disguise my concern at what seems to be a hardening of attitudes in departments. The bad habit of citing exemptions for the first time at a very late stage of an investigation has reappeared. In some cases it has taken literally months to obtain replies to correspondence. I am seriously concerned at these developments, which not only undermine the Code but also call into question the authority and standing of my office. If they are not reversed, they will raise serious doubts as to whether it is appropriate for the Ombudsman to continue to investigate complaints under the Code.

8.4.3   Evaluation

All in all, the system appears to operate fairly well within its restricted sphere of operation, but there are major areas where it could be improved. The more important of the criticisms levelled at the PCA relate to:

- the retention of Members of Parliament as filters of complaints. It is generally accepted that there is no need for such a filter mechanism. At one level, it represents a sop to the idea of parliamentary representation and control. Yet at the practical level, PCAs have referred complaints made to them directly to the constituent's Member of Parliament, in order to have them referred back to them in the appropriate form. It is suggested that there is no longer any need or justification for this farce;

- the restrictive nature of the definition of maladministration. It is possible to argue that any procedure that leads to an unreasonable decision must involve an element of maladministration and that, therefore, the definition as currently stated is not overly restrictive. However, even if such reverse reasoning is valid, it would still be preferable for the definition of the scope of the PCA's investigations to be clearly stated, and be stated in wider terms than at present;

- the jurisdiction of the PCA. This criticism tends to resolve itself into the view that there are many areas that should be covered by the PCA but which are not. For example, as presently constituted, the Ombudsman can only investigate the *operation* of general law. It could be claimed, and not without some justification, that the process of *making* law in the form of delegated legislation could equally do with investigation;

- the lack of publicity given to complaints. It is sometimes suggested that sufficient publicity is not given either to the existence of the various Ombudsmen or to the results of their investigations. The argument is that if more people were aware of the procedure and what it could achieve, then more people would make use of it, leading to an overall improvement in the administration of governmental policies;

- the reactive role of the Ombudsman. This criticism refers to the fact that the Ombudsmen are dependent upon receiving complaints before they can initiate investigations. It is suggested that a more *proactive* role, under which the Ombudsmen would be empowered to initiate investigation on their own authority, would lead to an improvement in general administration as well as increase the effectiveness of the activity of the Ombudsmen. This criticism is related to the way in which the role of the Ombudsmen is viewed. If they are simply a problem solving dispute resolution institution, then a *reactive* role is sufficient; if, however, they are seen as the means of improving general administrative performance, then a more *proactive* role is called for.

In his Hamlyn Lecture, the former Lord Chancellor, Lord Mackay, approvingly categorised the Ombudsman as:

> Popularly representing justice for the small against the great – justice that is quick, inexpensive and unfettered by legalistic procedures – acceptance of the institution of ombudsman now extends well beyond central and local government administration. The concept is widely viewed as a desirable, and even necessary, avenue to fairness wherever the individual is perceived to be at the mercy of an impenetrable administrative system.

8.5 Mediation and conciliation

The final alternative dispute mechanisms to be considered, mediation and conciliation, are the most informal of all.

8.5.1 Mediation

Mediation is the process whereby a third party acts as the conduit through which two disputing parties communicate and negotiate, in an attempt to reach a common resolution of a problem. The mediator may move between the parties, communicating their opinions without their having to meet, or alternatively the mediator may operate in the presence of the parties, but in either situation, the emphasis is on the parties themselves working out a shared agreement as to how the dispute in question is to be settled.

In his Hamlyn Lecture, Lord Mackay considered three alternative systems of mediation and examined the possibility of annexing such schemes to the existing court system. One, involving lawyers advising parties as to the legal strengths of their relative positions, he rejected on the grounds that it merely duplicated, without replacing or extending, what was already available in the courts. A second, based on judges adopting the role of mediators, he rejected on the ground that it might be seen as undermining the traditional impartiality of the judiciary. The third type, and the one that found most favour with him, broadened the issues beyond the legal, to explore solutions that were not available to the court. His approval, however, did not extend to financing such a system; the implication being that public money should, and does, finance the civil justice system and that any benefits that flow from a different system should be financed privately.

In March 1998, the LCD reported that take-up of voluntary mediation procedures offered in pilot schemes had been fairly low. As regards the pilot scheme established in the Central London county court, a monitoring report found that only 5% of cases referred to the ADR scheme actually took it up. However, in a more positive mode, the report did find that, in cases that did go to mediation, 62% settled during the process without going on to court. The conclusion of the report was that mediation was capable of dealing with a wider range of cases than might have been expected, including personal injury cases. It also reported that those who participated found the process satisfying and led to outcomes that the parties generally thought acceptable.

8.5.2 Mediation in divorce

Mediation has an important part to play in family matters, where it is felt that the adversarial approach of the traditional legal system has tended to emphasise, if not increase, existing differences of view between individuals and has not been conducive to amicable settlements. Thus, in divorce cases, mediation has traditionally been used to enable the parties themselves to work out an agreed settlement rather than having one imposed on them from outside by the courts.

This emphasis on mediation was strengthened in the Family Law Act 1996, but it is important to realise that there are potential problems with mediation. The assumption that the parties freely negotiate the terms of their final agreement in a less than hostile manner may be deeply flawed, to the extent that it assumes equality of bargaining power and knowledge between the parties to the negotiation. Mediation may well ease pain, but unless the mediation procedure is carefully and critically monitored, it may gloss over and perpetuate a previously exploitative relationship, allowing the more powerful participant to manipulate and dominate the more vulnerable and force an inequitable agreement. Establishing entitlements on the basis of clear legal advice may be preferable to apparently negotiating those entitlements away in the non-confrontational, therapeutic, atmosphere of mediation.

Under the Divorce Reform Act 1969, the concept of 'no fault' divorce was introduced for those couples who had been separated for two years, and it was assumed that this would provide the main grounds for divorce applications. This has not proved to be the case and it is commonly accepted that, because of the two year delay involved, 75% of those seeking divorces still applied on the basis of adultery or unreasonable behaviour, permitting them to complete the procedure in between three and six months.

The Family Law Act 1996 proposed to introduce real 'no fault' divorce by abolishing the grounds of adultery and unreasonable behaviour, but couples would have to wait a minimum of 12 months before their divorce was confirmed. Instead of filing a divorce petition, the person seeking to be divorced would merely be required to submit a statement certifying that their marriage had broken down. The process of divorce would require that the parties attend an informal meeting three months before they made their statement of marital breakdown. They would then have to wait a further nine months for their divorce, during which time they should reflect on whether the marriage could be saved, have an opportunity for reconciliation and consider arrangements relating to finance, property and children. The Act encouraged the use of mediation in appropriate cases, and allowed the court, after it had received a statement of marital breakdown, to direct the parties to attend a meeting with a mediator for an explanation of the mediation process. The role of the mediator was restricted to sorting out the aspects of the divorce relating to finance and children, and they should have referred the case to an appropriate counsellor if it appeared that the parties to the marriage might be open to reconciliation. During the 'cooling off period', State funding would be available for meetings with marriage guidance counsellors for those eligible for public funding, and others would be encouraged to take advantage of such marriage support services.

Although the Family Law Act was passed in 1996, the proposed reforms were not implemented immediately and trials were conducted as to the appropriateness of the new procedures. Also, the fact that the Family Law Act was passed under the previous Conservative administration, and as a consequence of the strenuous endeavours of the then Lord Chancellor, Lord Mackay, did not prevent the incoming Labour administration's continued support for the proposed reforms. As Lord Chancellor Irvine stated:

> ... in government, we have continued to encourage the use of mediation, most notably in the area of family law, where it is a central tenet of divorce law reform. The importance of mediation and ADR in family law cases can scarcely be understated, given the high incidence of family breakdown and the appalling social consequences which result [Lord Chancellor Irvine, speech to Faculty of Mediators, 1999].

However, in June 1999, Lord Irvine announced that the government would not be implementing the new proposals in the Family Law Act in the year 2000 as had been previously intended. It has to be said that much academic and legal practitioner opinion was dubious about, if not hostile to, the way in which the mediation procedure would operate. It was accepted generally that mediation might work in relation to children, but it was thought less likely to work where money was concerned and, in those circumstances, it was suggested that people would still be likely to look for their own personal legal representative rather than submit to mediation. It would appear that the results of the trials support such scepticism. Lord Irvine stated that the results of the mediation pilot schemes were disappointing, in that fewer than 10% of divorcing couples in the pilot areas were willing to make use of the preliminary information meetings which would become compulsory under the Family Law Act proposals. Of those attending the meetings, only 7% were successfully encouraged to opt for mediation, and only 13% took up the offer to see a marriage counsellor. Almost 40% of those attending the meetings stated that they were more convinced of the need to see an independent lawyer to protect their legal rights.

Lord Irvine's announcement was merely as to the postponement of the implementation of the divorce law reforms. Many, however, believed that this postponement was merely a precursor to their future abandonment.

In March 1998, the LCD reported that take up of the voluntary mediation procedure offered in the pilot schemes had been fairly low.

In a speech at the UK Family Law Conference in London on 25 June 1999, Lord Irvine recognised that his decision to postpone the implementation of Part II of the Family Law Act raised a question mark over its future, but he went on to say that the final decision depended on the outcome of the current and future research into the area. Unfortunately, at least for proponents of 'no fault' divorce, the outcome of the research proved disagreeable to the LCD (see *Report on Information Meetings*. On 16 January 2001, Lord Irvine announced the government's intention to repeal Part II of the Family Law Act 1996. Six versions of the compulsory information meetings, intended to help couples either to save their marriages or to end them with minimum distress and acrimony, had been tested in pilot schemes over a period of two years. The research showed that, although those attending such meetings valued the information gained, it actually tended to incline those who were uncertain about their marriage towards divorce. The Lord Chancellor, however, stated that his concerns did not only relate to information meetings, as the complex procedures in Part II would be likely also to lead to significant delay and uncertainty in resolving arrangements for the future. The government concluded that such delay would not be in the best interests of either couples or their children.

It is important to realise that the repealing of Part II of the Family Law Act does not mean the end of mediation. Both the Lord Chancellor and the government remain strongly committed to advancing the role of mediation in family breakdown and also, in January 2001, launched a publicity campaign to increase awareness of family mediation.

8.5.3   Conciliation

Conciliation takes mediation a step further and gives the mediator the power to suggest grounds for compromise and the possible basis for a conclusive agreement. Both mediation and conciliation have been available in relation to industrial disputes under the auspices of the government funded ACAS. One of the statutory functions of ACAS is to try to resolve industrial disputes by means of discussion and negotiation or, if the parties agree, the Service might take a more active part as arbitrator in relation to a particular dispute.

The essential weakness in the procedures of mediation and conciliation lies in the fact that, although they *may* lead to the resolution of a dispute, they do not *necessarily* achieve that end. Where they operate successfully, they are excellent methods of dealing with problems, as essentially the parties to the dispute determine their own solutions and therefore feel committed to the outcome. The problem is that they have no binding power and do not always lead to an outcome.

ARBITRATION, TRIBUNAL ADJUDICATION AND ALTERNATIVE DISPUTE RESOLUTION

Alternative dispute resolution

ADR has many features that make it preferable to the ordinary court system in many areas.

Its main advantage is that it is less antagonistic than the ordinary legal system, and is designed to achieve agreement between the parties involved.

Arbitration

This is the procedure whereby parties in dispute refer the issue to a third party for resolution, rather than take the case to the ordinary law courts. Arbitration procedures can be contained in the original contract or agreed after a dispute arises. The procedure is governed by the Arbitration Act 1996. The Act follows the Model Arbitration Law adopted by the United Nations Commission on International Trade Law (UNCITRAL). Arbitration awards are enforceable in the ordinary courts. They must be carried out in a judicial manner and are subject to judicial review.

Advantages over the ordinary court system are: privacy; informality; speed; lower cost; expertise; and it is less antagonistic.

Small claims procedure in the county court is a distinct process, although referred to as arbitration. Although still called small claims, the upper limit for such proceedings is the not inconsiderable sum of £5,000. This has raised some doubts as to the future operation of the system.

Administrative tribunals

These deal with cases involving conflicts between the State, its functionaries and private citizens. Domestic tribunals deal with private internal matters within institutions. Tribunals may be seen as administrative but they are also adjudicative in that they have to act judicially when deciding particular cases. Tribunals are subject to the supervision of the Council on Tribunals, but are subservient to, and under the control of, the ordinary courts.

Usually, only the chair of a tribunal is legally qualified.

Examples of tribunals are the: employment tribunal; social security appeals tribunal; mental health review tribunal; Lands Tribunal; Rent Assessment Committee.

Advantages of tribunals over ordinary courts relate to: speed; cost; informality; flexibility; expertise; accessibility; privacy.

Disadvantages relate to: appeals procedure; lack of publicity; the lack of public funding in most cases.

Ombudsmen

The role of Ombudsmen is to investigate complaints of maladministration in various areas of State activity. Members of the public must channel complaints through a Member of Parliament.

The powers of the Parliamentary Commissioner for Administration to investigate complaints are similar to those of a High Court Judge. The Ombudsman has no direct enforcement powers as such.

On conclusion of an investigation, he submits reports to the Member of Parliament who raised complaint and to the principal of the government office which was subject to the investigation. He can also report to Parliament.

Shortcomings in the procedure: the Member of Parliament filter; uncertain if not narrow jurisdiction; lack of publicity; the reactive rather than proactive nature of the role.

Mediation and conciliation

Mediation: the third party only acts as a go-between. The Family Law Act 1996 proposed a greater role for mediation in relation to divorce. However, following adverse trials, the Lord Chancellor announced in January 2001 that Part II of the Family Law Act would be repealed.

Conciliation: the third party is more active in facilitating a reconciliation or agreement between the parties.

CHAPTER 9

THE CRIMINAL PROCESS: (1) THE INVESTIGATION OF CRIME

9.1 General introduction to the criminal process

9.1.1 The criminal justice system in the 21st century

The criminal justice system has recently been the subject of widespread heated debate in Parliament, the broadcast media and the print media, and in academic and professional journals. The British Crime Survey (BCS) (*Crime in England and Wales* 2001/2002, Jon Simmons, Home Office, 2002) estimates there were just over 13 million crimes against adults living in households in 2001. The long term trend shows that the gradual rise in BCS crime during the 1980s and the steeper rise during the early 1990s have now been reversed. Even so, the number of crimes counted by the BCS is still a third higher than in 1981. There also appears to be a disproportionate increase in the number of serious crimes. Gun crime is a good example. In 1997/98, there were 4,903 crimes involving firearms (excluding air weapons). In 2001/02, there were 9,974. Half of these offences were associated with robberies; 35% involved violence against the person (Ford, 'Crimes with firearms increase to 61 a day' (2003) *The Times*, 10 January).

This chapter and the following one refer to the 'criminal justice system'. This has been for many years an accepted descriptive term used by social scientists, journalists and occasionally lawyers. Officially, however, there is no such thing as the 'criminal justice system'. Governmental responsibilities, for example, overlap in this area. The Home Secretary is responsible for the Metropolitan Police, criminal statistics, the probation service and the Crown Prosecution Service (CPS) (and, more broadly, for 'law and order'), while the Lord Chancellor is responsible for all the criminal law courts, the appointment of magistrates and the judges. Nonetheless, in recent times, there has been increasing governmental recognition of something called the 'criminal justice system'. On 30 December 1998, for example, a single official statement entitled 'Joint Press Release on the Criminal Justice System Public Service Agreement' was issued on behalf of the Home Office, the Lord Chancellor's Department (LCD) and the Attorney General's Office. It stated:

> The overarching aims, objectives and performance measures for the criminal justice system have been published for the first time in a cross departmental Public Service Agreement. The three Departments, and their respective services, will be working more closely than ever before to ensure that the criminal justice system protects the public and delivers justice. Inter-agency co-operation will be promoted at regional, local, as well as at the national level.

Ministers believe that these arrangements are a good example of 'joined-up government' in practice.

The significance of such a pronouncement is that it reveals an attempt to make co-ordinated policy in respect of each of these branches of operation. In fact, the statement goes on to become quite explicit:

The three ministers have set two overarching aims to provide a strategic direction for the system as a whole. They have made clear that every part of the criminal justice system (including the police, courts, Crown Prosecution Service, prison and probation services) should work together so as to best serve and protect the public.

The two overarching aims are:

- to reduce crime and the fear of crime and their social and economic costs; and

- to dispense justice fairly and efficiently and to promote confidence in the rule of law.

Supporting the aims are the following eight objectives:

In support of the first aim:

(1) to reduce the level of actual crime and disorder;

(2) to reduce the adverse impact of crime and disorder on people's lives;

(3) to reduce the economic costs of crime.

In support of the second aim:

(4) to ensure just processes and just and effective outcomes;

(5) to deal with cases throughout the criminal justice process with appropriate speed;

(6) to meet the needs of victims, witnesses and jurors within the system;

(7) to respect the rights of defendants and to treat them fairly;

(8) to promote confidence in the criminal justice system.

In pursuit of these general aims, and in a more recent manifestation of the desire on the part of the government to treat the system as an integrated whole, in February 2001, the Home Office, the LCD and the Attorney General's Office jointly published *Criminal Justice: The Way Ahead* (Cmnd 5074, 2001). There, the government set out its vision for a modern, efficient criminal justice system to help police, prosecutors, courts, prisons and probation officers deal more effectively with offenders, provide a professional service to the general public and step up support for victims and witnesses. The paper proposes that, in order to deliver a new criminal justice 'service', every part of the existing system, from detection, prosecution and punishment to resettlement of prisoners, will be subject to reform and modernisation. Proposals include:

- improved policing – enhanced detective capability, a police service-wide strategic approach to information technology, scientific and technical developments, more officers, greater police visibility and accessibility;

- more effective prosecution – increased investment in the CPS, a specialist body of prosecutors to deal with organised and serious crime, a new consolidated criminal code;

- punishments to fit the criminal as well as the crime – continued oversight and intervention by the criminal justice system of drug addicted offenders, more regard to crime reduction and reparation with new, more flexible community sentences, increase in severity of punishments for persistent offenders, improved supervision and support of short sentence prisoners after release from prison;

- improvements in the experience of victims and witnesses in the criminal justice system – court familiarisation visits and improved court waiting facilities, introduction of victim personal statements enabling victims to indicate the effect of the crime on their lives, better information on progress of the case from the CPS, a possible 'Victim's Fund' to ensure victims are more swiftly compensated, possible introduction of a Victims' Ombudsman to champion victims' interests and the opportunity for victims to report minor crime online.

9.2 Mistrust of the system

There exists mistrust of the criminal justice system from both those who believe innocent people have been convicted and those who think guilty people escape justice. The number of exposed miscarriages of justice involving malpractice and disastrous errors by agencies of the criminal justice system has grown rapidly. On 19 March 1991, the day the Birmingham Six were released from prison having wrongly served 16 years in jail, the Home Secretary announced a Royal Commission on Criminal Justice to examine the system with a view to reducing the chances of wrongful conviction. The Commission published its report with 352 recommendations in July 1993. Some of these recommendations have been implemented in subsequent legislation (like the establishment of the Criminal Cases Review Commission (CCRC) by the Criminal Appeal Act (CAA) 1995). For a useful discussion of these issues, see Annabelle James, 'Miscarriages of justice in the 21st century' (2002) 66(4) Journal of Criminal Law, pp 326–37. Great concern has been expressed by pressure groups about the government's rejection of the Royal Commission's findings in relation to the so called 'right to silence'. This right was effectively undermined by ss 34–37 of the Criminal Justice and Public Order Act (CJPOA) 1994, and this change will arguably increase the chances of miscarriages occurring rather than reduce them. Confidence in the criminal justice system appears to be in decline. In a national survey for the 1962 Royal Commission on the Police (Cmnd 1728, 1962, HMSO), 83% of respondents indicated that they had 'a great deal of respect' for the way the police operated. In a national poll in 1993, conducted by MORI for *The Sunday Times* and the Police

Federation, under 50% of respondents indicated that they had 'a great deal of respect' for the way the police operated. The poll also showed that one in six adults (7 million people) actually distrust the police ((1993) *The Sunday Times*, 25 July). In another nationwide poll ((1993) *The Independent*, 21 June), 28% of respondents indicated that they would be 'concerned at what might be going to happen' if stopped by the police, with only 36% of respondents indicating they would be confident that they would be treated fairly.

Public confidence in the police continued to fall in the late 1990s (see, for example, 'Lack of trust at heart of attitude problem' (1999) *The Guardian*, 25 February; 'One in four say police racist' (1999) *The Guardian*, 9 February). This drop in confidence plummeted with particular sharpness after the publication of the Macpherson Report into the racist killing of the black London teenager, Stephen Lawrence. The Report identified various fundamental operational failings of the police and, more significantly, 'institutional racism'. According to a recent survey, 75% of respondents believed that the police did 'a very good' or 'fairly good' job. Of these, 14% thought the police did a 'very good job'. Twenty years earlier, 43% of respondents to a similar survey had answered in this way. Although 76% of respondents were 'confident' or 'fairly confident' that the rights of defendants were respected, 56% believed that the criminal justice system was 'fairly ineffective' or 'totally ineffective'. The survey also revealed widespread dissatisfaction with the sentencing of offenders: 76% believed that sentences were too lenient while only 3% thought they were too severe (Tendler, 'Justice system is failing victims of crime say public' (2003) *The Times*, 10 January).

9.2.1   The Macpherson Report

Following the stabbing of Stephen Lawrence, a black teenager from south London, by a group of racist thugs in 1993, defects in several aspects of the English legal system failed to bring his killers to justice. There was a catalogue of profoundly incompetent errors in the way the police handled events. These included: the failure to administer proper first aid at the scene of the attack; a failure to properly search for evidence and suspects; a failure to properly log and investigate tip-offs about the identity of the killers; and a failure to treat the family of Stephen Lawrence with proper respect and sensitivity. A judicial inquiry headed by a former High Court Judge, Sir William Macpherson, was set up by the government in 1997 and its report was published in February 1999 (Cm 4262-I, The Stationery Office).

The Report accused the Metropolitan Police (in London) of 'institutional racism'. Its recommendation that the police and several other public services should now be brought fully within the Race Relations Act 1976, has been acted upon by amendments to the 1976 Act contained in the Race Relations (Amendment) Act 2000. The Act now makes it unlawful for a public authority (including the police) to discriminate against a person on racial grounds in carrying out any of its public functions. It also imposes a general duty on specified public authorities (including the police), in carrying out their functions, to have due regard for the need to eliminate unlawful discrimination and to promote equality of opportunity and good relations between persons of different racial groups.

Another recommendation in the Report would, if enacted, end the ancient principle against 'double jeopardy', whereby a person cannot be tried more than once for the same, or substantially the same, crime. There is arguably a good case for change here. The rule, which prevents anyone from being charged more than once in respect of the same crime, arose in an ancient era when there existed none of today's multifarious checks and balances against the abuse of official power (committal proceedings, independent magistrates and judges, random juries, stringent laws of evidence; see Chapter 10). At the time of the origin of the rule against double jeopardy, powerful aristocrats could, effectively, terrorise individual enemies with the threat of repeated prosecutions. By contrast, in today's setting, provided some form of high level and independent authorisation were to be required before a second prosecution could be brought, there would be no real risk that the threat of re-prosecution would constantly hang over an acquitted defendant's head. Only those fearful of new, viable incriminating evidence for serious crimes would have reason to worry.

The recommendation arose from one twist in the developments in the Lawrence case, in which three suspects were sent for trial at Crown Court after a private prosecution brought by Stephen's father. The trial was stopped by the judge, who ruled that there was insufficient evidence to proceed and ordered the jury to acquit the defendants. The rule of double jeopardy (*autrefois acquit* – the person has been otherwise acquitted) will now prevent any further prosecution being brought against the main suspects, even if strong evidence against them is subsequently found. The feeling that the guilty have got away with such a serious and repulsive crime is widespread. One national newspaper, beneath the banner headline 'Murderers', printed the names and photographs of the five chief suspects of the killing.

The Report recommends (Recommendation 38) that the Court of Appeal should have the power to permit prosecution after acquittal 'where fresh and viable evidence is presented'.

The Home Secretary referred this issue to the Law Commission, which recommended (Law Com 267, 2001) that the rule against double jeopardy should be subject to an exception where new evidence, which appears reliable and compelling as to the accused's guilt, is discovered after acquittal. The exception should apply retrospectively. However, the exception should apply only to murder cases and to genocide cases involving the killing of any person (and also to reckless manslaughter cases should proposals for reform of the law on involuntary manslaughter be enacted). The Law Commission also recommended extending the grounds for quashing a tainted acquittal (currently, acquittals resulting from conduct which is an offence involving interference with or intimidation of jurors, witnesses or potential witnesses) to include an offence involving interference with or intimidation of a judge, magistrate or magistrates' clerk. In both instances, the power to quash the acquittal should lie with the Court of Appeal (Criminal Division).

The Report's other recommendations include:

(1) that a ministerial priority be established for all police services 'to increase trust and confidence in policing among minority ethnic communities'.

Comment: Unfortunately, only days after this Report was published, it came to light that a special report commissioned 15 months *previously* showed that 17 out of the 43 police forces of England and Wales did not have any community and race relations policy, despite having been urged to establish one ((1999) *The Times*, 2 March).

(9) that a Freedom of Information Act should apply to all areas of policing, subject only to a 'substantial harm' test for withholding information.

Comment: Both during the investigation and at various stages after the failed public prosecution, the friends and relatives of Stephen Lawrence found it impossible to get clear and accurate information from the police about how the case had been handled and was being taken forward. The more open and transparent a system, the more likely it is to carry public confidence. It seems more likely that this hope will be realised by establishing a role for the CPS in keeping victims informed of the progress of the case (in accordance with the proposals in *Criminal Justice: The Way Ahead*) than by resort to the rather limited rights of access to information given by the Freedom of Information Act 2000.

(11) that the Race Relations Acts should apply to police officers and that Chief Constables should be vicariously liable for the acts and omissions of their officers in this area.

Comment: This proposal would help focus police attention on what might otherwise be unconscious or unintended racist behaviour and has been implemented by amendments to the 1976 Act made by the Race Relations (Amendment) Act 2000.

(33) that the CPS should, in deciding whether to prosecute a racist crime, consider that once the 'evidential test' is satisfied (that is, that there is a 'realistic prospect of conviction'), there is a rebuttable presumption that the public interest test is in favour of prosecution.

Comment: Racism in a crime is currently a factor which should strengthen the chances of a prosecution according to the Code for Crown Prosecutors; the change would make a prosecution more certain in such circumstances. The Code was issued in a revised form in October 2000. It has not been amended to state this proposition specifically but, commenting on the relationship between the evidential and public benefit tests, the Director of Public Prosecutions (DPP), Sir David Calvert-Smith, remarked that the Code creates 'a general presumption in favour of prosecution for all cases in which there is sufficient evidence, unless there are public interest factors that clearly outweigh those in favour of prosecution' ((2000) 150 NLJ 1495). The public interest factor in favour of prosecution relating to (*inter alia*) racist crime has been amended so that it extends beyond an actual racial motivation to encompass a demonstration of hostility towards the victim based on such a factor.

(34) that the police and CPS should take particular care to recognise and to include any evidence of a racial motivation in a crime. The CPS should take care to ensure that any such motivation is referred to at trial and in the sentencing process. No plea bargaining should ever exclude such evidence.

Comment: This highlights that racism is a serious aggravating factor in any crime, as it shows that the innocent victim has been specially and vindictively selected for a reason that is irrational, and therefore, especially terrifying. The Crime and Disorder Act (CDA) 1998 contains provisions which make the committing of various non-fatal offences, harassment, criminal damage and some public order offences separate and more serious offences where they are *racially aggravated* (ss 28–32). It also provides that in all offences, racial aggravation is to be taken into account when determining sentence (s 82). The CPS Annual Report for 1999–2000 on racial incident monitoring tends to reveal a mixed picture. There was a dramatic rise in the number of cases in which defendants faced allegations of racist incidents, about half of all cases being CDA 1998 cases, but there were significant variations in recording and reporting by different police forces. Note: the Anti-Terrorism, Crime and Security Act (ACSA) 2001 broadened the scope of s 28 of the CDA. It now refers to 'racially and religiously aggravated offences'.

(41) that consideration be given to the proposition that victims or victims' families should be allowed to become 'civil parties' to criminal proceedings, to facilitate and to ensure the provision of all relevant information to victims and their families.

Comment: Unlike civil litigation, it is the State that prosecutes where there has been a crime; the victim neither determines whether to prosecute nor, if someone is convicted, can they influence the sentence for the crime. Recommendation 41 is therefore a controversial proposal, as there has traditionally been great resistance to permitting citizens to participate in the prosecution of crimes. The essentially communicative role suggested here, however, is arguably different from an influential role.

(42) that there should be advance disclosure of evidence and documents as of right to parties who have leave from a coroner to appear at an inquest.

Comment: Presently, relatives often only discover the terrible details of the death of their loved ones at the inquest in open court, as some coroners will not release any information even to bereaved next of kin before the hearing.

(43) that consideration be given to the provision of legal aid to victims or the families of victims to cover representation at an inquest in appropriate cases.

Comment: This is a recommendation that has been made for many years by various bodies and committees. There is a very strong case for bereaved people *in extremis*, who cannot afford to have representation at the inquest of their loved one, to receive public funding.

Britain is a multi-cultural and ethnically diverse community. Its policing is based on consent rather than sheer strength: there are 60 million citizens and only 127,000 police officers, so it can only work on consent. At the heart of the debate about policing, the law and the criminal justice system in the wake of the Macpherson Report, is the question of whether ethnic minorities, especially visible minorities, can quickly be made to feel confident about the way they are treated by the English legal system.

A recent report produced by the Metropolitan Police Service (MPS) entitled *Stop and Search: Reviewing the Tactic* and two Home Office research papers, *Entry into the Criminal Justice System: A Survey of Police Arrests and their Outcomes* (1998) and *Statistics on Race and the Criminal Justice System* (1998), recognise the disproportionate use of stop and search powers against black people (see Cragg, 'Stop and search powers: research and extension' (1999) Legal Action 3, February). Cragg argues that, 'with the figures already showing that almost 90% of those stopped are not arrested (and therefore, the implication must be that there were, in fact, no grounds to stop and search these people), the training and management strategy proposed by the MPS "to manage the tactic more fairly and effectively" must be rigorously imposed and monitored if it is to have any chance of success'. A study by Miller, Quinton and Bland (Police Research Series Papers 127–32, September 2000) examined the disproportionate use of stops and searches by measuring populations 'available' to be stopped and searched by the police (those in public places where and when stops or searches are carried out). It found that in areas with high stop and search activity, young men and people from minority ethnic backgrounds tended to be over-represented in the available population. On the other hand, the findings suggested that, within the available population, no general pattern of bias against people from minority ethnic groups was evident, either as a whole or for particular groups. Comparing statistics on stops and searches with available populations showed that white people tended to be over-represented, Asian people tended to be under-represented (with some exceptions), and black people's representation varied (with examples of both over and under-representation). However, the report concluded that, despite these findings, the possibility of discrimination by officers in their use of stops and searches could not be dismissed. The exercise of stop and search powers by the police is governed by the revised Code of Practice A (see 9.3.14, below), which states that it is important that these powers are used fairly and responsibly. It warns, 'any misuse of the powers is likely to be harmful to policing and can lead to mistrust of police'.

9.2.2 Lack of confidence in the system

In 2001–02, the police in England and Wales recorded a total of 5,527,199 offences (*Crime in England and Wales 2001–2002*, Jon Simmons, 2002, Home Office). This figure is 7% higher than the one for 2000–01 (if changes in recording practice are taken into account the underlying increase is about 2%). Certain types of offence, like domestic burglary, theft of and from vehicles and vandalism against vehicles and other household and personal property, have greatly vexed large sections of the population. Just over 10 million BCS crimes are comparable with those recorded by police statistics. However, a large proportion of crime is unrecorded, as many offences are not reported to the police. Approximately 42% of the BCS crimes were reported to the police. Of these, an estimated 60% were recorded by the police.

9.2.3 A contradiction

There is a friction between the sort of policies that these two concerns generate, that is, people seem to want the police to have greater powers to combat crime, and yet contradictorily want greater controls on the police and evidence so as to avoid more miscarriages of justice. It is argued that if we wish to avoid unjust convictions like those of the Winchester Three, the Guildford Four, the Birmingham Six, the Maguire Seven, the Tottenham Three, Stefan Kiszko, Judith Ward and the Bridgewater Three ((1997) *The Guardian*, 21, 22 February), we should tighten the rules of evidence and procedure that govern the investigation and prosecution of crime. Against this, it has been argued (for example, by Charles Pollard, Chief Constable of the Thames Valley Police: letter (1995) *The Times*, 12 April; article (1995) *The Sunday Times*, 9 July) that the police should have greater powers and that the trial process should be tilted less in favour of the defendant. The rules on disclosure of evidence in criminal trials, for example, have been radically changed by the Criminal Procedure and Investigations Act (CPIA) 1996. In particular, the material the prosecution has to disclose to the defence is now staged and brought within a more restrictive framework and now, for the first time, the defence has a duty to disclose its case in advance of trial.

One problem, therefore, in this area of the English legal system is that as the growing problems of crime, and the fear of crime, become more important concerns of government, there are emerging two lobbies for change, lobbies which are diametrically opposed.

The criminal process is examined here in two chapters. This chapter considers the law relating to important pre-trial matters up to and including the admissibility of confession evidence in court. Chapter 10 looks at institutional and procedural aspects of prosecution and matters relating to bail, the classification of offences, trials, plea bargaining and the jury. In examining all these topics, it is important to keep in mind the various aims of the criminal justice system and the extent to which the existing law serves these aims. Amongst the aims to be borne in mind are the following:

- to detect crime and convict those who have committed it;
- to have rules relating to arrest, search, questioning, interrogation and admissibility of evidence which do not expose suspects to unfair treatment likely to lead to unjust convictions;
- to have rules as above which do not unnecessarily impede the proper investigation of crime;
- to ensure that innocent persons are not convicted;
- to maintain public order;
- to maintain public confidence in the criminal justice system;
- to properly balance considerations of justice and fair procedure with those of efficiency and funding.

9.2.4 Contemporary issues

The criminal justice system is bearing signs of strain as it tries to cope with a society in the throes of major transitions: changes in the pattern of family life; changes in the nature of employment expectations; and a revolution in information and communications technology.

In 1993, the prison population of England and Wales was 42,000 (this includes those incarcerated in young offender institutions). By 14 March 2003 this had risen to 72,806. The prison population is currently near capacity and rising at a rate of approximately 400 per month.

The Police and Magistrates' Courts Act 1994 amended the Police Act 1964, permitting Home Secretaries now to 'determine objectives for the policing of all of the areas of all police authorities'. Under this power, a new police mission statement was announced in 1999. The purpose of the police according to this is 'to help secure a safe and just society in which the rights and responsibilities of individuals, families and communities are properly balanced'. This raises many contentious issues, as the determination of, for example, what is a 'just society' becomes something which is more overtly a matter for policing policy than in previous times when the police role was more simply (in the words of Robert Peel, the 19th century founder of modern policing) to 'prevent and detect crime'.

Yet, can 127,000 police officers do well enough to retain credibility in a society of 60 million people undergoing all sorts of social upheavals? In 1998, the police had to respond to 17.8 million incidents and 7.5 million 999 calls. The racist canteen culture revealed in the wake of the Stephen Lawrence Inquiry (see 9.2.1, above) and the recognition in 1998 by the Commissioner for the Metropolitan Police that he probably had 250 corrupt officers on his force did not help raise public confidence.

It is not clear yet what is the main thrust of governmental policy in relation to the criminal justice system. Thus far, we have seen an unusual cocktail consisting of several privatisation measures and a good dose of centralisation.

Criminal justice has historically been regarded by government as a matter for the State. Recently, however, first under the Conservative government in the early 1990s and now under Labour, various parts of the system have been privatised. Such moves have not generally been seen as runaway successes. In November 1998, there was public scandal at the extent of injury to prison officers and trainers and damage to the premises of the country's leading private institution for young offenders. It was revealed that over £100,000 of damage had been wrought by wild 12–14 year olds at the Medway Secure Training Centre in Kent. After more than one fiasco, privatised prison escort services have come in for severe criticism, and a provision of the CJPOA 1994 allowing for private sponsorship of police equipment has been a boon for satirical cartoonists.

By contrast, there are several ways in which aspects of the criminal justice system, historically all independent from each other and detached from governmental control, have been drawn within the influence of central government. It has, for example, been a hallowed precept of the British constitution that police forces are local and not governmental agencies. Yet, under Conservative legislation, the Home Secretary became allowed to 'determine objectives for the policing of the areas of all police authorities'.

More worryingly, there has been a notable governmental move to integrate different organisational functions. The CPS has been restructured so that its erstwhile 13 regions are turned into 42 to match the 43 police forces of England and Wales. This is a remarkable swerve from previous policy. Close and often cosy relations between police officers and the lawyers who used to prosecute their cases (sometimes with atrocious malpractice) were the very reason for the establishment of the CPS.

However, moves towards criminal justice system unification go further than this. The Lord Chancellor announced in 1997 (*Ministerial Statement to the House of Lords*, 29 October 1997) that the 96 Magistrates' Courts Committees (which administer the courts dealing with 95% of all criminal cases) should enjoy much greater alignment with the police and the CPS.

Most disturbing of all for some are the foundations for the Criminal Defence Service (CDS) (laid in the Access to Justice Act 1999 and finally established in April 2001) which will give the government greater control over legal representation. The Law Society has pointed out that campaigning lawyers like Gareth Pierce, who represented the Guildford Four, and Jim Nicol, who represented the appellants in the Carl Bridgewater case, could be avoided by the new body.

There is also reason for disquiet about the law contained in the Terrorism Act 2000, which makes the opinion of a police officer admissible evidence in court – proof of membership of a proscribed organisation may be based in part upon the opinion of a senior police officer. In the wake of considerable evidence (from miscarriage of justice cases, especially those involving suspects of terrorism from Northern Ireland) that some police officers were apparently prepared to lie and falsify evidence to secure convictions, the new law has caused some people to become alarmed at the prospect that a person could be convicted of a serious offence on evidence taken mainly from the opinion of a police officer.

Proactive 'intelligence-led' policing has become increasingly commonplace in recent years, especially in relation to drugs and organised crime. Such techniques inevitably involve deception by police officers and their informers (see C Dunnighan and C Norris, 'A risky business: the recruitment and running of informers by English police officers' (1996) 19 Police Studies 1). This may involve testing whether a person is willing to commit an offence. Although English law has never recognised a defence of entrapment, entrapment may be a mitigating factor and a ground for excluding evidence; *R v Looseley; Attorney General's Reference (No 3 of 2000)* (2002). See Andrew Ashworth, 'Re-drawing the boundaries of entrapment' [2002] Crim LR 161–79.

9.3 Arrest

According to AV Dicey, 'individual rights are the basis not the result of the law of the constitution' (*Law of the Constitution*, 6th edition, p 203; cited by Judge LJ in *R v Central Criminal Court ex p The Guardian, The Observer and Bright* (2002)). *Before* considering the rights of the citizen and the law governing arrest and detention, what happens in the police station and what evidence is admissible in court, it is appropriate to look first at what the citizen can do if those rights are violated.

9.3.1 Remedies for unlawful arrest

Like other areas of law where the liberty of the subject is at stake, the law relating to arrest is founded upon the principle of *justification*. If challenged, the person who has attempted to make an arrest must justify his actions and show that the arrest was lawful. Failing this, the arrest will be regarded as unlawful.

There are three possible remedies:

- The person, or someone on his behalf, can bring proceedings of habeas corpus. This ancient prerogative writ used to begin with the words 'habeas corpus', meaning 'you must have the body'. It is addressed to the detainer and asks him to bring the detainee in question before the court at a specified date and time. The remedy protects the freedom of those who have been unlawfully detained in prison, hospital, police station or private custody. The writ is applied for from a judge in chambers and can, in emergencies, be made over the telephone. It must be issued if there is *prima facie* evidence that the detention is unlawful. As every detention is unlawful, the burden of proof is on the detainer to justify his conduct. If issued, the writ frees the detainee and thus allows him to seek other remedies (below) against the detainer.

- To use the illegality of the detention to argue that any subsequent prosecution should fail. This type of argument is very rarely successful as illegally obtained evidence is not, *ipso facto, automatically rendered* inadmissible. The House of Lords ruled in *R v Sang* (1979) that no discretion existed to exclude evidence simply because it had been illegally or improperly obtained. A court could only exclude relevant evidence where its effect would be 'unduly prejudicial'. This is reflected in s 78(1) of the Police and Criminal Evidence Act (PACE) 1984. This perhaps surprising rule was supported by the Royal Commission on Criminal Justice (although the argument there was chiefly focused on the admissibility of confession evidence). Professor Zander, however, in a note of dissent, contested the idea that a conviction could be upheld despite serious misconduct by the prosecution if there is other evidence against the convicted person. He states: 'I cannot agree. The moral foundation of the criminal justice system requires that, if the prosecution has employed foul means, the defendant must go free if he is plainly guilty ... the conviction should be quashed as an expression of the system's repugnance'. Since the Human Rights Act (HRA) 1998 became fully operative in October 2000, it has no longer been possible to treat such issues merely as involving interpretation of s 78(1) of PACE 1984 itself. Additionally, any court must take Art 6 of the European Convention on Human Rights (ECHR) into account in appropriate circumstances. For further discussion of this aspect, see 9.5.26, below.

- An action for damages for false imprisonment. In some cases, the damages for such an action would be likely to be nominal if the violation by the detainer does not have much impact on the detainee. Consider cases under this heading like *Christie v Leachinsky* (1947). Damages can, however, be considerable. In *Reynolds v Commissioner of Police for the Metropolis* (1982), a jury awarded £12,000 damages to the plaintiff. She had been arrested in the early hours in connection with charges of arson for gain, that is, that insured houses, which had been set alight deliberately, would be the subject of 'accidental fire' insurance claims. She was taken by car to a police station, a journey which took two and a half hours. She was detained until about 8 pm when she was told there was no evidence against her. She arrived home about 11 pm. The judge, Caulfield J, ruled that the police had no reasonable grounds for suspecting the plaintiff of having committed an arrestable offence and he directed the jury in relation to damages. The jury awarded £12,000 and the defendant's appeal against this sum as excessive was dismissed.

  In a review of trends in actions against the police, Sadiq Khan and Matthew Ryder ((1998) Legal Action 16, September) comment on two cases in relation to damages. In *Goswell v Commissioner of Police for the Metropolis* (1998), a jury awarded damages totalling £302,000 to Mr Goswell, comprising £120,000 for assault, £12,000 for false imprisonment and £170,000 exemplary damages. On appeal, Simon Brown LJ held that £100 was an appropriate award for basic damages for false imprisonment for 20 minutes. He allowed for the fact that the unlawfulness of the detention was a consequence of a breach of s 28 of PACE and expressed the opinion that the case 'does not in the fullest sense involve a wrongful deprivation of liberty'. Basic damages were assessed at £22,500, aggravated damages at £10,000 and £15,000 for exemplary damages. Overall, the figure was reduced from £302,000 to £47,500. In a second case against the police, *Commissioner of Police for the Metropolis v Gerald* (1998), an initial award by a jury of £125,000 for assault, false imprisonment and malicious prosecution was reduced to £50,000 on appeal by the Commissioner.

Apart from the question of civil remedies, it is important to remember the following:

- If the arrest is not lawful, there is the right to use reasonable force to resist it: *R v Waterfield* (1964); *Kenlin v Gardner* (1967). This is a remedy, however, of doubtful advisability, as the legality of the arrest will only be properly tested after the event in a law court. If a police officer was engaged in what the courts decide was a lawful arrest or conduct, then anyone who uses force against the officer might have been guilty of an offence of assaulting an officer in the execution of his duty, contrary to s 89(1) of the Police Act 1996.

- That, for our purposes in considering the consequences for an unlawfully arrested person faced with prosecution, s 78 of PACE 1984 states:

78(1) In any proceedings, the court may refuse to allow evidence on which the prosecution proposes to rely to be given if it appears to the court that, having regard to all the circumstances, including the circumstances in which the evidence was obtained, the admission of the evidence would have such an adverse effect on the fairness of the proceedings that the court ought not to admit it.

9.3.2 General powers of arrest

In *Spicer v Holt* (1977), Lord Dilhorne stated:

Whether or not a person has been arrested depends not upon the legality of the arrest, but on whether he has been deprived of his liberty to go where he pleases.

So, a person detained by the police against his will is arrested. Whether this arrest is lawful will depend on whether the conditions for a lawful arrest have been satisfied.

Lawful arrests are those: (1) under warrant; (2) without warrant at common law; or (3) without warrant under legislation.

9.3.3 Arrest under warrant

The police lay a written information on oath before a magistrate that a person 'has, or is suspected of having, committed an offence' (s 1 of the Magistrates' Courts Act 1980). The Criminal Justice Act (CJA) 1967 provides that warrants should not be issued unless the offence in question is indictable or is punishable with imprisonment.

Until recently, complex extradition arrangements existed between the Member States of the European Union (EU). In December 2001, the EU agreed in principle to introduce European arrest warrants. The decision was formally adopted in June 2002. The traditional approach (found in extradition agreements) embodied the principle of 'dual criminality'; that is, a person would not be extradited from one State to another unless his alleged offence was an extraditable crime in both countries. This requirement has now been removed from a list of 32 offences. The inclusion of 'racism and xenophobia' has aroused some controversy. See Susie Allegre, 'The myth and the reality of a modern European judicial space' (2002) 152 NLJ 986–87.

9.3.4 Common law arrests

The only power to arrest at common law is where a breach of the peace has been committed and there are reasonable grounds for believing that it will be continued or renewed, or where a breach of the peace is reasonably apprehended. Essentially, it requires *conduct* related to violence, real or threatened. A simple disturbance does not, in itself, amount to a breach of the peace unless it results from violence, real or threatened.

In 1981, two cases decided within months of each other offered definitions of a breach of the peace, in an attempt to bring some clarification to an area of law that previously was in doubt. In *R v Howell* (1981), the defendant was arrested after being involved in a disturbance at a street party in the early hours of the morning. Watkins LJ, who delivered the judgment of the court, observed that there was a power of arrest for anticipated breach of the peace provided the arrestor had been witness to the earlier shouting and swearing of H, and therefore had reasonable grounds for belief, and did believe at the time, that the defendant's conduct, either alone or as part of a general disturbance, was likely to lead to the use of violence by the defendant or someone else in the officer's presence.

The court adopted the following definition of 'breach of the peace' – it occurs:

> Wherever harm is actually done or is likely to be done to a person or in his presence his property or a person is in fear of being so harmed through an assault, an affray, a riot, unlawful assembly or other disturbance.

In the second of the two cases, *R v Chief Constable of the Devon and Cornwall Constabulary ex p Central Electricity Generating Board (CEGB)* (1981), Lord Denning MR suggested that breach of the peace might be considerably wider than this. This case involved a group of protesters who had occupied private land in order to prevent CEGB employees from carrying out a survey to assess its suitability for a nuclear power station. The protest was intended to be peaceful and non-violent. Lord Denning MR suggested that:

> There is a breach of the peace whenever a person who is lawfully carrying out his work is unlawfully and physically prevented by another from doing it ... If anyone unlawfully and physically obstructs the worker, by lying down or chaining himself to a rig or the like, he is guilty of a breach of the peace.

He appears to have been saying (Feldman, *Civil Liberties and Human Rights in England and Wales* (1993), pp 788–89) not that a breach of the peace is automatic in such circumstances, but that in the context of the *CEGB* case, any obstruction or unlawful *resistance* by the trespasser could give the police a reasonable apprehension of a breach of the peace, in the sense of violence.

However, in cases that have followed (such as *Parkin v Norman* (1982); *Percy v DPP* (1995); and *Foulkes v Chief Constable of Merseyside Police* (1998)), it is the definition in *R v Howell* that has been preferred. Despite earlier doubts, argues Parpworth ('Breach of the peace: breach of human rights?' (1998) 152 JP 6, 7 November), the recent decision of the European Court of Human Rights (ECtHR) in *Steel and Others v UK* (1998) brings clear and authoritative clarification to this area of law. This case represents 'a clear endorsement by a court largely unfamiliar with the common law concept of a breach of the peace that such a concept is in accordance with the terms of the European Convention on Human Rights'.

At common law, a constable may arrest a person for conduct which he genuinely suspects might be likely to cause a breach of the peace even on private premises where no member of the public is present: *McConnell v Chief Constable of Manchester* (1990). Although mere shouting and swearing alone will not constitute a breach of the peace, it is an offence under s 28 of the Town Police Causes Act 1847 and could lead to an arrest under s 25 of PACE (general arrest conditions). If it causes harassment, alarm or distress to a member of the public, it may constitute an offence under s 5 of the Public Order Act 1986.

9.3.5 Arrest under legislation

The right to arrest is generally governed by s 24 of PACE 1984. This provides that the police may arrest without a warrant for 'arrestable offences' and certain other offences. An arrestable offence is one for which the sentence is fixed by law (there are very few of these, life imprisonment for murder being the most common); any offence for which a person could be liable to a sentence of five years' imprisonment or more on first conviction; any one of the offences listed in s 24(2); any attempt to commit any of the above. The offences listed in s 24(2) involve Customs and Excise, the Official Secrets Acts, indecent assaults on women, taking a motor vehicle without authority and going equipped for stealing, and since 1995, certain offences relating to obscenity and indecent photographs and pseudo-photographs of children.

There are differences between the powers of arrest given by s 24 of PACE 1984 to police constables and ordinary citizens:

(4) Any person may arrest without a warrant:
    (a) anyone who is in the act of committing an arrestable offence;
    (b) anyone whom he has reasonable grounds for suspecting to be committing such an offence.

(5) Where an arrestable offence has been committed, any person may arrest without a warrant:
    (a) anyone who is guilty of the offence;
    (b) anyone whom he has reasonable grounds for suspecting to be guilty of it.

(6) Where a constable has reasonable grounds for suspecting that an arrestable offence has been committed, he may arrest without a warrant anyone whom he has reasonable grounds for suspecting to be guilty of the offence.

(7) A constable may arrest without a warrant:
    (a) anyone who is about to commit an arrestable offence;
    (b) anyone whom he has reasonable grounds for suspecting to be about to commit an arrestable offence.

A police officer is given additional powers under s 25, which states:

> 25(1) Where a constable has reasonable grounds for suspecting that an offence which is not an arrestable offence has been committed or attempted, or is being committed or attempted, he may arrest the relevant person if it appears to him that service of a summons is impracticable or inappropriate because any of the general arrest conditions is satisfied.

The general arrest conditions are specified in s 25(3). They are: that the officer does not know and cannot find out the suspect's name and address (or he has reasonable grounds to think that he has been given a false name or address); or has reasonable grounds for believing that an arrest is necessary to prevent someone causing physical harm to himself or someone else; or loss of or damage to property; or an offence against public decency; or an obstruction of the highway.

9.3.6   *G v DPP* (1989)

In *G v DPP* (1989), the appellant (G) with other juveniles, including a co-accused, Gill, went to a police station to complain about being ejected from a public service vehicle. On being asked for their names and addresses by the officer, G, the appellant, refused to do so; some of the others gave false particulars, but Gill gave his real name and address. The officer did not accept that Gill's particulars were correct because in his experience people who committed offences did not give correct details (even though the juveniles had only gone to the police station to complain about the way they had been treated on the bus). The juveniles would not accept the officer's advice about their complaint and became threatening and abusive. Gill was arrested for 'disorderly behaviour in a police station' and he struggled and resisted; the appellant joined in, punching the officer and causing him to lose hold of Gill. Both Gill and G were convicted of assaulting a police officer in the execution of his duty. The Divisional Court quashed their convictions. The offence of 'violent behaviour' or 'disorderly behaviour' under the Town Police Causes Act 1847 was not an arrestable offence. The only power the officer therefore had to arrest Gill was under s 25(3) of PACE 1984 if there were genuine doubts about Gill's name and address. But the ground given by the officer – about people who commit offences not giving their proper name, etc – was not a proper ground because there was no evidence that the youths had committed any offences; they had gone to the police simply to complain. Therefore, in purporting to arrest Gill, the officer had not been acting in the execution of his duty and the appellant could not, therefore, have been guilty of obstructing him in the performance of such duty.

It should be noted in particular that, under s 24(6), no offence need actually have been committed. All that is required is that the police officer reasonably believes that an arrestable offence has been committed.

The differences in the powers of arrest in s 24 are based on whether an offence:

- *is being* committed: anyone may make the arrest; see s 24(4);
- *has been* committed: anyone may make the arrest; see s 24(5) or the wider powers of the police (s 24(6)) who can arrest where they have 'reasonable grounds for suspecting that an arrestable offence has been committed' whether one has in fact been committed or not;
- is *about to be* committed: only a police officer may act here; see s 24(7).

PACE 1984 preserves an old common law distinction in respect of the powers of constables and private individuals when making such arrests. Where an arrest is being made *after* an offence is thought to have been committed, then PACE 1984 confers narrower rights upon the private individual than on the police officer.

9.3.7 *Walters v WH Smith & Son Ltd* (1914)

In *Walters v WH Smith & Son Ltd* (1914), the defendants had reasonably suspected that Walters had stolen books from a station bookstall. At his trial, Walters was acquitted, as the jury believed his statement that he had intended to pay for the books. No crime had therefore been committed in respect of any of the books. Walters sued the defendants, *inter alia*, for false imprisonment, a tort which involves the wrongful deprivation of personal liberty in any form, as he had been arrested for a crime which had not in fact been committed. The Court of Appeal held that, to justify the arrest, a private individual had to show not only reasonable suspicion but also that the offence for which the arrested person was given over into custody had in fact been committed, even if by someone else. A police officer making an arrest in the same circumstances could legally justify the arrest by showing 'reasonable suspicion' alone without having to show that an offence was, in fact, committed.

This principle is now incorporated in s 24 of PACE 1984. It is worthy of note that the less prudent arrestor who acts against a suspect when the latter is suspected of being in the act of committing an arrestable offence (s 24(4)) can justify his conduct simply by showing that there were 'reasonable grounds' on which to base the suspicion. They need not show that an offence was in fact being committed. If the arrestor waits until he thinks the crime has been committed, then, whereas a police officer will only have to show 'reasonable grounds for suspecting that an arrestable offence has been committed' (s 24(6)), a citizen can only justify his behaviour if an offence 'has been committed' (s 24(5)).

9.3.8 *R v Self* (1992)

This analysis is supported by the decision in *R v Self* (1992). The defendant was seen by a store detective in Woolworths to pick up a bar of chocolate and leave the store without paying. The detective followed him out into the street and, with the assistance of a member of the public, she arrested the suspect under the powers in s 24(5) of PACE 1984. The suspect resisted the arrest and assaulted both his arrestors. He was subsequently charged with theft of the chocolate and with offences of assault with intent to resist lawful apprehension or detainer, contrary to s 38 of the Offences Against the Person Act 1861. At his trial, he was acquitted of theft (apparently for lack of *mens rea*) but convicted of the assaults. These convictions were quashed by the Court of Appeal on the grounds that, as the arrest had not been lawful, he was entitled to resist it. The power of arrest conferred upon a citizen (s 24(5)) in circumstances where an offence is thought to *have been committed* only applies when an offence *has* been committed, and as the jury decided that Mr Self had not committed any offence, there was no power to arrest him.

9.3.9 *John Lewis & Co v Tims* (1952)

In *John Lewis & Co v Tims* (1952), Mrs Tims and her daughter were arrested by store detectives for shoplifting four calendars from the appellant's Oxford Street store. It was a regulation of the store that only a managing director or a general manager was authorised to institute any prosecution. After being arrested, Mrs Tims and her daughter were taken to the office of the chief store detective. They were detained there until a chief detective and a manager arrived to give instructions whether to prosecute. They were eventually handed over to police custody within an hour of arrest. In a claim by Mrs Tims for false imprisonment, she alleged that the detectives were obliged to give her into the custody of the police immediately upon arrest. The House of Lords held that the delay was reasonable in the circumstances as there were advantages in refusing to give private detectives a 'free hand' and leaving the determination of such an important question as whether to prosecute to a superior official.

9.3.10 What is the meaning of 'reasonable grounds for suspecting'?

Many of the powers of the police in relation to arrest, search and seizure are founded upon the presence of reasonable 'suspicion', 'cause' or 'belief' in a state of affairs, usually that a suspect is involved actually or potentially in a crime.

In *Castorina v Chief Constable of Surrey* (1988), detectives reasonably concluded that the burglary of a company's premises was an 'inside job'. The managing director told them that she had recently dismissed someone (the plaintiff), although she did not think it would have been her, and that the documents taken would be useful to someone with a grudge. The detectives interviewed the plaintiff, having found out that she had no criminal record, and arrested her under s 2(4) of the Criminal Law Act (CLA) 1967 (which has now been replaced by s 24(6) of PACE 1984). She was detained at the police station for almost four hours, interrogated and then released without charge. On a claim for damages for wrongful arrest and detention, a jury awarded her £4,500. The trial judge held that the officers had had a *prima facie* case for suspicion, but that the arrest was premature. He had defined 'reasonable cause' (which the officers would have needed to show they had when they arrested the plaintiff) as 'honest belief founded upon reasonable suspicion leading an ordinary cautious man to the conclusion that the person arrested was guilty of the offence'. He said an ordinary man would have sought more information from the suspect, including an explanation for any grudge on her part. In this he relied on the *dicta* of Scott LJ in *Dumbell v Roberts* (1944) that the principle that every man was presumed innocent until proved guilty also applied to arrests. The Court of Appeal allowed an appeal by the Chief Constable. The court held that the trial judge had used too severe a test in judging the officers' conduct.

Purchas LJ said that the test of 'reasonable cause' was objective and therefore the trial judge was wrong to have focused attention on whether the officers had 'an honest belief'. The question was whether the officers had had reasonable grounds to suspect the woman of the offence. There was sufficient evidence that the officers had had sufficient reason to suspect her.

Woolf LJ thought there were three things to consider in cases where an arrest is alleged to be unlawful:

- Did the arresting officer suspect that the person who was arrested had committed the offence? This was a matter of fact about the officer's state of mind.

- If the answer to the first question is yes, then was there reasonable proof of that suspicion? This is a simple objective matter to be determined by the judge.

- If the answers to the first two questions are both yes, then the officer did have a discretion to arrest, and the question then was whether he had exercised his discretion according to *Wednesbury* principles of reasonableness.

This case hinged on the second point and, on the facts, the Chief Constable should succeed on the appeal.

Note: The *Wednesbury* principles come from *Associated Provincial Picture Houses Ltd v Wednesbury Corp* (1948). Lord Greene MR laid down principles to determine when the decision made by a public authority could be regarded as so perverse or unreasonable that the courts would be justified in overturning that decision. The case actually concerned whether a condition imposed by a local authority on cinemas operating on Sundays was reasonable. Lord Greene MR said:

> ... a person entrusted with a discretion must, so to speak, direct himself properly in law. He must call his own attention to matters which he is bound to consider. He must exclude from his consideration matters which are irrelevant to what he has to consider. If he does not obey those rules, he may be truly said, and often is said, to be acting 'unreasonably'.

Sir Frederick Lawton, the third judge in the Court of Appeal in *Castorina*, agreed. The facts on which 'reasonable cause' was said to have been founded did not have to be such as to lead an ordinary cautious man to conclude that the person arrested *was* guilty of the offence. It was enough if they could lead an ordinary person to *suspect* that he was guilty.

This allows quite a latitude to the police. Additionally, the House of Lords has decided in *Holgate-Mohammed v Duke* (1984) that, where a police officer reasonably suspects an individual of having committed an arrestable offence, he may arrest that person with a view to questioning him at the police station. His decision can only be challenged on *Wednesbury* principles if he acted improperly by taking something irrelevant into account. The police arrested a former lodger for theft of jewellery from the house where she had lived in order to question her at the police station. The trial judge awarded her £1,000 damages for false imprisonment. The Court of Appeal set aside the award and the decision was upheld by the House of Lords. The following passage from a judgment in the Court of Appeal in *Holgate-Mohammed* was approved in the House of Lords:

> As to the proposition that there were other things which [the police officer] might have done. No doubt there were other things which he might have done first. He might have obtained a statement from her otherwise than under arrest to see how far he could get. He might have obtained a specimen of her handwriting and sent that off for forensic examination against a specimen of the writing of the person who had obtained the money by selling the stolen jewellery, which happened to exist in the case. All those things he might have done. He might have carried out finger print investigations if he had first obtained a print from the plaintiff. But, the fact that there were other things which he might have done does not, in my judgment, make that which he did do into an unreasonable exercise of the power of arrest if what he did do, namely, to arrest, was within the range of reasonable choices open to him.

It has been forcefully contended, however, that, in some circumstances, a failure to make inquiries before making an arrest could show that there were insufficient grounds for the arrest. See Clayton and Tomlinson, 'Arrest and reasonable grounds for suspicion' (1988) Law Soc Gazette, 7 September.

Note, however, that the powers are *discretionary*. See *Simpson v Chief Constable of South Yorkshire Police* (1991).

9.3.11 Detention short of arrest

For there to be an arrest, the arrestor must regard his action as an arrest. If he simply detains someone to question him without any thought of arrest, the action will be unlawful. It is often reported in criminal investigations that a person is 'helping police with their inquiries'. In *R v Lemsatef* (1977), Lawton LJ said:

> It must be clearly understood that neither customs officers nor police officers have any right to detain somebody for the purposes of getting them to help with their inquiries.

There is no police power to detain someone against his will in order to make inquiries about that person. See also *Franchiosy* (1979). This is confirmed by s 29 of PACE 1984, which states that where someone attends a police station 'for the purpose of assisting with an investigation', he is entitled to leave at any time unless placed under arrest. He must be informed at once that he is under arrest 'if a decision is taken by a constable to prevent him from leaving at will'. There is, however, no legal duty on the police to inform anyone whom they invite to the station to help with their inquiries that he may go.

9.3.12 Suspects stopped in the street

In *Kenlin v Gardiner* (1967), a police officer took hold of the arm of a boy he wanted to question about the latter's suspicious conduct. The boy did not believe the man was a policeman, despite having been shown a warrant card, and punched the officer in order to escape. The other boy behaved similarly but their convictions for assaulting an officer in the execution of his duty were quashed by the Divisional Court. The court held that the boys were entitled to act as they did in self-defence as the officer's conduct in trying to physically apprehend them had not been legal. There is no legal power of detention short of arrest. As Lawton LJ observed in *R v Lemsatef* (see above), the police do not have any powers to detain somebody 'for the purposes of getting them to help with their inquiries'.

It is important, however, to examine the precise circumstances of the detaining officer's conduct, because there are cases to suggest that if what the officer does amounts to only a *de minimis* interference with the citizen's liberty, then forceful 'self-defence' by the citizen will not be justified. In *Donnelly v Jackman* (1970), an officer approached a suspect to ask some questions. The suspect ignored the request and walked away from the officer. The officer followed and made further requests for the suspect to stop and talk. He tapped the suspect on the shoulder and the suspect reciprocated by tapping the officer on the shoulder and saying 'Now we are even, copper'. The officer tapped the suspect on the shoulder again which was replied to with a forceful punch. Mr Donnelly's conviction was upheld and the decision in *Kenlin v Gardiner* was distinguished as, in the earlier case, the officer had actually taken hold of the boys and detained them. The court stated that, 'it is not every trivial interference with a citizen's liberty that amounts to a course of conduct sufficient to take the officer out of the course of his duties'.

In *Bentley v Brudzinski* (1982), the facts were very close to those in question. A constable stopped two men who had been running barefoot down a street in the early hours. He questioned them about a stolen vehicle as they fitted the description of suspects in an earlier incident. They waited for about 10 minutes while the officer checked their details over a radio and then they began to leave. Another constable, who had just arrived on the scene, then said, 'Just a minute', and put his hand on the defendant's shoulder. The defendant then punched that officer in the face. Unlike the decision in *Donnelly v Jackman*, the Divisional Court held that the officer's conduct was more than a trivial interference with the citizen's liberty and amounted to an unlawful attempt to stop and detain him. The respondent was thus not guilty of assaulting an officer in the execution of his duty.

Note, also, that a person may be arrested for being silent or misleading under s 25 of PACE 1984 if the officer has reasonable doubts about the suspect's name and address or whether the summons procedure can be used at the address given.

9.3.13 Stop and search

PACE 1984 gives the police power to search 'any person or vehicle' and to detain either for the purpose of such a search (s 1(2)). A constable may not conduct such a search 'unless he has reasonable grounds for suspecting that he will find stolen or prohibited articles' (s 1(3)). Any such item found during the search can be seized (s 1(6)). An article is 'prohibited' if it is either an offensive weapon or it is 'made or adapted for use in the course of or in connection with burglary, theft, taking a motor vehicle without authority or obtaining property by deception or is intended by the person having it with him for such use by him or by some other person' (s 1(7)). An offensive weapon is defined as meaning 'any article made or adapted for use for causing injury to persons or intended by the person having it with him for such use by him or by some other person' (s 1(9)). This definition is taken from the Prevention of Crime Act 1953. It has two categories: things that are offensive weapons *per se* (that is, in themselves), like a baton with a nail through the end or knuckle-dusters, and things that are not offensive weapons, like a spanner, but which are intended to be used as such. If the item is in the first category, then the prosecution need prove only that the accused had it with him to put the onus onto the accused to show that he had a lawful excuse. Stop and search powers can now also be exercised under s 8A regarding items covered by s 139 of the CJA 1988. These items are any article which has a blade or is sharply pointed, except folding pocket knives with a blade of less than three inches. It is an offence to possess such items without good reason or lawful authority, the onus of proof being on the defendant. The courts will not accept the carrying of offensive weapons for generalised self-defence unless there is some immediate, identifiable threat.

Under s 2 of PACE 1984, a police officer who proposes to carry out a stop and search must state his name and police station, and the purpose of the search. A plain clothes officer must also produce documentary evidence that he is a police officer. The officer must also give the grounds for the search. Such street searches must be limited to outer clothing; the searched person cannot be required to remove any article of clothing other than a jacket, outer clothes or gloves. The officer is required to make a record of the search immediately, or as soon as is reasonably practicable afterwards (s 3). The record of the search should include the object of the search, the grounds of the search and its result (s 3). A failure to give grounds as required by s 2(3)(c) will render the search unlawful (*R v Fennelley* (1989)).

A recent case involved a protester who wore a skeleton-type mask at a demonstration. A police officer asked her to remove it. When she failed to do so, he tried to remove it himself. The protester responded by hitting him in the face. She was charged with assaulting a police officer in the course of his duty. The charge was dismissed by magistrates (partly because the policeman had failed to give his name, the location of his police station, or the reason why he wanted the mask to be removed). The Divisional Court took the view that an assault had been committed: *DPP v Avery* (2002).

9.3.14 The Code of Practice for the exercise of statutory powers of stop and search

In view of the wide powers vested in the police in the exercise of stop and search, Code A has been revised to reflect the new legislation and to clarify how searches under stop and search powers are to be conducted. The most recent edition of the revised Code came into effect on 1 April 2003 and supersedes earlier editions of Code A. The primary purpose of stop and search powers is to enable officers to allay or confirm suspicions about individuals without exercising their powers of arrest.

The Code applies to powers of stop and search and states at para 2.1(a) that these are 'powers which require reasonable grounds for suspicion before they may be exercised; that articles unlawfully obtained or possessed are being carried'.

Reasonable suspicion can never be supported on the basis of personal factors alone. For example, 'a person's race, age, appearance, or the fact that the person is known to have a previous conviction' cannot be used alone or in combination with each other as the reason for searching that person (para 2.2). Paragraph 2.6 states that:

> Where there is reliable information or intelligence that members of a group or gang habitually carry knives unlawfully or weapons or controlled drugs, and

wear a distinctive item of clothing or other means of identification to indicate their membership of the group or gang, that distinctive item of clothing or other means of identification may provide reasonable grounds to stop and search.

Other means of identification might include jewellery, insignias, tattoos or other features which are known to identify members of the particular gang or group (Note 9).

Any search involving the removal of more than an outer coat, jacket, gloves, headgear or footwear, or any other item concealing identity, may only be made by an officer of the same sex as the person searched and may not be made in the presence of anyone of the opposite sex unless the person being searched specifically requests it (para 3.6). All searches involving exposure of intimate parts of the body shall be conducted in accordance with para 11 of Annex A to Code C. All stops and searches must be carried out with courtesy, consideration and respect for the person concerned. Every reasonable effort must be made to reduce to the minimum the embarrassment that a person being searched may experience (para 3.1).

The revised Code A at para 2.15 introduces new powers to require removal of face coverings. These powers were added by s 60A of the Criminal Justice and Public Order Act 1994. Paragraph 2.15 states:

> The officer exercising the power must reasonably believe that someone is wearing an item wholly or mainly for the purpose of concealing identity. There is also a power to seize such items where the officer believes that a person intends to wear them for this purpose. There is no power for stop and search for disguises. An officer may seize any such item which is discovered when exercising a power of search for something else, or which is being carried, and which the officer reasonably believes is intended to be used for concealing anyone's identity.

Where there may be religious sensitivities about asking someone to remove headgear using a power under s 45(3) of the Terrorism Act 2000, the police officer should offer to carry out the search out of public view (for example, in a police van or police station if there is one nearby) (Note 8).

9.3.15 Search of arrested persons

The power to search after arrest somewhere other than at the police station is governed by s 32 of PACE 1984 (searches of detained persons are dealt with by s 54 and Code C, para 4.1). Section 32(1) allows the police to search someone arrested where there are grounds for believing that he may present a danger to himself or to others; s 32(2) allows a search for anything that might be used to effect an escape or which might be evidence relating to any offence. Additionally, s 32(2)(b) gives the police power to enter and search the premises in which he was when arrested, or immediately before he was arrested, for evidence relating to the offence for which he was arrested. Unlike the power to search under s 18, this is not limited to arrestable offences, nor do the searched premises need to be occupied or controlled by him. Such searches, however, are only lawful where there are reasonable grounds for believing that the search might find something for which a search is permitted under s 18(5) and (6). Random or automatic searching is not lawful. Section 32(4) states that a person searched in public cannot be required to take off more than outer garments like coats, jackets and gloves.

9.3.16 Search on detention

Section 54 of PACE 1984 and Code C, para 4.1 require the custody officer (a particular officer with special responsibilities in police stations) to take charge of the process of searching detainees. He must make sure a record is made of all the suspect's property unless he is to be detained for only a short time and not put in a cell. The person detained can be searched to enable this to happen, but the custody officer needs to believe it to be necessary; it is not an automatic right (s 54(6)). Anything the detainee has can be seized and retained, although clothes and personal effects can only be kept if the custody officer *believes* that the detained person *may* use them to escape, interfere with evidence, or cause damage or injury to himself, to others or to property. The police are not permitted, however, to retain anything protected by legal professional privilege, that is, private legal communications between the detainee and his legal adviser. The police can also seize things they *reasonably believe* to be evidence of an offence. A search must be carried out by a constable and only one who is the same sex as the person to be searched. Strip searches can only be made where the custody officer thinks it necessary to get some item that the detainee would not be allowed to keep; the officer must make a record of the reason for the search and its result.

9.3.17 Procedure on arrest

At common law (that is, before PACE 1984), it was necessary for the arrestor to make it clear to the arrestee that he was under compulsion either: (a) by physical means, such as taking him by the arm; or (b) by telling him, orally, that he was under compulsion. There was a danger, where words alone were used, that they might not be clear enough. Consider *Alderson v Booth* (1969). Following a positive breathalyser test, the officer said to the defendant: 'I shall have to ask you to come back to the station for further tests.' D did accompany the officer to the station. Lawful arrest was a condition precedent to anyone being convicted of driving with excess alcohol in their blood. At his trial, the defendant said he had not been arrested. He was acquitted and the prosecution appeal failed. Compulsion is a necessary element of arrest and the magistrates were not convinced that it was present in this case. The Divisional Court was not prepared to contradict the factual finding of the magistrates.

Additionally, where words alone were used, it was necessary for the arrestee to accede to the detention. There was no arrest where the arrestor said 'I arrest you' and the arrestee ran off before he could be touched (see *Sandon v Jervis* (1859)).

These principles remain good law after PACE 1984; see, for example, *Nichols v Bulman* (1985).

According to s 28(3) of PACE 1984, no arrest is lawful unless the arrestee is informed of the ground for the arrest at the time of, or as soon as reasonably practicable after, the arrest. Where a person is arrested by a constable, this applies (s 28(4)) regardless of whether the ground for the arrest is obvious.

The reasons for this rule were well put by Viscount Simon in *Christie v Leachinsky* (1947):

> ... a person is *prima facie* entitled to personal freedom [and] should know why for the time being his personal freedom is being interfered with ... No one, I think, would approve of a situation in which when the person arrested asked for the reason, the policeman replied 'that has nothing to do with you: come along with me' ... And there are practical considerations ... If the charge ... is then and there made known to him, he has the opportunity of giving an explanation of any misunderstanding or of calling attention to other persons for whom he may have been mistaken, with the result that further inquiries may save him from the consequences of false accusation ...

An arrest, however, becomes lawful once the ground is given. In *Lewis v Chief Constable of the South Wales Constabulary* (1991), the officers had told the plaintiffs of the fact of arrest but delayed telling them the grounds for 10 minutes in one case and 23 minutes in the other. The Court of Appeal said that arrest was not a legal concept but arose factually from the deprivation of a person's liberty. It was also a continuing act and therefore what had begun as an unlawful arrest could become a lawful arrest. The remedy for the plaintiffs was the damages they had been awarded for the 10 minutes and 23 minutes of illegality: £200 each.

In *DPP v Hawkins* (1988), the Divisional Court held that an exception to the rule requiring information to be given to the arrestee exists where the defendant makes it impossible (for example, by his violent conduct) for the officer to communicate the reasons for the arrest to him. In that situation, the arrest is lawful and remains lawful until such a time as the reasons should have been given. The fact that the reasons were not given then does not invalidate the original arrest. The arrest would only become unlawful from the moment when the reasons for it should have been given to the arrested person.

In *R v Telfer* (1976), a police officer knew that the defendant was wanted for questioning about certain burglaries. The officer checked that the suspect was wanted, but not for which particular burglaries. He then stopped the defendant and asked him to come back to the station; when the defendant refused, he was arrested 'on suspicion of burglary'. The arrest was held to be unlawful. The person arrested was entitled to know the particular burglary of which he was suspected.

In *Nicholas v Parsonage* (1987), N was seen riding a bicycle without holding the handlebars by two police officers. They told him twice to hold the bars and then he did so. When they drove off, N raised two fingers. They then stopped N and PC Parsonage asked him for his name, telling him it was required as he had been riding his bicycle in a dangerous manner. N refused. P then informed him of his powers under PACE 1984 and requested N's name and address. N again refused. P then arrested him for failing to give his name and address. N attempted to ride off and a struggle ensued. N was subsequently convicted of, *inter alia*, assaulting a police officer in the execution of his duty contrary to s 51(1) of the Police Act 1964. His appeal was dismissed by the Divisional Court, which held that the arrest under s 25 of PACE 1984 had been lawful as a constable exercising power under s 25(3) was not required to say why he wanted the suspect's name and address. N had been adequately informed of the ground of arrest under s 28(3) of PACE 1984. N was not arrested for failing to give his name and address, he was arrested because, having committed the minor offence of 'riding in a dangerous manner', it then became necessary to arrest him because the conditions in s 25(3)(a) and (c) were satisfied. These conditions were that an arrest for a minor offence is possible where the officer believes that the service of a summons is impracticable because he has not been given a proper name and address.

As to the extent of the explanation that has to be given on arrest under s 28 of PACE 1984, *Christie v Leachinsky* (above) was considered in *R v Chalkley and Jeffries* (1998). In this case, an arrest for an alleged credit card fraud was made for an ulterior motive, namely, to place recording equipment in the arrested defendant's house in order to record his discussions about planned robberies. The Court of Appeal held that, as there were reasonable grounds for suspecting the arrested defendant's involvement in the credit card frauds, and given that the police had informed him of this, the trial judge had been correct to rule that the arrest was lawful notwithstanding the ulterior motive.

Is it necessary for an arrestor to indicate to the arrestee the grounds on which his 'reasonable suspicion' was based? In *Geldberg v Miller* (1961), the appellant parked his car outside a restaurant in London while he had a meal. He was asked by police officers to move the car. He refused, preferring to finish his meal first. On being told that the police would remove the car, he removed the rotor arm from the distributor mechanism. He also refused to give his name and address or show his driving licence and certificate of insurance. He was arrested by one of the officers for 'obstructing him in the execution of his duty by refusing to move his car and refusing his name and address'. There was no power to arrest for obstruction of the police as no actual or apprehended breach of the peace was involved. The court held, however, that the arrest was valid for 'obstructing the thoroughfare', an offence under s 56(6) of the Metropolitan Police Act 1839, an offence the officer had not mentioned. Lord Parker CJ said:

In my judgment, what the appellant knew and what he was told was ample to fulfil the obligation as to what should be done at the time of an arrest without warrant.

An arrest will be unlawful, however, where the reasons given point to an offence for which there is no power of arrest (or for which there is only qualified power of arrest) and it is clear that no other reasons were present in the mind of the officer: *Edwards v DPP* (1993). This principle was confirmed in *Mullady v DPP* (1997). A police officer arrested M for 'obstruction', an offence with the power of arrest only if the defendant's conduct amounted to a breach of the peace (for which there is a common law power of arrest) or if one of the general arrest conditions as set out in s 25 is satisfied. The police argued that the officer could have arrested M for a breach of the peace and merely gave the wrong reason. The Divisional Court held that the officer had acted unlawfully and that it would be wrong for the justices to go behind the reason given and infer that the reason for the arrest was another lawful reason.

In some circumstances, the court may infer a lawful reason for an arrest if the circumstantial evidence points clearly to a lawful reason (*Brookman v DPP* (1997)). However, if there is insufficient evidence to determine whether a lawful or unlawful reason was given for the arrest, then the police will fail to show that the arrest was lawful (*Clarke v DPP* (1998)). The issue seems to be what degree of evidence is necessary to allow the court to infer a lawful reason for arrest (see further, Khan and Ryder (1998) Legal Action 16, September).

9.3.18 Police powers under s 60 of the Criminal Justice and Public Order Act 1994

Section 60 of the CJPOA 1994 provides for a stop and search power in anticipation of violence, and was introduced to deal with violent conduct, especially by groups of young men. The section provides that, where authorisation for its use has been granted:

(4) A constable in uniform may:

   (a) stop any pedestrian and search him or anything carried by him for offensive weapons or dangerous instruments;

   (b) stop any vehicle and search the vehicle, its driver and any passenger for offensive weapons or dangerous instruments.

(5) A constable may, in the exercise of those powers, stop any person or vehicle and make any search he thinks fit whether or not he has any grounds for suspecting that the person or vehicle is carrying any weapons or articles of that kind.

(6) If, in the course of such a search under this section, a constable discovers a dangerous instrument or an article which he has reasonable grounds for suspecting to be an offensive weapon, he may seize it.

The authorisation required by s 60 must be given by a police officer of, or above, the rank of superintendent (or a chief inspector or inspector where such an officer reasonably believes that incidents involving serious violence are imminent and no superintendent is available). The authorising officer must reasonably believe that:

(a) incidents involving serious violence may take place in any locality in his area; and

(b) it is expedient to grant an authorisation to prevent their occurrence.

Such an authorisation, which must be in writing, will permit the exercise of stop and search powers within that locality for a period up to 24 hours. The authorisation could conceivably be given in fear of a single incident, even though the CJPOA 1994 requires fear of 'incidents'. This is because s 6 of the Interpretation Act 1978 states that the plural includes the singular unless a contrary intention is shown.

There are several aspects of this section which have been drafted in what appears to be a deliberately vague way. 'Serious violence' is not defined and this will be very much within the judgment of the senior officer concerned, provided of course that his view is based upon reasonable belief. Richard Card and Richard Ward, in a commentary on the Act (*The Criminal Justice and Public Order Act 1994* (1994)), have noted that the dictionary includes 'force against property' as within the definition of violence, and this may well become an important matter for decision by the courts.

The word 'locality' is left undefined in the CJPOA 1994. It could be an area outside a particular club or pub, or it might extend to a large estate. The courts have the power to declare an authorisation invalid because of an over-expansive geographical area; they are unlikely to substitute their own view for that of the operational officer.

9.3.19 Other aspects of s 60 of the Criminal Justice and Public Order Act 1994

'Offensive weapon' (s 60(4), (11)) means the same as for s 1(9) of PACE 1984. It is: (a) any article made or adapted for use for causing injury to persons; or (b) intended by the person having it with him for such use by him or some other person. There is no provision for reasonable excuse for the possession of such weapons.

'Dangerous instruments' (s 60(4)) will often be caught within the definition of offensive weapons, but the definition extends to cover instruments which have a blade or are sharply pointed (s 60(11)).

The authorising officer must reasonably believe that it is 'expedient' to give an authorisation in order to prevent the occurrence of incidents of serious violence. Thus, the authorisation need not be the only way in which such incidents may be prevented. Various policing factors may have to be balanced, including the ability of the police force to remain effective and efficient if it were to use other methods.

There is no power to detain especially conferred on officers by s 60 in order to carry out the search but it does make failure to stop a summary offence. As it stands, there is nothing in s 60 which would permit an officer to use any force to conduct a non-consensual search. It is possible that the courts will imply such a power. When conducting the search, the officer must give the suspect his name, the police station to which he is attached, the authorisation for the search and the reason for the search. It seems that failure to comply with these conditions will make the search unlawful (see *Fennelley* (1989), a case where the defendant was not told why he was stopped, searched and arrested in the street. Evidence from the search, some jewellery, was excluded at the trial. Evidence of drugs found on him at the police station was also excluded).

The scope of s 60 and police powers to stop and search are being incrementally extended through various Acts of Parliament. They include the following: s 8 of the Knives Act 1997 amended s 60 to allow *initial* authorisations by an inspector or above thus obviating the need for an officer of at least the rank of superintendent; s 60(1)(b) extends the criteria under which an authorising officer may invoke this power to include reasonable belief that incidents involving serious violence may take place or that such instruments of weapons are being carried in a particular area; and s 60(3) provides that authorisations may be extended up to 24 hours instead of six, although only an officer of the rank of superintendent or above may do this. A new sub-s 11A was inserted under s 60 by s 8 of the Knives Act 1997 and states that, 'for the purposes of this section, a person carries a dangerous instrument or an offensive weapon if he has it in his possession'.

'Offensive weapon' means the same as for s 1(9) of PACE 1984 (see 9.3.13, above). 'Dangerous instruments' means instruments which have a blade or are sharply pointed.

These amendments are intended to deal with anticipated violence in situations where gangs or persons may be 'tooled-up' and travelling through various police areas en route to an intended scene of confrontation. Thus, the power may be invoked even where it is believed that the actual anticipated violence may occur in another police jurisdiction, for example, by football hooligans travelling to and from matches.

Further amendments to s 60 have been made under the CDA 1998. This is mainly to deal with the problem of troublemakers deliberately wearing facial coverings to conceal their identities, especially when the police are using CCTV cameras. Section 25 of the CDA 1998 inserted a new sub-s 4A under s 60, which conferred a power on any constable in uniform to demand the removal of, or seize, face coverings where an authority had been given under s 60, if the officer reasonably believed that the face covering was being worn or was intended to be used to conceal a person's identity. The Anti-Terrorism, Crime and Security Act 2001 replaced s 60(4A) with s 60AA. This is broader than the earlier sub-section and provides for the removal of 'disguises'. Section 25 also extends s 60(8) and makes it a summary offence if a person fails to stop, or to stop a vehicle or to remove an item worn by him when required by the police in the exercise of their powers under s 60. This is punishable by a term of imprisonment not exceeding one month and/or a maximum fine of £1,000. Section 60A inserted by s 26 of the CDA 1998 provides that things seized under s 60 may be retained in accordance with regulations made by the Secretary of State. (See L Jason-Lloyd (1998) 162 JP 836, 24 October.)

9.3.20 Accountability and s 60 of the Criminal Justice and Public Order Act 1994

There are dangers that the powers under s 60 could be misused, as no reasonable suspicion is required and the requirements for authorisation are rather nebulous.

The safeguards against misuse include the fact that the admissibility of evidence gained through the use of a dubious stop and search event may be in doubt if there are serious breaches of the revised Code A. Someone charged with obstructing a police officer in the exercise of duty may raise breaches of the Code in defence. Unlawful search or seizure may also provide a basis for an application for exclusion of evidence thus obtained under s 78 of PACE 1984.

As the police have a common law power to take whatever action is necessary in order to prevent an imminent breach of the peace (*Moss v Mclachlan* (1985)), then, even if a challenge to the use of a s 60 power is technically successful, the police conduct in question may often be thus justified.

9.3.21 The Terrorism Act 2000

The Terrorism Act 2000 gives exceptional powers of stop and search to uniformed police constables. A person of at least the rank of commander or assistant chief constable, who considers it expedient to do so for the prevention of acts of terrorism, may issue an authorisation specifying a particular area or place (to last for not more than 28 days). This gives a constable powers to stop vehicles and pedestrians within that area or place and search the vehicle, driver, passengers, pedestrian (and anything with them) for articles of a kind which could be used in connection with terrorism. These powers may be exercised whether or not the constable has grounds for suspecting the presence of articles of that kind. The constable may seize and retain an article which he discovers in the course of such a search and which he reasonably suspects is intended to be used in connection with terrorism (ss 44 and 45). By s 47, it is an offence to fail to stop a vehicle when required to do so, fail to stop when required to do so, and wilfully to obstruct a constable in the exercise of these powers. The offences are punishable with six months' imprisonment and/or a fine of up to £5,000.

These provisions are not confined to terrorism in connection with Northern Ireland or international terrorism. 'Terrorism' means the use or threat of action involving serious violence against a person, serious damage to property, endangering the life of a person other than the 'terrorist', creating a serious risk to the health or safety of the public or a section of the public, or designing seriously to interfere with or seriously to disrupt an electronic system. The above action(s) must be designed to influence the government or to intimidate the public or a section of the public, and made for the purpose of advancing a political, religious or ideological cause. However, where the use or threat of action involves the use of firearms or explosives, it need not be designed to influence the government or to intimidate the public or a section of the public.

Clearly, these are extensive powers which are available for activities which go well beyond political terrorism and may be used in the struggle to control various kinds of disaffected groups. Perhaps the most obvious example might be the animal rights groups, some of which have resorted to significant violence against those carrying on commercial activities involving animal experiments.

9.3.22 The use of force to effect an arrest

The use of force by a member of the public when arresting someone is governed by s 3 of the CLA 1967. This states:

(1) A person may use such force as is reasonable in the circumstances in the prevention of crime, or in effecting or assisting in the lawful arrest of offenders or suspected offenders or of persons unlawfully at large.

Reasonable force will generally mean the minimum necessary to effect an arrest.

The use of force by police officers is governed by s 117 of PACE 1984. This states:

Where any provision of this Act:

(a) confers a power on a constable; and

(b) does not provide that the power may only be exercised with the consent of some person, other than a police officer,

the officer may use reasonable force, if necessary, in the exercise of the power.

9.3.23 Duties after arrest

A person arrested by a constable, or handed over to one, must be taken to a police station as soon as is 'practicable', unless his presence elsewhere is 'necessary in order to carry out such investigations as it is reasonable to carry out immediately' (s 30(1), (10) of PACE 1984). Where a citizen makes an arrest, he 'must, as soon as he reasonably can, hand the man over to a constable or take him to the police station or take him before a magistrate', *per* Lord Denning in *Dallison v Caffery* (1965). There is no requirement, however, that this be carried out immediately: *John Lewis & Co v Tims* (see 9.3.9, above).

9.4 Entry, search and seizure

Powers of search and seizure consequent upon the exercise of general stop and search powers under PACE 1984, the CJPOA 1994 and the Terrorism Act 2000 have already been considered, though it must be remembered that other powers are available, conferred by statutes such as the Misuse of Drugs Act 1971. Apart from stop and search powers, there are various other powers involving entry into property and subsequent search and seizure. Once again, general powers of this nature are contained in PACE. Powers of search and seizure must be used proportionately. They are generally inappropriate when less intrusive routes to the same goals are available. 'Seize and sift' operations (where officers remove numerous items for examination away from the premises) are controversial: *R v Chesterfield Justices ex p Bramley* (2001). Although permitted by Part II of the Criminal Justice and Police Act (CJPA) 2001, these powers should only be exercised when there is no practicable alternative.

Note: PACE 1984 came into force on 1 January 1986. The Act was accompanied by four Codes of Practice: Code A on Stop and Search; Code B on Search of Premises; Code C on Detention, Questioning and Treatment of Persons in Custody; and Code D on Identification. Codes E and F, on the tape-recording and visual recording of interviews respectively, were added later. The Codes were produced after consultation with a wide range of interested groups and people, and were debated and approved by both Houses of Parliament before being promulgated. The first revised versions of Codes A–D came into force in April 1991. The Codes have been subjected to review and amendment. The most recent revised versions of Codes A–E came into force on 1 April 2003. The Codes are not technically law and s 67(10) of PACE 1984 states that a breach of them can lead to neither a claim for damages nor a criminal prosecution against police officers. A breach of the Codes is, however, automatically a disciplinary offence (s 67(8)).

The chief significance of a breach of the Codes is that a judge may exclude otherwise relevant evidence if it has been obtained in such a way and an appeal court may quash a conviction where a trial judge has not excluded such evidence (s 67(7)).

9.4.1 Entry of premises under the common law

Premises can be searched by consent. Here, the constable must get written consent from the occupier of the premises on a special 'Notice of Powers and

Rights' form before the search takes place. The officer must make inquiries to ensure that the person concerned is in a position to give that consent. Before seeking the consent, the officer in charge must state the purpose of the proposed search and inform the person concerned that he is not obliged to consent, that anything seized may be produced in evidence, and if such is the case, that he is not suspected of any offence. These propositions come from the governing *Code of Practice (B) for the Searching of Premises by Police Officers and the Seizure of Property found by Police Officers on Persons or Premises*. An officer cannot enter and search, or continue to search premises by consent, if the consent is given under duress or is withdrawn before the search is completed (Code B, para 5.3). Consent need not be sought if this would cause disproportionate inconvenience to the occupiers of premises, for example, where the police wish to briefly check a number of gardens on a suspected escape route.

Police officers may enter premises with permission or under implied permission, but then must leave when required unless remaining under some particular power. In *Davis v Lisle* (1936), Sidney Davis was a member of a firm that occupied a railway arch as a garage. Two police officers entered the garage to ask about a lorry that had been obstructing the highway. The lorry had since been moved into the garage. D, using obscene language and abuse, told the officers to leave. L was in the act of producing his warrant card when D struck him in the chest and stomach, damaging his tunic. The convictions of D for assaulting and obstructing a police officer in the execution of his duty were quashed by the Divisional Court. Lord Hewart CJ held that the officers were not acting in the course of their duty once they had remained on premises, having been told in forthright terms by the occupiers to leave: 'From that moment on, while the officers remained where they were, it seems to me that they were trespassers.'

9.4.2 Entry of premises to prevent an offence being committed

There is a common law right for police officers to enter a building to deal with or prevent a breach of the peace. In *Thomas v Sawkins* (1935), the Divisional Court held that police officers were entitled to enter and remain on premises, despite being asked by the occupiers to leave, in circumstances where the officers believed that certain offences (seditious speeches, incitements to violence) would be committed if they were not present. Lord Hewart CJ said:

> I am not at all prepared to accept the doctrine that it is only where an offence has been, or is being, committed, that the police are entitled to enter and remain on premises. On the contrary, it seems to me that a police officer has, *ex virtute officii*, full right so to act when he has reasonable grounds for believing that an offence is imminent or is likely to be committed.

Section 17(5) and (6) of PACE 1984 abolishes all common law powers of entry except to deal with or prevent a breach of the peace.

Note, however, that a licensee must be given a reasonable time to leave premises before his continued presence on the land constitutes a trespass, unless he makes it clear that he will not leave voluntarily (*Robson v Hallet* (1967)).

The power has even extended to private homes. In *McGowan v Chief Constable of Kingston upon Hull* (1967), the Divisional Court held that the police were entitled to enter and remain in a private dwelling where they feared there would be a breach of the peace arising out of a private quarrel.

9.4.3   Entry and search of premises to make an arrest

This is governed by s 17 of PACE 1984, which says that a constable may enter and search premises for the purposes of arresting someone for an arrestable offence or under warrant, recapturing a person unlawfully at large whom he is pursuing, saving life or limb or preventing serious damage to property. This power can only be exercised if the constable has 'reasonable grounds' for believing that the person whom he is seeking is on the premises.

A police officer exercising his power to enter premises by the use of reasonable force to arrest a person for an arrestable offence (pursuant to ss 17 and 117 of PACE 1984) should, unless circumstances make it impossible, impracticable or undesirable, announce to the occupier the reason why he is exercising that power. In *O'Loughlin v Chief Constable of Essex* (1998), a police officer who had a lawful right to enter premises but failed to announce why he was entering when it was practicable and possible to do so was held to be acting unlawfully. In such circumstances, the occupier is entitled to use reasonable force to prevent the entry.

The relevant powers here are those discussed below under ss 18 and 32 of PACE 1984. In practice, the police act routinely under s 18 and rarely under s 32.

Section 18 of PACE 1984 gives a constable power to enter and search:

> ... any premises occupied or controlled by a person who is under arrest for an arrestable offence, if he has reasonable grounds for suspecting that there is on the premises evidence other than items subject to legal privilege that relates (a) to the offence; or (b) to some other arrestable offence which is connected with or similar to that offence.

If, therefore, the police suspect that evidence of other unconnected offences is to be found at the address, then they must get a search warrant or seek the householder's consent to the search. The search of someone's address after they have been arrested normally requires written permission from an officer of the rank of inspector or above (s 18(4)). Section 18(5) makes an exception when the arrested person is taken straight to the address rather than to the police station. A search must not go beyond what is normally required to find the particular item(s) being sought; no general search is permitted (s 18(3)). The time constraint when the police use s 32 (the search has to be made at the time of the arrest) (see below) does not appear to apply to a s 18 search (see *R v Badham* (1987), below). It is perhaps because of this and the comparative narrowness of s 32 in respect of searches of premises (see below) that s 18 is much more frequently used by police. Research by Ken Lidstone, for example, found that in a survey of two city forces, s 18 accounted for 75% of searches compared with 2% for s 32: 'Entry, search and seizure' (1989) 40 NILQ 333, p 355, n 67.

Section 32(2)(b) gives the police power to enter and search premises in which the suspect was when arrested, or immediately before he was arrested, for *evidence relating to the offence for which he was arrested*. Unlike the power to search under s 18, this is not limited to arrestable offences, nor do the searched premises need to be occupied or controlled by him. Such searches, however, are only lawful where there are reasonable grounds for believing that the search might find something for which a search is permitted under s 32(5) and (6). Random or automatic searching is not lawful.

Section 32(7) states that where a person is arrested in premises consisting of two or more separate dwellings, only the premises in which he was arrested or was in immediately beforehand and any common parts (like stairways and common corridors) can be searched.

The powers here are narrower than those given under s 18 to enter and search the premises of an arrested person. Under s 18, the police may enter and search for evidence of the offence for which the person was arrested or *any* offence which is 'connected with or similar to that offence'. Section 32 only covers searches for evidence relating to the actual offence for which the suspect was arrested. The police can, however, under s 32, search the person himself for evidence of any offence. It was held in *R v Badham* that s 32 only applies to a search made at the time of the arrest. It does not permit the police to return to the premises several hours after the arrest.

In *R v Churchill* (1989), the defendant was arrested on suspicion of burglary and placed in a police car. The police asked him to hand over the keys to the car he had been in so that they could lock it, thus keeping it safe for a later scientific examination. C was convicted of assault when, after refusing to hand over the keys, a struggle ensued and he hit an officer. On appeal, he contended that the police had no power to take the keys since they had no evidence of any crime. The court quashed the conviction, saying that the case could have been argued on the basis of the officer's duty to preserve the property, but the prosecution had not used that argument. The police could, alternatively, have searched the car under s 32 as that section confers a power to search any 'premises' the defendant was in immediately before arrest and this includes a vehicle (s 23(a)).

9.4.4 Seizure of articles from searches

Seizure of articles from searches is controlled by s 19 and Code B, para 7. These state that an officer who is lawfully on any premises has power to seize anything which is on the premises if he has reasonable grounds to believe that an item has been obtained in consequence of the commission of an offence, or that it is evidence in relation to an offence, and that it is necessary to seize the item in order to prevent that item being concealed, lost, disposed of, altered, damaged, destroyed or tampered with (s 19(2) and (3) and para 7.1(b)). Items exempted from seizure are those reasonably believed to be subject to legal professional privilege (s 19(6)). The scope of the seizure rights is therefore quite wide and Zander has argued that the insistence since *Entick v Carrington* (1765) that general warrants are unlawful must now be qualified by the knowledge that, once the police have entered premises lawfully, it is difficult to hold them to a search restricted to the specific purpose of the search. The only serious restraint is the requirement in s 16(8) that a search under warrant must be carried out in a manner consistent with the items being looked for and in Code B, para 6.9, which states that 'premises may be searched only to the extent necessary to achieve the object of the search having regard to the size and nature of whatever is sought'.

9.4.5 Search warrants and safeguards

Section 8 of PACE 1984 provides for the issue of warrants by magistrates to enter and search premises for evidence of serious arrestable offences. This gives justices of the peace the power, on written application from a constable, to issue a search warrant where he is satisfied that there are reasonable grounds for believing that a 'serious arrestable offence' has been committed. A 'serious arrestable offence' (as distinct from an 'arrestable offence' defined by s 24) is defined by s 116 of and Sched 5 to PACE 1984. The definition divides offences into two categories. One category comprises offences so serious that they are always 'serious arrestable offences'; they are listed in Sched 5 and include treason, murder, manslaughter, rape, kidnapping, incest and possession of firearms with intent to injure, and attempts or conspiracies are treated as if they were completed. Any other arrestable offence is serious only if its commission has led, or is likely to lead, to any of the consequences specified in s 116(6), namely:

(a) serious harm to the security of the State or public order;

(b) serious interference with the administration of justice or with the investigation of offences;

(c) the death of anyone;

(d) serious injury to anyone;

(e) substantial financial gain to anyone;

(f) serious financial loss to anyone in the sense that, having regard to all the circumstances, it is serious for the person suffering loss (the seriousness of the loss is therefore to be measured by the financial position of the potential loser).

The magistrate must also be satisfied that:

- there is material on the premises likely to be of substantial value to the investigation (s 8(1)(b));

- it is likely to be relevant evidence (s 8(1)(c));

- it does not include 'excluded material' (for example, human tissue taken for medical diagnosis and held in confidence); journalistic material held in confidence (see s 11), or 'special procedure material' (for example, confidential business/professional material, see s 14); or material subject to legal privilege (s 10); and

- any of the conditions in s 8(3) applies. These are, essentially, that it is not practicable to gain entry to the premises in question without a search warrant or that the reasons for the search would be frustrated if the constable did not gain immediate entry upon arrival.

Section 15 incorporates proposals made by the Philips Royal Commission on Criminal Procedure (Cmnd 8092, 1981, HMSO) to protect against warrants being too easily obtained. Clearly, it is highly contentious at what point there is the correct, desirable balance between the State's concern to prevent and detect crime and the interests of the public at large in having the civil liberty of freedom from speculative entry into their homes by the police. If police officers could legally enter any home at any time without permission from anyone, then the detection of crime would arguably be easier than now, but there would be a significant price to pay in the consequential public resentment against the police and the probably profound loss of faith in the legal and political system.

An application for a search warrant must now state the grounds for making the application, the statutory authority under which the claim is made and the object of the proposed search in as much detail as possible. Research by Lidstone (see 9.4.3, above) has shown a tendency for informations (the applications) and warrants to use very generalised terms like 'electrical goods', which he argues is not desirable. The applications are normally made *ex parte* (that is, from one side – the police, without the presence of the person whose premises are to be searched) and the information must be made in writing by an officer who must answer any questions (from the magistrate) under oath. Lidstone's research also suggests that, both before and after PACE 1984, there is evidence of reliance on formulaic informations, for example, 'As a result of information received from a previously reliable source ...', and a lack of any probative questioning by magistrates on such informations. The warrant may only be used to gain entry on one occasion; if the police find nothing relevant and wish to return, they must apply for another warrant. On each search, the occupier must be given a copy of the warrant authorising entry.

One part of s 15 has caused some difficulty for the courts. It relates to the word 'it' in s 15(1), which states that 'an entry on or search of premises under a warrant is unlawful unless it complies with this section and s 16 below'.

What must comply – the warrant or the whole entry and search? In *R v Longman* (1988), Lord Lane CJ said, *obiter*:

> With some hesitation, we are inclined to think it probably refers to the warrant, but the real probability is that the intention of the framers of the Act was to provide that the warrant should comply with the terms of s 25 and the entry and search should comply with s 16. But, unhappily, that is not what it says. So, we leave that problem unresolved.

Section 16 and Code B govern the actual search of premises and seek to ensure that warrants are executed in a proper and reasonable manner. Section 16 states that any constable, not just the one named in the warrant, may execute that warrant (s 16(1)) and it must be carried out within one month of its date of issue (s 16(3)). The search must be at a 'reasonable hour' unless 'it appears to the constable executing it that the purpose of a search may be frustrated on an entry at a reasonable hour' (s 16(4)). Notice that here the test is subjective; it is what 'appears to the constable' that is critical, not whether such a belief is reasonable or not. If the occupier is present, he must be given a copy of the warrant (s 16(5)); if he is not there, then a copy must be left in a prominent place (s 16(7)). A constable executing a warrant must identify himself and, if he is not in uniform, he must produce documentary evidence that he is a constable, even if he is not asked (s 16(5)).

In *R v Longman* (above), a plain clothes police officer posed as a delivery girl from Interflora to gain entry to premises without alerting the occupants. She had come to the premises with other officers with a warrant to search for drugs. It was not the first time that the premises had been searched and the officers knew that entry would be very difficult. When the door was opened, the officers burst in. They did not, therefore, properly identify themselves as officers according to s 16(5), nor had they shown the householder their search warrant as required by para 5.5 of the 1991 revision of Code B. The Court of Appeal held that force or subterfuge could lawfully be used for the purposes of gaining entry with a search warrant. The warrant was 'produced' for the purposes of s 16(5) when the occupier was given the opportunity of inspecting it. In this case, the occupier had not attempted to look at the warrant, he had shouted a warning to others on the premises and then tried to stab the officers with a knife. The court held that it would be prepared to overlook failures to comply with the precise provisions of ss 15 and 16 regarding production of the warrant whenever circumstances made it wholly inappropriate, such as a search for drugs or in a terrorism case. In any event, it was not necessary that the formalities set out in s 16(a)–(c), on identification of the searcher as a police officer and production of the warrant, be carried out before *entry* but only before the search begins. The revised Code B states that the officer shall first attempt to get access by asking the occupier unless (Code B, para 6.4(iii)):

> ... there are reasonable grounds for believing that alerting the occupier or any other person entitled to grant access would frustrate the object of the search or endanger officers or other people.

A search under a warrant 'may only be a search to the extent required for the purpose of which the warrant was issued' (s 16(8)). In *Chief Constable of the Warwickshire Constabulary ex p Fitzpatrick* (1998), the Divisional Court disapproved of the police practice of using a warrant phrased in broad terms to seize every possible item that could broadly fall within those terms. They should ensure both that the material seized falls within the terms of the warrant and, because such a warrant is granted to search for material of evidential value, that there are reasonable grounds for believing so and that such material is likely to be of substantial value in the investigation. In this case, in relation to one of the warrants, the police officers went on a 'fishing expedition' and seized a large selection of documents not on their face related to the offence under investigation. In doing so, they exceeded the ambit of the warrant. Thus, the entire search was a trespass and unlawful under ss 16(8) and 15(1) of PACE (see further, Khan and Ryder, 'Police and the law' (1998) Legal Action 16, September).

A search warrant does not entitle the executing officers to search persons on the premises. Such persons may only be searched if arrested or if there is a specific power in the warrant, for example, as in warrants issued under s 23 of the Misuse of Drugs Act 1971 (Home Office Circular on PACE 1984, 1985, No 88/1855).

9.5 Interrogation, confession and admissibility of evidence

Before moving into the specific provisions of PACE 1984 and the Codes of Practice, it is important to be aware of the general issues at stake in this area of law. Are the rights of suspects being interrogated by the police sufficiently protected by law? Is there scope for abuse of power by the police? Are the police burdened by too many legal requirements when trying to induce a suspect to confess to a crime? What effects are likely to flow from the undermining of the right to silence (see ss 34–37 of the CJPOA 1994, 9.5.17, below)?

Once again, it is also necessary to bear in mind the significance of the ECHR in this context. Unless impossible because of conflicting primary legislation, English courts must interpret rules of law so as to be compatible with obligations under the ECHR. Article 5 guarantees a right to liberty. To justify depriving a person of his liberty before conviction for an offence, for example,

Art 5 requires that there be a lawful arrest or detention for the purpose of bringing the person before a competent authority on a reasonable suspicion of having committed an offence, or that arrest or detention is considered reasonably necessary to prevent him from committing an offence. Moreover, every person arrested shall be informed promptly in a language which he understands of the reasons for his arrest and of any charge against him, shall be brought promptly before a judge and shall be entitled to trial within a reasonable time or to release pending trial. Clearly, PACE requirements in relation to arrest and detention must be measured against Art 5. Equally, Art 6 requires a fair trial and declares a presumption of innocence, matters which bear on the conduct of the trial, the evidence presented, and the obligation to offer explanations or risk the consequences of adverse inferences being drawn from silence.

9.5.1 Time limits on detention without charge

Under s 42 of PACE 1984, a suspect can be held without being charged for 24 hours before any further authorisation needs to be given. At this point, the situation must be reviewed and further detention must be authorised by an officer of at least the rank of superintendent. The period is measured from arrival at the police station. If he is arrested by another force, the time runs from his arrival at the station of the area where he is wanted. If further detention is authorised, this can continue for up to the 36 hour point. After 36 hours from the beginning of the detention, there must be a full hearing in a magistrates' court with the suspect and, if he wishes, legal representation (s 43). The magistrates can grant a warrant of further detention for up to a further 60 hours – making a total of 96 hours (ss 43 and 44). However, the police could not be granted the 60 hour period as a whole because the maximum extension that a magistrates' court can grant at one time is 36 hours (ss 43(12), 44). The magistrates can only grant such extensions if the offence being investigated is a serious arrestable offence (s 116), is being investigated diligently and expeditiously, and provided that the further detention is necessary to secure or preserve evidence relating to an offence for which the suspect is under arrest or to obtain such evidence by questioning him (s 43(4)).

Section 38 states that, *after being charged*, the arrested person must be released with or without bail, unless:

- it is necessary to hold him so that his name and address can be obtained; or
- the custody officer reasonably thinks that it is necessary to hold him for his own protection or to prevent him from causing physical injury to anyone or from causing loss of or damage to property; or

- the custody officer reasonably thinks that he needs to be held because he would otherwise fail to answer bail or to prevent him from interfering with witnesses or otherwise obstructing the course of justice; or

- if he is a juvenile and ought to be held 'in his own interests'.

If the suspect is charged and not released, he will have to be brought before a magistrates' court 'as soon as practicable' and not later than the first sitting after being charged (s 46(2)).

9.5.2 Searches of detained persons

Searches of people detained at police stations are governed by s 54 and Code C. The Act also allows 'speculative searches' in which fingerprints, samples or information in respect thereof can be checked against other similar data held by the police. Section 82 of the CJPA 2001 retrospectively amended s 64 of PACE, giving the police the right to retain DNA samples and fingerprints. The Court of Appeal has decided that this does not contravene Arts 8 or 14 of the ECHR: *R v Chief Constable of South Yorkshire* (2002). For an analysis of this decision, see Charles Bourne, 'Retaining fingerprints and DNA samples' (2002) 152 NLJ 1693.

A person may only be searched if the custody officer considers this necessary in order to make a complete list of his property (s 54(6)). There is no automatic right to search all suspects as a matter of routine. The police can, however, search anyone to ascertain whether he has with him anything which he could use to cause physical injury, damage property, interfere with evidence or assist him to escape (s 55, as amended). Section 65 deals with intimate searches:

> ... a search which consists of the physical examination of a person's body orifices other than the mouth.

A physical examination of the mouth is therefore allowed in the circumstances where a non-intimate search of the person may occur, subject to the ordinary safeguards (Code of Practice A, para 3; Code C, para 4). A search of the mouth for drugs is not the taking of a sample as defined by s 65 of PACE 1984, so the restrictions which apply to the taking of samples do not apply here. A search of an arrested person's mouth may thus be carried out by a police officer at the station, subject to the safeguards in Code C. The officer carrying out the search must be of the same sex as the arrested person (s 54(9)). Nonetheless, an officer of either sex may search the arrested person's mouth at the time of the arrest if he has reasonable grounds to believe that the arrested person is concealing therein evidence related to the offence (s 32(2)(b)).

Intimate searches must be authorised by an officer of the rank of superintendent or above, on the basis of reasonable belief that the arrested person in police detention has concealed on him anything which could be used to cause physical injury to himself or to others and that he might so use it.

Intimate searches for weapons can, if a doctor or registered nurse is not available, be carried out by a police officer of the same sex as the suspect. If the search is for drugs, it can only be carried out by a doctor or registered nurse and it cannot be carried out at a police station (s 55(4)). Intimate searches for drugs are limited to those for hard drugs, defined as Class A drugs in Sched 2 to the Misuse of Drugs Act 1971.

9.5.3 The right to have someone informed when arrested

The effect of s 56 and Code C is that when a detainee is under arrest and is being held in custody in a police station, he is entitled, if he so requests, to have 'one friend or relative or other person who is known to him or who is likely to take an interest in his welfare' to be told as soon as practicable that he is under arrest and his whereabouts (s 56(1), Code C, para 5.1). If such a person cannot be contacted, the Code allows for two alternates to be nominated, following which any further alternates can be called at the discretion of the custody officer. Delay is only permissible in the case of a 'serious arrestable offence' (see s 116) and only if authorised by an officer of at least the rank of superintendent. The grounds for delaying appear in Annex B. They are essentially that there are reasonable grounds for believing that telling the named person of the arrest will lead to interference with, or harm to, evidence of witnesses or the alerting of others involved in such an offence; or will hinder the recovery of property obtained as a result of the offence. No one, however, may be prevented from notifying someone outside the police station for longer than 36 hours after 'the relevant time' (s 41(2)), usually the time that he arrived at the station. Unless the reasons for a lawful delay (see Annex B) exist, Code C states that the detainee should be allowed to speak on the telephone 'for a reasonable time to one person' (para 5.6) and that this privilege is in addition to the right to phone someone under para 5.1 to inform him or her of the arrest or under para 6.1 to obtain legal advice. Children and young persons are afforded additional rights by s 57; the section says that the police should contact a person 'responsible for his welfare' to inform the person about the arrest.

9.5.4 The right to consult a solicitor

Section 58(1) of PACE 1984 states that, 'A person who is in police detention shall be entitled, if he so requests, to consult a solicitor privately at any time'. The rules relating to persons held under suspicion of terrorist offences are different and will not be covered here. Where the detained person is a juvenile, mentally disordered or otherwise vulnerable, then 'the appropriate adult' may exercise the right to ask for legal advice. There is effectively a human right to custodial legal advice. This is guaranteed by Art 6(3)(c) of the ECHR: *Murray v UK* (1996); *Averill v UK* (2000); *Condron and Condron v UK* (2000). See Ed Cape, 'Incompetent police station advice and the exclusion of evidence' [2002] Crim LR 471–83.

Where the detainee has been allowed to consult a solicitor, and the solicitor is available, the solicitor must be allowed to sit in on any interview the police hold with the detainee (Code C, para 6.8). Normally, the request must be allowed as soon as practicable (s 58(4)).

9.5.5 Notifying the suspect of the right to free legal advice

There is clearly the danger that a person's right to legal advice can be effectively curtailed if he is not aware of it. Code C therefore goes to some lengths to ensure the detainee is aware of the right. The custody officer is required (para 3.5), when he authorises a person's detention in the police station, to make sure that the detainee signs the custody record signifying whether he wishes to have legal advice at that point.

The Code stipulates that police stations must advertise the right to free legal advice in posters 'prominently displayed in the charging area of every police station' (para 6.3). The Code also gives precise rules concerning at what point and in what form a person should be notified of the right to get free legal advice. For example, a person who comes to the station *under arrest* must be told immediately both orally and in writing (paras 3.1, 3.2). A person who comes to the police station voluntarily (that is, someone who is helping the police with their inquiries) is to be given a leaflet if he requests information, but strangely there is no police duty to notify if that person does not ask.

A person who asks for legal advice should be given the opportunity to consult a specific solicitor (for example, his own) or the duty solicitor (see 9.5.6, below). Alternatively, he should be given an opportunity to choose one from a list of those available to give advice. Ultimately, the custody officer has discretion to allow further requests if the others are unsuccessful. The advice may be given by a solicitor or other accredited representative. The revised Code C carries the provision that 'No police officer should, at any time, do or say anything with the intention of dissuading a detainee' (para 6.4) and that reminders of the right to consult legal advice should be given at specified times, for example, on commencement and re-commencement of interviews.

The revised Code also states (para 6.15) that if a solicitor arrives at the station to see a particular person, that person must (unless Annex B applies) be informed of the solicitor's arrival and asked whether they would like to see the solicitor. This applies even if the person concerned has already declined legal advice. This would be important, for example, where the lawyer had been sent by a friend or family member.

Under Code C, para 3.1(ii), the detainee must be told that they have the right to consult privately with a solicitor and that free independent legal advice is available. The solicitor or other accredited representative is paid from public funds. At his discretion, a solicitor may give the advice over the telephone. The

Law Society advises the solicitor when he is considering whether the telephone is a suitable medium to have regard to certain issues, for example, whether the detainee would be likely to be inhibited from speaking freely by fear of being overheard and whether the detainee has already been charged and no further police interview is proposed.

There has been notable judicial concern that the suspect's rights to be informed about the availability of legal advice is enforced. In *R v Absolam* (1989), the Court of Appeal quashed a conviction for the supply of cannabis and substituted one for simple possession because the defendant had not been informed of his right to see a solicitor before he had been questioned. The trial judge had held that the series of preliminary questions and answers did not amount to an 'interview', but the Court of Appeal disagreed; the questions were an 'interview' within the meaning of the Code because they were directed at a suspect with the aim of obtaining admissions on which a prosecution could be based. The reference in s 58(4) to seeing a solicitor 'as soon as practicable' was not relevant to the suspect's right to be informed of his right to legal advice from the outset of his detention.

In *R v Beycan* (1990), the defendant was arrested in connection with a charge of supplying heroin. He was taken to a police station where he was asked, 'Are you happy to be interviewed in the normal way we conduct these interviews without a solicitor, friend or representative?'. The Court of Appeal held that this did not amount to informing him of his right to legal advice and it quashed his conviction which was based on his subsequent confession.

9.5.6 Duty solicitors

The Duty Solicitor Schemes at police stations and magistrates' courts are run locally but organised under the auspices of the Legal Services Commission (LSC) acting through the CDS. At police stations, the duty solicitor is contacted through a special national telephone network provided by a company, Air Call plc. When a detainee asks for a duty solicitor (at any time of the day or night), a call is made to Air Call who then contact either the rota duty solicitor or telephone duty solicitors on the panel until, in the latter case, one is found who is able and willing to attend. In rota schemes, there is always (in theory) someone on duty; in panel schemes, the panellists are called one after the other on a list beginning with the name after the last solicitor to have come out.

It will be apparent that when a detainee at a police station requests legal advice, that advice may be provided by a number of different categories of advisers. Broadly speaking, the advice may be supplied as a result of a choice of adviser made by the suspect himself, or as a result of using the duty solicitor. Where the suspect makes his own choice of adviser, that person may be a solicitor or an accredited, probationary or non-accredited representative who may not be a solicitor. Under the new arrangements, public funding for such advice will only be available where the advice supplied by a firm which has a contract with the CDS to do criminal work and the advice is given by a solicitor, an accredited representative or a probationary representative. An accredited representative will be registered on the police station register and will have successfully undergone testing, including producing a portfolio and completing written tests. A probationary representative will be registered, but will not yet have completed the relevant tests. A probationary representative cannot give advice in connection with an indictable only offence. Any adviser who is a duty solicitor will have fulfilled the requirements for publicly funded advice. Eventually, such advice should also be available from salaried defenders engaged by the CDS.

Since PACE was enacted, the precise arrangements for who may give advice at police stations have altered significantly. In the early days of the operation of the Duty Solicitor Scheme, considerable disquiet was expressed about advice given to suspects at the police station. This disquiet tended to focus on delay in receiving advice, the lack of availability of a solicitor, the provision of advice over the telephone rather than in person, and the quality of advice and advisers, including advice from unqualified advisers (for a review of the evidence, see Sanders and Bridges, 'The right to legal advice', in *Miscarriages of Justice*, 1999). For example, the Runciman Royal Commission on Criminal Justice noted the problem of inadequate professional advice in some cases. Its Report states (para 69):

> The Legal Aid Board should commission occasional empirical research as a means of checking on the quality of performance of legal advisers at police stations.

The inadequacy of much legal advice given to suspects was highlighted when Stephen Millar, one of the Cardiff Three, had his conviction quashed on appeal ((1992) *The Times*, 11 December). In his judgment, the Lord Chief Justice criticised the defence solicitor for not intervening to halt the questioning. In his research for the Royal Commission on Criminal Justice, Professor John Baldwin analysed 600 police interviews (see 9.5.25, below) and found that in 66.5% of them, the adviser said nothing at all ((1993) 33 British J of Criminology 3). In one recent unreported case, a defence solicitor repeatedly claimed during interviews that his client was being untruthful. He apparently said: 'I'd better shut up or I'll be accused of prosecuting the case!' The Court of Appeal concluded that the solicitor had 'evinced a quite open hostility' towards his client: *R v M* (2000), cited by Ed Cape and Jane Hickman, 'Bad lawyer, good defence' (2002) 152 NLJ 1194–95. Confession evidence may be excluded under s 76(2)(b) of PACE if rendered unreliable by a person other than the suspect.

Following significant criticism, including that in the Runciman Report, The Law Society and Legal Aid Board introduced a scheme for the accreditation of non-solicitor representatives, which was implemented progressively from 1995 and which paved the way for the current arrangements described above.

9.5.7 Delaying access to legal advice

The police have no right to delay a detainee's access to legal advice except in the case of a serious arrestable offence (Annex B to Code C). If the detainee is being held in connection with a serious arrestable offence (s 116), he can be delayed access to legal advice, but the delay must be authorised by an officer of the rank of superintendent and only where he has reasonable grounds for believing that the exercise of the right:

- will lead to interference with, or harm to, evidence connected with a serious arrestable offence or interference with or physical harm to other persons; or

- will lead to the alerting of other persons suspected of having committed such an offence but not yet arrested for it; or

- will hinder the recovery of any property obtained as a result of such an offence.

If a delay is authorised, the suspect must be told the reason for it and the reason must be recorded in the custody record. The maximum period of delay is 36 hours (Annex B, para 6).

9.5.8   *R v Samuel* (1988)

In *R v Samuel* (1988), the defendant was arrested on suspicion of robbery and taken to a police station. During that day and the following day, he was interviewed several times about the robbery and other offences. He asked for a solicitor during the second interview. His request was refused by a superintendent on the grounds that two of the offences under investigation were serious arrestable offences and there would be a danger of accomplices being inadvertently alerted. At the fourth interview, Samuel confessed to two burglaries. A little later, a solicitor instructed by the family was notified of the charges, but he was refused access to the suspect. Shortly after that, Samuel confessed to the robbery charge. The trial judge admitted evidence of the last interview. Samuel was convicted of robbery and sentenced to 10 years' imprisonment. The Court of Appeal quashed the conviction. Two important issues were clarified:

- The police were not entitled to deny a suspect access to a solicitor after he has been charged, even if other charges are still being investigated. This follows from the plain and natural meaning of Annex B (para 1), which states that the right to legal advice can be delayed where:

  > ... the person is in police detention ... in connection with a serious arrestable offence, has not yet been charged with an offence and an officer of superintendent rank or above, or inspector rank or above ... has reasonable grounds for believing ...

- The right of access to a solicitor was a 'fundamental right of a citizen' and if the police sought to justify refusing that right, they must do so by reference to specific aspects of the case; it was insufficient to suppose that giving the suspect access to a solicitor *might* lead to the alerting of accomplices. The officer had to believe that it probably would and that the solicitor would either commit the criminal offence of alerting other suspects, or would be hoodwinked into doing so inadvertently or unwillingly. Either belief could only be genuinely held by an officer on rare occasions. The belief that a solicitor would commit the criminal offence had to be based on knowledge of that particular solicitor. It could not be advanced successfully in relation to solicitors generally. As to the other point, Hodgson J observed (p 626):

> But, what is said is that the detained person will be able to bring about one or more of the happenings (a) to (c) [in Annex B] by causing the solicitor to pass on unwittingly some form of coded message. Whether there is any evidence that this has or may have happened in the past we have no way of knowing. Solicitors are intelligent, professional people; persons detained by the police are frequently not very clever and the expectation that one of (a) to (c) will be brought about in this way seems to contemplate a degree of intelligence and sophistication in persons detained, and perhaps a naïveté and lack of common sense in solicitors which we doubt often occurs.

This is not perhaps a view of offenders and solicitors which would be immediately agreed with by all those whose work brings them into contact with either group. Hodgson J said there were two tests. First, did the officer have the belief? This was a subjective question. Secondly, was that belief reasonable? This is an objective matter. In this case, the solicitor was well known and highly respected. He was unlikely to be hoodwinked by a 24 year old. The suspect's mother had been informed of her son's arrest hours before the solicitor was refused access to the son. If anyone was to have been alerted, it could easily have been done already. The solicitor would have advised his client to have said nothing at that stage. Samuel would not have made his admission having been denied his 'fundamental freedom' to consult with a solicitor. The evidence of the admission should, therefore, have been excluded under s 78.

9.5.9   *R v Alladice* (1988)

In *R v Alladice* (1988), the Court of Appeal allowed the evidence of an admission made during an interview where the suspect had had access to a solicitor delayed. The decision has been regarded as based on the narrow facts of the case. Alladice had made admissions of involvement in an armed robbery and was convicted, but argued on appeal that the evidence should have been excluded because there had been no valid reason for delaying his access to a solicitor. He argued that the real reason for the delay was that the police believed that a solicitor would have advised him to remain silent and that, as the Code and *Samuel* showed, this was not a valid reason. The court found that, on the facts, there had been a breach of s 58, but that this did not mean that the evidence obtained in breach of the section should automatically be excluded. There was no suggestion of oppression nor was there evidence of bad faith on the part of the police. The court took the view that it would be wrong to regard the admission as having resulted from the refusal to grant access to a solicitor. Alladice had stated that he understood the caution, that he was aware of his rights and that he was able to cope with the interview. He argued that the alleged admissions had not been made, although that argument was rejected by the judge. In any event, it seemed to the Court of Appeal that the presence of a solicitor would not have made any difference to the suspect's knowledge of his rights. There was no causal link between the absence of Alladice's solicitor and the admission.

9.5.10 *R v Davidson* **(1988)**

In *R v Davidson* (1988), the trial judge stated that *Samuel* meant that, in order for the police to validly delay access to advice, they had to be 'nearly certain' that the solicitor granted access to a suspect would warn an accomplice or get rid of the proceeds of the crime. Davidson had been arrested for handling a stolen ring, the fruit of an armed robbery. The power to delay access to a solicitor could not be exercised until D had nominated a particular lawyer. As this had not been done when the superintendent came to consider the matter, he could not have had a reasonable fear that the lawyer would pass a message to another person involved in the crime. The suspect had already spoken to his wife twice, so the reality of the police fears that he would use the lawyer as a messenger had to be doubted. The court excluded the crucial confessions and the prosecution's case collapsed.

9.5.11 *R v Parris* **(1989)**

In *R v Parris* (1989), the court quashed a conviction for armed robbery because of breaches of s 58. The police arrested Parris for armed robbery and took him to the station where he was kept incommunicado (under s 56). He asked to see a solicitor at his first interview and was refused. He refused to answer any questions. During his second interview, he agreed to answer some questions, provided nothing was written down. He then allegedly made oral admissions although, at trial, he denied these took place. The Crown did not deny that there had been a breach of s 58(8) as there had been no valid reason for refusing access to a solicitor; the incommunicado order under s 56 was wrongly assumed to also exclude access to a solicitor under s 58. Had there been a solicitor present at the second interview, he would probably have advised

Parris not to speak; at the least he would have discouraged the alleged fabrication of admissions. The appeal succeeded.

9.5.12 Interviewing before solicitor arrives

The police have a right to start questioning detainees before a solicitor has arrived at the police station if the situation is an emergency or the solicitor is not likely to arrive for a considerable period. The power is governed by Code C, para 6.6, which states:

> A detainee who wants legal advice may not be interviewed or continue to be interviewed until they have reached such advice unless:
>
> (a) Annex B applies, when the restriction on drawing adverse inferences from silence in Annex C will apply because the detainee is not allowed an opportunity to consult a solicitor; or
>
> (b) an officer of superintendent rank or above has reasonable grounds for believing that:
>
>   (i) the consequent delay might:
>
>   • lead to interference with, or harm to, evidence connected with an offence;
>
>   • lead to interference with, or physical harm to, other people;
>
>   • lead to serious loss of, or damage to, property;
>
>   • lead to alerting other people suspected of having committed an offence but not yet arrested for it;
>
>   • hinder the recovery of property obtained in consequence of the commission of an offence;
>
>   (ii) when a solicitor, including a duty solicitor, has been contacted and has agreed to attend, awaiting their arrival would cause unreasonable delay to the process of investigation.

It will not normally be appropriate to begin an interview if the solicitor has said he is on his way (Note 6A). Another exception is where the solicitor cannot be contacted or declines to attend and the detainee, having been told about the Duty Solicitor Scheme, declines to ask for the duty solicitor or the duty solicitor is unavailable.

9.5.13 Answering police questions and the right to silence

The police are free to ask anyone any questions. The only restriction is that all questioning is supposed to cease once a detainee has been charged. Code C, para 11.6 states that:

> The interview or further interview of a person about an offence with which that person has not been charged or for which they have not been informed they may be prosecuted must cease when the officer in charge of the investigation:

(a) is satisfied all the questions they consider relevant to obtaining accurate and reliable information about the offence have been put to the suspect, this includes allowing the suspect an opportunity to give an innocent explanation and asking questions to test if the explanation is accurate and reliable, eg, to clear up ambiguities or clarify what the suspect said;

(b) has taken account of any other available evidence; and

(c) the officer in charge of the investigation, or in the case of a detained suspect, the custody officer, see *paragraph 16.1*, reasonably believes there is sufficient evidence to provide a realistic prospect of conviction for that offence if the person was prosecuted for it. See Note 11B.

This paragraph does not prevent officers in revenue cases or acting under the confiscation provisions of the Criminal Justice Act 1988 or the Drug Trafficking Act 1994 from inviting suspects to complete a formal question and answer record after the interview is concluded.

There is no obligation on a citizen to answer police questions. A person cannot be charged, for example, with obstructing the police in the execution of their duty simply by failing to answer questions. Although a judge or prosecutor cannot suggest to the jury that such silence is evidence of guilt, adverse inferences might be drawn in court from a defendant's earlier refusal to answer police questions (s 34 of the CJPOA 1994). Judges seem to have interpreted this section rather narrowly. Lord Bingham CJ, for example, said in *R v Bowden* (1999):

> Proper effect must of course be given to these provisions ... But since they restrict rights recognised at common law as appropriate to protect defendants against the risk of injustice, they should not be construed more widely than the statutory language allows.

It could be argued that s 34 is difficult to reconcile with the fair trial guarantees found in Art 6 of the ECHR. The Strasbourg Court has said, for example, that 'the very fact that an accused is advised by his lawyer to maintain his silence must be given appropriate weight by the domestic court. There may be good reason why such advice is given'; *Condron and Condron v UK* (2001). See generally, Ian Dennis, 'Silence in the police station: the marginalisation of section 34' [2002] Crim LR 25–38 and 9.5.15, below.

In *Rice v Connolly* (1966), the appellant was seen by officers in the early hours of the morning behaving suspiciously in an area where house-breaking had taken place on the same evening. On being questioned, he refused to say where he was going or where he had come from. He refused to give his full name and address, though he did give a name and the name of a road which were not untrue. He refused to accompany the officer to a police box for identification purposes, saying: 'If you want me, you'll have to arrest me.' He was arrested and charged with wilfully obstructing a police officer contrary to s 51(3) of the Police Act 1964.

His appeal against conviction succeeded. Lord Parker CJ noted that the police officer was acting within his duty in inquiring about the appellant and that what the appellant did was obstructive. The critical question, though, was whether the appellant's conduct was 'wilful' within the meaning of s 51. Lord Parker CJ, in the Divisional Court, took that word to mean 'intentional [and] without lawful excuse'. He continued:

> It seems to me quite clear that, though every citizen has a moral duty or, if you like, a social duty to assist the police, there is no legal duty to that effect, and, indeed, the whole basis of the common law is the right of the individual to refuse to answer questions put to him by persons in authority, and to refuse to accompany those in authority to any particular place; short, of course, of arrest.

The court was unanimous, although one judge, James J, cautioned that he would not go as far as to say that silence coupled with conduct could not amount to obstruction. It would depend on the particular facts of any given case.

In *Ricketts v Cox* (1982), two police officers who were looking for youths responsible for a serious assault approached the defendant and another man in the early hours of the morning. The justices found that the officers acted in a proper manner in putting questions to the men. The defendant was abusive, unco-operative and possibly hostile to the officers, using obscene language calculated to provoke and antagonise the officers, and tried to walk away. The justices were satisfied that this conduct amounted to an obstruction for the purposes of a charge under s 51(3) of the Police Act 1964. The defendant's appeal was dismissed by the Divisional Court which found that the case raised the point reserved by James J in *Rice v Connolly* – the combination of silence and hostility without lawful excuse. As Zander has observed, the state of the law here is now unclear.

9.5.14 Duties to answer

There are certain circumstances where the citizen is under a duty to answer police questions. Where a constable has reasonable grounds for believing that a vehicle has been involved in an accident and he seeks the particulars of the driver, he may arrest that person if the information is not given. With the Home Secretary's consent, and on the authority of a chief constable, coercive questioning (that is, where a suspect's silence can be used in evidence against him) can be used in matters under s 11 (as amended) of the Official Secrets Act 1911. There are also wide powers under the Companies Act 1985 to require officers and agents of companies to assist inspectors appointed to investigate the company. Refusal to answer questions can be sanctioned as a contempt of court (s 431) and as a criminal offence (s 447). A person can also be required to answer questions put to him by a liquidator of a company (*Bishopsgate Management Ltd v Maxwell Mirror Group Newspapers* (1993)).

Under s 2 of the CJA 1987, the Director of the Serious Fraud Office (SFO) (dealing with frauds worth over £5 million) can require anyone whom he has reason to think has relevant information to attend to answer questions and to provide information including documents and books. Such statements, however, cannot be used in evidence against the persons who make them unless they go into the witness box and give inconsistent testimony. Even this power, though, does not require the breach of legal professional privilege. Failure to comply with s 2 requests is a criminal offence and can result in an application for a magistrates' search warrant. These powers have been widely used. The SFO Annual Report for 1991–92 revealed that a total of 793 notices had been given during that year. In *R v Director of the Serious Fraud Office ex p Smith* (1993), the House of Lords held that the SFO could compel a person to answer questions relating to an offence with which he had already been charged. It followed that in relation to such questions, the suspect did not have to be further cautioned.

Other powers to compel answers on pain of penalties for refusal exist under the Terrorism Act 2000, and refusal to answer certain allegations from the prosecutor can be treated as acceptances of them under the Drug Trafficking Act 1994.

The closest English law comes to creating a duty to give one's name and address is the power given to the police under s 25(3) of PACE 1984. This is the power to arrest for a non-arrestable offence where the officer cannot find out the suspect's particulars for the purpose of serving a summons on him.

There is no duty to offer information about crime to the police. However, s 19 of the Terrorism Act 2000 makes it an offence for a person who believes or suspects that another person has committed an offence under any of ss 15–18 (offences involving funding of terrorism), and bases his belief or suspicion on information which comes to his attention in the course of a trade, profession, business or employment to not disclose to an officer as soon as is reasonably practicable his belief or suspicion and the information on which it is based. Additionally, s 5 of the CLA 1967 creates the offence of accepting money or other consideration for not disclosing information that would lead to the prosecution of an arrestable offence. The House of Lords has also held that it is the duty of every citizen in whose presence a breach of the peace is being committed to attempt to stop it, if necessary by detaining the person responsible. It is, however, except in the case of a citizen who is a police officer, 'a duty of imperfect obligation' (*Albert v Lavin* (1982), *per* Lord Diplock).

9.5.15 What can be said in court about silence in the face of police questioning

There is an established common law rule that neither the prosecution nor the judge should make adverse comment on the defendant's silence in the face of questions. The dividing line, however, between proper and improper judicial comment was a matter of great debate. There are many reasons why a suspect might remain silent when questioned (for example, fear, confusion, reluctance to incriminate another person) and the 'right to silence' enjoyed the status of a long established general principle in English law. Thus, in *R v Davis* (1959), a judge was ruled on appeal to have misdirected the jury when he told them that 'a man is not obliged to say anything but you are entitled to use your common sense ... can you imagine an innocent man who had behaved like that not saying anything to the police ... He said nothing'.

An exception, though, was that some degree of adverse suggestion was permitted where two people were speaking on equal terms and one refused to comment on the accusation made against him by the other. In *R v Parkes* (1974), the Privy Council ruled that a judge could invite the jury to consider the possibility of drawing adverse inferences from silence from a tenant who had been accused by a landlady of murdering her daughter. The landlady and tenant, for the purposes of this encounter, were regarded as having a parity of status unlike a person faced with questions from the police. It was held in *R v Chandler* (1976) that the suspect was on equal terms with the police officer where the former was in the company of his solicitor. Chandler had refused to answer some of the questions he had been asked by the police officer before the caution, and the judge told the jury that they should decide whether the defendant's silence was attributable to his wish to exercise his common law right or because he might incriminate himself. The Court of Appeal quashed Chandler's conviction since the judge had gone too far in suggesting that silence before a caution could be evidence of guilt.

It was proper for the judge to make some comment on a defendant's reticence before being cautioned provided that the jury were directed that the issue had to be dealt with in two stages: (i) was the defendant's silence an acceptance of the officer's allegations?; and, if so, (ii) could guilt of the offence charged be reasonably inferred from what the defendant had implicitly accepted? The court said that it did not accept that a police officer always had an advantage over a suspect. Everything depended on the circumstances. In an inquiry into local government corruption, for example, a young officer might be at a distinct disadvantage when questioning a local dignitary. That type of interview was very different from a 'tearful housewife' being accused of shoplifting.

The Court of Appeal's decision in *Chandler* asserted that silence might only be taken as acquiescence to police allegations before a caution. The court excluded silence after the caution as being something from which anything adverse can be inferred, because a suspect could not be criticised for remaining silent having been specifically told of that right. This, however, seemed like an irrational dichotomy. If the suspect did, in fact, have a legal right to silence whether or not he had been cautioned, it is very odd that full enjoyment of the right could only be effective from the moment of it being announced by the police. Additionally, any questioning of a suspect at a police station prior to a caution being given is probably in contravention of Code C, para 10, which requires a caution to be given at the beginning of each session of questioning. Violation of the Code affords grounds for an appeal under s 78 of PACE 1984. Cautions need not be given according to para 10.1:

... if questions are for other necessary purposes, eg:

(a) solely to establish their own identity or ownership of any vehicle;

(b) to obtain information in accordance with any relevant statutory requirement, see *paragraph 10.9*;

(c) in furtherance of the proper and effective control of a search, eg, to determine the need to search in the exercise of powers of stop and search or to seek co-operation while carrying out a search ...

9.5.16 Right to silence in courts

Before the changes to the right to silence that were eventually made by the CJPOA 1994, the value of maintaining the traditional approach was subjected to considerable scrutiny. Since 1988, the right to silence was effectively abolished in Northern Ireland. It became possible for a court to draw adverse inferences from a defendant's silence when he was arrested. Adverse inferences could also be drawn from the defendant's failure to provide an explanation for any 'object, substance or mark' on his clothing, footwear or in his possession which the arresting officer found suspicious and questioned the suspect about (Criminal Justice (Evidence etc) (Northern Ireland) Order 1988).

Similar recommendations were made by the Home Office Working Group on the Right to Silence in 1989. The question was also considered by the Runciman Royal Commission on Criminal Justice. It had to decide whether to adopt a practice like the Northern Ireland system and the one recommended by the Home Office, or whether to retain the right to silence, as the Philips Royal Commission on Criminal Procedure had recommended in 1981. In evidence to the Runciman Royal Commission, the proposal to retain the right to silence was supported by The Law Society, the Bar Council and the Magistrates' Association. It was opposed by the police, the CPS, HM Council of Circuit Judges and senior judges.

Professor Michael Zander's research on this issue suggested that the role of the right to silence in the real workings of the criminal justice system was in fact not as significant as often argued. In one of his studies, 'Investigation of crime' [1979] Crim LR 211, he looked at 150 cases randomly drawn from those heard at the Old Bailey. According to police statements, of the 286 defendants (in many cases, there was more than one defendant), only 12 were said to have relied on their right to silence when confronted by police accusations. Of these, nine were convicted. Zander has also made the following points:

- Most defendants plead guilty, so the right to silence is unimportant in such a context.

- Common law rules permit the judge to *mention* the defendant's silence and, in some limited circumstances, to comment on it.

- In any event, the jury may draw adverse conclusions about the defendant's silence to police questions, that is, whether the judge is permitted to comment on this or not.

In a study commissioned by the LCD, only 2% of 527 suspects exercised their right to silence; see Sanders *et al*, *Advice and Assistance at Police Stations and the 24 Hour Duty Solicitor Scheme*, 1989, LCD.

In a study by Stephen Motson, Geoffrey Stephenson and Tom Williamson ((1992) 32 British J of Criminology 23–40), the researchers looked at 1,067 CID interviews carried out in nine London police stations in 1989. By carefully matching cases where the right to silence had been exercised with like cases where it had not and then comparing the outcomes, the researchers found that decisions as to whether to prosecute were based on factors like the strength of the evidence against the suspect and the seriousness of the offence; they were not correlated with whether the suspect responded to questions or not. There was no evidence that silence at the police station gave the suspect any advantage at court. They commented:

> The high proportion of silence cases who ultimately plead guilty might be taken to suggest that the use of silence is a ploy – adopted for the most part by previously convicted offenders, [it] is abandoned in favour of a guilty plea when prosecution, probable conviction and (especially) sentencing are nigh.

The Runciman Royal Commission eventually decided to recommend retaining the right to silence. Its Report (1993) states (para 82):

> The majority of us believe that adverse inferences should not be drawn from silence at the police station and recommend retaining the present caution and trial direction.

The Commission did, however, recommend (para 84) the retention of the current law regarding silence in investigations of serious and complex fraud under which adverse consequences can follow from silence. The Report notes that a large proportion of those who use the right to silence later plead guilty. The majority of the Commission felt that the possibility of an increase in convicting the guilty by abolishing the right would be outweighed by the considerable extra pressure on innocent suspects in police stations. The Commission did, however, meet the police and CPS concern about 'ambush defences', where a defence is entered late in a trial, thus leaving the prosecution no time to check and rebut the defence. The Commission recommends that if the defence introduces a late change or departs from the strategy it has disclosed in advance to the prosecution, then it should face adverse comment (para 136). Professor Zander, however, issued a note of dissent that the principle must remain that the burden of proof always lies with the prosecution. He states:

> The fundamental issue at stake is that the burden of proof throughout lies with the prosecution. Defence disclosure is designed to be helpful to the prosecution and, more generally, to the system. But, it is not the job of the defendant to be helpful either to the prosecution or the system.

Since the abolition of the court of Star Chamber in 1641, no English court has had the power to use torture or force to exact confessions from suspects. The so called 'right to silence' really meant that a suspect could remain silent when questioned by police or in court without prosecution counsel or the judge being allowed to make adverse comment to the jury about such a silence. Traditionally, silence could not be used in court as evidence of guilt.

In support of the old rule, it could be said that:

• people are innocent until proven guilty of a crime by the State; and that

• people should never be under force to condemn themselves; and that

• there are several reasons other than genuine guilt why someone may wish to remain silent in the face of serious accusations – they might be terrified, confused, retarded, wish to protect someone else or fear that the truth would get them in some other type of trouble. The 11th Report of the Criminal Law Revision Committee (1972) gives several examples. The accused might be so shocked at an accusation that he forgets a vital fact which would acquit him of blame; his excuse might be embarrassing, like being in the company of a prostitute; or he may fear reprisals from another party;

• the 'right' is widely protected in other aspects of society: the police, for example, when facing internal disciplinary charges, are not bound to answer questions or allegations put to them.

9.5.17 Effective abolition of the right to silence

The government ignored the recommendations of the Runciman Commission and, in ss 34–37 of the CJPOA 1994, effectively abolished the right to silence. 'Abolished' may be too strong a word because everyone still has the right to remain silent in the same circumstances as they did before the CJPOA 1994; what has changed is the entitlement of a judge or prosecuting counsel to make adverse comment on such a silence.

Notwithstanding the 1994 Act, therefore, any person may refuse to answer questions put to him out of court. There are only a few exceptions to this (as with s 2 of the CJA 1987, which concerns the investigation of serious fraud, and requires certain questions to be answered under pain of punishment for refusal) and they existed before the Act. The CJPOA 1994 does not alter the position of the accused person as a witness – he remains a competent but not compellable witness in his own defence (s 35), although now the prosecution as well as the judge may comment upon such a failure to give evidence (s 168).

Except in so far as the new law makes changes, the old law still applies.

In enacting ss 34–37 of the CJPOA 1994, the government was adopting a particular policy. The general purpose of the Act was to assist in the fight against crime. The government took the view that the balance in the criminal justice system had become tilted too far in favour of the criminal and against the public in general, and victims in particular. The alleged advantage of the change in law is that it helps convict criminals who, under the old law, used to be acquitted because they took advantage of the right to keep quiet when questioned without the court or prosecution being able to comment adversely upon that silence. Introducing the legislation, the Home Secretary said that change in law was desirable because 'it is professional criminals, hardened criminals and terrorists who disproportionately take advantage of and abuse the present system'.

Section 34 states that where anyone is questioned under caution by a police officer, or charged with an offence, then a failure to mention a fact at that time which he later relies on in his defence will allow a court to draw such inferences as appear proper about that failure. Inferences may only be drawn if, in the circumstances, a suspect could reasonably have been expected to mention the fact when he was questioned. The inferences which can be drawn can be used in determining whether the accused is guilty as charged. The section, however, permits adverse inferences to be drawn from silence in situations that do not amount to 'interviews' as defined by Code C of PACE 1984, and thus which are not subject to the safeguards of access to legal advice and of contemporaneous recording which exist where a suspect is interviewed at the police station. The caution to be administered by police officers is as follows (with appropriate variants for ss 36 and 37):

> You do not have to say anything. But, it may harm your defence if you do not mention when questioned something which you later rely on in court. Anything you do say may be given in evidence.

Section 58 of the Youth Justice and Criminal Evidence Act (YJCEA) 1999 amends s 34 by adding a new s 34(2A). This restricts the drawing of inferences from silence in an interview at a police station (or similar venue) where the suspect was not allowed an opportunity to consult a solicitor prior to being questioned or charged (see Code D, Annex C). This amendment is intended to meet the ruling of the ECtHR in *Murray v UK* (1996) that delay in access to legal advice, even if lawful, could amount to a breach of Art 6, given the risk of adverse inferences being drawn.

Section 35 allows a court or jury to infer what appears proper from the refusal of an accused person to testify in his own defence, or from a refusal without good cause to answer any question at trial. In the *Practice Direction (Criminal: Consolidated)* (2002), para 44, the Lord Chief Justice indicated that where the accused is legally represented, the following should be said by the judge to the accused's lawyer at the end of the prosecution case if the accused is not to give evidence:

> Have you advised your client that the stage has now been reached at which he
> may give evidence and, if he chooses not to do so or, having been sworn,
> without good cause refuses to answer any question, the jury may draw such
> inferences as appear proper from his failure to do so?

If the lawyer replies to the judge that the accused has been so advised, then the
case will proceed. If the accused is not represented, and still chooses not to give
evidence or answer a question, the judge must give him a similar warning,
ending: '... the jury may draw such inferences as appear proper. That means
they may hold it against you.'

Section 36 permits inferences to be drawn from the failure or refusal of a
person under arrest to account for any object, substances or mark in his
possession, on his person, in or on his clothing or footwear, or in any place at
which he is at the time of arrest. Section 37 permits inferences to be drawn from
the failure of an arrested person to account for his presence at a particular place
where he is found.

Thus, as the late Lord Taylor, the then Lord Chief Justice, observed, the legal
changes do not, strictly speaking, abolish the right to silence:

> If a defendant maintains his silence from first till last, and does not rely on any
> particular fact by way of defence, but simply puts the prosecution to proof, then
> [ss 34–37] would not bite at all.

The change has been widely and strongly opposed by lawyers, judges and
legal campaign groups. Liberty, for example, has said that drawing adverse
inferences from silence would undermine the presumption of innocence.
Silence is an important safeguard against oppressive questioning by the police,
particularly for the weak and vulnerable.

John Alderson, former chief constable of Devon and Cornwall (1973–82)
and a respected writer on constitutional aspects of policing, has written of the
impending danger when police are able to 'exert legal and psychological
pressure on individuals held in the loneliness of their cells'. He stated ((1995)
The Independent, 1 February) that:

> History tells us that, when an individual has to stand up against the entire
> apparatus of the modern State, he or she is very vulnerable. That is why, in
> criminal cases, the burden of proof has always rested on the State rather than on
> the accused. The Founding Fathers of America amended their constitution to
> that effect in 1791.

Undermining the right to silence may constitute a significant constitutional
change in the relationship between the individual and the State. It may be
doubted whether the majority of suspects should be put under greater
intimidation by the system because of the conduct of a few 'hardened
criminals' – the justification for the legislation given by the Home Secretary
when he introduced it.

Two points should be noted, however, to put the debate in its proper historical context. First, it should not be forgotten that there were, prior to the Act, several instances in English law where there was already a legal obligation for a suspect to answer questions. These included the obligation to speak under s 2 of the CJA 1987 (see above); the obligations under ss 431–41 of the Companies Act 1985 (concerning investigations in respect of company officers and agents whose companies are being investigated by the Department of Trade and Industry); and the obligations under ss 22 and 131 of the Insolvency Act 1986 (concerning inquiries upon the winding up of companies). Note, however, that in *Saunders v UK* (1997), the ECtHR held that where evidence obtained under compulsion is subsequently used in a trial, this amounts to a breach of the right to a fair trial in Art 6. Consequently, s 59 of and Sched 3 to the YJCEA 1999 amend the various existing statutes to provide that, in any criminal proceedings, the prosecution will not be able to introduce evidence of, or put questions about, answers given under compulsion unless the evidence is first introduced or a question is asked by or on behalf of the accused in the proceedings.

Secondly, in the few cases where the right to silence was used under the pre-Act law, we need to ask how far juries were genuinely sympathetic to the judge's directions that they could not assume guilt from silence. Juries convicted in half of such cases, so there is evidence that jurors were suspicious and sceptical about people who exercised the right, just as they may be today where someone exercises the right (that is, remains silent from arrest until the jury retires without relying on any fact he could have mentioned earlier).

In research undertaken in 1995 and 1996, Bucke, Street and Brown (Home Office Research Study 199, 2000) found that the provisions had had a marked impact on various aspects of the investigation and trial of criminal offences, including suspects' use of silence at the police station, police practices in relation to interviewing and disclosure, the advice given at police stations by legal advisers and the proportion of defendants testifying at trial. However, they concluded that there was no discernible increase in charges or convictions and reported that there was considerable scepticism about the effect on professional criminals. For an interesting account of these controversial reforms, see Ian Dennis, 'The Criminal Justice and Public Order Act 1994: the evidence provisions' [1995] Crim LR 4. For a more detailed discussion, see S Easton, *The Case for the Right to Silence*, 2nd edn (1998).

9.5.18 Directions to the jury on silent defendants

Following the enactment of the CJPOA 1994, there has been a steady stream of case law as to correct judicial practice when directing the jury about the drawing of adverse inferences under s 34 and s 35.

In *R v Cowan* (1995), the Court of Appeal considered what should be said in the summing up if the defendant decides not to testify. The jury must be directed that (as provided by s 38(3) of the CJPOA 1994) an inference from failure to give evidence could not on its own prove guilt. The jury had to be satisfied (on the basis of the evidence called by the prosecution) that the prosecution had established a case to answer before inferences could be drawn from the accused's silence. The jury could only draw an adverse inference from the accused's silence if it concluded that the silence could only be sensibly attributed to the accused having no answer to the charge or none that could stand up to cross-examination.

The difficult issue as to correct judicial practice when the accused remains silent during interview on the advice of his solicitor was considered in *R v Condron* (1997) and *R v Argent* (1997). These cases make it clear that such advice was only one factor to be taken into consideration, along with all the other circumstances, in any jury determination as to whether adverse inferences could be drawn from a 'no comment' interview. In *Condron*, the Court of Appeal considered the guidelines set out in *Cowan* (above) and concluded that they were equally applicable to failure to answer questions (s 34) and failure to testify (s 35).

Stuart-Smith LJ, giving the judgment of the court, went on to say that it was desirable to direct the jury that if, despite any evidence relied upon to explain the failure (to answer questions), or in the absence of such evidence, it concluded that the failure could only sensibly be attributed to the accused having fabricated the evidence subsequently, the jury might draw an adverse inference.

More detailed guidance was given in *Argent*, where Lord Bingham set out the conditions that had to be met before s 34 could operate. They include:

(a) the failure to answer had to occur before the defendant was charged;

(b) the alleged failure must occur during questioning under caution;

(c) the questioning must be directed at trying to discover whether and by whom the offence has been committed;

(d) the failure must be a failure to mention any fact relied on in the person's defence;

(e) the fact the defendant failed to mention had to be one which this particular defendant could reasonably be expected to have mentioned when being questioned, taking account of all the circumstances existing at that time (for example, the time of day, the defendant's age, experience, mental capacity, state of health, sobriety, personality and access to legal advice).

The Court of Appeal in *Argent* took a similar view to that of the Judicial Studies Board (JSB) as regards the relevance of legal advice to remain silent. This, of course, puts the solicitor who attends the interview under some difficulty, especially as The Law Society guidelines suggest that to remain silent is inappropriate when the police have made less than full disclosure of the evidence available. However, Lord Bingham in *Argent* added that the jury is neither concerned with the correctness of the solicitor's advice, nor with whether it complies with the Law Society guidelines, but with the reasonableness of the defendant's conduct in all circumstances.

The court approved the trial judge's direction to the jury:

> You should consider whether or not he is able to decide for himself what he should do or having asked for a solicitor to advise him he would not challenge that advice [at p 34].

Finally, in *R v Daniel (Anthony Junior)* (1998), it was held that the *dicta* of Stuart-Smith LJ in *Condron* (1997) need not be confined to a subsequent fabrication. In addition to the JSB specimen direction, it is desirable for the judge in an appropriate case to include a passage to the effect that, if the jury conclude that the accused's reticence could only sensibly be attributed to his unwillingness to be subjected to further questioning, or that he had not thought about all the facts, or that he did not have an innocent explanation to give, they might draw an adverse inference. This was upheld soon after by the Court of Appeal in *R v Beckles and Montague* (1999), when the defendant gave a 'no comment' interview on legal advice. It was held that the proper inference under s 34 was not limited to recent fabrication.

Where, however, a judge concludes that the requirements of s 34 have not been satisfied and therefore that it is not open to him to leave to the jury the possibility of drawing adverse inferences, he must direct the jury that it should not in any way hold against the accused the fact that he did not answer questions in interview (*R v McGarry* (1998)).

The provisions as to silence must now also meet the requirements of Art 6 of the ECHR. The ECtHR had already held in *Murray v UK* that this right is not absolute and that a system under which inferences could be drawn from silence did not in itself constitute a breach of Art 6, though particular caution when drawing inferences was necessary. This was re-affirmed in *Condron v UK* (2000), where the Court asserted that though silence could not be the only or even the main basis for any conviction, it was right that it should be taken into account in circumstances which clearly called for an explanation from the accused (examples might be having to account for presence at the scene of the crime, or having to account for the presence of fibres on clothing). It should be noted that although the specimen direction issued by the JSB and used by judges emphasises that silence cannot be the only basis for a conviction, it does not make any reference to whether it can be the main basis for conviction. Thus, there is a possible conflict between the approach under the ECHR and that currently adopted in English courts.

The ECtHR considers that legal advice is of great significance in this system. Thus, both *Murray v UK* and *Condron v UK* stressed the importance of access to legal advice at the time of any interview. As explained earlier, the finding in *Murray v UK* that denial of access to legal advice, in conjunction with the drawing of inferences, amounted to a breach of Art 6 led to the amendment to the CJPOA 1994 contained in s 34(2A). However, access in itself is not the end of the matter. The question which then arises is whether the drawing of inferences may be improper under the ECHR where silence results from legal advice. The approach of the English courts to this aspect has been discussed above. The ECtHR has held in both *Condron v UK* and *Averill v UK* (2000) that legal advice may be a proper reason for declining to answer questions and that it may not be fair to draw adverse inferences in such cases.

9.5.19 Tape-recording of interrogations

The police were initially very hostile to the recommendation of the Philips Royal Commission on Criminal Procedure that there should be tape-recording of interviews with suspects. After a while, however, the police became more enthusiastic when it became apparent that the tape-recording of the interrogations increased the proportion of guilty pleas and reduced the challenges to prosecution evidence. Tape-recording of interviews is conducted in accordance with Code of Practice E. The tapes are time-coded so that they cannot be interfered with. It is now compulsory for all police stations to record all interviews with suspects interrogated in connection with indictable offences.

9.5.20 Confessions and the admissibility of evidence

It was long established by the common law that a confession would not be admitted in evidence if it was 'involuntary' in the sense that it was obtained by threat or promise held out by a person in authority. This would include 'even the most gentle, if I may put it that way, threats or slight inducements', *per* Lord Parker CJ in *R v Smith* (1959). In that case, a sergeant major had put the whole company on parade and told them no one would be allowed to move until one of them gave details about which of them had been involved in a fight resulting in a stabbing. A confession resulting from this incident was ruled to have been something that should not have been admitted (although the conviction was not quashed as there was other evidence against the defendant).

In *R v Zavekas* (1970), a conviction was quashed where it had resulted from an improper promise. Z was told that the police were arranging an identification parade and that he would be free to go if he was not picked out. He asked whether he could be allowed to go at once if he made a statement. The officer agreed and then Z made a statement admitting guilt. The admission was given in evidence and Z was convicted. His conviction was quashed even though the inducement had not been proffered by the police. Similarly, the Court of Appeal regarded it a 'fatal inducement' for a police officer to have agreed to a request by the defendant, in *R v Northam* (1968), for a second offence to be taken into account at a forthcoming trial rather than tried as a separate matter.

Apart from threats and promises, 'oppression' leading to a confession would render such a statement inadmissible. The Judges Rules were a set of guidelines made by Divisional Court judges for excluding unreliable evidence, but they left it as discretionary whether violation of the rules should result in the exclusion of any resultant evidence.

There had been a significant change in the approach of the courts by the 1980s. The new approach was to ask, even where there had been promises or threats, as a matter of fact and causation, had there been an involuntary confession? In *R v Rennie* (1985), Lord Lane CJ stated that even where a confession was made 'with a hope that an admission may lead to an earlier release or a lighter sentence' and the hope was prompted by something said or done by a person in authority, the confession would not automatically be regarded as involuntary. The same applied where, as in the present case, a confession was prompted by a fear that otherwise the police would interview and perhaps charge the defendant's sister and mother. The judge should apply his 'common sense' and assume that voluntary meant 'of one's own free will'.

This approach was much criticised as it was often impossible for even trained psychologists to realise which pressures on a suspect being questioned were the ones that prompted him to confess.

The law is now contained in s 76 of PACE 1984, which renders inadmissible any confession (i) obtained as a result of oppression (s 76(2)(a)) or (ii) which was obtained in consequence of something 'likely in the circumstances to render unreliable any confession which might be made by the accused in consequence thereof' (s 76(2)(b)). 'Oppression' is defined by s 76(8) to include 'torture, inhuman or degrading treatment, and the use or threat of violence'.

9.5.21 Oppression

The judge rules on whether evidence is admissible on these lines: if it is admitted, then the jury decides whether to believe it. There should be a 'trial within a trial' – without the jury – to determine whether the evidence is admissible (*R v Liverpool Juvenile Court ex p R* (1988)).

The courts have not found much evidence of 'oppression' in police questioning. In *Miller* (1986), a paranoid schizophrenic had confessed to killing his girlfriend. He had admitted the killing in an interview which contained both reliable and unreliable matter. He later retracted his confession. It was argued for him at trial that the confession should be excluded under s 76(2)(a) – that it had been obtained by 'oppression of the person who made it', as it had come as the result of protracted and oppressive interviews which had caused him to suffer an episode of 'schizophrenic terror'. Medical evidence was given that the style and length of questioning had produced a state of voluntary insanity in which his language reflected hallucinations and delusion. The judge would not exclude the evidence and the defendant was convicted of manslaughter. The Court of Appeal held that the mere fact that questions triggered off hallucinations in the defendant was not evidence of oppression.

In *R v Fulling* (1987), the Court of Appeal held that it was not oppression for the police to tell the defendant that her lover had been having an affair with another woman, which so affected her that she made a confession. The word 'oppression', the court held, should be given its ordinary dictionary meaning as stated in the *Oxford English Dictionary*:

> The exercise of authority or power in a burdensome, harsh or wrongful manner; unjust or cruel treatment of subjects, inferiors, etc; the imposition of unreasonable or unjust burdens.

9.5.22 Unreliability

Evidence of a confession can be excluded if it was given:

> ... in consequence of anything said or done which was likely in the circumstances existing at the time, to render unreliable any confession which might be made by him in consequence thereof ... [s 76(2)(b)].

The phrase 'anything said or done' means by someone other than the suspect. In *R v Goldenberg* (1988), G, a heroin addict, was arrested on a charge of conspiracy to supply diamorphine. He requested an interview five days after his arrest and during this he gave information about a man whom he said had supplied him with heroin. It was argued for G at trial that he had given the statement to get bail and thus to be able to feed his addiction; that the words 'in consequence of anything said or done ...' included things said or done by the suspect and that the critical thing here was the things G had said and done, namely, requested the interview and given any statement that would be likely to get him out of the station. G was convicted and his appeal was dismissed. Neill LJ stated:

> In our judgment, the words 'said or done' in s 76(2)(b) of the 1984 Act do not extend so as to include anything said or done by the person making the confession. It is clear from the wording of the section and the use of the words 'in consequence' that a causal link must be shown between what was said or done and the subsequent confession. In our view, it necessarily follows that 'anything said or done' is limited to something external to the person making the confession and to something which is likely to have some influence on him.

The reasoning in cases like *Zavekas* (see 9.5.20, above) has now clearly been rejected. This view is confirmed by Code C – that if a suspect asks an officer what action will be taken in the event of his answering questions, making a statement or refusing to do either, the officer may inform him what action he proposes to take in that event 'provided that the action is itself proper and warranted' (para 11.3).

9.5.23 *R v Heaton* (1993)

In *R v Heaton* (1993), the appellant was convicted of manslaughter of his 26 day old son. The evidence of the mother, who was of limited intelligence, was that the appellant had shaken the child hard to quieten him and that the child subsequently went limp and breathless. She had also said that she had given the child Calpol (a children's medicine containing paracetamol).

Due to difficulties in contacting the appellant's solicitor, he had been in custody overnight for some 15 and a half hours by the time he was able to see a solicitor. As he said he had been ill, he was examined by a doctor who said he was fit to be interviewed. He was interviewed for about 75 minutes in the presence of the solicitor and the interview was tape-recorded. The first part of the interview dealt with his background details. When asked about the events leading up to the child's death, he at first denied that he had held the child. Later, he admitted holding the child but denied holding him up in the air. Under further questioning, he admitted holding the child up in the air and finally conceded that he had shaken the child about four times to and fro to keep him quiet and that the child's head was flopping.

The defence case was that the death could have been caused solely by the administration of the wrong drug by the mother; although she claimed to have given the child Calpol, which contained paracetamol, no evidence of any paracetamol was found in the child's body on postmortem. However, promethazine was found in the blood and was the active ingredient of Phenergen, a drug which the mother also had in the house for the older children. In his evidence, the appellant said that he came downstairs to find the baby purplish in the face and breathless and had seen the mother giving him some medicine, following which she became hysterical and shook the baby. In the interview, he had been upset and as the police would not believe what he was saying, in the end he had told them that he had shaken the child. He denied that he had done so violently or in order to quieten the child.

On the *voir dire* (the trial within a trial where the judge, having asked the jury to go out, decides a dispute between counsel as to whether certain evidence is admissible), the defence sought to exclude the evidence of the appellant's interview under ss 76 and 78 of PACE 1984. An application was made to call a psychiatrist, Dr Z, on the *voir dire*. The trial judge ruled against admitting Dr Z's evidence and that the interview should be admitted.

On appeal, it was argued on the appellant's behalf that the trial judge was wrong to exclude the evidence of Dr Z, and that the trial judge should have excluded the interview because the officers concerned had applied pressure to the appellant, raising their voices and repeating their questions.

9.5.24 The Court of Appeal's decision

The Court of Appeal dismissed the appeal, holding:

- The trial judge had considered Dr Z's report, which was based upon a single interview with the appellant, sight of the case papers, hearing of the interview tapes and a conversation with the probation officer. Dr Z had noted in particular: 'My impression is that he is not exceptionally bright and is possibly of dull normal intelligence and is very suggestible.' In *R v Turner* (1975), Lawton LJ said at p 83:

  > ... an expert's opinion is admissible to furnish the court with scientific information which is likely to be outside the experience and knowledge of a judge or jury. If, on the proven facts, a judge or jury can form their own conclusions without help, then the opinion of an expert is unnecessary. In such a case, if it is given dressed up in scientific jargon, it may make judgment more difficult. The fact that an expert witness has impressive scientific qualifications does not, by that fact alone, make his opinion on matters of human nature or behaviour within the limits of normality any more helpful than that of the jurors themselves; but there is a danger that they may think it does.

  In the more recent case of *R v Raghip, Silcott and Braithwaite* (1991), the Court of Appeal had drawn a distinction between psychiatric or psychological evidence going to *mens rea* and such evidence going to the reliability of a confession, but had not criticised the general principle laid down in *Turner*. The court had rejected a 'judge for yourself' approach by the judge in respect of the jury and, it would seem, in respect of his own task on a *voir dire*, where there was expert evidence which would have been of assistance in assessing the defendant's mental condition. In that case, Alliott J said:

  > ... the state of the psychological evidence before us ... is such that the jury would have been assisted in assessing the mental condition of Raghip and the consequent reliability of the alleged confessions. Notwithstanding that Raghip's IQ was at 74 just in the borderline range, a man chronologically aged 19 years seven months at the date of the interview with a level of functioning equivalent to that of a child of nine years, and the reading capacity of a child of six years, cannot be said to be normal. It would be impossible for the layman to divide that data from Raghip's performance in the witness box, still less the abnormal suggestibility of which [the expert witness] spoke.

- There was in *Heaton* no suggestion of mental handicap or retardation; the appellant was within the normal range of intelligence, albeit towards the duller end of it. There was nothing more than Dr Z's bare impression that the appellant was very suggestible; there was no data on which to found that assertion nor was it clear that 'very suggestible' was outside the normal range. The judge expressly indicated that he should be told if there was anything more to Dr Z's evidence than was contained in his report and he was not informed of anything else. In those circumstances, he concluded that there was nothing in the doctor's impression which complied with the tests laid down in *Turner* and illustrated by *Raghip*; in the court's judgment, he was justified in ruling as he did. Unless the medical evidence sought to be introduced on an issue of this kind was truly based on some scientific data or expert analysis outside the experience of judge and jury, a mere impression, even of a highly qualified doctor, that the defendant 'is not exceptionally bright' or was 'very suggestible' was not admissible for the reasons set out by Lawton LJ.

- The court had read the transcript of the interview and heard the tape-recordings. The appellant had a full opportunity to consult with a solicitor before the interview and the solicitor was present throughout. A doctor had examined the appellant and pronounced him fit to be interviewed. The questioning lasted in all only some 75 minutes and much of the first two tapes was concerned merely with taking the appellant's history. Voices were slightly raised but there was no shouting and no oppressive hostility; the pace of the interview was slow and the appellant was given time to consider his replies. Some questions were repeated several times but not inappropriately. In *R v Paris, Abdullahi and Miller* (1994), where similar arguments were raised, the court said:

> Of course, it is perfectly legitimate for officers to pursue their interrogation of their suspect with a view to eliciting his account or gaining admissions. They are not required to give up after the first denial or even after a number of denials.

In that case, the questioning had continued for some 13 hours and the tapes had shown hostility and bullying on the part of the interviewing officers. In the present case, the situation was wholly different, with the appellant changing his story gradually over a comparatively short period and providing further details without the police putting them in. The judge had been right to conclude that the prosecution had discharged the burden upon them to exclude oppression and the possibility that the circumstances might have rendered the admission unreliable.

In a commentary on *Heaton* in the Criminal Law Review, it is pointed out that the law on confessions is developing in a number of ways to prevent, as far as is possible, the conviction of weak minded and suggestible persons on the basis of their own unreliable statements. In addition to the exclusionary rule in s 76(2)(b) of PACE 1984 and the discretion in s 78, defendants labouring under a 'significant degree of mental handicap' are protected by the rule in *McKenzie* (1994), which requires an unconvincing case based solely on confessions to be withdrawn from the jury.

'Confessions' made to fellow prisoners are particularly controversial. In 1996, Lin, Megan and Josie Russell were attacked while taking their dog for a walk. Lin and Megan were killed; Josie suffered serious injuries. Michael Stone was arrested and charged with the murders. He was then remanded into custody. At his trial in 1998, two fellow inmates, Damien Daley and Harry Thompson, were called as witnesses. Both alleged that Stone had 'confessed' to them. Stone was convicted. The next day Thompson contacted national newspapers. He said that he had lied in court because of police pressures. In 2001, Stone's convictions were quashed by the Court of Appeal. At his re-trial, the prosecution used Daley's evidence and Stone was re-convicted. A strong argument could be made for excluding such dubious evidence under s 78 of PACE. The central problem has been described by Gwyn Morgan, 'Cell confessions' (2002) 152 NLJ 453:

> There may be a strong incentive for 'grasses' to come up with their incriminating stories. Deals may be done with the police as to the withdrawal of charges. Even where this is not the case, those on remand may well feel – even if they are wrong – that giving evidence for the prosecution will ease the way when their own cases come up. And where the grasses are already convicted, they may be anxious (again rightly or wrongly) to give a favourable impression to the prison authorities or the parole board. What's more, in contrast to most witnesses, coming to court does not adversely interfere with their lives; it's a day out.

9.5.25 Research findings

In an interesting study of police interview techniques ('Police interview techniques: establishing truth or proof?' (1993) 33 British J of Criminology 3), John Baldwin analysed 400 videoed police interviews with suspects – 100 from each of four police stations – and 200 audio-taped interviews taken from two busy stations. As he observes, an interrogation leading to a confession can be of great importance to the police, as it can provide an alternative to a time-consuming investigation of the crime. Baldwin did not find much evidence of oppression, but rather of deficiency in questioning technique:

> ... coercion or belligerence in police interviews strike the observer much less frequently than feebleness and ineptitude. Instances of heavy handedness were much less common than unduly timorous questioning. It must, nonetheless, be acknowledged that the boundaries between officers acting, say, upon an assumption of guilt, or failing adequately to listen to suspects' responses, and exerting undue pressures to induce a confession, are thoroughly blurred.

Baldwin concludes that, evaluated as a search for 'the truth', most police interviews are 'thoroughly deficient'. But such a judgment would be to miss the point of interrogation, a central feature of which is concerned with the future rather than past events. Interrogations are, he argues, conducted with an eye to any subsequent trial:

> A main purpose of the interrogation is thus to seek to limit, close down, or pre-empt the future options available to the subject. It will be very difficult for suspects to claim in court that, say, goods were taken by accident or that they

were not at the scene when precisely the opposite was established in an earlier taped interview.

9.5.26 Evidence illegally or improperly obtained

There is an overlap between the subject of this discussion and that above because sometimes the illegally or improperly obtained evidence will be a confession, in which case the rules above will also apply.

There was for a long time a judicial discretion to exclude otherwise admissible evidence on the basis that it would be unfair to the defendant. The *dictum* of Lord Goddard CJ on this was often cited. He said: 'If, for instance, some admission or piece of evidence, for example, a document, had been obtained from a defendant by a trick, no doubt the judge might properly rule it out.' (See *Kuruma Son of Kaniu v R* (1955), a Privy Council case dealing with an appeal from Kenya. It held that, if evidence was relevant, it did not matter how it was obtained.)

In *R v Sang* (1979), the House of Lords took a very restrictive view of the discretion, holding that it could not be used to exclude evidence merely on the basis that it was given by an *agent provocateur*. The defendant claimed he had been induced to commit an offence by an informer acting on the instructions of the police. All the judges ruled that there was no defence of entrapment in English law. They were also unanimous in ruling that (except for confessions or issues of self-incrimination) no discretion existed to exclude evidence simply on the basis that it had been improperly or illegally obtained. Such illegality might lead to civil proceedings or disciplinary action within the police, but not to the exclusion of evidence. The only basis for excluding relevant evidence was if its prejudicial effect outweighed its probative value. This reasoning has been reconfirmed by the Court of Appeal in *R v Spurthwaite and Gill* (1993).

The approach of s 78 of PACE 1984 is to widen the discretion. It does not go so far as the system in the USA where improperly obtained evidence is inadmissible – the doctrine that the fruit of the poisoned tree should not be eaten. It states that the court *may* refuse to allow evidence on which the prosecution proposes to rely:

> ... if it appears to the court that, having regard to all the circumstances, including the circumstances in which the evidence was obtained, the admission of the evidence would have such an adverse effect on the fairness of the proceedings that the court ought not to admit it.

The courts have been persuaded on many occasions to exclude evidence using this section. In fact, Zander has suggested that 'the judges have forged the somewhat ambiguous words of s 78 into a powerful weapon to hold the police accountable for breaches of the law and the Codes of Practice'. Most cases have involved access to solicitors or the law relating to interrogations. In *R v Absolam* (1989), the Court of Appeal quashed a conviction for supplying cannabis where

A, in contravention of the Code, had not been told of his right to a solicitor and rules about the tape-recording of interviews were broken.

Unlike the rule applying to s 76 (see 9.5.22, above), there does not need to be a trial within a trial under s 78 to determine whether the evidence is admissible. The admissibility of a confession can be opposed under both s 76 and s 78. The court will be less willing to exclude evidence where there were technical breaches but the defendant had experience of police stations. In *R v Dunford* (1991), the Court of Appeal refused to quash a conviction in spite of a serious breach of s 58 (see 9.5.4, above) because D, who had several previous convictions, answered 'No comment' to awkward questions by the police and refused to sign a record of the interview. The court thought it was extremely doubtful 'whether the solicitor's advice would have added anything to [his] knowledge of his rights'.

Since the HRA became fully operative in October 2000, it has no longer been possible to treat such issues merely as involving interpretation of s 78(1) of PACE 1984 itself. Additionally, Art 6 of the ECHR must be taken into account by any court in appropriate circumstances. Article 6 guarantees the right to a fair trial, and a trial may not be fair if there are irregularities in the investigative process which result in evidence being unlawfully obtained. It has already been seen that the Court of Appeal has wavered over whether a lack of fairness in a trial contrary to Art 6 should essentially require a conviction to be quashed as being unsafe (see 4.5.2). In the context currently under consideration, the interesting issue may well be whether the illegal or improper manner of obtaining the evidence means that its use in the trial renders the trial itself unfair. If it does not, then Art 6 clearly has no effect. In *Khan* (1996), it was held by the House of Lords that evidence obtained from a secret listening device planted by the police, and which was the only evidence on which the accused was convicted of drug-dealing, was rightly admitted. Since the authority to engage in such conduct was not properly established by legal rules, this form of covert surveillance was a breach of the right to respect for private life, home and correspondence as guaranteed by Art 8. When, in *Khan v UK* (2000), the accused subsequently argued before the ECtHR that his Convention rights had been violated, the Court agreed in respect of Art 8, but denied that that meant that his right to a fair trial had been violated under Art 6, even though the conviction was based only on that evidence. Criticising this approach, Ashworth has argued strongly that when exercising the discretion to exclude evidence under s 78, English courts should give extra weight to the fact that the evidence was obtained in breach of a Convention right, rather than in breach of domestic law ([2000] Crim LR 684).

9.5.27 Runciman Royal Commission proposals

The Commission's recommendations in this area are of particular interest, as it was set up in the wake of a number of grave miscarriages of justice in which people had been wrongly convicted on the basis of subsequently discredited confession evidence. The Commission was announced on the day the Birmingham Six were released from jail having served 16 years for crimes which later scientific evidence showed they could not have confessed to in the way the police alleged.

9.5.28 Confession evidence

The Commission said:

- (para 85) when PACE 1984 is next revisited, attention should be given to the fact that s 77 (judge's duty to caution the jury of the need for care in cases where mentally handicapped people have made confessions without independent witnesses) is limited to the 'mentally handicapped' and does not include the 'mentally ill' or other categories of the 'mentally disordered';

- (para 86) the law should be changed so that a judge may stop any case if the prosecution evidence is demonstrably unsafe or unsatisfactory or too weak to be allowed to go to the jury;

- (para 87) wherever a confession has allegedly been made to the police outside the police station, whether tape-recorded or not, it should be put to the suspect at the beginning of the first tape-recorded interview at the station. Failure to do this may render the alleged confession inadmissible, but, if the suspect does not confirm the confession on the tape, it should not automatically be inadmissible;

- (para 88) an alleged confession to an investigating official should be allowed to go before the jury even if not tape-recorded, provided it meets the tests contained in PACE 1984 and the judge believes the jury could safely consider it.

9.5.29 Corroboration of confessions

The Commission recommended that:

- (para 89) there should be a judicial warning in cases where confession evidence is involved. The precise terms of the warning should depend on the circumstances of the case. If it remains possible for a confession to be admitted without other supporting evidence, the jury should be warned that great care is needed before convicting on the basis of the confession alone;

- (para 90) the majority of the Commission believed that where a confession is credible and has passed the tests laid down in PACE 1984, the jury should be able to consider it even in the absence of other evidence. The judge should in all such cases give a strong warning to the jury. The other evidence which the jury should be advised to look for should be supporting evidence (that is, of a different kind) in the *R v Turnbull* (1977) sense.

There was considerable disquiet among defence lawyers and civil liberty groups that the Commission had not recommended the automatic inadmissibility of uncorroborated confessions. (See, for example, (1993) *The Guardian*, 7 July.) Consider, for example, the case of the Guildford Four. Three men and a woman were jailed for life in 1975 after being convicted of bombing pubs in 1974, which killed five people. The evidence against them amounted to confessions they were alleged to have made. Fourteen years after conviction, a rough set of typed notes was discovered with handwritten addenda which matched one of the men's supposedly contemporaneously recorded interview. The Lord Chief Justice, Lord Lane, concluded that the police officers involved must have lied. The three former officers, however, were acquitted later on charges of attempting to pervert the course of justice. Alistair Logan, solicitor for two of the men, has pointed out that the men would not necessarily have been saved by Runciman's recommendations, because these accept the possibility of uncorroborated confessions going to the jury.

The Commission's Report notes that it is now generally accepted that people do on occasions confess to crimes they have not committed, perhaps due to a desire for notoriety, to protect somebody else, or for immediate advantage like wanting to get out of the police station. The long held belief that people will not make false statements against themselves can no longer be sustained. The Report advocates the introduction of continuous video-recording of all police custody suites at a cost of about £9 million. The Report states (para 50):

> Continuous video-recording (including sound track) of all the activities in the custody office, the passages and stairways leading from the custody office to the cells and, if feasible, the cell passage and the doors of individual cells of all police stations designated under PACE 1984 as suitable for detaining suspects should be introduced as soon as practicable.

John Baldwin has argued ('Power and police interviews' (1993) 143 NLJ 1194, 14 August) that the Royal Commission's Report was sadly lacking in not providing recommendations for a better legal regulation of police questioning of suspects. He says in the Report:

> There is little new thinking or analysis; rather, the emphasis is upon re-working old ideas and offering encouragement to those professional groups which are striving to improve their own procedures.

The problem needing to be addressed, argues Baldwin, is basically one of power:

> Legal advisers and their clients are bound to be relatively powerless in a situation in which it is police officers who decide when an interview takes place, how it is to be conducted and for how long. Interviews take place on police territory and on police terms. Police officers can even determine who sits where

in the interview room and they may deliberately prevent eye contact between legal representatives and their clients by physically bolting the chairs to the floor. Their power to eject troublesome advisers from the interview room [Code of Practice C, para 6.9], though very infrequently exercised, underlines still further who is in charge.

9.6   Revised PACE Codes

In April 2003, revised PACE Codes of Practice A–E came into force. Although the essential structure remains substantially intact, there are numerous amendments.

Code A – stop and search. It is anticipated that the revised Code A will make it clear beyond doubt that searches must not take place unless the necessary legal power exists. Police officers will also be expected to record encounters which do not involve searches. If an officer asks a member of the public to account for his 'actions, behaviour, presence in the area or possession of anything', a record must be made. The person stopped will be entitled to a copy.

Code B – entry and search of premises. Paragraph 1.3 states:

> The right to privacy and respect for personal property are key principles of the Human Rights Act 1998. Powers of entry, search and seizure should be fully and clearly justified before use because they may significantly interfere with the occupiers' privacy. Officers should consider if the necessary objectives can be met by less intrusive means.

Paragraph 7.7 states:

> The Criminal Justice and Police Act 2001, Part 2, gives officers limited powers to seize property from premises or persons so that they can sift or examine it elsewhere. Officers must be careful they only exercise these powers when it is essential and they do not remove any more material than necessary. The removal of large quantities of material, much of which may not ultimately be retainable, may have serious implications for the owners ... Officers must carefully consider if removing copies or images of relevant material or data would be a satisfactory alternative to removing originals.

Code C – treatment and questioning in the police station. The revised version of Code C restricts the drawing of adverse inferences by a detainee's decision to remain silent until he has received legal advice. This has implications for the cautioning of suspects. The revisions are largely a response to *Murray v UK* (1996).

Code D – identification procedures. These have been amended partly to take account of the increasing use of video evidence.

Code E – tape recordings. Revisions to Code E largely reflect changes to cautioning procedures.

THE CRIMINAL PROCESS: (1) THE INVESTIGATION OF CRIME

Legal advisers and their clients are bound to be relatively powerless in a situation in which it is police officers who decide when an interview takes place, how it is to be conducted and for how long. Interviews take place on police territory and on police terms. Police officers can even determine who sits where in the interview room and they may deliberately prevent eye contact between legal representatives and their clients by physically bolting the chairs to the floor. Their power to eject troublesome advisers from the interview room (Code of Practice C, para 6.9), though very infrequently exercised, underlines still further who is in charge.

At the beginning of the 21st century, we can see the first governmental recognition of something called a 'criminal justice system'. The police, the probation service, the prison service, the magistracy, the Crown Courts and other elements have all been grouped within the system. This means that rules or policy relating to one element can be evaluated in terms of their impact in relation to another part of the system. Conflicting public desires arise in this area. On the one hand, there is a general mistrust of certain sorts of policing, and a desire for more protective civil liberties law, while on the other hand, there is a desire for more offenders to be captured and punished, and the belief that, in order for this to succeed, civil liberties need to be reduced. The Macpherson Report following the stabbing of Stephen Lawrence has given a significant impetus for reform of the law relating to policing.

Remedies

Remedies for unlawful arrest include: (1) an action for habeas corpus; (2) that any subsequent prosecution arising from the arrest should fail – s 78 of the Police and Criminal Evidence Act (PACE) 1984; and (3) a claim for damages for false imprisonment. If the arrest is not lawful, then reasonable force may be used to resist it.

Arrest

Arrest can be: (1) under police warrant; (2) under common law for breach of the peace; or (3) under legislation, principally PACE 1984. The details in ss 24 and 25 of PACE 1984 and connected cases are very important.

Detention

Detention short of arrest does not exist. Note this confirmation by s 29 of PACE 1984.

Suspects stopped in the street

Suspects stopped in the street are not legally obliged to help police with enquiries. Note the distinction between *Kenlin v Gardiner* (1967) and *Donnelly v Jackman* (1970). Note also that a person may be arrested for being silent or misleading under s 25 if the officer has reasonable doubts about the suspect's name and address, or whether the summons procedure can be used at the address given. Note the newly enlarged powers of stop and search under s 60.

Procedure on arrest

Procedure on arrest involves the arrestor having to inform the suspect of the grounds for arrest (s 28(3)). Note, though, that an arrest becomes lawful from when the information is given. The extent of the required information to the suspect is important (see *Geldberg v Miller* (1961); *R v Telfer* (1976)).

The use of force

The use of force to effect an arrest must be 'reasonable in all the circumstances' (s 3 of the Criminal Law Act 1967 (citizens); s 117 of PACE 1984 (police officers)).

Stop and search

Stop and search is governed by s 1 and Code A of PACE 1984. The judge can exclude evidence obtained in breach of the Codes (s 67(7) of PACE 1984). There are legal obligations on an officer conducting a search (ss 2 and 3 of PACE 1984). Note that the Code is quite specific about what indices can be grounds for reasonable suspicion and which, individually or combined, may not.

Section 60 of the Criminal Justice and Public Order Act (CJPOA) 1994 has provided a new stop and search power in anticipation of violence. Under it, with authorisation, an officer can stop any pedestrian and search him for offensive weapons or dangerous instruments, or even stop vehicles. The authorising officer must reasonably believe that incidents involving serious violence may take place in the area. Section 81 of the same Act creates a new power of stop and search of people and vehicles where it is expedient to do so to prevent certain acts of terrorism.

Search of arrested persons

Search of arrested persons is governed by s 32 of PACE 1984. The person arrested cannot be required to take off more than outer garments. The place where he was arrested, or where he was immediately before, can also be searched under s 32. Note the differences between this power and those under s 18 regarding premises.

Search on detention

Search on detention is governed by s 54 of PACE 1984 and Code C, para 4.1, which require the custody officer to take charge of the process of searching the detained person.

Premises

Premises can be entered by police: (1) with permission; or (2) to prevent a breach of the peace; or (3) pursuant to s 18 or s 32 of PACE 1984. The differences between these provisions are important. They are:

	Section 18 (entry and search after arrest)	Section 32 (search of premises has to be at time of arrest)
Search of person: (only s 32)		for weapons, means to escape, evidence relating to 'an offence', that is, any offence
Search of premises:	the police may enter and search the arrestee's premises to look for evidence relating to the offence for which the person was arrested or some other arrestable offence connected with that or similar to that offence for which he was arrested.	to enter and search premises where D was when arrested or immediately before arrest for evidence relating to *the offence for which the person was arrested*. They need not be his premises but the power must be based on reasonable belief that the officer will find something for which a search is permitted.

Powers of seizure of articles from searches

Powers of seizure of articles from searches under s 19 and Code B, para 6 are quite wide, including items from any offence. The exemptions, like items under legal professional privilege, are important.

Search warrants and safeguards

Search warrants and safeguards issued under s 8 of PACE 1984 require the magistrate to be satisfied of four things. Note the difficulty of balancing the interests of effective policing with those of civil liberties. Note the ambiguity in s 15 and the way it was resolved in *R v Longman* (1988).

Interrogation, confession and admissibility of evidence

The main problem here is for the law to strike the proper balance between giving the police sufficient power to interrogate and protecting the interests of suspects. Too few rules governing how the police can conduct an interrogation and too few rules restricting the sort of evidence that can be put to a jury might easily lead to oppressive behaviour by the police interviewing suspects. Too many restrictive rules, conversely, will thwart the police in their endeavours to prosecute offenders successfully.

The right to have someone informed

The right to have someone informed after arrest is given (s 56(1), Code C, para 5.1) to all suspects after arrest. It can be delayed, however, under s 116. The case must involve a 'serious arrestable offence' and it must be authorised by a superintendent on certain grounds, for example, the arrested person would alert others involved in a crime.

Access to legal advice

Access to legal advice is provided for under s 58 and Code C. The notification must accord with details set out in Code C. Note the criticisms of the Duty Solicitor Scheme. Is it adequately staffed? Note also the circumstances in which legal advice can be delayed under s 116, Code C, Annex B. In certain circumstances, questioning can begin before the detainee's legal advisor arrives (Code C, para 6.6).

Time limits

Note ss 42 and 38 of PACE 1984 for time limits operational before and after charges. Delayed access to legal advice is possible in cases of serious arrestable offences. A suspect can be held for up to 24 hours without being charged; longer with authorisation from the superintendent and up to 96 hours with magistrates' permission.

The right to silence

The right to silence means that a person cannot be charged with obstructing the police in the execution of their duty simply by failing to answer questions. Note the important difference between *Rice v Connolly* (1966) and *Ricketts v Cox* (1982). There are some circumstances where the suspect does have to answer on pain of penalty (s 2 of the Criminal Justice Act 1987).

What could be said in court before April 1995 about the defendant's silence varied according to whether the questions were put by an officer or someone on equal terms with the questioned person. Generally, no adverse inferences could be invited, although the judge could comment on reticence prior to cautioning. Most defendants did not use the right and of those who did, few seemed, according to research, to benefit from it.

Now, after ss 34–37 of the CJPOA 1994, certain adverse inferences may be drawn from a suspect's failure to answer police questions, or his failure to answer them in court.

Confessions

Confessions must be voluntary and given without oppression being used to extract them; they must also not come from any circumstances likely to make them unreliable (s 76).

Evidence illegally obtained

Evidence illegally or improperly obtained is not automatically inadmissible, but it may be excluded under s 78 if it appears to a court that in all the circumstances, the admission of the evidence 'would have such an adverse effect on the fairness of the proceedings that the court ought not to admit it'.

Runciman Royal Commission recommendations

The Runciman Royal Commission recommendations included:

- that the law should be changed so that a judge may stop any case if the prosecution evidence is demonstrably unsafe or unsatisfactory or too weak to be allowed to go to the jury;

- that wherever a confession has allegedly been made to the police outside the police station, whether tape-recorded or not, it should be put to the suspect at the beginning of the first tape-recorded interview at the station. Failure to do this may render the alleged confession inadmissible, but if the suspect does not confirm the confession on the tape, it should not automatically be inadmissible;

- that there should be a judicial warning in cases where confession evidence is involved. The precise terms of the warning should depend on the circumstances of the case. If it remains possible for a confession to be admitted without other supporting evidence, the jury should be warned that great care is needed before convicting on the basis of the confession alone;

- that where a confession is credible, and has passed the tests laid down in PACE 1984, the jury should be able to consider it even in the absence of other evidence. The judge should in all such cases give a strong warning to the jury. The other evidence which the jury should be advised to look for should be supporting evidence of a different kind.

CHAPTER 10

THE CRIMINAL PROCESS: (2)
THE PROSECUTION

The classification of offences and matters relating to transfers for trial, summary trial and trial on indictment are dealt with in Chapter 4.

Until 1986, England was one of only a few countries which allowed the police to prosecute rather than hand over this task to a State agency like the district attorney in the USA. The Crown Prosecution Service (CPS) was established by the Prosecution of Offences Act (POA) 1985 and the police now play no part in prosecutions beyond the stage of charging the suspect.

There have been many problems with the new system and some writers like Zander have argued that the change could represent a considerable setback for the criminal justice system (Zander, *Cases and Materials on the English Legal System* (1996)). There used to be five different forms of prosecution, those by:

- the police, who prosecuted most offences;

- the Attorney General/Solicitor General, whose permission was needed to prosecute for many serious crimes and who could enter a *nolle prosequi* to stop certain prosecutions or give a *fiat* to disallow them to begin;

- the Director of Public Prosecutions (DPP), who prosecuted in very serious cases and cases brought to him by the government;

- public bodies like local authorities. These used to amount to about 25% of all prosecutions, most being by the Post Office for television licence offences;

- private prosecutions, which involved having to persuade a magistrate of the propriety in issuing a summons. The Attorney General and the DPP both had the power to take over a private prosecution and then drop it for reasons of public policy. Private bodies like stores and the RSPCA most regularly brought prosecutions. A study in 1980 showed that only 2.4% of prosecutions were private (Lidstone, *Prosecutions by Private Individuals and Non-police Agencies* (1980)).

10.1 The Crown Prosecution Service

The move to establish a CPS was precipitated by a report from JUSTICE, the British section of the International Commission of Jurists, in its 1970 Report, *The Prosecution Process in England and Wales*. It argued that the police were not best suited to be prosecutors because they would often have a commitment to winning a case even where the evidence was weak. They were also not best placed to consider the public policy aspects of the discretion not to prosecute. The police were firmly opposed to such a change. They argued that statistics showed that the police were not given to pursuing cases in a way which led to a high rate of acquittal. They also showed that in cases involving miscarriages of justice, the decision to prosecute had been taken by a lawyer.

The question was referred to the Philips Royal Commission on Criminal Procedure, which judged the then existing system according to its fairness, openness and accountability. It proposed a new system based on several distinct features, including the following:

- that the initial decision to charge a suspect should rest with the police;
- that thereafter all decisions as to whether to proceed, alter or drop the charges should rest with another State prosecuting agency;
- this agency would provide advocates for all cases in the magistrates' courts apart from guilty pleas by post. It should also provide legal advice to the police and instruct counsel in all cases tried on indictment.

The POA 1985 established a national prosecution service under the general direction of the DPP. The 1985 Act gives to the DPP and the CPS as a whole the right to institute and conduct any criminal proceedings where the importance or difficulty of the case make that appropriate (s 3(2)(b)). This applies to cases that could also be started by the police or other bodies like local authorities. It can also, in appropriate circumstances, take over and then discontinue cases. The CPS relies on the police for the resources and machinery of investigation.

In the period following its launch, the CPS experienced severe problems of staff shortage related to the general funding of the service. This improved over the years, and by March 1993, the full lawyer staff establishment had almost been met. It was apparently difficult to recruit staff of an adequate standard for the available pay and there has been considerable use of agents, that is, lawyers in private practice working for the CPS on a fee-for-case basis.

As employed solicitors or barristers, Crown prosecutors were originally unable to conduct cases in the higher courts. Changes to the rules on rights of audience in the higher courts for employed lawyers, introduced by the Access to Justice Act 1999, now permit them to do so. Consequently, any Crown prosecutor who is qualified to appear before the higher courts is able to do so. This involves having rights of audience as a barrister or as a solicitor advocate. The CPS Annual Report for 2001–2002 indicates that by the end of March 2002, 301 higher court advocates had been fully trained.

Additionally, changes to the POA 1985 introduced by the Crime and Disorder Act (CDA) 1998 permit some lower court work to be undertaken by designated caseworkers who are not Crown prosecutors. To be able to do so, they must have undergone specified training and have at least three years' experience of casework or have a legal qualification. They are able to review and present straightforward magistrates' court cases which raise no technical issues and which are uncomplicated in terms of fact and law. Essentially, this will involve cases where there is an anticipated guilty plea, or minor road traffic offences where the proof in absence procedure is used. They cannot deal with cases such as indictable-only offences, contested trials, where there is election for jury trial, and cases which raise sensitive issues. At the end of March 2001, there were 222 designated caseworkers. Another 25 had been trained by March 2002.

From its inception, the CPS was criticised for a variety of alleged faults, principally that it was inefficient and had a low success rate in prosecutions. Many police officers expressed doubts about the rigour with which cases were handled by the CPS, and dubbed it the 'Criminal Prosecution Society'. The Bar Council passed a motion in 1993 condemning the service for being too ready to abandon cases 'fearing defeat or cost'.

The former Director of Public Prosecutions, Barbara Mills QC, who headed the CPS until April 1998, laid much of the responsibility for poor conviction rates at the door of the police. In one public statement, she blamed lack of proper preparation by the police for two-fifths of the 185,824 cases dropped in the magistrates' court in 1992–93. Another 8,046 were dropped at the Crown Court. Mrs Mills claimed that in a quarter of cases that had to be dropped, CPS lawyers had no option because witnesses were missing or refused to give evidence, or because the case was being considered elsewhere in the justice system so the 'double jeopardy' rule applied. Between 1994 and 1997, crime figures fell, but arrest rates remained static, reflecting what police claim was increasing success against offenders. However, the percentage of magistrate level cases discontinued by the CPS crept up. Again, the reasoning for dropping or downgrading cases was found wanting.

To answer criticism, the CPS commissioned an analysis of a sample 10,000 cases that it had to drop in 1992–93. The results show that 43% were abandoned on the ground of insufficient evidence to provide a realistic prospect of conviction. In 31% of cases, prosecutors abandoned them because it was 'not in the public interest' to proceed, for example, where the defendant had already been convicted and sentenced on another matter (9%) or only a nominal penalty was likely (6%). Much criticism of the CPS has come from police officers who object to the CPS continuing not to pursue cases for these very reasons.

A highly critical report published by a review body headed by Sir Iain Glidewell in June 1998 concluded that the CPS had failed to achieve the expected improvements in the prosecution system since it was set up in 1986 and had become bureaucratic and over-centralised. The report depicted a service where charges were thought to be 'inappropriately downgraded' and a disproportionately large number of serious violent crimes were not prosecuted. Proposals for a complete overhaul of the CPS were strongly backed by many in the criminal justice system ((1998) *The Times*, 2 June).

As a result of the Glidewell Report, the CPS underwent a major structural re-organisation in 1999. Its operation was decentralised so as to realign the CPS areas to match the boundaries of police forces – there were previously 13 CPS areas and now there are 42 to match the 43 police forces of England and Wales (there are two police forces for London, the Metropolitan Police and the City of London police). New Chief Crown Prosecutors (CCPs) for the 42 areas were appointed in 1999. As its case workload is so large, London has three CCPs. The new DPP, David Calvert-Smith QC, stated that:

> The new postholders will, in effect, be local DPPs with the power to act on their own initiative and to take their own decisions. They will be placing a priority on prosecution work which will benefit the local communities they serve [CPS, Official Statement, 109/99, 8 March 1999].

The CCPs will be accountable to their local communities, and the CPS contends that a localised service will enable good working relationships with the other agencies in the criminal justice system, including the police, the courts and the judiciary (CPS, Official Statement, 113/99, 12 April 1999).

In its 2001–2002 Annual Report, the CPS states that, in the year under review, it dealt with 1.36 million cases in the magistrates' courts and around 115,000 in the Crown Court. Of these, 53,506 cases in the magistrates' courts and 18,956 cases in the Crown Court were contested. The Report notes that in the magistrates' courts, the overall conviction rate was 98.3%, exactly the same as in 2000–01 and 1999–2000. The conviction rate in the Crown Court was 88.8% compared with 87.9% in 2000–01 and 88.6% in 1999–2000. These figures, though, represent cases which end up in court and they include guilty pleas. The number of discontinuances in both sorts of court is high. Discontinuances occur where witnesses fail to attend or attend and change their evidence. In 2001–02, there were 171,381 cases discontinued by the CPS in the magistrates' courts (13.1% compared with 13% in 2000–01 and 12.2% in 1999–2000), and 11,825 cases not proceeded with in the Crown Court (14% of all cases brought) compared with 10,145 in 2000–01. In 1997, only 7.7% of Crown Court cases were not proceeded with.

The CPS states that the continuing rise in the number of Crown Court cases which are not proceeded is due, in part, to the implementation of s 51 of the CDA 1998 (with effect from January 2001). As indictable-only cases are now sent directly to the Crown Court, it is no longer possible to test witnesses in advance at committal hearings.

The CPS Annual Report 1999 notes that, during the year under review, the CPS dealt with proportionally more serious crime, with indictable-only cases – the most serious – rising to 30% of the total Crown Court caseload.

The proportion of indictable-only offences in the Crown Court rose from 18.2% in 1991–92 to 26% in 1997–98 and 38.7% in 2001–02. The rise has been influenced by the plea before venue procedure for either way cases, which means that such cases are not unnecessarily committed to the Crown Court.

Pilot schemes aimed at reducing delays in criminal courts have led to more efficient and speedier justice, with more cases dealt with at the first hearing, cases which go to trial being heard more quickly and a reduction in bureaucracy.

The CPS shares key performance targets for the criminal justice system with the Home Office and Lord Chancellor's Department (LCD). These included halving the time from arrest to sentence for persistent young offenders from 142 to 71 days by 31 March 2002. By September 2001, the time had been reduced to 70 days (see CPS Annual Report 2001–02).

By October 2000, the average time to process such cases was calculated at 94 days, with Youth Court cases taking an average of 81 days and Crown Court cases an average of 230 days. However, averages can conceal some wide variations between individual courts, as a study in 2000 reveals. In an inspection conducted jointly by the Inspectorates of the Constabulary, the CPS and the Magistrates' Courts Service, the comparable figures were 93, 74 and 185 days. Yet the lowest for a Youth Court, for example, was 44 days and the highest 130 days.

10.1.1 The Code for Crown Prosecutors

This Code (The Code for Crown Prosecutors, CPS, revised 2001) is issued under s 10 of the POA 1985. It explains the principles used by the CPS in its work. It says that 'police officers should take account of the principles of the Code when they are deciding whether to charge a defendant with an offence'.

10.1.2 The discretion to prosecute

The police have a very significant discretion as to what to do when a crime has possibly been committed. They could turn a blind eye, caution the suspect or charge the suspect, in which case, they must decide for what. As is very cogently argued by McConville, Sanders and Leng in *The Case for the Prosecution* (1991), prosecution cases are constructed from the evidence and testimony of many people including lay witnesses, victims, the police, CPS lawyers and expert witnesses. Each of these parties is fallible and prone to perceive events in line with their own sorts of experience. The net result of this is that the prosecution case is normally nothing more than an approximation of 'the truth'. The most influential role is that of the police, as it is they who ultimately decide whether to charge anyone, if so, whom and for what. Once these discretions have been exercised, there is a relatively narrow band of data on which the CPS can work.

In 1951, the Attorney General, Lord Shawcross, noted that:

It has never been the rule in this country – I hope it never will be – that suspected criminal offences must automatically be the subject of prosecution [House of Commons Debates, vol 483, col 681, 29 January 1951].

This *dictum* has been almost universally accepted within the criminal justice system.

There is evidence, however, that the police do (for operational or social reasons) tend to focus their attention on particular types of conduct. Research, for example, by Andrew Sanders has shown a tendency for there to be a bias in favour of prosecuting working class offenders as opposed to middle class offenders. He compared the police response to offences with that of the Factory Inspectorate's response to violation of the Health and Safety laws, and found that the police were much more likely to initiate prosecutions against working class suspects than were the factory inspectors against businesses and business executives. For the police, there was an institutional bias in favour of prosecution reflected in the principle 'let the court decide', whereas with the Factory Inspectorate, prosecution was only a last resort after an attempt at negotiated compliance had failed. In 1980, there were 22,000 serious cases of tax evasion, but only one in 122 cases was prosecuted. By contrast, there were 107,000 social security frauds, of which one in four was prosecuted. Tax evasion resulted in a loss to the public purse 30 times larger than that caused by social security fraud, yet there was more State money spent on prosecuting people for social security fraud. (See Sanders, 'Class bias in prosecutions' (1985) 24 Howard J 176.) There is also evidence that the Environment Agency has a 'bottom heavy' enforcement policy, that is, it is more concerned to prosecute minor offenders than large companies. (See M Watson, 'Low fines for environmental offences? Blame the regulators not the courts' (2003) 167 Justice of the Peace 50.)

10.1.3 Police cautioning of offenders

Prior to changes introduced by the Crime and Disorder Act (CDA) 1998, cautioning of both adult and young offenders was a possible alternative to prosecution and was particularly encouraged in the case of the latter. Following implementation of the changes introduced by the 1998 Act, cautions are now available only for adult offenders, with a new system of reprimands and warnings applying to young offenders.

Cautioning of adults

The Home Office provided guidance on when to caution in 1990 and 1994 (see Home Office Circulars 1990/59 and 1994/18). A caution is not a conviction, but it remains on an offender's record for a minimum of five years and may be used at the sentencing stage if he is subsequently convicted of another offence.

A caution must be administered by an officer of the rank of inspector or above, and attendance at the police station is usually required. Three conditions must be met:

- There must be sufficient evidence to have justified a prosecution.
- The offender must admit guilt.
- The offender must agree to the procedure.

Cautioning may be particularly appropriate where an offender is old or infirm, mentally ill, suffering from severe physical illness, or suffering from severe emotional distress.

Reprimands and warnings for young offenders

Sections 65–66 of the CDA 1998 introduced a new scheme which includes police reprimands and warnings, accompanied by intervention to reduce the likelihood of re-offending. A first offence can result in a reprimand, final warning or criminal prosecution, depending on its seriousness. A further offence following a reprimand will lead to a warning or a charge. A further offence after a warning will normally lead to a charge, a second warning only being possible in limited circumstances where the latest offence is not serious and more than two years have elapsed since the first warning was given. Reprimands and warnings will be issued at a police station and a police officer may only issue them either where:

- there is sufficient evidence for prosecution;
- guilt is admitted;
- there are no previous convictions; or
- prosecution is not in the public interest.

After a warning has been issued, the young offender will be referred to a youth offending team (as established by s 39 of the CDA 1998), which will assess the offender to determine whether a rehabilitation programme to prevent re-offending is appropriate, and to provide one where it is. Conditional discharge of a young offender who commits an offence within two years of receiving a warning is not possible unless there are exceptional circumstances relating to the offence or the offender. Any reprimand, warning or recorded non-compliance with a rehabilitation programme may be cited in court in the same way as previous convictions.

10.1.4 CPS guidelines

The Code for Crown Prosecutors (promulgated on behalf of the DPP) sets out the official criteria governing the discretion to prosecute.

The revised Code issued in 2001 requires two tests to be satisfied before a prosecution is brought: there must be a 'realistic prospect of conviction' (the evidential test); and the prosecution must be 'in the public interest'.

The evidential test requires prosecutors to predict what a jury or bench, properly directed, would be likely to decide. The guidelines require prosecutors to assess the reliability of evidence, not just its admissibility, hence the questions (para 5.3b): 'Is there evidence which might support or detract from the reliability of a confession? Is the reliability affected by factors such as the defendant's age, intelligence or level of understanding?'

As Glanville Williams ([1985] Crim LR 115)) and Andrew Sanders ((1994) 144 NLJ 946) have argued, this test favours people who are well respected in society – like police officers and businessmen – in whose favour juries and magistrates might be biased. It disfavours the sort of victims who are unlikely to make good witnesses. Sanders proposes a better test: whether, on the evidence, a jury or bench ought (on the balance of probabilities) to convict.

The public interest must be considered in each case where there is enough evidence to provide a realistic prospect of conviction. In cases of any seriousness, a prosecution will usually take place unless there are public interest factors tending against prosecution which clearly outweigh those tending in favour.

The Code lists some 'public interest factors in favour of prosecution' (para 6.4) and some against (para 6.5). The former include cases where:

- a conviction is likely to result in a significant sentence;
- a weapon was used or violence was threatened during the commission of the offence;
- the offence was committed against a person serving the public, like a police officer or a nurse;
- the offence, although not serious in itself, is widespread in the area where it was committed;
- there is evidence that the offence was carried out by a group;
- the offence was motivated by any form of discrimination against the victim's ethnic or national origin, sex, religious beliefs, political views or sexual orientation; or the suspect demonstrated hostility towards the victim based on any of those characteristics.

A prosecution is less likely to proceed, we are told, where:

- the court is likely to impose a very small or nominal penalty;
- the offence was committed as a result of a genuine mistake or misunderstanding (judged against the seriousness of the offence);
- the loss or harm can be described as minor and was the result of a single incident, particularly if it was caused by a misjudgment;

- a prosecution is likely to have a very bad effect on the victim's physical or mental health, always bearing in mind the seriousness of the offence;
- details could be made public that could harm sources of information, international relations or national security.

Crown prosecutors must balance factors for and against prosecution carefully and fairly. Deciding on the public interest is, the Code says (para 6.6), 'not simply a matter of adding up the number of factors on each side'.

Barbara Mills has stated that the Attorney General has commended the Code to other prosecutors. This may help to correct inconsistent approaches between the police and CPS on the one hand and, on the other, prosecutors like the Inland Revenue and Health and Safety Executive. As Sanders (see above) has observed, if you illegally gain a fortune or maim someone, you will probably be treated more leniently than ordinary disposals for such offences if the crimes are, technically, tax evasion and operating an unsafe place of work. (See also D Bergman, 'Boardroom GBH' (1999) 149 NLJ 1656.)

10.1.5 CPS independence from the police

The CPS is institutionally separate from the police. The police are no longer in a client-lawyer relationship with the prosecutor, able to give instructions about how to proceed. The police are still, however, in the most influential position as it is only once they have taken the decision to charge a suspect that the CPS will be called on to look at the case. The CPS in practice exercises no supervisory role over the police investigation of cases; it simply acts on the file presented after the investigation by the police. The power of the CPS to discontinue prosecutions (under s 23 of the POA 1985), or the continuing power to withdraw or offer no evidence, is an important feature of its independence. An argument that 'The system is dominated throughout its stages by the interests and values of the police, with the CPS playing an essentially subordinate and reactive role' is put by McConville in *The Case for the Prosecution* (1991).

The Report of the Runciman Royal Commission on Criminal Justice (1993) recommended that the CPS should play a greater role in the investigative process. It stated (para 93):

> The police should seek the advice of the CPS at the investigation stage in appropriate cases in accordance with guidelines to be agreed between the two services.

The Report also stated (para 95):

> Where a chief officer of police is reluctant to comply with a request from the CPS to investigate further before a decision on discontinuance is taken, HM Chief Inspector of Constabulary in conjunction with the Director of Public Prosecutions should bring about a resolution of the dispute.

Oddly, however, the rationale underlying the establishment of the CPS (independence from the police) appears to have been undermined since 1998, when many police stations have had CPS liaison officers working in the stations themselves.

Further evidence of encouragement of the relationship between the CPS and the police appears in the response to recommendations made by the Glidewell Committee in 1998. The Committee recommended that the CPS should take responsibility for the prosecution process immediately following charge. There should be a single integrated unit to assemble and manage case files, combining the current police Administrative Support Units and those parts of the CPS branch which deal with file preparation and review. The Committee proposed as a model a 'Criminal Justice Unit' in the charge of a CPS lawyer with mainly CPS staff, although many of these might be the civilian police staff currently employed in Administrative Support Units. The Committee suggested that such a unit would need to be able to call on the police to take action in obtaining more evidence and so a senior police officer would need to be part of the unit, which would be housed in or near the relevant police station. The unit would deal with fast track cases in their entirety and with simple summary cases, that is, with both the file preparation and the necessary advocacy. The CPS should primarily be responsible, in the magistrates' courts, for the timely disposal of all cases prosecuted by its lawyers, and share with the court one or more performance indicators related to timeliness. The Committee recommended the formation of Trial Units to deal with advocacy in some trials in the magistrates' courts and the management and preparation of all cases in the Crown Court, the hope being to lead to a shift in the centre of gravity of the CPS towards the Crown Court.

These recommendations were put into effect in six pilot areas and a report by the Glidewell Working Group in February 2001 found that, following a study carried out in September and October 2000, they: eliminated unnecessary work through improved communications; speeded up notification of proposed discontinuance; improved notification of case results to victims and witnesses; freed up staff to take on additional functions; and established a single contact point for the public on the prosecution of magistrates' court cases.

The following letter to *The Times* (6 August 1999) raises several noteworthy points on the other side of the argument:

From His Honour Judge Barrington Black

Sir, You report (3 August) that staff from the Crown Prosecution Service are to work with police officers in police stations to speed justice, and save £20 million a year.

Twenty years, and many millions of pounds ago, prior to the creation of the CPS, in the city where I practised, and throughout the country, the county prosecutor and his staff occupied an office above police headquarters.

They were available for consultations with police officers at any time, and they knew about the details of a case as it progressed. The police officer was responsible for the main papers and ensuing witness attendance. Defence solicitors also had direct contact with someone who could make decisions.

The words 'plea bargaining' are now forbidden but, in those days, a calculated assessment of the evidence and an indictment appropriate to that evidence were often determined to the benefit of the victim, the defendant, the public purse and justice.

I am delighted to hear that a system which was tried, tested and worked is to be revived.

Yours truly,

BARRINGTON BLACK

Harrow Crown Court

There may, however, be serious problems in developing too cosy a relationship between the police and the prosecuting authorities, as sometimes the former have to come under the professional consideration of the latter. In August 1999, the CPS came under severe criticism in an official report into decisions not to prosecute police officers in circumstances where people had died in police custody. The report, *Inquiry into Crown Prosecution Service Decision Making in Relation to Deaths in Custody and Related Matters,* by His Honour Judge Gerald Butler QC (HMSO) states that the way the CPS responded to such cases was 'inefficient and fundamentally unsound'. It led to a 'thoroughly unsatisfactory situation' which needed to be urgently rectified. Following the criticisms in the Butler Report and further analysis by the CPS Inspectorate, the relevant decision making processes were revised.

10.1.6 Judicial control of prosecution policy

There is a very limited way in which the courts can control the exercise of prosecutorial discretion by the police. Lord Denning MR gave the example in one case of a Chief Constable issuing a directive to his men that no person should be prosecuted for stealing goods worth less than £100 (over £1,000 in 1993 prices), and said 'I should have thought the court could countermand it. He would be failing in his duty to enforce the law'. More generally, the courts had no control (*per* Lord Denning MR, *R v Metropolitan Police Commissioner ex p Blackburn* (1968)):

> For instance, it is for the Commissioner of Police of the Metropolis, or the Chief Constable, as the case may be, to decide in any particular case whether inquiries should be pursued, or whether an arrest should be made or a prosecution brought. It must be for him to decide on the disposition of his force and the concentration of his resources on any particular crime or area. No court can or should give him directions on such a matter.

Apart from this, there is the doctrine of constabulary independence (see *Fisher v Oldham Corp* (1930)), which regards the constable as an independent office-holder under the Crown who cannot be instructed by organisational superiors or by governmental agency about how to exercise his powers. The constable is accountable only to law.

An interesting instance of the courts being used to attack a use of police discretion is *R v Coxhead* (1986). The appellant was a police sergeant in charge of a police station. A young man was brought into the station to be breathalysed and the sergeant recognised him as the son of a police inspector at that station. The sergeant knew the inspector to be suffering from a bad heart condition. In order not to exacerbate this condition, the sergeant did not administer the test and allowed the motorist to go free. The sergeant was prosecuted and convicted for conduct tending and intended to pervert the course of justice. The sergeant's defence was that his decision came within the legitimate scope of discretion exercised by a police officer. The trial judge said the matter should be left for the jury to determine; they must decide the extent of any police discretion in accordance with the facts. The jury convicted the sergeant and this was upheld by the Court of Appeal. In minor cases, the police had a very wide discretion whether to prosecute, but in major cases they had no discretion or virtually none. Thus, in a serious case like drink driving, there was no discretion which the sergeant could have been exercising legitimately. It is odd, however, that this is left for the jury to decide after the event rather than being subject to clear rules.

10.1.7 State prosecutors in the Crown Courts

Reference has already been made to the fact that Crown prosecutors are now able to appear in the higher courts if they are suitably qualified. This has caused a great deal of concern in some quarters. The basis of the worry is that, as full time salaried lawyers working for an organisation, CPS lawyers will sometimes be tempted to get convictions using dubious tactics or ethics because their own status as employees and prospects of promotion will depend on conviction success rates. Where, as now, barristers from the independent Bar are used by the CPS to prosecute, there is (it is argued) a greater likelihood of the courtroom lawyer dropping a morally unsustainable case.

Section 42 of the Access to Justice Act 1999 tries to overcome the possible difficulties with a provision (amending s 27 of the Courts and Legal Services Act (CLSA) 1990) that every advocate 'has a duty to the court to act with independence in the interests of justice', in other words, a duty which overrides any inconsistent duty, for example, one to an employer. Professor Michael Zander QC has contended, however, that these are 'mere words'. He has said (letter to *The Times*, 29 December 1998) that they are unlikely to exercise much sway over CPS lawyer employees concerned with performance targets set by their line managers, and that:

> The CPS as an organisation is constantly under pressure in regard to the proportion of discontinuances, acquittal and conviction rates. These are factors in the day-to-day work of any CPS lawyer. It is disingenuous to imagine they will not have a powerful effect on decision making.

The Bar is also very wary of this change, an editorial in Counsel (the journal of the Bar of England and Wales) saying:

> ... we are gravely concerned about the extent to which prosecutions will be done in-house by the CPS when the need for independent prosecutors is so well established in our democracy [(1999) Counsel 3, February].

It is important to set the arguments in a wider context. What are the social, economic or political debates surrounding this issue of how best to run a system of courtroom prosecutors? The change to having Crown Court prosecutions carried out by salaried CPS lawyers will be more efficient (as the whole prosecution can be handled in-house without engaging the external service of an independent barrister), and will, ultimately, cost the State less than is currently spent on prosecutions. Some will argue that justice is being sacrificed to the deity of cost cutting. On the other hand, it could be argued that justice and efficiency are not mutually exclusive phenomena.

10.2 Bail

Bail is the release from custody, pending a criminal trial, of an accused on the promise that money will be paid if he absconds. All decisions on whether to grant bail therefore involve delicate questions of balancing interests. A person is presumed innocent of a criminal charge unless he is proved guilty of it; this implies that no one should ever be detained unless he has been found guilty. For several reasons, however, it can be regarded as undesirable to allow some accused people to go back to society before the case against them is tried in a criminal court. Indeed, about 12% of offenders who are bailed to appear in court fail to appear for their trials (P Wintour, 'Threat of jail to cut court delays' (2002) *The Guardian*, 5 October).

To refuse bail to an accused might involve depriving someone of liberty who is subsequently found not guilty or convicted but given a non-custodial sentence. Such a person will probably have been kept in a police cell or in a prison cell for 23 hours a day. Unlike the jurisdictions in the Netherlands,

Germany and France, no compensation is payable in these circumstances. On the other hand, to allow liberty to the accused pending trial might be to allow him to abscond, commit further offences, interfere with witnesses and obstruct the course of justice. The difficulties involved in finding the proper balance have been highlighted by several cases of serious assault and rape being committed by persons who were on bail, and by the fleeing of Asil Nadir to Northern Cyprus in May 1993. Mr Nadir skipped his £3.5 million bail to travel to a jurisdiction which would not extradite him to England. He claimed that he would not be given a fair trial for the offences of theft and false accounting with which he was charged, and went on the public record as saying that his sureties would not suffer hardship as he would repay those who had put up bail for him.

The basic way in which the law currently seeks to find the right balance in such matters is by operating a general presumption in favour of bail, a presumption which can be overturned if one or more of a number of indices of suspicion exist in respect of a particular defendant. Even where bail is granted, it may be subject to certain conditions to promote public safety and the interests of justice.

10.2.1 The Criminal Justice and Public Order Act 1994

Over recent years, the government took the view that bail was too easily granted and that too many crimes were being committed by those on bail who deserved to be in custody while awaiting trial. The Bail (Amendment) Act 1993 and the Criminal Justice and Public Order Act (CJPOA) 1994 (ss 25–30) emanate from that philosophy, their aim being to restrict the granting of bail. A case which caught public sympathy for this view involved a young man who had many convictions for car crime and joyriding. Whilst on bail, he was joyriding in a vehicle when he smashed into a schoolgirl. She clung to the bonnet but he shook her off and thus killed her. The Home Secretary commented publicly that the new legislative measures would prevent such terrible events.

Each year (prior to the Acts), about 50,000 offences were committed by people on bail. A study by the Metropolitan Police in 1988 indicated that 16% of those charged by that force were already on bail for another offence. Another study in 1993, from the same force, showed that, of 537 suspects arrested in one week during a clampdown on burglary, 40% were on bail. Some had been bailed 10 or 15 times during the preceding year. (Figures from Robert Maclennan MP, HC Committee, col 295, 1994.) A recent survey revealed that males in prison for motor vehicle theft who had previous experience of bail claimed on average to have committed a similar offence *each month* while on bail (*Justice for All*, Cm 5563, 2002, The Stationery Office).

In the criminal process, the first stage at which bail is raised as an issue is at the police station. If a person is arrested on a warrant, this will indicate whether he is to be held in custody or released on bail. If the suspect is arrested without a warrant, then the police will have to decide whether to release the suspect after he has been charged. After a person has been charged, s 38(1)(a) of the Police and Criminal Evidence Act (PACE) 1984 states that a person must be released unless: (a) his name and address are not known; or (b) the custody officer reasonably thinks that his detention is necessary for his own protection; or (c) to prevent him from injuring someone or damaging property or because he might abscond or interfere with the course of justice. Most arrested people are bailed by the police. In 1990, 83% of those arrested in connection with indictable offences and 88% of those arrested for summary offences (other than motoring offences) were released. This area has been amended by s 28 of the CJPOA 1994. A custody officer can now, in the case of an imprisonable offence, refuse to release an arrested person after charge if the officer has reasonable grounds for believing that the detention of that person is necessary to prevent him from committing any offence. Previously, many cases were caught by (b) (above), but some likely conduct, for example, drink driving, was not.

Section 27 of the CJPOA 1994 amends PACE 1984 (ss 38, 47) so as to allow the police to grant conditional bail to persons charged. The conditions can be whatever is required to ensure that the person surrenders to custody, does not commit an offence while on bail, or does not interfere with witnesses or otherwise obstruct the course of justice. The new powers of the custody officer, however, do not include a power to impose a requirement to reside in a bail hostel. By amending Part IV of PACE 1984, s 29 of the CJPOA 1994 gives the police power to arrest without warrant a person who, having been granted conditional police bail, has failed to attend at a police station at the appointed time.

The Bail Act (BA) 1976 created a statutory presumption of bail. It states (s 4) that, subject to Sched 1, bail shall be granted to a person accused of an offence and brought before a magistrates' court or a Crown Court and to people convicted of an offence who are being remanded for reports to be made. The court must therefore grant bail (unless one of the exceptions applies) even if the defendant does not make an application. Schedule 1 provides that a court need not grant bail to a person charged with an offence punishable with imprisonment if it is satisfied that there are substantial grounds for believing that, if released on bail, the defendant would:

- fail to surrender to custody;
- commit an offence while on bail; or
- interfere with witnesses or otherwise obstruct the course of justice.

The court can also refuse bail if it believes that the defendant ought to stay in custody for his own protection, or if it has not been practicable, for want of time, to obtain sufficient information to enable the court to make its decision on bail, or he has previously failed to answer to bail (Sched 1, Part I, paras 2–6).

When the court is considering the grounds stated above, all relevant factors must be taken into account, including the nature and seriousness of the offence, the character, antecedents, associations and community ties of the defendant, and his record for satisfying his obligations under previous grants of bail.

If the defendant is charged with an offence not punishable with imprisonment, Sched 1 provides that bail may only be withheld if he has previously failed to surrender on bail and if the court believes that, in view of that failure, he will fail again to surrender if released on bail.

Section 25 of the CJPOA 1994 provided that in some circumstances, a person who had been charged with or convicted of murder, attempted murder, manslaughter, rape or attempted rape must not be granted bail. The circumstances were simply that the conviction must have been within the UK, and that, in the case of a manslaughter conviction, it must have been dealt with by way of a custodial sentence. The word 'conviction' is given a wide meaning and includes anyone found 'not guilty by way of insanity'.

There was debate about whether the changes wrought by s 25 were justifiable. A Home Office Minister, defending the section, stated that it would be worth the risk if it prevented just one murder or rape, even though there might be a few 'hard cases', that is, people eventually acquitted of crime, who were remanded in custody pending trial. (David Maclean MP, Minister of State, Home Office, HC Committee, col 282, 1994.) As Card and Ward remarked in a commentary on the CJPOA 1994, the government when pushed was unable to cite a single case where a person released on bail in the circumstances covered by s 25 re-offended in a similar way. There is no time limit on the previous conviction and there is no requirement of any connection between the previous offence and the one in question. Card and Ward suggest that there is a world of difference between a person who was convicted of manslaughter 30 years ago on the grounds of complicity in a suicide pact and who is now charged with attempted rape (of which he must be presumed innocent), and the person who was convicted of rape eight years ago and now faces another rape charge. The first person is not an obvious risk to society and it is, they argue, regrettable that bail will be denied to him. There is also argument to be had with the contents of the s 25 list. Why should some clearly dangerous and prevalent crimes like robbery be omitted from it? In any case, it might have been better had the offences in the list raised a strong presumption against bail as opposed to an absolute ban, as the former could be rebutted in cases where there was, on the facts, no risk.

A further significant difficulty with this approach was that it appeared to be incompatible with the requirements of Art 5(3) of the European Convention on Human Rights (ECHR), decisions of the court on which make it clear that the decision to remand a defendant in custody before trial must be a decision of the court based on the merits after a review of the facts. By precluding bail in the specified circumstances, s 25 denied the court the opportunity to take a decision based on the merits. Thus, in *CC v UK* (1999) (subsequently confirmed by the European Court of Human Rights (ECtHR) in *Caballero v UK* (2000)), the European Court found that s 25 violated rights under Art 5(3) where the claimant had been denied bail on a rape charge in 1996 because of a conviction for manslaughter in 1987.

Anticipating this decision, s 25 was amended by the CDA 1998 to provide that bail should only be granted in homicide and rape cases if the court is 'satisfied that there are exceptional circumstances which justify it'. However, doubts have been expressed by the Law Commission and others about whether this change achieves compliance with obligations under the ECHR (all the more important now that the Human Rights Act (HRA) 1998 is fully in force). The argument is that the presumption required by the ECHR is innocence and therefore that the defendant should be released, whilst that required by the amended s 25 is that the defendant should not be released.

When the Criminal Justice Bill is enacted, it will attempt to establish a presumption against bail where a defendant is charged with an imprisonable offence *and* tests positive for Class A drugs *and* refuses treatment. Although such a presumption might enjoy considerable public support, it may be difficult to reconcile it with Art 5 of the ECHR. 'One happy consequence will be yet more Class A drug addicts in prison, not receiving treatment' (F Fitzgibbon, 'Trial and error?' (2003) 147 SJ 8).

Bail can be granted as conditional or unconditional. Where it is unconditional, the accused must simply surrender to the court at the appointed date. Failure to appear without reasonable cause is an offence under the BA 1976 (s 6) and can result, if tried in a Crown Court, in a sentence of up to 12 months' imprisonment or a fine. Conditions can be attached to the granting of bail where the court thinks that it is necessary to ensure that the accused surrenders at the right time and does not interfere with witnesses or commit further offences. There is no statutory limit to the conditions the court may impose, and the most common include requirements that the accused reports daily or weekly to a police station, resides at a particular address, surrenders his passport or does not go to particular places or associate with particular people.

Section 7 of the BA 1976 gives the police power to arrest anyone on conditional bail whom they reasonably suspect is likely to break the conditions or has already done so. Anyone arrested in these circumstances must be brought before a magistrate within 24 hours. The magistrate may then reconsider the question of bail.

Personal recognisances, by which the suspect agreed to pay a sum if he failed to surrender to the court, were abolished by the BA 1976 (s 3(2)) except in cases where it is believed that he might try to flee abroad. The Act did retain the court's right to ask for sureties as a condition of bail. By putting sureties in a position where they can have large sums of money 'estreated' if the suspect does not surrender to the court, significant pressure (not using the resources of the criminal justice system) is put on the accused. The proportion of those who do not answer to bail is very small – consistently about 4% of those given bail. Section 9 of the BA 1976 strengthens the surety principle by making it a criminal offence to agree to indemnify a surety. This sort of thing could happen, for example, if the accused agreed to reimburse the surety in the event that the accused skipped bail and the surety was requested to pay.

The CDA 1998 makes further changes to the law relating to bail. Section 54, which amended ss 3 and 3A of the BA 1976, provides for increased powers to require security or impose conditions (by taking away the requirement that the defendant must appear unlikely to remain in Great Britain). The amendment also allows courts to be able to require defendants to attend interviews with a legal representative as a condition of bail.

10.2.2 Appeals and re-applications

The rules which govern how someone who has been refused bail might re-apply and appeal have also been framed with a view to balancing the interests of the accused with those of the public and justice. The original refusal should not be absolute and final but, on the other hand, it is seen as necessary that the refusals are not reversed too easily.

If the court decides not to grant the defendant bail, then Sched 1, Part IIA (inserted by s 154 of the Criminal Justice Act (CJA) 1988) provides that it is the court's duty to consider whether the defendant ought to be granted bail at each subsequent hearing. At the first hearing after the one at which bail was first refused, he may support an application for bail with any arguments, but at subsequent hearings, the court need not hear arguments as to fact or law which it has heard before. The CJA 1988 enables a court to remand an accused, in his absence, for up to three successive one week remand hearings provided that he consents and is legally represented. Such repeated visits are costly to the State and can be unsettling for the accused, especially if he has to spend most of the day in a police cell only to be told the case has been adjourned again without bail. If someone does not consent, they are prevented from applying for bail on each successive visit if the only supporting arguments are those that have been heard by the court before (*R v Nottingham JJ ex p Davies* (1980)).

To avoid unproductive hearings, that is, to promote courts being able to adjourn a case for a period within which reasonable progress can be made on it, s 155 of the CJA 1988 allows for adjournments for up to 28 days provided the court sets the date for when the next stage of the proceedings should take place. What began as an experiment under this section has now by statutory order (SI 1991/2667) been extended to all courts.

The interests of the accused are also served by the variety of appeals he may make if bail has been refused. If bail has been refused by magistrates then, in limited circumstances, an application may be made to another bench of magistrates. Applications for reconsideration can also be made to a judge in chambers (through a legal representative) or to the Official Solicitor (in writing). Appeal can also be made to a Crown Court in respect of bail for both pre-committal remands and where a defendant has been committed for trial or sentence at the Crown Court.

Section 3 of the BA 1976 allows for an application to vary the conditions of court bail to be made by the person bailed, the prosecutor or a police officer. Application may also be made for the imposition of conditions on unconditional court bail. As amended by the CJPOA 1994, s 3 of the BA 1976 now allows for the same thing in relation to police bail, although the new provisions do not allow the prosecutor to seek reconsideration of the decision to grant bail itself. Under the Bail (Amendment) Act 1993, however, the prosecution does now have a right to appeal against the grant of bail by a court. This right applies to offences which carry a maximum sentence of imprisonment of five years or more, and to offences of taking a vehicle without consent (joyriding). When this right of appeal is exercised, the defendant will remain in custody until the appeal is heard by a Crown Court judge who will decide whether to grant bail or remand the defendant in custody within 48 hours of the magistrate's decision. Parliament was concerned that this power could be abused and has stated that it should be reserved 'for cases of greatest concern, when there is a serious risk of harm to the public' or where there are 'other significant public interest grounds' for an appeal. When the Criminal Justice Bill is enacted, the prosecution will probably gain the right to appeal against grants of bail relating to all imprisonable offences.

Section 67(1) of the CJA 1967 states that time spent in custody pre-trial or pre-sentence can generally be deducted from the ultimate sentence (if the relevant provisions of ss 87 and 88 of the Powers of Criminal Courts (Sentencing) Act 2000 are brought into force, s 67 will be repealed). No compensation, however, is paid to people who have been remanded in custody but are subsequently found not guilty. Several European countries, like France and Germany, will sometimes offer compensation in similar circumstances.

Although this area of law was subject to a comprehensive revision after a Home Office special working party reported in 1974, and has been legislatively debated and modified twice since the BA 1976, it is still a matter of serious concern both to those civil libertarians, who consider the law too tilted against the accused, and to the police and commentators, who believe it too lenient in many respects. This criticism of the law from both sides to the debate might indicate a desirable state of balance reached by the current regulatory framework:

- *Opposition to the current arrangements – civil libertarian perspective*

  It is a cause for concern that, in the 1990s, of those dealt with summarily after being remanded in custody, about 50% received non-custodial sentences and a further 25% were acquitted.

  There are wide variations in the local policies of different courts; one study has shown, for instance, that the number of indictable custodial remands per 1,000 indictable proceedings was 111 in Brighton as against 313 in Bournemouth (B Gibson, 'Why Bournemouth?' (1987) 151 JP 520, 15 August).

  The last decade has seen a disturbing rise in the remand prison population. In 1980, it accounted for 15% of the average prison population. By 1990, it had risen to over 10,000 prisoners, 22% of the average prison population.

- *Opposition to the current arrangements – a police/public perspective*

  There are arguments which point to the numbers of people who commit offences whilst out on bail. A study conducted in Bristol, for example, showed that over one-third of all defendants charged with burglary were on bail for another offence at the time of their arrest. Following some dreadful cases of serious offences being committed whilst the perpetrator was on bail, s 153 of the CJA 1988 required magistrates to give reasons if they decided to grant bail against police objections in cases of murder, manslaughter or rape.

  The percentage of people who skip bail is too high, especially for the more minor offences. Note: the annual figure, however, of those who do not answer to bail is consistently under 4%.

Positive developments in recent years have been the use of Bail Information Schemes (BIS) for courts (about 100 courts now operate such schemes) and government concern to increase the number of bail hostels. The BIS resulted from pilot schemes organised by the Vera Institute of Justice of New York. They give courts verified information from the probation service about defendants' accommodation or community ties. The evidence suggests that the courts using such schemes make greater use of bail than those which do not have the schemes.

10.3 Plea bargaining

'Plea bargaining' has been defined as 'the practice whereby the accused enters a plea of guilty in return for which he will be given some consideration that results in a sentence concession' (Baldwin and McConville, *Negotiated Justice: Pressures on Defendants to Plead Guilty* (1977)). In practice, this can refer to:

- a situation either where there has been a plea arrangement for the accused to plead guilty to a lesser charge than the one with which he is charged (for example, charged with murder, agrees to plead guilty to manslaughter). This is sometimes called 'charge bargaining'; or

- where there is simply a sentencing discount available on a plea of guilty by the accused. This is sometimes called a 'sentence bargain'.

10.3.1 *R v Turner* (1970)

A plea of guilty by the accused must be made freely. The accused must only be advised to plead guilty if he has committed the crime in question. In *R v Turner* (1970), Lord Parker CJ set out guidelines on plea bargaining. He stated that:

(1) it may sometimes be the duty of counsel to give strong advice to the accused that a plea of guilty with remorse is a mitigating factor which might enable the court to give a lesser sentence (displays of remorse following a not guilty plea tend to be unconvincing);

(2) the accused must ultimately make up his or her own mind as to how to plead;

(3) there should be open access to the trial judge and counsel for both sides should attend each meeting, preferably in open court; and

(4) the judge should never indicate the sentence which he is minded to impose, nor should he ever indicate that on a plea of guilty he would impose one sentence, but that on a conviction following a plea of not guilty he would impose a severer sentence.

The judge could say what sentence he would impose on a plea of guilty (where, for example, he has read the depositions and antecedents) but without mentioning what he would do if the accused were convicted after pleading not guilty. Even this would be wrong, however, as the accused might take the judge to be intimating that a severer sentence would follow upon conviction after a guilty plea. The only exception to this rule is where a judge says that the sentence will take a particular form, following conviction, whether there has been a plea of guilty or not guilty.

10.3.2 Court of Appeal *Practice Direction*

These guidelines were subsequently embodied in a Court of Appeal *Practice Direction* [1976] Crim LR 561, which are now included in *Practice Direction*

(Criminal: Consolidated) [2002] 1 WLR 2870, para 45. A number of difficulties have been experienced in applying these principles. Perhaps the greatest problem has resulted from the fact that, although the principles state (No 45.4) that a judge should never say that a sentence passed after a conviction would be more severe than one passed after a guilty plea, it is a generally known rule that guilty pleas lead to lesser sentences. In *R v Cain* (1976), it was stressed that, in general, defendants should realise that guilty pleas attract lesser sentences. Lord Widgery said, 'Any accused person who does not know about it should know about it'. The difficulty is that the trial judge must not mention it, otherwise he could be construed as exerting pressure on the accused to plead guilty.

In *R v Turner*, the defendant pleaded not guilty on a charge of theft. He had previous convictions and during an adjournment he was advised by counsel in strong terms to change his plea. After having spoken with the judge, whom the defendant knew, counsel advised that in his opinion a plea of guilty would result in a non-custodial sentence, whereas if he persisted with a not guilty plea and thereby attacked police witnesses, there was a real possibility of receiving a custodial sentence. The defendant changed his plea to guilty and then appealed on the ground that he did not have a free choice in changing his plea. His appeal was allowed on the basis that he might have formed the impression that the views being expressed to him by his counsel were those of the judge, particularly as it was known by the accused that counsel had just returned from seeing the judge when he gave his advice to the accused.

The advantages for the prosecution in gaining a guilty plea are obvious, but justice demands that the court should be able to pass a proper sentence consistent with the gravity of the accused's actions, and if a plea is accepted, then the defendant can only be sentenced on the basis of the crime that he has admitted. It is noteworthy that the judge is not bound to accept a plea arrangement made between the sides. The Farquharson Committee on the Role of Prosecuting Counsel thought that there is a general right for the prosecution to offer no evidence in respect of any particular charge, but that where the judge's opinion is sought on whether it is desirable to reassure the public at large that the right course is being taken, counsel must abide by the judge's decision. Where the judge thinks that counsel's view to proceed is wrong, the trial can be halted until the DPP has been consulted and given the judge's comments. In the notorious case of *R v Sutcliffe* (1981), the 'Yorkshire Ripper' case, the prosecution and defence had agreed that Sutcliffe would plead guilty to manslaughter on the grounds of diminished responsibility, but the trial judge rejected that agreement and, after consultations with the DPP, Sutcliffe was eventually found guilty of murder.

10.3.3 *R v Pitman* **(1991)**

The extent of the difficulties in framing rules on plea bargaining which achieve clarity and fairness can be judged by the remark of Lord Lane CJ in the case of *R v Pitman* (1991):

> There seems to be a steady flow of appeals to this court arising from visits by counsel to the judge in his private room. No amount of criticism and no amount of warnings and no amount of exhortation seems to be able to prevent this from happening.

In this case, on counsel's advice, the appellant pleaded not guilty to causing death by reckless driving. On Cup Final day in 1989, he had driven, having been drinking all afternoon, in a car without a rear view mirror. He had crashed into another car, killing one of its passengers, whilst having double the permitted level of alcohol in his blood.

During the trial, the judge called both counsel to his room and stated that he did not think there was a defence to the charge. Counsel for the appellant explained that although the appellant had admitted that his carelessness caused the accident, the advice to plead not guilty was based on the fact that the prosecution might not be able to prove the necessary recklessness. The trial judge replied that the appellant's plea was a matter for the appellant himself and not counsel, and that if the appellant accepted responsibility for the accident, he ought to plead guilty and if he did so, he would receive 'substantial credit' when it came to sentencing.

Counsel for the appellant then discussed this with the appellant who changed his plea to guilty and was sentenced to nine months' imprisonment and disqualified from driving for four years. His appeal was allowed as the judge had put undue pressure on the appellant and his counsel to change his plea to guilty, as the remarks suggested that his chances of acquittal were slight if he pleaded not guilty and that if he was found guilty, he would certainly be sentenced to imprisonment. Lord Lane CJ emphasised that a judge should not initiate discussions in private and that where, at the behest of counsel, they are absolutely necessary, they should be recorded by shorthand or on a recording device.

Another problem here concerns framing the guidelines so that they are sufficiently permissive to allow counsel access to the judge in his private room in deserving instances, but avoiding the problems of confidentiality. As Mustill LJ said in *R v Harper-Taylor and Barker* (1988): 'The need to solve an immediate practical problem may combine with the more relaxed atmosphere of the private room to blur the formal outlines of the trial.' There is a risk that counsel and solicitors may hear something said to the judge which they would rather not hear, putting them into a state of conflict between their duties to their clients and their obligations to maintain the confidentiality of the private room. Reviewing the current state of the law, Curran has written that the effect of cases like *R v Bird* (1977) and *R v Agar* (1990) (the latter not a plea bargaining case but one which hinged on a judge's ruling in his private room as complied with by counsel to the appellant's detriment) is that defence counsel has a duty to disclose to his client any observations made by the judge in his room which significantly affect the client's case, whether or not the judge expresses them to be made confidentially.

The difficulties in this area of law stem largely not from deficient rules, but rather from the wish that the rules should achieve diverse aims. As Zander has observed, the fundamental problem is that the Court of Appeal wants to have it both ways: 'On the one hand, it wants defendants to appreciate that, if they plead guilty, they will receive a lesser sentence. On the other hand, it does not want judges to provide defendants with solid information as to how great the discount will be.'

10.3.4 Royal Commission recommendations

A more open system of plea bargaining was advocated by the Runciman Royal Commission on Criminal Justice (para 156). The Report argued that this would do much to alleviate the problem of 'cracked trials' in which defendants do not plead guilty until the last moment, wasting the time of witnesses, the police, the CPS and the court. In a system where the vast majority of cases in the Crown Court and magistrates' courts result in guilty pleas (79% and 81.5%, respectively), the operation of the plea bargain becomes very important.

The Commission research indicated that 'cracked trials' accounted for more than one-quarter of all cases. The Commission also noted that sentence discounts of between 25% and 30% for guilty pleas have been long established practice in the Crown Court. The Commission suggested that higher discounts should be available for those who plead guilty earlier in the process. The Report stated:

> The most common reason for defendants delaying a plea of guilty until the last minute is a reluctance to face the facts until they are at the door of the court. It is often said too that a defendant has a considerable incentive to behave in this way. The longer the delay, the more the likelihood of witnesses becoming intimidated or forgetting to turn up or disappearing.

It recommended (para 157):

> At the request of defence counsel on instructions from the defendant, judges should be able to indicate the highest sentence that they would impose at that point on the basis of the facts as put to them.

On the issue of charges, it recommended (para 161):

> Discussions on the level of charge (charge bargaining) should take place as early as possible in order to minimise the need for cases to be listed as contested trials.

Requests made to the judge could be made at a preparatory hearing, at a hearing called especially for the purpose or at the trial itself. The Report denied that such a system was at all near the American scheme, which is widely regarded as promoting injustice as it acts as a wholesale plea bargaining system in which the prosecution can suggest the appropriate sentence. Lord Runciman stated that: 'We agree that to face defendants with a choice between what they might get on an immediate plea of guilty and what they might get if found guilty by the jury does amount to unacceptable pressure.'

Research conducted by Professor Zander for the Royal Commission on Criminal Justice (Zander and Henderson, *The Crown Court Study*, Royal Commission on Criminal Justice Study 19, 1993, p 145) found that, in a study of 900 Crown Court cases, 90% of barristers and two-thirds of judges were in favour of formalising plea bargaining based on sentence discounts. The study suggested that 11% of those who pleaded guilty in fact maintained their innocence but wanted to secure a reduction in sentence.

The Court of Appeal has consistently indicated that the information should not be given to defendants because that might put undue pressure on them to plead guilty, but sentence discounts are legally recognised. In DA Thomas (ed), *Current Sentencing Practice*, para A8 2(b) states that: 'a guilty plea attracts a lighter sentence, the extent of the reduction is usually between one-quarter and one-third of what would have otherwise been the sentence.' Moreover, Lord Widgery has stated (see 10.3.2, above) that defendants should know about them. The pressure could scarcely be increased by providing a defendant with details rather than leaving it to his general knowledge. If anything, Zander has argued, it would diminish the pressure by making it clear that the defendant's fears about the penalty for pleading not guilty are exaggerated.

In a detailed research report on this issue, the reform group JUSTICE has cast serious doubt on many aspects of the system, which could soon be adopted if the Runciman Royal Commission proposals are enacted. In *Negotiated Justice: A Closer Look at the Implications of Plea Bargaining* (1993), it is argued that, although favoured in some form by 90% of barristers and 60% of judges, plea bargaining can not only lead to unjust convictions, but also to inaccurate and unfair sentences. The latter occur because when the trial judge is making an offer of a reduced penalty, the defendant is still at that stage formally protesting his innocence, so it is extremely difficult for his lawyer to present a plea in mitigation of sentence. The reform body JUSTICE argues that the earlier withdrawal of weak prosecution cases, better liaison between defence and prosecution, and earlier contact between defendant and barrister would result in greater efficiency and fairness.

There is, though, reason for anxiety with such a call for more openness. Sanders and Young ((1994) 144 NLJ 1200) regard it as 'an idealistic notion' that one can improve the effectiveness of the system in convicting the guilty without also increasing its effectiveness in convicting the innocent. They say that one simply has to make a 'value choice' about the weight to be given to protecting the innocent relative to other important values, such as repressing crime and economy in the use of scarce resources. In one Home Office study (*Magistrates' Court or Crown Court? Mode of Trial Decisions and Sentencing*, Home Office Study No 125, 1992), Hedderman and Moxon found that 65% of those pleading guilty in Crown Court cases said that their decision had been influenced by the prospect of receiving a discount in sentence, and nearly one-third claimed to have pleaded guilty as a direct result of a charge bargain. Even the Royal Commission recognised that not all those pleading guilty are in fact guilty; some may have just capitulated to the pressure of taking the reduced sentence rather than run the risk of the full sentence. As Sanders and Young contend, this issue goes to the heart of constitutional principles. Only if the State acts properly in collecting and presenting evidence can punishment be justified according to commonly accepted principles. Even the guilty are entitled to due process of law. A system of plea bargaining may undermine such principles, as it allows the State to secure convictions based on unproven allegations.

Informal plea bargaining is obviously open to abuse: P Darbyshire, 'The mischief of plea bargaining' [2000] Crim LR 895; C Dyer, 'Making a pact with the Devil' (2000) *The Guardian*, 30 October. The recent White Paper, *Justice for All*, states (4.42–4.43):

> We ... intend to introduce a clearer tariff of sentence discount, backed up by arrangements whereby defendants could seek advance indication of the sentence they would get if they pleaded guilty ... We do not take lightly the danger of putting innocent defendants under pressure to plead guilty ... The defendant, through their legal advisers ... should initiate the request. It should be made formally in court sitting in private ... It should be fully recorded. All relevant information about the offence and defendant should be put to the judge, who would indicate the maximum sentence on a guilty plea made at that stage (but not what the sentence might be were a contested trial to result in a guilty verdict).

10.4 The jury

It is generally accepted that the jury of '12 good men and true' lies at the heart of the British legal system. The implicit assumption is that the presence of 12 ordinary lay persons, randomly introduced into the trial procedure to be the arbiters of the facts of the case, strengthens the legitimacy of the legal system. It supposedly achieves this end by introducing a democratic humanising element into the abstract impersonal trial process, thereby reducing the exclusive power of the legal professionals who would otherwise command the legal stage and control the legal procedure without reference to the opinion of the lay majority.

According to EP Thompson:

> The English common law rests upon a bargain between the law and the people. The jury box is where the people come into the court; the judge watches them and the jury watches back. A jury is the place where the bargain is struck. A jury attends in judgement not only upon the accused but also upon the justice and humanity of the law [*Writing by Candlelight*].

Few people have taken this traditional view to task but, in a thought-provoking article in the Criminal Law Review ([1991] Crim LR 740), Penny Darbyshire did just that. In her view, the jury system has attracted the most praise and the least theoretical analysis of any component of the criminal justice system. As she correctly pointed out, and as will be shown below, juries are far from being either a random or a representative section of the general population. In fact, Darbyshire goes so far as to characterise the jury as 'an anti-democratic, irrational and haphazard legislator, whose erratic and secret decisions run counter to the rule of law'. She concedes that while the 20th century lay justices are not representative of the community as a whole, neither is the jury. She points out that jury equity, by which is meant the way in which the jury ignores the law in pursuit of justice, is a double-edged sword which may also convict the innocent; and counters examples such as the *Clive Ponting* case with the series of miscarriages of justice relating to suspected terrorists in which juries were also involved.

Darbyshire is certainly correct in taking to task those who would simply endorse the jury system in an unthinking, purely emotional manner. With equal justification, she criticises those academic writers who focus attention on the mystery of the jury to the exclusion of the hard reality of the magistrates' court. It is arguable, however, that she goes to the other extreme. Underlying her analysis and conclusions is the idea that 'the jury trial is primarily ideological' and that 'its symbolic significance is magnified beyond its practical significance by the media, as well as academics, thus unwittingly misleading the public'. Whilst one might not wish to contradict the suggestion that the jury system operates as a very powerful ideological symbol, supposedly grounding the criminal legal system within a framework of participative democracy and justifying it on that basis, it is simply inadequate to reject the practical operation of the procedure on that basis alone. Ideologies do not exist purely in the realm of ideas, they have real, concrete manifestations and effects; in relation to the jury system, those manifestations operate in such a way as to offer at least a vestige of protection to defendants. In regard to the comparison between juries and the summary procedure of the magistrates' courts, Darbyshire puts two related questions. First, she asks whether the jury system is more likely to do justice and get the verdict right than the magistrates' courts; then she goes on to ask why the majority of defendants are processed through the magistrates' courts. These questions are highly pertinent; it is doubtful, however, whether her response to them is equally pertinent. Her answers would likely be that the jury does not perform any better than the magistrates and, therefore, it is immaterial that the magistrates deal with the bulk of cases. Her whole approach would seem to be concentrated on denigrating the performance of the jury system. A not untypical passage from her article admits that, in relation to the suspect terrorist miscarriages of justice, juries 'were not to blame for these wrongful convictions'. However, she then goes on in the same sentence to accuse the juries of failing 'to remedy the lack of due process at the pre-trial stage', and thus blames them for not providing 'the brake on oppressive State activity claimed for the jury by its defenders'.

Although there is most certainly scope for a less romantic view of how the jury system actually operates in practice, Darbyshire's argument seems to be that the magistrates are not very good but then neither are the juries; and as they only operate in a small minority of cases anyway, the implication would seem to be that their loss would be no great disadvantage. Others, however, would maintain that the jury system does achieve concrete benefits in particular circumstances and would argue further that these benefits should not be readily given up. Amongst the latter is Michael Mansfield QC who, in an article in response to the Runciman Report, claimed that the jury 'is the most democratic element of our judicial system' and the one which 'poses the biggest threat to the authorities'. (These questions will be considered further in relation to the Report of the Runciman Commission and the Criminal Justice (Mode of Trial) Bills, at 10.8, below.)

It should be noted that the jury system influences court procedure and the admissibility of evidence. Character evidence is an obvious example. (See J McEwan, 'Previous conduct at the crossroads: which "way ahead"?' [2002] Crim LR 180–91.) The alleged ability of defence lawyers to manipulate the system has been criticised by the Association of Chief Police Officers: see I Francis, 'Letting the frogs out of the kitchen' (2002) 152 NLJ 83. This may change in the near future. The recent White Paper, *Justice for All*, states (4.57):

> ... where a defendant's previous convictions, or other misconduct, are relevant to an issue in the case, then unless the court considers that the information will have a disproportionate effect, they should be allowed to know about it. It will be for the judge to decide whether the probative value of introducing this information is outweighed by its prejudicial effects.

Having defended the institution of the jury generally, it has to be recognised that there are particular instances which tend to bring the jury system into disrepute. For example, in October 1994, the Court of Appeal ordered the re-trial of a man convicted of double murder on the grounds that four of the jurors had attempted to contact the alleged victims using a Ouija board in what was described as a 'drunken experiment' (*R v Young* (1995)). A second convicted murderer appealed against his conviction on the grounds of irregularities in the manner in which the jury performed its functions. Amongst the allegations levelled at the jury was the claim that they clubbed together and spent £150 on drink when they were sent to a hotel after failing to reach a verdict. It was alleged that some of the jurors discussed the case against the express instructions of the judge and that on the following day, the jury foreman had to be replaced because she was too hungover to act. One female juror was alleged to have ended up in bed with another hotel guest.

A truly remarkable case came to light in December 2000 when a trial, which had been going on for 10 weeks, was stopped on the grounds that a female juror was conducting what were referred to as 'improper relations' with a male member of the jury protection force that had been allocated to look after the jury during the trial. The relationship had become apparent after the other members of the jury had found out that they were using their mobile phones to send text messages to one another during breaks in the trial. That aborted trial was estimated to have cost £1.5 million, but it emerged that this was the second time the case had had to be stopped on account of inappropriate behaviour on the part of jury members. The first trial had been abandoned after some of the jury were found playing cards when they should have been deliberating on the case.

Another example of the possible criticisms to be levelled against the misuse of juries occurred in Stoke-on-Trent, where the son of a court usher and another six individuals were found to have served on a number of criminal trial juries. Whilst one could praise the public spirited nature of this dedication to the justice process, especially given the difficulty in getting members of jury panels (see 10.6 and 10.7, below), it might be more appropriate to condemn the possibility of the emergence of a professional juror system connected to court officials. Certainly, the Court of Appeal was less than happy with the situation, and overturned a conviction when the Stoke practice was revealed to it.

Over the past 10 years, the operation of the jury system has been subject to one Royal Commission (Runciman), one review (Auld) and several statutory attempts to alter it. An examination of these various endeavours will be postponed until the end of this chapter; for the moment, attention will be focused on the jury system as it currently functions.

10.5 The role of the jury

It is generally accepted that the function of the jury is to decide on matters of fact, and that matters of law are the province of the judge. Such may be the ideal case, but most of the time, the jury's decision is based on a consideration of a mixture of fact and law. The jurors determine whether a person is guilty on the basis of their understanding of the law as explained to them by the judge.

The oath taken by each juror states that they 'will faithfully try the defendant and give a true verdict according to the evidence', and it is contempt of court for a juror subsequent to being sworn in to refuse to come to a decision. In 1997, Judge Anura Cooray sentenced two women jurors to 30 days in prison for contempt of court for their failure to deliver a verdict. One of the women, who had been the jury foreman, claimed that the case, involving an allegation of fraud, had been too complicated to understand, and the other had claimed that she could not ethically judge anyone. Judge Cooray was quoted as justifying his decision to imprison them on the grounds that:

> I had to order a re-trial at very great expense. Jurors must recognise that they have a responsibility to fulfil their duties in accordance with their oath.

The women only spent one night in jail before the uproar caused by Cooray's action led to their release and the subsequent overturning of his sentence on them.

It should be appreciated that serving on a jury can be an extremely harrowing experience. Jurors are the arbiters of fact, but the facts they have to contend with can be horrific. Criticisms have been levelled at the way in which the jury system can subject people to what in other contexts would be pornography, of either a sexual or violent kind, and yet offer them no counselling when their jury service comes to an end. Many jurors fear reprisals from defendants and their associates. In April 2003, two illegal immigrants, Baghdad Meziane and Brahim Benmerzouga, were convicted of various offences under the Terrorism Act 2000. It appears that they had raised hundreds of thousands of pounds for Al Qa'ida and other radical Islamic organisations. The trial at Leicester Crown Court became a 'drama unprecedented in legal history' (S Bird, 'Jurors too scared to take on case' (2003) *The Times*, 2 April):

> The case began in February, amid extraordinary security arrangements. A jury was sworn in and retired overnight … The next morning one frightened female juror had worked herself up into such a state that she vomited in the jury room. Two others burst into tears … The jury was dismissed – as was a second after a male juror expressed fears for his family's safety.

The third jury was down to nine when it was time to deliver a verdict. Jurors receive inadequate protection and support. The only recognition currently available is that the judge can exempt them from further jury service for a particular period. Many would argue that such limited recognition of the damage that jurors might sustain in performing their civic duty is simply inadequate.

10.5.1 The jury's function in trials

Judges have the power to direct juries to acquit the accused where there is insufficient evidence to convict them, and this is the main safeguard against juries finding defendants guilty in spite of either the absence, or the insufficiency, of the evidence. There is, however, no corresponding judicial power to instruct juries to convict (*DPP v Stonehouse* (1978)). That being said, there is nothing to prevent the judge summing up in such a way as to make it evident to the jury that there is only one decision that can reasonably be made, and that it would be perverse to reach any other verdict but guilty.

What judges must not do is overtly put pressure on juries to reach guilty verdicts. Finding of any such pressure will result in the overturning of any conviction so obtained. The classic example of such a case is *R v McKenna* (1960), in which the judge told the jurors, after they had spent all of two and a quarter hours deliberating on the issue, that if they did not come up with a verdict in the following 10 minutes, they would be locked up for the night. Not surprisingly, the jury returned a verdict; unfortunately for the defendant, it was a guilty verdict; even more unfortunately for the judicial process, the conviction had to be quashed on appeal for clear interference with the jury.

In the words of Cassels J:

> It is a cardinal principle of our criminal law that in considering their verdict, concerning, as it does, the liberty of the subject, a jury shall deliberate in complete freedom, uninfluenced by any promise, unintimidated by any threat. They stand between the Crown and the subject, and they are still one of the main defences of personal liberty. To say to such a tribunal in the course of its deliberations that it must reach a conclusion ... is a disservice to the cause of justice ... [*R v McKenna* (1960)].

Judges do have the right, and indeed the duty, to advise the jury as to the proper understanding and application of the law that it is considering. Even when the jury is considering its verdict, it may seek the advice of the judge. The essential point, however, is that any such response on the part of the judge must be given in open court, so as to obviate any allegation of misconduct (*R v Townsend* (1982)).

In criminal cases, even perversity of decision does not provide grounds for appeal against acquittal. There have been occasions where juries have been subjected to the invective of a judge when they have delivered a verdict with which he disagreed. Nonetheless, the fact is that juries collectively, and individual jurors, do not have to justify, explain or even give reasons for their decisions. Indeed, under s 8 of the Contempt of Court Act 1981, it would be a contempt of court to try to elicit such information from a jury member in either a criminal or a civil law case.

In *Attorney General v Associated Newspapers* (1994), the House of Lords held that it was contempt of court for a newspaper to publish disclosures by jurors of what took place in the jury room while they were considering their verdict, unless the publication amounted to no more than a re-publication of facts already known. It was decided that the word 'disclose' in s 8(1) applied not just to jurors, but to any others who published their revelations.

In an interview for *The Times* in January 2001, the Lord Chief Justice, Lord Woolf, expressed himself very strongly in favour of lifting the ban on jury research, though he emphasised that great care was needed in the conduct of any such research. Fresh impetus may be given to this proposal by the concerns about juries engendered by the decision of the Court of Appeal in *Grobbelaar v News Group Newspapers* (see 10.7.1, below).

These factors place juries in a very strong position to take decisions that are 'unjustifiable' in accordance with the law, for the simple reason that they do not have to justify the decisions. Thus, juries have been able to deliver what can only be described as perverse decisions. In *R v Clive Ponting* (1985), the judge made clear beyond doubt that the defendant was guilty, under the Official Secrets Act 1911, of the offence with which he was charged: the jury still returned a not guilty verdict. Similarly, in the case of Pat Pottle and Michael Randall, who had openly admitted their part in the escape of the spy George Blake, the jury reached a not guilty verdict in open defiance of the law.

In *R v Kronlid* (1996), three protestors were charged with committing criminal damage, and another was charged with conspiracy to cause criminal damage, in relation to an attack on Hawk Jet aeroplanes that were about to be sent to Indonesia. The damage to the planes allegedly amounted to £1.5 million and they did not deny their responsibility for it. They rested their defence on the fact that the planes were to be delivered to the Indonesian State, to be used in its allegedly genocidal campaign against the people of East Timor. On those grounds, they claimed that they were in fact acting to prevent the crime of genocide. The prosecution cited assurances, given by the Indonesian government, that the planes would not be used against the East Timorese, and pointed out that the UK government had granted an export licence for the planes. As the protestors did not deny what they had done, it was apparently a mere matter of course that they would be convicted as charged. The jury, however, decided that all four of the accused were innocent of the charges laid against them. A government Treasury minister, Michael Jack, subsequently stated his disbelief at the verdict of the jury. As he stated:

> I, and I am sure many others, find this jury's decision difficult to understand. It would appear there is little question about who did this damage. For whatever reason that damage was done, it was just plain wrong [(1996) *The Independent*, 1 August].

It is perhaps just such a lack of understanding, together with the desire to save money on the operation of the legal system, that has motivated the government's expressed wish to replace jury trials in relation to either way offences (see 10.8). In any event, juries continue to reach perverse decisions where they are sympathetic to the causes pursued by the defendants. Thus, in September 2000, 28 Greenpeace volunteers, including its executive director Lord Melchett, were found not guilty of criminal damage after they had destroyed a field containing genetically modified maize. They had been found not guilty of theft in their original trial in April of that year. Although Judge David Mellor told the jury:

> It is not about whether GM crops are a good thing for the environment or a bad thing. It is for you to listen to the evidence and reach honest conclusions as to the facts.

The jury seemed to have adopted a different approach.

A non-political example of this type of case can be seen in the jury's refusal to find Stephen Owen guilty of any offence after he had discharged a shotgun at the driver of a lorry that had killed his child. And, in September 2000, a jury in Carlisle found Lezley Gibson not guilty on a charge of possession of cannabis after she told the court that she needed it to relieve the symptoms of the multiple sclerosis from which she suffered. The tendency of the jury occasionally to ignore legal formality in favour of substantive justice is one of the major points in favour of its retention, according to its proponents.

10.5.2 Appeals from decisions of the jury

In criminal law, it is an absolute rule that there can be no appeal against a jury's decision to acquit a person of the charges laid against him.

Although there is no appeal as such against acquittal, there does exist the possibility of the Attorney General referring the case to the Court of Appeal, to seek its advice on points of law raised in criminal cases in which the defendant has been acquitted. This procedure was provided for under s 36 of the CJA 1972, although it is not commonly resorted to. It must be stressed that there is no possibility of the actual case being reheard or the acquittal decision being reversed, but the procedure can highlight mistakes in law made in the course of Crown Court trial and permits the Court of Appeal to remedy the defect for the future. (See *Attorney General's Reference (No 1)* (1988) for an example of this procedure, in the area of insider dealing in relation to shares on the Stock Exchange. This case is also interesting in relation to statutory interpretation. See also *Attorney General's Reference (No 3 of 1999)*, considered at 6.2.)

In civil law cases, the possibility of the jury's verdict being overturned on appeal does exist, but only in circumstances where the original verdict was perverse, that is, no reasonable jury properly directed could have made such a decision.

10.5.3 Majority verdicts

The possibility of a jury deciding a case on the basis of a majority decision was introduced by the CJA 1967. Prior to this, the requirement was that jury decisions had to be unanimous. Such decisions are acceptable where there are:

- not less than 11 jurors and 10 of them agree; or
- there are 10 jurors and nine of them agree.

Where a jury has reached a guilty verdict on the basis of a majority decision, s 17(3) of the Juries Act (JA) 1974 requires the foreman of the jury to state in open court the number of jurors who agreed and the number who disagreed with the verdict. See *R v Barry* (1975), where failure to declare the details of the voting split resulted in the conviction of the defendant being overturned. In *R v Pigg* (1983), the House of Lords held that it was unnecessary to state the number who voted against where the foreman stated the number in favour of the verdict, and thus the determination of the minority was a matter of simple arithmetic.

However, in *R v Mendy* (1992), when the clerk of the court asked the foreman of the jury how a guilty decision had been reached, he replied that it was 'by the majority of us all'. The ambiguity of the reply is obvious when it is taken out of context and this was relied on in a successful appeal. It was simply not clear whether it referred to a unanimous verdict, as the court at first instance had understood it, or whether it referred to a real majority vote, in which case, it failed to comply with the requirement of s 17(3) as applied in *R v Barry*. The Court of Appeal held that in such a situation, the defendant had to be given the benefit of any doubt and he was discharged.

The Court of Appeal adopted a different approach in *R v Millward* (1999). The appellant had been convicted, at Stoke-on-Trent Crown Court, of causing grievous bodily harm. Although the jury actually had reached a majority decision, the foreman in response to the questioning of the clerk of the court mistakenly stated that it was the verdict of them all. The following day, the foreman informed the judge that the verdict had in fact been a majority verdict of 10 for guilty and two against.

The Court of Appeal met the subsequent challenge with the following exercise in sophisticated reasoning. The court at first instance had apparently accepted a unanimous verdict. Therefore, s 17 had not been brought into play at all. And, bearing in mind s 8 of the Contempt of Court Act 1981, discouraging the disclosure of votes cast by jurors in the course of their deliberations, the issue had to be viewed under the policy of the law. It would set a very dangerous precedent if an apparently unanimous verdict of a jury delivered in open court, and not then challenged by any juror, was re-opened and subjected to scrutiny. It would be difficult to see how the court could properly investigate a disagreement as to whether jurors had dissented or not.

In the instant case, there was a proper majority direction and proper questions asked of the jury and apparently proper and unambiguous answers given without challenge. Therefore, there should be no further inquiry.

There is no requirement for the details of the voting to be declared in a majority decision of not guilty.

10.5.4 Discharge of jurors or the jury

The trial judge may discharge the whole jury if certain irregularities occur. These would include the situation where the defendant's previous convictions are revealed inadvertently during the trial. Such a disclosure would be prejudicial to the defendant. In such a case, the trial would be ordered to commence again with a different jury. Individual jurors may be discharged by the judge if they are incapable of continuing to act through illness 'or for any other reason' (s 16(1) of the JA 1974). Where this happens, the jury must not fall below nine members.

10.6 The selection of the jury

In theory, jury service is a public duty that citizens should readily undertake. In practice, it is made compulsory, and failure to perform one's civic responsibility is subject to the sanction of a £1,000 fine.

10.6.1 Liability to serve

According to statistics produced by the LCD, around 250,000 people sit as jurors in any year. The JA 1974, as amended by the CJA 1988, sets out the law relating to juries. Prior to the Juries Act, there was a property qualification in respect to jury service which skewed jury membership towards middle class men. Now, the legislation provides that any person between the ages of 18 and 70, who is on the electoral register and who has lived in the UK for at least five years, is qualified to serve as a juror.

The procedure for establishing a jury is a threefold process:

- An officer of the court summons a randomly selected number of qualified individuals from the electoral register.
- From that group, panels of potential jurors for various cases are drawn up.
- The actual jurors are then randomly selected by means of a ballot in open court.

As has been pointed out, however, even if the selection procedure were truly random, randomness does not equal representation. Random juries, by definition, could be: all male, all female, all white, all black, all Conservative or all members of the Raving Loony Party. Such is the nature of the random process; the question that arises from the process is whether such randomness is necessarily a good thing in itself, and whether the summoning officer should take steps to avoid the potential disadvantages that can result from random selection.

As regards the actual random nature of the selection process, a number of problems arise from the use of electoral registers to determine and locate jurors:

- Electoral registers tend to be inaccurate. Generally, they misreport the number of younger people who are in an area simply because younger people tend to move about more than older people and therefore tend not to appear on the electoral role of the place in which they currently live.

- Electoral registers tend to under-report the number of members of ethnic minorities in a community. The problem is that some members of the ethnic communities, for a variety of reasons, simply do not notify the authorities of their existence.

- The problem of non-registration mentioned above was compounded by the disappearance of a great many people from electoral registers in order to try to avoid payment of the former poll tax. It is a matter of some doubt whether such people have registered with the passing of that particular tax or whether they will simply cease to exist for the purpose of jury service. The Runciman Commission, not surprisingly, suggested that every endeavour should be made to ensure that electoral registers are accurate.

10.6.2 Exceptions, excusals and disqualifications

In 2001, almost a third of the people summoned for jury trial were excused jury service ('Jury excuses' (2002) 152 NLJ 780). The general qualification for serving as a juror is subject to a number of exceptions. A number of people are deemed to be ineligible to serve on juries on the basis of their employment or vocation. Amongst this category are judges; justices of the peace; members of the legal profession; police and probation officers; and members of the clergy or religious orders. The reason for excluding those involved in the administration of justice is understandable, but less so is the exclusion of clergy. The Runciman Report recommended that the clergy and members of religious orders should be eligible to serve on juries, but that members of such orders which have beliefs that are incompatible with jury service should be excused. The latter recommendation was introduced by s 42 of the CJPOA 1994.

In an endeavour to maintain the unquestioned probity of the jury system, certain categories of persons are disqualified from serving as jurors. Amongst these is anyone who has been sentenced to a term of imprisonment or youth custody of five years or more. In addition, anyone who, in the past 10 years, has served a sentence or has had a suspended sentence imposed on them, or has had a community service order made against them, is also disqualified. Finally, with respect to people with criminal records, anyone who has been placed on probation within the previous five years is also disqualified. Those on bail in criminal proceedings are disqualified from serving as a juror in the Crown Court. (See the recommendations of the Runciman Commission, below.) The final category of people disqualified from serving as jurors are the mentally ill.

Certain people are excused as of right from serving as jurors on account of their jobs. Amongst these are members of the medical professions, Members of Parliament and members of the armed forces. In 2001, 32,321 people were excused jury service as of right. Others may be excused from current jury service on the basis of past service. There is additionally a discretionary power given to the court to release a person from jury service, or alternatively to defer their service to some time in the future, if they show grounds for such treatment. Grounds for such excusal or deferral are supposed to be made only on the basis of good reason, but there is at least a measure of doubt as to the rigour with which such rules are applied.

A Practice Note issued in 1988 (now *Practice Direction (Criminal: Consolidated)* [2002] 1 WLR 2870, para 42) stated that applications for excusal should be treated sympathetically and listed the following as good grounds for excusal:

(a) personal involvement in the case;

(b) close connection with a party or a witness in the case;

(c) personal hardship;

(d) conscientious objection to jury service.

Lord Justice Auld's recent review of the criminal justice system recommended that virtually everyone (except the mentally ill) should be eligible for jury service. This proposal is likely to be implemented when the Criminal Justice Bill is enacted.

The previous, somewhat antiquated procedure for selecting potential jury members, with its accompanying disparity of treatment, is in the process of being modernised by the introduction of a Central Summoning Bureau based at Blackfriars Crown Court Centre in London. Progressively from October 2000, the new Bureau is using a computer system to select jurors at random from the electoral registers and issue the summonses, as well as dealing with jurors' questions and requests. It is intended to link the jury summoning system to the national police records system to allow checks to be made against potentially disqualified individuals. However, severe doubts have been expressed as to the accuracy of the police national computer (PNC), which might not only render the checks on juries inaccurate, but might actually contravene the Data Protection Act 1998. When the Metropolitan Police conducted an audit of the PNC in 1999, it was found to have 'wholly unacceptable' levels of inaccuracy, with an overall error rate of 86%. In one case in 2000 at Highbury Corner magistrates' court in north London, a man charged with theft of £2,700 was granted bail on the grounds that the PNC showed that he had no previous convictions. In fact, he was a convicted murderer released from prison on licence.

The aim of the new procedure is to ensure that all jurors are treated equally and fairly and that the rules are enforced consistently, especially in regard to requests to be excused from service and thus to reduce at least some of the potential difficulties mentioned above.

10.6.3 Physical disability and jury service

It is to be hoped that the situation of people with disabilities has been altered for the better by the CJPOA 1994, which introduced a new s 9B into the JA 1974.

Previously, it was all too common for judges to discharge jurors with disabilities, including deafness, on the assumption that they would not be capable of undertaking the duties of a juror.

Under the new provision, where it appears doubtful that a person summoned for jury service is capable of serving on account of some physical disability, that person, as previously, may be brought before the judge. The new s 9B, however, introduces a presumption that people should serve and provides that the judge shall affirm the jury summons unless he is of the opinion that the person will not be able to act effectively.

It would appear, however, that the CJPOA does not improve the situation of profoundly deaf people who could only function as jurors with the aid of a sign language interpreter. That was the outcome of a case decided in November 1999, that profoundly deaf Jeff McWhinney, chief executive of the British Deaf Association, could not serve as a juror. For him to do so would have required that he had the assistance of an interpreter in the jury room and that could not be allowed as, at present, only jury members are allowed into the jury room.

10.6.4 Challenges to jury membership

That juries can be 'self-selecting' provides grounds for concern as to the random nature of the jury, but the traditional view of the jury is further and perhaps even more fundamentally undermined by the way in which both prosecution and defence seek to influence its constitution.

Under s 12(6) of the JA 1974, both prosecution and defence have a right to challenge the array where the summonsing officer has acted improperly in bringing the whole panel together. Such challenges are rare, although an unsuccessful action was raised in *R v Danvers* (1982), where the defendant tried to challenge the racial composition of the group of potential jurors.

10.6.5 Challenge by the defence

Until the CJA 1988, there were two ways in which the defence could challenge potential jurors:

- *Peremptory challenge*

  The defence could object to any potential jury members, up to a maximum number of three, without having to show any reason or justification for the challenge. Defence counsel used this procedure in an attempt to shape the composition of the jury in a way they thought might best suit their client, although it has to be said that it was an extremely inexact process, and one that could upset or antagonise rejected jurors. In spite of arguments for its retention on a civil liberties basis, the majority of the Roskill Committee on Fraud Trials (January 1986, HMSO) recommended that the right be abolished, and abolition was provided for in the CJA 1988.

- *Challenge for cause*

  The defence retains the power to challenge any number of potential jurors for cause, that is to say that there is a substantial reason why a particular person should not serve on the jury to decide a particular defendant's case. A simple example would be where the potential juror has had previous dealings with the defendant or has been involved in the case in some way. There may be less obvious grounds for objection, however, which may be based on the particular juror's attitudes, or indeed political beliefs. The question arises whether such factors provide grounds for challenge. In what is known as *The Angry Brigade* case in 1972 (see (1971) *The Times*, 10–11 December; (1972) *The Times*, 12–15 December), a group of people was charged with carrying out a bombing campaign against prominent members of the Conservative government. In the process of empanelling a jury, the judge asked potential jurors to exclude themselves on a variety of socio-political grounds, including active membership of the Conservative Party. As a consequence of the procedure adopted in that case, the Lord Chief Justice issued a practice direction in which he made it clear that potential jurors were not to be excluded on account of race, religion, politics or occupation. Since that practice direction, it is clear that the challenge for cause can only be used within a restricted sphere, and this makes it less useful to the defence than it might otherwise be if it were to operate in a more general way.

It has been argued that the desire of civil libertarians to retain the right of the defence to select a jury that might be more sympathetic to its case is contradictory, because although in theory they usually rely on the random nature of the jury to ensure the appearance of justice, in practice they seek to influence its composition. When, however, the shortcomings in the establishment of panels for juries is recalled, it might be countered that the defence is attempting to do no more than counter the inbuilt bias that ensues from the use of unbalanced electoral registers.

10.6.6 Challenge by the prosecution

If the defence attempts to ensure that any jury will not be prejudiced against its case, if not predisposed towards it, the same is true of the prosecution. However, the prosecution has a greater scope to achieve such an aim. Whilst the prosecution has the same right as the defence to challenge for cause, it has the additional option of excluding potential jury members by simply asking them to stand by until a jury has been empanelled. The request for the potential juror to stand by is only a provisional challenge and, in theory, the person stood by can at a later time take their place on the jury if there are no other suitable candidates. In practice, of course, it is unlikely in the extreme for there not to be sufficient alternative candidates to whom the prosecution do not object and prefer to the person stood by.

When the Roskill Committee recommended the removal of the defence's right to pre-emptive challenge, it recognised that, in order to retain an equitable situation, the right of the Crown to ask potential jurors to stand by should also be withdrawn. Unfortunately, although the government of the day saw fit to follow the Committee's recommendation in relation to the curtailment of the defence rights, it did not feel under the same obligation to follow its corresponding recommendation to curtail the rights of the prosecution. Thus, the CJA 1988 made no reference to the procedure and, in failing to do so, established a distinct advantage in favour of the prosecution in regard to selecting what it considered to be suitable juries.

The manifest unreasonableness of this procedure led to the Attorney General issuing a practice note (1988) to the effect that the Crown should only exercise its power to stand by potential jurors in the following two circumstances:

- To prevent the empanelment of a 'manifestly unsuitable' juror, with the agreement of the defence. The example given of 'manifest unsuitability' is an illiterate person asked to sit in a highly complex case. It is reasonable to doubt the ability of such a person to follow the process of the case involving a number of documents, and on that basis they should be stood by.

- In circumstances where the Attorney General has approved the vetting of the potential jury members and that process has revealed that the particular juror in question might be a security risk. In this situation, the Attorney General is also required to approve the use of the 'stand by' procedure.

10.6.7 Jury vetting

Jury vetting is the process by which the Crown checks the background of potential jurors to assess their suitability to decide particular cases. The procedure is clearly contrary to the ideal of the jury being based on a random selection of people, but it is justified on the basis that it is necessary to ensure that jury members are not likely to divulge any secrets made open to them in the course of a sensitive trial or, alternatively, on the ground that jurors with extreme political views should not be permitted the opportunity to express those views in a situation where they might influence the outcome of a case.

The practice of vetting potential jurors developed after the *Angry Brigade* trial in 1972, but it did not become public until 1978. In that year, as a result of an Official Secrets Act case, known by the initials of the three defendants as the ABC trial, it became apparent that the list of potential jurors had been checked to establish their 'soundness'. As a consequence of that case, the Attorney General published the current guidelines for vetting jury panels. Since that date, the guidelines have been updated and the most recent guidelines were published in 1988. These guidelines maintain the general propositions that jury members should normally be selected at random from the panel and should be disqualified only on the grounds set out in the JA 1974. The guidelines do, however, make reference to exceptional cases of public importance where potential jury members might properly be vetted. Such cases are broadly identified as those involving national security, where part of the evidence may be heard on camera, and terrorist cases.

Vetting is a twofold process. An initial check into police criminal records and police Special Branch records should be sufficient to reveal whether a further investigation by the security services is required. Any further investigation requires the prior approval of the Attorney General.

In addition to vetting properly so called, the Court of Appeal in *R v Mason* (1980) approved the checking of criminal records to establish whether potential jurors had been convicted of criminal offences in the past and therefore were not eligible to serve as jurors. The Runciman Commission recommended that this process of checking on those who should be disqualified on the basis of previous criminal conviction should be regularised when the collection and storage of criminal records is centralised. This was achieved when the Criminal Records Bureau was established as a result of Part V of the Police Act 1997.

10.6.8 The racial mix of the jury

In *R v Danvers* (1982), the defence had sought to challenge the array on the basis that a black defendant could not have complete confidence in the impartiality of an all white jury. The question of the racial mix of a jury has exercised the courts on a number of occasions. In *R v Ford* (1989), the trial judge's refusal to accept the defendant's application for a racially mixed jury was supported by the Court of Appeal on the grounds that, 'fairness is achieved by the principle of random selection' as regards the make up of a jury, and that to insist on a racially balanced jury would be contrary to that principle, and would be to imply that particular jurors were incapable of impartiality. A similar point was made in *R v Tarrant* (1997), in which a person accused of drug-related offences was convicted by a jury that had had been selected from outside the normal catchment area for the court. The aim of the judge had been to minimise potential jury intimidation, but nonetheless, the Court of Appeal overturned the conviction on the grounds that the judge had deprived the defendant of a randomly selected jury.

To deny people the right to have their cases heard by representatives of their own race, on the basis of a refusal to recognise the existence of racial discriminatory attitudes, cannot but give the appearance of a society where such racist attitudes are institutionalised. This has particular resonance given the findings of the Macpherson Inquiry that the police force were 'institutionally racist'. Without suggesting that juries as presently constituted are biased, it remains arguable that if, in order to achieve the undoubted appearance of fairness, jury selection has to be manipulated to ensure a racial mix, then it should at least be considered.

An interesting case study in this respect is the trial in 1994 of Lakhbir Deol, an Asian who was accused of the murder of a white youth in Stoke-on-Trent in 1993. Mr Deol's lawyers sought to have the case moved from Stafford to Birmingham Crown Court on the grounds that Stafford has an almost completely white population, whereas Birmingham has an approximately 25% ethnic minority population. Mr Justice McKinnon repeatedly refused the request and the trial was heard in Stafford as scheduled. Mr Deol was acquitted, so his fears were proved groundless, but surely the worrying fact is that he had those fears in the first place.

It is heartening to note that the Runciman Commission fully endorsed the views expressed above and recommended that either the prosecution or the defence should be able to insist that up to three jury members be from ethnic minorities, and that at least one of those should be from the same ethnic minority as the accused or the victim. Sir Robin Auld, in his review of the criminal courts, also recommended that provision should be made to enable ethnic minority representation on juries where race is likely to be relevant to an important issue in the case.

It is of interest, if not concern, to note that the former Lord Chief Justice, Lord Taylor, whilst recognising that the criminal justice system was:

> ... failing blacks and Asians, by tolerating racist attitudes and allowing ethnic minorities to believe that they were beyond the protection of the law ...,

was equally sure that proposals for ethnically balanced juries, and indeed, the new offence of racially motivated attacks, were:

> Attractive sounding, but deeply flawed proposals.

He went on to criticise the Runciman proposals as:

> ... the thin edge of a particularly insidious wedge ...

And, somewhat ironically, given subsequent proposals by the recent Home Secretaries, he asserted that:

> We must on no account introduce measures which allow the State to start nibbling away at the principle of random selection of juries [speech to NACRO reported in *The Guardian*, 1999].

In *R v Smith* (2003), the Court of Appeal re-affirmed the traditional view in holding that it had not been unfair for Smith to be tried by a randomly selected all white jury. In addition, however, the court held that the selection process had not infringed Smith's rights under Art 6 of the ECHR.

Another case which raised a human rights issue was *R v Mushtaq* (2002), in which the defendant appealed against his conviction for conspiracy to defraud. He had admitted to police that he had played a minor part in the conspiracy, but later claimed that his confession had been obtained by oppression. The judge ruled during the trial that M's confession had not been obtained by oppression and was therefore admissible, and in his summing up to the jury, he emphasised that the confession was central and crucial to the case. Mushtaq claimed that the judge's direction to the jury was in breach of Art 6 of the ECHR and that the jury, *as a separate and distinct public authority*, had a duty to protect his rights. The Court of Appeal dismissed the appeal, holding that the separate functions allocated to the judge and the jury in relation to disputed confessions had significant advantages for ensuring that justice was done. The admissibility of a confession was a matter for the judge and if the prosecution failed to satisfy the judge that a confession was not obtained by oppression, the jury would not hear it. This division of function between judge and jury complied with the requirement to provide an adequate safeguard for a defendant's Art 6 rights, and it could not be said that the jury was a separate public authority having a distinct and separate duty from the judge to protect M's rights. In a criminal trial, it was the court acting collectively that had the shared responsibility of ensuring a fair trial.

10.6.9 Racial bias in juries

If the law does not allow for the artificial creation of ethnic balance in juries, then it must ensure that ethnically unbalanced juries do not become ethnically biased ones.

In May 2000, the ECtHR held by a majority of 4:3 that the right of a British Asian to be tried by an impartial tribunal had been violated on the basis of alleged racism within the jury that had convicted him. Kuldip Sander had been charged with conspiracy to commit fraud and was tried at Birmingham Crown Court in March 1995. During the trial, one of the jurors sent a note to the judge stating:

> I have decided I cannot remain silent any longer. For some time during the trial I have been concerned that fellow jurors are not taking their duties seriously. At least two have been making openly racist remarks and jokes and I fear are going to convict the defendants not on the evidence but because they are Asian. My concern is the defendants will not therefore receive a fair verdict. Please could you advise me what I can do in this situation.

The judge adjourned the case, but kept the juror who had written the letter apart from the other jurors whilst he listened to submission from counsel in open court. The defence asked the judge to dismiss the jury on the ground that there was a real danger of bias. The judge, however, decided to call the jury back into court, at which stage the juror who had written the complaint joined the others. The judge read out the complaint to them and told them the following:

I am not able to conduct an inquiry into the validity of those contentions and I do not propose to do so. This case has cost an enormous amount of money and I am not anxious to halt it at the moment, but I shall have no compunction in doing so if the situation demands ... I am going to ask you all to search your conscience overnight and if you feel that you are not able to try this case solely on the evidence and find that you cannot put aside any prejudices you may have will you please indicate that fact by writing a personal note to that effect and giving it to the jury bailiff on your arrival at court tomorrow morning. I will then review the position.

The next morning, the judge received two letters from the jury. The first letter, which was signed by all the jurors including the juror who had sent the complaint, refuted any allegation of racial bias. The second letter was written by a juror who appeared to have thought himself to have been the one who had been making the jokes. The juror in question stated that he was sorry if he had given any offence, that he had many connections with people from ethnic minorities and that he was in no way racially biased.

The judge decided not to discharge the jury and it went on to find the applicant guilty, although it acquitted another Asian defendant. The applicant's appeal, partly on the grounds of bias on the part of the jury, was dismissed by the Court of Appeal.

The majority of the ECtHR, however, held that the trial was conducted contrary to Art 6(1) of the ECHR. The Court considered that the allegations contained in the note were capable of causing the applicant and any objective observer to have legitimate doubts as to the impartiality of the court, which neither the collective letter nor the redirection of the jury by the judge could have dispelled.

In reaching its decision, the Court distinguished the decision in the similar case of *Gregory v UK* (1998). In the *Gregory* judgment, there was no admission by a juror that he had made racist comments, in the form of a joke or otherwise; there was no indication as to who had made the complaint and the complaint was vague and imprecise. Moreover, in the present case, the applicant's counsel had insisted throughout the proceedings that dismissing the jury was the only viable course of action.

The Court accepted that, although discharging the jury might not always be the only means to achieve a fair trial, there were certain circumstances where this was required by Art 6(1) of the ECHR. As the Court stated:

Given the importance attached by all Contracting States to the need to combat racism, the Court considers that the judge should have reacted in a more robust manner than merely seeking vague assurances that the jurors could set aside their prejudices and try the case solely on the evidence. By failing to do so, the judge did not provide sufficient guarantees to exclude any objectively justified or legitimate doubts as to the impartiality of the court. It follows that the court that condemned the applicant was not impartial from an objective point of view.

The Court, however, refused his claim for compensation of some £458,000, which suggests that it was not convinced that a substitute jury would not have convicted him as well.

It has already been seen that s 8 of the Contempt of Court Act 1981 prevents investigation into what occurs in the privacy of the jury room and such prohibition applies equally to judges. In *R v Qureshi* (2001), the defendant had been convicted of arson and of attempting to attain property by deception. Three days after the verdict, a juror in the trial informed the court that some members of the jury had been racially prejudiced against Qureshi and had decided he was guilty from the outset of the trial. Qureshi's application for permission to appeal against his conviction was rejected by the Court of Appeal on the grounds that the complaint did not arise during the trial, but only after an apparently regular verdict had been delivered. In order to pursue the allegation, the court would have had to investigate what had happened in the jury room and that was precluded by s 8 of the Contempt of Court Act. In reaching this decision, the Court of Appeal distinguished *Sander*, where the complaint arose during the trial, and followed *R v Miah* (1997), where the complaint arose after the event. In the latter case, it was stated that the rule against breaching jury secrecy applied to 'anything said by one juror to another about the case from the moment the jury is empanelled, at least provided what is said is not overheard by anyone who is not a juror'. It has to be asked whether such a rule is acceptable, especially when it conceals possible injustice. For a detailed analysis of these cases, see P Robertshaw, 'Responding to bias amongst jurors' (2002) 66(1) Journal of Criminal Law 84–95.

10.7 The decline of the jury trial

Many direct attempts have been made in the recent past to reduce the operation of the jury system within the English legal system. These particular endeavours, however, have to be understood in the context of the general historical decline in the use of the jury as the mechanism for determining issues in court cases. Perhaps the heat engendered in the current debate is a consequence of the fact that the continued existence of the jury as it is presently constituted cannot be taken for granted.

10.7.1 The jury trial in civil procedure

There can be no doubt as to the antiquity of the institution of trial by jury, nor can there be much doubt as to its supposed democratising effect on the operation of the legal system. Neither, unfortunately, can there be any grounds for denying the diminishment that has occurred in the fairly recent past in the role of the jury as the means of determining the outcome of trials, nor can the continued existence of the jury as it is presently constituted be taken for granted.

In respect of civil law, the use of juries has diminished considerably and automatic recourse to trial by jury is restricted to a small number of areas and, even in those areas, the continued use of the jury is threatened. Prior to 1854, all cases that came before the common law courts were decided by a judge and jury. The Common Law Procedure Act of that year provided that cases could be settled without a jury where the parties agreed, and since then, the role of the jury has been gradually curtailed until, at present, under s 69 of the Supreme Court Act 1981, the right to a jury trial is limited to only four specific areas: fraud, defamation, malicious prosecution and false imprisonment. (Similar provisions are contained in the County Courts Act 1984.)

Even in these areas, the right is not absolute and can be denied by a judge under s 69(i) where the case involves 'any prolonged examination of documents or accounts or any scientific or local investigation which cannot conveniently be made with a jury'. (See *Beta Construction Ltd v Channel Four TV Co Ltd* (1990) for an indication of the factors that the judge will take into consideration in deciding whether a case should be decided by a jury or not.)

The question of whether or not juries should be used in libel cases gained wider consideration in the case involving McDonalds, the fast food empire, and two environmentalists, Dave Morris and Helen Steel. McDonalds claimed that their reputation was damaged by an allegedly libellous leaflet issued by members of an organisation called London Greenpeace including Morris and Steel, which linked McDonalds' products to heart disease and cancer as well as the despoilation of the environment and the exploitation of the Third World. In a preliminary hearing, later confirmed by the Court of Appeal, it was decided that the evidence to be presented would be of such scientific complexity that it would be beyond the understanding of a jury. (See (1997) *The Times*, 10 June.)

The right to jury trial in defamation cases has been the object of particular criticism. In 1975, the Faulks Committee on the Law of Defamation recommended that the availability of jury trial in that area should be subject to the same judicial discretion as all other civil cases. In its conclusions, the Faulks Report shared the uncertainty of the Court of Appeal in *Ward v James* (1965) as to the suitability of juries to determine the level of damages that should be awarded. Support for these views has been provided by a number of defamation cases decided since then, such as *Sutcliffe v Pressdram Ltd* (1990), in which the wife of a convicted serial killer was awarded damages of £600,000. She eventually settled for £60,000 after the Court of Appeal stated that it would reassess the award.

In *Aldington v Watts and Tolstoy* (1990), damages of £1.5 million were awarded. This huge award was subsequently held by the ECtHR to be so disproportionate as to amount to a violation of Tolstoy's right to freedom of expression under Art 10 of the ECHR (*Tolstoy Miloslavsky v UK* (1995)). Domestic law has also sought to deal with what could only be seen as excessive awards of damages in defamation cases, even prior to the HRA, which makes the ECtHR *Tolstoy* decision and Art 10 of the ECHR binding in UK law.

Section 8 of the CLSA 1990 gave appeal courts the power to alter damages awards made by juries to a level that they felt to be 'proper'. Nonetheless, the question of what actually constitutes a proper level of damages continued to present problems for juries, which continued to award very large sums. The problem arose from the limited guidance that judges could give juries in making their awards. In *Rantzen v Mirror Group Newspapers* (1993), the Court of Appeal stated that judges should advise juries, in making their awards, to consider the purchasing power of the award and its proportionality to the damage suffered to the reputation of the plaintiff, and should refer to awards made by the courts under s 8 of the CLSA (Rantzen's original award of £250,000 was reduced to £110,000). Still, extremely large awards continued to be made, and in *John v MGN Ltd* (1996), the Court of Appeal stated that past practice should be altered to allow juries to refer to personal injury cases to decide the level of award, and that the judge could indicate what sort of level would be appropriate (John's awards of £350,000 for the libel and £275,000 in exemplary damages were reduced to £75,000 and £50,000 respectively).

In 1996, statute law intervened in the form of the Defamation Act, which was designed to simplify the procedure of defamation cases. The main provisions of the Act are:

(a) a new one year limitation period for defamation claims;

(b) a new statutory defence based on responsibility for publication. This replaces the common law defence of innocent dissemination;

(c) an updating of defences in relation to privilege, that is, reporting on the proceedings and publications of, for example, the courts and government;

(d) a new streamlined procedure for dealing with a defendant who has offered to make amends. This would involve paying compensation, assessed by a judge, and publishing an appropriate correction and apology;

(e) new powers for judges to deal with cases without a jury. Under this provision, the judge can dismiss a claim if he considers it has no realistic prospect of success. Alternatively, if he considers there to be no realistic defence to the claim, he can award summary relief. Such relief can take the form of a declaration of the falsity of the statement; an order to print an apology; an order to refrain from repeating the statement; and damages of up to £10,000.

It is a matter of constitutional interest that s 13 of the Defamation Act 1996, altering the operation of s 9 of the Bill of Rights 1689, was specially introduced to allow the former Conservative MP, Neil Hamilton, to bring a defamation action against *The Guardian* newspaper which had accused him of accepting money for asking questions in the House of Commons. The Bill of Rights had granted qualified privilege to MPs, but *The Guardian* had successfully argued that, as they could not sue Hamilton in regard to parliamentary matters, he in turn could not sue them. Unusually, as Law Lords are not supposed to involve themselves in party political matters, s 13 of the Defamation Act, which allowed MPs to waive their privilege, was moved by Lord Hoffmann, apparently at the behest of the then Lord Chancellor, Lord Mackay. Hamilton's action against *The Guardian* subsequently collapsed and he lost his parliamentary seat in the 1997 election. Lord Hoffmann went on to demonstrate his lack of political grasp in the infamous *Pinochet* case (see Chapter 6).

The most significant elements of the Defamation Act came into effect at the end of February 2000, but in January 2001, the Court of Appeal used its common law powers to completely overturn the award of damages in the case of *Grobbelaar v News Group Newspapers Ltd* (2001). Grobbelaar, an ex-football player, had been accused of accepting money to fix football matches. He had been found not guilty in a criminal case and had been awarded £85,000 damages for defamation in a related civil case against *The Sun* newspaper. On appeal, the Court of Appeal held that the newspaper could not rely on the defence of limited qualified privilege, as recently recognised in *Reynolds v Times Newspapers Ltd and Others* (1999), and could be held to account for such defamatory statements as could not be proved true. However, although the court stated that it would be most reluctant to find perversity in a jury's verdict, it had such jurisdiction and, therefore, duty to consider that ground of appeal. The court then went on to conclude that no reasonable jury could have failed to be satisfied on the balance of probabilities, and to a relatively high degree of probability, that Grobbelaar had been party to corrupt conspiracies. The court considered that the evidence led inexorably to the view that Grobbelaar's story was 'quite simply incredible. All logic, common sense and reason compelled one to that conclusion'.

As regards overturning the decision of the jury, in the words of Thorpe LJ:

> I recognise and respect the unique function of a jury that heard all of the evidence over some 16 days of trial, nevertheless it would be an injustice to the defendants to allow the outcome to stand.

On further appeal, the House of Lords held that the Court of Appeal was correct in holding that the jury's decision was open to review on the grounds of perversity. However, it found that the Court of Appeal had been wrong to overturn the jury's verdict on the grounds of perversity in this instance, as the verdict could have been explained in such a way that did not necessarily require the imputation of adversity. Grobbelaar's victory, however, was pyrrhic in the extreme; due to his breach of his legal and moral obligations, the damages awarded by the jury were quashed and substituted by the award of nominal damages of £1, with no costs awarded.

The extent of damages and, in particular, exemplary damages awarded against the police in a number of civil actions has also been problematic (see 7.9 for a consideration of types of damages). These actions have arisen from wrongful arrest, false imprisonment, assault and malicious prosecution and usually have involved connotations of racist behaviour on the part of the police. In setting the level of damages, juries have wished signally to demonstrate their disapproval of such police behaviour, but as the courts have correctly pointed out, any payments made come from the public purse, not from the individuals involved. The issue came to a head in *Thompson and Another v Commissioner of Police for the Metropolis* (1997), in which the Court of Appeal considered awards made to two plaintiffs. The first had been assaulted in custody and false evidence was used against her in a criminal trial during which she was held in prison. In a civil action, she was awarded £51,500 damages, of which £50,000 were exemplary damages. The second plaintiff was physically and racially abused by police when they broke into his house and arrested him. In a consequential civil action, he was awarded £220,000 for wrongful arrest, false imprisonment and assault, of which £200,000 were exemplary damages. On appeal, the Court of Appeal stated that in such cases, the judge should direct the jury that:

(i) damages, save in exceptional circumstances, should be awarded only as compensation and in line with a scale which keeps the damages proportionate with those payable in personal injury cases;

(ii) where aggravated damages are appropriate, they are unlikely to be less than £1,000, or to be more than twice the basic damages except where those basic damages are modest;

(iii) in relation to the award of exemplary damages the jury should be told of the exceptional nature of the remedy, and told that the basic and aggravated damages together must be insufficient to punish the defendant before any exemplary damages can be considered. Where exemplary damages are appropriate they are unlikely to be less than £5,000. Conduct must be particularly deserving of condemnation to warrant an award of £25,000 and the absolute maximum should be £50,000. It would be unusual for such damages to be more than three times the basic damages being awarded unless those basic damages are modest.

In the two cases in question, the first exemplary award was reduced from £50,000 to £25,000; and in the second, the exemplary component was reduced from £200,000 to £15,000.

The reasoning in the *Thompson* case was followed in *Hill v Commissioner of Police for the Metropolis* (1998), where the plaintiff was awarded £45,600 for wrongful arrest, false imprisonment, assault and malicious prosecution. The most contentious award was that of exemplary damages, the bracket having been set by the judge as between £5,000–£15,000, but the jury awarded the plaintiff £20,000. The Court of Appeal held that the jury had only gone beyond the guidelines to a limited extent and it was clear that they had taken a poor view of the police officers' conduct. In those circumstances, although the total award was high and might be seen to be out of proportion to awards made in personal injury cases, it was not seen as manifestly excessive in relation to Thompson's case.

If the extent of damages has been a particular problem in relation to defamation claims, especially when they are compared to the much smaller awards made in relation to personal injury, it should also be noted that public funding is not normally available in defamation cases, although it is available in relation to malicious falsehood. This effectively has made defamation a rich person's claim. As a consequence, people without the necessary wealth to finance legal proceedings find it extremely difficult to gain redress when they have suffered from what subsequently turns out to be false and damaging press coverage of their affairs. It is to be hoped that the new summary procedure, under the Defamation Act 1996, will redress this situation. But of equal concern is the way some wealthy people were able and allowed to abuse the system. One example was the late and notorious publisher, Robert Maxwell, who often used libel proceedings or the threat of them to silence critics. As it turned out, much of what Mr Maxwell sought to prevent from becoming public knowledge was in fact illegal and harmful business conduct.

In all other civil cases, there is a presumption against trial by jury although, under s 69(3), the judge has the discretion to order a trial by jury. (See *Ward v James* (1965), where the court decided that a jury should be used in civil cases only in 'exceptional circumstances', although no exhaustive list as to what amounted to exceptional circumstances was provided.)

10.7.2 Juries in criminal trials

It has to be borne in mind that the criminal jury trial is essentially the creature of the Crown Court, and that the magistrates' courts deal with 95% of criminal cases. In practice, juries determine the outcome of less than 1% of the total of criminal cases for the reason that, of all the cases that are decided in the Crown Court, 60% of defendants plead guilty on all counts and therefore have no need of jury trial. It can be seen, therefore, that in absolute and proportional terms, the jury does not play a significant part in the determination of criminal cases.

If trial by jury is not statistically significant, it cannot be denied that it is of major significance in the determination of the most serious cases. Even this role, however, has not gone without scrutiny, as will be seen below.

It should not be forgotten that the right to jury trial has been abolished in Northern Ireland since 1973. In response to the problem of the intimidation of jury members, the *Report of the Commission to Consider Legal Procedures to Deal with Terrorist Activities in Northern Ireland*, headed by Lord Diplock, recommended that cases be decided without juries in particular situations. The so called 'Diplock courts' operate in relation to certain 'scheduled offences', particularly, but not exclusively, associated with terrorism.

10.8 Jury reform

10.8.1 Roskill Committee

In 1986, the Roskill Committee on Fraud Trials critically examined the operation of the jury in complex criminal fraud cases. Its report recommended the abolition of trial by jury in such cases. The Roskill Committee did not go as far as to recommend that all fraud cases should be taken away from juries, only the most complex, of which it was estimated that there were about two dozen or so every year. It was suggested that these cases would be better decided by a judge assisted by two lay persons drawn from a panel with specialist expertise. The government declined to implement the recommendations of the Roskill Committee, and instead introduced procedures designed to make it easier to follow the proceedings in complex fraud cases.

After being found not guilty of a £19 million fraud charge, George Walker, the former chief executive of Brent Walker, said: 'Thank God for the jury. It would be madness to lose the jury system.' This enthusiastic endorsement of the jury system is in no little way undercut, however, by the fact that Walker is reported as going on to state that he was sure the jury had not properly understood much of the highly detailed material in the trial, as he admitted: 'I didn't understand a lot of it, so I can't see how they could.'

Mr Walker's enthusiasm perhaps was not shared by his co-accused, Wilfred Aquilina, who was found guilty, on a majority verdict, of false accounting.

In February 1998, the Home Office issued a Green Paper entitled *Juries in Serious Fraud Trials*. The Consultation Paper suggested the need for a new procedure in relation to complex fraud trials, due to the fact that 'the detection, investigation and trial of serious criminal fraud offences have presented certain difficulties not commonly found amongst other types of offences'. A variety of possible alternatives were put forward:

- Special juries: these would be made up of qualified people and might be drawn from a special pool of potential jurors. Alternatively, ordinary jurors would have to be assessed as to their competency to sit on the case.

- Judge run trials: specially trained judges, either singly or in a panel, and possibly with the help of lay experts.

- Fraud tribunals: following Roskill, these would be made up of a judge and qualified lay members with the power to question witnesses.

- Verdict only juries: in this situation, the judge would hear the evidence and sum up the facts, leaving the jury simply to vote on guilt or innocence.

- A special juror: here, 11 of the jury would be selected as normal, but the 12th would be specially qualified in order to be able to assist the others on complex points.

With respect to these alternatives, the government stated that it had no particular preference.

Under the proposals, a judge would decide at a pre-trial hearing if the case would be heard by an ordinary jury, or under whichever of the possible new procedures was finally selected. The Green Paper estimated that, at most, 85 cases each year would be subject to the new procedure, but significantly, it was also estimated that adopting the new procedures would cut costs by up to 25%.

Subsequently, in April 1998, the Home Secretary requested the Law Commission to carry out a review of fraud trials, focusing particularly on whether the existing law was:

- readily comprehensible to juries;
- adequate for effective prosecution;
- fair to defendants; and
- able to cope with changes in technology.

However, in its response in Consultation Paper No 155, *Fraud and Deception* (1999), the Law Commission addressed only the issues of possible criminal offences and did not deal with any procedural issues. The recent White Paper, *Justice for All*, states (4.30) that each year about 15–20 of the most complex fraud trials should be dealt with by a judge sitting alone. For a useful discussion, see D Corker, 'Trying fraud cases without juries' [2002] Crim LR 283–94. The proposals relating to fraud trials contained in the Criminal Justice Bill 2002 will be considered at 10.8.5, below.

10.8.2 The Runciman Commission

The Report of the Royal Commission on Criminal Justice made numerous recommendations relating to juries. Indeed, the very first recommendation made by it was that s 8 of the Contempt of Court Act 1981 should be repealed to enable research to be conducted into juries' reasons for their verdicts. At present, s 8 makes it an offence to obtain, disclose or solicit any particulars of statements made, opinion expressed, arguments advanced or votes cast by members of a jury in the course of their deliberations in any legal proceedings.

In relation specifically to the selection of juries, the Commission addressed itself to many of the problems that were considered above and made the following recommendations:

- Every endeavour should be made to ensure that the electoral rolls are comprehensive and include everybody who ought to be included.

- Clergymen and members of religious orders should be eligible, but practising members of religious sects which object to jury service should be excluded.

  This was supported by Auld LJ in his 2001 report (see www.criminal-courts-review.org.uk).

- Potential jurors should be given alternative dates if they cannot sit on the date originally suggested.

- The rates of financial allowances for those on jury service should be reviewed as a matter of urgency.

  This is a clear recognition of the fact that it costs people money to serve on juries and that, as a consequence, people try to avoid their social and legal duty to serve.

- Jury summoning officers should try to make sure that potential jury members do not know each other or the accused.

The Commission made some recommendations designed to improve the operation of the existing disqualification procedure:

- When the national criminal record system is fully operational, courts should arrange for that agency to screen jurors on a routine basis to discover any disqualifying convictions they might have.

- Jurors should be required to positively affirm that they have no disqualifying convictions, and should be open to conviction if they provide false information.

There were, however, some recommendations that were less obviously justified or needed and which give some cause to suspect the underlying purpose of the Commission's report in general. These are as follows:

- People currently on bail should be disqualified from serving.

  One is immediately prompted to ask why such people should be disqualified. By definition, they have not been convicted of the offence of which they stand charged, and may not be. Is disqualifying them on no other ground than that they have been charged with an offence, not tantamount to pre-judging the case against them?

  In any case, the proposal was effected by s 40 of the CJPOA 1994 and, consequently, any person on bail in criminal proceedings is disqualified from serving as a juror in the Crown Court. The disqualification does not cover service in civil proceedings.

- Once s 8 of the Contempt of Court Act is repealed, it is recommended that research be carried out into the possible influence of jurors with criminal records on the decisions of juries.

It would appear to be an implicit assumption that such people have a deleterious effect on the operation of juries. The further implication is that such research would be conducted to prove the point, as the first step to disqualifying them as potential jurors. Thus, the apparently praiseworthy procedure of opening up the jury process to investigation may have the ulterior motive of intending to discredit its operation.

In relation to the ethnic origin of jurors, the Runciman Commission addressed the difficulties looked at above (see 10.6.8) and made the following recommendations:

- In exceptional cases, it should be possible for either the prosecution or the defence to apply to the trial judge to have the jury selected in such a way as to ensure that it contains three people from ethnic minority communities.

- It should also be open for the prosecution or defence to argue the need that one of these three be of the same ethnic minority as the defendant or the victim.

It should be noted that these two measures would not just operate in cases where the accused was a member of an ethnic minority, but could also be used in relation to trials involving white accused, perhaps charged with racist offences. In either situation, the intention would be to provide a signal indication of the impartiality of the procedure.

As regards the conduct of trials, most of the proposals made in this section relate to ensuring that jurors are fully aware of what is going on in the court and what is expected of them. There are a couple of recommendations that are worthy of closer consideration:

- Every effort should be made to protect jurors from intimidation. Guidance should be given to jurors on what to do if they feel intimidated, and in sensitive cases, the public gallery should be sited in such a way as to preclude the possibility of intimidation of the jury.

  In the context of this chapter, it is worth noting that claims about intimidation have been used to justify the removal of jury trials in Northern Ireland. This proposal, however, appears to be a reasonable and practical suggestion designed to curtail the problem without undermining the jury system. Section 51 of the CJPOA 1994 introduced the offence of jury intimidation in furtherance of this aim.

- With specific regard to fraud trials, it was recommended that s 10(3) of the CJA 1988 should be amended to permit judges to put the issues before the jury at the outset of the trial.

  This proposal recognises the particular difficulties faced by jurors in fraud trials but, in the light of the controversy considered below in cases triable 'either way', it is interesting to note that the Commission did not suggest the removal of the jury from such cases.

The general proposals of the Runciman Commission in relation to juries were not without an element of controversy, but it was, without doubt, the Commission's proposal to limit the role of the jury in the criminal process that generated the most debate. This particular recommendation, number 114 out of a total 352, stimulated more response than any other single proposal; by and large, that response was hostile.

In order to understand the full implications of the recommendation, it is necessary to reconsider points that have been discussed previously in Chapters 4 and 6.

It is essential to appreciate the distinction between offences to be tried only by summary procedure, offences to be tried only on indictment and offences triable 'either way'. Summary offences are those which are triable only in the magistrates' courts and cases which, as has been noted previously, magistrates decide on their own without the assistance of a jury. There are literally hundreds of summary offences; given the limitations on the sentencing powers of magistrates, they are by necessity the least serious of criminal acts, such as road traffic offences and minor assault. The most serious offences, such as major theft, serious assault, rape, manslaughter and murder, have to be tried on indictment before a jury in the Crown Court. There is, however, a third category, offences triable 'either way' which, as the name suggests, may be tried either summarily or on indictment. It was the Runciman Commission's recommendation in relation to this third category that gave rise to most controversy.

The current way of determining how an offence triable 'either way' is actually heard is set out in the Magistrates' Courts Act (MCA) 1980. Under s 19 of that Act, the magistrates' court has to decide whether the offence is more suitable for summary trial or trial on indictment. In reaching that decision, the magistrates must take into account the nature of the case, its seriousness, whether the penalty they could impose would be adequate, and any other circumstances which appear to the court to make it more suitable for the offence to be tried one way rather than the other. If the magistrates decide that the case is suitable for summary hearing, they are required by s 20 of the MCA 1980 to inform the defendant of their decision and also to inform him that if he pleads guilty or is found guilty on the summary hearing, he may still be committed to the Crown Court for sentencing if the magistrates are of the opinion that their powers of sentencing are inadequate. If the accused agrees to a summary hearing, the trial goes ahead in the magistrates' court. If, however, the defendant objects to the summary procedure, the case goes on indictment to the Crown Court and the magistrates merely act as examining justices. It is this latter right, the right of the defendant in cases triable 'either way' to elect for/insist on a trial by jury, that the Runciman Commission recommended should be removed.

The Commission's Report stated that defendants should not 'be able to choose their court of trial solely on the basis that they think that they will get a fairer hearing at one level than another' (see para 6.18 of the Report). The conclusion of the Commission seems to be that, because defendants do not trust the magistrates' court, and there is some justification for this in respect of the rates of acquittal, and do have more faith in the Crown Court than is warranted in terms of sentencing, then they should be forced to use the magistrates' court. As the report stated: 'Magistrates' courts conduct over 93% of all criminal cases and should be trusted to try cases fairly' (see para 6.18 of the Report). It is at least arguable that in this conclusion, the Commission is missing the point. Put starkly, the evidence supports the conclusion that defendants do not trust magistrates' courts. Indeed, the evidence as to the number of people changing their plea to guilty in the Crown Court would seem to support the conclusion, not so much that defendants trust juries, but more that they do not trust magistrates. This lack of trust in the magistracy is further highlighted by the fact that those who do not plead guilty would rather have their guilt or innocence determined by a jury.

Simply forcing such people to use the magistrates' courts does not address the underlying problem, let alone solve it.

It would have been possible for the Commission to have achieved its end by simply recommending that particular offences that are defined as triable 'either way' at present should be re-categorised as offences only open to summary procedure. That it did not do so further indicates the weakness of the underlying logic of its case for removing the right to insist on trial on indictment. The Commission rejected the reclassification of offences partly because of the difficulty and uncertainty inherent in the task. Additionally, and more importantly, however, it rejected this approach because it wished to leave available the possibility of the defendant successfully insisting on trial on indictment in the case of first offenders, where the consequences of loss of reputation would be significant. In the words of the Commission: 'Loss of reputation is a different matter, since jury trial has long been regarded as appropriate for cases involving that issue. But, it should only be one of the factors to be taken into account and will often be relevant only to first offenders' (see para 6.18 of the Report).

There are two assumptions in this proposal. First, there is the surely objectionable, assumption that the reputation of anyone with a previous conviction is not important. But of even more concern is the fact that it is recognised that in the cases of first offenders, they should be permitted access to the jury. The question has to be asked: why should this be the case if juries do no more than magistrates do? It appears that in the instance of first offenders, it is recognised that juries do offer more protection than magistrates. Again, this demands the question: why should the extra protection not be open to all? Thus, once more the economic imperative that motivated the

Commission comes into question, and once again the pursuit of lower cost takes over from the need to be clearly seen to provide justice.

It has been claimed that this proposal comes dangerously close to advocating a two tier system of criminal justice, with the cheaper version being reserved for the punishment of the 'criminal classes'. Opposition to it has been voluble and former Lord Chief Justice Taylor stated his personal disapprobation. Also, the former Vice President of The Law Society, Charles Elly, stated the Society's strong opposition to this particular proposal and expressed the view that it 'can only have been based on the interests of cost-cutting, not of justice'. The then Chairman of the Criminal Bar, whilst approving of the rest of the Report, was equally outspoken about this proposal. As he saw it, the abolition of the right to jury trial in such cases was: '... likely to involve unequal treatment of defendants, favouring those whom society views as more respectable than others.' Or, as Michael Mansfield QC put the matter: 'If the Commission has its way we are racing towards middle class justice.'

10.8.3 Criminal Justice (Mode of Trial) Bills

The Runciman Commission Report was produced under the auspices of a Conservative government operating under an economic imperative to reduce costs. If those who were opposed to its findings found comfort in the election of a New Labour government in 1997, they were soon to be disabused when the new (now former) Home Secretary, Jack Straw, announced his intention to reduce the rights to jury trials, essentially to the same end as the Runciman proposals. Thus, the first Criminal Justice (Mode of Trial) Bill was introduced in the parliamentary session of 1999–2000. This Bill sought to amend the MCA 1980 by introducing sections which gave the magistrates, rather than the accused, the power to decide whether a case should be tried summarily or on indictment. As Runciman's Report had been, so the new Bill was solicitous of the protection of those accused whose reputation 'would be seriously damaged as a result of conviction'. The Bill was generally criticised as an illiberal measure by civil liberties organisations and the legal professions, but was particularly attacked for the manner in which it sought to protect the rights of individuals with reputations to protect. Such solicitude for those with reputations to protect, apparently as opposed to the common majority of people, was seen as inherently unjust and dangerously class based. The opposition to the Bill outside Parliament was matched, and more importantly so in relation to its legislative progress, by equal opposition within the House of Lords, which voted against its passage.

Undaunted by the rejection of his Bill, the Home Secretary re-introduced a reformed version of it in the Criminal Justice (Mode of Trial) (No 2) Bill. In acknowledgment of criticisms of the earlier Bill, the (No 2) Bill made it clear that the reputation, or any other personal characteristic, of the accused was not something to be taken into account by the magistrates in deciding on the mode of trial. Nonetheless, the Bill was once again defeated in the House of Lords in 2001.

Although the newly re-elected government insisted that it retained the power to use the Parliament Acts to force a mode of trial Bill through the House of Lords, its approach altered following the publishing of the report on the criminal courts conducted by Sir Robin Auld.

10.8.4 The Auld Review

In his extensive *Review of the Criminal Courts,* Sir Robin Auld LJ included recommendations which were aimed specifically at the current operation of the jury within the criminal justice system. In summary, he recommended the following points:

- Jurors should be more widely representative than they are of the national and local communities from which they are drawn. Qualification for jury service should remain the same, save that entitlement to, rather than actual, entry on an electoral role should be a criterion. Potential jurors should be identified from a combination of a number of public registers and lists.

- No one in future should be ineligible for, or excusable as of right from, jury service. While those with criminal convictions and mental disorder should continue to be disqualified, any claimed inability to serve should be a matter for discretionary deferral or excusal.

- Provision should be made to enable ethnic minority representation on juries where race is likely to be relevant to an important issue in the case.

- The law should not be amended to permit more intrusive research than is already possible into the workings of juries, though in appropriate cases, trial judges and/or the Court of Appeal should be entitled to examine alleged improprieties in the jury room.

- The law should be declared, by statute if need be, that juries have no right to acquit defendants in defiance of the law or in disregard of the evidence.

- If the jury's verdict appears to be perverse, the prosecution should be entitled to appeal on the grounds that the perversity is indicative that the verdict is likely to be unfair or untrue.

- The defendant should no longer have an elective right to trial by judge and jury in 'either way' cases.

- Trial by judge and jury should remain the main form of trial of the more serious offences triable on indictment, that is, those that would go to the Crown Division, subject to four exceptions:
  (i) defendants should be entitled, with the court's consent, to opt for trial by judge alone;

(ii) in serious and complex frauds, the nominated trial judge should have the power to direct trial by himself and two lay members drawn from a panel established by the Lord Chancellor for the purpose (or, if the defendant requests, by himself alone);

(iii) a Youth Court, constituted by a judge of an appropriate level and at least two experienced youth panel magistrates, should be given jurisdiction to hear all grave cases against young defendants;

(iv) legislation should be introduced to require a judge, not a jury, to determine the issue of fitness to plead.

10.8.5 Criminal Justice Bill 2002

Within this extremely extensive piece of proposed legislation, the Criminal Justice Bill did focus on aspects of the jury system:

- Jury service will be widened by abolishing all exemptions from jury service, apart from those suffering from a mental illness. Thus, judges, lawyers, the police and all others will be required to serve as jurors. The aim is to make the jury representative of the community in reality, rather than merely in theory, as is currently the case.

- The proposed legislation will allow trial by a judge alone in the following circumstances:

  (i) where the accused has requested such a trial. It is thought that this proposal might be used in sex-related cases. Any application will have to be approved by the court;

  (ii) cases relating to complex or lengthy commercial/financial cases. This proposal actually goes further than Auld or previous recommendations in reducing the role of juries in fraud trials;

  (iii) where there is a serious risk of jury intimidation.

- The sentencing powers of magistrates will be increased from 6 to 12 months, with the Home Secretary being given the authority to increase that limit to 18 months. It has been suggested that this proposal will obviate the need to introduce more contentious measures such as the previous Mode of Trial Bills, as it will directly increase the powers of magistrates without the need to re-categorise either way offences.

10.8.6 Conclusion

It has been repeatedly suggested by those in favour of abolishing, or at least severely curtailing, the role of the jury in the criminal justice system that the general perception of the jury is romanticised and has little foundation in reality. Runciman did not actually make this point explicitly, but it is implicit in his assessment of the jury system as against the magistrates' courts. Others have been more explicit; thus, the Roskill Committee expressed the view that:

> Society appears to have an attachment to jury trial which is emotional or
> sentimental rather than logical [para 8.21].

A similar point had been made previously by the Faulks Committee, but that
report also recognised the source of the public's opinion and was careful not to
dismiss it as unimportant:

> Much of the support for jury trials is emotional and derives from the undoubted
> value of juries in serious criminal cases where they stand between the
> prosecuting authority and the citizen [para 496].

The jury system certainly commands considerable public support. A recent
survey asked 903 members of the public how they felt about the restrictions to
trial by jury proposed by Lord Justice Auld; 66% of respondents opposed the
proposals and only 28% were in favour.

The ideological power of the jury system should not be under-estimated. It
represents the ordinary person's input into the legal system and it is at least
arguable that in that way, it provides the whole legal system with a sense of
legitimacy. It is argued by some civil libertarians that the existence of the non-
jury Diplock courts in Northern Ireland brings the whole of the legal system in
that province into disrepute.

As Lord Devlin noted (*Trial By Jury*, 1966):

> The first object of any tyrant in Whitehall would be to make Parliament utterly
> subservient to his will; and the next to overthrow or diminish trial by jury, for
> no tyrant could afford to leave a subject's freedom in the hands of 12 of his
> countrymen.

It should also be noted that most jurors seem to be reasonably happy with the
system despite the stress and inconvenience it can impose on them. In 2000, the
Court Service carried out a 'Jury Satisfaction Survey' (unpublished). This
revealed that 95% of those questioned were satisfied or very satisfied with their
treatment by the criminal justice system.

THE CRIMINAL PROCESS: (2)
THE PROSECUTION

The Crown Prosecution Service

The Crown Prosecution Service (CPS) was introduced in 1986, and it is important to understand the five types of prosecution which existed before this time and how the CPS was supposed to resolve the criticisms of the old system. What sort of biases can occur in the use of prosecutorial discretion and why? Why were the police regarded as not the most suitable agency to exercise the prosecutorial discretion? What were the police defences to those criticisms? The police argued that conviction rates vindicated the way they exercised their discretion. The Code for Crown Prosecutors (2000) specifies factors which should weigh for and against a prosecution.

Cautioning offenders

Cautioning offenders is now applicable only to adults, with a new system of reprimands and warnings applying to young offenders. The CPS guidelines on prosecution require a 'realistic prospect of conviction' and that the 'public interest' is served by any prosecution. What difficulties are caused by such formulae?

Judicial control

Judicial control of prosecution policy is very limited and amounts to being able to correct only flagrantly irrational decisions by senior officers (*R v Metropolitan Police Commissioner ex p Blackburn* (1968)).

Bail

Bail is the release from custody, pending a criminal trial, of an accused on the promise that money will be paid if he absconds. The important issue raised here is how best the regulations should be framed so as to balance the conflicting interests of public safety and civil liberty. Public safety would perhaps be best served by keeping in custody everyone accused of a crime until their trial; this, though, would clearly be unnecessarily draconian. Conversely, civil liberty might be best served by allowing every suspect to remain free, however heinous the crime of which they have been accused and whatever their past record. The important statutory provisions are s 38 of the Police and Criminal Evidence Act 1984 and ss 3, 4 and 6 of and Sched 1 to the Bail Act 1976.

Changes made by the Bail (Amendment) Act 1993 and the Criminal Justice and Public Order Act 1994 allow prosecutors to appeal against the granting of bail, restrict some aspects of it being granted, and afford greater opportunities for police bail.

Plea bargaining

Plea bargaining is the practice where the accused enters a plea of guilty in return for which he will be given a sentence concession. It can also refer to 'plea arrangements' where the accused agrees to plead guilty to a lesser charge than the one with which he is, or is to be, charged. Note the recommendation of the Runciman Commission to introduce sentence discounting as a means to avoid 'cracked trials'. Dangers arising from such procedures include innocent persons being pressurised to 'take a plea' and serious offenders being processed for minor offences. In a system where the vast majority of cases in the Crown Court and magistrates' courts result in guilty pleas (79% and 81.5%, respectively), the operation of the plea bargain becomes very important.

The jury

The jury has come under close public scrutiny since the Runciman Commission's recommendation to curtail the right to jury trial. It is important to know the standard arguments in favour of the jury and also the arguments showing it to be not truly random and representative. The detail of the jury's function in a trial and the extent to which its verdict can be appealed against are important. In what ways can the membership of the jury be challenged? What arguments were adopted by the Runciman Commission when recommending fewer jury trials? Juries lie at the heart of the English criminal justice system. There is debate about whether juries provide any better justice than magistrates' courts or whether the role is purely symbolic. The recommendations in Auld LJ's report on the criminal courts are important; they include the proposal to make juries more widely representative of national and local communities.

The role of the jury

To decide matters of fact – judges decide matters of law. Judges can instruct juries to acquit but not to convict. Juries do not have to give reasons for their decision. There is no appeal against an acquittal verdict, although points of law may be clarified by an Attorney General's reference. Civil cases can be overturned if perverse – but not criminal cases. Verdicts can be delivered on the basis of majority decisions. The use of juries has declined in relation to criminal and civil law.

Selection of juries

Random in theory – selective in practice. All on the electoral register are liable to serve, but the registers tend to be inaccurate. Service is subject to exemption, excusal and disqualification. Defence and prosecution can challenge for cause. Prosecution can ask jurors to stand by. Jury vetting is checking that jurors are suitable to hear sensitive cases. If Runciman is followed, juries may be required to have a racial mix.

The Runciman Report

Section 8 of the Contempt of Court Act 1981 should be amended. Attempts should be made to improve the representative nature of juries. The operation of disqualification procedures should be tightened and extended to those on bail. The ethnic mix of a jury should be open to adjustment. In complex fraud trials, judges should be permitted to explain the matters involved at the outset of the trial. Magistrates should have the final say in where offences triable 'either way' are heard.

CHAPTER 11

LEGAL SERVICES

11.1 Introduction

We are concerned here with a number of issues related to the provision and organisation of legal services, and issues of public access to legal services. The delivery of legal services at the outset of the 21st century looks very different from the way things were as recently as 1970. The legal profession has undergone a series of major changes as a result of the Courts and Legal Services Act (CLSA) 1990; the provision of public funding, advice and assistance has been drastically altered as a result of changes introduced in 1999. The introduction of the 'conditional fee arrangement' (no win, no fee) in 1995 was another contentious issue in this area. In the 1950s, only a minute proportion of the population used lawyers to solve problems. Now, in the 2000s, a great many individuals, small businesses and organisations are using lawyers often as a matter of course.

In several respects, the delivery of legal services is working effectively and is set on a path of improvement in respect of both the nature and extent of what is being offered. In 2003, for example, the Chairman of the Bar of England and Wales noted:

> We have a strong Bar. In 1980, there were 4,589 barristers in practice. By 1986 that number had risen to 5,489. By 1990 there were 6,579 in practice. Today there are 10,207 in private practice plus 3,300 in employed practice [ie, working for companies or organisations not from chambers]. That growth in numbers shows a steadily increasing demand for the services which the Bar has to offer [Matthias Kelly QC, *Counsel*, February 2003].

The Law Society, whose membership has also risen steadily over the same period (from about 58,000 members in 1986 to 80,000 in 2003), presents the following among its 'Key Objectives' for the period 2002–04:

> ... to provide prompt redress for consumers and effective enforcement and disciplinary mechanisms; to reinforce the Law Society's role as a promoter of equal opportunities and diversity within the profession; to establish the Law Society as an authoritative voice on law reform in the public interest; to promote effective justice for all; to champion the unique role of the solicitor in society ... to help solicitors break into new markets and new areas of employment ... [The Law Society, *The Corporate Plan, Annual Report*, 2002].

According to The Law Society's annual statistical report for 2001, the law firms of England and Wales generate £10.5 billion a year, and if the rate of growth in the profession continues at the rate at which it has been expanding since the 1970s (Neil Rose, 'The way we are' (2002) *The Gazette*, 19 September, p 22) then by 2055, we shall have one million lawyers. Whether such a development is an index of a healthy, rights-conscious society or an unhealthy, disputatious society is an interesting question. The global lawyer-population ratio is 1:2,370, whereas in England and Wales it is 1:600.

There are, however, many aspects of the provision of legal services that are problematic. In a consultative document published by the Lord Chancellor's Department, *Legal Advice Services: A Pathway Out of Social Exclusion* (Lord Chancellor's Department, 16 November 2001), the result of a collaboration between the Lord Chancellor's Department and the Law Centres Federation, the problem of providing legal services to poor, marginal or insecure people is addressed. Case studies in the report show how legal and advice services can help in a variety of situations and can link with the objectives of other government departments. The case studies cover homelessness, mental health problems, debt and money problems, welfare benefit issues, family and relationship difficulties, education problems and diversity issues. In all of them legal and advice services can play an important role alongside other agencies in helping to bring social justice to the socially excluded. It is clear that early and appropriate legal help can save much worry and hardship for a large group of people, and legal and advice services are an effective partner for other agencies helping the socially excluded. Social exclusion is what happens when people or areas suffer from a combination of linked problems such as lack of access to services, unemployment, poor skills, low incomes, poor housing, crime, poor health and family breakdowns. These problems are bad enough on their own, but, as the report notes, the problems are made worse through the way they are often interlinked, which compounds the deprivation which many people face in their everyday lives. Social exclusion can affect anyone. But certain groups, such as those growing up in low income households or with family conflict, those who do not attend school and some minority ethnic communities, are particularly at risk. These groups tend to get their services from any of the wide range of providers of legal and advice services, and while solicitors' firms make up the largest number of legal service providers, there are a growing number of other sources of help, such as Law Centres, Citizens Advice Bureaux, independent advice centres and local authority services.

In 2001, the Office of Fair Trading (OFT) published a report by the Director General of Fair Trading entitled *Competition in Professions*. That report was accompanied by a detailed report from the OFT consultants, Law and Economics Consulting Group (LECG). The paper touches on matters like conveyancing, multi-disciplinary partnerships and the QC system.

It is to be noted that restrictions on competition may be justified if, for example, they are in the public interest. The OFT report highlighted some of the potential anti-competitive restrictions found in the legal professions, like the requirement for a consumer to use a solicitor and a barrister in some cases where the work could, apparently, be adequately executed by a single expert. The OFT did not, however, examine justifications of restrictions (for example, countervailing consumer benefits). As was noted by another committee investigating legal services:

> In examining restrictive practices, a balance has to be struck between de-regulation on the one hand and the need to safeguard consumers on the other [*A Time for Change* – the Marre Committee report on the future of the legal professions, 1988].

The government's aim is to ensure that the professions are properly subject to competition. In most cases, the theory of modern capitalism is that open and competitive markets are the best way to ensure that consumers get the best possible service. On all the issues raised in this consultation, the government's position was that the market should be opened up to competition unless there existed strong reasons why that should not be the case, such as evidence that real consumer detriment might result from such a change. A number of questions in the document sought information about the likely level of demand from other potential providers of legal services. This information will be useful in gauging the speed with which change in the market might take place, but evidence of low demand would not in itself, the government stated, be sufficient reason to justify a decision not to open up the market. The Lord Chancellor's Department will consider what further steps might be needed in respect of the market for legal services to ensure that competition issues are fully addressed.

It is important when considering all the elements of this chapter to ask yourself questions about the aims of all the systems and proposed changes to them. What is their immediate aim? Is such an immediate aim part of a wider legal or social objective? How does the funding of any given component operate and what do its critics say is wrong or undesirable about it or the way it works?

11.2 The legal profession

The English legal system is one of only three in the world to have a divided legal profession where a lawyer is either a solicitor or a barrister. Each branch has its own separate traditions, training requirements and customs of practice. It is important to remember that not only lawyers regularly perform legal work. As one text notes (Bailey and Gunn, *Smith & Bailey on the Modern English Legal System* (1991), p 105):

> ... many non-lawyers perform legal tasks, some of them full time. For example, accountants may specialise in revenue law, trade union officials may appear regularly before industrial tribunals on behalf of their members, and solicitors may delegate work to legal executives. Conversely, many of the tasks performed by lawyers are not strictly 'legal'.

11.3   Solicitors

The solicitor can be characterised as a general practitioner: a lawyer who deals with clients direct, and when a particular specialism or litigation is required, will engage the services of counsel, that is, a barrister. Looking at the solicitor as a legal GP and the barrister as a specialist, however, can be misleading. Most solicitors, especially those in large practices, are experts in particular areas of law. They may restrict their regular work to litigation or commercial conveyancing or revenue work. Many barristers on the other hand might have a quite wide range of work including criminal, family matters and a variety of common law areas like tort and contract cases. The origins of the solicitor go back to the attornatus, or later the 'attorney', a medieval officer of the court whose main function was to assist the client in the initial stages of the case. One group of people practising in the Court of Chancery came to be known as 'solicitors'. Originally, they performed a variety of miscellaneous clerical tasks for employers such as landowners and attorneys. Their name was derived from their function of 'soliciting' or prosecuting actions in courts of which they were not officers or attorneys. Eventually, neither of these groups was admitted to the Inns of Court (where barristers worked); they merged and organised themselves as a distinct profession.

It was not, however, until 1831 that 'The Society of Attorneys Solicitors Proctors and Others not being Barristers Practising in the Courts of Law and Equity in the UK' was given its Royal Charter. This body emerged as the governing body of solicitors, the term 'attorney' falling from general use.

According to the latest Law Society figures available in March 2003 (*Key Facts 2002: The Solicitors' Profession*), there are 113,372 solicitors 'on the Roll', that is, people qualified to work as solicitors, of whom 89,045 have a current practising certificate (pc). This represents a growth of about 10% during the last 10 years. The number of women solicitors with pcs has increased by 120% from 15,563 to 34,366. The percentage of pc holders drawn from minority ethnic groups has increased from 2.2% to 8.2%. Just over half of all solicitors with a practising certificate are aged 40 or under. The geographical distribution of solicitors leaves much room for improvement. Of the 9,231 law firms in England and Wales, 26% are in London, and approaching one-half of all firms are in a single region: the south east. Firms in London employ 42% of the 70,571 solicitors in private practice.

One very significant area of development and concern for solicitors at the beginning of the 21st century is the extent to which their monopolies of certain sorts of practice have been eroded. They have already lost their monopoly on conveyancing (although only a solicitor is authorised to give final endorsement to such work if carried out by a licensed conveyancer). Then, in 1999, the Access to Justice Act (see Chapter 12) introduced the provision that the Lord Chancellor would in future be able to authorise bodies other than The Law Society to approve of their members carrying out litigation. This, however, should be seen in the wider context of the policy to break down the historical monopolies of both branches of the legal profession. Thus, we can note the growth, since the CLSA 1990, of solicitors' rights of audience in court, and a corresponding anxiety at the Bar when these rights were granted.

The 1999 Act provides that every barrister and every solicitor has a right of audience before every court in relation to all proceedings. The right, however, is not unconditional. In order to exercise it, solicitors and barristers must obey the rules of conduct of the professional bodies and must have met any training requirements that have been prescribed, like the requirement to have completed pupillage in the case of the Bar, or to have obtained a higher courts advocacy qualification in the case of solicitors who wish to appear in the higher courts.

11.3.1 Training

The standard route to qualification is a law degree followed by a one year Legal Practice Course (LPC) and then a term as a trainee solicitor which, like the barrister's pupillage, is essentially an apprenticeship. Non-law graduates can complete the Postgraduate Diploma in Law in one year and then proceed as a law graduate. All newly admitted solicitors must now undergo regular continuing education, which means attendance at non-examined legal courses designed to update knowledge and improve expertise. After completion of the LPC and traineeship, a trainee solicitor may apply to The Law Society to be 'admitted' to the profession. The Master of the Rolls will add the names of the newly qualified to the roll of officers of the Supreme Court. To practise, a solicitor will also require a practising certificate (£700 in 2003) issued by The Law Society, and will be required to make a contribution to the compensation fund run by The Law Society to pay clients who have suffered loss through the misconduct of a solicitor. Additionally, solicitors have to pay an annual premium for indemnity insurance.

11.3.2 The Law Society

This is the profession's governing body controlled by a council of elected members and an annually elected President. Its powers and duties are derived from the Solicitors Act 1974. Complaints against solicitors used to be dealt with by the Solicitors' Complaints Bureau and the Solicitors' Disciplinary Tribunal, the latter having power to strike from the roll the name of an offending solicitor. It had been sometimes seen as worrying that the Society combined two roles with a possible conflict of interests: maintenance of professional standards for the protection of the public, and as the main professional association to promote the interests of solicitors. Consider a rather basic example. Acting for its members, The Law Society should perhaps try to ensure that insurance policies against claims for negligence are always available for solicitors even if they have been sued for this several times. For such insurance to be granted to someone with such a questionable professional record is, however, clearly not in the best interests of the public who use solicitors.

Office for the Supervision of Solicitors

From 1 September 1996, the Solicitors' Disciplinary Tribunal continued to work as before, but the Office for the Supervision of Solicitors (OSS) took over the work of the Solicitors' Complaints Bureau, and the old organisation was abolished. The OSS, based in Leamington Spa, has more than 200 staff and employs solicitors, accountants, qualified mediators and administrative support staff. The Office is divided into two parts, one of which deals with client-related matters and the other with regulation. All new cases are examined upon arrival and directed to one or other of them. Staff work in small teams, and one member of staff will follow a complaint through from start to finish.

A Remuneration Certificate Department carries out free reviews of solicitors' bills to ensure that they are fair and reasonable. The Office for Professional Regulation (a part of the OSS) ensures that solicitors comply with the regulations that govern them, like the Solicitors' Investment Business Rules.

The Compensation Fund was set up in 1941 by The Law Society to protect the clients of dishonest solicitors. The fund is supervised by the OSS. In matters of professional misconduct, the OSS can either impose an internal disciplinary sanction or prosecute the most serious cases before the Solicitors' Disciplinary Tribunal. In cases of inadequate professional services, the OSS can order a solicitor to forgo all or part of his fees and can award compensation of up to £5,000. The mission statement of the OSS states that, 'our aim is to work for excellence and fairness in guarding the standards of the solicitors' profession'. How far that aim is achieved must be judged in the light of developments over the next couple of years.

Members of the public with criticisms about solicitors' work will receive an initial response within 24 hours under the new practice of the OSS. Staff have been asked to be more open with the public, make greater use of telephones in contacting complainants and to write letters in plain English rather than in legalistic language. Advertisements were placed in the media for 10 lay people to join a committee dealing with the supervision of the profession.

The OSS is, however, funded by The Law Society, so a serious question arises as to whether this body will be seen as sufficiently independent by the public. Its efficiency has also come into question. Asked about the effectiveness of the OSS during Lord Chancellor's Department questions in the House of Commons, minister Rosie Winterton said, 'We are not satisfied that the OSS is currently working as effectively as it should' ((2003) The Gazette, 13 February, p 3). The Society's independent commissioner, Sir Stephen Lander, has said that the problem with the OSS is that it takes 'an approach which looks at the consumer through the prism of the Society's own regulations and jurisdiction', something he termed 'an insider view' ((2003) *The Gazette*, 6 February, p 1). He explained that he thought 'the OSS should not, of course, favour the client over the solicitor, or stop approaching each case strictly on its merits. Those remain the most important requirements', but rather the OSS should explicitly respond to the layman when things have gone wrong with a solicitor, regardless in the first instance of the cause or context. In a survey conducted by The Law Society's regulation directorate in 2002, of 209 firms chosen at random, only 35% had a satisfactory complaints procedure ((2002) *The Gazette*, 7 November, p 39). In an effort to improve the standards of firms, The Law Society's practice standards unit (PSU) will inspect all of the 1,100 firms that have three or more outstanding complaints against them ((2002) *The Gazette*, 17 October).

In *Wood v Law Society* (1995), the claimant (W) alleged that she was the victim of continuing misconduct by a firm of solicitors. She complained that H, a partner in a law firm, wrongly acted for both sides when arranging a series of loans for W on the security of W's home, and that H failed to disclose that H's husband was a director of one of the lenders. H's firm acted for the lenders in issuing court proceedings and obtained possession of the cottage for them. After many complaints to them by W, The Law Society conceded, after much delay, that it had been 'unwise' for H's firm to act for the lenders and that this was 'conduct unbefitting a solicitor'. The Society issued a formal rebuke. W sought damages from The Law Society, arguing that, as a result of the Society's incompetence and delay, she lost the chance of avoiding repossession of her home and suffered anxiety and distress.

The Court of Appeal held that if there was a duty owed to W by the Society, *it did not include a duty to provide peace of mind or freedom from distress*. Even though the Society appeared not to have lived up to the standards reasonably to be expected of it, there was no prospect of establishing that its failure to properly or timely investigate her complaints could have any sounding in damages. The loss suffered by W was not directly caused by The Law Society's incompetence and delay.

Another case dealing with the liability of solicitors is *White v Jones* (1995). This decision arguably widened the liability of solicitors. The House of Lords decided that a solicitor owes a duty of care to the intended beneficiary of a will when instructed by the testator to draw up that will. A firm of solicitors had been instructed by a client to change his will so that his daughters (whom he had previously cut out of an inheritance) should each receive £9,000. The firm did not act promptly on these instructions and the father eventually died before the will had been changed. Thus, the daughters received nothing. The person actually acting in the matter was a legal executive, not a solicitor, but it was the liability of the firm which was in issue. The Court of Appeal allowed an appeal by the plaintiffs, and granted that they should be awarded damages from the firm of solicitors to cover the loss, that is, the amounts they would have inherited had the firm acted professionally. The House of Lords upheld this decision.

The case is an interesting illustration of the judicial development of the common law. There was no obvious way in which the claimants had an action. They could not sue the firm in contract because they had made no contract with the firm; only their father had done so. The daughters were outside of the arrangements between their father and his solicitors; they were third parties and the law did not at that time recognise a *ius quaesitum tertio* (a contractual right for the benefit of a third party). The precedents in the tort of negligence did not provide much assistance because, unlike the facts of those cases, the daughters here were not people who had relied upon the firm (as in a case like *Ross v Caunters* (1979)).

The leading opinion was given by Lord Goff who decided that there was a need to give people like the claimants a remedy in this sort of situation, a remedy which was not available according to technical rules of law. He thus favoured 'practical justice', recognising that:

> ... cases such as these call for an appropriate remedy and that the common law
> is not so sterile as to be incapable of supplying that remedy when it is required
> [at p 777].

By a majority of 3:2, the Lords extended the duty of care owed by professionals as it had been expressed in *Hedley Byrne v Heller* (1963). They said that, where the loss suffered by the victim was purely economic, it would be possible to bring an action where the professional had given negligent advice or made negligent statements, but also extended this to the general principle that the provider of professional services could be liable for pure economic loss where his skills were being relied upon.

11.3.3 The Institute of Legal Executives

The Institute of Legal Executives (ILEX) represents over 22,000 legal executives employed in solicitors' offices. They are legally trained (the Institute runs its own examinations) and carry out much of the routine legal work which is a feature of most practices. The Institute was established in 1963 with the support of The Law Society. The Managing Clerks' Association, from which ILEX developed, recognised that many non-solicitor staff employed in fee earning work, and in the management of firms, needed and wanted a training route which would improve standards and award recognition for knowledge and skills. The education and training facilities ILEX offers have developed in number and diversity so that ILEX is able to provide a route to a career in law which is open to all.

Legal executives are, in the phrase of the ILEX website (www.ilex.org.uk) qualified lawyers specialising in a particular area of law. They will have passed the ILEX Professional Qualification in Law in an area of legal practice to the same level as that required of solicitors. They will have at least five years' experience of working under the supervision of a solicitor in legal practice or the legal department of a private company or local or national government. Fellows are issued with an annual practising certificate, and only Fellows of ILEX may describe themselves as 'Legal Executives'. Specialising in a particular area of law, their day-to-day work is similar to that of a solicitor.

Legal executives might handle the legal aspects of a property transfer; assist in the formation of a company; be involved in actions in the High Court or county courts; draft wills; advise clients accused of serious or petty crime, or families with matrimonial problems; and many other matters affecting people in their domestic and business affairs. Legal executives are fee earners – in private practice their work is charged directly to clients – making a direct contribution to the income of a law firm. This is an important difference between legal executives and other types of legal support staff who tend to handle work of a more routine nature. In March 2000, six legal executives qualified to become the first legal executive advocates under the Courts and Legal Services Act 1990. The advocacy certificates were approved by the ILEX Rights of Audience Committee. The advocates now have extended rights of audience in civil and matrimonial proceedings in the county courts and magistrates' courts. In some circumstances, Fellows of ILEX can instruct barristers directly. BarDIRECT (the Bar Council's scheme by which barristers can be directly instructed by some professional and voluntary organisations, rather than by solicitors) enables legal executives to access a wide choice of legal advice and representation for their clients and their employers.

11.4 Barristers

The barrister is often thought of as primarily a court advocate, although many spend more time on drafting, pleadings (now called statements of case) and writing advices for solicitors. Professional barristers are technically competent to perform all advocacy for the prosecution or defence in criminal cases, and for a claimant or defendant in a civil claim. More generally, however, established barristers tend to specialise in particular areas of work. Over 60% of practising barristers work in London.

In 2002, there were 10,334 barristers in independent practice in England and Wales, of whom 7,573 were men and 2,761 were women. There were 1,078 Queen's Counsel, of whom 991 were men and 87 were women (Bar Council, 2003).

The Bar had been organised as an association of the members of the Inns of Court by the 14th century. Today, there are four Inns of Court (Inner and Middle Temples, Lincoln's Inn and Gray's Inn), although there were originally more, including Inns of Chancery and Sergeants' Inns, the latter being an association of the king's most senior lawyers. Until the CLSA 1990, the barrister had a virtual monopoly on advocacy in all the superior courts (in some cases solicitors could act as advocates in the Crown Court). In most situations, they cannot deal direct with clients but must be engaged by solicitors (but see 11.8, below).

11.4.1 Training

Entry to the Bar is now restricted to graduates and mature students. An aspirant barrister must register with one of the four Inns of Court in London. Commonly, a barrister will have a law degree and then undertake professional training for one year leading to the Bar Examinations. Alternatively, a non-law graduate can study for the Common Professional Examination for one year and, if successful in the examinations, proceed to the Bar Examinations. The successful student is then called to the Bar by his or her Inn of Court. It is also a requirement of being called that, during study for the vocational course, the student attends his or her Inn to become familiar with the customs of the Bar. The student then undertakes a pupillage, essentially, an apprenticeship to a junior counsel. Note that all barristers, however senior in years and experience, are still 'junior counsel' unless they have 'taken silk' and become Queen's Counsel (QCs). Barristers who do not intend to practise do not have to complete the pupillage.

11.4.2 The Inns of Court

The Inns of Court are administered by their senior members (QCs and judges) who are called Benchers. The Inns administer the dining system and are responsible for calling the students to the Bar.

11.4.3 The General Council of the Bar

The General Council of the Bar of England and Wales and of the Inns of Court (the Bar Council) is the profession's governing body. It is run by elected officials. It is responsible for the Bar's Code of Conduct, disciplinary matters and representing the interests of the Bar to external bodies like the Lord Chancellor's Department, the government and The Law Society. According to its own literature, this Council:

> ... fulfils the function of what might be called a 'trade union', pursuing the interests of the Bar and expanding the market for the Bar's services and is also a watchdog regulating its practices and activities.

11.4.4 Education

The Bar Council Education and Training Department regulates education and training for the profession.

11.4.5 Queen's Counsel

Queen's Counsel (QCs) are senior barristers of special merit. In 2003, the Bar had 1,078 QCs in practice, the status being conferred on about 45 barristers each year. They are given this status (known as 'taking silk' because a part of the robe they are entitled to wear is silk) by the Queen on the advice of the Lord Chancellor. There are annual invitations from the Lord Chancellor for barristers to apply for this title. Applicants need to show at least 10 years of successful practice at the Bar. If appointed, the barrister will become known as a 'Leader' and he or she will often appear in cases with a junior. The old 'Two Counsel Rule' under which a QC always had to appear with a junior counsel, whether one was really required or not, was abolished in 1977. He or she will be restricted to high level work (of which there is less available in some types of practice) so appointment can be financially difficult but, in most cases, it has good results for the QC as he or she will be able to considerably increase fee levels. The first report by Sir Colin Campbell, First Commissioner of the Commission for Judicial Appointments, published at the end of 2002, revealed serious deficiencies in the current system of appointment. The report upheld four complaints against the Lord Chancellor's Department and invited the Lord Chancellor (who is a member of the Cabinet, and thus could be seen as 'political') to reconsider his role in the appointments system. However, only 10 individuals made formal complaints from well over 3,000 unsuccessful applicants for judicial posts or for 'silk' (QC). Complaints were upheld on behalf of four people and rejected for two others. The four complaints were upheld on the basis of procedural and administrative failings, but did not go to the merits of any particular substantive decision. More staff were committed to the 2002 'Silk' competition and more still will be committed for 2003. The guidance of the new competition requires the comments of consultees on candidates to be supported by detailed reasons and to be based on recent experience. In addition, the 'sift panel' will include an independent assessor. In 2002, for the first time, the names of 55 commercial law firms who were consulted by the LCD about the suitability of applicants for silk were released. This sort of consultation has been used since 1999. There are, though, calls for even wider consultation of law firms, and even calls for all solicitors to be consulted (see (2002) *The Gazette*, 10 October, p 29).

11.4.6 The barrister's chambers

Barristers are not permitted to form partnerships (except with lawyers from other countries); they work in sets of offices called chambers. Most chambers are run by barristers' clerks who act as business managers, allocating work to the various barristers and negotiating their fees. Imagine the situation where a solicitor wishes to engage a particular barrister for a case on a certain date and that barrister is already booked to be in another court three days before that date. The clerk cannot be sure whether the first case will have ended in time for the barrister to be free to appear in the second case. The first case might be adjourned after a day or, through unexpected evidential arguments in the early stages in the trial, it might last for four days. If the barrister is detained, then his brief for the second case will have to be passed to another barrister in his chambers very close to the actual trial. This is known as a late brief. Who will be asked to take the brief and at what point is a matter for the clerk. The role of the barrister's clerk is thus a most influential one. From 2003, lay clients will be able to enjoy direct access to barristers in some cases. It is currently possible for barristers to accept instructions from some licensed organisations (as opposed to the normal practice of being briefed by solicitors), but the new plans will permit ordinary people to instruct barristers in some situations (see 11.8, below).

11.5 Professional etiquette

The CLSA 1990 introduced a statutory committee, the Lord Chancellor's Advisory Committee on Legal Education and Conduct (ACLEC) which, until recently, had responsibilities in the regulation of both branches of the profession.

As part of the government's reforms of legal services, generally and publicly funded legal advice specifically, the Access to Justice Act 1999 (s 35) has replaced the ACLEC (considered by some as slow and ponderous) with the Legal Services Consultative Panel, launched at the beginning of 2000. The Consultative Panel has: (a) the duty of assisting in the maintenance and development of standards in the education, training and conduct of persons offering legal services and, where appropriate, making recommendations to the Lord Chancellor; and (b) the duty of providing to the Lord Chancellor, at his request, advice about particular matters relating to any aspect of the provision of legal services (including the education, training and conduct of persons offering legal services).

The Law Society and the Bar Council exercise tight control over the professional conduct of their members. Barristers can only meet the client when the solicitor or his or her representative is present. This is supposed to promote the barrister's detachment from the client and his or her case, and thus lend greater objectivity to counsel's judgment. Barristers and solicitors must dress formally for court appearances, although solicitors, when appearing in the Crown, county or High Court, are required to wear robes but not wigs. A barrister not wearing a wig and robe cannot be 'seen' or 'heard' by the judge.

Traditionally, lawyers were not permitted to advertise their services, although this area has been subject to some deregulation in the light of recent trends to expose the provision of legal services to ordinary market forces. Solicitors can, subject to some regulations, advertise their services in print and on broadcast media.

11.5.1 Immunity from negligence claims

Until recently barristers could not be sued by their clients for negligent performance in court or for work which was preparatory to court work (*Rondel v Worsley* (1969)); this immunity had also been extended to solicitors who act as advocates (*Saif Ali v Sidney Mitchell* (1980)). The client of the other side, however, may sue for breach of duty (*Kelly v London Transport Executive* (1982)). This was changed in a major case in 2000.

Advocates' liability

Arthur JS Hall and Co v Simons and Other Appeals (2000)

Background

Lawyers are, for the general public, the most central and prominent part of the English legal system. They are, arguably, to the legal system what doctors are to the health system. For many decades, a debate had grown about why a patient injured by the negligence of a surgeon in the operating theatre could sue for damages, whereas a litigant whose case was lost because of the negligence of his advocate could not sue. It all seemed very unfair. Even the most glaringly obvious courtroom negligence was protected against legal action by a special advocates' immunity. The claim that this protection was made by lawyers (and judges who were lawyers) for lawyers was difficult to refute. In this House of Lords' decision, the historic immunity was abolished in respect of both barristers and solicitor-advocates (of whom there are now over 1,787 with higher courts rights of audience), and for both civil and criminal proceedings.

Facts

In three cases, all conjoined on appeal, a claimant raised a claim of negligence against a firm of solicitors, and in each case, the firms relied on the immunity attaching to barristers and other advocates from claims in negligence. At first instance, all the claims were struck out. Then, on appeal, the Court of Appeal said that the claims could have proceeded. The solicitors appealed to the Lords and two key questions were raised: should the old immunity rule be maintained and, in a criminal case, what was the proper scope of the principle against 'collateral attack'? A 'collateral attack' is when someone convicted in a criminal court tries to invalidate that conviction outside the criminal appeals process by suing his trial defence lawyer in a civil court. The purpose of such a 'collateral attack' is to win in the civil case, proving negligence against the criminal trial lawyer, and thus by implication showing that the conviction in the criminal case was unfair.

Held

The House of Lords held (Lord Hope, Lord Hutton and Lord Hobhouse dissenting in part) that, in the light of modern conditions, it was now clear that it was no longer in the public interest in the administration of justice that advocates should have immunity from suit for negligence for acts concerned with the conduct of either civil or criminal litigation.

Lord Hoffmann (with Lord Steyn, Lord Browne-Wilkinson and Lord Millett delivering concurring opinions) said that over 30 years had passed since the House had last considered the rationale for the immunity of the advocate from suit in *Rondel v Worsley*. Public policy was not immutable and there had been great changes in the law of negligence, the functioning of the legal profession, the administration of justice and public perceptions. It was once again time to re-examine the whole matter. Interestingly, Lord Hoffmann chose to formulate his opinion in a creative mode to reflect public policy, rather than in the tradition of what can be seen as slavish obedience to the details of precedent:

> I hope that I will not be thought ungrateful if I do not encumber this speech with citations. The question of what the public interest now requires depends upon the strength of the arguments rather than the weight of authority.

The point of departure was that, in general, English law provided a remedy in damages for a person who had suffered injury as a result of professional negligence. It followed that any exception which denied such a remedy required a sound justification. The arguments relied on by the court in *Rondel v Worsley* as justifying the immunity had to be considered. One by one, these arguments are evaluated and rejected.

Advocate's divided loyalty

There were two distinct versions of the divided loyalty argument. The first was that the possibility of being sued for negligence would actually inhibit the lawyer, consciously or unconsciously, from giving his duty to the court priority over his duty to his client. The second was that the divided loyalty was a special factor that made the conduct of litigation a very difficult art and could lead to the advocate being exposed to vexatious claims by difficult clients. The argument was pressed most strongly in connection with advocacy in criminal proceedings, where the clients were said to be more than usually likely to be vexatious.

There had been recent developments in the civil justice system designed to reduce the incidence of vexatious litigation. The first was r 24.2 of the Civil Procedure Rules, which provided that a court could give summary judgment in favour of a defendant if it considered that 'the claimant had no real prospect of succeeding on the claim'. The second was the changes to the funding of civil litigation introduced by the Access to Justice Act 1999, which would make it much more difficult than it had been in the past to obtain legal help for negligence claims which had little prospect of success.

There was no doubt that the advocate's duty to the court was extremely important in the English justice system. The question was whether removing the immunity would have a significantly adverse effect. If the possibility of being held liable in negligence was calculated to have an adverse effect on the behaviour of advocates in court, one might have expected that to have followed, at least to some degree, from the introduction of wasted costs orders (where a court disallows a lawyer from being able to claim part of a fee for work which is regarded as unnecessary and wasteful). Although the liability of a negligent advocate to a wasted costs order was not the same as a liability to pay general damages, the experience of the wasted costs jurisdiction was the only empirical evidence available in England to test the proposition that such liability would have an adverse effect upon the way advocates performed their duty to the court, and there was no suggestion that it had changed standards of advocacy for the worse.

The 'cab rank'

The 'cab rank' rule provided that a barrister could not refuse to act for a client on the ground that he disapproved of him or his case. The argument was that a barrister who was obliged to accept any client would be unfairly exposed to vexatious claims by clients for whom any sensible lawyer with freedom of action would have refused to act. Such a claim was, however, in the nature of things intuitive, incapable of empirical verification and did not have any real substance.

The witness analogy

The argument started from the well established rule that a witness was absolutely immune from liability for anything that he said in court. So were the judge, counsel and the parties. They could not be sued for libel, malicious falsehood or conspiring to give false evidence. The policy of the rule was to encourage persons who took part in court proceedings to express themselves freely. However, a witness owed no duty of care to anyone in respect of the evidence he gave to the court. His only duty was to tell the truth. There was no analogy with the position of a lawyer who owed a duty of care to his client. The fact that the advocate was the only person involved in the trial process who was liable to be sued for negligence was because he was the only person who had undertaken such a duty of care to his client.

Collateral attack

The most substantial argument was that it might be contrary to the public interest for a court to re-try a case which had been decided by another court. However, claims for negligence against lawyers were not the only cases that gave rise to a possibility of the same issue being tried twice. The law had to deal with the problem in numerous other contexts. So, before examining the strength of the collateral challenge argument as a reason for maintaining the immunity of lawyers, it was necessary to consider how the law dealt with collateral challenge in general.

The law discouraged re-litigation of the same issues except by means of an appeal. The Latin maxims often quoted were *nemo debet bis vexari pro una et eadem causa* and *interest rei publicae ut finis sit litium*. The first was concerned with the interests of the defendant: a person should not be troubled twice for the same reason. That policy had generated the rules which prevented re-litigation when the parties were the same: *autrefois acquit* (someone acquitted of a crime cannot be tried again for that crime); *res judicata* (a particular dispute decided by a civil court cannot be re-tried); and issue estoppel (a person cannot deny the fact of a judgment previously decided against him).

The second policy was wider: it was concerned with the interests of the State. There was a general public interest in the same issue not being litigated over again. The second policy could be used to justify the extension of the rules of issue estoppel to cases in which the parties were not the same, but the circumstances were such as to bring the case within the spirit of the rules. Criminal proceedings were in a special category, because although they were technically litigation between the Crown and the defendant, the Crown prosecuted on behalf of society as a whole. So, a conviction had some of the quality of a judgment *in rem*, which should be binding in favour of everyone.

Not all re-litigation of the same issue, however, would be manifestly unfair to a party or bring the administration of justice into disrepute. Sometimes there were valid reasons for re-hearing a dispute. It was therefore unnecessary to try to stop any re-litigation by forbidding anyone from suing their lawyer. It was 'burning down the house to roast the pig; using a broad-spectrum remedy without side effects could handle the problem equally well'.

The scope for re-examination of issues in criminal proceedings was much wider than in civil cases. Fresh evidence was more readily admitted. A conviction could be set aside as unsafe and unsatisfactory when the accused appeared to have been prejudiced by 'flagrantly incompetent advocacy': see *R v Clinton* (1993). After conviction, the case could be referred to the Court of Appeal if the conviction was on indictment, or to the Crown Court, if the trial was summary, by the Criminal Cases Review Commission.

It followed that it would ordinarily be an abuse of process for a civil court to be asked to decide that a subsisting conviction was wrong. That applied to a conviction on a plea of guilty as well as after a trial. The resulting conflict of judgments was likely to bring the administration of justice into disrepute. The proper procedure was to appeal, or if the right of appeal had been exhausted, to apply to the Criminal Cases Review Commission. It would ordinarily be an abuse, because there were bound to be exceptional cases in which the issue could be tried without a risk that the conflict of judgments would bring the administration of justice into disrepute.

Once the conviction has been set aside, there could be no public policy objection to a claim for negligence against the legal advisers. There could be no conflict of judgments. On the other hand, in civil, including matrimonial, cases, it would seldom be possible to say that a claim for negligence against a legal adviser or representative would bring the administration of justice into dispute. Whether the original decision was right or wrong was usually a matter of concern only to the parties and had no wider implications. There was no public interest objection to a subsequent finding that, but for the negligence of his lawyers, the losing party would have won.

But again, there might be exceptions. The claim for negligence might be an abuse of process on the ground that it was manifestly unfair to someone else. Take, for example, the case of a defendant who published a serious defamation which he attempted unsuccessfully to justify. Should he be able to sue his lawyers and claim that if the case had been conducted differently, the allegation would have been proved to be true? It seemed unfair to the claimant in the defamation claim that any court should be allowed to come to such a conclusion in proceedings to which he was not a party. On the other hand, it was equally unfair that he should have to join as a party and rebut the allegation for a second time. A man's reputation was not only a matter between him and the other party; it represented his relationship with the world. So, it might be that in such circumstances, a claim for negligence would be an abuse of the process of the court.

Having regard to the power of the court to strike out claims which had no real prospect of success, the doctrine was unlikely in that context to be invoked very often. The first step in any application to strike out a claim alleging negligence in the conduct of a previous action had to be to ask whether it had a real prospect of success.

Lord Hope, Lord Hutton and Lord Hobhouse delivered judgments in which they agreed that the immunity from suit was no longer required in relation to civil proceedings, but dissented to the extent of saying that the immunity was still required in the public interest in the administration of justice in relation to criminal proceedings.

Comment

This decision is of major and historic importance in the English legal system for several reasons. It can be seen as a bold attempt by the senior judiciary to drag the legal profession (often a metonymy for the whole legal system) into the 21st century world of accountability and fair business practice. In his judgment, Lord Steyn makes this dramatic observation:

> ... public confidence in the legal system is not enhanced by the existence of the immunity. The appearance is created that the law singles out its own for protection no matter how flagrant the breach of the barrister. The world has changed since 1967. The practice of law has become more commercialised: barristers may now advertise. They may now enter into contracts for legal services with their professional clients. They are now obliged to carry insurance. On the other hand, today we live in a consumerist society in which people have a much greater awareness of their rights. If they have suffered a wrong as the result of the provision of negligent professional services, they expect to have the right to claim redress. It tends to erode confidence in the legal system if advocates, alone among professional men, are immune from liability for negligence.

The case raises and explores many key issues of the legal system, including: the proper relationship between lawyers and the courts; the proper relationship between lawyers and clients; the differences between criminal and civil actions; professional ethics; the nature of dispute resolution and the circumstances under which the courts should make new law. Above all, however, the case has one simple significance: 'it will', in the words of Jonathan Hirst QC, a former Chairman of the Bar Council, 'mean that a claimant who can prove loss, as the result of an advocate's negligence, will no longer be prevented from making a claim. We cannot really say that is wrong' ((2000) *Bar News*, August, p 3).

11.6 Fusion

The division of the legal profession into two branches can be seen as problematic in some respects. Even before the changes wrought by the CLSA 1990, solicitors did a reasonable amount of advocacy in the lower courts and in tribunals. On the other hand, barristers quite often give advice to clients, albeit through solicitors. Both barristers and solicitors do pleadings and drafting work. For many years, there was a strong movement for fusion of the two branches. Submissions made to the Benson Royal Commission on Legal Services argued that the necessity of a member of the public employing a barrister as well as a solicitor for certain work (for example, litigation) was like insisting on a taxi traveller hiring two taxis at once when one would be sufficient to get him to his destination. The legal need to hire two lawyers when one will do causes inefficiency (failures in communication, delay, return of briefs by barristers who are fully booked), damages the client's confidence in the legal process (as barristers are regarded as too remote and often insufficiently prepared), and is more expensive than simply engaging a single lawyer.

Fusion was strongly opposed by The Law Society and the Bar Council in their submissions to the Benson Commission (1979). It was argued that fusion would lead to a fall in the quality of advocacy. The leading barristers in a single-profession environment would simply join the major law firms and thus be unavailable for general engagement. Smaller firms would be unlikely to generate enough litigation to keep a barrister as a partner, and then would find it increasingly challenging to brief counsel of equal standing with that of an opponent. This would create an overall pattern of larger firms expanding and smaller ones – those serving small towns, etc – going out of business.

There would be a reduced number of specialist advocates because, whereas with the divided profession a specialist barrister could 'sell' his specialism to a queue of solicitors from different firms, under the fused profession, he would be pressured into working at one firm. Another opposition hinged on two features of the English court process: orality and single, continuous hearings designed to make the best use of judicial time but at the expense of practitioners. It has been argued that barristers are better placed organisationally to meet both such requirements.

Additionally, unlike the American system, judges do not have researchers or much time to prepare themselves for cases. The judge relies on the parties to present the case thoroughly. In such circumstances, it was argued, there is a critical need for the judge to have confidence in the competency of the advocates appearing in the case. This can only be properly achieved in the system which cultivates the barrister as a separate professional branch.

The Benson Royal Commission on Legal Services unanimously rejected the idea of fusion. The report conceded that fusion might lead to some saving, but only in the smaller cases, and in larger cases, the expense could be even greater. Using two lawyers did not necessarily entail duplicated work.

It is arguable now that fusion has effectively been organised covertly and gradually. Solicitors' monopolies over conveyancing and the right to conduct litigation have been technically removed (by the CLSA 1990 and the Access to Justice Act 1999, respectively), and the Bar's monopoly over rights of audience, even in the higher courts, has also been removed (by the same legislation). Specialism thus becomes a *de facto* matter more than an automatic function of one branch of the profession. We begin the new century with specialist criminal law solicitor-advocates operating from dedicated offices in some cities (a sort of solicitors 'chambers'), and barristers who are effectively working as in-house lawyers in companies doing work which seems very like the traditional work of solicitors. There are still, however, some suggestions for further mergers between the branches of the profession. In January 2003, the chairman of the Bar Council, Matthias Kelly QC, called for all advocates, including solicitor-advocates, to be regulated by the Bar Council. He said, 'That is a logical position. The present position is that the Bar Council regulates all barristers, even those employed in solicitors offices, in the same way as The Law Society regulates sole practitioner solicitor-advocates' ((2003) *The Gazette*, 9 January, p 5).

11.7 The Courts and Legal Services Act 1990

Both branches of the legal profession have traditionally enjoyed monopolies in the provision of certain legal services (for example, advocacy was reserved almost exclusively to barristers, while conveyancing was reserved to solicitors). In the 1980s, Lord Mackay, the then Lord Chancellor, argued that these monopolies did not best serve the users of legal services as they entailed unnecessarily limited choice and artificially high prices. The Courts and Legal Services Act (CLSA) 1990 was introduced to reform the provision of legal services along such lines. Today, many of the old monopolies have been broken. Thus, we have solicitor-advocates and non-solicitor licensed conveyancers.

In 1990 in the CLSA, the government broke the solicitors' conveyancing monopoly by allowing licensed conveyancers to practise. There was initially evidence that this increased competition resulted in benefits to the consumer. From 1985, The Law Society had permitted solicitors to sell property, like estate agents, so as to promote 'one-stop' conveyancing. The Consumers' Association estimated that solicitors' conveyancing prices fell by a margin of 25–33% before licensed conveyancers actually began to practise.

Under the CLSA 1990, apart from allowing the Bar Council and The Law Society to grant members rights of audience as before, The Law Society is able to seek to widen the category of those who have such rights. Applications are made to the Lord Chancellor, who refers the matter to his Advisory Committee. If the Committee favours the application, it must also be approved by four senior judges (including the Master of the Rolls and the Lord Chief Justice), each of whom can exercise a veto. The Director General of the Office of Fair Trading must also be consulted by the Lord Chancellor. All those who consider applications for extended rights of audience or the right to conduct litigation must act in accordance with the 'general principle' in s 17.

11.7.1 Section 17

The principle in s 17 states that the question whether a person should be granted a right of audience or to conduct litigation is to be determined only by reference to the following four questions:

- Is the applicant properly qualified in accordance with the educational and training requirements appropriate to the court or proceedings?

- Are applicants members of a professional or other body with proper and enforced rules of conduct?

- Do such rules have the necessary equivalent of the Bar's 'cab rank rule', that is, satisfactory provision requiring its members not to withhold their services: on the ground that the nature of the case is objectionable to them or any section of the public; on the ground that the conduct, opinions or beliefs of the prospective client are unacceptable to them or to any section of the public; on any ground relating to the prospective client's source of financial support (for example, public funding)?

- Are the body's rules of conduct 'appropriate in the interests of the proper and efficient administration of justice'?

Subject to the above, those who consider applications must also abide by s 17's 'statutory objective' of 'new and better ways of providing such services and a wider choice of persons providing them, while maintaining the proper and efficient administration of justice'.

Successful applications were made by The Law Society, the Head of the Government Legal Service and the Director of Public Prosecutions (DPP). The Advisory Committee, whilst rejecting the idea of an automatic extension of solicitors' rights of audience upon qualification (for example, guilty plea cases in Crown Courts), accepted the principle that they should qualify for enlarged rights after a course of advocacy training. Non-lawyers can also apply for rights of audience in the courts: the Chartered Institute of Patent Agents successfully applied for rights to conduct litigation in the High Court. Under s 11 of the CLSA 1990, the Lord Chancellor will use his power to enable lay representatives to be used in cases involving debt and housing matters in small claims procedures. Similarly, under ss 28 and 29 of the CLSA 1990, the right to conduct litigation is thrown open to members of any body which can persuade the Advisory Committee, the Lord Chancellor and the four senior judges that its application should be granted as the criteria set out in s 17 (above) are satisfied.

The historic monopoly of barristers to appear for clients in the higher courts was formally ended in 1994 when the Lord Chancellor approved The Law Society's proposals on how to certify its members in private practice as competent advocates. The innovation is likely to generate significant change in the delivery of legal services, especially in the fields of commercial and criminal cases. The prospective battle between solicitors and barristers for advocacy work can be simply characterised.

11.7.2 Solicitors' rights of audience

In February 1997, the Lord Chancellor, Lord Mackay, and the four designated judges (Lord Bingham, Lord Woolf, Sir Stephen Brown and Sir Richard Scott; see s 17 of the CLSA 1990) approved The Law Society's application for rights of audience in the higher courts for employed solicitors, but subject to certain restrictions.

Under The Law Society's 1998 regulations approved by the Lord Chancellor's Department, some solicitors (those who are also barristers or part time judges) are granted exemption from the new tests of qualification for advocacy. Others need to apply for the grant of higher courts qualifications, either in civil proceedings, criminal proceedings or in both. A holder of the higher courts (criminal proceedings) qualification has rights of audience in the Crown Court in all proceedings (including its civil jurisdiction) and in other courts in all criminal proceedings. A holder of the higher courts (civil proceedings) qualification may appear in the High Court in all proceedings and in other courts in all civil proceedings. Applicants for these qualifications must have practised as a solicitor for at least three years. The qualifying scheme is designed only for solicitors who are already lower court advocates. The three elements which must be demonstrated by an applicant are:

- two years' experience of advocacy in the lower courts and experience of the procedures of the relevant higher court;
- competency in a written test on evidence and procedure; and
- satisfactory completion of an advocacy training course.

Large city firms of solicitors already have their litigation lawyers trained to qualify for advocacy in the High Court. One problem, however, for these large firms is that they have found it very difficult for their applicants (for audience rights) to meet The Law Society's requirement for county court advocacy experience. Although the expansion of this court's jurisdiction under the CLSA 1990 (in particular commercial litigation involving sums up to £50,000) has given more county court work to large firms, they generally do very little of this. Large firms have had to take on perhaps hundreds of county court cases just to get the ones that will go to trial, and even then, these would only be a means to an end, namely the qualification to appear in the High Court.

One benefit for law firms is that those which offer advocacy training are likely to attract the best graduates. This is a worry for the commercial Bar, as some graduates will see a training contract with an advocacy element as a better option than the less secure Bar pupillage. The Bar is determined that it will not lose any significant ground in the face of this new competition. Its representatives claim that solicitors will not be able to compete with barristers because of their much higher overheads.

From 2000, there have been three routes to qualification: the 'development' route leading to the all proceedings qualification; the 'accreditation' route appropriate for solicitors who have significant experience of the higher civil and/or higher criminal courts; and the 'exemption' route which has existed under both the 1992 and 1998 regulations. The accreditation and exemption routes will be phased out by 2005 leaving only the development route. The development route has three stages: training and assessment in procedure, evidence and ethics in the higher civil and higher criminal courts; training and assessment in advocacy skills; and experience of either civil or criminal proceedings, some of which may take place pre-admission. Trainee solicitors, therefore, can get training and assessment and up to six months' experience behind them during their training contract. However, this new fast track for novice lawyers has left The Law Society open to criticism of lowering standards and allowing inexperienced advocates into the higher courts without the necessary competence. The Law Society, however, recognises the need to maintain standards and believes that its proposals not only maintain standards, but have the capacity to enhance standards through the provision of advocacy services.

The figures show there has been a steady increase in the number of solicitor-advocates, which in 2003 amounted to a total of 1,787. This is made up of 384 qualified for all proceedings, 430 with the civil qualification and 973 with the criminal qualification, including 400 Crown Prosecution lawyers. With commercial firms increasingly bringing low end work in-house, and a streamlined qualification procedure, these figures, especially on the civil side, are now likely to increase. A solicitor-advocate chambers in Birmingham called Midlands Solicitor Chambers is already a model for such developments elsewhere. The larger firms are finding it propitious to create general or specialist advocacy units, a point the significance of which is best seen when the influence of the large firms is appreciated. It is clear that the face of advocacy is changing. When the relevant part of the Access to Justice Act 1999 (see 11.7.3, below) came into force, even employed solicitors gained the right to present cases in the higher courts.

Many barristers are very worried about the threat to their traditional work. A potentially significant development is BarDIRECT, a pilot scheme set up in 1999 that enables certain professions and organisations to have direct access to barristers without referral through a solicitor. While this initiative could be one of the keys to the continuing success of the Bar, it is argued that it makes barristers no different from solicitors and could even encroach on the solicitors' market. However, Bruce Holder QC, chairman of the Bar Public Affairs Committee, does not see it as an attempt to deprive solicitors of work, but merely as trying to reduce unnecessary restrictive practices. He argues ((2000) *The Gazette*, 10 January) that BarDIRECT will benefit a few specific organisations such as police forces, trades unions, professional organisations and doctors' defence bodies, who would not traditionally be using solicitors anyway and who require a specialised opinion from a barrister, but are currently forced to go through a solicitor to get one.

11.7.3 The Access to Justice Act 1999 and rights of audience

Lawyers' rights of audience before the courts were further addressed in Part III of the Access to Justice Act 1999. It replaces the Lord Chancellor's Advisory Committee on Legal Education and Conduct with a new Legal Services Consultative Panel:

- It provides that, in principle, all lawyers should have full rights of audience before any court, subject only to meeting reasonable training requirements.
- It reforms the procedures for authorising further professional bodies to grant rights of audience or rights to conduct litigation to their members; and for approving changes to professional rules of conduct relating to the exercise of these rights.

The Act also contains sections which:

- simplify procedures for approving changes to rules and the designation of new authorised bodies;
- give the Lord Chancellor power, with the approval of Parliament, to change rules which do not meet the statutory criteria set out in the CLSA 1990 as amended by these sections;
- establish the principle that all barristers and solicitors should enjoy full rights of audience; and
- establish the primacy of an advocate's ethical duties over any other civil law obligations.

The legislation enables employed advocates, including Crown Prosecutors, to appear as advocates in the higher courts if otherwise qualified to do so, regardless of any professional rules designed to prevent their doing so because of their status as employed advocates.

Background

The background to these proposals is set out in a Consultation Paper issued by the Lord Chancellor's Department in June 1998 – *Rights of Audience and Rights to Conduct Litigation in England and Wales: The Way Ahead.*

Rights to appear as an advocate in court (rights of audience) and rights to do the work involved in preparing cases for court (rights to conduct litigation) are governed by the CLSA 1990. The 1990 Act left it to 'authorised bodies' (currently the Bar Council, The Law Society and the Institute of Legal Executives) to set the rules which govern the rights of their members, subject to a statutory approval process in which new or altered rules were submitted for the approval of the Lord Chancellor and the four 'designated judges' (the Lord Chief Justice, Master of the Rolls, President of the Family Division and Vice Chancellor). Before making their decisions, the Lord Chancellor and designated judges were to receive and consider the advice of the Lord Chancellor's Advisory Committee on Legal Education and Conduct (ACLEC) and of the Director General of the Office of Fair Trading. Applications for the designation of new authorised bodies were subject to a similar procedure, but the designation of the new body was made by Order in Council subject to approval by both Houses.

The government argued that the old approval procedures were convoluted and slow, and that rights of audience were too restrictive. Some applications for approvals took several years to be processed, in part due to the need for applications to meet the approval of several parties. Rights of audience in the higher courts (the House of Lords, Court of Appeal, High Court and Crown Court) remain restricted to barristers and a small number of solicitors in private practice.

The 1999 Act simplified and expedited the approval procedure. The ACLEC was replaced by a smaller and less expensive committee, the Legal Services Consultative Panel. The functions of the Panel were not prescribed in detail in the statute, and its composition was left to the Lord Chancellor to determine, although in appointing members, he was required to have regard to specified criteria setting out appropriate knowledge and experience.

The 1999 Act provides that every barrister and every solicitor has a right of audience before every court in relation to all proceedings. These general rights were not present for solicitors in the 1990 Act. The Act also restates the current position that all solicitors have rights to conduct litigation before all courts. These rights are not unconditional; in order to exercise them, solicitors and barristers must obey the rules of conduct of the professional bodies and must have met any training requirements that may be prescribed (such as the requirement to complete pupillage in the case of the Bar, or to have obtained a higher courts advocacy qualification in the case of solicitors who wish to appear in the higher courts).

Section 38 of the Access to Justice Act 1999 provides that advocates and litigators employed by the Legal Services Commission can provide their services to members of the public. Without this clause, they might be prevented from doing so by professional rules.

Section 40 of the 1999 Act gives the General Council of the Bar and ILEX the power to grant their members rights to conduct litigation.

Section 42 of the 1999 Act gives statutory force to the existing professional rules, which make it clear that the overriding duties of advocates and litigators are their duty to the court to act with independence in the interests of justice, and their duty to comply with their professional bodies' rules of conduct. Those duties override any other civil law obligation which a person may be under, including the duty to the client or a contractual obligation to an employer or to anyone else. A barrister, solicitor or other authorised advocate or authorised litigator must refuse to do anything required, either by a client or by an employer, that is not in the interests of justice (for example, suppress evidence). The purpose of this clause is to protect the independence of all advocates and litigators.

11.7.4 Partnerships and transnational firms

By virtue of s 66 of the CLSA 1990, solicitors are enabled to form partnerships with non-solicitors (multi-disciplinary partnerships or MDPs), and the section confirms that barristers are not prevented by the common law from forming such relationships. They are, however, prohibited from doing so (unless with a foreign lawyer) by the Bar. Solicitors are able, under s 89 of the CLSA 1990 (Sched 14), to form multi-national partnerships (MNPs). The arrival of MNPs over the coming years will raise particular problems concerning the maintenance of ethical standards by The Law Society over foreign lawyers. MDPs also raise potentially serious problems, as even in arrangements between solicitors and others, it will be likely that certain work (for example, the conduct of litigation) would have to be performed by solicitors.

In a move to pave the way towards allowing MDPs, The Law Society has devised a scheme, 'legal practice plus', which would allow non-solicitor partners (NSPs) to join firms and enter into a contract with The Law Society agreeing to be bound by its professional rules. There are, however, concerns over the scheme's viability, particularly over the preservation of legal professional privilege.

Accountants are doing more legal work and solicitors are doing more accountancy work than ever before, but the two professional bodies do not allow their members to join a single practice. The main obstacle is rule 7 of the Solicitors Practice Rules, which prohibits solicitors from sharing fees with non-solicitor professionals. There is a build up of pressure for this obstacle to be removed, see, for example, Nigel S Cobb (2002) 152 NLJ 1341.

The business organisation called the limited liability partnership (LLP) was introduced by the Limited Liability Partnership Act 2000. The new business form seeks to amalgamate the advantages of the company's corporate form with the flexibility of the partnership form. Although called a 'partnership', the new form is, in fact, a distinct legal entity that enjoys an existence apart from that of its members. The LLP can enter into agreements in its own name, it can own property, sue and be sued. Traditional partnerships by contrast entail liability for the partners as individuals. Although the LLP enjoys corporate status, it is not taxed as a separate entity from its members. Solicitors do not seem to have been keen to adopt these as their preferred form of firm. Of those formed so far (and there were, in 2002, fewer than 100 from the then existing 8,300 law firms), most were formed because of international constraints in mergers, that is, the foreign firm could not merge with the British one unless the British one became an LLP. One perceived risk that seems to be important to many lawyers is that an LLP can be sued itself rather than proceedings being launched against only one or two partners (Mark Smulian, 'Doing the dirty deed' (2002) *The Gazette*, 31 October, p 23).

Law firms

There is, however, a widening gap between the work and remuneration of the top few hundred commercial firms and the 10,000 smaller High Street firms.

A recent series of mergers has created a few relatively huge law firms, and the merger of an English firm with an American one has produced the world's first billion dollar practice. Partners at Clifford Chance voted to merge with the USA's Rogers & Wells to form a firm employing 5,800 people in 30 offices worldwide. The new firm generates over one billion dollars in turnover a year. The firm specialises in corporate finance, commercial property, anti-trust law and litigation. Keith Clark, senior partner at Clifford Chance, has explained that the aim of the merger was to create a truly international firm capable of offering an integrated legal service to an increasingly global business community. He has said, 'Clients don't want all the time delays and inefficiencies of dealing with half a dozen legal firms around the world. What they want is one firm which has the capacity to be a one-stop shop for all their corporate needs' ((1999) *The Times*, 12 July). In the context of legal and social theory, it is of interest to some that these events can be seen as illustrative of the theory of dialectical materialism – the interaction between ideas, action and the material world. During the 1980s, law firms, by doing all the legal work on mergers for commercial companies (for example, telecommunications, energy and manufacturing) helped to create a new environment of transnationals operating on a world basis. Now, that new material environment has affected the very law firms who helped to create it. These law firms are now themselves changing into global firms in order to do the ordinary legal work for the new commercial giants. By contrast, law firms that gave a public funding service to under-privileged groups are progressively reducing such activity. As Paula Rohan has noted, 'After almost 60 years of giving the most disadvantaged members of society access to legal advice, the system is on its last legs – at least according to a major *Gazette* survey' (see (2003) *The Gazette*, 23 January, p 1, and 30 January, 'A Dying Breed', p 20). As a consequence of very low rates of remuneration making even a break-even policy virtually impossible, and political attacks on public funding lawyers, 78% of the 291 firms who responded to the survey were considering cutting down on their public funding work, and 91% stated they were dissatisfied with the current system.

11.7.5 Employed solicitors

This is the fastest growing area of practice with more than a fifth of those holding a practising certificate working outside private practice. Employed solicitors are professionals who work for salaries as part of a commercial firm, private or public enterprise, charity or organisation, as opposed to solicitors in private practice who take instructions from various clients. As Janet Paraskeva, The Law Society chief executive, notes: 'In-house lawyers can provide cost-effective legal advice, and have an increasingly important role in corporate governance. [They] often act as co-ordinators for the outsourcing of legal work and become involved with public affairs, risk management and general business analysis' ((2003) *The Gazette*, 20 February). In the decade 1992–2002, the numbers of employed solicitors grew from 9,778 to 18,474 – an 89% increase. In fact, the number of solicitors working in the employed sector is likely to be much higher because the figures come from The Law Society list of those with practising certificates but, because of their employed status, many lawyers are not required to have such a certificate. In-house solicitors often enjoy more flexible working terms than their private practice counterparts, so it is probably no accident that 42.4% of solicitors holding practising certificates in commerce and industry are women, while only 35.2% of practising certificate holders in private practice are women (*Key Facts 2002: The Solicitors' Profession*).

11.7.6 Monopoly conveyancing rights

Historically, barristers, solicitors, certified notaries and licensed conveyancers enjoyed statutory monopolies, making it an offence for any other persons to draw up or prepare documents connected with the transfer of title to property for payment. The CLSA 1990 broke this monopoly by allowing any person or body not currently authorised to provide conveyancing services to make an application to the Authorised Conveyancing Practitioners Board (established by s 34) for authorisation under s 37. The Board must be satisfied, before granting authorisation, that the applicant's business is, and will be, carried on by fit and proper persons, and must believe that the applicant will establish or participate in the systems for the protection of the client specified in s 37(7) including, for example, adequate professional indemnity cover and regulations made under s 40 concerning competence and conduct. Banks and building societies were in a privileged position (s 37(8)) since they were already regulated by statute. These institutions did not initially appear enthusiastic to compete with solicitors by establishing in-house lawyers. They have preferred instead to use panels of local practitioners.

The solicitors' monopoly on the grant of probate has also been abolished. Under ss 54–55 of the CLSA 1990, probate services were opened up to be available from approved bodies of non-lawyers. Grant of probate is the legal proof that a will is valid, which is needed for a person to put the will into effect. New probate practitioners directly compete with solicitors for probate work. The grant of probate is only a small part of the probate process, but when it was restricted as business which only a solicitor could perform, it effectively prevented others, except some banks, from being involved in probate. The banks seem best placed to take up work in this area as they already have trustee and executor departments. Like the slow take-up to do conveyancing work (there are still only relatively few commercial licensed conveyancers handling among them about 5% of all conveyancing), enthusiasm to break into the probate business has been hard to detect.

In its Green Papers published in 1989, the government stated that the means it favoured to produce the most efficient and effective provision of legal services would be 'the discipline of the market'. This technique, however, has not been without its problems. There was not a rush to use the conveyancing services of solicitors who had made their prices very competitive in the wake of competition from licensed conveyancers. In one survey, The Law Society found that only 8% of clients had opted for cheaper services ((1993) *The Lawyer*, 12 October). More worrying is the allegation that a significant number of those offering 'cut-price' conveyancing are not producing a respectable quality of service. Tony Holland, a former president of The Law Society, has argued that this is a result of a rush of inadequately trained persons to make money from that part of solicitors' erstwhile monopoly which has been thrown open to non-lawyers ((1994) 144 NLJ 192). He noted, however, that at the time of writing the article he was engaged in giving expert testimony in no fewer than 19 actions for negligence arising from incompetent conveyancing.

Nevertheless, research published by the Department of the Environment, Transport and the Regions showed that conveyancing in England and Wales was the cheapest of the 10 European countries surveyed, even though it was the slowest. It takes an average of six to eight weeks for a contract to be exchanged in England and Wales, while in the USA and South Africa the average is a week. Even so, while the legal fee for conveyancing on a £60,000 house in England and Wales is about £1,500, the same service in France costs about £3,600 and in Portugal, it is about £6,000 (see News in Brief, 'Cheap conveyancing' (1998) 148 NLJ 8). The Lord Chancellor's Department's 2002 Consultation Paper on legal services, *In the Public Interest*, suggested that the introduction of the licensed conveyancer system has not worked well because licensed conveyancers are handling only 5% of conveyancing services. The system has not, therefore, succeeded in providing real competition. There is a growing concentration of conveyancing into a small number of polarised firms (see, for example, Nigel S Cobb (2002) 152 NLJ 1340) according to some observers of conveyancing.

11.7.7 The Legal Services Ombudsman

An Ombudsman (a name taken from Sweden where the post has existed for over 170 years) is a person independent of the government or a given field of activity who investigates complaints of maladministration. The post of Legal Services Ombudsman (LSO) was created in 1990 by s 21 of the CLSA 1990 and covers England and Wales. The Act provides that the LSO must not be a lawyer. The Access to Justice Act 1999 gave the LSO powers to make orders rather than recommendations requiring the legal professional bodies and individual practitioners to pay appropriate compensation to complainants. Zahida Manzoor, the LSO for England and Wales, said when she was appointed in March 2003, that she would take a robust stance to ensure that the legal professions had fair, open and efficient complaints handling systems that met public needs. In the period March 2002–March 2003, she observed that the Office of the Legal Services Ombudsman had received 1,750 new cases from members of the public who remained dissatisfied with the way their complaint had been handled by the lawyers' own professional bodies. She said that there was a lot to be done regarding the professional bodies' complaints handling systems, especially in relation to the Office for the Supervision of Solicitors, part of The Law Society. She observed that the number of cases being referred to her Office was continuing to rise:

> Not only is this unacceptable but it may only be the tip of the iceberg. It is highly likely that these cases only reflect those people who are aware of their rights and have the perseverance to pursue their complaints. There may be many more people who are unhappy at the level of service they have received from the legal profession but are unaware of their rights to get redress.

The number of complaints should always be seen in the context of the number of practising lawyers and the number of transactions during the period under review. There are, altogether, over 90,000 solicitors and barristers in England and Wales, who between them work on over two million contentious and non-contentious cases each year.

This Ombudsman is empowered by s 22 of the 1990 Act to 'investigate any allegation which is properly made to him and relates to the manner in which a complaint made to a professional body with respect to an authorised advocate, authorised litigator, licensed conveyancer, recognised body or notary who is a member of that professional body; or any employee of such a person, has been dealt with by that professional body'. The LSO cannot normally investigate any complaint whilst it is being investigated by a professional body, nor if it has been dealt with by a court or the Solicitors' Disciplinary Tribunal or the disciplinary tribunal of the Council of the Inns of Court, since the procedures in such tribunals satisfy the need for public accountability.

Upon completing an investigation, the LSO must send a copy of her reasoned conclusions to the complainant and the person or body under investigation. The report can make any of the following recommendations:

- that the complaint be reconsidered by the professional body;

- that the professional body should consider its powers in relation to the person who was the subject of complaint;

- that the person complained about, or any person connected to him or her, should pay compensation to the complainant for loss suffered or inconvenience or distress caused;

- that the professional body concerned should pay such compensation;

- that a separate payment be made to the complainant in respect of costs related to the making of the allegation.

The person or body to whom these recommendations are sent must reply within three months explaining what action has been, or is proposed to be, taken to comply with the recommendation(s) made.

11.8   Lawyers and fair trading

If you want your car's electrical wiring repaired, you can approach an auto-electrician and ask for the work to be done. You do not have to first ask a car mechanic to engage the services of the auto-electrician on your behalf and then pay them both. Yet in law there is often a situation in which a client has to pay for both a solicitor and a barrister when it is only the barrister who does the job the client wants done. The Office of Fair Trading (OFT) has asked the government to put an end to the restrictive practice whereby the public has to pay for both a solicitor and barrister, in some circumstances, when in fact it is the services of only one person that are required. Clients' bills are thus increased unnecessarily (*Competition in Professions*, 2002, OFT, www.oft.gov.uk).

OFT investigators were particularly concerned that under the Bar's code of conduct, barristers can only be approached directly by a member of the public after first 'instructing' a solicitor. The report concludes that this rule is an unnecessary and costly obstacle to access to legal services. Ministers are now expected to implement the OFT's recommendation.

In response, the Bar Council stated that it welcomed any proposal which improved choice for the consumer. The Council, however, has cautioned that a wholesale change would not work to the client's advantage in all cases. Its stance has been that there is no benefit, for example, to a person who has been arrested in going to a chamber for help when a solicitor is in a much better position to advise them at the police station.

The government is now considering whether it is best to remove the 'double lawyer' obligation in the Bar's rules or to develop the BarDIRECT scheme which currently licenses specified organisations and public bodies, such as police forces and trade unions, to leapfrog the solicitor and go directly to a barrister. In 2002, the Bar Council published an agreed response to the OFT report (www.barcouncil.org.uk). The key proposals put to the OFT were as follows:

- From 2003, a relaxation of the Bar's rules limiting direct access by lay clients, subject to safeguards to protect the client.

- A further liberalisation of the Bar's rules to allow comparative advertising on fees, but not on so called 'success rates'.

- A robust defence of the Bar's ban on partnerships, on the grounds that this promotes competition between 10,000 barristers in private practice, and preserves their fundamental independence which is at the core of the justice system.

- A firm rejection of the suggestion that private practice barristers should be able to conduct litigation, on the basis that the rules preventing this have no adverse effects on competition and promote specialisation by the Bar in advocacy and advice.

- An acceptance that the system for appointing Queen's Counsel should be kept under review, but a strong assertion of the value of QCs to purchasers in the legal services market.

- Strong support for upholding legal professional privilege (under which communications between lawyer and client are secret and cannot be accessed by others or used against them), on the grounds that the protection this provides is a fundamental human right for the client.

As it stands, the Bar is a professional grouping with a common system of education, training, professional rules and standards, and discipline. There are those who think that allowing experts from various professions to combine to form single businesses is desirable, as these would produce helpful one-stop shops for clients (especially corporate clients). By contrast, others take the view that the standards of the Bar would be compromised by such changes.

When solicitors acquired rights of audience in the higher courts, the Bar responded with the BarDIRECT scheme, but that was limited to barristers accepting work directly from licensed organisations that had satisfied the Bar that they could provide the same service to barristers that solicitors usually performed. There is some opposition among barristers to the scheme being extended so as to allow barristers to accept instructions directly from lay people – a scheme that will be introduced in late 2003. David Mason, a barrister from Newcastle Upon Tyne, puts the case against such change very clearly ('Will direct access work?' (2003) 153 NLJ 332). The public, Mason argues, are likely to be very positive about the possibility of having direct access to a barrister, but in practice, there will be much disappointment:

Barristers cannot conduct litigation in the way that solicitors do. The rules will not allow them to correspond with the other side, instruct expert witnesses, take witness statements other than from their lay client, handle clients' money, or undertake many of the activities that the public expects from solicitors. The cost may be less because only one professional person is engaged, but the product the client will be buying will be very different, and will undoubtedly disappoint.

Mason argues that, in fact, large areas of practice, like crime and family work, will be excluded because the Legal Services Commission has indicated that it will not fund such direct access work. The cases where it might have some uptake are criminal appeals where no new evidence is likely to be involved. In family cases, clients are often stressed and anxious and want immediate and constant contact with solicitors, and the same is often true of commercial and corporate clients, but barristers might be caught up in court for days or weeks without being able to get back to the client. The clerks to chambers are there to serve the barristers and deal with solicitors' requests, not to assuage the anxieties of clients. Mason concludes that 'many direct access arrangements will flounder and end in tears over this sort of issue'.

LEGAL SERVICES

The main area of debate on this theme is the best approach to supplying the highest number and widest range of people with legal services appropriate to what citizens need. How can the legal profession become more user friendly? Have the changes made under the CLSA 1990 to increase competition in the provision of legal services been successful? Have the restrictive professional monopolies been properly broken and, if so, will the quality of services offered by non-lawyers (for example, conveyancing, probate, litigation) be reduced? Will the exclusion of millions of people from public funding eligibility have any serious consequences?

The impact of the conditional fee arrangements, the 1995 Green Paper on legal aid, and franchising are of special importance, but to deal with these issues properly, you need to be familiar with the details of how legal services are delivered in general.

The legal profession

The legal profession, although not fused, comprises solicitors and barristers whose work is becoming increasingly similar in many respects. Additionally, the ending of monopolies on litigation, probate and conveyancing has meant that lawyers' traditional work is increasingly becoming blurred with that of other professionals. The liabilities of lawyers for errors and negligence are key issues. Another is the way in which complaints are handled by the professions.

The Courts and Legal Services Act 1990

The CLSA 1990 was passed 'to see that the public has the best possible access to legal services and that those services are of the right quality for the particular needs of the client'. The detail by which the Act sought to do this is very important, especially s 17 (general principle, litigation and rights of audience); s 11 (lay representatives); ss 28–29 (right to conduct litigation); s 66 (multi-disciplinary partnerships); s 89 (multi-national partnerships); ss 34–37 (conveyancing); ss 21–26 (the Legal Services Ombudsman); and s 58 (conditional fee arrangements).

The Access to Justice Act 1999

The 1999 Act makes many changes which will have an impact upon the professions. It articulates the principle that all lawyers should have full rights of audience before all courts, provided they have passed the relevant examinations. Also, by reforming the procedures for authorising further professional bodies to grant rights of audience, it signals a widening of those rights in the future.

CHAPTER 12

THE FUNDING OF LEGAL SERVICES

12.1 Introduction

Legal aid (now called public funding) was introduced after World War II to enable people who could not otherwise afford the services of lawyers to be provided with those services by the State. The system grew and extended its reach and range of services enormously over the decades. Costs to the government were gigantic. The system underwent various restrictions and cutbacks during the late 1990s and was replaced by other systems like the Community Legal Service (2000) and the Criminal Defence Service (2001). The term 'legal aid' is still used as a descriptive, non-technical term to refer to State-funded services.

Two factors combined in the early 1990s to cause great change in the way that legal services are funded. The first factor was the spiralling cost of legal aid to the State during a period of recession. The money available to the government was insufficient to meet the rising cost of maintaining the level and extent of legal services previously available. The second factor was the professed aim of the government in general and Lord Mackay, the then Lord Chancellor, in particular to reduce the State's role in the provision of legal services. There is some evidence that, given the aim of the reforms, the project has not been entirely successful. In 2003, the legal aid budget went into the red by £100 million (Paula Rohan, 'LCD reveals £100 legal aid overspend' (2003) *The Gazette*, 13 February).

Over 10 million people were taken out of the bracket of legal aid eligibility as a result of governmental changes to the eligibility criteria (see Smith, *Shaping the Future: New Directions in Legal Services* (1995), Legal Action Group). To try to compensate for this exclusion of millions of people from the effective right to use the law, other schemes have been promoted and developed. These include the use of 'no win, no fee' arrangements, the use of non-lawyer legal services, and legal services private insurance.

The legal aid budget for 1996–97 was £1.48 billion. It was in that context that the White Paper *Striking the Balance: the Future of Legal Aid in England and Wales* (HMSO) was published in 1996. The paper proposed the most radical changes to the legal aid system since its launch in 1951. The main aims of the White Paper in relation to funding legal services were: (a) to impose cash limits on the legal aid scheme (instead of allowing it to have a demand-led budget); (b) to require some form of payment from all users; and (c) to operate a separate budget for major, expensive cases.

There are several State-funded schemes to facilitate the provision of aid and advice. Each scheme has different rules relating to its scope, procedures for application and eligibility. Because of the importance of justice and access to the legal machinery, the idea behind legal aid is to give people who could otherwise not afford professional legal help the same services as more wealthy citizens. This raises important social, political and economic questions. Do poorer people deserve the same quality of legal advice as that which can be afforded by wealthy people? If so, how should such schemes be funded?

12.2 A brief historical overview

The legal aid system was introduced under the Legal Aid and Advice Act 1949 by the Labour government after World War II to allow poor people to have access to the justice system. Before this time, such people had to rely on charity if they went to court. The system was seen by the government as the 'second arm of the Welfare State' (the first one being the National Health Service). The system expanded throughout the 1950s and 1960s. It moved from just covering the higher courts to covering the lower courts, and from just civil courts to criminal courts. The present scheme was introduced by the Access to Justice Act 1999 following the government White Paper, *Modernising Justice*, published on 2 December 1998. The old scheme was contained in the Legal Aid Act 1988. Under the 1988 Act, the term 'legal aid' strictly referred to only representation in court. In fact, it covered a wide range of subsidised or free services. There were three main types of legal aid, which were Legal Advice and Assistance, Civil Legal Aid and Criminal Legal Aid.

Legal Advice and Assistance, also known as the Green Form scheme, enabled a solicitor to undertake ordinary legal work (excluding court work) up to a limit, initially, of three hours' worth of work for a client who passed the relevant means test administered by the solicitor. The amount of work could be extended with the permission of the local Legal Aid Area Committee. Assistance by way of representation (ABWOR), also means tested, was an extension of the Legal Advice and Assistance scheme which covered court appearances where advice or letter writing had not solved a problem. It was available for domestic proceedings in magistrates' courts proceedings, before mental health review tribunals, representations under the Police and Criminal Evidence Act (PACE) 1984 for warrants of further detention and representation in certain child care proceedings. The scheme covered the cost of a solicitor preparing a case and representing a client in most civil cases in magistrates' courts, now known as Family Proceedings Courts. These cases included separation, maintenance (except child maintenance where the Child Support Agency has jurisdiction), residence/contact, paternity and defended adoption proceedings.

The Green Form scheme and ABWOR were the most widely used of the legal aid schemes prior to the Access to Justice Act. At the beginning of the 1990s, the take-up was stable at around one million acts of assistance per year, but then the scheme began to grow, reaching a peak of 1.6 million acts of assistance in 1993–94. This growth was principally fuelled by increased demand for advice on social and economic matters, such as housing, debt and welfare benefits, although advice on personal injuries, employment and immigration matters also grew during that period (Legal Aid Board, *Annual Report*, 1998–99, section 3, p 117). From 1996, the volume of Green Form cases paid for by the Legal Aid Board started to rise again, due largely to the introduction of standard fees for Criminal Legal Aid in the magistrates' courts in 1993, but a renewed demand for advice on civil, non-matrimonial matters, especially immigration and nationality and welfare benefits, led to the peak of 1994 being reached again in 1998 (*Annual Report*, 1998–99, p 120).

Civil Legal Aid was available for many types of action but not, notably, for proceedings in coroners' courts or tribunals (except the Lands Tribunal and the Employment Appeal Tribunal), nor for proceedings involving libel or slander. From 1989, Civil Legal Aid was run by the Legal Aid Board. An applicant had to satisfy two tests: a means test and a merits test. The means test used the concepts of 'disposable capital' and 'disposable income', which are still applied. The former includes savings, jewellery and the value of the house you live in (although any equity of up to a specified sum was excluded); the latter involved actual income less income tax, national savings, money for dependants, necessaries, travel to work, etc. Disability Living Allowance, Attendance Allowance, Constant Attendance Allowance, Council Tax Benefit, Housing Benefit payments made under the Earnings Top-up scheme or the Community Care Direct Payment scheme are not counted as income. If an applicant's income and/or capital was below a certain amount, representation was free; if it was above that amount, then a contribution would be payable on a sliding scale, but with a ceiling figure above which the applicant would not be eligible for financial assistance. Under the merits test, the applicant had to show the Board that he had reasonable grounds for taking, defending or being party to an action, but the applicant could be refused aid if it appeared to the Board unreasonable to grant representation.

Criminal Legal Aid covered the cost of case preparation and representation in criminal cases. The decision as to whether to grant legal aid was made by the court clerk according to criteria in the Legal Aid Act 1988. In the event of a refusal, there was a statutory right of appeal to Criminal Legal Aid committees run by The Law Society. As with Civil Legal Aid, the applicant had to pass a merits and a means test. The merits test was simply whether it was in the 'interests of justice', with the following factors being taken into account:

(a) Whether the offence was such that if proved it would be likely that the court would impose a sentence that would deprive the defendant of his liberty or lead to his loss of livelihood or serious damage to his reputation.

(b) If the determination of the case might involve consideration of a substantial question of law.

(c) If the defendant had linguistic difficulties or other disability.

(d) If the defence required expertise like cross-examination.

(e) Whether it was in the interests of another party that the accused be represented. This was usually satisfied by defendants in the Crown Court – the success rate was about 98%.

The means test was normally carried out by court clerks and was similar to the test for Civil Legal Aid, although the threshold amounts differed.

In addition to these schemes, some solicitors were prepared to give a free or fixed-fee interview without carrying out any means test related to the interviewee's income or capital. Duty Solicitor Schemes are available at most magistrates' courts and police stations. Solicitors can give *free* legal advice to someone who is being questioned by the police whether or not such a suspect has been arrested; advice and free representation can also be given for someone's first appearance for a particular offence at a magistrates' court. A number of historical and economic factors combined to reduce the scope of the system from the mid-1970s. By the 1990s, the system applied to a much smaller section of the community than it had done in previous decades. In the 1950s, about 80% of the population were covered by the legal aid system, whereas by 1998, less than 40% of the population were covered.

The scope of eligibility had expanded quickly in the 1970s. As a result, more lawyers were setting up practices catering for legal aid clients. Divorces were becoming much more common (as the result of social factors and legislation which made divorce easier), and divorce accounted for a very large part of Civil Legal Aid. Alongside all this, the economy was going into recession, and this had two effects: (a) it resulted in there being less money in government funds from which to finance legal aid; and (b) it generated waves of economically related problems (unemployment, family break-ups, welfare problems) which needed legal services for people who could not afford to pay for them.

From the mid-1980s, successive Lord Chancellors were engaged in a series of measures to try to reduce public expenditure on the legal system. A common feature of the Civil and Criminal Legal Aid schemes was that expenditure on them was demand-led. Any lawyer could do legal aid work for a client who passed the relevant means test (if any) and whose case passed the statutory merits test (in the case of Civil Legal Aid) or the 'interests of justice' test (in the case of Criminal Legal Aid). Lawyers were paid on a case by case basis for each individual case or other act of assistance, usually at rates or fees set in regulations, but in some cases on the same basis as a privately funded lawyer.

This, in the government's view, meant that there were few mechanisms or incentives for promoting value for money or assuring the quality of the services provided, and that neither the government nor the Legal Aid Board was able to exert adequate control over expenditure or determine the priorities for that expenditure.

From August 1994, the Legal Aid Board operated a voluntary quality assurance scheme, known as franchising. Solicitors who met certain management criteria were devolved certain administrative powers, enabling them to undertake cases in one or more of the 10 subject categories in which they are awarded (criminal, family, personal injury, housing, etc) a contract, without obtaining prior approval from what was the Legal Aid Board. These practices received certain fiscal benefits such as a lump sum payment from the Legal Aid Board on account, immediately upon the approval of a case. In relation to these firms, the Legal Aid Board moved from being an approving body to a quality control organisation. This has become the main method of delivery of legal aid under the Access to Justice Act 1999, in spite of fears amongst many lawyers and commentators that this trend will lead to seriously reduced access to legal services. The fear was based on the notion that, because the smaller firms would find it too difficult to satisfy the management criteria, and would become uncompetitive, a number would go out of business.

12.3 The new legal aid scheme

The Access to Justice Act 1999 set up a new legal aid system and made provisions about rights to supply legal services (see Chapter 11), court procedure (see Chapter 7), magistrates and magistrates' courts (see Chapter 4). The provisions in the Act form part of the wide-ranging programme of reforms to legal services and the courts, described in the government's White Paper, *Modernising Justice*, published on 2 December 1998. Except where noted, the Act only affects England and Wales.

Part I of the 1999 Act established a Legal Services Commission (LSC) to maintain and develop the Community Legal Service (CLS) and the Criminal Defence Service (CDS) which replaced the Civil and Criminal Legal Aid schemes respectively. The Act also enabled the Lord Chancellor to give the Commission orders, directions and guidance about how it should exercise its functions. The Community Legal Service Fund replaced the legal aid fund in civil and family cases. The Commission uses the resources of the fund in a way that reflects priorities set by the Lord Chancellor, and its duty to secure the best possible value for money, to procure or provide a range of legal services. The Commission also has a duty to liaise with other funders of legal services to facilitate the development of co-ordinated plans for making the best use of all available resources. The strategy is to develop a network of legal service providers of assured quality, offering the widest possible access to information and advice about the law, and assistance with legal problems. The CDS is intended to ensure that people suspected or accused of a crime are properly represented, while securing better value for money than was possible under the legal aid scheme.

12.3.1 Controlled and licensed work

As noted at 12.2, above, legal aid funding was granted on a case by case basis until the system of franchising was introduced in August 1994, where firms of solicitors meeting certain requirements were able to contract to undertake certain cases without prior approval, and claim funding on a more advantageous basis than previously. This franchise or 'contract' system has formed the basis of the new legal aid scheme. Under this new scheme, funded services fall under the headings of 'controlled work' and 'licensed work'. Controlled work comes under the contract system and consists of all legal help and legal representation. The decision about whether to provide services in a particular case is made by the supplier, who is either a solicitor or a not-for-profit organisation, such as a law centre or Citizens Advice Bureau (discussed at 12.8, below). They bid for a contract to provide legal services funded by the LSC to the Regional Legal Services Committees. Under the contract, the number of cases that may be undertaken by the suppliers is limited. Licensed work is the equivalent of the case by case approval granted for all State-funded legal work prior to 1994 and all non-franchised work prior to the establishment of the LSC. Licensed work is administered through a certification process requiring the Commission's initial approval of the cost, timing and scope of each case. Once the licence is granted, it covers all legal representation before the courts, except for very expensive cases referred to as 'very high cost cases' (VHCC) which are managed under individual case contracts with the Commission. The VHCC are those in which a solicitor is instructed with a criminal case that is likely to last 25 days or more at trial, or is likely to accrue more than £150,000 defence costs, then he notifies the Criminal High Cost Case (CHCC) Unit of the Commission and special arrangements are made in respect of the funding of the case.

12.3.2 Contracting

The work that may be undertaken by a supplier, whether a solicitor or a not-for-profit organisation, has been divided into the following categories: crime, family, personal injury, clinical negligence, housing, immigration, welfare benefit, employment, mental health, debt, consumer and general contract, education, community care, actions against police, public law. A General Civil Contract under the CLS or a General Criminal Contract under the CDS may be awarded to allow a supplier to undertake work within one or more categories. The contract will state the categories and terms under which the supplier may provide legal advice and representation. The purpose of specifying categories in respect of civil contracts is to ensure an appropriate distribution of legal and advice services to meet demand in each region. In order to assess demand and ensure that the right kind of services are available to meet the needs of a region, Community Legal Service Partnerships (CLSPs) have been set up. The service provided may be at different levels depending on the case. The different levels of service are:

Legal Help: this is the provision of initial advice and assistance.

Help at Court: this enables a solicitor or adviser to speak on behalf of a person at certain court hearings without formally acting for that person in the whole proceedings.

Approved Family Help: this is the provision of help in relation to family disputes including the resolution of the matter by negotiation or otherwise. This covers initial advice and assistance, issuing proceedings and representation where necessary in order to obtain disclosure of information from another party or to obtain a consent order when matters in dispute have been agreed. It is available in two forms: Help with Mediation where a person is attending mediation sessions and General Family Help.

Family Mediation: this covers mediation for a family dispute, including finding out whether mediation is suitable or not.

Legal Representation: under this, a person can be represented in court. It is available in two forms:

(i) *Investigative Help*: funding is limited to investigation of the strength of a claim.

(ii) *Full Representation*: funding is provided to represent people in legal proceedings.

Support Funding: this provides partial funding for very expensive cases which are otherwise funded privately. It is available in two forms:

(i) *Investigative Support*: funding is limited to investigation of the strength of a claim with a view to a conditional fee agreement.

(ii) *Litigation Support*: this provides partial funding of high cost proceedings under a conditional fee agreement.

12.3.3 Quality Mark

In order to be a supplier under either the CLS or the CDS, the solicitor or not-for-profit organisation must achieve the minimum standards under the respective Quality Marks. There are three kinds of Quality Mark: information, general help and specialist help, with a supplier displaying an appropriately endorsed logo on its premises. A supplier of information will typically be a library and provide leaflets, reference material and access to the CLS or CDS *Directory of Services*. A supplier of general help will provide information and advice and will be a Citizens Advice Bureau or other advice agency. A supplier of specialist information will be a solicitor, a law centre, or some Citizens Advice Bureaux, and it will be able to give information and advice on a complex problem in a specialist legal area which will be shown next to the supplier's entry in the CLS or CDS *Directory*.

12.4   The Legal Services Commission

As from 1 April 2000, the Legal Services Commission replaced the Legal Aid Board. It was considered necessary to establish a new body to reflect the fundamentally different nature of the CLS when compared to Civil Legal Aid. Within the broad framework of priorities set by the Lord Chancellor, the Commission is responsible for taking detailed decisions about the allocation of resources. It is also required to liaise with other funders to develop the CLS more widely. The Commission has a wider role in respect of the CDS than the Legal Aid Board did in respect of Criminal Legal Aid. The Board had very limited responsibilities for legal aid in the higher criminal courts. Membership of the Commission differs from that of the old Legal Aid Board, to reflect a shift in focus from the needs of providers to the needs of users of legal services. Also, the Commission is smaller than the Board: 7–12 members rather than 11–17. This is intended to facilitate 'focused decision making'.

12.5   The Community Legal Service

The LSC has two main duties in respect of the CLS:

• First, it manages a CLS Fund (ss 4–11 of the 1999 Act), which has replaced legal aid in civil and family cases. The CLS Fund is used to secure the provision of appropriate legal services within the resources made available to it, and according to priorities set by the Lord Chancellor and by regional and local assessments of need. A Funding Code, drawn up by the Commission and approved by the Lord Chancellor, sets out the criteria and procedures for granting contracts and deciding whether to fund individual cases. As spending has been brought under better control, it has been possible to expand the scope of the fund into areas that were not covered by legal aid, in particular to alternatives to lawyers and courts, like mediation and advice agencies. Mediation is already a requirement in family matters (see Part III of the Family Law Act 1996).

- Secondly, as part of a wider CLS, the Commission has, in co-operation with local funders and interested bodies, developed local, regional and national plans to match the delivery of legal services to identified needs and priorities.

12.5.1 Community Legal Service contract

In carrying out the first duty of managing the CLS, the LSC developed the General Civil Contract to introduce contracting within the statutory framework created by the Access to Justice Act 1999, with effect from 1 January 2000. There are two versions of the General Civil Contract, one for solicitors and one for not-for-profit agencies, because of the differences in the terminology and methods of delivery used by these types of suppliers. An important aspect of the new scheme is that the right kind of services should be available to meet the needs of a region. In furtherance of this aim, the Commission published a Consultation Paper in 2002, setting out its proposals for establishing regional priorities for civil contracting through the production of Regional Legal Services Committees' reports, Regional Directors' contracting strategies and CLSPs. Following this consultation, the Commission has put in place a new process for the regional prioritisation of needs. As a result, new bid rules for the award of General Civil Contracts for Controlled Work apply as from 1 January 2003, although these will be further revised as from 1 April 2004 to reflect regional priorities and to hold a wider bidding process.

The new term for litigants who obtain LSC funding is 'LSC funded clients', and the fund out of which litigants who obtain LSC funding is referred to as the CLS Fund. Section 7 of the 1999 Act allows the Lord Chancellor, using regulations, to set financial eligibility limits. Therefore, an applicant must be able to show that his capital *and* income are within the current financial limits.

12.5.2 Financial eligibility test

The Community Legal Service (Financial) Regulations 2000, as amended under the Community Legal Service (Financial) (Amendment No 3) Regulations 2001, sets out the thresholds for financial eligibility. The test uses the basic concepts of 'disposable income', that is, income available to a person after deducting essential living expenses; and 'disposable capital', that is, the assets owned by a person after essential items like a home. If a person could sell her home, pay off the mortgage and still have more than £100,000 left (called 'equity'), then she will not qualify for aid.

Certain services are free regardless of financial resources, such as services consisting exclusively of the provision of general information about the law, legal system and availability of legal services, legal representation in some cases involving the Children Act 1989 and related proceedings, and representation at a mental health review tribunal. Some services are non-contributory and a client is either eligible or not, whereas others are contributory in accordance with a sliding scale dependent on how much a client's income or capital exceeds a given threshold. There is a cap amount over which a person is ineligible for legal aid. In summary, the financial eligibility amounts for applications on or after 5 August 2002 are as follows:

- For all levels of service, there is (as of April 2003) a gross income cap of £2,288 per month. This cap may be increased by £145 per month for each child in excess of four. A client who is directly or indirectly in receipt of Income Support or income-based Job Seeker's Allowance automatically satisfies the gross income test for all levels of service.

- For the service of Legal Help, Help at Court and Legal Representation before Immigration Adjudicators and the Immigration Appeal Tribunal, the disposable income must not exceed £621 per month and there is a capital limit of £3,000.

- For the service of Family Mediation, Help with Mediation and other Legal Representation (which may be subject to a contribution from income and capital), the disposable income must not exceed £707 per month and there is a capital limit of £8,000.

When assessing gross income and disposable income, State benefits under the Social Security Contributions and Benefits Act 1992 (Disability Living Allowance, Attendance Allowance, Constant Attendance Allowance, Invalid Care Allowance, Severe Disablement Allowance, Council Tax Benefit, Housing Benefit and any payment out of the social fund), back to work bonuses under the Job Seekers Act 1995, war and war widows' pensions and fostering allowances are disregarded.

The only level of service assessed by the supplier for which contributions can be sought is Legal Representation in Specified Family Proceedings. However, provided that the client's gross income is below the prescribed limit, clients with a disposable income of £267 or below per month will not need to pay any contributions from income, but may still have to pay a contribution from capital. A client with disposable income in excess of £267 and up to £707 per month will be liable to pay a monthly contribution of a proportion of the excess over £268, assessed in accordance with the following bands:

Band	Monthly disposable income	Monthly contribution
A	£268 to £393	Quarter of income in excess of £263
B	£394 to £522	£32.50 + third of income in excess of £393
C	£523 to £707	£75.50 + half of income in excess of £522

A client whose disposable capital exceeds £3,000 is required to pay a contribution of either the capital exceeding that sum or the likely maximum costs of the funded service, whichever is the lesser.

For example, if disposable income is £408 per month, the contribution will be in Band B, the excess income is £15 (£408 – £393), the monthly contribution would therefore be £37.50 (£32.50 + £5).

Provided it is not disregarded as subject matter of the dispute, a client's main or only dwelling in which he resides must be taken into account as capital, subject to the following rules:

(a) The dwelling should be valued at the amount for which it could be sold on the open market.

(b) The amount of any mortgage or charge registered on the property must be deducted, but the maximum amount that can be deducted for such a mortgage or charge is £100,000.

(c) The first £100,000 of the value of the client's interest after making the above mortgage deduction must be disregarded.

The original proposal was that homeowners with £3,000 equity in their homes would be liable to make contributions to the cost of their legal aid. This was dropped following outrage by practitioners and legal interest groups, as it was said that such a move would effectively abolish legal aid for virtually all homeowners.

12.5.3 The Funding Code

In addition to financial eligibility, an applicant's case must also satisfy a new merits test. The Commission has prepared a Code which will replace, and is intended to be more flexible than, the merits test that was used for Civil Legal Aid. The Code sets out the criteria for determining whether services funded by the CLS Fund should be provided in a particular case and, if so, what services it is appropriate to provide. The Code also sets out the procedures for making applications. In drafting the Code, the Commission was required to consider the extent to which the criteria for assessment should reflect the following factors (s 8 of the Access to Justice Act 1999):

(a) The likely cost of funding the services and the benefit which may be obtained by their being provided.

(b) The availability of sums in the CLS Fund for funding the services and, having regard to the present and likely future demands on that Fund, the appropriateness of applying them to fund the services.

(c) The importance of the matters in relation to which the services would be provided for the individual.

(d) The availability to the individual of services not funded by the Commission and the likelihood of his being able to avail himself of them.

(e) If the services are sought by the individual in relation to a dispute, the prospects of his success in the dispute.

(f) The conduct of the individual in connection with services funded as part of the CLS (or an application for funding) or in, or in connection with, any legal proceedings.

(g) The public interest.

(h) Such other factors as the Lord Chancellor may by order require the Commission to consider.

The Code is required to reflect the principle that in many family disputes, mediation is more appropriate than court proceedings. This is intended to reinforce the development, under the Family Law Act 1996, of mediation as a means of resolving private law family disputes in a way that promotes as good a continuing relationship between the parties concerned as is possible in the circumstances. The government has argued that mediation is more constructive than adversarial court proceedings, and that litigation in these cases usually serves only to reinforce already entrenched positions and further damage the relationship between the parties. In addition, the cost of court proceedings is higher than that of mediation, and additional costs have to be borne by the property of the family, reducing the amount available to the parties and their children in future. The credibility of mediation as an appropriate forum for family matters in general took a blow in 1999, when the government abandoned plans to introduce the scheme related to divorce after pilot studies failed to produce good results.

The Commission revised the merits test for Controlled Legal Representation and issued guidance which came into force on 16 December 2002. The reform of the merits test, which regulates the demand that qualifies for help, is said by the government to complement the reforms of the supply of services – with the intention of creating a flexible system for deploying resources to meet a range of priorities within a controlled budget.

The Funding Code sets out general criteria in relation to services for all categories except very expensive cases, judicial review, claims against public authorities, clinical negligence, housing, family, mental health and immigration, for which there are criteria specific to the particular category. The Code defines which factors are relevant in a given category, how they should be taken into account, and what weight should be given to them. For example, standard criteria for the service of legal representation include: whether there is alternative funding available; whether there are alternatives to litigation; or whether the case could be allocated to the small claims track. For services in most categories, consideration must be given to whether there is sufficient benefit to the client in receiving a particular service and what the prospect of success is. Where this is a consideration, cases are put into one of six categories according to their chances of success as follows: very good (80% or better chance of success); good (60–80%); moderate (50–60%); borderline (50%); poor (less than 50%) or unclear. The considerations are not the same for all services, categories or types of case within those categories, for example, prospects of success will not be a relevant factor in cases about whether a child should be taken into local authority care.

12.5.4 Legal services provided

Section 4 of the 1999 Act describes the services that may be provided under the CLS. These range from the provision of basic information about the law and legal services to providing help towards preventing or resolving disputes and enforcing decisions which have been reached. The scheme encompasses advice, assistance and representation by lawyers (which have long been available under the legal aid scheme), and also the services of non-lawyers. It will extend to other types of service including, for example, mediation in family or civil cases where appropriate.

Under Sched 2, restrictions are specified in respect of other services for certain categories. Only basic information and advice will be available for:

- disputes involving allegations of negligent damage to property or the person ('personal injury'), apart from those about clinical negligence. These cases are generally considered suitable for conditional fees;

- allegations of defamation or malicious falsehood. Generally, legal aid was not available for representation in defamation, but it was sometimes possible to get legal aid by categorising the case as one of malicious falsehood. The government's view is that these cases do not command sufficient priority to justify public funding; in any event, they may often be suitable for a conditional fee;

- disputes arising in the course of business. Legal aid was not available for firms and companies, but a sole trader could get legal aid to pursue a business dispute. Businessmen have the option of insuring against the possibility of having to take or defend legal action. The government does not believe that the taxpayer should meet the legal costs of sole traders who fail to do so;

- matters concerned with the law relating to companies or partnerships;

- matters concerned with the law of trusts or trustees; boundary disputes. The government does not consider that these command sufficient priority to justify public funding. In addition, funding for representation at proceedings before the Lands Tribunal or Commons Commissioners is no longer available. Other services, including assistance with preparing a case, continue to be available.

For some categories, subject to local priorities, a full range of services will be available, whereas for others, all services except representation at court by a lawyer may be obtained.

The Lord Chancellor can make directions bringing cases that would be excluded within the provisions of the Act in exceptional circumstances. For example, the Lord Chancellor may direct that personal injury cases (which are generally excluded by Sched 2, because most such cases are suitable for conditional fees) be funded by the CLS fund where exceptionally high investigative or overall costs are likely to be necessary, or where issues of wider public interest are involved. The Consultation Paper, *Access to Justice with Conditional Fees* (Lord Chancellor's Department (LCD), 1998), notes that it will be necessary to decide what should constitute public interest (para 3.31). For example, a test case about a novel point of law might have no more than a 50% chance of success, but the decision could impact on numerous future cases (in the way that recent cases involving sporting injuries have extended the duty of care owed by officials wider than was previously accepted: see *Vowles v Evans and Welsh Rugby Union* (2003)), or a claim for a relatively small sum in damages might benefit a large number of other people with a similar claim. Examples might be claims arising out of the use of pharmaceutical products and pollution of water supplies or the atmosphere. Very expensive cases often include this type of public interest aspect: they are expensive because they are novel and complex, or because their wide potential impact means that they are hard fought.

12.5.5 The CLS Fund

The CLS Fund, as established under s 5 of the 1999 Act, is not uncapped, as was the old Legal Aid Fund. In the pre-1999 system, if more money was needed after the initial budgeting by the government, supplementary funding could be found. Today, the amount of the Fund is to be fixed each year by the Lord Chancellor, who takes account of the receipts from contributions (for example, from local authorities) with the balance from money voted by Parliament. The Lord Chancellor is able to direct the Commission to use specified amounts within the Fund to provide services of particular types (s 5(6)). The Lord

Chancellor divides the Fund into two main budgets, for providing services in: (i) family; and (ii) other civil cases, while allowing the Commission limited flexibility to switch money between the two areas. The Lord Chancellor may set further requirements within these two budgets, by specifying the amount, or the maximum or minimum amount, that should be spent on, say, services from the voluntary advice sector, mediation or cases involving a wider public interest. The idea here is that in this way, it will be possible to ensure that resources are allocated in accordance with the government's priorities.

The Commission may use the CLS Fund to provide services (s 6(3)). These include making contracts with, or grants to, service providers, or employing staff to provide services directly to the public. These flexible powers are intended to give effect to one of the principal objectives of the reform of publicly funded legal services: that is, the ability to tailor the provision of services, and the means by which services are delivered, to the needs of local populations and particular circumstances. The Commission is allowed to test new forms of service provision through pilot projects such as the Family Advice and Information Networks Pilot Project (FAINS) and telephone advice service. The Commission is under a duty to obtain the best value for money – a combination of price and quality – when using the resources of the Fund to provide services; and as part of the government's Best Value initiative, local authorities that are able to demonstrate success in developing community legal services are awarded a CLS Beacon Award. To date, eight local authorities have been given this status.

In line with the principle of flexibility, it may be possible to exclude further categories which can generally be funded privately, as conditional fees, legal expenses insurance and other forms of funding develop more widely. Equally well, as resources become available through the greater control of spending and value for money provided by the new scheme and the development of private alternatives, it may be possible to extend the scheme's scope to cover services that are excluded now because, although they would command some priority, they are unaffordable.

12.5.6 Extension of financial conditions on an assisted party

The 1999 Act extends the potential scope of financial conditions imposed on an assisted party in two ways, although there are no immediate plans to use either of these powers:

- It will be possible to make the provision of services in some types of cases subject to the assisted person agreeing to repay an amount in excess of the cost of the services provided, in the event that their case is successful (s 10(2)). This might make it possible to fund certain types of case on a self-financing basis, with the additional payments from successful litigants applied to meet the cost of unsuccessful cases. It would also be possible to mix public funding with a private conditional fee arrangement, subject to the same conditions about the uplift to the costs in the event of a successful outcome. The government has suggested that this might be appropriate, for example, where a case could not be taken under a wholly private arrangement, because the solicitors firm was not large enough to bear the risk of the very high costs likely to be involved.

• It will be possible (s 10(3), (4)) to require the assisted person to repay, over time and with interest, the full cost of the service provided (for example, through continuing contributions from income). This will make it possible to provide services in some categories of case in the form of a loan scheme.

Section 11 of the 1999 Act establishes limits on the liability of the person receiving funded services to pay costs to the unassisted party. The costs he must pay cannot go above what is 'reasonable' (s 11(1)), taking into account the financial resources of all parties. It also provides that regulations may specify the principles that are to be applied in determining the amount of any costs awarded against the party receiving funded services, and the circumstances in which a costs order may be enforced against the person receiving funded services.

Today, the regulations that limit the circumstances in which the costs order may be enforced against the person receiving funded services (or the liability of the Commission to meet any costs order on behalf of the person receiving funded services) are made on a more flexible basis. Previously, protection from costs was seen by governments to create too great an advantage in litigation for the person receiving legal aid.

12.5.7 Matching delivery with needs and priorities

The fulfilment of the second duty of the Commission, to match the delivery of legal services to identified needs and priorities at a local level, is dependent in practice on the formation of CLSPs in each local authority area. The CLSPs are intended to provide a forum, in each local authority area, for the local authority and the LSC, and if possible other significant funders, to come together to co-ordinate funding and planning of local legal and advice services, to ensure that delivery of services better matches local needs. The Commission and the CLSPs are intended to encourage innovation by the voluntary sector in the delivery of advice, through increased use of information technology and mobile 'outreach' services providing help to people in remote communities.

Overall, the intention is to:

• make best use of all the resources available for funding legal services, by facilitating a co-ordinated approach to planning;

• improve value for money through contracting and the development of quality assurance systems;

- establish a flexible system for allocating central government funding, in a rational and transparent way within a controlled budget, so as to provide legal services where they are judged to be most needed; and

- ensure that the scheme is capable of adapting to meet changing priorities and opportunities.

The establishment of CLSPs is ahead of schedule. Partnerships now cover in excess of 99% of the population of England and Wales, and 100% coverage is expected to be achieved well in advance of the spring 2004 target.

12.5.8 Relative success of the scheme

When the scheme was proposed, government plans appeared so vague that some lawyers questioned the credibility of the service and warned that it ran the risk of being a 'leafleting service' (News, 'The legal profession and the Community Legal Service' (1999) 149 NLJ 1195). However, a report from the National Audit Office (NAO), *Community Legal Service: the Introduction of Contracting* (HC 89 2002–2003), identifies significant improvements that have taken place in the administration of Civil Legal Aid, with better control, targeting and scrutiny of suppliers by the LSC since the CLS was created in April 2000 (see www.nao.gov.uk). In 2001–02, net expenditure borne by the CLS Fund totalled £734 million, with expenditure on licensed work totalling £476 million and expenditure on controlled work totalling £258 million. These positive points, though, should be read in the context of the general overspend on legal services cited at the outset of this chapter (12.1).

The report also identifies some problems in the new system. There is cause for concern about the volume of suppliers opting out of contracting in family work and the need for additional supply in high priority categories of law, such as community care, housing and mental health. Since the introduction of new contracting arrangements, there has been a decline in the number of solicitors firms providing legal aid services from 4,866 in January 2000 to 4,427 by July 2002. However, the number of not-for-profit firms providing services rose from 344 to 402 over the same period. The reduction in the supplier base is partly a deliberate move away from reliance on a large number of generalist support firms towards a smaller number of specialist quality-assured providers. However, the reduction also reflects concern amongst some firms about the level of remuneration offered on Civil Legal Aid work. The Commission has identified gaps in provision in some parts of the country, particularly in rural areas, and in some areas of law, for example, family law, but has had some success in attracting suppliers to immigration work.

The government says that while there is no immediate threat to the supply of services in most areas, there is a need for action to relieve pressure in the medium to long term. Initiatives such as the 'Developing Legal Aid Solicitors' scheme might help address this. Under this scheme, the LSC provides grants to meet the tuition fees of students on the Legal Practice Course (LPC) and grants to support the provision of training contracts for successful LPC students. This has led to better scrutiny of suppliers by the LSC and to a greater degree of control over the Civil Legal Aid budget. The report to Parliament notes that the Commission has, in some cases, disallowed a significant proportion of the costs claimed on help and advice work, although in some cases, these amounts have been reinstated after mediation with the supplier. Audits conducted by the Commission of case files kept by suppliers suggest that 35% of suppliers were over-claiming in excess of 20%, although some suppliers have complained about the basis of some of these decisions. The 2001–02 audit results suggest that there has been some improvement in suppliers' performance over the previous year. However, a significant minority of suppliers have not improved. The Commission has stated its intention to remove suppliers who persistently over-claim on controlled work. The removal process currently takes a minimum of around 18 months and could be reduced, although there are risks in what are relatively new procedures.

12.6 The Criminal Defence Service

The CDS Commission is under a duty to secure the provision of advice, assistance and representation, according to the interests of justice, to people suspected of a criminal offence who are arrested and held in custody or facing criminal proceedings (s 12(2) of the Access to Justice Act 1999). Criminal proceedings are defined in the Act as including criminal trials, appeals and sentencing hearings, extradition hearings, binding over proceedings, appeals on behalf of a convicted person who has died, and proceedings for contempt in the face of any court (s 13(1)). The Act allows the Lord Chancellor to add further categories by regulation. This power will be used, for example, to prescribe Parole Board reviews of discretionary life sentences. Advice and assistance is provided to people subject to criminal investigations or proceedings by duty solicitors at a magistrates' court, at a solicitor's office, and to a 'volunteer' at a police station.

Section 13(2) enabled the Commission to comply with this duty by securing advice and assistance through entering into contracts; by paying non-contracted lawyers on a case by case basis; by making payments to persons or bodies; by making grants or loans to persons or bodies; by establishing and maintaining bodies; by making grants to individuals; by providing them through salaried defenders employed by non-profit-making organisations; or by doing anything else which the Commission considers appropriate for funding advice and assistance except providing it itself. It also enabled the Commission to secure the provision of advice and assistance by different means in different areas in England and Wales and in relation to different descriptions of cases. All contractors are expected to meet quality assurance standards and contracts will, where possible, cover the full range of services from arrest until the case is completed. (The old arrangements for Criminal Legal Aid were widely seen as fragmented: a person could receive assistance in respect of the same alleged offence under several separate schemes, each resulting in a separate payment for the lawyers involved.)

Applications for publicly funded representation are made by way of a form supplied by the court (Form A for magistrates' court proceedings and Form B for the Crown Court). The appropriate officer, usually the court clerk, will grant or refuse the application. If the application is refused, the court must give reasons and a renewed application may be made. If an application is granted, a Representation Order will be issued. Failure to complete details of a defendant's means on the form could lead to a Recovery of Defence Costs Order (RDCO) (see further below) being made in relation to Crown Court proceedings.

The legislation provides that defendants granted a Representation Order can choose their representative. However, s 15 enables this right to be restricted by regulations. The Criminal Defence Service (General) (No 2) Regulations 2001, which took effect from 2 April 2001, limited the choice of representative to those holding contracts with the Commission. In serious fraud cases, the defendant's choice is further limited to representatives from a panel of firms or individual advocates who specialise in a particular type of case. Membership of a panel depends on meeting pre-determined criteria. In this way, the Commission can ensure that defendants facing charges in these exceptional cases are represented by those with the necessary expertise, experience and resources. In addition, s 15(2)(a) of the 1999 Act enables the Lord Chancellor to make regulations defining circumstances where defendants will not have a right to a choice of representative, but will instead have a representative assigned to them.

As under the old system, the courts will grant representation under the scheme to defendants according to 'the interests of justice'. However, the courts will no longer have to conduct a means test as well before granting representation, although a financial eligibility test is applied for advice and assistance. Under the old Criminal Legal Aid scheme, most defendants (about 95%) were not required to make a contribution to their defence costs. Those who did contribute and were acquitted usually had their contributions returned. The cost of means testing and enforcing contribution orders was high in relation to the contributions recovered. In 1997–98, Criminal Legal Aid contributions totalled £6.2 million, while the direct cost of administering the system was about £5 million. Means testing also led to delays in cases being brought to court, because cases had to be adjourned when the evidence required to conduct the test was not produced.

Instead of means testing, s 17 of the 1999 Act and the Criminal Defence Service (Recovery of Defence Costs Orders) Regulations 2001 give the trial judge at the end of a case in the Crown Court power to make an RDCO. The scheme is an arrangement to collect costs incurred where an individual has been granted publicly funded representation in criminal proceedings before any court except the magistrates' court. It applies to all other proceedings other than committals for sentence and appeals against sentence. The judge has a duty to consider making an RDCO at the end of the case after all other financial orders or penalties have been made. In exercising the duty, the judge must consider whether it is reasonable in all the circumstances to make such an RDCO, including the means of the defendant and his or her partner. Generally, an order will not be made against the first £3,000 of any capital, and although the defendant's house may be considered as capital, the property will be assessed at market value less any mortgage and the first £100,000 of any equity will be disregarded. RDCOs will be usually made on the basis of capital and income will not be considered unless gross annual income is in excess of £24,000. The Order is not dependent on the defendant being convicted and does not form part of the sentence, although an Order against an acquitted defendant will be exceptional. The Order can be for any amount up to the full costs incurred not only in the court making the RDCO, but also in other courts. The court may refer a case to the Special Investigations Unit of the Commission to investigate the defendant's means where the defendant is considered to have complex financial affairs. The judge may require the solicitor acting for the defendant to provide an estimate of the costs likely to be incurred in the proceedings. If,after the making of the RDCO, it is an over-estimate, the balance must be repaid. The RDCO will specify the amount of the costs to be paid and the terms of payment. In addition, the court has powers to make an order freezing the defendant's assets where appropriate to ensure payment of an RDCO. Payment is made to the Commission who may enforce the Order as a civil debt.

As mentioned above, advice and assistance (including advocacy assistance), other than by way of legal representation, is subject to a financial eligibility test. The Criminal Defence Service (General) Regulations 2001 provide that advice and assistance may be granted without reference to the financial resources of an individual for the following:

- advocacy assistance before a magistrates' court or Crown Court; or
- for advice and assistance (including advocacy assistance) provided by a court duty solicitor; or
- for police station advice and assistance to a client who is arrested and held in custody or who is a volunteer or who is in military custody; or
- advocacy assistance on an application for a warrant for further detention or an extension of that warrant.

In all other cases, the client's disposable income and disposable capital must be below certain limits. The limits (as at April 2003) are:

Advice and Assistance	Income limit	£91 per week Allowances for dependants: Partner £31.10 Child 15 or under £38.50 Child 16 or over £38.50
	Capital limit	No dependants £1,000 One dependant £1,335 Two dependants £1,535 Plus £100 for each additional dependant
Advocacy Assistance	Income limit	£192 per week Allowances for dependants: Partner £31.10 Child 15 or under £38.50 Child 16 or over £38.50
	Capital limit	No dependants £3,000 One dependant £3,335 Two dependants £3,535 Plus £100 for each additional dependant

Clients automatically qualify if they are in receipt of Income Support, income-based Job Seeker's Allowance, or Working Tax Credit, unless their disposable capital exceeds £1,000. Unlike the CLS, the CDS is a demand-led scheme and s 18 of the Access to Justice Act requires the Lord Chancellor to provide the necessary funding, but may seek to secure the best possible value for money.

12.7 Public Defender Service

The Commission is piloting its own Public Defender Service (PDS). Section 13(2)(f) of the 1999 Act contains powers to enable the Commission to provide services through lawyers in its own employment. These powers are intended to provide flexibility if, for example, there is limited coverage by private lawyers in rural areas. Using employed lawyers should also, the government has argued, provide the Commission with better information about the real costs of providing these services. The Commission in its Annual Report for 2001–02 states that the PDS has been established to:

- provide independent, high quality value for money criminal defence services to the public;
- provide examples of excellence in the provision of criminal defence services nationally and locally;

- provide benchmarking information to be used to improve the performance of the contracting regime for private practice suppliers;

- raise the level of understanding within government and all levels and areas of the Commission of the issues facing criminal defence lawyers in providing high quality services to the public;

- provide an additional option for ensuring the provision of quality criminal defence services in geographical areas where existing provision is low or of a poor standard;

- recruit, train and develop people to provide high quality criminal defence services, in accordance with the PDS's own business needs which will add to the body of such people available to provide criminal defence services generally; and

- share with private practice suppliers best practice in terms of forms, systems, etc, developed within the PDS to assist in the overall improvement of CDS provision locally.

Under the four year pilot, which began in 2001, six offices have been established, comprising staff directly employed by the Commission. The pilot will form the basis of research into the merits of a mixed (private practice and employed) CDS. The final results of the research will be published in 2005.

The offices are situated in Birmingham, Liverpool, Middlesbrough, Swansea, Cheltenham and Pontypridd. The individual offices will operate and run crime files as they would if they were in the private sector, and will take their turn on the duty solicitor rotas and compete with private suppliers in that area. The Public Defender offices offer a full range of services, from police station advice to representation in court, and instruct agents in the same way as private suppliers. It is believed that clients will be attracted and retained by word of mouth recommendation arising from the quality of service provided. It is anticipated that as the pilot progresses, individual offices may develop specialisms such as youth work. This is likely to be a natural development based on the location of the particular office and, at least initially, the skills of the people recruited.

Independence of lawyers in the PDS is a major concern. The government aims to achieve independence for the PDS lawyers by the appointment of a professional head of service and the effective implementation of a Code of Conduct. Section 16 of the 1999 Act requires salaried defenders employed by the LSC to be subject to a Code guaranteeing minimum standards of professional behaviour. A Code has been approved by Parliament following consultation and includes the following duties: to avoid discrimination; to protect the interests of the individuals for whom services are provided; to avoid conflicts of interest and of confidentiality. In particular, the Code of Conduct contains a clause specifically designed to ensure that public defenders are not 'too ready to plea bargain'. It says: 'A professional employee shall not put a client under pressure to plead guilty and, in particular, shall not advise a client that it is in his interests to plead guilty unless satisfied that the prosecution is able to discharge the burden of proof.'

12.8 The voluntary sector

There are over 1,500 not-for-profit advice agencies in England and Wales. They receive their funding – over £150 million a year in total – from many different sources, mainly local authorities, but also charities including the National Lottery Charities Board, central government and the LSC. The provision of advice services is not spread consistently across the country. Some areas appear to have relatively high levels of both legal practitioners and voluntary outlets, while others have few or none. For example, the LSC's South East Area has one Citizens Advice Bureau per 46,000 people, but, in the East Midlands, 138,000 people share a Citizens Advice Bureau. The government believes that the fragmented nature of the advice sector obstructs effective planning and prevents local needs for legal advice and help from being met as rationally and fully as possible.

12.8.1 Law Centres

There are 51 Law Centres in England and Wales staffed by salaried solicitors, trainee solicitors and non-lawyer experts in other areas like debt management. They are funded by local and central government and charity. They have 'shop front' access and aim to be user-friendly and unintimidating. They are managed by committees and represented by the Law Centres Federation. The report of the Rushcliffe Committee on Legal Aid and Advice (1945) had recommended a nationwide network of State salaried lawyers providing advice for a low, fixed fee. There was provision in the Legal Aid and Advice Act 1949 for this, but it was never implemented. The first centre was established in England in North Kensington in July 1970 in the face of great opposition from The Law Society. Since then, the Society has developed a more tolerant stance to the centres as it acknowledges that they can confer benefits to local law firms through the referrals of clients.

Law Centres take on individual cases, providing, for example, advice on landlord and tenant matters and representing people at tribunals. Some centres also take on group work since quite often the problems of one client are part of a wider problem. This sort of work is controversial.

How far is it correct for lawyers to become involved in socio-legal problems in an effort to combat the disadvantages of the poor? In 1974, in a collective statement of purpose, the Law Centres supported American statements such as one which claimed that the effective solution of the problems of the poor may require the lawyer 'to direct his attention away from the particular claim or grievance to the broader interests and policies at stake'. Such campaigns could deal, for example, with slum clearance or matters concerning roads and pavements. The Benson Commission rejected this sort of work for its proposed Citizens' Law Centres (CLCs), taking the view that community action tends to involve only one section of the community and that the independence of a centre can be compromised if it becomes a base for campaigns.

The Commission's proposed CLCs seemed to be an attempt to win back for private practitioners the large number of clients who were being assisted by Law Centres, as the CLCs would have been operated under the control of The Law Society and Bar Council and users would pay on the same basis as publicly funded clients of private practitioners. This would have increased the burden on the Legal Aid Fund, though, when the government was keen to make retrenchments, so the proposal was rejected.

12.8.2 Other voluntary advice

There are now 700 Citizens Advice Bureaux with 1,313 outlets in total. They deal with a high number of cases (over six million a year) and a very wide range of problems of which between one-third and one-half are legal problems. There are, however, very few trained lawyers working for the Bureaux.

The Bar Council supports a Free Representation Unit for clients at a variety of tribunals for which legal aid is not available. Most of the representation is carried out by Bar students supported and advised by full time caseworkers. A special Bar unit based in London was formed in 1996 through which more senior barristers provide representation. Some colleges and universities also offer advice. For example, the College of Law in London operates a free advice service in which vocational students give advice on such matters as personal injury cases and employment law.

Both barristers and solicitors operate 'pro bono' (from the Latin phrase *pro bono publico*, meaning for the public good) schemes under which legal work is done without charge or at reduced cost for members of the public ineligible for legal aid from the LSC but with limited means, or charitable and other non-profit making organisations. Examples of *pro bono* activities include: solicitors attending advice sessions at Citizens Advice Bureaux or other free services, free advice to members of organisations, for example, trade union general advice schemes, secondment to Law Centres and free advice to charitable organisations.

12.9 Conditional fee arrangements

As part of the scheme to expose the provision of legal services to the full rigour of market forces, the then Lord Chancellor chose to devote an entire Green Paper in 1989 to *Contingency Fees*. Following a recommendation from the Civil Justice Review, the paper had sought opinion on the funding of litigation on a contingent fee basis. This provides that litigation is funded by the claimant only if he wins, in which event, the lawyer claims fees as a portion of the damages payable to the claimant. The response to this idea was largely hostile.

The traditional opposition to contingency fees in the English legal system was that they were 'maintenance' (the financial support of another's litigation) and 'champerty' (taking a financial interest in another's litigation). Champerty occurs when the person maintaining another takes as his reward a portion of the property in dispute. It taints an agreement with illegality and renders it void (for a discussion of the principle, see *Grovewood Holding plc v James Capel & Co Ltd* (1995)). Section 14 of the Criminal Justice Act 1967 abolished maintenance and champerty as crimes and torts, but kept the rules making such arrangements improper for solicitors.

English litigation uses the Indemnity Rule, by which the loser pays the costs of the winner and thus puts him, more or less, in the position he enjoyed before the damage was done. Objectors to contingency fee agreements pointed out that such things were incompatible with the Indemnity Rule because, although the winner's costs would be paid for him by the other side, he would still have to pay for his lawyer from his damages (calculated to put him in the position he would have enjoyed if no wrong had been done to him) so he would not really be 'made whole' by his award. The position is different in the USA, where contingency agreements are common in personal injury cases, because there each side bears its own costs.

It was further contended by objectors to the contingency fee that the legal aid system adequately catered for those who were too poor to afford an ordinary private action. Even if there were people who were just above the legal aid financial thresholds but still too poor to pay for an action, this should be dealt with simply by changing the threshold.

Section 58 of the Courts and Legal Services Act (CLSA) 1990 permitted the Lord Chancellor to introduce conditional fee arrangements, although these cannot apply to criminal cases, family cases or those involving children (s 58(10)). However, there are a number of different arrangements for conditional fees, so one issue to be addressed was the type of conditional fee system that should be applied in England and Wales. The Scottish model, for which initially there was reasonable support, is that of the 'speculative fee', whereby the solicitor can agree with his client that he would be paid his ordinary taxed costs only if he won the case. Two other forms of contingency fee were rejected during the consultation period as being unsuitable. The first was a restricted contingency fee system in which the fee payable in the event of a successful action would be a *percentage of the damages*, but where the actual levels of recovery would be governed by rules. The second was an unrestricted contingency arrangement, similarly based on a percentage of damages, but at uncontrolled levels. These plans were rejected because it was thought that to give the lawyer a stake in the claimant's damages would be likely to create unacceptable temptations for the lawyer to behave unprofessionally in order to secure his fee.

The system eventually adopted is that where conditional fees are based on an 'uplift' from the level of fee the lawyer would normally charge for the sort of work in question. Originally, the maximum uplift was to be 20% in order to induce lawyers to take on potentially difficult cases and to help finance lawyers' unsuccessful conditional fee cases. This would have meant they could charge the fee that they would normally charge for a given type of case, plus an additional fifth.

In August 1993, after a long process of negotiation with the profession, Lord Mackay, the then Lord Chancellor, finally announced that he would allow the conditional fee to operate on a 100% uplift. Thus, solicitors receive no fee if they lose a case, but double what they would normally charge if they win the case. The Law Society had campaigned vigorously against the proposed 20% uplift, arguing that such risks as the no win, no fee arrangement entailed would not be regarded as worth taking by many solicitors simply on the incentive that their fee for winning the case would be 20% more than they would normally charge for such a case. The LCD originally decided to restrict the scheme to cases involving personal injury, insolvency and the European Court of Human Rights.

The system came into effect in June 1995. Such agreements are now legal, provided that they comply with any requirements imposed by the Lord Chancellor and are not 'contentious business agreements'. These are defined under s 59 of the Solicitors Act 1974 as agreements between a solicitor and his client made in writing by which the solicitor is to be remunerated by a gross sum, or a salary, at agreed hourly rates or otherwise, and whether higher or lower than that at which he would normally be remunerated.

In 1998, the Lord Chancellor produced another Consultation Paper, *Access to Justice with Conditional Fees*, where he proposed that insurance premiums supporting conditional fee arrangements should be recoverable between the parties. The Legal Aid Board was in favour of this change. It said in its response document (para 2.7) that 'this would make conditional fee agreements more viable and more attractive for clients and lawyers without unduly penalising opponents'.

The Law Society was less enthusiastic, pointing out that there is still a risk of a 'perverse incentive' operating – defendants with meritorious defences might end up paying higher premiums than those with no real defence. This is because an insurance company backing a defendant with a good defence will realise that the case will last longer than one where the defendant only has a mediocre defence. If the defendant then loses after a long case, he will have a bigger bill to pay for the other side's costs than in a shorter case. This leads to the paradox that the stronger the case you have as a defendant, the higher the premium you will have to pay, as your case will last longer. Weak defendants get defeated early on in proceedings. If a losing defendant has to pay not only the other side's lawyer's fee, but also the other side's insurance premium, the paradox above is worsened because a strong defendant will mean that a claimant's premium will be high, and if the claimant's premium is high, and the defendant might end up having to cover that cost if he loses, then the defendant's premium will also be raised!

'Pursuit' is the name of a legal expenses insurance policy offered by Royal Sun Alliance. Under the policy, the premium is only paid if the case is won, although there is a £200 non-refundable assessment fee. The government has endorsed this policy, although The Law Society and the Bar have been more reserved. The Law Society Vice President, Robert Sayer, said: 'No insurance product, this included, will provide a solution to the removal of legal aid' ((1999) Law Soc Gazette, 24 March).

The right to use 'no win, no fee' agreements to pursue civil law claims was extended by the Conditional Fee Agreements Order 1998. The Order allowed lawyers to offer conditional fee agreements to their clients in all civil cases excluding family cases. Speaking in the House of Lords on 23 July, the Lord Chancellor, Lord Irvine, said:

> These agreements will result in a huge expansion of access to justice. Today, only the very rich or the very poor can afford to litigate. In future, everyone with a really strong case will be able to secure his rights free of the fear of ruin if he loses. They will bring the majority of our people into access to justice.

Conditional fees have been the means by which at least 60,000 personal injury cases have been brought, and many, in all likelihood, would not have been brought but for the existence of conditional fees. The Order retains the old rule that the maximum uplift on the fees lawyers can charge is 100%. Thus, a lawyer may take on a claim against an allegedly negligent employer whose carelessness has resulted in the client being injured. The lawyer, who might normally charge £2,000 for such a case, can say 'I shall do this work for nothing if we lose, but £3,000 if we win'. In fact, as the price uplift can be up to 100% of the normal fee, he can stipulate for up to £4,000 in this example. The Law Society has recommended an additional voluntary cap of 25% of damages, and this has been widely accepted in practice.

The real problems continued to be:

(a) that the new system, designed really to help the millions who have been regulated out of the legal aid system, does not help people whose cases stand only a limited chance of success, as lawyers will not take their cases; and

(b) the difficulties of a claimant getting insurance to cover the costs that he will have to pay, if he loses the claim, for the other side's lawyers. Where a personal injury claim arises from a road traffic incident, it is almost always clear to a solicitor where blame and legal liability probably lie. Risks are therefore calculable by insurance companies, so one can presently insure against having to pay the other side's costs in the event of losing an action on a personal injury case for about £100 in a 'no win, no fee' arrangement. There are, however, many areas, and medical negligence cases are good examples, where the chances of success are notoriously difficult to predict. Thus, insurance against having to pay the other side's costs is prohibitively high, running into many thousands of pounds in some cases. It is quite unrealistic to assume that all such cases, arising often from highly distressing circumstances, will be dealt with in future on a 'no win, no fee' basis. Lawyers will generally not want to take on such cases on such a basis, and even where they do, clients will often not be able to afford the necessary insurance. As insurance to cover client costs in medical 'no win, no fee' cases has proven so expensive, legal aid continues to cover clinical negligence cases.

One possible development with the conditional fee system is the use of the arrangement by a litigant in order to improve his bargaining power when trying to negotiate a settlement with an opponent. This is based on the idea that because no win, no fee arrangements are only taken on by solicitors if they believe that they have a good chance of winning, a no win, no fee client should be able to face his opponent with some confidence. However, as one very experienced litigator has observed, the no win, no fee arrangement is 'not a piece of advice to the client which the client can then use for his own negotiating purposes. Rather it is the solicitor's own approach to the commercial transaction with the client and it can be changed on re-consideration and reflection' (Richard Harrison, 'Conditional fees and conflicts of interest' (2002) 152 NLJ 1505).

12.9.1 Access to Justice Act 1999

The Access to Justice Act 1999 (ss 27–31), together with the Conditional Fee Arrangements Regulations 2000 and the Collective Conditional Fee Arrangements Regulations 2000, reformed the law relating to conditional fees to enable the court to order a losing party to pay, in addition to the other party's normal legal costs, the uplift on the successful party's lawyers' fees and, in any case where a litigant has insured against facing an order for the other side's costs, any premium paid by the successful party for that insurance. The intention was to:

- ensure that the compensation awarded to a successful party is not eroded by any uplift or premium. The party in the wrong will bear the full burden of costs;

- make conditional fees more attractive, in particular to defendants and to claimants seeking non-monetary redress (these litigants can rarely use conditional fees now, because they cannot rely on the prospect of recovering damages to meet the cost of the uplift and premium);

- discourage weak cases and encourage settlements;
- provide a mechanism for regulating the uplifts that solicitors charge. In future, unsuccessful litigants will be able to challenge unreasonably high uplifts when the court comes to assess costs.

In the first version of conditional fee arrangements, only people who expected to win money from their case could benefit from conditional fees. This was the only way that most people could afford to pay the success fee. There were also available insurance policies which could be taken out by someone contemplating litigation to cover the costs of the other party and the client's own costs (including, if not a conditional fee case, a client's solicitor's fees) if the case was lost. However, it meant that a successful litigant would not receive all the money he was awarded, so the government made provision in the Access to Justice Act 1999 to make it possible for the winning party to recover the success fee and any insurance premium from the losing party. This came into effect on 1 April 2000 and ensures that it is the person or organisation that has committed the legal wrong who pays, and it allows defendants and claimants (other than in family law cases) whose case is not about money to use conditional fee arrangements. However, these measures were primarily designed for the High Street solicitor. The Conditional Fee Arrangements Regulations 2000 require that before an agreement is made, the legal representative must inform the client of the circumstances in which the client may be liable for the legal representative's costs, and advise the client as to whether and how the costs might be covered by insurance or by other methods of finance. In addition, the conditional fee agreement must specify the particular proceedings to which the arrangement relates and the circumstances in which the legal representative's fees and expenses are payable. If the agreement provides for a success fee, then it must briefly specify the reasons for setting the percentage increase at the level stated in the agreement.

Collective conditional fee arrangements

A further development is a set of regulations (www.lcd.gov.uk) enabling the bulk purchase and provision of legal services through collective conditional fee agreements, which came into effect on 30 November 2000. The collective conditional fee agreements are designed specifically for mass providers and purchasers of legal services, such as trade unions, insurers or commercial organisations. A collective conditional fee agreement will enable a trade union to enter into a single agreement with solicitors to govern the way in which cases for its members will be run and paid for; by simplifying the process, it will reduce the cost of pursuing separate individual cases. The scheme will also benefit commercial organisations which will be able to enter collective conditional fee agreements to pursue or defend claims arising in the course of business.

12.9.2 The advantages of conditional fee arrangements

For claimants, the advantages can be summarised as being:

- that lawyers acting in any case will be confident (they will have had to weigh carefully the chances of success before taking the case as their fee depends on winning) and determined;
- there will be freedom from the anxiety of having to pay huge fees;
- there will be no need to pay fees in advance; and
- there will be no delays or worries with legal aid applications.

For defendants there will be advantages too, as the contingency fee system will probably reduce the number of spurious claims. In a period where legal aid is being cut back so drastically, preventing so many people from going to law, this system can be seen as a way of preserving at least some limited access to the legal process. Losing parties will still be liable to pay the other side's costs, so it will be unlikely that people will take action unless they consider they have a good chance of success.

The taxpayer can also be given the advantage in the form of a significant reduction in the funding of the legal aid system. Furthermore, practitioners who are competent to assess and willing to take the risks of litigation will arguably enjoy a better fee paying basis, increased fee income and overall business, fewer reasons for delay and more satisfied clients with fewer complaints.

Consider two examples. First, a middle class couple consult their solicitor about injuries received in a road accident. Their joint income and savings put them outside the legal aid scheme. The proposed litigation is beset with uncertainties as the other driver's insurers have denied liability. The couple have to worry about their own expenses and the possibility under the Indemnity Rule of paying for the defendant's costs. Secondly, a young man who has been injured at work wants to sue his employer. The case will turn on some difficult health and safety law on which there are currently conflicting decisions. He is eligible for legal aid, but he will have to make substantial contributions because of his level of income, and if his claim fails, he will have to pay the same sum again towards the expenses of his employers. In both cases, the prospective litigants might well drop any plan to litigate. Both cases, however, might proceed expeditiously if they found a lawyer to act on a no win, no fee basis.

12.9.3 The disadvantages of conditional fee arrangements

Critics of the system argue that it encourages the sort of speculative actions that occur frequently in the USA, taken up by the so called 'ambulance chasing' lawyers. It can be argued that the system of contingency fees creates a conflict of interest between the lay client and the lawyer, with a consequential risk of exploitation of the client. Where a lawyer's fee depends on the outcome of a case, there is a greater temptation for him to act unethically. When the Royal Commission on Legal Services (1979) rejected the idea of contingent fees, it stated that such a scheme might lead to undesirable practices by lawyers including, 'the construction of evidence, the improper coaching of witnesses, the use of professionally partisan expert witnesses, especially medical witnesses, improper examination and cross-examination, groundless legal arguments designed to lead the courts into error and competitive touting'. If the case was won, the lawyer claimed a significant part of the damages, but there was also a real danger that lawyers would be pressured to settle too readily to avoid the costs of preparing for a trial that could be lost and therewith the fee. An example would be where an insurance company admits liability but contests the level of damages. The claimant might stand to get substantially higher compensation by contesting the case. Under the new system, however, his solicitor will have a strong interest in advising him to settle. A settlement would guarantee the solicitor's costs and the agreed 'mark up' (up to 100% more than a normal fee for such work), both of which would be completely lost if the case was fought and lost. This would not occur outside of a conditional fee arrangement. Although the conventional system of payment was not without problems, as Walter Merricks, then of The Law Society, has stated:

> ... when a lawyer is being paid by the hour, he may have a financial interest in encouraging his client to go on with an open-and-shut case, increasing his own fees.

The Law Society has argued that the system, if not properly regulated, could promote the sort of 'ambulance chasing' practised by American lawyers in the wake of the 1984 Bhopal disaster, in which over 2,500 people were killed by escaping gas from a US company (Union Carbide Corporation) plant in India. American lawyers flew out to act for victims and their relatives and some were reported to be taking fees of 50% of the claimants' damages.

It was argued by some that by allowing lawyers to *double* their normal fee for certain cases, the Lord Chancellor risked eliminating any benefit speculative fees might bring. If the successful client was not to be able to recover the *uplift* from the other side, he would have to fund it himself out of the damages he had been awarded. In effect, this often resulted in his damages being halved. The uplift can now be recovered, subject to taxation (that is, court official approval), following changes made by the Access to Justice Act 1999.

It is not even clear that the main claim made for the system – that it increases access to the courts – is correct. The Scottish experience is that speculative cases do not exceed 1% of the cases in the caseload of the Faculty of Advocates. One firm opponent of the system is Lord Justice Auld. He has argued that the system will eventually endanger the esteem in which lawyers are held by the public. He has doubted whether the scheme will produce greater commitment by lawyers to their cases: 'There is a distinction to be drawn between the lawyer's commitment to the case and his anxiety to recover his fees. The two do not always correspond.'

12.9.4 The operation of conditional fee arrangements

The workings of conditional fee agreements in England and Wales have been of particular concern to those looking at how the English legal system is managing to provide access to legal services to those (perhaps 60% of the adult population) who are too poor to pay full legal fees but too rich to get State-funded services from the CLS. A major study of the conditional fee system (Yarrow (1997)) commissioned by the Lord Chancellor's Advisory Committee on Legal Education and Conduct, assessed how widely and in what ways conditional fees were being used. The research was based on a survey of 120 firms of solicitors and an analysis of 197 conditional fee cases begun in the personal injury field. The research found evidence of considerable inconsistency in the size of the 'success fee' calculated for cases with similar chances of success. Moreover, the fee appeared to be too high in up to six cases in 10 which had 'very good' chances of winning.

Yarrow found that a surprisingly high proportion of cases were regarded as having relatively low chances of success given that personal injury cases usually have an extremely high success rate. This could indicate that some solicitors could be over-estimating the chances of failure and therefore charging a higher 'success fee'. Yarrow concludes that such concerns could cast doubt over the entire system. Overall, the average 'success fee' charged by solicitors was 43% but, for one in 10 cases, it was close to the maximum of 100%. However, the voluntary 25% cap on the proportion of damages that can be swallowed up by the 'success fee' recommended by The Law Society is used by almost all solicitors.

Further research in 1999 by Yarrow and Abrams into the client's experience of conditional fee agreements reported widespread confusion and a general lack of understanding of the arrangements, which were so complex that solicitors found it difficult to explain to their clients how they worked. The University of Westminster Report, *Nothing to Lose?*, said that the recoverability proposals of the success fee and the insurance premium under the Access to Justice Act, while benefiting clients, would add another layer of complication to the arrangements. Of the 40 clients interviewed in the study, only one understood the conditional fee agreement scheme in its entirety, but he had 'considerable' experience of law. The majority, however, said they were satisfied with the outcome of their case, which they would otherwise have been unable to pursue.

Since the introduction of conditional fees, the common law has been developed in two decisions by the courts (*Thai Trading Co (A Firm) v Taylor* (1998) and *Bevan Ashford v Geoff Yeandle (Contractors) Ltd* (1998)). In the first of these cases, the Court of Appeal held that there were no longer public policy grounds to prevent lawyers agreeing to work for less than their normal fees in the event that they were unsuccessful, provided that they did not seek to recover more than their normal fees if they were successful (the latter was only permissible in those proceedings in which conditional fee agreements were allowed). In *Bevan Ashford*, the Vice Chancellor held that it was also lawful for a conditional fee agreement to apply in a case which was to be resolved by arbitration (under the Arbitration Act 1996), even though these were not court proceedings, provided all the requirements specified by regulations as to the form and content of the agreement were complied with.

Following the decision in *Thai Trading Co (A Firm) v Taylor*, r 8 of the Solicitors' Practice Rules was amended in January 1999 to allow any arrangement already permitted under statute or common law. At the time, this appeared to permit solicitors to enter into *Thai Trading* types of agreements referred to as 'conditional normal fee arrangements' (that is, a normal fee if successful, a reduced fee if not successful).

However, the case law was not settled. The decision of the Court of Appeal in *Geraghty v Awwad* (2000) created confusion over the enforceability of *Thai Trading* types of arrangements. In *Geraghty v Awwad*, it was argued that at the time the agreement was entered into in 1993, the Solicitors' Practice Rules did not allow such agreements. The Court of Appeal considered itself bound by the House of Lords' decision in *Swain v The Law Society* (1983), which had not been considered in *Thai Trading Co (A Firm) v Taylor*, and held that the Practice Rules had the effect of statute. The argument that by 1993 the common law allowed for such agreements was also rejected. Accordingly, in *Geraghty v Awwad*, the agreement was held to be unenforceable as being both contrary to legislation and the common law. (In *Thai Trading Co (A Firm) v Taylor*, it was argued that just because the Solicitors' Practice Rules prohibited a certain practice, this did not in itself render that practice illegal.)

On 1 April 2000, the new Conditional Fee Agreements Regulations 2000 came into effect under s 27 of the Access to Justice Act 1999, permitting a number of different arrangements as conditional fee agreements, including acting speculatively without a success fee or at a discounted rate in a losing case. Thus, *Thai Trading* type of agreements entered into after 1 April 2000 are now enforceable provided they comply with the new Regulations, dispelling any confusion created by the case law.

Recently, there have been a number of difficulties arising from conditional fee agreements. First, the House of Lords in *Callery v Gray* (2002) expressed concern that conditional fee agreements are open to abuse, with excessive claims being pursued for base costs, insurance premiums and success fees (uplift), as claimants are acting without risk and, because there is no market restriction on costs, lawyers are able to set off the cases they lose against those they win. Secondly, differing views are taken by the courts as to what is considered to be a 'reasonable success fee' for particular types of work. In

Callery v Gray, 20% was thought permissible in a modest and straightforward road traffic accident claim. However, in *Halloran v Delaney* (2002), 5% was thought an appropriate figure.

Thirdly, the courts have been required to consider the extent to which a conditional fee agreement must comply with reg 4 of the Conditional Fee Agreements Regulations 2000 in order to be enforceable. The regulation requires the solicitor to explain the agreement. However, in *English v Clipson* (Peterborough county court, unreported, 5 August 2002), the explanation was given by the representative of an organisation called The Accident Group (a scheme of claimant representatives). He was not a solicitor, so therefore the Regulations had not been complied with and the conditional fee agreement was not enforceable. By contrast, it was held in *Sharratt v London Central Bus Co* (Supreme Court Cost Office, 27 November 2002) that it was possible for a solicitor to delegate the explanation to such a person.

Fourthly, the terms of the conditional fee agreement and its validity are of critical importance to the defendant, as it is he who will have to pay the costs if the claimant is successful. In *Worth v McKenna* (Liverpool County Court, unreported, 2002), it was claimed that the agreement was privileged and therefore the defendant was not entitled to see it. The circuit judge held that it was a privileged document although it could be disclosed if put in issue, for example, by questioning the claimant solicitor's bill of costs. However, there is an argument that disclosure should be permitted earlier in proceedings, as the contents of the agreement could affect the manner in which the case is conducted. As already noted, the conditional fee arrangement does not sit comfortably with the indemnity principle in the English system, under which the unsuccessful party pays the costs of the successful party, and it may be appropriate that limitation should be put on what might be included in the indemnity. For example, the unsuccessful party might be obliged to pay the base fee which is the usual fee for such work, but any 'uplift' or insurance premiums could be paid out of the damages awarded.

An alternative to the conditional fee arrangement is the fixed fee. These are being considered by the Civil Justice Council (which monitors the civil justice system) as a means of keeping costs down in certain cases. The rationale behind fixed fees is that costs should be more certain and affordable in order to increase access to justice. The cases in which they are considered to be appropriate are road traffic accident claims which are settled without negotiation between the claimant's solicitors and the insurers and without the need for court proceedings, and which are limited in value to £10,000. For a scheme to operate effectively, the fees must be certain and in proportion to the work required. There must also be an opportunity for claimants to opt out of the scheme and pursue their claims in court if justice requires. The fees must be reasonable and regularly reviewed or solicitors will not be prepared to undertake the work, and there must be sanction for those parties who do not pay promptly as such payment is an advantage of the system. In December

2002, at the second Costs Forum, comprising representatives of the legal profession, insurance industry, judiciary and academics, the following was agreed for claims of £10,000 or less:

- the basic cost, being the minimum that could be charged for such work, was £800;

- a percentage of the damages awarded, which should be 20% for amounts up to £5,000 and 15% for those between £5,000 and £10,000;

- a success fee (uplift) of 5% (if payable);

- plus VAT and disbursements.

The matter now has to be considered by the Civil Justice Council with a view to its inclusion in the Civil Procedure Rules. The question that then follows is to what extent can fixed fees be applied to other areas of work?

12.10 Unmet legal need

Since the early 1970s, there have been many published research papers and texts which cast doubt on how effectively the legal profession provides for the needs of the whole community. It has been argued that whilst presenting itself as available to give service to everyone on the full range of matters which are capable of being effectively resolved by law, the truth is that lawyers are generally only used by a narrow social group for a narrow range of services. Many problems people suffer which are susceptible to legal resolution are not taken to lawyers for their advice and assistance. The reasons for this appear to be multifarious, but are broadly to do with:

(a) the inaccessibility of lawyers;

(b) the failure of sufferers to perceive their problem as something a lawyer could help to solve;

(c) the failure of lawyers to market themselves as being able to help with as wide a range of problems as the law could help solve; and

(d) financial barriers (real or apparent).

Early American research by Mayhew and Reiss ('The social organisation of legal contacts' (1969) 34 American Sociological Rev 311) surveyed American residents and found that while seven out of 10 had seen a lawyer at least once, and one in four had visited one in the last five years, only 39% had ever sought advice on a matter other than property. They concluded:

> The association between income and legal contacts is in part an organisational effect. The legal profession is organised to serve business and property interests. The social organisation of business and property is highly legalised. Out of this convergence emerges a pattern of citizen contact with attorneys that is heavily orientated to property ...

The results of a mass observation study in England, in which the legal experiences of 2,004 people were examined, showed similar results to the Detroit study. Eighty one per cent of respondents said they had never come into contact with a solicitor. Of those who did consult solicitors, 45% went about a property matter (see Zander, 'Who goes to solicitors?' (1969) 16 Law Soc Gazette 174, March).

It is appropriate first to consider the nature of a 'legal' problem. The basic premise of pioneering research on this subject is that it is wrong to define as 'legal problems' simply those predicaments which are usually taken to lawyers to solve. Such a definition excludes problems which could be solved by legal means but are not dealt with by lawyers. Solicitors have been criticised for the restricted view they have of their work, but there is evidence to suggest that the public has an even narrower perception of the sort of thing a solicitor could help them with than do solicitors themselves (Morris, White and Lewis (1973)). As far as the solicitors themselves are concerned, some of their narrow-minded approaches might be attributable to their legal education. Subjects like welfare law, for example, are only optional and are not widely available to undergraduates. In any event, the subjects which offer more lucrative career paths, like revenue law or company law, have always been more popular than welfare subjects. The Marre Report on the future of the legal profession (*A Time for Change*, 1988) made a specific call for a better response from lawyers to problems involving housing and immigration law.

The largest survey of what lawyers do and for whom was conducted for the Benson Royal Commission on Legal Services (*Survey of Users and Non-users of Legal Services in England and Wales*, RCLS, Vol 2). The sample was based on 2,026 consultations in 1977, which involved 1,770 people out of 7,941 households interviewed. It found that some 15% of adults used a lawyer's service in 1977. It also found that of 27 categories of work used by the survey, just seven accounted for over 80% of all the work taken to solicitors: domestic conveyancing, probate, wills, divorce and matrimonial, motoring and other offences, personal injury cases and property matters. A survey conducted for The Law Society in 1989 confirmed this general pattern.

There has been much debate as to the true significance of these research findings. Do they reflect a restricted public perception of what solicitors deal with, or simply a failure to approach solicitors for other reasons like, for example, perceived costs? The Commission found that, during 1977, a solicitor was used by 25% of the professional class, 21% of employers and managers, but only 10% of unskilled workers. Michael Zander has argued that the results of the survey demonstrate that the use of lawyers is 'problem connected' even more than it is 'type-of-person connected'. That is, that although people from different socio-economic backgrounds use solicitors to a different extent, it is not simply their background that provides the best explanation. In fields of work involving property (for example, conveyancing, probate), those with property use lawyers much more than those who have none. As this is the largest single source of work for the solicitors' profession, it explains why lawyer use appears to reflect the differences between classes. Zander has argued that this impression is misleading: 'If one looks at non-property types of work, the use of lawyers is relatively even as between members of different socio-economic backgrounds.'

One main reason for people not using solicitors is ignorance that the lawyer could be useful. Genn ('Who claims compensation', in Harris *et al*, *Compensation and Support for Illness and Injury* (1984)) has shown how many people fail to pursue proper claims because their first line of inquiry to another body (for example, employers, police, trade union) results in misleading advice. Apathy in prospective litigants is also a significant factor. The rules permitting solicitors to advertise, made in 1983, and their further relaxation in 1987, will perhaps bring more people into solicitors' offices. This will only help, however, to the extent that the apathy is not as a result of fear of costs. All research on the matter, including that of Genn (1984) and the Marre Committee (1988), has demonstrated that costs have a deterrent effect on seeking legal advice. Widespread ignorance of the legal aid schemes must also be relevant to this point.

The image of lawyers has sometimes been identified as a barrier to a greater range of customers. The Marre Committee (1988) focused on the facts that most solicitors' offices are inaccessible and unwelcoming and that they do not cater for many needs like those of linguistic minorities. The results of the most recent population census of 2001 show that 7.9% of the population is from ethnic minorities (*Britain 1998*, 1998, Office for National Statistics, p 39), and whilst that figure does not represent those who are not conversant in English, it suggests that there might be a real problem for many people who are perhaps likely to have problems that lawyers could help to solve. The Law Society survey (1989) found that the image of solicitors amongst the general public is 'good but not outstanding'. Compared with bank managers, accountants, NHS doctors and estate agents, although they were found to be easier to talk to than all the others bar doctors, solicitors were regarded as 'after your money' only less than estate agents. In 1999, it found its image was poor enough in the public eye to warrant spending £60,000 on a public relations exercise to improve the way lawyers are perceived.

In *Rethinking Legal Need: the Case of Criminal Justice* (1991), Paul Robertshaw rejects normative definitions of need, arguing that these rely too heavily on the assumptions of whoever is doing the defining, tend to be lawyer orientated and result in other people's problems being redefined by experts. He also rejects self-defined notions of 'legal need', as they are too uncertain and subject to methodological difficulties. Instead, he uses a concept of comparative need and tries to establish a negative definition of need by comparing outcomes: '... if those in receipt of the [legal] service are not significantly better off than those without them, there can be no need.' He analyses existing research data on the outcomes of legally aided representation and non-legally aided cases and concludes that the general assumption that people assisted by representation need it because they get a better outcome by using it is not proven. There are several problems with such reasoning, as Ed Cape has demonstrated (1994). Basically, Robertshaw equates the provision of legal services with 'representation', whereas in fact representation is only a part of any legal service. If one just measures the outcome of representation as opposed to the whole legal service, the result is likely to be very misleading. A suspect may well need legal advice at a police station, and such advice may well result in the police deciding not to charge the suspect.

12.10.1 Does it matter if such needs remain unmet?

In the Dimbleby Lecture 1992, the late Lord Chief Justice Taylor observed that there might be very serious social problems, even resulting in 'unrest', if the law did not become more accessible.

The true extent of unmet need might be less than is apparent simply by asking questionnaire respondents whether they have consulted solicitors about certain matters. This is because people might be making use of other sources of advice, for example, Citizens Advice Bureaux, accountants, building societies, licensed conveyancers, in circumstances where they might otherwise have consulted lawyers.

The greater the level of unmet need, the worse the social implications. It is, though, notoriously difficult to ascertain the extent of the unmet need. Similar problems affect different people to different degrees. When does a person *need* legal advice? The pioneering research by Abel-Smith, Zander and Brooke adopted a partly subjective test of 'need'. They used a test of what would constitute 'a risk of substantial loss or disadvantage which would be important for the individual concerned'. This standard differed for each category of problem. Zander, writing five years later, acknowledged that these tests for need were highly artificial.

On the whole, poor people use lawyers much less than do rich people. Although, as Zander has argued, the current picture of unmet need has come from researchers who have concentrated on the poor, not the whole population, and Genn has found that people from the higher socio-economic groups are less likely to make a claim consequent upon personal injury (Genn (1984)), it is not difficult to see that the poor are legally disadvantaged by their lack of legal awareness, influence and resources like energy and time.

THE FUNDING OF LEGAL SERVICES

Legal aid

The scheme prior to the Access to Justice Act 1999 was contained in the Legal Aid Act 1988. A common feature of the Civil and Criminal Legal Aid schemes was that expenditure on them was demand-led. Any lawyer could do legal aid work for a client who passed the relevant means test (if any), and whose case passed the statutory merits test (in the case of Civil Legal Aid) or the interests of justice test (in the case of Criminal Legal Aid). Lawyers were (and will continue to be under the transitional arrangements) paid on a case by case basis for each individual case or other act of assistance, usually at rates or fees set in regulations, but in some cases on the same basis as a privately funded lawyer.

This, in the government's view, meant that there were few mechanisms or incentives for promoting value for money or assuring the quality of the services provided.

The new legal aid scheme

The Access to Justice Act 1999 replaces the legal aid system with two new schemes, and makes provisions about rights to supply legal services, appeals, and court procedure, magistrates and magistrates' courts.

The provisions in the Act form part of the wide-ranging programme of reforms to legal services and the courts, described in the government's White Paper, *Modernising Justice*, published in 1998.

The 1999 Act established a Legal Services Commission (LSC) to run the Community Legal Service (CLS), which replaces the legal aid fund in civil and family cases, and the Criminal Defence Service (CDS), which replaces the legal aid scheme in criminal cases, to secure the provision of publicly funded legal services for people who need them. It also enabled the Lord Chancellor to give the Commission orders, directions and guidance about how it should exercise its functions.

The Commission must use the resources of the CLS Fund in a way that reflects priorities set by the Lord Chancellor and its duty to secure the best possible value for money, to procure or provide a range of legal services. The Commission also has a duty to liaise with other funders of legal services to facilitate the development of co-ordinated plans for making the best use of all available resources. The intention is to develop a network of legal service providers of assured quality, offering the widest possible access to information and advice about the law, and assistance with legal problems.

The CDS is intended to ensure that people suspected or accused of a crime are properly represented, while securing better value for money than was possible under the legal aid scheme.

The Legal Services Commission

The 1999 Act established the new LSC and makes provision for appointments to it. The Commission replaces the Legal Aid Board. It was considered necessary to establish a new body to reflect the fundamentally different nature of the CLS compared to Civil Legal Aid. Within the broad framework of priorities set by the Lord Chancellor, the Commission will be responsible for taking detailed decisions about the allocation of resources.

The Community Legal Service

The LSC has two main duties in respect of the CLS.

First, it manages a CLS Fund, which replaces legal aid in civil and family cases. The CLS Fund is used to secure the provision of appropriate legal services, within the resources made available to it, and according to priorities set by the Lord Chancellor and by regional and local assessments of need through Community Legal Service Partnerships. A Funding Code has been drawn up by the Commission and approved by the Lord Chancellor, and sets out the criteria and procedures for deciding whether to fund individual cases.

Secondly, as part of a wider CLS, the Commission, in co-operation with local funders and interested bodies, develops local, regional and national plans to match the delivery of legal services to identified needs and priorities.

Overall, the intention is to:

- make best use of all the resources available for funding legal services, by facilitating a co-ordinated approach to planning;
- improve value for money through contracting and the development of quality assurance systems.

The Access to Justice Act 1999 describes the services which may be provided under the CLS. These range from the provision of basic information about the law and legal services, to providing help towards preventing or resolving disputes and enforcing decisions which have been reached. The scheme encompasses advice, assistance and representation by lawyers (which had long been available under the legal aid scheme), and also the services of non-lawyers. It extends to other types of service, including, for example, mediation in family or civil cases where appropriate.

The Commission uses the CLS Fund to provide services by contracting with service providers, employing staff or making grants to provide services directly to the public. These flexible powers are intended to give effect to one of the principal objectives of the reform of publicly funded legal services, that is, the ability to tailor the provision of services, and the means by which services are to be delivered, to the needs of local populations and particular circumstances. The Commission also tests new forms of service provision through pilot projects.

Subject to exceptions that the Lord Chancellor makes by direction, only basic information and advice will be available for:

- disputes involving allegations of negligent damage to property or the person ('personal injury'), apart from those about clinical negligence. These cases are generally considered suitable for conditional fees;

- allegations of defamation or malicious falsehood. Generally, legal aid is not currently available for representation in defamation, but it is sometimes possible to get legal aid by categorising the case as one of malicious falsehood. The government's view is that these cases do not command sufficient priority to justify public funding and, in any event, they may often be suitable for a conditional fee.

The Lord Chancellor, using regulations, has set financial eligibility limits for people to receive services funded by the CLS Fund. Different conditions, or no conditions, are set for different circumstances or types of case or service.

The funding assessment under the Code replaces the merits test for Civil Legal Aid with a more flexible assessment, applying different criteria in different categories according to their priority.

The Code reflects the principle that, in many family disputes, mediation is more appropriate than court proceedings. This is intended to reinforce the development, under the Family Law Act 1996, of mediation as a means of resolving private law family disputes in a way that promotes as good a continuing relationship between the parties concerned as is possible in the circumstances.

The 1999 Act extends the potential scope of financial conditions in two ways, although there are no immediate plans to use either of these powers:

- it will be possible to make the provision of services in some types of cases subject to the assisted person agreeing to repay an amount in excess of the cost of the services provided, in the event that their case is successful. This might make it possible to fund certain types of case on a self-financing basis, with the additional payments from successful litigants applied to meet the cost of unsuccessful cases;

- it will be possible to require the assisted person to repay, over time and with interest, the full cost of the service provided (for example, through continuing contributions from income). This will make it possible to provide services in some categories of case in the form of a loan scheme.

The Act establishes limits on the liability of the person receiving funded services to pay costs to the unassisted party.

The Criminal Defence Service

The purpose of the CDS is to secure the provision of advice, assistance and representation, according to the interests of justice, to people suspected of a criminal offence or facing criminal proceedings.

The Commission is empowered to secure these services through contracts with lawyers in private practice, or by providing them through salaried defenders employed by non-profit making organisations. This will necessarily mean that suspects' and defendants' choice of representative is limited to contracted or salaried defenders, although the intention is to maintain an element of choice in all but exceptional cases.

The Access to Justice Act 1999 places a duty on the Commission to fund representation for individuals granted a right to representation. It enables the Commission to comply with this duty in the same ways as for advice and assistance. The courts will grant representation under the scheme to defendants according to 'the interests of justice', but will no longer have to conduct a means test before granting representation, although a financial eligibility test is applied for advice and assistance and assisted advocacy. Instead of means testing, the trial judge at the end of a case in the Crown Court has a duty to consider whether it is reasonable in all the circumstances, taking into account the means of the defendant, to make a Recovery of Defence Costs Order. The Order can be for any amount up to the full costs incurred.

Public Defender Service

The Commission is piloting its own Public Defender Service to provide services through lawyers in its own employment. The Public Defender offices offer a full range of services from police station to representation in court. It is believed that clients will be attracted and retained by recommendation arising from the quality of service provided.

Conditional fees

The 1999 Act reforms the law relating to conditional fees to enable the court to order a losing party to pay, in addition to the other party's normal legal costs, the uplift on the successful party's lawyers' fees and, in any case where a litigant has insured against facing an order for the other side's costs, any premium paid by the successful party for that insurance. The intention is to ensure that the compensation awarded to a successful party is not eroded by any uplift or premium. The party in the wrong will bear the full burden of costs. It is also the intention to make conditional fees more attractive, in particular to defendants and to claimants seeking non-monetary redress.

CHAPTER 13

THE EUROPEAN CONTEXT

13.1 Introduction

As was stated in Chapter 2, it is unrealistic and indeed impossible for any student of English law and the English legal system to ignore the UK's membership of the European Union (EU) and European Communities (EC). Nor can the impact of the European Court of Human Rights (ECtHR) be ignored, especially now that the Human Rights Act (HRA) 1998 has made the Articles of the European Convention on Human Rights (ECHR) directly applicable in the UK. However, it has to be recognised that placing the English legal system in its European context does make some demands on the individual. For one thing, although the Treaty on European Union 1992 (the Maastricht Treaty) established the Union of its title, it did not dissolve its constituent communities which therefore continue in existence, distinct from that Union. There are said to be three pillars to the EU:

(a) European Community, consisting of not only its treaties but wider aspects relating to citizenship and, indeed, economic and monetary union.

(b) Common foreign and security policy.

(c) Home affairs and justice.

It is particularly important to note, however, that the EU does not share the same legal institutional form as the EC and that it is, therefore, still appropriate to talk about Community law rather than Union law.

It is also essential to distinguish between the two different courts that operate within the European context: the European Court of Justice (ECJ), which is the court of the EC, sitting in Luxembourg; and the ECtHR, which deals with cases relating to the ECHR and sits in Strasbourg.

The long term process leading to the, as yet still to be attained, establishment of an integrated EC was a response to two factors: the disasters of World War II; and the emergence of the Soviet Bloc in Eastern Europe. The aim was to link the separate European countries, particularly France and Germany, together in such a manner as to prevent the outbreak of future armed hostilities. The first step in this process was the establishment of a European Coal and Steel Community. The next step towards integration was the formation of the European Economic Community (EEC) under the Treaty of Rome in 1957. The UK joined the EEC in 1973. The Treaty of Rome has subsequently been amended in the further pursuit of integration as the Community has expanded. Thus, the Single European Act (SEA) 1986 established a single economic market within the EC and widened the use of majority voting in the Council of Ministers. The Maastricht Treaty further accelerated the move towards a federal European supranational State, in the extent to which it recognised Europe as a social and political – as well as an economic – community. Previous Conservative governments of the UK resisted the emergence of the EU as anything other than an economic market and objected to, and resiled from, various provisions aimed at social, as opposed to economic, affairs. Thus, the UK was able to opt out of the Social Chapter of the Treaty of Maastricht. The present Labour administration in the UK has had no such reservations and, as a consequence, the Treaty of Amsterdam 1997 incorporated the European Social Charter into the EC Treaty which, of course, applies to the UK (see below). One of the consequences of the Amsterdam Treaty was a renumbering of all the Articles in the various EC Treaties. This chapter will adopt the new numbering, but list the old numbers in brackets.

As the establishment of the single market within the European Community progressed, it was suggested that its operation would be greatly facilitated by the adoption of a common currency, or at least a more closely integrated monetary system. Thus, in 1979, the European Monetary System (EMS) was established, under which individual national currencies were valued against a nominal currency called the ECU and allocated a fixed rate within which they were allowed to fluctuate to a limited extent. Britain was a member of the EMS until 1992, when financial speculation against the pound forced its withdrawal. Nonetheless, other members of the EC continued to pursue the policy of monetary union, now entitled European Monetary Union (EMU), and January 1999 saw the installation of the new European currency, the Euro, which has now replaced national currencies within what is now known as the Eurozone. The UK did not join the EMU at its inception and the question as to whether or not it should join remains one of the most pressing of current political issues.

The general aim of the EU is set out in Art 2 (number unchanged) of the Treaty of Rome, as amended by the Maastricht Treaty, as follows:

> The Community shall have as its task, by establishing a common market and an economic and monetary union and by implementing the common policies or activities referred to in Article 3, to promote throughout the Community a harmonious and balanced development of economic activities, sustainable and non-inflationary growth respecting the environment, a high degree of convergence of economic performance, a high level of employment and of social protection, the raising of the standard of living and quality of life, and economic and social cohesion and solidarity among Member States.

Amongst the policies originally detailed in Art 3 (number unchanged) were included:

- the elimination between Member States of custom duties and of quantitative restrictions on the import and export of goods;
- the establishment of a common customs tariff and a common commercial policy towards third countries;

- the abolition between Member States of obstacles to the freedom of movement for persons, services and capital;

- the adoption of a common agricultural policy;

- the adoption of a common transport policy;

- the harmonisation of laws of Member States to the extent required to facilitate the proper functioning of the single market;

- the creation of a European Social Fund in order to improve the employment opportunities of workers in the Community and to improve their standard of living.

Article 3 has subsequently been extended to cover more social, as opposed to purely economic, matters and now incorporates policies relating to education, health, consumer protection, the environment and culture generally. In 1989, the Community adopted a Charter of Fundamental Social Rights of Workers, although the UK government under the leadership of the then Prime Minister Margaret Thatcher declined to sign it, seeing it as representing an unacceptable interference in the free operation of the market. The Treaty on European Union, the Maastricht Treaty, had originally contained a 'Social Chapter', based on the earlier Social Charter and designed to further the 'promotion of employment, improved living and working conditions, proper social protection, dialogue between management and labour, the development of human resources with a view to lasting high employment and the combating of exclusion'. Once again, the UK government, this time under the leadership of John Major, refused to accede to such provisions, and in order to save the rest of the Treaty, the Social Chapter had to be removed and appended as a protocol binding on the then other 11 members of the Community, but not the UK. It is of perhaps signal importance that one of the very first measures taken by the new Labour administration, led by Prime Minister Tony Blair, was to declare its intention to sign up to the Social Chapter. Consequent upon the agreement of the UK government, the Treaty of Amsterdam 1997 was able to incorporate the European Social Chapter into the EC Treaty.

In December 2000, the European Council met in Nice in the south of France. The Council consists of the Heads of State or government of the Member Countries of the EU, and is the body charged with the power to make amendments to EU treaties. The purpose of the meeting was to prepare the Union for expansion from its current 15 to 27 members by the year 2004. New members will range from the tiny Malta with a population of 370,000 to Poland with its population of almost 39 million people. In order to accommodate this large expansion, it was recognised that significant changes had to be made in the institutions of the current Union, paramount amongst those being the weighting of the voting power of the Member States. Although parity was to be maintained between Germany, France, Italy and the UK at the new level of 29 votes, Germany and any two of the other largest countries gained a blocking power on further changes, as it was accepted that no changes, even on the basis of a qualified majority vote, could be introduced in the face of opposition from countries constituting 62% of the total population of the Union. The recognition of such veto power was seen as a victory for national as against supra-national interests within the Union and a significant defeat for the Commission. However, the number of matters subject to qualified majority voting was increased, although a number of countries, including the UK, refused to give up their veto with regard to the harmonisation of national and corporate tax rates. Nor would the UK, this time supported by Sweden, agree to give up the veto in relation to social security policy. Core immigration was another area in which the UK government retained its ultimate veto.

At the same time as these changes were introduced, the members of the Council of Europe also signed a new charter of fundamental rights. Amongst the rights recognised by the charter are included:

- right to life;
- respect for private and family life;
- protection of family data;
- right to education;
- equality between men and women;
- fair and just working conditions;
- right to collective bargaining and industrial action;
- right not to be dismissed unjustifiably.

It is significant that the charter was not included within the specific Treaty issues at Nice at the demand of the UK. The UK had also ensured that some of the references, particularly to employment matters, were subject to reference to domestic law. In a publicity release on the new charter, the government stated that:

> It reflects the range of rights enjoyed by European citizens and is fully compatible with the European Convention. On social and economic issues the charter sets out principles from national and European legislation but *does not assert new legal rights*.

The government's position in this regard is somewhat contradictory in that if, as it and the charter itself states, the charter contains no new rights, then why should it not be included in the Treaty? No doubt the apparent lack of consistency can be explained by its political fear of domestic anti-European press coverage at the time of the then upcoming General Election in June 2001. Perhaps of more relevance, however, is the fact that, in spite of what the charter states about not creating law, the ECJ will no doubt refer to it in interpreting other EC law. So, it may have an impact on that law.

In June 2001, Ireland caused a furore within the EU when its voters declined to ratify the Nice Treaty in a referendum. Perhaps not surprisingly, given the sensitivity of the issue, Ireland was the only Member State which made ratification a matter for its electorate, all the other Member States preferring to ratify the Treaty through their Parliaments. Following the vote, strong pressure was placed on the Irish government to ensure ratification at a later date, and at the Gothenburg summit meeting in the same month, the leaders of the EU made it clear that the expansion of the EU was irreversible. In 2002, the Irish electorate ratified the Treaty.

Notice should also be taken of the *Convention on the Future of Europe*, which was established in February 2002 under the leadership of former French President Valery Giscard d'Estaing. The purpose of the 105 member Convention is to consider the future of the European project, and to come up with proposals to make the Union more popular, democratic and effective.

13.1.1 Parliamentary sovereignty, European Community law and the courts

The doctrine of parliamentary sovereignty has already been considered with respect to the relationship between Parliament and the courts (see 1.4.1), and similar issues arise with regard to the relationship between EC law and domestic legislation. It has already been seen that the doctrine of parliamentary sovereignty is one of the cornerstones of the UK constitution. One aspect of the doctrine is that, so long as the appropriate procedures are followed, Parliament is free to make such law as it determines. The corollary of that is that no current Parliament can bind the discretion of a later Parliament to make law as it wishes. The role of the court, as also has been seen, is merely to interpret the law made by Parliament. Each of these constitutional principles is revealed as problematic in relation to the UK's membership of the EU and the relationship of domestic and EC law.

Before the UK joined the EU, its law was just as foreign as law made under any other jurisdiction. On joining the EU, however, the UK and its citizens accepted, and became subject to, EC law. This subjection to European law remains the case even where the parties to any transaction are themselves both UK subjects. In other words, in areas where it is applicable, European law supersedes any existing UK law to the contrary. The European Communities Act (ECA) 1972 gave legal effect to the UK's membership of the EEC, and its subjection to all existing and future Community law was expressly stated in s 2(1), which provides:

> All such rights, powers, liabilities, obligations and restrictions from time to time created or arising by or under the Treaties, and all such remedies and procedures from time to time provided for by or under the Treaties, as in accordance with the Treaties *are without further enactment to be given legal effect or used in the UK* shall be recognised and available in law, and be enforced, allowed and followed accordingly [emphasis added].

Such statutory provision merely reflected the approach already adopted by the ECJ:

> By contrast with ordinary international treaties, the EC Treaty has created its own legal system which ... became an integral part of the legal systems of the Member States and which their courts are bound to apply [*Costa v ENEL* (1964)].

The impact of Community law on, and its superiority to, domestic law was clearly stated by Lord Denning MR thus:

> If on close investigation it should appear that our legislation is deficient or is inconsistent with Community law by some oversight of our draftsmen then it is our bounden duty to give priority to Community law. Such is the result of s 2(1) and (4) of the European Communities Act 1972 [*Macarthys Ltd v Smith* (1979)].

Thoburn v Sunderland CC (2002) appeared a simple enough case, but it raised some fundamental constitutional issues. It concerned a Sunderland greengrocer who sold fruit only by imperial weight. He was given a conditional discharge after his conviction under an Order in Council implementing a European Directive. He appealed by way of case stated, arguing that the Weights and Measures Act 1985 took precedence over European law or Orders in Council. His appeal failed, but in deciding the issue, Laws LJ rejected the argument that the overriding force of European law in the UK depends on its own principles as enunciated by the European Court in *Costa v ENEL*. Laws LJ stated that EC law could not entrench itself, because when Parliament enacted the ECA in 1972, it could not and did not bind subsequent Parliaments. The British Parliament, being sovereign, could not abandon its sovereignty, and there are no circumstances in which the jurisprudence of the Court of Justice could elevate Community law to a status within the corpus of English domestic law to which it could not aspire by any route of English law itself.

However, he went on, the traditional doctrine of parliamentary sovereignty has been modified by the common law, which has in recent years created classes of legislation that cannot be repealed by mere implication, that is, without express words to that effect. There now exists a clear hierarchy of Acts of Parliament – 'ordinary' statutes, which may be impliedly repealed, and 'constitutional' statutes, clearly including the ECA, which may not. The ECA is a constitutional statute and cannot be impliedly repealed, but that truth derives not from EU law but from the common law. In summary, the appropriate analysis of the relationship between EC and domestic law required regard to four propositions:

(i) Each specific right and obligation provided under EC law was, by virtue of the 1972 Act, incorporated into domestic law and took precedence. Anything within domestic law which was inconsistent with EC law was either abrogated or had to be modified so as to avoid inconsistency.

(ii) The common law recognised a category of constitutional statutes.

(iii) The 1972 Act was a constitutional statute which could not be impliedly repealed.

(iv) The fundamental legal basis of the UK's relationship with the EU rested with domestic rather than European legal powers.

Thus does Laws LJ maintain balance between the supremacy of EU law in matters of substantive law, and the supremacy of the UK Parliament in establishing the legal framework within which EU law operates.

An example of EC law invalidating the operation of UK legislation can be found in the *Factortame* cases. The Common Fishing Policy established by the EEC had placed limits on the amount of fish that any Member country's fishing fleet was permitted to catch. In order to gain access to British fish stocks and quotas, Spanish fishing boat owners formed British companies and re-registered their boats as British. In order to prevent what it saw as an abuse and an encroachment on the rights of indigenous fishermen, the British government introduced the Merchant Shipping Act 1988, which provided that any fishing company seeking to register as British would have to have its principal place of business in the UK and at least 75% of its shareholders would have to be British nationals. This effectively debarred the Spanish boats from taking up any of the British fishing quota. Some 95 Spanish boat owners applied to the British courts for judicial review of the Merchant Shipping Act 1988 on the basis that it was contrary to Community law.

The High Court decided to refer the question of the legality of the legislation to the ECJ under Art 234 (formerly 177) (see 13.3.6, below), but in the meantime granted interim relief, in the form of an injunction disapplying the operation of the legislation to the fishermen. On appeal, the Court of Appeal removed the injunction, a decision which was confirmed by the House of Lords. However, the House of Lords referred the question of the relationship of Community law and contrary domestic law to the ECJ. Effectively, they were asking whether the domestic courts should follow the domestic law or Community law. The ECJ ruled that the Treaty of Rome required domestic courts to give effect to the directly enforceable provisions of Community law and, in doing so, such courts are required to ignore any national law that runs counter to Community law. The House of Lords then renewed the interim injunction. The ECJ later ruled that in relation to the original referral from the High Court, the Merchant Shipping Act 1988 was contrary to Community law and therefore the Spanish fishing companies should be able to sue for compensation in the UK courts. The subsequent claims also went all the way to the House of Lords before it was finally settled in October 2000 that the UK was liable to pay compensation, which was estimated at between £50 million and £100 million.

The foregoing has demonstrated the way in which, and the extent to which, the fundamental constitutional principles of the UK are altered by its membership of the EU. Both the sovereign power of Parliament to legislate in any way it wishes and the role of the courts in interpreting and applying such legislation are now circumscribed by Community law. There remains one hypothetical question to consider and that relates to the power of Parliament to withdraw from the EU. Whilst ECJ jurisprudence might not recognise such a power, it is certain that the UK Parliament retains such a power in UK law. If Community law receives its superiority as the expression of Parliament's will in the form of s 2 of the European Communities Act, as suggested by Lord Denning in *Macarthys*, it would remain open to a later Parliament to remove that recognition by passing new legislation. Such a point was actually made by the former Master of the Rolls in his judgment in that very case:

> If the time should come when our Parliament deliberately passes an Act with the intention of repudiating the Treaty or any provision in it or intentionally of acting inconsistently with it and says so in express terms then I should have thought that it would be the duty of our courts to follow the statute of our Parliament.

Article 10 (formerly 5) requires:

> Member States to take all appropriate measures, whether general or particular, to ensure fulfilment of the obligations arising out of this Treaty or resulting from action taken by the institutions of the Community. They shall facilitate the achievement of the Community's tasks. They shall abstain from any measure which could jeopardise the attainment of the objectives of this Treaty.

This Article effectively means that UK courts are now Community law courts and must be bound by, and give effect to, that law where it is operative. The reasons for the national courts acting in this manner are considered by John Temple Lang, Director in the Competition Directorate General, in an article entitled 'Duties of national courts under Community constitutional law' [1997] EL Rev 22. As he writes:

> National courts are needed to give companies and individuals remedies which are as prompt, as complete and as immediate as the combined legal system of the Community and of Member States can provide. Only national courts can give injunctions against private parties for breach of Community law rules on, for example, equal pay for men and women, or on restrictive practices. Private parties have no standing to claim injunctions in the Court of Justice against a Member State; they can do so only in a national court. In other words, only a national court could give remedies to individuals and companies for breach of Community law which are as effective as the remedies for breach of national law.

13.2 Sources of European Community law

Community law, depending on its nature and source, may have direct effect on the domestic laws of its various members; that is, it may be open to individuals to rely on it without the need for their particular State to have enacted the law within its own legal system (see *Factortame*).

There are two types of direct effect. Vertical direct effect means that the individual can rely on EC law in any action in relation to their government, but cannot use it against other individuals. Horizontal direct effect allows the individual to use the EC provision in an action against other individuals. Other EC provisions only take effect when they have been specifically enacted within the various legal systems within the Community.

The sources of Community law are fourfold:

- internal treaties and protocols;
- international agreements;
- secondary legislation;
- decisions of the ECJ.

13.2.1 Internal treaties

Internal treaties govern the Member States of the EU, and anything contained therein supersedes domestic legal provisions. The primary treaty is the Treaty of Rome as amended by such legislation as the SEA 1986 or the Maastricht Treaty on European Union and the Amsterdam Treaty. Upon its joining the Community, the Treaty of Rome was incorporated into UK law by the ECA 1972.

As long as treaties are of a mandatory nature and are stated with sufficient clarity and precision, then they have both vertical and horizontal effect (*Van Gend en Loos* (1963)).

13.2.2 International treaties

International treaties are negotiated with other nations by the European Commission on behalf of the EU as a whole and are binding on the individual members of the EU.

13.2.3 Secondary legislation

Secondary legislation is provided for under Art 249 (formerly 189) of the Treaty of Rome. It provides for three types of legislation to be introduced by the European Council and Commission:

- *Regulations* apply to, and within, Member States generally, without the need for those States to pass their own legislation. They are binding and enforceable from the time of their creation and individual States do not have to pass any legislation to give effect to regulations. Thus, in *Macarthys Ltd v Smith* (1979), on a referral from the Court of Appeal to the ECJ, it was held that Art 141 (formerly 119) entitled the plaintiff to assert rights that were not available to her under national legislation, the Equal Pay Act 1970, that had been enacted before the UK had joined the EEC. Whereas the national legislation clearly did not include a comparison between former and present employees, Art 141's reference to 'equal pay for equal work' did encompass such a situation. Smith was consequently entitled to receive a similar level of remuneration to that of the former male employee who had done her job previously. The horizontal direct effect of regulations was confirmed by the ECJ in *Munoz y Cia SA v Frumar Ltd* (2002), in which it was held that the claimant was entitled to bring a civil claim against the defendant for failure to comply with EU labelling regulations.

Regulations must be published in the *Official Journal* of the EU. The decision as to whether or not a law should be enacted in the form of a regulation is usually left to the Commission, but there are areas where the Treaty of Rome requires that the regulation form must be used. These areas relate to: the rights of workers to remain in Member States of which they are not nationals; the provision of State aid to particular indigenous undertakings or industries; the regulation of EU accounts and budgetary procedures.

- *Directives*, on the other hand, state general goals and leave the precise implementation in the appropriate form to the individual Member States. Directives, however, tend to state the means as well as the ends to which they are aimed and the ECJ will give direct effect to directives which are sufficiently clear and complete. See *Van Duyn v Home Office* (1974). Directives usually provide Member States with a time limit within which they are required to implement the provision within their own national laws. If they fail to do so, or implement the directive incompletely, then individuals may be able to cite and rely on the directive in their dealings with the State in question. Further, *Francovich v Italy* (1991) has established that individuals who have suffered as a consequence of a Member State's failure to implement Community law may seek damages against that State.

- *Decisions* on the operation of European laws and policies are not intended to have general effect but are aimed at particular States or individuals. They have the force of law under Art 249 (formerly 189).

- Additionally, Art 211 (formerly 155) provides for the Commission to issue *recommendations* and *opinions* in relation to the operation of Community law. These have no binding force, although they may be taken into account in trying to clarify any ambiguities in domestic law.

13.2.4 Judgments of the European Court of Justice

The ECJ is the judicial arm of the EU and, in the field of Community law, its judgments overrule those of national courts. Under Art 234 (formerly 177), national courts have the right to apply to the ECJ for a preliminary ruling on a point of Community law before deciding a case.

The mechanism through which Community law becomes immediately and directly effective in the UK is provided by s 2(1) of the ECA. Section 2(2) gives power to designated ministers or departments to introduce Orders in Council to give effect to other non-directly effective Community law.

13.3 The institutions of the European Union

The major institutions of the EU are: the Council of Ministers; the European Parliament; the European Commission; the ECJ.

13.3.1 The Council of Ministers

The Council is made up of ministerial representatives of each of the 15 Member States of the EU. The actual composition of the Council varies depending on the nature of the matter to be considered. When considering economic matters, the various States will be represented by their finance ministers or, if the matter before the Council relates to agriculture, the various agricultural ministers will attend. The organisation of the various specialist councils falls to the President of the Council and that post is held for six-monthly periods in rotation by the individual Member States of the EU. The Presidency of the Council is significant to the extent that the country holding the position can, to a large extent, control the agenda of the Council and thus can focus EU attention on areas that it considers to be of particular importance.

The Council of Ministers is the supreme decision making body of the EU and, as such, it has the final say in deciding upon EU legislation. Although it acts on recommendations and proposals made to it by the Commission, it does have the power to instruct the Commission to undertake particular investigations and to submit detailed proposals for its consideration.

Council decisions are taken on a mixture of voting procedures. Some measures only require a simple majority; in others, a procedure of qualified majority voting is used; and in yet others, unanimity is required. Qualified majority voting is the procedure in which the votes of the 15 Member countries are weighted in proportion to their population from 10 down to two votes each. There are a total of 87 votes to be cast and, in order to pass a vote on the basis of a qualified majority, a minimum of 62 votes in favour is required. The corollary of this is that it requires a total of 26 votes to block any proposal that can be decided on by qualified majority voting. It can be seen, therefore, that even qualified majority voting requires a substantial degree of agreement across the EU.

Prior to approving the enlargement of the EU, by the accession of Austria, Finland and Sweden on 1 January 1995, both the UK and Spain insisted on what is known as the Ioannina Compromise. The Compromise states that:

> ... if members of the Council representing a total of 23 to 25 votes indicate their intention to oppose the adoption by the Council of a decision by qualified majority, the Council will do all in its power to reach within a reasonable time and without prejudicing obligatory time limits laid down in the Treaties and by secondary law, such as Arts 251 and 252 [formerly, Arts 189B and 189C] of the Treaty establishing the European Community, a satisfactory solution that could be adopted by at least 65 votes.

The effectiveness of this Compromise is a matter of some doubt, especially given the Commission's subsequent declaration that it would call for a vote on the new basis, as soon as it considered that a reasonable time had elapsed.

The SEA (a European treaty legislated into UK law as the European Communities (Amendment) Act 1986) extended the use of qualified majority voting, but unanimity is still required in what can be considered as the more politically sensitive areas, such as those relating to the harmonisation of indirect taxation or the free movement of individuals. In addition to the need for unanimity in such sensitive areas, there is also the ultimate safeguard of what is known as the Luxembourg Compromise. This procedure, instituted at the behest of the French government in 1966, permits individual Member States to exercise a right of veto in relation to any proposals which they consider to be contrary to a 'very important interest' of theirs.

The meeting of the European Council at Nice in December 2000 approved the future enlargement of the Union (see 13.1). It also approved a further extension of qualified majority voting and a new procedure for taking such votes. Under the new system, with the extended membership of 27, the total number of votes available will be 345, ranging from 29 to 3 votes per country, the qualifying majority will be 258 and the blocking majority 88. This latter figure appears to require more than three of the four largest countries to defeat a proposal; however, the inclusion of a further blocking minority on the basis of population, that is, 62%, ensures that Germany and any of the two other largest countries can defeat any proposal.

As the format of particular councils fluctuates, much of its day-to-day work is delegated to a Committee of Permanent Representatives which operates under the title of COREPER.

Article 2 of the SEA 1986 provided that:

> The European Council shall bring together the Heads of State or of government of the Member States and the President of the Commission of the European

Communities. They shall be assisted by the Ministers for Foreign Affairs and by a member of the Commission. The European Council shall meet at least twice a year.

The European Council, now known as the Council of the European Union, can be seen, therefore, as a form of EU summit meeting. It is chaired by the head of government currently holding the Presidency of the Council. Although not originally recognised in the Treaty of Rome, the function of the European Council was clarified by Art D of the Treaty on European Union, which stated that it 'shall provide the union with the necessary impetus for its development and shall define the general political guidelines thereof'.

13.3.2 The European Parliament

The European Parliament is the directly elected European institution and, to that extent, it can be seen as the body which exercises democratic control over the operation of the EU. As in national Parliaments, members are elected to represent constituencies, the elections being held every five years. There are a total of 626 members divided amongst the 15 Member States, approximately in proportion to the size of their various populations. Members of the European Parliament do not sit in national groups, but operate within political groupings.

The preparations for the increase in membership approved at Nice also provided for changes in the level of representation in the Parliament. The new total will rise to 732, but as the number of countries is increasing by 10 as from 1 May 2004, this overall increase actually requires a reduction in the number of members returned by all of the present Member countries except Germany. In recognition that it has by far the largest population, it will keep the right to send 99 members to the Parliament. The UK, France and Italy will go down to 72. At the lowest end of representation, Malta will have 5 members and Luxembourg, Estonia and Cyprus 6 each.

The European Parliament's general secretariat is based in Luxembourg, and although the Parliament sits in plenary session in Strasbourg for one week in each month, its detailed and preparatory work is carried out through 18 permanent committees which usually meet in Brussels. These permanent committees consider proposals from the Commission and provide the full Parliament with reports of such proposals for discussion.

13.3.3 Powers of the European Parliament

The powers of the European Parliament (the Parliament), however, should not be confused with those of national Parliaments, for the European Parliament is not a legislative institution and, in that respect, it plays a subsidiary role to the Council of Ministers. Originally its powers were merely advisory and supervisory.

In pursuance of its advisory function, the Parliament always had the right to comment on the proposals of the Commission and, since 1980, the Council has been required to wait for the Parliament's opinion before adopting any law. In its supervisory role, the Parliament scrutinises the activities of the Commission and has the power to remove the Commission by passing a motion of censure against it by a two-thirds majority.

The legislative powers of the Parliament were substantially enhanced by the SEA 1986. Since that enactment, it has had a more influential role to play, particularly in relation to the completion of the internal market. It can now negotiate directly with the Council as to any alterations or amendments it wishes to see in proposed legislation. It can also intervene to question and indeed alter any 'joint position' adopted by the Council on proposals put to it by the Commission. If the Council then insists on pursuing its original 'joint position', it can only do so on the basis of unanimity.

The SEA 1986 also required the assent of Parliament to any international agreements to be entered into by the EU. As a consequence, it has ultimate control not just in relation to trade treaties, but also as regards any future expansion in the EU's membership.

The European Parliament is, together with the Council of Ministers, the budgetary authority of the EU. The budget is drawn up by the Commission and is presented to both the Council and the Parliament. As regards what is known as 'obligatory' expenditure, the Council has the final say, but in relation to 'non-obligatory' expenditure, the Parliament has the final decision whether to approve the budget or not. Such budgetary control places the Parliament in an extremely powerful position to influence EC policy, but perhaps the most draconian power the Parliament wields is the ability to pass a vote of censure against the Commission, requiring it to resign en masse.

The events of 1998–99 saw a significant shift in the relationship between the Parliament and the Commission. In December 1998, as a result of sustained accusations of mismanagement, fraud and cover ups levelled against the Commission, the Parliament voted not to discharge the Commission's accounts for 1996. Such action was, in effect, a declaration that the Community's budget has not been properly handled and was tantamount to a vote of no confidence in the Commission. In January 1999, the Community's Court of Auditors delivered what can only be described as a devastating report on fraud, waste, mismanagement and maladministration on the part of the Commission. It was found that the Commission had understated its financial obligations by £3.3 billion, and was so lax in its control that it had not even noticed that its banks were not paying any interest on huge amounts of money they were holding. The report of the Court of Auditors led to a vote of no confidence in the Commission in early January 1999 and, although the Commission survived the vote by a majority of 293 to 232, it had to accept the setting up of a 'committee of wise persons' to investigate and report on its operation. At the time, the appointment of this committee was thought to be a diplomatic fudge, allowing the Commission to carry on under warning as to its future conduct. However, when the committee submitted its report, it was so damning that it was immediately obvious that the Parliament would certainly use its power to remove the Commission. To forestall this event, the Commission resigned en masse.

However, by the first week of July 1999, a new Commission had been proposed and gained the approval of the European Parliament later that month. In what new President Romano Prodi said was to be a reforming Commission, the senior UK Commissioner, Neil Kinnock, was appointed as Vice President with the specific remit of reforming the EU. It cannot be claimed, however, that the fiscal regulation of the EU budget has greatly improved, and it is still the cause of discontent. For example, in November 2001, the Court of Auditors, in its report on the previous year's activity, stated that around 5% of the EU budget was unaccounted for. A new financial embarrassment arose in September 2002, with the announcement of the suspension by Neil Kinnock of the European Commission's senior accountant, Marta Andreason, following her public allegation of sloppy accounting by the body, including the claim that it had less secure accountancy procedures than Enron. Then in March 2003, it was announced that Edith Cresson, a former French Prime Minister and European Commissioner, and seven current and former EU officials were to be charged in the Belgian courts with fraud during her time at the Commission.

13.3.4 Economic and Social Committee

If the Parliament represents the directly elected arm of the EU, then the Economic and Social Committee represents a collection of unelected, but nonetheless influential, interest groups throughout the EU. This Committee is a consultative institution and its opinion must be sought prior to the adoption by the Council of any Commission proposal. The Economic and Social Committee represents the underlying 'corporatist' nature of the EU, to the extent that it seeks to locate and express a commonality of view and opinion on proposals from such divergent interests groups as employers, trade unions and consumers. It is perhaps symptomatic of the attitude of recent British governments to this underlying corporatist, essentially Christian Democratic, strand within the EU that it dispensed with its own similar internal grouping, the National Economic Development Council, in 1992.

13.3.5 The European Commission

The European Commission is the executive of the EU and, in that role, it is responsible for the administration of EU policies. There are 20 Commissioners chosen from the various Member States to serve for renewable terms of four years. Commissioners are appointed to head departments with specific responsibility for furthering particular areas of EU policy. Once appointed, Commissioners are expected to act in the general interest of the EU as a whole rather than in the partial interest of their own home country.

As a result of the Nice summit, the five largest countries, which currently each appoint two Commissioners, agreed to give up one of their appointees in 2005, and a system of rotation will be implemented for the benefit of the smaller Member countries, whilst preventing an increase in the number of Commissioners to match the new membership.

In pursuit of EU policy, the Commission is responsible for ensuring that Treaty obligations between the Member States are met and that Community laws relating to individuals are enforced. In order to fulfil these functions, the Commission has been provided with extensive powers both in relation to the investigation of potential breaches of Community law and the subsequent punishment of offenders. The classic area in which these powers can be seen in operation is competition law. Under Arts 81 and 82 (formerly 85 and 86) of the Treaty of Rome, the Commission has substantial powers to investigate and control potential monopolies and anti-competitive behaviour, and it has used these powers to levy what, in the case of private individuals, would amount to huge fines where breaches of Community competition law have been discovered. In November 2001, the Commission imposed a record fine of £534 million on a cartel of 13 pharmaceutical companies which had operated a price-fixing scheme within the EU in relation to the market for vitamins. The highest individual fine was against the Swiss company Roche, which had to pay £288 million, whilst the German company BASF was fined £185 million. The lowest penalty levelled was against Aventis, which was only fined £3 million due to its agreement to provide the Commission with evidence as to the operation of the cartel. Otherwise its fine would have been £70 million. The Commission took two years to investigate the operation of what it classified as a highly organised cartel, holding regular meetings to collude on prices, exchange sales figures and co-ordinate price increases.

In the following month, December 2001, Roche was again fined a further £39 million for engaging in another cartel, this time in the citric acid market. The total fines imposed in this instance amounted to £140 million.

The Commission also acts, under instructions from the Council, as the negotiator between the EU and external countries.

In addition to these executive functions, the Commission has a vital part to play in the EU's legislative process. The Council can only act on proposals put before it by the Commission. The Commission therefore has a duty to propose to the Council measures that will advance the achievement of the EU's general policies.

13.3.6 The European Court of Justice

The ECJ is the judicial arm of the EU, and in the field of Community law its judgments overrule those of national courts. It consists of 15 judges, assisted by nine Advocates General, and sits in Luxembourg. The role of the Advocate General is to investigate the matter submitted to the Court and to produce a report, together with a recommendation, for the consideration of the Court. The actual Court is free to accept the report or not as it sees fit.

The SEA 1986 provided for a new Court of First Instance to be attached to the existing Court of Justice. The jurisdiction of the Court of First Instance is limited mainly to internal claims by employees of the Community and to claims against fines made by the Commission under Community competition law. The aim is to reduce the burden of work on the Court of Justice, but there is a right of appeal, on points of law only, to the full Court of Justice. In July 2000, an appeal against a fine imposed by the Commission in 1998 against Europe's biggest car producer Volkswagen (VW) was successful to the extent that the ECJ reduced the amount of the fine by £7.5 million. Unfortunately for VW, it upheld the essential finding of the Commission and imposed a fine of £57 million on it. VW were found guilty of 'an infringement which was particularly serious, the seriousness being magnified by the size of the Volkswagen group'. What the company had done was to prevent essentially German and Austrian customers from benefiting from the weakness of the Italian lira between 1993 and 1996 by instructing the Italian dealers not to sell to foreign customers on the false basis that different specifications and warranty terms prevented cross-border sales. Not only had VW instructed that this should happen, but it threatened that Italian dealers would lose their franchises if they failed to comply.

The Court of Justice performs two key functions:

(a) It decides whether any measures adopted, or rights denied, by the Commission, Council or any national government are compatible with Treaty obligations. Such actions may be raised by any EU institution, government or individual. In October 2000, the Court of Justice annulled EU Directive 98/43, which required Member States to impose a ban on advertising and sponsorship relating to tobacco products, because it had been adopted on the basis of the wrong provisions of the EC Treaty. The Directive had been adopted on the basis of the provisions of the Treaty relating to the elimination of obstacles to the completion of the internal market, but the Court decided that under the circumstances, it was difficult to see how a ban on tobacco advertising or sponsorship could facilitate the trade in tobacco products.

Although a partial prohibition on particular types of advertising or sponsorship might legitimately come within the internal market provisions of the Treaty, the Directive was clearly aimed at protecting public health and it was therefore improper to base its adoption on the freedom to provide services (*Germany v European Parliament and EU Council* (Case C-375/98)).

A Member State may fail to comply with its Treaty obligations in a number of ways. It might fail or indeed refuse to comply with a provision of the Treaty or a regulation; alternatively, it might refuse to implement a directive within the allotted time provided for. Under such circumstances, the State in question will be brought before the ECJ, either by the Commission or another Member State or indeed, individuals within the State concerned.

In 1996, following the outbreak of 'mad cow disease', BSE, in the UK, the European Commission imposed a ban on the export of UK beef. The ban was partially lifted in 1998 and, subject to conditions relating to the documentation of an animal's history prior to slaughter, from 1 August 1999, exports satisfying those conditions were authorised for despatch within the Community. When the French Food Standards Agency continued to raise concerns about the safety of British beef, the Commission issued a protocol agreement, which declared that all meat and meat products from the UK would be distinctively marked as such. However, France continued in its refusal to lift the ban. Subsequently, the Commission applied to the ECJ for a declaration that France was in breach of Community law for failing to lift the prohibition on the sale of correctly labelled British beef in French territory. In December 2001, in *Commission of the European Communities v France*, the ECJ held that the French government had failed to put forward a ground of defence capable of justifying the failure to implement the relevant Decisions and was therefore in breach of Community law.

(b) It provides authoritative rulings, at the request of national courts, under Art 234 (formerly 177) of the Treaty of Rome, on the interpretation of points of Community law. When an application is made under Art 234, the national proceedings are suspended until such time as the determination of the point in question is delivered by the ECJ. Whilst the case is being decided by the ECJ, the national court is expected to provide appropriate interim relief, even if this involves going against a domestic legal provision, as in the *Factortame* case.

This procedure can take the form of a preliminary ruling where the request precedes the actual determination of a case by the national court.

Article 234 provides that:

> The Court of Justice shall have jurisdiction to give preliminary rulings concerning:
>
> (a) the interpretation of treaties;
>
> (b) the validity and interpretation of acts of the institutions of the Union and of the European Central Bank;

(c) the interpretation of the statutes of bodies established by an act of the Council, where those statutes so provide.

Where such a question is raised before any court or tribunal of a Member State, that court or tribunal may, if it considers that a decision on the question is necessary to enable it to give judgment, request the Court of Justice to give a ruling thereon.

Where any such question is raised in a case pending before a court or tribunal of a Member State against whose decision there is no judicial remedy under national law, that court or tribunal shall bring the matter before the Court of Justice.

The question as to the extent of the ECJ's authority arose in *Arsenal Football Club plc v Reed* (2003), which dealt with the sale of football souvenirs and memorabilia bearing the names of the football club and consequently infringing its registered trade marks. On first hearing, the Chancery Division of the High Court referred the question of the interpretation of the Trade Marks Directive (89/104) in relation to the issue of trade mark infringement to the ECJ. After the ECJ had made its decision, the case came before Laddie J for application, who declined to follow that decision. The grounds for so doing were that the ambit of the ECJ's powers was clearly set out in Art 234. Consequently, where, as in this case, the ECJ makes a finding of fact which reverses the finding of a national court on those facts, it exceeds its jurisdiction and it follows that its decisions are not binding on the national court. The Court of Appeal later reversed Laddie J's decision on the ground that the ECJ had not disregarded the conclusions of fact made at the original trial and, therefore, he should have followed its ruling and decided the case in Arsenal's favour. Nonetheless, Laddie J's general point as to the ECJ's authority remains valid.

It is clear that it is for the national court and not the individual parties concerned to make the reference. Where the national court or tribunal is not the 'final' court or tribunal, the reference to the ECJ is discretionary. Where the national court or tribunal is the 'final' court, then reference is obligatory. However, there are circumstances under which a 'final' court need not make a reference under Art 234 (formerly 177). These are:

- where the question of Community law is not truly relevant to the decision to be made by the national court;

- where there has been a previous interpretation of the provision in question by the ECJ so that its meaning has been clearly determined;

- where the interpretation of the provision is so obvious as to leave no scope for any reasonable doubt as to its meaning.

This last instance has to be used with caution given the nature of Community law; for example, the fact that it is expressed in several languages using legal terms which might have different connotations within different jurisdictions. However, it is apparent that where the meaning is clear, no reference need be made.

Reference has already been made to cases that have been referred under the Art 234 procedure. Thus, the first case to be referred to the ECJ from the High Court was *Van Duyn v Home Office* (1974), the first case to be referred from the Court of Appeal was *Macarthys Ltd v Smith* (1979), and the first from the House of Lords was *R v Henn* (1982).

Reference has already been made in Chapter 5 to the methods of interpretation used by courts in relation to Community law. It will be recalled that, in undertaking such a task, a purposive and contextual approach is mainly adopted, as against the more restrictive methods of interpretation favoured in relation to UK domestic legislation. The clearest statement of this purposive, contextualist approach adopted by the ECJ is contained in its judgment in the *CILFIT* case:

> Every provision of Community law must be placed in its context and interpreted in the light of the provisions of Community law as a whole, regard being had to the objectives thereof and to its state of evolution at the date on which the provision in question is to be applied.

It can be appreciated that the reservations considered previously in regard to judicial creativity and intervention in policy matters in the UK courts apply *a fortiori* to the decisions of the ECJ.

Another major difference between the ECJ and the court within the English legal system is that the former is not bound by the doctrine of precedent in the same way as the latter is. It is always open to the ECJ to depart from its previous decisions where it considers it appropriate to do so. Although it will endeavour to maintain consistency, it has, on occasion, ignored its own previous decisions, as in *European Parliament v Council* (1990), where it recognised the right of the Parliament to institute an action against the Council.

The manner in which European law operates to control sex discrimination through the Equal Treatment Directive is of significant interest and, in *Marshall v Southampton and West Hampshire Area Health Authority* (1993), a number of the points that have been considered above were highlighted. Ms Marshall had originally been required to retire earlier than a man in her situation would have been required to do. She successfully argued before the ECJ that such a practice was discriminatory and contrary to Community Directive 76/207 on the equal treatment of men and women.

The present action related to the level of compensation she was entitled to as a consequence of this breach. UK legislation, the Sex Discrimination Act 1975, had set limits on the level of compensation that could be recovered for acts of sex discrimination. Marshall argued that the imposition of such limits was contrary to the Equal Treatment Directive and that, in establishing such limits, the UK had failed to comply with the Directive.

The Court of Appeal referred the case to the ECJ under Art 234 (formerly 177) and the latter determined that the rights set out in relation to compensation under Art 5 of the Directive were directly effective, and that, as the purpose of the Directive was to give effect to the principle of equal treatment, that could only be achieved by either reinstatement or the awarding of adequate compensation. The decision of the ECJ therefore overruled the financial limitations placed on sex discrimination awards and effectively overruled the domestic legislation.

P v S and Cornwall CC (1996) extended the ambit of unlawful sex discrimination under the Directive to cover people who have undergone surgical gender reorientation (sex change). However, in *Grant v South West Trains Ltd* (1998), the ECJ declined to extend the Directive to cover discrimination on the grounds of sexual orientation (homosexuality), even though the Advocate General had initially supported the extension of the Directive to same-sex relationships. Whilst *Grant* was in the process of being decided in the ECJ, a second case, *R v Secretary of State for Defence ex p Perkins (No 2)* (1998), had been brought before the English courts arguing a similar point, that discrimination on grounds of sexual orientation was covered by the Equal Treatment Directive. Initially, the High Court had referred the matter, under Art 234 (formerly 177), to the ECJ for decision, but on the decision in *Grant* being declared, the referral was withdrawn. In withdrawing the reference, Lightman J considered the proposition of counsel for Perkins to the effect that:

> ... there have been a number of occasions where the ECJ has overruled its previous decisions; that the law is not static; and, accordingly, in a dynamic and developing field such as discrimination in employment there must be a prospect that a differently constituted ECJ may depart from the decision in *Grant* ... But, to justify a reference, the possibility that the ECJ will depart from its previous decision must be more than theoretical: it must be a realistic possibility. The decision in *Grant* was of the full Court; it is only some four months old; there has been no development in case law or otherwise since the decision which can give cause for the ECJ reconsidering that decision ... I can see no realistic prospect of any change of mind on the part of the ECJ.

It could be pointed out that there could be no change in case law if judges such as Lightman J refused to send similar cases to the ECJ, but there may well be sense, if not virtue, in his refusal to refer similar cases to the ECJ within such a short timescale.

13.3.7 The Court of Auditors

Given the part that the Court of Auditors played in the 1998–99 struggle between the Parliament and the Commission, the role of this body should not be under-estimated.

As its name suggests, it is responsible for providing an external audit of the Communities' finances. It examines the legality, regularity and soundness of the management of all the Communities' revenue and expenditure. The following passage from its statement of assurance relating to the budget for the year 1996–97 provides a flavour of its findings:

> ... as in previous years, the incidence of errors affecting the transactions underlying the Commission's payments is too high for the Court to provide assurance about their legality and regularity.
>
> Many of the errors found in the payments provide direct evidence of failure to implement the control mechanisms foreseen in the regulations or to apply requisite checks before payments are made ... there were, again, many formal errors affecting payments. These are, essentially, cases where there was a failure to comply with the applicable regulations ... in many cases, formal errors involve specific systems weaknesses, notably failure to implement the control procedure required to ensure the eligibility of the recipients and the accuracy of the amounts paid.

From this passage may well be seen the reason why the Parliament sought to establish some control over the operation of the Commission.

It would seem, however, that matters have not progressed as rapidly as might be hoped, as the Court of Auditors' report for the year 1998–99 still found:

> ... an unacceptable incidence of errors which affected the legality and the regularity of payments from the budget.

13.4 The European Court of Human Rights

It has to be established and emphasised from the outset that the substance of this section has absolutely nothing to do with the EU as such; the Council of Europe, of which the ECtHR is the legal institution, is a completely distinct organisation and, although membership of the two organisations overlap, they are not the same. The Council of Europe is concerned not with economic matters but with the protection of civil rights and freedoms.

It is gratifying, at least to a degree, to recognise that the ECHR and its Court (the ECtHR) are no longer a matter of mysterious external control, the HRA having incorporated the ECHR into UK law, making the ECtHR the supreme court in matters related to its jurisdiction. Much attention was paid to the ECHR and the HRA in Chapter 1 (see 1.7), so it only remains to consider the structure and operation of the ECtHR. Two points should be emphasised at this juncture. First, although the number of domestic cases relating to the ECHR will continue to increase and consequently domestic human rights jurisprudence will emerge and develop, it should be borne in mind that in relation to these cases, the ultimate court of appeal remains the ECtHR. Secondly, as has been considered at 1.7, s 2 of the HRA requires previous decisions of the ECtHR to be taken into consideration by domestic courts, and this means *all* decisions of the ECtHR, not just the cases that directly involve the UK. Consequently, it remains imperative that students of the UK legal system be aware of, and take into consideration, the decisions of that court.

The Convention originally established two institutions:

(a) The European Commission of Human Rights. This body was charged with the task of examining, and if need be investigating the circumstances of, petitions submitted to it. If the Commission was unable to reach a negotiated solution between the parties concerned, it referred the matter to the Court of Human Rights.

(b) The ECtHR. The ECHR provides that the judgment of the Court shall be final and that parties to it will abide by the decisions of the Court. This body, sitting in Strasbourg, was, and remains, responsible for all matters relating to the interpretation and application of the current Convention.

However, in the 1980s, as the ECHR and its Court became more known and popular as a forum for asserting human rights, so its workload increased. This pressure was exacerbated by the break up of the old Communist Eastern Bloc and the fact that the newly independent countries, in both senses of the words, became signatories to the Convention. The statistics support the view of the incipient sclerosis of the original structure.

Applications registered with the Commission

Year	Number of applications registered
1981	404
1993	2,037
1997	4,750

Cases referred to the Court

Year	Number of cases referred
1981	7
1993	52
1997	119

As a consequence of such pressure, it became necessary to streamline the procedure by amalgamating the two previous institutions into one Court. In pursuit of this aim, Protocol 11 to the Convention was introduced in 1994. The new ECtHR came into operation on 1 November 1998, although the Commission continued to deal with cases which had already been declared admissible for a further year. The current President of the ECtHR, Luzius Wildhaber, has also emphasised the need for reform to deal with the apparently ever-increasing caseload. As he stated in his opening address at the commencement of the judicial year in January 2003:

The Court has discussed the issues both in its Sections and in plenary administrative session. A number of ideas have been put forward including an accelerated procedure for repetitive cases and the setting up of a fifth Section with specific and exclusive competence for unmeritorious cases, on the one hand, and repetitive or clone cases, on the other. Judges have generally expressed themselves to have been in favour of abandoning a purely chronological approach to processing cases and giving priority to important cases. Whichever way you look at it, hard choices will have to be made, as indeed they already have been to some extent with regard to the Court's internal procedure and work processes. At the risk of repeating myself, the key word is, as I said last year, effectiveness: effectiveness in terms of internal efficiency, but also effectiveness in terms of attaining the aims of the ECHR in a rapidly changing world.

Following the reconstruction, however, applications to the new court continued to rise as follows:

1998	5,981
1999	8,396
2000	10,486
2001	13,858
2002	28,257

The former President of the French *Conseil constitutionnel*, Robert Badinter, has proposed turning the ECtHR into a supreme court and creating a second tier of regional human rights courts as a possible way of dealing with the Court's apparently ever-increasing workload.

The ECtHR consists of 41 judges, representing the number of signatories to the ECHR, although they do not have to be chosen from each State and, in any case, sit as individuals rather than representatives of their State. Judges are elected, by the Parliamentary Assembly of the Council of Europe, generally for six years, but arrangements have been put in place so that one-half of the membership of the judicial panel will be required to seek renewal every three years.

Structure of the Court

The Plenary Court elects its President, two Vice Presidents and two Presidents of Section for a period of three years. It is divided into four Sections, whose composition, fixed for three years, is geographically and gender balanced and takes account of the different legal systems of the Contracting States. Each Section is presided over by a President, two of the Section Presidents being at the same time Vice Presidents of the Court. Committees of three judges within each Section deal with preliminary issues and, to that extent, they do the filtering formerly done by the Commission. Cases are actually heard by Chambers of seven members chosen on the basis of rotation. Additionally, there is a Grand Chamber of 17 judges made up of the President, Vice Presidents and Section Presidents and other judges by rotation. The Grand Chamber deals with the most important cases that require a reconsideration of the accepted interpretations of the ECHR. Again, the Grand Chamber is established with a view to geographical balance and different legal traditions. The Section President and the judge elected in respect of the State concerned sit in each case. Where the latter is not a member of the Section, he sits as an *ex officio* member of the Chamber.

Procedure before the Court

Any individual or Contracting State may submit an application alleging a breach by a Contracting State of one of the ECHR rights. Individuals can submit applications themselves, but legal representation is recommended and is required for hearings. Although a legal aid scheme has been set up by the Council of Europe for applicants who cannot fund their cases, recovery is usual from any award of monetary compensation.

Hearings are public, unless the Chamber decides otherwise on account of exceptional circumstances, and all documents filed with the Court's Registry are accessible to the public. It is, however, quite common for negotiations towards a friendly settlement to take place during proceedings, with the Registrar acting as intermediary, and such negotiations are confidential.

Admissibility procedure

Each application is assigned to a Section whose President designates a rapporteur, who examines it and decides whether it should be dealt with by a three member Committee or by a seven member Chamber.

If passed to a Committee, it may decide, by unanimous vote, to declare inadmissible or strike out an application without further examination.

If not struck out, the case goes on to a Chamber for hearing on both admissibility and merits. The initial decisions of the Chamber on admissibility are taken by majority vote. They must contain reasons and be made public. The Chamber's decision to admit an application leads to a hearing as to the merits of the case.

Procedure on the merits

The President of the Chamber may grant leave, or invite any Contracting State which is not party to the proceedings or any person concerned who is not the applicant, to submit written comments and, in exceptional circumstances, to make representations at the hearing. A Contracting State whose national is an applicant in the case is entitled to intervene as of right.

The Chamber hearing the case may at any time remit it to the Grand Chamber where it is concerned that it raises an important issue relating to the interpretation of the ECHR or a major extension of previous precedent.

In practice, only a minority of registered applications result in a judgment on the merits of the case. Other applications are completed at an earlier stage by being declared inadmissible, being otherwise struck out or following a friendly settlement. For example, in 2000, the Court delivered 695 judgments, 6,769 applications were struck out and 1,082 were declared inadmissible. The remainder of applications received remained to be dealt with.

Examples of such friendly procedures are *Cornwell v UK* and *Leary v UK*, both reported in 2000. These cases both involved men whose wives died, leaving them solely responsible for their children. Had they been women in similar situations, they would have received benefits, namely, a Widowed Mother's Allowance and a Widow's Payment, payable under the Social Security and Benefits Act 1992. The applicants complained that the lack of benefits for widowers under British social security legislation discriminated against them on grounds of sex, in breach of Art 14 (prohibition of discrimination) of the ECHR, taken in conjunction with both Art 8 (right to respect for private and family life) and Art 1 of Protocol No 1 (protection of property) of the ECHR. The cases were struck out following a friendly settlement in which Cornwell and Leary received back payment of monies due and further payments until the Welfare Reform and Pensions Act 1999 came into force, which equalised the position.

Judgments

Chambers decide by a majority vote and usually reports give a single decision. However, any judge in the case is entitled to append a separate opinion, either concurring or dissenting.

Within three months of delivery of the judgment of a Chamber, any party may request that a case be referred to the Grand Chamber if it raises a serious question of interpretation or application, or a serious issue of general importance. Consequently, the Chamber's judgment only becomes final at the expiry of a three month period, or earlier if the parties state that they do not intend to request a referral. If the case is referred to the Grand Chamber, its decision, taken on a majority vote, is final. All final judgments of the Court are binding on the respondent States concerned. Responsibility for supervising the execution of judgments lies with the Committee of Ministers of the Council of Europe, which is required to verify that States have taken adequate remedial measures in respect of any violation of the ECHR.

In deciding cases, the ECtHR makes use of two related principles: the doctrine of the margin of appreciation; and the principle of proportionality.

Margin of appreciation

This refers to the fact that the ECtHR recognises that there may well be a range of responses to particular crises or social situations within individual States, which might well involve some legitimate limitation on the rights established under the ECHR. The Court recognises that in such areas, the response should be decided at the local level, rather than being imposed centrally. The most obvious, but by no means the only, situations that involve the recognition of the margin of appreciation are the fields of morality and State security. For example, *Wingrove v UK* (1997) concerned the refusal of the British Board of Film Classification to give a certificate of classification to the video film, *Visions of Ecstasy*, on the grounds that it was blasphemous, thus effectively banning it. The applicant, the director of the film, claimed that the refusal to grant a certificate of classification to the film amounted to a breach of his rights to free speech under Art 10 of the ECHR. The Court rejected his claim, holding that the offence of blasphemy, by its very nature, did not lend itself to precise legal definition. Consequently, national authorities 'must be afforded a degree of flexibility in assessing whether the facts of a particular case fall within the accepted definition of the offence'. In reaching its decision, the Court clearly set out how the doctrine was to operate and its justifications. It also explained the different ranges of the margin of appreciation that will be allowed in different areas. Thus:

> Whereas there is little scope under Article 10 para 2 of the Convention (Art 10-2) for restrictions on political speech or on debate of questions of public interest a wider margin of appreciation is generally available to the Contracting States when regulating freedom of expression in relation to matters liable to offend intimate personal convictions within the sphere of morals or, especially, religion. Moreover, as in the field of morals, and perhaps to an even greater degree, there is no uniform European conception of the requirements of 'the protection of the rights of others' in relation to attacks on their religious convictions. What is likely to cause substantial offence to persons of a particular religious persuasion will vary significantly from time to time and from place to place, especially in an era characterised by an ever growing array of faiths and denominations. By reason of their direct and continuous contact with the vital forces of their countries, State authorities are in principle in a better position than the international judge to give an opinion on the exact content of these requirements with regard to the rights of others as well as on the 'necessity' of a 'restriction' intended to protect from such material those whose deepest feelings and convictions would be seriously offended.

In *Civil Service Unions v UK* (1988), it was held that national security interests were of such paramount concern that they outweighed individual rights of freedom of association. Hence, the unions had no remedy under the ECHR for the removal of their members' rights to join and be in a trade union.

It should also be borne in mind that States can enter a derogation from particular provisions of the ECHR, or the way in which they operate in particular areas or circumstances. The UK entered such derogation in relation to the extended detention of terrorist suspects without charge under the Prevention of Terrorism (Temporary Provisions) Act 1989, subsequently replaced and extended by the Terrorism Act 2000. Those powers had been held to be contrary to Art 5 of the ECHR by the ECtHR in *Brogan v UK* (1989). The UK also entered a derogation in relation to the Anti-Terrorism, Crime and Security Act 2001, which was enacted in response to the attack on the World Trade Center in New York on 11 September of that year. The Act allows for the detention without trial of foreign citizens suspected of being involved in terrorist activities (see *A v Secretary of State for the Home Department* (2002) at 1.7.1.5, above).

One point to note in relation to the operation of the margin of appreciation is that, by definition, it is a rule of international law, in that it recognises the different approaches of distinct States. Consequently, it is limited in operation to the supranational ECtHR and not to national courts. The latter may follow precedents based on the doctrine, but it is difficult to see how they could themselves apply it in a national context, although it would appear that the domestic courts' development of the doctrine of deference achieves similar ends to those allowed under the margin of appreciation.

Proportionality

Even where States avail themselves of the margin of appreciation, they are not at liberty to interfere with rights to any degree beyond what is required, as a minimum, to deal with the perceived problem within the context of a democratic society. In other words, there must be a relationship of necessity between the end desired and the means used to achieve it.

As the ECtHR stated in *Chorherr v Austria* (1994):

> The margin of appreciation extends in particular to the choice of the reasonable and appropriate means to be used by the authority to ensure that lawful manifestation can take place peacefully.

Proportionality has already been mentioned in relation to judicial review, where it was suggested that it might infiltrate the English legal system (see 6.9.3). However, in relation to the HRA, proportionality is central to the jurisprudence of the ECtHR and as such is now central to the jurisprudence of the UK courts in relation to human rights issues. It is suggested that it will not be restricted to this limited sphere for long and that it will expand into judicial review and other areas as the HRA becomes increasingly understood and used.

It also has to be recognised that the ECHR as a legal document is not fixed text. As Luzius Wildhaber has stated:

On the question of evolutive interpretation, it is precisely the genius of the Convention that it is indeed a dynamic and a living instrument, which has shown its capacity to evolve in the light of social and technological developments that its drafters, however far sighted, could never have imagined. The Convention has shown that it is capable of growing with society; and in this respect its formulations have proved their worth over five decades. It has remained a live and modern instrument. The 'living instrument' doctrine is one of the best known principles of Strasbourg case law, the principle that the Convention is interpreted 'in the light of present day conditions', that it evolves, through the interpretation of the Court.

The recognition of this approach may be seen in the Court's legal recognition of transsexuals' new sexual identity in *Goodwin v UK* (2002). Until that decision, the Court had found that there was no positive obligation for the States to modify their civil status systems so as to have the register of births updated or annotated to record changed sexual identity. However, in *Goodwin*, the Court finally reached the conclusion that the fair balance now favoured the recognition of such rights, and ruled accordingly.

13.4.1 The genesis of the Regulation of Investigatory Powers Act 2000

An examination of the list of cases decided by the ECtHR provides some interesting insights into the potential impact of the HRA now that it is open to UK courts to use the European Convention as a basis for their decisions.

One particular topic that has repeatedly drawn the attention of the ECtHR concerns the power of the police and security forces to collect incriminating information.

In *Malone v UK* (1984), the ECtHR decided that telephone tapping by the police, authorised by the UK government and condoned under common law powers by the High Court was in breach of Art 8 of the ECHR, which guarantees the right to respect for private life. The Article provides:

There shall be no interference by a public authority with the exercise of this right except such as is in accordance with the law and is necessary in a democratic society in the interests of national security ...

The ECtHR held that the tapping was in breach of Art 8(2), because it was not 'in accordance with law', but was rather governed by an unregulated discretion. It could not be 'necessary in a democratic society' as there were no constitutional safeguards against misuse of the power. The government reacted by introducing legislation to control telephone tapping by the police. The Interception of Communications Act (IOCA) 1985 limits telephone tapping to cases where the Home Secretary has issued a warrant and, to safeguard against arbitrary use, the warrant can only be issued in three specified circumstances, one of which is the prevention of serious crime. Further safeguards are provided by a tribunal to investigate complaints about the use of these powers and by the establishment of a commissioner to review annually how the Home Secretary has exercised his powers.

However, perhaps the most surprising aspect of *Malone* was the recognition in the UK courts that telephone tapping could not be unlawful in the UK, as there was no right of privacy at common law that could be breached. And of course, the right of respect for private life provided by the European Convention was not justiciable in the UK courts at that time (*Malone v Metropolitan Police Commissioner* (1979)).

At least somewhat surprisingly, the IOCA only applied to interceptions on public telecommunications systems and did not regulate private systems such as internal works systems. As a consequence, the UK was also found in breach of Art 8 in *Halford v UK* (1997), where such a private system was abused to record conversations.

Even more surprising, not to say complacent, was the way in which the flaws inherent in the procedure relating to the interception of communication were not remedied in relation to the use of covert listening devices, commonly referred to as 'bugging'. Thus, a very similar situation, and corresponding decision, occurred in *Khan v UK* (2000). In *Khan*, the ECtHR held unanimously that there had been violations of Art 8 (right to respect for private and family life) and Art 13 (right to an effective remedy) of the ECHR, after the claimant had been convicted of drug dealing on the basis of evidence improperly obtained by a secret listening device installed by the police. As in *Malone*, the ECtHR held that, at the time in point, there was no statutory system to regulate the use of covert listening devices. As the Home Office Guidelines, which regulated such recordings, were neither legally binding nor publicly accessible, any such recording was consequently not 'in accordance with the law', as required by Art 8(2) of the ECHR. Khan had been arrested in 1993, but it was not until the enactment of the Police Act 1997 that a statutory basis for the authorisation of such surveillance operations was properly constituted, and that may have been instigated by a European Commission finding in *Govell v UK* (1997) that no existing statutory system governed the use of covert listening devices. Consequently, in the *Khan* case, there had been a breach of Art 8 of the ECHR because the tape-recording could not be considered to be 'in accordance with the law' as required by Art 8(2). The ECtHR found, however, that the use at the applicant's trial of the secretly taped material did not conflict with the requirements of fairness guaranteed by Art 6(1) of the ECHR. As the last court in the UK, the approach of the House of Lords is of some interest and reveals the frustration that the court felt in relation to the case, which no doubt it was aware would eventually be decided in a contrary manner by the ECtHR. As it stated, in English law, a breach of the provisions of Art 8 was not determinative of the outcome, and the judge's discretion to admit or exclude such evidence under s 78 of the Police and Criminal Evidence Act (PACE) 1984 was subject to common law rules that relevant evidence which was obtained improperly, or even unlawfully, remained admissible. As Lord Nolan expressed the situation:

> The sole cause of this case coming to your Lordship's House is the lack of a statutory system regulating the use of surveillance devices by the police. The absence of such a system seems astonishing, the more so in view of the statutory framework which has governed the use of such devices by the Security Service since 1989, and the interception of communications by the police as well as by other agencies since 1985. I would refrain from other comment because counsel for the respondent was able to inform us, on instructions, that the government proposes to introduce legislation covering the matter in the next session of Parliament.

One can almost hear the additional words 'and not before time', but unfortunately it was too late in the *Khan* case, which had to make its protracted way to the ECtHR.

All of the preceding cases required action on the part of the UK government, and to that end the Regulation of Investigatory Powers Act (RIPA) was enacted in July 2000. That Act was specifically introduced to ensure that the investigatory powers of State authorities are used in accordance with human rights, but in so doing, it significantly increased the State's power in relation to surveillance. The regulated powers relate to:

- the interception of communications;
- the acquisition of communications data (for example, billing data);
- intrusive surveillance (on residential premises/in private vehicles);
- covert surveillance in the course of specific operations;
- the use of covert human intelligence sources (agents, informants, undercover officers);
- access to encrypted data.

For each of these powers, the Act ensures that the law clearly covers:

- the purposes for which they may be used;
- which authorities can use the powers;
- who should authorise each use of the power;
- the use that can be made of the material gained;
- independent judicial oversight;
- a means of redress for the individual.

Unfortunately, the RIPA was introduced too late to prevent the UK being found to be in breach of Art 8 of the ECHR in *Allan v UK* in 2002, which arose from covert bugging actions taken by the police.

13.5 The European Convention and the European Union

Having started this section by stressing the fundamental distinction between the ECJ and the ECtHR, it is necessary to end it by blurring it and pointing out the various ways in which the EC, and then Union, have expressly recognised the rights provided in the ECHR and the decisions made by the ECtHR. Thus, in a joint declaration delivered in 1997, the European Parliament, the Council and the Commission emphasised the prime importance they attached to the protection of fundamental rights:

> ... as derived particularly from the constitution of the Member States and the European Convention for the Protection of Human Rights and Fundamental Freedoms [(1977) OJ C103].

Article 6 (formerly Art F(2)), which was introduced by the Maastricht Treaty, expressly states that:

> The Union shall respect fundamental rights, as guaranteed by the European Convention for the Protection of Human Rights and Fundamental Freedoms ... as general principles of Community law.

The ECJ, in the same way as English courts, has equally been guided by the Convention where Community law is silent. It still remains possible, however, for cases to be brought to either or both judicial forums. Issues relating to discrimination are an ideal case in point, by being potentially both in breach of employment law regulated by the EC, and fundamental human rights regulated by the ECHR. It is also an unfortunate fact that it is possible for at least a degree of incompatibility between the decisions of the two courts in relation to very similar matters (for example, see *SPUC v Grogan* (1991) and *Open Door and Well Women v Ireland* (1992)). Such possibilities would be precluded if, following the recent action of the UK, the EU, as a body, were formally to incorporate the Convention. The likelihood of such a course of action was indicated with approval by the current President of the ECtHR, Luzius Wildhaber, in his opening address at the commencement of the judicial year in January 2003. As he said:

> One aspect of [the] future will be the system's relationship with the European Union and particularly the enlarged Union. Again this is a recurring topic and I make no apologies for reiterating my call for the Union to accede to the Convention. On this front the latest news is encouraging. In his report to the Copenhagen summit on 12 December last year the Chairman of the Convention, Mr Giscard d'Estaing, spoke of a 'very strong tendency' in favour of accession within the Convention on the future of Europe ... On the basis of cogent argument, the working group comes down unanimously in favour of inserting into the new European Union Treaty a constitutional clause allowing accession.

THE EUROPEAN CONTEXT

The European Union

UK law is now subject to Community law in particular areas.

In practice, this has led to the curtailment of parliamentary sovereignty in those areas.

Sources of European Community law

The sources of EC law are:

- internal treaties and protocols;
- international agreements;
- secondary legislation; and
- decisions of the European Court of Justice.

Secondary legislation takes three forms:

- regulations which are directly applicable;
- directives which have to be given statutory form;
- decisions are directly applicable.

Major institutions

The major institutions of the European Union (EU) are:

- the Council of Ministers;
- the European Parliament;
- the Commission; and
- the European Court of Justice.

The European Court of Human Rights

The European Council, the European Commission of Human Rights and the European Court of Human Rights are distinct institutions whose purpose is to regulate the potential abuse of human rights. They are not part of the EU structure.

Since the enactment of the Human Rights Act 1998, the European Convention on Human Rights has been incorporated into UK law. It remains to see what effect this has on domestic UK law, but it cannot but be significant.

FURTHER READING

GENERAL READING

Alderson, J, 'Modern policing' (1995) *The Independent*, 1 February

Allen, T, Aikenhead, H and Widdison, R, 'Computer simulation of judicial behaviour', http://webjcli.ncl.ac.uk/1998/issue3/allen3.html

Archbold (Richardson, PJ (ed)), *Criminal Pleading, Evidence and Practice*, 2003, London: Sweet & Maxwell

Ashworth, A, *Sentencing and Criminal Justice*, 2000, London: Butterworths

Bailey, SH and Gunn, MJ, *Smith & Bailey on The Modern English Legal System*, 3rd edn, 1996, London: Sweet & Maxwell

Baldwin, J, 'Police interview techniques: establishing truth or proof?' (1993) 33 British J of Criminology 3

Baldwin, J, 'Power and police interviews' (1993) 143 NLJ 1194

Baldwin, J and Hill, S, *The Operation of the Green Form Scheme in England and Wales*, 1988, London: LCD

Baldwin, J and McConville, M, *Negotiated Justice: A Closer Look at the Implications of Plea Bargaining*, 1993, London: Martin Robertson

Baldwin, J and McConville, M, *Negotiated Justice: Pressures on Defendants to Plead Guilty*, 1977, London: Martin Robertson

Barnard, M, 'All bar none' (1999) 96/26 Law Soc Gazette 20

Bennion, F, 'A naked usurpation?' (1999) 149 NLJ 421

Bennion, F, 'Statute law obscurity and drafting parameters' (1978) British JLS 235

Bennion, F, *Statutory Interpretation*, 2nd edn, 1992, London: Butterworths

Bindaman, D, 'Crown duals' (1999) Law Soc Gazette, 31 March

Bindman, G, 'Lessons of *Pinochet*' (1999) 149 NLJ 1050

Blackstone's Civil Procedure (Plant, C (ed)), 2003, Oxford: OUP

Broadbent, G, 'Offensive weapons and the Criminal Justice Act' (1989) Law Soc Gazette, 12 July

Burns, R, 'A view from the ranks' (2000) 150 NLJ 1829–30

Burrow, J, 'Pre-committal custody time limits' (1999) 149 NLJ 330

Cane, P (ed), *Atiyah's Accidents, Compensation and the Law*, 6th edn, 1999, London: Butterworths

Cape, E, 'Police interrogation and interruption' (1994) 144 NLJ 120

Card, R and Ward, R, *The Criminal Justice and Public Order Act 1994*, 1994, Bristol: Jordans

Clayton, R and Tomlinson, H, 'Arrest and reasonable grounds for suspicion' (1988) 32 Law Soc Gazette 22

Cragg, S, 'Stop and search powers: research and extension' (1999) Legal Action 3

Craig, P and de Búrca, G, *EU Law: Text, Cases and Materials*, 3rd edn, 2003, Oxford: OUP

Crawford, L, 'Race awareness training and the judges' (1994) Counsel 11

Croall, H, *Crime and Society in Britain*, 1998, London: Longman

Darbyshire, P, 'The lamp that shows that freedom lives – is it worth the candle?' [1991] Crim LR 740

De Sousa Santos, B, *Toward a New Common Sense*, 2002, London: Butterworths

Devlin (Lord), *Trial by Jury*, 1966, London: Stevens

Diamond, D, 'Woolf reforms hike costs' (1999) The Lawyer 2

Dicey, AV, *An Introduction to the Study of the Law of the Constitution* (1885), 10th edn, 1959, London: Macmillan

Dixon, D, Coleman, C and Bottomley, K, 'Consent and legal regulation of policing' (1990) 17 JLS 345

Exall, G, 'Civil litigation brief' (1999) SJ 32

Exall, G, 'Civil litigation brief' (1999) SJ 162

Exall, G, 'Civil litigation brief' (1999) SJ 270

Feldman, D, *Civil Liberties and Human Rights in England and Wales*, 1993, Oxford: OUP

Flemming, J, 'Judge airs concerns over Woolf reforms' (2000) Law Soc Gazette, 10 February

Frenkel, J, 'Offers to settle and payments into court' (1999) 149 NLJ 458

Frenkel, J, 'On the road to reform' (1998) Law Soc Gazette, 16 December

Genn, H, *Hard Bargaining: Out of Court Settlement in Personal Injury Claims*, 1987, Oxford: OUP

Genn, H and Genn, Y, *The Effectiveness of Representation at Tribunals*, 1989, London: LCD

Gibb, F, 'Plaintiff cries as law goes native' (1999) *The Times*, 27 April

Gibb, F, 'Rude judges must mind their language' (1999) *The Times*, 29 June

Gibb, F, 'Thatcher furious at "vindictive" Pinochet decision' (1999) *The Times*, 16 April

Gibson, B, 'Why Bournemouth?' (1987) 151 JP 520

Glasser, C, 'Legal aid and eligibility' (1988) Law Soc Gazette, 9 March

Glasser, C, 'Legal services and the Green Papers' (1989) Law Soc Gazette, 5 April

Gold, S, 'Woolf watch' (1999) 149 NLJ 718

Goodhart, A, 'The *ratio decidendi* of a case' (1959) 22 MLR 117

Goodrich, P, *Reading the Law*, 1986, Oxford: Basil Blackwell

Grainger, I and Fealy, M, *An Introduction to the New Civil Procedure Rules*, 1999, London: Cavendish Publishing

Griffith, JAG, *The Politics of the Judiciary*, 5th edn, 1997, London: Fontana

Griffiths, C, 'Jury trial' (1999) Counsel 14

Hamer, P, 'Complaints: a new strategy' (1999) 149 NLJ 959

Harris, D *et al*, *Compensation and Support for Illness and Injury*, 1984, Oxford: Clarendon

Harrison, R, 'Appealing prospects' (2000) NLJ 1175–76

Harrison, R, 'Cry Woolf' (1999) 149 NLJ 1011

Harrison, R, 'Why have two types of civil court?' (1999) 149 NLJ 65

Hart, H, *The Concept of Law*, 1961, Oxford: OUP

Hayek, FA, *The Road to Serfdom* (1971), 1994, London: Routledge and Kegan Paul

Hedderman, C and Moxon, C, *Magistrates' Court or Crown Court? Mode of Trial Decisions and Sentencing*, Home Office Study No 125, 1992, London: HMSO

HM Magistrates' Courts Service Inspectorate, *Annual Report 1997–98*, London: HMSO

Holdsworth, W, *A History of English Law*, 1924, London: Methuen

Holland, T, 'Cut price conveyancing' (1994) 144 NLJ 192

Irvine (Lord), 'Community vision under fire' (1999) Law Soc Gazette, 26 May

Jason-Lloyd, L, 'Section 60 of the Criminal Justice and Public Order Act 1994' (1998) 162 JP 836

JUSTICE, *Professional Negligence and the Quality of Legal Services – An Economic Perspective*, 1983, London: JUSTICE

Kairys, D, *The Politics of Law: A Progressive Critique*, 1982, New York: Pantheon

Keating, D, 'Upholding the Rule of Law' (1999) 149 NLJ 533

Khan, S and Ryder, M, 'Police and the law' (1998) Legal Action 16

Law Society Civil Litigation Committee, 'Unravelling the enigma of *Thai Trading*' (2000) Law Soc Gazette, 9 June

Lee, S, *Judging Judges*, 1988, London: Faber & Faber

Legal Services Ombudsman, *Demanding Progress*, 1999–2000 Annual Report, London: HMSO

Lidstone, K, 'Entry, search and seizure' (1989) 40 NILQ 333

Lidstone, K (ed), *Prosecutions by Private Individuals and Non-Police Agencies*, 1980, London: HMSO

Lidstone, K and Palmer, C, *The Investigation of Crime*, 1996, London: Butterworths

Lord Chancellor's Department, *Judicial Statistics 2000*, Cm 3980, London: HMSO

Loughlin, M, *Sword and Scales*, 2000, Oxford: Hart

MacCallum, V, 'Learning lessons' (2001) Law Soc Gazette, 10 January

MacCormick, N, *Legal Rules and Legal Reasoning*, 1978, Oxford: Clarendon

Mackay (Lord), *The Administration of Justice*, 1994, Hamlyn Lectures, London: Sweet & Maxwell

Malleson, K, *The New Judiciary – The Effect of Expansion and Activism*, 1999, Aldershot: Ashgate

Mansell, W and Meteyard, B, *A Critical Introduction to Law*, 2nd edn, 1999, London: Cavendish Publishing

Mayhew, L and Reiss, A, 'The social organisation of legal contacts' (1969) 34 American Sociological Rev 311

McConville, M, Sanders, A and Leng, R, *The Case for the Prosecution*, 1991, London: Routledge

McGrath, P, 'Appeals against small claims track decisions' (1999) 149 NLJ 748

McLaughlin, E and Muncie, J, *Controlling Crime*, 2001, London: Sage and the Open University

Money-Kyrle, R, 'Advocates' immunity after *Osman*' (1999) 149 NLJ 945 and 981

Montesquieu, C, *De l'Esprit des Lois* (1748), 1989, Cambridge: CUP

Morris, P, White, R and Lewis, P, *Social Needs and Legal Action*, 1973, London: Robertson

Motson, S, Stephenson, G and Williamson, T, 'The effects of case characteristics on suspect behaviour during police questioning' (1992) 32 British J of Criminology 23

Murphy, M, 'Civil legal aid eligibility' (1989) Legal Action 4

Napier, M, 'Conditional fees' (1995) 92/16 Law Soc Gazette 1626

News, 'The legal profession and the Community Legal Service' (1999) 149 NLJ 1195

News in Brief, 'Cheap conveyancing' (1998) 148 NLJ 8

Oliver, D and Drewry, G, *The Law and Parliament*, 1998, London: Butterworths

Pannick, D, *Advocates*, 1992, Oxford: OUP

Pannick, D, *Judges*, 1987, Oxford: OUP

Parker, C, 'Judicial decision making' (1999) 149 NLJ 1142

Parpworth, N, 'Breach of the peace: breach of human rights?' (1998) 152 JP 6

Payne, R, 'To counsel, not confront: the law on ADR' (1999) Counsel 30

Purchas, F (Sir), 'What is happening to judicial independence' (1994) 144 NLJ 1306

Raz, J, 'The Rule of Law and its virtue' (1977) 93 LQR 195

Reid (Lord), 'The judge as law maker' (1972) 12 JSPTL 22

Reiner, R, *Crime, Order and Policing*, 1994, London: Routledge

Reiner, R, 'Responsibilities and reforms' (1993) 143 NLJ 1096

Reiner, R, *The Politics of the Police*, 2nd edn, 2000, Oxford: OUP

Richardson, J *et al*, *Archbold on Criminal Evidence, Pleading and Practice*, 1995, London: Sweet & Maxwell

Robertshaw, P, *Rethinking Legal Need: The Case of Criminal Justice*, 1991, Aldershot: Dartmouth

Robertson, G, 'The Downey Report: MPs must realise they are not above the law' (1997) *The Guardian*, 4 July

Rutherford, A, 'Judicial training and autonomy' (1999) 149 NLJ 1120

Rutherford, A, 'Preserving a robust independence' (1999) 149 NLJ 908

Sanders, A, 'Class bias in prosecutions' (1985) 24 Howard J 17

Sanders, A, 'The silent code' (1994) 144 NLJ 946

Sanders, A and Young, R, *Criminal Justice*, 1995, London: Butterworths

Sanders, A and Young, R, 'Plea bargaining and the next Criminal Justice Bill' (1994) 144 NLJ 1200

Sanders, A *et al*, *Advice and Assistance at Police Stations and the 24 Hour Duty Solicitor Scheme*, 1989, London: LCD

Scrivener, A, 'The birth of a new language in the court room: English' (1999) *The Independent*, 26 April

Sedley, S (Sir), 'Human rights: a 21st century agenda' [1995] PL 386

Simpson, A, 'The *ratio decidendi* of a case' (1957) 20 MLR 413

Skordaki, E, *Judicial Appointments*, Law Society Research Study No 5, 1991, London: HMSO

Slapper, G, 'English legal system' (1999) 26 SLR 31

Smith, JC, 'Criminal appeals and the Criminal Cases Review Commission' (1995) 145 NLJ 534

Smith, R, 'Judicial statistics: questions and answers' (1994) 144 NLJ 1088

Smith, R, 'Politics and the judiciary' (1993) 143 NLJ 1486

Smith, R (ed), *Achieving Civil Justice*, 1996, London: LAG

Smith, R (ed), *Shaping the Future: New Directions in Legal Services*, 1995, London: LAG

St Luce, S, 'Cutting the lifeline' (1999) 149 NLJ 398

Steyn (Lord), 'The weakest and least dangerous department of government' [1997] PL 84

Temple Lang, J, 'The duties of national courts under Community constitutional law' [1997] EL Rev 22

Thomas, DA (ed), *Current Sentencing Practice*, 1999, London: Sweet & Maxwell

Thompson, P (ed), *The Civil Court Practice*, 1999, London: Butterworths

Trent, M, 'ADR and the new Civil Procedure Rules' (1999) 149 NLJ 410

Turner, AJ, 'Inferences under s 34 of the Criminal Justice and Public Order Act 1994: Part One' (1999) 163 JP, 27 March

Turner, AJ, 'Inferences under s 34 of the Criminal Justice and Public Order Act 1994: Part Two' (1999) 163 JP, 24 April

Twining, W, *Globalisation and Legal Theory*, 2000, London: Butterworths

Twining, W and Meirs, D, *How To Do Things With Rules*, 4th edn, 1999, London: Butterworths

Unger, R, *In Law and Modern Society*, 1976, New York: Free Press

Verkaik, R, 'Opinions on counsel' (1998) 95/04 Law Soc Gazette 22

von Hayek, FA, *The Road to Serfdom* (1971), 1994, London: Routledge and Kegan Paul

Wadham, J and Arkinstall, J, 'Human rights and crime' (1999) 149 NLJ 703

Watson, A, 'The right to elect trial by jury: the issue reappears' (1998) 163 JP 636

Weber, M, *Economy and Society (Wirtschaft und Gesellschaft)*, 1968, Roth, G and Widttich, C (trans), Berkeley: California UP

Wendel Holmes, O, *The Common Law* (1881), 1968, London: Macmillan

Williams, G, 'Letting off the guilty and prosecuting the innocent' [1985] Crim LR 115

Wolchover, D and Heaton-Armstrong, A, 'Jailing psychopaths and prison cell confessions' (1999) 149 NLJ 285

Woolf (Lord), 'Judicial review – the tensions between the executive and the judiciary' (1998) 114 LQR 579

Yarrow, S, *The Price of Success*, 1997, Grantham: Grantham

Yarrow, S and Abrams, P, *Nothing to Lose? Clients' Experiences of Using Conditional Fees*, Summary Report, 1999, London: University of Westminster

Zander, M, *A Matter of Justice*, 1989, Oxford: OUP

Zander, M, *Cases and Materials on the English Legal System*, 8th edn, 1999, London: Butterworths

Zander, M, 'Costs of litigation – a study in the Queen's Bench Division' (1975) Law Soc Gazette, 25 June

Zander, M, 'How does judicial case management work?' (1997) 147 NLJ 353

Zander, M, 'Investigation of crime' [1979] Crim LR 211

Zander, M, *Legal Services for the Community*, 1978, London: Temple Smith

Zander, M, 'The trouble with fast track fixed costs' (1997) 147 NLJ 1125

Zander, M, 'The Woolf Report: forwards or backwards for the new Lord Chancellor' (1997) 16 Civil Justice Quarterly 208

Zander, M, 'Who goes to solicitors?' (1969) 66 Law Soc Gazette 174

Zander, M, 'Woolf on Zander' (1997) 147 NLJ 768

Zander, M and Henderson, P, *The Crown Court Study*, Royal Commission on Criminal Justice Study 19, 145, 1993, London: HMSO

FURTHER READING BY CHAPTER

Chapter 1   Law and Legal Study

Barnett, H, *Constitutional and Administrative Law*, 4th edn, 2002, London: Cavendish Publishing

Bradney, A *et al*, *How to Study Law*, 3rd edn, 1995, London: Sweet & Maxwell

Clinch, P, *Using a Law Library*, 2nd edn, 2001, London: Blackstone

Fitzpatrick, P (ed), *Dangerous Supplements*, 1991, London: Pluto

Holmes, N and Venables, D, *Researching the Legal Web*, 2nd edn, 1999, London: Butterworths

Social and legal order

Mansell, W and Meteyard, B, *A Critical Introduction to Law*, 2nd edn, 1999, London: Cavendish Publishing

Roberts, S, *Order and Dispute*, 1979, Harmondsworth: Penguin

Legal language

Friedman, L, 'On interpretation of laws' (1988) 11(3) Ratio Juris 252

Goodrich, P, *Reading the Law*, 1986, Oxford: Basil Blackwell

Jackson, B, *Making Sense in Law*, 1995, London: Deborah Charles

Law, politics and the Rule of Law

Bennion, F, 'A naked usurpation?' (1999) 149 NLJ 421

Dicey, AV, *Introduction to the Law of the Constitution*, 1897, London: Macmillan

Feldman, D, 'The Human Rights Act and constitutional principles' (1999) 19(2) JLS, June

Fine, R, *Democracy and the Rule of Law*, 1984, London: Pluto

Hill, C, *Liberty Against the Law*, 1996, Harmondsworth: Penguin

Horowitz, MJ, 'The Rule of Law: an unqualified good?' (1977) 86 Yale LJ 561

Kairys, D (ed), *The Politics of Law: A Progressive Critique*, 1990, London: Pantheon

Keating, D, 'Upholding the Rule of Law' (1999) 149 NLJ 533

Laws, J (Sir), 'Law and democracy' [1995] PL 72

Locke, J, *The Treatises of Government*, 1988, Cambridge: CUP

Raz, J, 'The Rule of Law and its virtue' (1972) 93 LQR 195

Sedley, S (Sir), *Freedom, Law and Justice*, 1998, Hamlyn Lectures, London: Sweet & Maxwell

Sedley, S (Sir), 'Human rights: a 21st century agenda' [1995] PL 386

Steiner, H and Alston, P, *International Human Rights in Context*, 1996, Oxford: Clarendon

Thompson, A, 'Taking the right seriously: the case of FA Hayek', in Fitzpatrick, P (ed), *Dangerous Supplements*, 1991, London: Pluto

Thompson, E, *Whigs and Hunters*, 1977, Harmondsworth: Penguin

von Hayek, F, *The Road to Serfdom*, 1962, London: Routledge

Young, J, 'The politics of the Human Rights Act' (1999) 26(1) JLS 27

Chapter 2   Sources of Law

Boulton, C (ed), *Erskine May's Treatise on the Law, Privileges, Proceedings and Usage of Parliament*, 1989, London: Butterworths

Cross, R, *Cross, Harris and Hart, Precedent in English Law*, 4th edn, 1991, Oxford: Clarendon

Goodhart, A, 'The *ratio decidendi* of a case' (1959) 22 MLR 117

Holdsworth, W, 'Case law' (1934) 50 LQR 180

Jenkins, C, 'Helping the reader of Bills and Acts' (1999) 149 NLJ 798

MacCormick, N, *Legal Rules and Legal Reasoning*, 1978, Oxford: Clarendon

Simpson, A, 'The *ratio decidendi* of a case' (1957) 20 MLR 413; (1958) 21 MLR 155

The following are also relevant to the issues in Chapter 5:

Bates, T, 'The contemporary use of legislative history in the United Kingdom' (1995) 54(1) CLJ 127

Bell, J and Engle, G (Sir), *Cross: Statutory Interpretation*, 3rd edn, 1995, London: Butterworths

Bennion, F, 'Statute law: obscurity and drafting parameters' (1978) 5 British JLS 235

Bennion, F, *Statutory Interpretation*, 2nd edn, 1992, London: Butterworths

Committee on the Preparation of Legislation, *Renton Committee Report*, Cmnd 6053, 1975, London: HMSO

Eskridge, W, *Dynamic Statutory Interpretation*, 1994, Cambridge, MA: Harvard UP

Friedman, L, 'On interpretation of laws' (1988) 11(3) Ratio Juris 252

Chapter 3   The Civil Court Structure

Barnard, D and Houghton, M, *The New Civil Court in Action*, 1993, London: Butterworths

Fage, J and Whitehead, G, *Supreme Court Practice and Procedure*, 1992, London: Fourmat

Flemming, J, 'Judge airs concerns over Woolf reforms' (2000) Law Soc Gazette, 10 February

Greenslade, R, *Civil Court Practice*, 1997, London: Butterworths

Harrison, R, 'Appealing prospects' (2000) NLJ 1175–76

Harrison, R, 'Why have two types of civil court?' (1999) 149 NLJ 65

Judicial Statistics Annual Report 2002, Government Statistical Service, London: The Stationery Office

O'Hare, J and Hill, R, *Civil Litigation*, 10th edn, 2001, London: Sweet & Maxwell

Pedley, FH, 'The small claims process' (1994) 144 NLJ 1217

Pershad, R, 'Delay, listing and the county court' (1994) Counsel 16

Woolf (Lord), *Access to Justice – Final Report to the Lord Chancellor on the Civil Justice System in England and Wales*, 1996, London: HMSO

Chapter 4   The Criminal Court Structure

Carlen, P, *Magistrates' Justice*, 1976, Oxford: Martin Robertson

Grove, T, *The Magistrates' Tale*, 2002, London: Bloomsbury

Malleson, K, 'The Criminal Cases Review Commission: how will it work?' [1995] Crim LR 928

Matthews, P and Foreman, J (eds), *Jervis: On the Office and Duties of Coroners*, 1993, London: Sweet & Maxwell

Moxon, D and Hedderman, C, 'Mode of trial decisions and sentencing differences between courts' (1994) 33(2) Howard J of Criminal Justice 97

Richardson, PJ (ed), *Archbold on Criminal Pleading, Evidence and Practice*, 2003, London: Sweet & Maxwell

Smith, JC, 'The Criminal Appeal Act 1995: appeals against conviction' [1995] Crim LR 921

Chapter 5   Judicial Reasoning

Bell, J and Engle, G (Sir), *Cross on Statutory Interpretation*, 1995, London: Butterworths

Bennion, F, *Statutory Interpretation*, 1992, London: Butterworths

Bindman, G, 'Lessons of *Pinochet*' (1999) 149 NLJ 1050

Denning (Lord), *Due Process of Law*, 1980, London: Butterworths

Denning (Lord), *The Discipline of Law*, 1979, London: Butterworths

Manchester, C *et al*, *Exploring the Law*, 2000, London: Sweet & Maxwell

Parker, C, 'Judicial decision making' (1999) 149 NLJ 1142

Pickles, J, *Straight from the Bench*, 1987, London: Hodder and Stoughton

Reid (Lord), 'The judge as law maker' (1972) 12 JSPTL 22

Chapter 6   The Judiciary

Baldwin, J, 'The social composition of magistrates' (1976) 16 British J of Criminology 171

Browne-Wilkinson, N (Sir), 'The independence of the judiciary in the 1980s' [1988] PL 4

Crawford, L, 'Race awareness training and the judges' (1994) Counsel 11

Griffith, JAG, *The Politics of the Judiciary*, 5th edn, 1997, London: Fontana

Hailsham (Lord), 'The office of Lord Chancellor and the separation of powers' (1989) 8 Civil Justice Quarterly 308

Lee, S, *Judging Judges*, 1988, London: Faber & Faber

MacCormick, N, *Legal Rules and Legal Reasoning*, 1978, Oxford: Clarendon

Mackay (Lord), *The Administration of Justice*, 1994, London: Sweet & Maxwell

Malleson, K, *The New Judiciary – The Effect of Expansion and Activism*, 1999, Aldershot: Ashgate

McLachlin, B, 'The role of judges in modern Commonwealth society' [1994] LQR 260

Pannick, D, *Judges*, 1987, Oxford: OUP

Parker, H *et al*, *Unmasking the Magistrates*, 1989, Milton Keynes: OUP

Royal Commission on Criminal Justice, *Runciman Report*, Cm 2263, 1995, London: HMSO

Rutherford, A, 'Judicial training and autonomy' (1999) 149 NLJ 1120

Skordaki, E, *Judicial Appointments*, Law Society Research Study No 5, 1991, London: HMSO

Stevens, R, *The Independence of the Judiciary*, 1993, Oxford: OUP

See, in addition, reading for Chapter 2.

Chapter 7   The Civil Process

Blackstone's Civil Procedure (Plant, C (ed)), 2003, Oxford: OUP

Burns, R, 'A view from the ranks' (2000) NLJ 1829–30

Genn, H, *Hard Bargaining: Out of Court Settlements in Personal Injury Claims*, 1987, Oxford: OUP

Graham, T, 'CPR Part 36 offers' (2003) 153 NLJ 354

Grainger, I and Fealy, M, *The Civil Procedure Rules in Action*, 2nd edn, 2000, London: Cavendish Publishing

Harrison, R, 'Cry Woolf' (1999) 149 NLJ 1011

Iller, M, *Civil Evidence: The Essential Practitioner's Guide*, 2002, London: Cavendish Publishing

Lawton, F, 'Court experts' (1995) SJ 793

Miller, F, 'The adversarial myth' (1995) 145 NLJ 743

Stewart, N (QC), 'Civil procedure: recovery' (2003) 153 NLJ 463

Thompson, P (ed), *The Civil Court Practice*, 1999, London: Butterworths

Trent, M, 'ADR and the new Civil Procedure Rules' (1999) 149 NLJ 410

Woolf (Lord), *Access to Justice – Final Report to the Lord Chancellor on the Civil Justice System in England and Wales*, 1996, London: HMSO

Zander, M, 'Are there any clothes for the emperor to wear?' (1995) 145 NLJ 154

Zander, M, 'The trouble with fast track fixed costs' (1997) 147 NLJ 1125

Zander, M, 'The Woolf Report: forwards or backwards for the new Lord Chancellor' (1997) 16 Civil Justice Quarterly 208

Zuckerman, AAS, 'A reform of civil procedure – rationing procedure rather than access to justice' (1995) 22 JLS 156

Chapter 8   Arbitration, Tribunal Adjudication and Alternative Dispute Resolution

Abel, R, 'The comparative study of dispute institutions in society' (1973) 8 Law and Society Rev 217

Baldwin, J, *The Small Claims Procedure and the Consumer*, 1995, London: Office of Fair Trading

Beale, H and Dugdale, T, 'Contracts between businessmen: planning and the use of contractual remedies' (1975) 2 British JLS 45

Genn, H and Genn, Y, *The Effectiveness of Representation at Tribunals*, 1989, London: LCD

JUSTICE, *Industrial Tribunals*, 1987, London: JUSTICE

Mackay (Lord), *The Administration of Justice*, 1994, London: Sweet & Maxwell

Michaelson, J, 'An A–Z of ADR' (2003) 153 NLJ 101, 181 and 232

Payne, R, 'To counsel, not confront: the law on ADR' (1999) Counsel 30

Pedley, FH, 'The small claims process' (1994) 144 NLJ 1217

The Annual Report of the Council on Tribunals, HC 114, 1995–96, London: HMSO

The Annual Report of the Council on Tribunals, 1996–97, London: HMSO

Chapter 9   The Criminal Process: (1) The Investigation of Crime

Ashworth, A, *Serious Crime, Human Rights and Criminal Procedure*, 2002, London: Sweet & Maxwell

Baldwin, J, *The Conduct of Police Investigation*, 1992, London: HMSO

Baldwin, J and McConville, M, *Jury Trials*, 1979, Oxford: Clarendon

Bevan, V and Lidstone, K, *The Investigation of Crime*, 2nd edn, 1996, London: Butterworths

Burrow, J, 'Pre-committal custody time limits' (1999) 149 NLJ 330

Committee on Fraud Trials, *Roskill Report*, 1986, London: HMSO

Darbyshire, P, 'The lamp that shows that freedom lives – is it worth the candle?' [1991] Crim LR 740

Dennis, I, 'The Criminal Justice and Public Order Act 1994: the evidence provisions' [1995] Crim LR 4

Devlin, P, *Trial by Jury*, 1956, London: Stevens

Dixon, D, Coleman, C and Bottomley, K, 'PACE in practice' (1991) 141 NLJ 1586

Doran, S and Jackson, J, 'The case for jury waiver' [1997] 155 Crim LR

Findlay, M and Duff, P, *The Jury Under Attack*, 1988, London: Butterworths

Greer, S, 'The right to silence: defence disclosure and confession evidence' (1994) 21 JLS 103

Herbert, P, 'Racism, impartiality and juries' (1995) 145 NLJ 146

Royal Commission on Criminal Justice, *Runciman Report*, Cm 2263, 1995, London: HMSO

Sanders, A and Young, R, *Criminal Justice*, 2000, London: Butterworths

Wadham, J and Arkinstall, J, 'Human rights and crime' (1999) 149 NLJ 703

Wolchover, D and Heaton-Armstrong, A, 'Jailing psychopaths and prison cell confessions' (1999) 149 NLJ 285

Zander, M, *The Police and Criminal Evidence Act 1994*, 3rd edn, 1995, London: Sweet & Maxwell

Zander, M, 'The Joint Review of PACE' (2003) 153 NLJ 204

Chapter 10   The Criminal Process: (2) The Prosecution

Ashworth, A and Fionda, J, 'The new code for crown prosecutors: prosecution, accountability and the public interest' [1994] Crim LR 894

Baldwin, J and McConville, M, *Negotiated Justice: Pressures on Defendants to Plead Guilty*, 1977, Oxford: Martin Robertson

Bindaman, D, 'Crown duals' (1999) Law Soc Gazette 22–28

Cockburn, JS and Green, TA, *Twelve Good Men and True*, 1988, Guilford: Princeton UP

CPS, *The Code for Crown Prosecutors*, rev edn, June 1994, London: CPS

Devlin, P, *Trial by Jury*, 1956, London: Stevens

Findlay, M and Duff, P, *The Jury Under Attack*, 1988, London: Butterworths

Griffiths, C, 'Jury trial' (1999) Counsel 14

Hastie, R, *Inside the Juror: The Psychology of Juror Decision Making*, 1993, Cambridge: CUP

Henderson, P and Nicholas, T, *Offending While on Bail*, Home Office Research Bulletin 32, 1992, London: Home Office Research Unit

Mahendra, B, 'Justice tarnished, tardy but triumphant' (2003) 153 NLJ, 7 February,

Rose, D, *In the Name of the Law – The Collapse of Criminal Justice*, 1996, London: Jonathan Cape

Rutherford, A, 'Preserving a robust independence' (1999) 149 NLJ 908, pp 908–10

Sanders, A, 'Class bias in prosecutions' (1985) 24 Howard J 176

Thompson, EP, *Writing by Candlelight*, 1980, London: Merlin

Uglow, S, Cheney, D and Dickson, L, *Criminal Justice*, 2nd edn, 2002, London: Sweet & Maxwell

Watson, A, 'The right to elect trial by jury: the issue reappears' (1998) 163 JP 636

Chapter 11   Legal Services

Abel, R, *The Legal Profession in England and Wales*, 1988, Oxford: Basil Blackwell

Barnard, M, 'All bar none' (1999) 96/26 Law Soc Gazette 20

Boxer, C, 'Conditional fees: lawyers courting disaster' (1995) 145 NLJ 1069

Cobb, N, 'Structural faults' (2003) 153 NLJ 744

Cocks, R, *Foundations of the Modern Bar*, 1983, London: Sweet & Maxwell

Editorial, 'Rights of audience' (1998) 162 JP 193

Genn, H and Genn, Y, *The Effectiveness of Representation at Tribunals*, 1989, London: LCD

Jackson, R, 'Disappointed litigants and doubtful actions' (1995) Counsel 16

Law Society Consultation Paper, *Supervision of Solicitors – The Next Decade*, July 1995, London: The Law Society

MacCallum, V, 'Learning lessons' (2001) Law Soc Gazette, 10 January

Mason, D, 'The changing landscape' (2003) 153 NLJ, 25 April

Money-Kyrle, R, 'Advocates' immunity after *Osman*' (1999) 149 NLJ 945 and 981

Powell, JL, 'Barristers' immunity – time to go' (1995) Counsel 11

St Luce, S, 'Cutting the lifeline' (1999) 149 NLJ 398

Verkaik, R, 'Opinions on counsel' (1998) Law Soc Gazette, 28 January

Chapter 12   The Funding of Legal Services

Bean, D, 'Surveying the new landscape' (1999) Counsel 8

Cobb, N, 'Resolving the funding black hole' (2003) 153 NLJ 427

Knafler, S, 'Litigation for the poor' (1994) SJ 256

Law Commission Consultation Paper, *Legal Aid – Targeting Need: The Future of Publicly Funded Help in Solving Legal Problems and Disputes in England and Wales*, Cm 2854, London: HMSO

Law Society Civil Litigation Committee, 'Unravelling the enigma of Thai Trading' (2000) Law Soc Gazette, 9 June

Marshall, D, 'The new CFA arrangements' (2003) 153 NLJ 833

Morgan, G, 'Notice of termination of the general criminal contract' (2003) 153 NLJ 653

Morris, P *et al*, *Social Needs and Legal Action*, 1973, Oxford: Martin Robertson

Peysner, J and Balen, P, 'Conditional fees' (1995) Law Soc Gazette, 31 August; (1995) Law Soc Gazette, 13 September

Underhill, N *et al*, 'Law for free' (2003) Counsel 14

Chapter 13   The European Context

Benoetvea, J, *The Legal Reasoning of the European Court of Justice: Towards a European Jurisprudence*, 1993, Oxford: Clarendon

Borgsmit, K, 'The Advocate General at the European Court of Justice: a comparative study' (1988) 13 EL Rev 106

Craig, P and de Búrca, G, *EU Law: Text, Cases and Materials*, 2nd edn, 1998, Oxford: OUP

Davies, K, *Understanding EU Law*, 2nd edn, 2003, London: Cavendish Publishing

Dickson, B, *Human Rights and the European Convention*, 1997, London: Sweet & Maxwell

Foster, N, *EC Legislation*, 13th edn, 2002, London: Blackstone

Harris, DJ *et al*, *Law of the European Convention on Human Rights*, 1995, London: Butterworths

Kennedy, T, *Learning European Law: A Primer and Vade-mecum*, 1998, London: Sweet & Maxwell

Lasok, KPE, *Law and Institutions of the European Union*, 7th edn, 2001, London: Butterworths

Neville Brown, L and Kennedy, T, *The Court of Justice of the European Communities*, 4th edn, 1994, London: Sweet & Maxwell

Shaw, J, *European Community Law*, 2nd edn, 1996, London: Macmillan

Tillotson, J and Foster, N, *EU Law: Text, Cases and Materials*, 4th edn, 2003, London: Cavendish Publishing

Ward, I, *A Critical Introduction to European Law*, 1996, London: Butterworths

Weatherill, S and Beamont, P, *EC Law*, 1993, London: Penguin

INDEX

Civil process

I

K

L

T